D0655213

Lionel Carley

Eastcote

28. i. 2004

Man & Music

THE LATE ROMANTIC ERA

Man & Music

THE LATE
ROMANTIC
ERA

From the mid-19th century to World War I

EDITED BY JIM SAMSON

M

© 1991 Granada Group and The Macmillan Press Ltd

All rights reserved. No reproduction, copy or transmission
of this publication may be made without written permission.
No paragraph of this publication may be reproduced, copied
or transmitted save with written permission or in accordance
with the provisions of the Copyright, Designs and Patents Act
1988, or under the terms of any licence permitting limited
copying issued by the Copyright Licensing Agency,
33–4 Alfred Place, London WC1E 7DP.
Any person who does any unauthorized act in relation to this
publication may be liable to criminal prosecution and civil
claims for damages.

First published in the United Kingdom 1991 by
The Macmillan Press Limited
London and Basingstoke

Associated companies in Auckland, Delhi, Dublin, Gaborone,
Hamburg, Harare, Hong Kong, Johannesburg, Kuala Lumpur, Lagos,
Manzini, Melbourne, Mexico City, Nairobi, New York, Singapore,
Tokyo.

British Library Cataloguing in Publication Data
Samson, Jim
 The late Romantic era from the mid 19th century to World
 War I. – (Man & Music).
 1. Western music, 1825–1900
 I. Title II. Series
 780.9034

ISBN 0-333-51602-8

Typeset by Florencetype Ltd, Kewstoke, Avon
Printed in Hong Kong

Contents

Abbreviations

Grove6	*The New Grove Dictionary of Music and Musicians*
GroveA	*The New Grove Dictionary of American Music*
JAMS	*Journal of the American Musicological Society*
ML	*Music and Letters*
MQ	*The Musical Quarterly*
NZM	*Neue Zeitschrift für Musik*
PRMA	*Proceedings of the Royal Musical Association*

Illustration
Acknowledgments

The publisher would like to thank the following institutions and individuals who have kindly provided material for use in this book:
Oxford Illustrators: 1, 38; Mary Evans Picture Library, London: 2, 7, 19, 20, 22, 25; Nationalarchiv der Richard-Wagner-Stiftung/Richard-Wagner-Gedenkstätte, Bayreuth: 3, 12; Bayerisches Staatsbibliothek, Munich: 4; Museum of Fine Arts (The Hayden Collection), Boston: 5; Bibliothèque de l'Opéra, Paris: 6; Deutsche Fotothek/Sächsische Landesbibliothek, Dresden: 8; Stadtarchiv, Aachen: 9; Germanisches Nationalmuseum, Nuremberg: 10; Kurt Hofmann, Hamburg: 11 (right); Österreichische Nationalbibliothek: (Bildarchiv), Vienna: 13, 16, 17, 68(a), 69, 72; Wiener Stadt- und Landesbibliothek: 14; Historisches Museum der Stadt Wien: 15; Musée de Luxembourg/photo ND-Viollet, Paris: 18; Concerts Colonne, Paris: 21; Musée d'Orsay, Paris/photo Réunion des Musées Nationaux: 23; Civica Raccolta Stampe 'Achille Bertarelli', Castello Sforzesco, Milan: 24, 27; photo Giancarlo Costa, Milan: 26, 28; Museo Teatrale alla Scala, Milan: 29; ARXIU-MAS, Barcelona: 30; Biblioteca de Catalunya, Barcelona: 31; Society for Cultural Relations with the USSR, London: 32 (Tretyakov Gallery, Moscow), 33, 37; Tchaikovsky House Museum, Klin: 34 (from *Pyotr Il'yich Tchaikovsky*, by K. J. Dawydowa, I. G. Sokolinskaja, P. J. Waidmann, VEB Deutscher Verlag für Musik, Leipzig, 1978); Trustees of the Theatre Museum, Victoria and Albert Museum, London: 36; Národni Muzeum, Prague/photo Olga Hilmerová: 39; Néprajzi Múzeum, Budapest: 41; Biblioteca Narodowa, Warsaw: 42; Mansell Collection, London: 43, 54; Bartók Archives, Budapest: 44; Ateneumin Taidemuseo, Helsinki: 45; Nationalhistoriska Museum på Frederiksborg, Hillerød/photo Robert Harding Picture Library, London: 46; Nationalmuseum, Stockholm: 47; Nasjonalgalleriet, Oslo: 48; Munch-Museet, Oslo: 49; Mrs Aivi Gallen-Kallella-Sirén/photo Museokuva, Helsinki: 50; Oxford University Press: 51, 52, 53(a); Henry Ford Museum and Greenfield Village (35.777.87): 57(a); New York Historical Society (Bella C. Landauer Collection), New York City: 57(b), 59, 61 (from *American Advertising Posters of the Nineteenth Century*, by Mary Black, Dover Publications Inc, 1976); Special Collections, Baker Library, Dartmouth College Hanover, New Hampshire: 60; Paul Oliver Collection, Oxford: 62; Teatro Colón, Buenos Aires: 63; Staatsoper, Dresden: 64(a); Museum der Geschichte der Stadt Leipzig: 65; Berlin Philharmonisches Orchester/photo R. Friedrich: 66; Stadtische Galerie im Lenbachhaus, Munich/© ADAGP, Paris and DACS, London: 67; Österreichische Galerie, Vienna: 68(b); Dr Dietrich Alfred Roller: 69; Collection of Lawrence and Ronald Schoenberg, and Nuria Schoenberg Nono: 71; Roger-Viollet, Paris: 18, 73, 74, 76, 78; Bibliothèque Nationale, Paris: 75, 77.

Preface

The *Man and Music* series of books – eight in number, chronologically
organized – were originally conceived in conjunction with the
television programmes of the same name, of which the first was shown
by Channel 4 in 1986 and distributed worldwide by Granada
Television International. These programmes were designed to
examine the development of music in particular places during particular periods in the history of Western civilization.

The books have the same objective. Each is designed to cover a
segment of Western musical history; the breaks between them are
planned to correspond with significant historical junctures. Since
historical junctures, or indeed junctures in stylistic change, rarely
happen with the neat simultaneity that the historian's or the editor's
orderly mind might wish for, most volumes have 'ragged' ends and
beginnings: for example, the Renaissance volume terminates, in Italy,
in the 1570s and 80s, but continues well into the seventeenth century
in parts of northern Europe.

These books do not, however, make up a history of music in the
traditional sense. The reader will not find technical, stylistic discussion in them; anyone wanting to trace the detailed development of
the texture of the madrigal or the rise and fall of sonata form should
look elsewhere. Rather, it is the intention in these volumes to show in
what context, and as a result of what forces, social, cultural, intellectual – the madrigal or sonata form came into being and took its
particular shape. The intention is to view musical history not as a
series of developments in some hermetic world of its own but rather as
a series of responses to social, economic and political circumstances
and to religious and intellectual stimuli. We want to explain not
simply *what* happened, but *why* it happened, and why it happened
when and where it did.

We have chosen to follow what might be called a geographical, or
perhaps a topographical, approach: to focus, in each chapter, on a
particular place and to examine its music in the light of its particular
situation. Thus, in most of these volumes, the chapters – once past
the introductory one, contributed by the volume editor – are each

devoted to a city or a region. This system has inevitably needed some modification when dealing with very early or very recent times, for reasons (opposite ones, of course) to do with communication and cultural spread.

These books do not attempt to treat musical history comprehensively. Their editors have chosen for discussion the musical centres that they see as the most significant and the most interesting: many lesser ones inevitably escape individual discussion, though the patterns of their musical life may be discernible by analogy with others or may be separately referred to in the opening, editorial chapter. We hope, however, that a new kind of picture of musical history may begin to emerge from these volumes, and that this picture may be more accessible to the general reader, responsive to music but untrained in its techniques, than others arising from more traditional approaches. In spite of the large number of lovers of music, musical histories have never enjoyed the appeal to a broad, intelligent general readership in the way that histories of art, architecture or literature have done: these books represent an attempt to reach such a readership and explain music in terms that may quicken their interest.

*

The television programmes and books were initially planned in close collaboration with Sir Denis Forman, then Chairman of Granada Television International. The approach was worked out in more detail with several of the volume editors, among whom I am particularly grateful to Iain Fenlon for the time he has generously given to discussion of the problems raised by this approach to musical history, and also to Alexander Ringer and James McKinnon for their valuable advice and support. Discussion with Bamber Gascoigne and Tony Cash, in the course of the making of the initial television programmes, also proved of value. Jim Samson and I are particularly grateful to Professor Edgar Yates for his generous advice and suggestions with regard to the chapters on Vienna and especially his valuable supplement of the bibliographical notes. I am grateful to Celia Thomson for drafting the chronologies that appear in each volume and to Elisabeth Agate for her invaluable work as picture editor in bringing the volumes to visual life.

London, 1991   STANLEY SADIE

Chapter I

Music and Society

JIM SAMSON

1848

Music has a double history, social and stylistic. A sociology of musical
language might hope to reveal that at very deep levels they are tightly
meshed, even that they make a single statement. Yet that is far from
obvious. This book is cautious about any assumptions of a closed and
unified cultural field, in which all opposing tendencies would be
related dialectically. Its authors have been content to outline areas
of interaction between musical life and musical language without
adopting at the outset any single explanatory theory. Such at least is
our starting-point. At the same time we recognize that areas of
interaction have a way of generating patterns and, as the patterns
multiply, some tentative notion of a deeper unity may present itself
after all – not a single statement, perhaps, but an intricate web of
intersecting causal threads.

   In examining context in nineteenth-century music we are struck at
least by parallels in periodization, suggesting that the threads linking
musical life and musical language extended also to wider movements
in political, social and intellectual history. It would clearly be naive to
identify the political turning-point of 1848 as a precise divider of
nineteenth-century music history. But it would be equally misguided
to ignore the evidence of a caesura around that time. The revolutions
were a milestone of social as well as political history. They marked the
end of a period of turbulence in the underlying social order of France
and central Europe and this in turn was reflected in a consolidation
of the structures of musical life. At the same time the mid-century
witnessed significant changes in intellectual climate, and their
influence on musical composition extended even to programmes for
renovation.

   The failure of the revolutions brought to an end a half-century
which has justly been termed 'the age of revolution'.[1] That period
was also the golden age of liberalism in political ideology and of
Romanticism in imaginative culture. It is tempting to seek generalized
connections between all three. In Romanticism a revolutionary
consciousness was indeed at work. Like the political revolutionary,

1

1. *Political map of Europe, 1871–1914*

the Romantic artist aimed to transform, not just to reflect or to analyse, existing realities. He would remake the world, in that 'fever of exultation which overthrows and overwhelms everything' (Géricault). Romanticism was also a cultural expression of the spirit of political liberalism, bound to it above all in its emphasis on the individual. 'Romanticism', wrote Hugo in the preface to *Hernani*, 'always inadequately defined . . . is in reality *liberalism* in literature'.[2]

It is perhaps no coincidence then that the end of the revolutionary era in 1848 also brought to a close the 'utopian' phase of political liberalism and the heyday of Romanticism in most areas of imaginative culture. The latter case is widely accepted in literature and the visual arts, less so in music. Yet even in music it has been sensibly argued that there was a major division around the mid-century.[3] About that time, an old guard of Romantic composers departed, or stopped composing (Chopin, Mendelssohn, Schumann), and a new, very different generation came to maturity (Brahms, Bruckner, Franck). For both Liszt and Wagner, moreover, the mid-century signalled new creative directions, with important consequences for the wider world of music.

For some commentators this change of tone has demanded and justified a change of label, in spite of obvious stylistic continuities. The term 'Romanticism' connotes ideas and motivations more clearly than styles. Above all it is grounded in the idea that the world may be more fully known through the power of the creative imagination than through conceptual thought or empirical observation; 'knowing through feeling' was Wagner's potent phrase. The vision or dream-world of the Romantic artist, informed and made aesthetically whole by his genius, would give the rest of us a privileged insight into reality. Such ideas belong mainly to the first half of the century. True, they survived in music much longer than in literature or the visual arts. Yet music was by no means impervious to the widespread changes in cultural climate which followed 1848, and a helpful periodization would reflect both its independence of, and its response to, those changes.

The term 'neo-Romanticism' has had some currency.[4] It draws a line between the two halves of the century while recognizing that the ideals of the Romantic movement were not lost in the music of the later nineteenth century, as they were to a greater extent in literature and painting. Rather there was a new and often selfconscious working-out of those ideals, an earnest preoccupation with forms, systems and theories, at times too an anti-subjectivism which was remote indeed from the exuberance and spontaneity of the early nineteenth century. These new creative directions were paralleled, moreover, by significant changes in the social history of music around the mid-century and in the climate of public taste.

If there really was a caesura in music history, it was not a direct response to the revolutions themselves. Uncomfortable as they were for musicians in the major cities, the disturbances of 1848 left the institutional framework of musical life – or at any rate the main pillars of that framework – largely intact. We learn more by examining underlying changes in social history, of which the failure of the revolutions was an important marker. One effect of that failure was a fundamental shift in middle-class political attitudes, in essence a separation of liberal and radical thought. The violence of the counter-revolution, notably in Paris and Vienna, drove a wedge between liberals and radicals, splitting uneasy alliances which had already been strained to breaking-point in Lamartine's Provisional Government and in the debates of the Frankfurt Parliament. The struggle went the way of the liberals, but in the process both the political profile of the bourgeoisie and the nature of liberalism were profoundly changed.

Social historians have been properly cautious about the identification of the 'middle class' as a homogeneous unit.[5] Yet it is clear that it became increasingly aware of itself as a class in the nineteenth century, defining itself not only through a political aspiration which complemented its economic status, but also through its growing influence on the formal culture of Europe. 1848 was a turning-point in the development of this selfconsciousness. Following it, the propertied bourgeoisie of France and Germany secured its position against the lower orders, turning its back on revolution. Its political aims were not fully realized in either country, but its dominant position in society was decisively confirmed and its social base was increasingly unified by the mode of production of high capitalism. No matter that the consolidation of middle-class power and influence had reached rather different stages in France and Germany. The important point is that the aftermath of 1848 revealed to the newly emancipated liberal bourgeoisie where its best interests lay.

Something of this reshaping of European society was reflected in the texture of musical life. A generous perspective on the century as a whole points up the contrast between its two halves, notably in the arena of the public concert. There were no sharp divisions here, but a perceptible change of emphasis none the less, as the colourful, dynamic and flamboyant concert life of the 1830s and 1840s gradually congealed into more stable, settled forms, reflecting the strengthening social structure at its foundation. The precise nature of the transformation was complex and had as much to do with the changing functions of music within the higher social classes as with changes in the social order itself.[6] But the broad picture at least may be sketched here.

Put baldly, the transformation was from the early nineteenth-century salon and benefit concert to the late nineteenth-century recital and subscription concert. Habeneck's Société des Concerts du Conservatoire in Paris, Mendelssohn's Gewandhaus concerts in Leipzig and the Philharmonic Society in London, all exclusive and exceptional when they were first established in the early nineteenth century, provided models for the kind of concert series that was to become increasingly prevalent in the second half of the century, with a permanent musical director, professional performers and a repertory centred on the Viennese Classics with a sprinkling of ambitious modern works. This central transformation carried with it, moreover, several related ones – from casual to ordered programming, from mixed to single media, from composer-virtuoso to composer and interpreter.

In Paris the structure of the transformation is particularly clear. Before 1848 the Concerts du Conservatoire remained an exclusive and highly élitist island of classical music, surrounded by salons and by ad hoc benefit and demonstration concerts. Attempts by Berlioz and others to establish rival series were largely unsuccessful. Then, in 1852, Pasdeloup founded his Société des Jeunes Artistes du Conservatoire; its popular blend of the 'classical' and the occasional 'modern' work (notably Wagner) not only successfully rivalled the Concerts du Conservatoire but formed the prototype for later nineteenth-century series like the Concerts Colonne (themselves an outgrowth of Pasdeloup's series) and the Concerts Lamoureux. Chamber music series, devoted mainly to Classical quartets, were also established at this time, with the Société Alard-Franchomme in 1848, the Société des Dernières Quatuors de Beethoven in 1851 and the Société Armingaud in 1856. And this pattern – the gradual consolidation of regular concert series and of a standard repertory – was repeated elsewhere: in London, where the New Philharmonic Society was established in 1852, in Vienna, where the Vienna Philharmonic was formed in 1860, and in the major cities of the German Confederation and the eastern Habsburg Empire.

The historic cities of Germany had of course very different traditions and they preserved their separate characters in some measure throughout the century. The leading courts were at Berlin, Dresden and Munich: Berlin, a garrison town but with an impressive court establishment; Dresden, a cultural centre with pronounced nationalist leanings; Munich, developed by Ludwig I as a 'renaissance city', but with its artistic pretensions utterly remote from the Bavarian peasant people. If we add Leipzig and tiny Weimar, with their reputations for progressive thought and art, and commercially and artistically active 'free' cities like Frankfurt and Hamburg, we may gain some impression of the thriving diversity of cultural life in the German states.

Yet in spite of this diversity, a middle-class concert life gradually

2. Bach bicentenary concert given by the choral society 'La Concordia' in the hall of the Paris Conservatoire; engraving from 'L'illustration' (2 May 1885)

took shape in Germany in the 1830s and 1840s, similar in many ways to that developing in Paris, London and Vienna. The persistence of patronal culture delayed it, but increasingly court institutions were transformed *de facto* into public institutions, with the court functioning as a promoter rather than a sponsor of culture for middle-class consumers. And as the middle-class cultural base widened, the federal differences gradually lessened, especially with the modernization of German society which followed 1848. Naturally there was no sudden break, but in the 1850s and 1860s concert life already had a structure recognizably similar to our own.

In this way the newly consolidated bourgeois class defined itself, institutionalizing its musical life in a manner independent of sacred and courtly life. It established its principal ceremony – the public concert – in the major cities of England, France and central Europe; it created a repertory of classical music, with related concert rituals, to confirm and authenticate the new status quo; it manipulated and changed the meaning of an outmoded style to give itself cultural roots; it created a fetishism, even indeed a sense, of the 'great work', which is still with us today.

In opera, no less than in concert life, the two halves of the century present very different profiles. For Italian opera the mid-century inaugurated an era dominated by the powerful achievements of a single composer involved in the creation of great works in a spirit far removed from that of the early nineteenth-century Italian masters. From *Rigoletto* onwards, Verdi sought to create a *dramma per musica* through a renovation and adaptation of Italian opera conventions, which had long since yielded their dramatic potential to the claims of *bel canto*. Moreover, just as the creative impulse in Italian opera was being channelled into a handful of ambitious, epic works by an innovatory genius, so the repertory of the major opera houses was becoming increasingly standardized, centred on a small number of popular masterpieces. Both developments were in tune with the age.

There were also changes in French opera at this time, and for all three of the principal companies in Paris. Grand opera, the achievement of Véron, Scribe and Meyerbeer, had taken its final form at Le Peletier after the bourgeois revolution of 1830 (the Opéra moved to the Boulevard des Capucines only towards the end of the Second Empire). In many ways grand opera came to embody the ideals of the July Monarchy, synthesizing business and artistic skills in a spirit of commercial enterprise and tailoring its product carefully to meet the demands of the new middle-class establishment. Meyerbeer's *Le prophète* of 1849, the last of his operas staged during his lifetime, was a symbolic turning-point. After *Le prophète*, grand opera consolidated its achievements, but with no more innovations. Indeed, many of its greatest successes of the 1850s and 1860s were conceived much earlier.[7]

7

The rival Théâtre Italien at the Salle Ventadour had catered during the July Monarchy for a rather different public, in which the disaffected Bourbon aristocracy was prominent, and it lost its specific audience, its prestige and much of its distinctive character after the change of régime. But it was the Opéra-Comique at the second Salle Favart (from 1840) that changed most, and in a way that tells us most about the age. Its role as a bridge between 'art' and 'entertainment' was lost after 1848. Indeed as a genre *opéra comique* virtually disappeared in the second half of the century, its traditions splitting into the 'serious' world of lyric opera and the 'popular' world of operetta.

The commercialization of opera, blatant in France from the beginning of the July Monarchy, was achieved more stealthily in the German states and the eastern Habsburg Empire, but the general direction was similar. Subsidies were still provided by such major courts as Vienna, Dresden and Munich, but even there the theatres depended increasingly on the box office and on the appointment of professional managers with entrepreneurial skills, a tendency that increased to a marked degree after the revolutions. Here the parallel with Paris ends. The turning-point in German opera in 1848 was of an essentially different order from that dictated by political and social change in France. It was forged above all by ideas and by creative genius.

The operatic repertory was cautious in the extreme during the post-Congress 'quiet years' in Germany, partly because of a ruthless régime of censorship which persisted until the fall of Metternich in 1849. That censorship accounts in some measure for the relatively low vitality of German opera between Weber and Wagner, whose own early operas, in theme and presentation, remain – just – within the framework of German Romantic opera. The transformation of German, and not only German, opera was effected by Wagner after his exile from Dresden in 1849. It was in Switzerland that he engaged in a fundamental rethinking of his art, a form of theorizing that responded to creative needs but that in turn informed creative process. At precisely the same time Liszt was theorizing in Weimar about the future of instrumental music, and he too was about to put his theories into practice in a series of pioneering symphonic poems. It is perhaps fitting that in Germany the caesura at mid-century should have been in part a matter of ideas.

LIBERALISM

Even as revolution and counter-revolution raged in the German states in 1848–9, issues of constitutionalism, national unity and human rights were aired in a parliament for all the states held at the 'free city' of Frankfurt. The Frankfurt Parliament proved hopelessly ineffective politically, but it was the major platform for liberal debate in 1848 and its collapse was a symbolic turning-point in the history of liberalism.

Underlying the political argument was a conceptual conflict between two very different understandings of the 'human rights' that liberalism espoused – in effect between freedom and contractualism. The former carried with it a notion of psychological egoism, a view of man in search of self-realization, free, isolated, striving. Its tone was idealist. The latter depended more on an exercise of reason and duty, on political concepts of consensus and the social contract. On this analysis it was considered the duty of the enlightened, educated and 'rational' to represent and speak for the unenlightened and under-privileged, who were themselves incapable of exercising rational choice, including electoral choice. Its tone was realist. Before 1848 the former view dominated the rhetoric, and was expressed on behalf of all. After 1848 it was the latter position, with its acceptance of privilege, that prevailed. It accorded well with a middle class which had climbed to dominance by means of the 'contractual state' and had bought its freedom through property ownership. These were the vested interests which had been threatened in 1848.

The shift of emphasis in liberal ideology and the closing of class ranks which accompanied it were reflected in the attitudes of creative artists, most of whom were from the educated middle class. By the 1830s the majority of leading writers and artists in France identified closely with the liberal cause and the reform movement. 'La bataille romantique' involved a search for political and social relevance in creative writing and took its stand on the belief that the poet, no less than the politician, could change history. A generation of writers publicized the liberal ideology of individual freedom both in explicit political terms and, more imaginatively, in the creation of its fictional archetype, the Romantic hero, independent and desiring. In some notable cases – Lamartine, Sand and (more ambivalently) Hugo – they stepped directly into the political arena. Through oratory, pamphleteering and direct political action, they helped shape the 'revolution of the intellectuals', opening the way for an unusually direct convergence of art and politics.

The 'social romanticism' of the pre-1848 years, with its lyrical blend of utopian socialism, illuminism and heady republicanism, was splintered totally in the aftermath of the 'June Days', as it became increasingly clear that the revolutions, far from marking the appearance of a new, regenerate mankind, had signalled only the rise to power of a rich, commercial middle class.[8] When Lamartine's government fell, leading writers and artists without exception retreated from political action and in most cases from revolutionary sympathies. The conclusion seemed clear. The poet could not change history.

The revolutions and their aftermath had a more ambivalent effect on the German artist, both disillusioning and liberating. As in France, idealist myths were shattered; but at the same time a more open political debate was made possible, at least for a time, by the collapse of Metternich. The 'blue-pencil' régime which followed the Carlsbad Decrees of 1819 had for three decades spread the net of intellectual repression across the German states and the Habsburg Empire and its effect on artists was naturally debilitating. Paris too had its censorship (it was re-established in 1835, following abolition in 1831), but it was relatively mild compared with the Habsburg-German model. In Prussia and Austria every town that had a printing works also had a censor (often the chief of police). Journals and pamphlets, especially those emanating from the universities, were the main victims, but the theatre was also carefully watched – and that included opera.

An obvious effect was the polarization of political attitudes among writers and artists in Germany and the Habsburg lands, where the 'indignant artist' was a less familiar figure than in Paris. Either the artist accepted the status quo, in which case critical comment would be confined to the mildly satirical (or the skilfully disguised), or he rejected it, coming into direct conflict with the authorities, as did the 'Young Germany' movement, banned in 1835, and the radical and short-lived playwright Georg Büchner.[9] For many the protest could be carried on only in exile.

Composers, like other creative artists, were generally on the reformist wing of politics in the early nineteenth century and they travelled a similar path from idealism to disillusionment. Berlioz, Liszt and Schumann all adopted radical, progressive attitudes in their early years, flirting with Saint-Simonian ideas and in the case of Schumann identifying closely with 'Young Germany'. In the end all three came to despise revolutionary activity. Before 1848 their stance had already become one of apolitical detachment, and this was decisively confirmed by their reaction to the revolutions themselves. The sequence was typical. César Franck declared that he was 'cured' of tendencies to extremism by the 'June Days'.

The essential point about this loss of idealism is that composers were strongly inclined to put their music before any programme of social and political reform; indeed such programmes were often espoused precisely because they seemed to offer a more conducive framework for the pursuit of music. Composers, then as now, sought stability before all else, and they came to view any form of political upheaval as inimical to their art. As Henry Raynor remarked: 'The artist may love freedom in theory, but he cannot exist without tradition'.[10]

The case of Wagner highlights the central issue. His early political activities – letters, speeches, heavily ideological artistic projects and direct action (of leading composers only Wagner and Spohr were

3. Set designed by Josef Hoffmann for the final scene of Act 3 in the 1876 Bayreuth production of Wagner's 'Götterdämmerung'

directly involved in the events of 1848) – were founded on the belief that there might be a causal chain leading from political revolution to artistic transformation and from there to a more general social regeneration, a belief articulated in *Die Kunst und die Revolution* of 1849. In exile, however, Wagner was quick to renounce his connection with the rising at Dresden. He too lost faith with revolution, or rather he separated the notions of political and cultural revolution, formerly fused in his mind. As we shall see, that change of thinking is in a sense encoded in the libretto of the *Ring*.

Opera was of course one of the few media through which music could make explicitly ideological statements in support of liberal ideas. But following the Carlsbad Decrees any such political comment had to be carefully veiled in the German-Habsburg lands, usually by means of a historical or geographical distance, or both – an exotic of time and space. Between Beethoven and Wagner German opera made little attempt at political critique, however indirect, retreating rather into the worlds of fairy-tale and Gothic fantasy. The historical dramas staged at the French Opéra could go rather further, but here the underlying motivation was seldom a passion for reform, and the political messages tended in any case to be fairly one-dimensional.

It remained for Wagner to give significant and sophisticated

11

operatic expression to reformist, even revolutionary, politics. George Bernard Shaw's interpretation of the *Ring* as social and political allegory was undoubtedly rooted in at least one layer of Wagner's original intention and it has been extended convincingly by Deryck Cooke.[11] In this analysis *Rheingold* emerges as a potent critique of the social and political world of mid-nineteenth-century Europe, specifically in its study of two types of power-seeker in conflict – the political (Wotan) and the economic (Alberich). In both cases the drive to power results in corruption and exploitation. Alberich, the capitalist plutocrat, enslaves his workers; Wotan, the authoritarian (originally constitutional) ruler, himself becomes a law-breaker.

As the conflict of the mythic drama unfolds in later operas, working itself out in human dramas of love and heroism, so too a further conflict arises, close to the heart of the liberal debate. It is a conflict between freedom and contractualism, between Wotan's need of a free hero to accomplish his will and the 'world of contracts' epitomized in his original contract with the giants. Significantly Wagner's first version of the libretto would have favoured the former, with Siegfried carried in triumph into Valhalla, and the subsequent change of intention resonates in liberal thought.

But there was an even more significant change of perspective, recognized by Wagner himself in a letter to August Röckel.[12] As Cooke pointed out, the political dimension of the *Ring* receded in importance as Wagner worked on the libretto. The original aim was explicitly didactic – to show the birth, development and disintegration of a civilization, from whose errors we might learn. But this political and social meliorism gave way to an apolitical metaphysical conclusion of Schopenhauerian pessimism, a recognition that the condition of *Rheingold* was the true and static condition of the phenomenal world. Significantly it is on the level of psychological rather than political interpretation that a positive theme emerges from the *Ring*: the centrality of love and compassion and their incompatibility with dominance over others. This transformation represents one artist's change of heart. At the same time it speaks of a more general withdrawal, on the part of composers and of artists, from politics to art, from engagement to detachment, from idealism to realism. It speaks too of the end of liberalism as a direct catalyst of European culture. The 'free' artist now turned inward, seeking self-realization in the subjective world of the emotions.

Only in music did liberalism continue to play an important, albeit indirect, role in art in the second half of the century. It did so through the powerful influence of Beethoven on leading composers of the period, an influence carrying a potent, if concealed, ideological element. The ideological layer of a musical work is naturally unstable – to say the least – when there is no recourse to dramatic action, poetic text or denotative title. But even in purely instrumental music the creative process may be influenced, if not actually determined, by a composer's ideological commitment. Bach and Mozart used musical codes as well as verbal texts to serve God and the ideals of freemasonry, drawing partly on connotative values established through convention and partly on privately conceived but publicly perceivable repertories of musical symbols. In the same way Beethoven's attempt to express through his music something of his commitment to the radical humanitarian thought of the age of revolution inspired a new quality in musical language.

That commitment was a primary cause of the elevated, exalted tone of his music, of its (areligious) ethical pretension and of its rhetorical insistence, which so often seems to invite a metaphorical interpretation of the forcefully articulated individual gesture as well as of basic musical processes – growth, transformation, antithesis, climax. There are more specific associations too, for Beethoven absorbed into his musical language something of the stylistic idiom of post-revolutionary public music – marches, funeral marches, overtures, hymns and theatre pieces by such composers as Lefèvre, Méhul and Gossec. And since that music drew heavily on popular genres, themselves grounded in specific social functions, it was already implicitly programmatic.

Beethoven was perhaps the only early nineteenth-century composer of stature who could be described as a truly 'committed' or 'engaged' artist. Even if his commitment was to a generalized, abstract and utopian notion of liberty, it was not something superimposed on his activity as a composer, but a shaping factor of that activity. As such it also helped to shape late nineteenth-century music, so crucial was Beethoven reception as a determinant of style. There were few major figures who remained untouched by his achievement, and it is significant that he was mentor to composers whose aesthetic was diametrically opposite, to those who sought a renewal of music through an appeal to the non-musical world and to those committed to the idea of absolute music. Even when the directly ideological motivation was either lost to formalism (Brahms, Bruckner) or diffused into autobiography and metaphysics (Berlioz, Mahler), it left its trace in the ambition and pretension of the musical work, its quest for an epic status. Beethoven promoted – and bequeathed to the later nineteenth century – an increasingly influential view of music as a discourse of ideas as much as an object of beauty.

Beethoven reception illustrates too that stylistic continuities can survive major changes in intellectual and artistic climate much more easily in music than in the other arts. They can do so for the obvious reason that the form and substance of a musical work may be more readily separated from any 'message' a composer may want to convey than they can in the representational media. This goes some way to explaining why music appears to be 'out-of-step' with literature and the visual arts in the late nineteenth century. It suggests too that the threads spun by early nineteenth-century liberalism were at once more slender and more durable in music than in any other art form.

TASTES AND REPERTORIES

In both France and Germany the consolidation of middle-class power and influence following 1848 took place initially within authoritarian, paternalistic and increasingly centralist régimes, loosely reformist in social policy. Political liberties were repressed, but economic liberalism was actively fostered. The two decades after the revolutions were years of economic progress and technological achievement, bringing relative stability to the wealthy, propertied bourgeoisie, whose interests were dependent, however indirectly, on the capitalist undertakings of a new economic order. Indeed, as Theodore Hamerow observed, the unity of the middle class during this period derived essentially from a community of interests rather than a community of origins.[13]

That unity was expressed in cultural life too. In music the patronal system lingered and a working-class culture began to glimmer, but it was the bourgeois world which financed and controlled the rapidly expanding and increasingly diversified and specialized musical establishment. That world could now sustain and absorb, without yet any serious threat to its internal coherence, several independent layers of music-making, their boundaries sharper and less fluid than in the early nineteenth century, as repertories were inexorably prised apart.

There was amateur music-making in the bourgeois home, demanding a contemporary repertory of songs (often *am Volkston*) and of short, manageable piano pieces (simple transcriptions, dance and 'character' pieces) – a *Trivialmusik* which formed the mainstay of the publisher's income. This was usually fairly close in style to the songs and piano pieces of contemporary art music. Indeed such eminent composers as Brahms and Tchaikovsky found no difficulty in moving from symphony to dance piece, from concert hall to drawing-room. But in lesser hands that very proximity of style brought its own dangers. The music of the bourgeois home constantly risked, and often seemed to court, infection from a nineteenth-century 'project of greatness', to which it was ill-suited. Sharing in the pretensions of high art, it would become literally pretentious.

There was collective music-making for amateurs in choral societies, orchestras and wind bands, flourishing in England, Germany, Bohemia and in French provincial cities. Much of it involved a wholesale appropriation of existing high-art repertories, as often as not transforming their meaning in the process, as in the massed-choir performances of Handel which began to proliferate in England

4. *Band playing at the Volksgarten, Vienna; engraving from the Leipzig 'Illustrirte Zeitung'*
(12 October 1889)

following the Crystal Palace festivals of the 1850s. In the working-
class milieu of the brass band, moreover, there was a similar but even
more radical and interesting transformation of high-art repertories; by
the simple act of transcription, both genre and style were changed
while the notes remained the same.

There was professionally transmitted 'light' music, a contemporary,
and increasingly specific, repertory directed to the ballroom, the
popular (including promenade) concert and the theatre. The polished,
elegant waltzes of the Strauss family are characteristic. So too are the
witty, neo-classical operettas of Offenbach. In both cases the music
was composed initially for professional performance, and it was far
removed in spirit from the vast corpus of ephemera produced for
amateurs in the bourgeois home. But it was united with that repertory
in its untroubled acceptance of the commodity status of music in the
post-Beethoven world – one governed increasingly by commercial
interests. Put crudely, all this music, contemporary and classical, was
'entertainment' before it was 'art'.

Other layers of music-making were characterized by a pointed
rejection of that commodity status, by a strong sense of the degeneration of the musical language of the market-place. There was the
professional concert series devoted mainly to classical music. Such
series were organized on a commercial basis, of course, but their
primary role was one of social legitimization and their repertory had
not yet succumbed to a manipulative culture industry. The growing

historicism of musical taste, demonstrated and promoted by these concerts, spawned moreover many ancillary changes in musical life, not least in pedagogy, journalism and performing practice.

Finally there were progressive composers, who, suspicious of dilettantism and the mass appeal of popular music, were initially sympathetic to the classical revivals but eventually came to feel threatened by them, so that they and their supporters took their stand

5. *Rehearsal of the Pasdeloup Orchestra at the Cirque d'Hiver, Paris; painting (1876) by John Singer Sargent*

increasingly against the conservative as well as the commercial. The clash of interests is well illustrated in Paris, where Pasdeloup's concerts, promoting modern as well as classical works, ran into difficulties with conservative taste of a kind (and with a rhetoric) all too familiar today. These two layers, increasingly at odds, were none the less united in their commitment to a project of greatness in music; music – contemporary and classical – was 'art' before it was 'entertainment'.

The middle ground was not entirely lost in the second half of the century. Benefit concerts and salons were on the decline, but far from extinct, and they continued to blend the lightweight and the substantial in their highly diversified programmes. Major composers, moreover, were by no means reluctant to turn their hand to *Trivialmusik* with an eye to their pocket. Above all opera, true to its traditions, continued to mediate between high art and popular entertainment. But the underlying trends were clear, even in opera. Significantly the major generic innovations – operetta and music drama – served to formalize a widening gap between the popular and the serious.

These were general trends. Within them there were essential differences between music-making in France and in Austro-Germany, no doubt reflecting differences of social and political profile and even of national temperament. It is worth giving some consideration to these differences and to their context. In the two decades separating their revolutions and their war, France and Prussia followed increasingly divergent political paths, especially in the second decade with the rise of Bismarck. Napoleon, under pressure, liberalized the Second Empire; Bismarck, in the ascendant, defeated his own liberal opposition. Napoleon championed the nationalisms of others; Bismarck consolidated and manipulated nationalism at home. Napoleon rushed into ill-considered foreign adventures; Bismarck used his wars economically and strategically to further Prussian interests. France, already heavily industrialized, confidently and carelessly enjoyed its status as the first power of Europe; Prussia, conservative and near-feudal in its social base, steadily mounted its strength, building an economic and military power which was second to none in Europe. The war, when it came, was Napoleon's last hope to save a crumbling empire; it was Bismarck's opportunity to unite, or as one historian put it, to conquer Germany.

Prussia gives inadequate measure of Germany as a whole during these two decades, but its traditional social organization delayed by only a little the transformation taking place all over the Confederation. In essence the static society of the 'quiet years' gave way to a powerfully dynamic one, as the rapidly expanding German population (in contrast to minimal growth in France) gravitated increasingly to the cities, themselves changing from a mixture of court establishment and rural village to something more akin to our modern industrial complex. The urban middle class, ambitious, frugal and hard-working, not only built Germany's economic might during these decades; it also strengthened and consolidated the cultural life of the German cities, taking over that role increasingly from a receding court patronage.

Commercial expansion and cultural development went hand in hand in German cities, and both proceeded in part from a sense of inferiority which was measured against French primacy of both the recent and the more distant past. The middle class set the tone in manners, fashion and culture from the mid-century, and it was an earnest and assertive rather than a flamboyant tone, blending the spirit of nationalism with a strong sense of cultural disadvantage.[14] The old 'Biedermeier' values persisted among the German bourgeoisie, in the northern cities especially. It was a sober, 'bookish' culture that was promoted, one that preferred literary 'evenings' to salons and that placed great store on an excellent education system within which music played a prominent role.

The major exception to this broad characterization was Vienna, a city of the Confederation but also, and more important, the seat of the Habsburg Empire, to whose interests developing German nationalism posed a direct threat. As the capital of an empire on the wane, Vienna was both a hotbed of underground political radicalism (much of it in support of German nationalism and opposed to the liberal bourgeois establishment) and a showcase for imperial display. In both respects it was closer to Paris than to the German cities. Indeed the two capitals had much in common during this period, not least in their parallel programmes of urban reconstruction. The boulevards and the Ringstrasse, and the impressive public buildings associated with them, affirmed and symbolized the bourgeois ascendancy. In both cities political corruption went hand in hand with the extravagance and heedless gaiety of cosmopolitan capitals, where the lavish entertainments of a pleasure-seeking demi-monde could barely conceal the real hardship below. For all their glories, Vienna and Paris were the shop windows of declining empires during these two decades. And it was in these cities, as the century drew to its close, that the crisis of a liberal bourgeois culture would be given its most acute expression.

Vienna and Paris had a musical life of unparalleled richness, yet curiously neither produced a major composer in the two decades after 1848. Berlioz was still active in Paris, but he was essentially a product of the pre-revolutionary era, while Bizet's star had not yet fully risen. Brahms, and later Bruckner, were attracted to Vienna, but as men and artists they were shaped by the provincial Germany of their earlier years. The true musical mirror of Viennese and Parisian 'society' was neither classical nor modern but a professional light

6. Poster by Jules Chéret for the revival of Offenbach's 'Orphée aux enfers' at the Théâtre Gaîté, Paris, on 5 May 1878

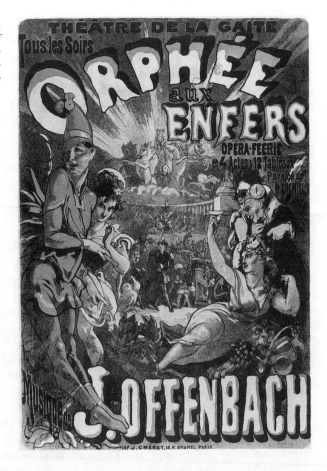

music just then reaching its zenith in Vienna in the 'classical' waltzes of Johann Strauss (ii).

There was a comparable dance music in Paris (indeed it supplied Vienna with the popular quadrille), but its composers never achieved the worldwide acclaim of the Strauss family. In Paris light music of quality was associated not with the ballroom but with the theatre, and especially with operetta, triumphantly launched by Offenbach when his *Ba-ta-clan* was produced at the Bouffes-Parisiens in 1855. Offenbach and his librettists tuned in to the contradictions and tensions of Second Empire society, satirizing its mores by exposing the hollowness of convention and appearance and at times extending their hard-hitting critique to directly political issues. *La Grande-Duchesse de Gérolstein* is characteristic in its portrayal of the irresponsible behaviour of the great, its suggestion that major affairs of state were determined largely by personal whims and desires and its clear message that a

19

sudden rise to eminence can be followed no less suddenly by a fall from grace.

La Grande-Duchesse was produced in 1867, and among the distinguished foreign visitors who saw it was Bismarck, three years before the war that brought the Second Empire to an end – and with it Offenbach's years of success in Paris. He had first come to the attention of the wider musical world when *Orphée aux enfers* was given at the Bouffes-Parisiens in 1858. A year later Wagner arrived in Paris, an event 'celebrated' by Offenbach with a wicked parody performed at the Carnaval des Revues. A year after that (1860), at the command of the emperor, *Tannhäuser* was produced at the Opéra, and its notorious disruption by the Jockey Club was in no small measure a political gesture directed against Napoleon himself.

These were interesting years for opera in Paris. Between the productions of *Orphée* and *Tannhäuser*, Gounod's *Faust* was given at the Théâtre Lyrique (1859). This was significant as an attempt to establish a new middle ground in response to the polarization of opera epitomized by Offenbach and Wagner. Gounod gave a lead in the creation of a 'drame lyrique' moulded to Second Empire tastes. Moreover it was a genuinely French creation. Not only were the greatest works given at the Opéra in these years by Wagner and Verdi, but the most characteristic works – *Le prophète* and *L'africaine* – were by a composer of German origin. Even Offenbach had been born in Cologne! The Théâtre Lyrique provided an antidote. Gounod followed *Faust* with *Philémon et Baucis* (1860), *Mireille* (1864) and *Roméo et Juliette* (1867). Ambroise Thomas wrote *Mignon* for the theatre in 1866 and Bizet contributed *Les pêcheurs de perles* and *La jolie fille de Perth*, both much indebted to Gounod, in 1863 and 1867 respectively. Yet for all its importance, the Théâtre Lyrique never successfully challenged the Opéra and the Opéra-Comique as the main centres of opera in Paris and it did not survive the collapse of the Second Empire. By then the traditional associations of operatic venues had changed radically. Ironically, the two greatest French operas of the period – *Les troyens* and *Carmen* – were given their premières not at the Opéra but at the Opéra-Comique.

Following the ill-fated production of *Tannhäuser* there was no Wagner production in Paris until *Rienzi* was given at the Théâtre Lyrique in 1869. But concert performances of his music were frequent in the 1860s and the French Wagner cult gained momentum during this decade. It was promoted much more by progressive artists and writers than by composers, and it was Wagner's ideas as much as his music that excited their interest, culminating in the appearance of the *Revue wagnérienne*.[15] It is striking that with the production of *Tannhäuser* Wagner's music was used to promote political interests and that in the 1860s it generated and fuelled an essentially literary debate. In both cases the music seemed to take a back seat. True, at the end of the century French music succumbed helplessly to Wagner's stylistic influence, but even then composers played little part in the controversies and debates aroused by his ideas.

Perhaps it is an over-simplification to view the attitude to Wagner in France as symptomatic of the peripheral status assigned to music within an essentially literary culture, as against the pre-eminence of music in Germany. It may at least be claimed that its status was very different in France – a craft to be cultivated excellently, and above all to be left to the professionals.[16] Amateur music-making had nothing like the same prominence in Paris as in large German cities, where choral societies were a prominent part of musical life (witness the careers and music of Brahms and Bruch), as indeed they were in Protestant England and Protestant Bohemia. The cultivation of music as a worthy, improving activity was indeed an important dimension of the bourgeois ethic in Germany. Quite apart from the choral movement there was a vast repertory of music designed for the home, fulfilling a social function very different from the Parisian salon repertory. Although often of little intrinsic merit, such music – especially the popular orchestral and operatic transcriptions – provided much of the educative foundation on which a solid musical culture could be built.

The centrality of music in late nineteenth-century German culture is shown too at the professional level. As in Paris, there were strident polemics about music, but here musicians were among the main participants, and they extended the discussion to embrace (however insecurely) the wider world of ideas. Indeed it is notable that music – its role and its meaning – was often at the heart of philosophical debate in Germany. The issue of national character is as treacherous in music as in any other sphere. But it does seem that for the German mind the blend of abstract thought and direct emotional expression is (or perhaps was) especially seductive, and it is precisely that blend which is achieved in musical language. The special significance of music is attested above all by the peculiarly German preoccupation with what Carl Dahlhaus called 'the idea of absolute music',[17] something of marginal importance in France until the 1870s, when its cultivation was in any case a direct response to German models. In that idea Western music celebrated an 'autonomy-character' specific to bourgeois society and yet in some senses implicit (through the development of notational and compositional systems) in its entire history.

THE CLIMATE OF IDEAS
'Never', said A. J. P. Taylor, 'has a revolution so discredited the power of ideas.'[18] Yet it was really the status rather than the power of

ideas that changed after 1848. From abstractions which had shaped, and might change, the world, they became the tools with which to gain an empirical understanding of it. The later nineteenth century stands out for its remarkable achievements in the natural sciences. The rise of industrialism both fed those achievements and was nourished by them, resulting in a rapid transformation of society through technological growth – in effect a revolution in machines, transport and communication which launched Europe breathless into the modern world.

The impact of science on the world of ideas was registered in many ways in the late nineteenth century. On one level the dual impulse of the industrial and scientific revolutions demanded new economic and social theories which might address the changing realities of life in a scientific, industrial age. Utilitarianism and Marxism were in their different ways responses to that demand. On another level a scientific modality increasingly penetrated and eventually came to dominate almost all other disciplines, as the 'isms' suggest. Metaphysical idealism gave way to positivism, a 'science' of society. Romanticism gave way to realism, an art of 'scientific' analysis and observation. Even history became a 'science'.

And music, the art least adept at representation, was touched by these changes too, in the positivist orientation of musical life and in the realist orientation of musical language. Realism was a central theme of aesthetic debate in the 1850s and 60s and it is not surprising that the term should have been widely applied to composers too, often pejoratively and usually loosely. Both Berlioz and Wagner were labelled 'realists' at one time or another, sometimes with reference to nothing more than the descriptive elements in their music.

Dahlhaus has demonstrated that the term may signify rather more.[19] Even where the music of the period might be described more plausibly as 'neo-Romantic' than as 'realist', it often shared with the other arts a loss of idealism and of subjectivism. In many cases it shared too a contempt for aesthetic norms and conventions, flaunting them carelessly in the interests of a greater 'reality'. We need not follow Eduard Kruger and later Ernst Bücken in calling Wagner a 'realist' to see that his music touches that aesthetic at numerous points. His graphic depictions of the natural world are perhaps the most obvious. But his sacrifice of conventional operatic forms to a 'realistic' musico-dramatic dialogue and of classical periodization to a heightened musical prose reflecting the 'reality' of speech can also be viewed in these terms.

In subject matter of course Wagner was no realist, at least not in any commonly understood sense of the term. Yet other composers followed their literary colleagues in this area too, widening the range of admissible content, breaking down the stylistic differentiations traditionally separating the social classes and locating high drama and tragedy in an 'everyday' setting. The movement crossed national boundaries, albeit taking very different forms in the process. In song it embraced Musorgsky's *The Nursery* and Wolf's Eichendorff lieder; in opera it ranged from Bizet's *Carmen* to Giordano's *Andrea Chenier*.

A different perspective on the rise of modern science would note other, less tangible evidence of its effect on the history of ideas. When Kant proposed that both facts and values might be grounded in the self, that the mind was itself the source of universal and necessary principles, he paved the way for two later developments. On the one hand he made possible a theory of being and knowledge which bound the self tightly to the world, a theory whose moral and aesthetic implications were explored by Fichte and Schelling respectively. In this way the individualism, political and cultural, of the Romantic age was philosophically predicated (Fichte's writings in particular were an important philosophical source for the concept of the Romantic). The second development flows from the first. By grounding the world in the self, Kant made possible, though he did not himself create, an evolutionary-dynamic model of reality – nature-in-the-making – to replace a worn-out mechanical-static model. It was Hegel who formalized this into a philosophical system and one that was perfectly in tune with the coming scientific revolution achieved by Darwin.

The biological simile of organic growth, together with its inflation as evolutionary theory, seemed relevant to many disciplines in the late nineteenth century, not least the understanding of history itself. The historicism of the age – its assumption of a single unified history, embracing many different 'histories' in a linear progression from simple to complex forms – was all-pervasive. 'A change has come over the spirit of enquiry', wrote G. H. Lewes in 1855, '. . . we are all now bent on tracing the phases of development. To understand the *grown* we try to follow the *growth*.'[20]

This was reflected in the developmental tendencies apparent in all the arts. It was an age when artists, including composers, disliked repeating themselves, let alone anyone else – when 'development', 'growth' and 'evolution' were the watchwords of the age. The biological simile was applied to the course of music history, to the unfolding of individual musical styles and even to the structure of musical works. Present-day discussions of organicism in late nineteenth-century music, of the integration of part and whole, are not just projections into history of current analytical concerns – though they are that too. They reflect preoccupations – in some cases obsessions – of the composers themselves. Thus Wagner, writing of Beethoven: 'At every point in the score he would have to look both before and after, seeing the whole in each part and each part as contributing to the whole'; and of the *Ring*: '[It] turned out to be a firmly entwined unity. There is scarcely a bar in the orchestral writing that doesn't develop out of preceding motives'.[21]

The primacy of science had one further consequence. It brought with it in many cases a decline in religious faith. This was not just a matter of traditional beliefs overturned in the face of new scientific evidence. Rather it concerned the nature of authority, as a 'rational' authority increasingly took precedence over an 'arbitrary' one. Since civilization had been founded on religious values, their apparent loss seemed to many an issue of grave consequence. As Nietzsche saw it, nineteenth-century bourgeois morality was a highly unstable halfway stage between Christian morality and the loss of any moral imperative, the pathway to a necessary nihilism.

In some ways the neo-classicism of the age can be viewed as a response to this development – a search for lost values, transplanting the past into the present to offset its insecurities. And the past assumed this stabilizing, justifying role all the more strongly following the collapse in 1848 of the promise held out by the ideals of the French Revolution. The past was no longer a nostalgic ideal, as in the Romantic age, but a necessary validation of bourgeois culture. Music reflected this development too, most obviously in the emergence of a classical repertory, but also in the historicist thrust of pedagogy and performing practice and even in an incipient neo-classicism in musical works, discernible in different ways in both Brahms and Bruckner (and not confined to them).

An alternative response to the loss of religious certainties was the drawing of values into the scientific domain. Where religion had once been the repository of facts as well as values, 'scientism' sought to effect a reversal – to make of science a repository of values as well as facts, in effect a secular metaphysic. For many nineteenth-century artists Goethe's *Faust* seemed to symbolize this development, representing man as a visionary whose quest for knowledge of the world and of himself would admit no constraining influence, however drastic the consequences. Faust, like Prometheus, challenged the Godhead. Unlike Marlowe's, moreover, Goethe's Faust would not appeal for redemption to 'Christ's blood streaming in the firmament'.

Until the nineteenth century, music composed in praise of God, however functional or occasional, was usually an expression of beliefs sincerely held. We need a broad definition of Christian doctrine to claim the same of sacred music by Beethoven, Berlioz or Brahms, music composed to celebrate the universal, but essentially human, qualities inherent in religion; at the very least the Godhead is democratized. There was in any case a drastic reduction in the output of religious music, and in this respect too Faust seemed to challenge God. Numerous musical works drew upon Goethe's masterpiece in the nineteenth century. Many of them are conventional settings or depictions of events in its narrative but some are more ambitious and it may be worth looking at the different approaches adopted in these.

In *La damnation de Faust* (1845–6) Berlioz preserved, however idiosyncratically, something of the main narrative of Goethe's poetic drama, weaving into it a character sketch of Faust the seeker, damned (without redemption) by his own weakness. Narrative continuity and characterization are achieved, however, at the expense of the more mystical, philosophical dimension of Goethe's drama, expressed above all in its second part. For that we must turn to Schumann, whose *Szenen aus Goethes Faust* were assembled over some nine years (1844–53). He did not eschew the metaphysical scenes, and his setting of the apotheosis (in Part 3), including the 'Chorus mysticus', is of a quiet, reflective intensity which comes very close to a musical equivalent of Goethe's elevated poetry.

Yet Schumann's 'scenes' are essentially disconnected meditations, with little attempt at narrative continuity. It was above all a new kind of musical continuity – the technique of thematic transformation – which enabled Liszt, in his *Faust-Symphonie* of 1854–7, to transcend both Berlioz's character sketching (by revealing the unity underlying different facets of character – Mephistopheles as Faust's 'darker self' or Jungian 'shadow') and Schumann's deeper spiritual insights (by making them integral to the entire work). It is worth noting that Wagner's *Ring*, which parallels Goethe in many ways, made its points by similar means. At the very end of our period, in Mahler's Eighth Symphony, we find the summation of these concerns. It is perhaps the most powerful and moving response to Goethe, but here – significantly – there is a parallel invocation to God: as elsewhere in the art of the *fin de siècle*, the spirit of Romantic idealism has been rekindled in a heightened, intensified form.

Long before Mahler composed his Eighth Symphony, the need for an idealist counterweight to the positivist–realist orientation of art and thought had made itself felt. To many the panaceas offered by neo-classicism and scientism seemed inadequate, the one producing forms without substance, the other facts without meaning. The extraordinary growth of interest in Schopenhauer from the mid-1850s is indicative of a search for new meaning, for an alternative idealist, but secular, mode of thought. It argues a disenchantment with the 'phenomenal' world analysed by science in favour of a 'noumenal' world proposed, but regarded as unknowable, by Kant. The noumenal was given a highly specific interpretation by Schopenhauer, identified as a single, undifferentiated drive, impersonal and destructive, which he called the 'will'.

In Book 3 of *Die Welt als Wille und Vorstellung* he outlined the special role of art as a means of penetrating beyond the phenomenal world to a knowledge of those mediating and representational 'ideas' in whose disinterested contemplation we are released temporarily from our enslavement to the will. For a permanent release we must await death. Music is given special privilege within Schopenhauer's system. As the only non-representational art, it speaks directly of the noumenal – is indeed its major representation in the world of phenomena. 'The composer', argued Schopenhauer, 'reveals the innermost nature of the world, and expresses its profoundest wisdom, in a language that his reasoning faculty does not understand.'

Schopenhauer's philosophy, ignored for most of his lifetime (he died in 1860), was congenial to many late nineteenth-century artists in its atheism, its pessimism, its 'discovery' of a sexually motivated unconscious, its attunement to Darwinian theory and in the leading role it assigned to art. In the 1850s it was already contributing to a fundamental change of direction in Wagner's work and thought, though it seems likely that Wagner's discovery of Schopenhauer was a recognition of something he already knew or sensed: the resulting change in his aesthetic, that music should embody rather than serve the drama, was less a total contradiction of earlier theory, let alone practice, than a shift of emphasis, a means of subsuming his earlier position into something larger.

Wagner's change of thinking under Schopenhauer's tutelage was articulated in such later writings as *Zukunftsmusik* (1860) and *Beethoven* (1870), but more significantly it was given glorious expression in the later stages of the *Ring*, in *Tristan* and in *Parsifal*. Bryan Magee points out not only that *Tristan* is: 'a sort of musical equivalent of Schopenhauer's doctrine that existence is an inherently unsatisfiable web of longings, willings and strivings from which the only permanent liberation is the cessation of being', but also that the work celebrates an affinity between the two involvements of ordinary life which, in Schopenhauer's philosophy, bring us close to the noumenal – sexual love and music.[22] Magee demonstrates further the extent to which the verbal imagery of Wagner's text is itself often poeticized Schopenhauer, 'a fusion of insights from a great philosopher with the art of a consummate musical dramatist'.

In due course the combined influence of Schopenhauer and Wagner would trigger the thought of Nietzsche, though Nietzsche's transformation of Schopenhauer's underlying concepts was radical to the point of being oppositional. There is a line of succession here – Schopenhauer, Wagner, Nietzsche – which had a most powerful impact on *fin de siècle* art. Each of them opened up new vistas for later artists, composers and writers. In certain instances, notably Thomas Mann and Gustav Mahler, the combined influence of all three was decisive in shaping their art as well as their beliefs.

Schopenhauer was not, of course, the first to assign privilege to music's non-representational character, but his influence was undoubtedly a factor in the idea's ascendancy in the late nineteenth century. Music was valued 'avant toute chose' for its 'suggestive indefiniteness', its mysterious affective power, its message 'too profound for words'. This notion of music's primacy developed towards extreme formulations at the end of the century, as in Nietzsche's remarks on the 'supreme revelation of music', beside which we feel the 'crudeness of all imagery and of every emotion that might be adduced by way of analogy'[23] or Pater's famous dictum that 'all art aspires towards the condition of music'.

Yet a contrary view developed in parallel. Schopenhauer's contemporary and rival Hegel had assigned a very different status to music within his philosophy. For Hegel too art was a mode of cognition and revelation, but his 'placing' of it was very different. Above all, art was a means of unveiling the absolute idea through a progressive illumination of its sensuous appearance, its beauty. As such it paralleled at a lower level the acquisition of knowledge through conceptual thought. The stages of progressive illumination were defined for Hegel not only through historical epochs but through a hierarchy within the art forms themselves, taking us from 'symbolic' art, characteristically represented by Egyptian architecture, through the 'classical' art of Greek sculpture to the 'Romantic' arts of painting, music and poetry, themselves arranged in a hierarchy that places music below poetry. Accordingly, and in direct antithesis to Schopenhauer, 'absolute' music was less revealing of the world than music allied to poetry.

Superficially the nineteenth century journeyed from Hegel's position to Schopenhauer's, from a point where the composer looked to poetry to one where the poet looked to music. But in reality both positions co-existed throughout the century, coming into sharp conflict in the debate between absolute and programme music, between formalism and expressivism. This was the central issue of late nineteenth-century music aesthetics, and it extended beyond such critics and historians as Karl Brendel and Eduard Hanslick to engage some of the leading composers of the age. They too contributed to the verbal polemic: Liszt, who sought a renewal of music through its 'inner connection with poetry'; Brahms, who defended the dignity of instrumental music; Wagner, who took his initial stand on a musico-poetic fusion (*Oper und Drama*) but later (*Zukunftsmusik, Beethoven*) affirmed the primacy of music.

There is indeed a reformulation in Wagner's later writings. Yet, as Dahlhaus has convincingly argued, the result was not two contradictory theories but a single 'two-fold' theory, a recognition that music may serve and be conditioned by the drama on a compositional level while determining and initiating it on a metaphysical one.[24] In this sense we might regard Wagner's later position as a reconciliation of competing nineteenth-century theories about the status of music.

Yet it was also a recovery of much more ancient insights. 'Rhythm and melody follow the words', said Plato. And at the same time, 'Rhythm and harmony find their way to the innermost places of the soul'.

AUTHORITY AND REFORM

The central issues in a social history of European music during this period may perhaps be focussed by considering two polemically related countries on the edge of Europe. Russia and England, an unlikely pairing in many respects, shared more than their imperial ambitions in the nineteenth century. They were the only major powers whose governments were stable enough to withstand the revolutionary pressures that came to a head elsewhere in 1848. The reasons were of course very different. Russia's stability derived from a tradition of autocratic control which had not yet been seriously challenged. Nineteenth-century Russia was still a feudal country, agrarian in economic base, localized as to civic law and government and with a court society and higher gentry isolated from the rest of the people. In England, on the other hand, the middle class was already an established political force which, following the constitutional rights achieved by the Reform Bill of 1832, had little inclination to foment a revolution.

A further parallel was a shared sense that they were on the periphery of European affairs. This was a shaping factor in the political, intellectual and cultural profiles of both countries, but again an opposition underlies the parallel. With established and respected traditions of philosophy and literature and a recent history of constitutional reform, England was the envy of many European intellectuals in the nineteenth century and had little reason to lack confidence. Indeed, the later Victorian years saw her long-standing tradition of national independence degenerate at times into an unhealthy chauvinism. English art and thought responded constantly to influences from Europe, but the nature of the response was again an assertion of independence. At its best it resulted in a unique synthesis of movements and positions which would have been incompatible on the European mainland; at its worst it reduced European achievements to the status of passing fashions – ideas to be tried for size.

Russia, by contrast, agonized over western Europe, wrestling with an inferiority complex which led her either to embrace the West uncritically or to reject it fiercely. Since the Petrine reforms, the question of a correct stance towards Europe dominated Russian thought and politics, culminating in the conflict between Slavophiles and Westernizers. The issues raised by Chaadayev's *Philosophical Letter* (published in 1836) and Kireevsky's *On the Character of Western*

Civilization and its Relationship to Russian Civilization (published in 1852) continued to reverberate through the 1860s, but inexorably the debate about Europe became fused with a more radical debate about social theory.[25] The 'men of the 60s', such as Chernishevsky and Herzen, may have taken their inspiration from a Western cult of reason, but they sought solutions far more uncompromising than those of the liberal bourgeoisie of the West. They were committed to a radical programme of social meliorism and engagement, and they expected art to play its part.

The artist was mostly ready to do so. The Russian intellectual, a figure largely created by the Petrine reforms and drawn mainly from the gentry, had adopted from the start a critical and alienated posture in relation to his society. And much more than in western Europe he was a figure of some importance – a visionary and prophet, a spokesman for his generation, the most powerful voice of opposition in a totalitarian and feudal state which would countenance no political opposition. The severity of the censor in Russia, as much a feature of the nineteenth century as of the twentieth, was really a reflection of the unusual importance attached to art and ideas.

The centrality of the poet and thinker was also argued in England, but mainly by poets and thinkers. The artist's role was inevitably less politically potent in a relatively free society whose reading public belonged mainly to a well-upholstered middle class. Censorship in England was directed less against the politically subversive than against the unpleasant or indecent in a society much imbued with an ethos of respectability.[26] It was religion that fuelled intellectual controversy in England. And it was religion too that tempered the indifference of the middle-class public towards the vast and ever-expanding ranks of the urban poor.

A proletariat in the modern sense was formed rather earlier in England than in France or Germany, and even as Victorian prosperity reached its height, the scientific-industrial advance was taking a high toll in squalor and deprivation. There was of course a critique. Both Carlisle and Ruskin supported the Chartists in 1848, and many of the novelists of the age addressed the social injustices that accompanied industrialization. But the dissenting voice was usually accommodated within an overriding confidence in progress, grounded in those middle-class values to which the Victorian artistic and literary establishments were firmly welded. There was little room for the more radical social critique, essentially disinterested, which emerged in Russia.

There are two broad themes here – the dialogue with Europe and the status and role of the artist in society – and they form a useful framework for the study of musical life in England and Russia. In Russia the Slavophile-Westernizer argument found a musical counterpart of sorts in the rivalry between Anton Rubinstein's Russian Musical Society and Mily Balakirev's circle, known as the 'Mighty Handful'. That rivalry may be understood at least partly through the 'blank page' concept of Russian history and culture which recurred constantly in the writings of Westernizers and Slavophiles alike, though they viewed it in very different ways. For the Westernizers the blank page was a drawback; for the Slavophiles it was an opportunity.

There was a comparable dual response to the 'blank page' of music history. Rubinstein was intent on filling it as rapidly as possible with an excellent copy of the best European models. Balakirev, on the other hand, sought to exploit the lack of tradition in a positive way – to draw a new picture. The Balakirev circle was committed, then, to modernism as well as to nationalism, or rather it took its stand on a fusion of the two. In short, the rivalry was centred as much on a conservative-modernist debate as on a cosmopolitan-nationalist debate.[27]

No such rivalry would have been conceivable in England, where the dialogue with Europe already had a lengthy history and where musical composition had settled into a comfortable acceptance of established European (specifically German) styles. Handel, Mendelssohn, Spohr and Brahms all called the tune at different times. Two things conspired to maintain this position: the aspiring composer in England had little choice but to travel abroad for an adequate training; and, even more important, music had been held in such low esteem for so long by the dominant classes that foreignness had come to be regarded as fashionable. Both these conditions obtained in Russia, too, but there they met with resistance.

And that is the nub of the matter. It has been argued that the German stranglehold on nineteenth-century English music is not an issue, since the German tradition was in reality a *lingua franca* available to all.[28] This view fails to recognize deeper changes which accompanied the expressive aesthetic of the Romantic era. Before the nineteenth century, great music could indeed arise from a stylistically derivative 'project of excellence', in harmony with the religious or political establishment. In the nineteenth century it demanded an (implicitly critical) 'project of greatness'. There was such a project, informed variously by social commitment, nationalist ideology and modernist ambition, in Russia, where the composer was integral to a wider intellectual world. It was conspicuously absent in England.

When we come to consider the status of the composer within these two societies, it may be worth noting that both Russia and England lacked that sense of a continuously evolving musical tradition which we find in Germany and France, for all their political disruption. In Germany music-making remained centred on court institutions well into the nineteenth century – even into the second half – and it was only gradually absorbed by a middle-class culture. In France the political and social transformation was more abrupt, of course, but the centralization of musical life meant that its institutions either survived political upheaval or soon resumed their activities 'under new management'. In both cases there was underlying stability and continuity for a musical establishment mindful as much of the composer as of the performer and listener.

In England a flourishing court and aristocratic patronage of music declined rather earlier than in France and Germany and well before a modern institutional framework had been built up. There was a gap in English musical life between the effective demise of aristocratic culture and the emergence of a fully fledged middle-class concert life. The composer in particular lost his place at the centre of an active and developing musical tradition. Accordingly music was more easily appropriated by, and contained within, a dominant middle-class culture than in either France or Germany. The modernization of musical life which took place from the late eighteenth century remained essentially a one-sided affair, favouring 'consumption' over 'production', cultivating the performer and the listener at the expense of the composer and accepting more or less uncritically the commodity status of the musical work.

Closely identified with the musical establishment, and accepting the bourgeois values it represented, the English composer seemed happy to submit to the modest demands of nineteenth-century public taste and had little contact with any wider, more critical, intellectual world. It is idle, though tempting, to speculate that in a different environment a composer of Sullivan's talent might have been a major creative figure. As it is, he is better known for *The Lost Chord* and the Savoy operas than for his more ambitious symphonic output. If *The Lost Chord* epitomizes the easy sentiment and pretension of the Victorian age, the Savoy operas celebrate its complacency and insularity, albeit in music of genuine wit and inventiveness.

Operas by Michael Balfe, Vincent Wallace and Julius Benedict had made some headway in England, registering something of the general growing interest in national opera in Europe round the mid-century, but their modest success was eclipsed totally by the collaboration of Gilbert and Sullivan. Musically their operettas owed much to Offenbach. Like him, they directed their satire both to the clichés of contemporary theatre and to the foibles of contemporary society; but they never attacked the basic structure of that society and they avoided the sensual and the vulgar – the 'improprieties' – which played a part in French operetta. In some ways the Savoy operas were the most important, and most representative, musical works of the Victorian age. They were entertainments directed to a conservative, and above all a respectable, middle-class audience whose values they mocked gently but in reality applauded.

For a radical critique of those values we need to look beyond the middle-class establishment to the new culture of the working class – increasingly literate (owing partly to adult education programmes, mechanics' institutes and lending libraries) and increasingly politicized. In nineteenth-century England a new kind of urban popular music developed, associated above all with industrial folksong and the rise of the music hall. There was an affirmative, propagandist art here too – much more jingoistic than anything in Gilbert and Sullivan – but equally there was a critical strand, capable of opposing the ruling ideology with a candour unavailable to official art. As the century drew to a close the music hall lost something of this critical edge, as well as much of its bawdiness. It became the *locus* for new social alignments between working- and middle-class audiences, rather as the public concert had brought together upper- and middle-class audiences a century before.[29]

In contrast, in Russia the trappings of a middle-class concert life were transplanted to a society without a middle class and the leading nationalist composers were members of the gentry following professions other than music. The absence of an industrial world, moreover, not only precluded an urban working-class culture but kept the remarkably rich and diverse rural folksong traditions of Russia relatively unpolluted by urban influence. Folksong was tapped by Balakirev's circle for ideological reasons, as one of several means of promoting a nationalist aesthetic. But the 'Russianness' of their music amounts to rather more than this: it rests on an association of potent national symbols and images (drawn from history and literature) with highly specific and innovatory musical gestures, some with roots in folksong and Orthodox chant, some drawing on a more recent tradition of art music (Glinka) and some making their point precisely through their defiant rejection of any kind of orthodoxy.

Russian composers were in the vanguard of musical nationalism in the nineteenth century. They also made some of the most powerful statements on behalf of social and political reform, notably through their contacts with such progressive intellectuals as Vladimir Stasov, a protégé of the influential writer and social critic Belinsky. Musorgsky in particular identified closely with the realist and populist movements of the later nineteenth century, sharing with Stasov, Chernishevsky and others a conviction that the primary role of art was to illuminate, and ultimately to change, social realities, and giving such views persuasive musical expression in works of the calibre of *Boris Godunov*. Musorgsky was indeed the supreme modernist of the late nineteenth century, not least because his quest for a new 'realism' in music resulted in a decisive break with (and not just a modification of) the norms and conventions of musical language. It is to Musorgsky that we must look for the first signs of those radical new methods which would become widespread in the early years of the twentieth century.

It is intriguing to consider the polarity of cultures represented by two countries on the edge of Europe – an 'advanced' industrialized one and a backward feudal one. England led the way in developing a middle-class musical establishment which of its nature encouraged the commodification of the art. Her major composers were part of the dominant culture, accepting of its values and even in some cases of the peripheral status it assigned to music. Russia, by contrast, 'borrowed' a middle-class musical establishment to which her major composers, as amateurs and aristocrats, did not fully belong. This made possible a more high-minded and serious, or alternatively a more iconoclastic, view of music; it also enabled the composer to take his place more centrally within the wider intellectual community, committed as it was both to nationalism and to modernism.

This polarity may help us to see in sharper focus some of the major developments taking place in Europe itself. England and Russia allow us to view separately, and with particular clarity, two strands held in dialectical opposition in France, Germany and to some extent central Europe, where they generated an increasingly explosive force-field. We have on one hand a musical life (and a music) which affirmed and legitimized, with no significant critical element, the bourgeois ascendancy; and on the other an aesthetic of modernism, a 'pioneering' music responsive neither to the professional establishment nor to public taste and taking as its sole authority the individual creative genius's urge for self-expression.

NATIONALISM
In the political life of Europe as a whole the decline of idealism after 1848 was related to an increasing cynicism in international relations – a so-called 'Realpolitik'. European arteries hardened after the revolutions, and a succession of wars of limited and specific goals ensued, after some 30 years of relative peace between, if not within, the nations. Underlying many of these struggles was increasing friction between the strengthening national identities of the Germans and the Slavs; and underlying that was an irreconcilable tension between nationalist aspirations and the long-established and still powerful dynastic principle. Even before German and Italian unification, the Habsburg Empire was beginning to split at the seams. Yet the forces of inertia were strong, and it was only with World War I that the dynasty finally collapsed, along with the Hohenzollerns and their neighbours the Romanovs, the first victims of a socialist revolution.

Liberalism was in essence replaced by nationalism as the driving political force of the later nineteenth century. Moreover the two ideologies, while stemming from the same root, were conceptually at odds as the nationalist demand for collective freedom clashed with the individual freedom to which liberalism still paid lip service, even after 1848. Ernest Gellner demonstrated in a penetrating study that the spirit of political nationalism has a solid underpinning in social history, and it is no coincidence that the second half of the nineteenth century was the highpoint both of bourgeois ambition and of nationalist aspiration.[30] Nationalism dominated the political arena and exerted an insistent cultural pressure too as the century turned. Just as early nineteenth-century artists had given cultural support to liberalism, so their successors gave their support to the nationalist cause. And that included composers.

Before the nineteenth century, specific compositional styles often had national (or more precisely, geographical) roots. But the shaping forces of these styles were social or regional rather than national, and the styles were seldom confined by national frontiers. Nor did this change totally in the later nineteenth century. There was still a measure of common currency in the musical language of leading composers from all over Europe, for the give-and-take of stylistic influence was no respecter of nations. Even when composers turned to folksong and folkdance, they usually did so for exotic local colour (Bizet) or beauty of melody (Bruch) rather than for nationalist publicity.

None the less the thrust of political and cultural nationalism played an increasingly important role in determining the profile of musical styles. This was not just a matter of promoting nationalist programmes, as did Verdi in *Nabucco* and *I lombardi*, Wagner in the *Ring* and *Die Meistersinger* and even Brahms (obliquely) in the *German Requiem*. It amounted to an increasing stylistic differentiation between national traditions and to a more possessive attitude to 'national' material. The Italian operatic tradition became more exclusively the preserve of the Italian composer, and it was clearly differentiated from French lyric opera and German Romantic opera. Puccini was the last major composer to earn his living as a repertory opera composer within the Italian tradition. By then nationalism in a belatedly industrialized Italy was encouraging on the one hand a selfconscious modernity (*verismo*) and on the other a wave of heritage gathering, associated both with folklorism and neo-medievalism (a movement inspired above all by D'Annunzio) and with a renewed interest in a 'golden age' of national music, especially that of Monteverdi. The underlying motivation for this later nationalism was arguably a loss of confidence in the primacy of Italian music, as Austro-German symphonism seemed to dominate almost every musical culture.

In the late nineteenth century the great sonata-symphonic succession was increasingly perceived as a national achievement, a triumphant expression of German culture, and that perception was in turn projected back to the Viennese Classical style. The notion of a continuously evolving national tradition was at least partly a constructed notion, and since the symphonic line was regarded, even at the time, as a mainstream, its ascendancy and privilege were also viewed in national terms. There were of course other ways in which the nationalist impulse asserted itself in German music. As in Italy, it involved the celebration of a heroic past (the motivations underlying the Breitkopf editions are symptomatic) as well as a glorious present (witness the Bayreuth Festival Theatre). Much more than in Italy, however, it was inseparably linked to the triumph of the bourgeois establishment, arguably given its culminating and most characteristic musical expression in the tone poems and operas of Richard Strauss.

At the turn of the century Strauss was regarded as the voice of the avant garde, the leading representative of the 'New German' music, and as such he was widely imitated by composers all over Europe. Yet in the end history has deemed Mahler a more truly innovatory figure. Like Puccini, Mahler was in some senses the end of a long and seminally important line; but unlike Puccini he also stood at the beginning of another line. It is perhaps ironic that the great symphonic tradition should have reached its apogee in the music of an Austrian Jew born in Bohemia, though that very fact has some explanatory power. Ultimately the anguish of Mahler's music is not just personal. Much more than in the works of Strauss, the crisis within liberal bourgeois culture was given its supreme musical expression in his output. Here, at the heart of a disintegrating symphonic heritage, were the birth-pangs of a new musical world.

Not surprisingly, emergent and reviving national movements elsewhere viewed the operatic and symphonic traditions of Italy and Germany first as models and then as imperialisms to be repelled. In the case of northern Europe (Scandinavia) the second stage was distinctly muted as the nationalist drive allied itself to a thoroughgoing renewal of the symphonic tradition, culminating in a magnificent 'second growth' of that tradition in the music of Nielsen and Sibelius – and to some extent beyond them. German symphonism was a well-established cultural import in Scandinavia in the later nineteenth century, but younger symphonists could also look to Russia for inspiration and seemed able to avoid the expressionist crisis that stifled the genre in Germany and central Europe. Intriguingly, the symphonic awakening on the northern edge of Europe was also able to recapture something of the lofty idealism and humanism of Beethoven, easily adopting a tone that no longer seemed available to composers in Austro-Germany.

The resurgence of French nationalism in the 1870s in some ways followed a more characteristic pattern. Born of anti-German feeling and fostered by the Commune and the Third Republic, it was expressed initially through a revival of instrumental music heavily indebted to German achievements before a new voice was found – or rather an old voice recovered. An ambivalence towards German music characterized a good deal of the music composed in France in the late nineteenth century and early twentieth. The music of Franck and his circle was the most obviously responsive to German influence. Significantly, however, it was d'Indy, one of Franck's most talented pupils, whose teaching did most to point a younger generation of composers towards an earlier age of French music and a possible source of renewal.

Ultimately this rediscovery of ancient roots proved a more fruitful way forward than Massenet's pursuit of the more immediate native inheritance of Gounod and Ambroise Thomas. If the concept of a 'French tradition' has any meaning, it describes something of the cool, poised, classical quality, essentially Latinate, which is reinstated in the music of Fauré and later of Ravel. There is no lack of intensity in their music; it can be exuberant and poignant. But its subjective emotional qualities are harnessed by the lucidity of its forms. There is above all an explicit rejection of the excessive emotionalism which these composers identified with German late Romanticism, and it is significant that neither had any truck with Wagner. By contrast Debussy inherited something of the more general French ambivalence towards German culture, especially Wagner, and the defiant assertion of national values in his later music was genuinely hard-won. His music in any case transcended the national perspective. In technical terms it embodied a synthesis that would prove of the greatest value for the later history of musical language, influencing profoundly an entire generation of composers from Russia, central Europe, England and Spain.

The appearance of national schools in England and Spain in the early twentieth century echoed the French pattern. Musical creativity in both countries was all but submerged by foreign influence in the late nineteenth century – German and Italian respectively. The 'renaissance' in each case took place in the 1890s and was expressed initially within the terms of existing stylistic norms (Elgar, Pedrell), before seeking new directions (Vaughan Williams, Falla). As in France, those new directions amounted in part to the rediscovery of earlier 'national' traditions, notably from the sixteenth century, but there were other factors. One was the example of modern French music, in which new tonal languages (involving modal modifications of classical tonality together with Russian-influenced chromatic symmetries) had already been achieved. Debussy's Spanish idiom was important not least for its impact on modern Spanish music (Albéniz and Granados as well as Falla), while the 'pastoral modality' of Vaughan Williams and Holst owed much to both Debussy and Ravel.

A further factor was the folksong revival of the early twentieth century. It had touched French nationalism too in the regional accents cultivated by d'Indy as well as by such lesser figures as Guy Ropartz and Déodat de Séverac. But for Vaughan Williams and Falla folk music became a means of reshaping rather than merely colouring or inflecting musical language. Folk music was regarded as the most potent, though by no means the only, musical symbol of the nation, and it was collected with a respect and concern for scientific accuracy in marked contrast to the revivalist (and revisionist) approach of nineteenth-century pioneers. The seed of this association between folksong and nationalism lay mainly in early nineteenth-century German thought, notably in Herder, but it bore musical fruit above all in eastern and central Europe.

By the 1860s the equation of nationalism and modernism in Russia had already created a powerful and radical alternative to the forms and conventions of west European music, the true value of which would become apparent only in the modernist movements of the early twentieth century. In east central Europe, on the other hand, emerging national styles initially preserved a much closer dialogue with the Austro-German tradition of which (in some cases) they had been an integral part. For much of the nineteenth century, organized musical life in these lands, especially in the eastern Habsburg Empire, was still responding to processes of social and cultural modernization which had swept rapidly eastwards from western Europe in the early years of the century. The cities of east central Europe were establishing, in short, the institutional base on which a thriving national music might later be built; but it was only in the Czech lands that there was a national 'school' that was in any sense a match for the achievements of the Russian nationalists.

Even in the Czech lands a middle course – still close to Austro-German norms – was largely adopted, at least until the advent of Janáček. Janáček's music was in turn part of a much more general 'renaissance' of music in east central Europe in the early twentieth century. In Hungary there were Bartók and Kodály, in Poland Szymanowski and in Romania Enescu. Each began by responding to and mastering the musical idiom of a powerful 'mainstream'. Distinctive national styles crystallized as they increasingly identified that mainstream with Austro-German hegemony and sought to break free from its powerful grip. The 'renaissance', then, involved an element of liberation, but by the early twentieth century there were other models available, notably the achievements of the Russian nationalists and of modern French music. Janáček's music is strikingly close to Musorgsky's in its underlying concerns though the question of direct influence is moot. Bartók, Szymanowski and Enescu each worked through a period of fascination with modern French music, and in all three cases the influence penetrated some way below the surface of their music.

In the end, though, it was folk music – discovered or rediscovered – that did most to help the younger generation of composers forge a new language. Bartók and Kodály turned to a Magyár peasant music largely overlooked by earlier Hungarian nationalists, including Liszt, and Bartók in particular went on to explore at the deepest level the meeting-points between that music and the most progressive techniques of Western art music. Enescu moved from an early conventional treatment of popular Romanian music, notably in his two Romanian Rhapsodies and the *Poème roumain* (stylistically similar to Dvořák's Slavonic Rhapsodies), towards a unique synthesis of Western techniques and indigenous features drawn from the rich veins of Romanian church and folk music. Szymanowski too, in an astonishing *volte face*, built his later music on the remarkable folk music of the Tatra mountains, responding in his own way to the celebratory nationalism of a newly independent Poland.

Nationalism was indeed the motivating force behind this awakening throughout east central Europe. Yet it is in the nature of things that national schools have a limited lifespan. They escape provincialism only by admitting the influence of the wider contemporary world. Aspiring towards the universal, they in turn lose touch with those indigenous qualities which had defined the ideological commitment in the first place. National styles retain their vitality only when the indigenous and the universal are held in balance, and it is worth noting that these pioneering figures of the early twentieth century achieved greatness in part by subsuming the nationalist impulse within a larger project, whether the realism of Janáček, the conquest of the exotic (of which the Tatra music was a variety) in Szymanowski or the East–West synthesis of Bartók and Enescu. Significantly, in the aftermath of these early twentieth-century awakenings, music in east central Europe lost touch with a nationalist aesthetic and entered the wider world.

In one country the nationalist impulse produced not only far-reaching changes in musical language, but a radical challenge to the aesthetic foundations that had underpinned European music since the Renaissance. The musical voice of modern urban America took shape not in the concert hall but in oral traditions with quite different ethnic roots and in no sense dependent on European notions of aesthetic autonomy, of 'great' or even of durable works. Unlike the industrial folk music of western Europe, an American popular idiom – jazz, blues and Tin Pan Alley – created its own, largely self-consistent musical culture, sharply defined and essentially separate from Western traditions. Unlike those traditions, moreover, it was a music willing to engage openly with modern mass culture and the culture industry. In due course it would reach Europe, beginning an American cultural imperialism that has since swept all before it.

In classical music too America challenged the assumptions underlying European music. Charles Ives was in the mould of European nationalists at least to the extent that he built his work round national images drawn from history, mythology and landscape and used vernacular musical material as a powerful symbol of the nation. But the 'American-ness' of his work arguably went some way beyond this. It was partly his 'frontier' spirit, but even more it was his untroubled acceptance of a stylistic pluralism which had no ironic intent and therefore questioned the notions of wholeness and unity which are a prerequisite of aesthetic autonomy, that essentially European project which set out to separate art from life. In Europe too these notions were being questioned, notably by Mahler, but there the process carried with it an enormous sense of loss.

In one important respect the music of Ives shared a good deal with that of Janáček, Bartók and other early twentieth-century nationalists. All these composers turned to folk and popular materials, with their own capacity to reset the norms of musical language, at the very time when existing norms were already beginning to disintegrate. Technically their music posed a direct challenge to the language of traditional tonality, sacrificing conventions which had survived intact for several centuries of Western music. They were not of course alone in this. The system of triadic tonality which had developed from the Renaissance onwards and which had been formalized in the Classical period was called into question by composers all over Europe and beyond at the turn of the century. Increasingly that system conceded to the explorations and experiments of modernism.

EARLY MODERNISM
The revolution in musical language in the early twentieth century was greater and more radical than at any earlier period in the history of Western music. Only at the turn of the fourteenth and fifteenth centuries had there been a remotely comparable break in continuity. In seeking to explain the rise of modernism in music we may at least begin by referring to immediate contextual factors. Music did not after all exist in a vacuum, and if it is true that in the later stages of bourgeois culture it came close to realizing its 'project of autonomy', then that autonomy was itself partly a social phenomenon. The early twentieth-century musical avant garde stood in a particular relation to the broad sweep of culture at a critical moment in history. Its very isolation was an implicit commentary on its political, social and intellectual contexts.

World War I and its outcome formalized politically the triumph of nineteenth-century nationalism, though it by no means quelled the continuing aspirations of the disadvantaged nor, for that matter, the imperialist ambitions of the successful. On one level music reflected the underlying political feeling, as strengthening Austro-German influences provoked nationalist movements throughout Europe, culminating in a crop of national styles in the early years of the century. The differentiation between these styles could easily be exaggerated, however. In reality their contribution was less to promote individual 'schools' than to allow a collective alternative to German late Romanticism.

In this respect the major impetus came from Russia. Russia preserved a genuine independence from Austro-German styles in the nineteenth century, and her achievement informed – in a precise, technical way – the new tonal languages developed by such early twentieth-century composers as Debussy, Bartók and Stravinsky. These new tonal languages were one manifestation of early modernism and they stood in clear opposition to the expressionistic atonality and serialism developed by the Second Viennese School. Viewed reductively, the musical legacy of nineteenth-century nationalism was above all the crystallization of these two polarized lines of development, each culminating in radical changes in musical language in the early twentieth century.

Yet underlying this divergence was a single, more generalized and all-embracing development: the questioning and ultimately the rejection of long-established norms of musical language. That development in the end crossed national boundaries and ignored political differences. Nor is this surprising, since the advance of political nationalisms, promoting separatism, could scarcely conceal the ever more homogeneous and international character of a modern urban bourgeois culture. Within this Europe-wide culture there was, however, a further division in musical style, more radical than the differentiation between national traditions. This was the increasing separation of 'serious' and 'popular' styles determined by the commodification of culture accompanying the age of capital, by the values and ideology of the ascendant middle class and by the increasing evidence of fragmentation and breakdown within that ascendancy.

The divergence between the popular and the significant is best explored in relation to an age-old tension between music's subservience to function and its desire for autonomy. That tension may exist within any work in any period, but different historical settings will prejudice the outcome. In general the history of Western music described an increasing autonomy. The development of 'rational' notational and compositional systems, disengaged from the non-musical world, made autonomous artistic statements possible, and this 'autonomy character' in turn encouraged a degree of social disengagement on the part of the composer, a process that reached a decisive stage in the nineteenth

7. *Edison's Improved Phonograph in the press gallery at Crystal Palace, recording 'Israel in Egypt' at the Handel Festival in 1888; engraving from the 'Illustrated London News' (21 April 1888)*

century. Yet even then autonomy remained an elusive goal. Middle-class concert life was almost as much a ritual or ceremony as the church service and as such made its own demands on the composer. His new-found independence was real enough, but it was not so much a total emancipation from social constraints as a more overtly critical, even defiant, attitude towards these constraints. And since defiance is itself a mode of dependency, the autonomy could only be partial.

At the very least we could claim that the 'project of autonomy'[31] found its most congenial historical setting in the bourgeois ascendancy of the nineteenth century. The project of autonomy in turn fostered a project of greatness and it was that which increasingly prised apart the popular and the significant. A differentiation between popular and 'refined' or 'subtle' art was not of course unique to the nineteenth century.[32] But there is a distinction between an *ars subtilior* which responds to an élitist-taste public and an avant garde which makes its own statement. In the second half of the nineteenth century some progressive music was beginning to take on the aspect of an avant garde.

Stylistically Wagner and Offenbach might be taken to represent this divergence within the musical world of a newly emancipated middle class. Wagner, together with the Liszt circle, established a programme (and rhetoric) of modernism whose ramifications for musical language extended beyond generic innovations (music drama and symphonic poem) to embrace major changes in the nature of musical continuity.[33] Few composers of the late nineteenth century and early twentieth were untouched by these technical changes, nor indeed by the avant-garde pretensions of a 'music of the future'. In due course the changes and the pretensions were the pathway to a music composed in blatant defiance of the market-place. Schoenberg's Society for Private Musical Performances was in this sense a powerfully symbolic moment in the development of the avant garde, shutting out the populace in the interests of preserving musical language from further degeneration.

Offenbach's aim was rather to look back, to recapture something of the character of eighteenth-century comic opera, and his musical language returned to the conventions of an earlier age in a spirit at once nostalgic and parodistic. His achievement was scarcely less influential than Wagner's, leaving its mark on English and Viennese operetta before eventually finding its way into the American musical of the twentieth century. And here the transition from a 'conventional' music responsive to public taste to one that succumbed to an ever more voracious 'culture industry', responsive only to an anonymous mass market with all its attendant apparatus, was already well under way.

The rise of an alienated avant garde in the early twentieth century would have been inconceivable without the parallel emergence of this 'culture industry', manipulative of conventional language. Indeed they were really two sides of the same coin, the one increasingly critical of the commodity status which the other increasingly affirmed. The polarized relation between them is even to an extent encoded stylistically. In the late nineteenth century, popular music drifted away from progressive art music while at the same time preserving a definable relationship to it, whether of parody, imitation or wholesale (but recontextualized) appropriation. But there was a more deep-seated common ground between the two kinds of music in the shared archetypes of march, popular dance and folksong.[34] Essentially popular music, these archetypes underpinned much of the high art repertory too, even when refined almost beyond recognition. As they diverged into modernism and mass culture, both kinds of music tended to lose touch with these underlying archetypes. In short, the divergence took place within a single middle-class culture, albeit an increasingly fragmented one.

If the profile of modernism comes into clear focus in relation to a commercial mass culture (in the mode of a connected antithesis), closer examination of that profile reveals that it is itself made up of sharply contrasting features. The economic expansion and technological revolution that characterized the last quarter of the nineteenth century effectively transformed the existing cultural order (that of the solid bourgeois world and its accompanying social relations) into our present more fragmented order of cultural modernity, an order that both extended bourgeois values and undermined them. This promoted on the one hand a probing, progressive art – literally an 'avant garde' – which continued the bourgeois faith in science and progress, and on the other an anarchic, iconoclastic art that opposed the bourgeois world with its commitment to rationality, albeit from within the confines of that world.

Modernism in the former sense was an aesthetic response to modernity. In music we might associate it with the pioneering figure of Busoni; but in very different ways this faith in progress was equally apparent in the innovations of Ives and of Schoenberg. Modernism in the latter sense was a model of dissent, a 'necessary nihilism' (Nietzsche), anti-bourgeois and anti-convention, even in some cases anti-modernity. In its more extreme formulations it was a retreat not only from science and positivism but from the entire inheritance of post-Renaissance European art. In music it was pioneered above all by Satie. (It touched other composers too in the early twentieth century, but it would be given its most comprehensive expression in the radical aesthetic developed by John Cage and others in the aftermath of World War II.)

Implicit in much of this discussion is the shaping role of geography. The primary context for modernism was of course the modern city, not only as the home of artistic institutions but as the 'frontier' of technological and intellectual development. And if the crisis in urban bourgeois culture was in essence Europe-wide, the expression of that crisis was influenced heavily by local contexts. Inevitably the modernisms of Berlin and Paris were very different in nature; and they were both different from the modernisms of St Petersburg and Vienna. It is easy to see that there was a political background for the 'progress-ive' music composed in Berlin – by Strauss as well as Busoni – and for the later (postwar) embrace of a socially engaged and socially committed art in that city. Equally the modern movement in St Petersburg – Skryabin as well as Stravinsky – owed much to the collision of two cultures which was peculiar to Russian intellectual and artistic circles at the turn of the century.

The crisis of modern culture was perhaps most acute in Paris and Vienna, and these cities afford us the sharpest contrast. Where modernism in Paris was eclectic, diversified, detached and experimental, in Vienna it took the form of an inward-looking crisis of expression, alienated from the public, jealous of the integrity of art and protective of its 'truthfulness'. These are broad generalizations, to be sure, but they point to a genuine difference in 'tone' and one that extended far beyond music. To a marked extent composers in both these cities were an integral part of wider intellectual communities. They participated in the cultural debate and took their place within the 'circles' that promoted new ideas in science and philosophy as well as in the arts. Above all they were responsive to a wave of artistic 'movements' (complete with manifestos) which were through their very existence – let alone their programmes – a selfconscious affirmation of the 'modern'.

Debussy and Schoenberg were the true revolutionaries in the musical worlds of Paris and Vienna, and both were shaped at least in part by the two cities' cultural ambiences. Debussy's revolution was closely attuned to the ideals of symbolist poets such as Verlaine and Mallarmé and impressionist painters such as Monet; his pursuit of mystery, suggestion and dream was in essence a quest for greater reality, both objective and psychological, a reality which registered the illusory nature of any categories designed to specify the world and which promoted rather the importance of the ephemeral, the immediate sense-impression, in our understanding both of nature and of ourselves. It was a form of 'aestheticism', and even when it acquired a moral tone, as in some of Debussy's later music, it never lost its emotional reticence, its discreet sense of aesthetic 'play' and its distance from the unfettered subjectivism of the late Romantics.

In a similar way, Schoenberg's concern to protect a logically, inevitably developing musical language from debasement finds a context in Viennese culture, notably in the campaigns against the corruption and distortion of verbal language which were wielded by Karl Kraus in *Die Fackel*. Equally it invites comparison with the deliberations of Wittgenstein and the 'Vienna circle' on the competence and limits of language, on the relationship between the 'word' and the world. More specifically, Schoenberg's explosion of traditional tonality by invoking an intensely subjective 'law of feeling' to replace the decaying conventions of tonal harmony closely paralleled the 'expressionism' of Oscar Kokoschka, just as his later containment of that law of feeling within a neo-classical frame recalls (though less obviously) the architectural principles of Adolf Loos.

The very mention of such names tempts us to propose Vienna as the major, though by no means the only, crucible of modernism. It was caught between the Germanic and the Slavonic worlds, and its rapid modernization in the late nineteenth century conjured into life much that was new in the history of ideas and of imaginative culture. Klimt, Schnitzler, Hugo von Hofmannsthal and the 'Ringstrasse' architects might be added to our earlier list. So too might Freud, whose achievement was both culture-specific – Viennese to the core – and at the same time magnificently expressive of the universal change in interpretative perspective which accompanied modernity.[35] That change in perspective – suppressing conventional causality, with its emphasis on the linear and sequential, and promoting instead a multi-layered, spatial causality – is everywhere apparent in modernist art, much of which openly cultivated the irrational, the immaterial and the inorganic, placing 'reality' in the realm of the imagination.[36]

Why, then, was Vienna so central to early modernism? Carl Schorske, in a wide-ranging analysis, has explained it partly in social and political terms, identifying in Vienna an early playthrough of the later much more widespread crisis and subsequent demise of the liberal bourgeois ascendancy in Europe.[37] But there is a parallel (or alternative) explanation, proposed by George Steiner, Steven Beller and others.[38] To a marked extent the pioneers of modern art and thought in Vienna, in almost every discipline including music, were Jews. Several ways of understanding this Jewish element have been proposed: Jewish alienation as a model of modernist alienation; the Jewish rebirth (following emancipation) as a model for modernist rebirth; and, more recently, the assimilationist transference of Jewish educational and religious practices into Western culture. However we understand it, there is a real issue here: the inescapable and intriguing fact that modernism in Vienna was predominantly a Jewish movement.

The changes in musical language in the early years of the century yield some of their meaning to an investigation of immediate conditioning factors – political, social and intellectual. At the same time the radical nature of those changes invites a more aggressive interpretation. It is problematical in any art of any period to rob it of its competence by explaining it solely in contextual terms. It is the more problematical in music, an essentially symbolic language, and during a period that espoused the idea of aesthetic autonomy. There need be no conflict between an acceptance of the specificity of art histories and the recognition that those histories are socially (and ideologically) informed, since there is an all-important gap separating the aesthetic response from the social cause.[39] Modernism in every art form involved a major displacement of language and immanent materials, in terms specific to itself. The aesthetic response was in part an opportunity – an invitation to create a new style, or to subvert an old one.

It is arguable that music focusses the problem of language more clearly than any other art form, because its capacity to register change in any other way (for example through its subject matter) is more limited. There is then an internal history to be traced, of increasing chromaticism and dissonance, and its outcome was the overthrow of conventions that had prevailed for several centuries, surviving with ease innumerable changes of style. Whatever the variety of different modernisms – Debussy, Bartók, Stravinsky, Schoenberg – they all had this powerful, if negative, feature in common. That has a bearing too on the periodization of musical modernism. The underlying attitudes associated with the movement – avant-garde pretension, dissent, withdrawal from the public, experimentalism and so forth – are not period-specific, though they increased exponentially from the 1850s. But the change in language, the essential defining feature of musical modernism, can be pinned down rather narrowly to the period from about 1890 to 1914, with the major 'break' occurring in 1907–9 in music by Schoenberg (and his pupils), Skryabin, Busoni and Bartók. And since the change was so fundamental, it is incumbent on cultural theory to investigate causality at a deeper level than the immediate context.

Such an investigation really lies beyond the brief of a 'social history' of music, but a few speculative pointers might nevertheless be offered, by way of a postlude to this chapter. We would take as a starting-point the growing autonomy of the aesthetic sphere in European history, which might be identified as the essential mark of the bourgeois cultural order, with both social and intellectual origins in the Enlightenment. That autonomy was supported by the development of independent artistic institutions which came with the bourgeois emancipation, and also by the progressive 'rationalization' of the institutions themselves and of the materials and language of art.[40] In music this process reached its ultimate goal in the 'idea of absolute music', at which point autonomy became itself the content of the musical work, and the imperative was to achieve 'unity' and 'wholeness', the prerequisites for a closed, independent statement of substance. The autonomy of the aesthetic sphere in turn enabled that sphere to criticize, even to oppose, the social sphere, and it is that critical stance which Adorno and others have taken as a defining characteristic of modernism.[41]

In a penetrating analysis of early twentieth-century culture, Peter Bürger goes a stage further.[42] He has suggested that an avant garde (as opposed to modernism) could arise only when this project of autonomy was finally complete and the ineffectiveness of its critique of society had become apparent. The avant garde, then, represented an attack not on society but on the 'institution of art', itself a bourgeois product whose basic mode was autonomy. The aim of the avant garde, argues Bürger (provocatively), was paradoxically a reintegration of art and society through a subversion of the form and language of an autonomous bourgeois art, and its principal tools were the fragment, the montage, the 'non-organic' work.

It is interesting to reflect on the possible application of such ideas to music. Analysis at this level presupposes of course that art, specifically music, is a mode of cognition, that it reveals the historical and social totality of which it is a part and that it encodes social and ideological change through its forms as well as its subject matter. Viewed in such terms the project of autonomy in European music takes on additional significance. That project was in effect a long-range, over-arching development, in which notational and compositional systems gradually acquired the capacity to create an independent order in time, given expression in the closed, unified musical work. Because of its internal cohesion the musical work could map our real existence in time on to an ideal, symbolic plane, which moreover enabled precisely that resolution and closure unavailable during our real existence. It is surely significant that the major strategies by means of which this ordering of time was achieved – a tonal structure based on triadic harmonies, a thematic argument based on the principle of development and a rhythmic process based on metric invariance – began to crystallize in the early Renaissance, fused into an indivisible whole in the style of Classical tonality and splintered again in the early modernist period.

The revolution in musical language which we identify as early modernism was in part, then, a subversion of the holistic strategies of European music. Structural harmony, thematic fragmentation (and subsequent reconstitution) and metre were all ways of shaping time, of relating part to whole and of generating direction in music. Their subversion, in a manner that harmonizes well with Bürger's remarks on the avant-garde aesthetic of the 'non-organic' work and the 'fragment', suggests an epochal change of direction in European music, notably in relation to its specifically European character.

At the same time it would be misleading to suggest that early modernism may be explained (away) as the end of the European era. The complexity of the modernist period is at least partly caused by the shadow of the old falling constantly on the new. Recent creative praxes suggest, moreover, that we may need to reappraise modernism from the perspective of our own so-called postmodern world – pluralist and decentred, involved with texts rather than works, with excellence rather than greatness. From this perspective (which will itself no doubt be subject to later review, modernism may well come to be understood less as the repudiation of bourgeois culture than as its culmination, the summation of an essentially Romantic enterprise in which a small handful of highly valued creators working largely within a single tradition spearheaded us into the future.

NOTES

[1] E. Hobsbawm, *The Age of Revolution* (London, 1977).

[2] For a detailed study of the links between Romanticism and liberalism, see N. J. Rosenblum, *Another Liberalism: Romanticism and the Reconstruction of Liberal Thought* (Cambridge, Mass., 1988).

[3] Notably in C. Dahlhaus, 'Neo-Romanticism', *Between Romanticism and Modernism*, trans. M. Whittall (Berkeley, Los Angeles and London, 1980), 1–18.

[4] Dahlhaus, op cit.

[5] See L. O'Boyle, 'The Middle Class in Western Europe', *American Historical Review*, lxxi (1966), 827–45.

[6] W. Weber, 'The Muddle of the Middle Classes', *19th-Century Music*, iii (1979–80), 175–85; see also Weber, *Music and the Middle Class* (London, 1975).

[7] K. Pendle, *Eugène Scribe and French Opera of the Nineteenth Century* (Ann Arbor, 1979).

[8] See F. P. Bowman, 'Illuminism, Utopia, Mythology', *The French Romantics*, ed. D. G.

Charlton (Cambridge, 1984), 76–112; also F. W. J. Hemmings, *Culture and Society in France 1848–1898* (London, 1971).

[9] For a useful discussion see A. Menhennet, *The Romantic Movement* (London, 1981).

[10] H. Raynor, *Music and Society since 1815* (New York, 1976), 33.

[11] D. Cooke, *I Saw the World End: a Study of Wagner's 'Ring'* (London, New York and Melbourne, 1979).

[12] See Cooke, op cit, 21.

[13] T. Hamerow, *Restoration, Revolution, Reaction: Economics and Politics in Germany, 1815–1871* (Princeton, 1958).

[14] E. Sagarra, *Tradition and Revolution: German Literature and Society, 1830–1890* (London, 1971).

[15] G. Turbow, 'Art and Politics', *Wagnerism in European Culture and Politics*, ed. D. C. Large and W. Weber (Ithaca, NY, and London, 1984), 134–66.

[16] R. Myers, *Modern French Music: its Evolution and Cultural Background from 1900 to the Present Day* (Oxford, 1971).

[17] C. Dahlhaus, *The Idea of Absolute Music*, trans. R. Lustig (Chicago and London, 1989).

[18] A. J. P. Taylor, *The Course of German History* (London, 1961).

[19] C. Dahlhaus, *Realism in Nineteenth-Century Music*, trans. M. Whittall (Cambridge, 1982).

[20] Quoted in the introduction (by A. S. Byatt) to the Penguin edition of George Eliot's *The Mill on the Floss* (London, 1979).

[21] Quoted in C. von Westernhagen, *The Forging of the Ring*, trans. A. and M. Whittall (Cambridge, 1976).

[22] B. Magee, *The Philosophy of Schopenhauer* (Oxford, 1983).

[23] F. Nietzsche, 'On Music and Words', trans. W. Kaufmann; pubd as an appendix to Dahlhaus, *Between Romanticism and Modernism*, 103–19.

[24] C. Dahlhaus, 'The Twofold Truth in Wagner's Aesthetics', *Between Romanticism and Modernism*, 19–39.

[25] See A. Walicki, *A History of Russian Thought from the Enlightenment to Marxism* (Oxford, 1980).

[26] See F. M. L. Thompson, *The Rise of Respectable Society: a Social History of Victorian Britain, 1830–1900* (London, 1988).

[27] For a full discussion see R. C. Ridenour, *Nationalism, Modernism and Personal Rivalry in Nineteenth-Century Russian Music* (Ann Arbor, 1977).

[28] N. Temperley in the introduction to *The Romantic Age 1800–1914*, ed. N. Temperley, Athlone History of Music in Britain (London, 1981).

[29] See D. Russell, *Popular Music in England 1840–1914: a Social History* (Manchester, 1987).

[30] E. Gellner, *Nations and Nationalism* (Oxford, 1983). More specific studies, for example of German nationalism, have argued rather that the origins of the nationalist impulse may be located in the persistence of old élites and the alleged failure of political modernization; for a discussion see H. James, *A German Identity: 1770–1900* (London, 1989).

[31] The phrase, used several times in this chapter, is J. Habermas's in 'Modernity: an Incomplete Project', *The Anti-Aesthetic: Essays on Postmodern Culture*, ed. H. Foster (Washington, DC, 1983); also *The Philosophical Discourse of Modernity: Twelve Lectures by Jurgen Habermas*, trans. F. Lawrence (Oxford, 1987).

[32] See W. Wiora, 'Of Art Music and Cultural Classes', *Music and Civilisation: Essays in Honour of Paul Henry Lang*, ed. E. Strainchamps and M. R. Maniates (New York and London, 1984), 472–7.

[33] For a discussion of the rhetoric of modernism in Wagner and Liszt, see W. Weber, 'Wagner, Wagnerism, and Musical Idealism', *Wagnerism in European Culture and Politics*, 28–71.

[34] See J. Marothy, *Music and the Bourgeois, Music and the Proletarian*, trans. E. Rona (Budapest, 1974).

[35] S. Marcus, *Freud and the Culture of Psychoanalysis* (Boston, 1984).

[36] In the introduction to *Modernism 1890–1930*, ed. M. Bradbury and J. McFarlane (Harmondsworth, 1976).

[37] C. Schorske, *Fin-de-siècle Vienna: Politics and Culture* (New York, 1981).

[38] G. Steiner, 'Le langage et l'inhumain', *Revue d'esthétique*, new ser., no.9 (1985), 65–70; S. Beller, *Vienna and the Jews 1867–1938: a Cultural History* (Cambridge, 1989); see also *Jews, Antisemitism and Culture in Vienna*, ed. I. Oxaal, M. Pollak and G. Botz (London, Boston and Henley, 1987).

[39] For a discussion of this issue see J. Wolff, *Aesthetics and the Sociology of Art* (London, 1983).

[40] M. Weber, *The Rational and Social Foundations of Music*, trans. and ed. D. Martindale, J. Riedel and G. Neuwirth (Illinois, 2/1958), examines the concept of rationalization in some of its

multiple meanings; Weber was a pioneer of systematic sociology, whose work ranged widely over economic systems, world religions and social institutions, and his music sociology should be viewed as part of a much broader project.

[41] Adorno's clearest formulation of these ideas is in his incomplete final work, *Aesthetic Theory*, trans. C. Lenhardt (London, 1984).

[42] P. Bürger, *Theory of the Avant-Garde*, trans. M. Shaw (Manchester and Minneapolis, 1984).

Chapter II

Germany: the 'Special Path'

JOHN DEATHRIDGE

It is generally agreed that the 1848–9 revolution was a pivotal event in German history. It is also agreed (or at least difficult to deny) that 1848–9 was a turning-point in German music. In February 1848 the overthrow of Louis-Philippe in France reverberated in parts of Germany on a scale unknown since the revolution of 1789. In the same month Franz Liszt left behind his career as a world-famous piano virtuoso and settled in Weimar where, among other things, he invented a new musical genre: the symphonic poem. Soon after the Paris uprising and the successful revolutions in Vienna and Berlin (March 1848) the Dresden royal Kapellmeister Richard Wagner began – earlier than is often realized – to plan an epoch-making work that eventually became the *Ring*.[1] Just over a year later Wagner was on the barricades. But the Dresden revolution (May 1849) ended in disarray and he was forced into exile for eleven years. Ironically, the revolution made him famous: his works were performed all over Germany and his writings widely read and debated. The critic Richard Pohl ruefully remarked in 1853, 'Wagner has made more of an impact on Germany by not being there than he ever did when he was'.[2]

Few German composers were not affected by the spirit of 1848–9. Lortzing wrote a revolutionary opera *Regina* that presents in the opening scene armed workers on strike for higher pay and, among other things, unruly buccaneers who rob the small daughter of a factory owner. These were not meant as gestures on behalf of the underprivileged of course, but as a warning that proletarian elements could unbalance what was in essence a revolution of the middle classes.[3] (*Regina* is one of Lortzing's worst operas and was mercifully never performed in his lifetime.) Spohr noted in his catalogue of works that his String Sextet in C (op.140) was written in March and April 1848 'at the time of the glorious revolution of the people for the liberty, unity and grandeur of Germany'. He helped the citizens' militia to man the barricades in Kassel and actually attended the Frankfurt National Assembly,[4] that talkative and ill-fated body of (mainly) upper-middle-class representatives who mistakenly thought

8. The ruins of the Zwinger and old opera house in Dresden after the revolution in May 1849; lithograph (1853) by W. Bassler after F. Brauer. 'Towards eleven o'clock in the morning [Sunday 6 May]', wrote Wagner, 'I saw the old opera house, in which I had conducted the last performance of Beethoven's Ninth Symphony a few weeks before, go up in flames'

that persuasion and consensus would win the day over military force. Even a shy and outwardly conservative man like Robert Schumann was not indifferent. 'I'm pleased', he wrote to the critic Franz Brendel on 17 June 1849, 'that you sometimes make people realize just how strongly my music is rooted in the present.' On the same day he wrote to his publisher that, if anything, his newly composed Four Marches (op.76) were 'republican', insisting on larger print than usual for the date (1849) on the title-page. 'For once', he wrote in a letter to Liszt, 'the date is significant.'[5]

However, it is one thing to say that the 1848–9 revolution left an indelible mark on the history of Germany and its music, and quite another to say what kind of mark it was. Schumann's caveat 'for once' in his letter to Liszt and the oversize date on the title-page of the Four Marches were meant to convey that the work was an exception. In fact by going out of his way to suggest that the connection of the music with events in the outside world was unusual, Schumann was as close to the world of the literary Romantics as he had always been. A theory of musical Romanticism has yet to be written and clearly it would diverge in many respects from its counterpart in literature. Still, Schumann, Liszt and Wagner, for all their interest in the revolution, never seem to be far from the illusion argued, so to speak, by Romantic poetry that only art can transcend a 'corrupting appropriation'[6] by politics. Wagner's assertion in 1851 that he had never 'really' been part of the failed Dresden uprising, but that his 'participation in the political world of appearances had by its very nature always been artistic'[7] may sound unbelievable – more a sop offered to the conservative forces in Germany he wanted to appease than a truthful account. Yet from the point of view of a Romantic idealist it was a perfectly logical claim.

The effect of the 1848–9 revolution on German society was no less paradoxical. A. J. P. Taylor's exasperating comment that with 1848 'German history reached its turning-point and failed to turn'[8] helped to set the agenda among historians after World War II for the theory of the so-called *Sonderweg* or 'special path'. In essence this is the idea that with the failure of the revolution, modern Germany embarked on a unique and fateful course that led inevitably to Hitler. At issue, according to more critical historians, are the alleged sins of omission of the German bourgeoisie; among others they include civic quietism and cultural pessimism, prompting the banal diagnosis that the German middle classes suffered from a 'star-struck and supine response to authority'.[9] Germany in other words lacked the allegedly typical 'Western' pattern of development historians claim to find in the liberal-democratic models of Anglo-American and French societies. In order to see the true complexity of German history, however, it is important to ask what did happen rather than what did not. The press, the back-room pressure groups, the network of voluntary associations (Vereine) and the vociferous debates between different bourgeois factions in the public arena were hardly signs that the middle classes had totally succumbed to the power of a military and aristocratic élite.

The point is well taken. If militarism and feudal authority managed to retain their hold over German society largely because of sharp divisions among the bourgeoisie that seemed to offer little hope of stability, this is not to say that the middle classes lacked initiative or that the legal and institutional changes they brought about amounted to a failure of nerve. On the contrary, even in the relatively small world of music the activities of men like the critics Franz Brendel and Louis Köhler, who founded the important Allgemeiner Deutscher Musikverein between 1859 and 1861, as well as more prominent figures like Wagner and Liszt, made heroic efforts to change the face of the music profession in Germany in the years after the 1848–9 revolution. When Wagner first wrote his lengthy *Plan for the Organization of a German National Theatre for the Kingdom of Saxony*[10] in 1848, this hard-headed and decidedly unromantic analysis of the relation between music and state was greeted with derision by court officials. When it was finally published in 1871, the year of the founding of the German Reich, it was as topical as ever and rightly seen as a precursor of the Allgemeiner Deutscher Musikerverband founded in

Berlin by Heinrich Thadewalt in 1872 – the first organization to represent the interests of professional musicians that was securely anchored by the legal reforms of the new Reich. (Wagner's *Plan* raises many issues, including the erosion of standards by business interests and the incompetence of unqualified heads of artistic institutions, that are perhaps even more relevant in the late twentieth century than they were in the mid-nineteenth.)

The famous partisan battle, too, between the admirers of Brahms on one hand and those of Wagner and Liszt on the other looks at first sight like yet another destabilizing controversy. Yet it at least drew the attention of sections of the public not normally interested in 'higher' artistic squabbles to the fact that German music was not just an imitation of foreign culture (most opera and publishing houses were dominated by French and Italian imports or imitations of them) but a serious and modern tradition in its own right, albeit one still under the shadow of feudal corporate patronage. With the foundation of the Reich in 1871 the controversy subsided, only to be replaced by calls for state subsidy (including the financing of Bayreuth) that largely fell on deaf ears. Still, the sloth of the new Reich in affairs of art in the 1870s and 1880s did not deter a figure like Hans von Bülow (who gave himself the sardonic title 'Court Pianist and Court Kapellmeister of the German People')[11] from energetic propaganda on behalf of German music as a cause in itself. Indeed, by declaring an allegiance to both the Brahms and the Wagner–Liszt parties (to the great annoyance of Wagner) Bülow deliberately set an example of constructive propaganda that was meant to reconcile serious differences of opinion and – whether in aesthetics or politics – to prove that unity of purpose was more important than internecine debate.

Even before World War II and the consolidation of the 'special path' theory, historians were inclined to be over-glum about the social context of nineteenth-century German music. In general, Ernest Newman wrote in the first volume of his Wagner biography, the professional composer at the turn of the century 'was held in the old patronising disesteem as a plebeian whose function it was to provide entertainment for his betters, to take orders from Court Intendants and speculative impresarios and be thankful for any bone that was flung to him'.[12] By mid-century, according to Newman, conditions for composers and performers were not much better:

> In all but two or three of the largest German cities the orchestral and vocal material and technique must have been quite inadequate for the performance of anything but the simplest works . . . As late as 1853, Liszt, after having produced at Weimar the earlier works of Wagner, had to complain to the Grand Duke Carl Alexander . . .

9. *Franz Liszt conducting the 35th Lower Rhine Music Festival in 1857; engraving. 566
performers took part in the Aachen festival which included performances of Handel's 'Messiah',
Schubert's 'Great' C major Symphony, Wagner's 'Tannhäuser' Overture and Liszt's Piano
Concerto in E♭ (soloist Hans von Bülow). Liszt's position, high on a podium in the middle of the
auditorium, is significant of the conductor's relationship to the different social groups in his audience
rather than to his performers (mostly out of sight in this illustration); the obviously more élite
members of the audience in the foreground are looking on with less than rapt attention*

that the forces at his disposal did not permit him to give the
representative operas of the day the kind of performances they
needed.[13]

There are more than a few echoes here of the Romantic notion of art
blighted by a philistine world. In fact the overall picture Newman
paints is so bleak that one wonders how musicians managed to do
anything enterprising at all. Sobering as the image is, however, it has
been overdrawn in many of its details to make the entrance of Wagner
into the world of German music, and his (in Newman's view) single-
handed struggle to 'save' German art from the forces of reaction, all
the more theatrically effective. The well-known 'fact' for instance that
Liszt conducted the first performance of *Lohengrin* in Weimar (1850)
with an orchestra of only 38 musicians – a ludicrously small number
considering the demands of the score – is a myth invented by
Newman.[14] Intent on seeing German art as a victim of feudal
backwardness, he quite forgot that Liszt had written to Wagner twice

(in the middle of July and on 12 August 1850) to say that the resident orchestra in Weimar was being augmented with outside musicians 'selon les exigences de la Partition'.[15]

With Liszt in Weimar, Spohr in Kassel, Franz Lachner in Munich and the lesser-known Joseph Strauss in Karlsruhe, some court theatres in Germany in the 1850s had varied and interesting repertories often built up with ingenuity in the face of the courts' conservatism. (After 1848–9 theatres under aristocratic patronage were modernized in the sense that they were run on more commercial lines, a change that made it doubly difficult to try out new and 'difficult' works.) A few bold spirits were less ready after the revolution, too, to sacrifice their independence on the altar of feudal authority. Spohr had the temerity to start legal proceedings against the Elector of Hesse in 1852 after he had been heavily fined for taking leave without permission (the case dragged on for nearly four years and in the end Spohr had to concede defeat). The fact that Liszt complained to the Grand Duke of Weimar at all is also a reminder that the relations of musicians with the court were not as one-sided as they used to be. Liszt was even arraigned in the conservative press for 'forgetting the duties imposed on him by his office'[16] as Grand Ducal Director of Music Extra-ordinary when, after conducting the first performance of Peter Cornelius's *Der Barbier von Bagdad* in front of an unsympathetic audience in 1858, he took it upon himself to applaud the composer and the singers. Worse, he persuaded the orchestra to applaud as well. Scarcely credible as this detail is now, the fact that the complaint was vigorously rebuffed by Franz Brendel in the progressive periodical *Neue Zeitschrift für Musik*[17] was a small sign that authoritarian cultural conservatism – a reflection of what has been called the politics of 'reaction' in Germany in the decade after the 1848–9 revolution[18] – was not suffered gladly by at least some sections of the middle classes.

MUSIC SOCIETIES AND VOLUNTARY ASSOCIATIONS

To see German music in the second half of the nineteenth century solely in terms of a prolonged battle between feudal villains and cultural heroes is to see it too much in terms of its own ideology: the valiant artist-philosopher locked in a desperate battle with the mighty Goliath of corporate philistinism; the creator of Promethean powers who can forge a timeless art of the future. These are just two scenarios in the Romantic imagination that have unconsciously influenced even sceptical observers who, surprisingly, have been reluctant to see German music in a more differentiated social context. Newman reserves only a few scathing words for the societies and voluntary associations (Gesellschaften and Vereine), for instance, that played a significant role in Germany's musical life, and one quite distinct from similar organizations in other countries, especially England. Another view is that, similar to the unfulfilled political aspirations of the bourgeoisie, musically active groups at a local level were unable to bridge the gap that separated them from imperial and civic authority; left in the lurch by state and city, their ideals merely 'drained away' into the social activities of the associations.[19]

The extent to which Germany's associative life has affected its political and cultural history since the latter part of the eighteenth century has admittedly only recently been realized. The associations provided the concrete link between individuals who had isolated themselves from their origins in the narrow confines of the traditional order and who felt attracted towards large and abstract groups – the Nation, the Educated, the Enlightened – that offered them a new identity.[20] The interests of the associations and those of the middle classes were not identical, but their interdependence is clear enough. Local studies of Augsburg, Hamburg and Weinheim, as well as more general accounts undertaken since, agree that the aspirations of the educated and propertied bourgeoisie, its family, personal and social ties, were crystallized by the associations at an informal, non-corporatist level. It has even been argued that through the varied activities of the associations – from charity and religion to sport and culture – the different groups of the bourgeoisie in Germany, in the absence of effective representation at state level, were actually able to come together as a class.[21]

Thus, far from being a poor substitute for state and municipal support, the associations that had been springing up since the beginning of the century to give some semblance of identity to groups of people who just wanted to get together and sing, or the music societies formed by philanthropic citizens to help local orchestras and conservatories, enjoyed greater independence and influence than is usually realized. Certainly, reliable contemporary observers were in no doubt that by mid-century this loosely structured and more or less informal promotion of music was significant. In 1855 the influential theorist A. B. Marx wrote:

> Now – after a lapse of half a century – there is scarcely a village without its singing association, and . . . almost every little town has two or three of them. In Berlin, there are some ten or twenty . . . Their tendencies and merits depend not only upon the qualification and views of their conductors, but also upon the fitness, perseverance, and energy of the members – a consideration which is . . . of still greater importance in respect to the aggregate meetings of the societies of different towns – those 'music festivals' which . . . have spread over the whole of Germany.[22]

It would be a mistake none the less to see the associative life that had begun to provide a widespread outlet for the musical aspirations of the

10. A procession at the National German Choir Festival held in Nuremberg in 1861; lithograph. The ambitious and well-rehearsed concerts that took place during such festivals were in a sense only a backdrop to the processions, flag-waving, speeches and gun salutes that accompanied them (the placards mark the individual choral societies, or 'singing associations', from all parts of Germany, particularly Bavaria)

middle classes by the middle of the nineteenth century as an arena for exclusively bourgeois interests. Indeed, the predominantly institutional character of music in the kingdoms, electorates, duchies and imperial free cities into which Germany was divided was probably why alternatives in the shape of informal collective musical activity within larger, and not only middle-class, groups outside the smaller ruling élites were more widespread in Germany than elsewhere. A. B. Marx's allusion to the 'tendencies' of the singing associations and the 'views' of their conductors also has political overtones. After 1848–9 the singing associations in particular were symbols of an endangered species of popular liberalism that consciously brought together all levels of society – including the inhabitants of rural areas and even occasionally members of the nobility – into a kind of democratic conviviality that meant more than just singing. This was not lost on the authorities who, in the reactionary climate of the 1850s, tried to hunt out the 'radical' elements. In 1851, for instance, the Prussian Ministry of the Interior received the following report which it acted upon immediately:

11. Title-page of Brahms's 'Ave Maria' (1861) for women's chorus and orchestral or organ accompaniment. The work was first performed in Hamburg (2 December 1859), under Brahms's direction, by his Frauenchor. The photograph (right) of four members of the choir, Laura Garbe, Betty and Marie Völckers and Marie Reuter, was still in Brahms's possession when he died

the demand for a democratic way of life lies at the root of many of these singing associations, especially as the personalities who are often at the helm of such associations offer no guarantees. Since radicalism is trying more and more to make its escape into the nooks and crannies of society where it is more difficult to hunt out, it would be highly desirable if, with governmental authority, these singing associations could be placed under observation.[23]

It is probably no exaggreation to say that the gradual transformation of the choral movement in Germany from a liberal into a decidedly reactionary force in the latter part of the nineteenth century was – in its initial stages at least – not unconnected with systematic government and police interference.

The reality of the societies and associations is not to be confused either with the nationalist sentiment and myth of community in such works as Wagner's *Die Meistersinger* and Brahms's *German Requiem* – a virtually irretrievable layer in these masterpieces that is hard to reconstruct now except in the most generalized terms. (It is no coincidence that they were first performed with great success in the late 1860s at a time of growing national consciousness culminating in the Franco-Prussian War of 1870.) The choral and social groupings in the last scene of *Die Meistersinger* could be interpreted as an affectionate parody in sixteenth-century costume of regular events like the Lower Rhine Music Festival – the most prestigious of the music festivals that had grown up in Germany by the second half of the nineteenth century.[24] And the sublime choral writing in the *German Requiem* is not as distant from the vocal style of worthy local singing associations as it might seem today. But Wagner spent valuable nervous energy in his last years thinking of ways to escape the clutches of the 'Verein-dolts' as he called them (implying not only the members of the notorious Wagner societies but the kind of person attracted to associations in general) and noted that in 'a business sense' an association 'is utterly unpractical: in a theoretic-moral sense there is nothing whatever to be said for it'.[25] Brahms's relations with choral societies (in Detmold and Hamburg for instance)[26] and every other kind of musical Verein were usually positive, if a little *gemütlich*; yet even he could bring himself to describe one of them, C. Riedel's singing association in Leipzig, as a 'swindle'.[27]

None the less Wagner well knew that to judge the societies and associations 'in a business sense' was to miss the point (though as far as the largely reactionary Wagner societies were concerned he was not mistaken about their questionable 'theoretic-moral' stance). In the absence of civic or commercial backing, the voluntary organization of interested parties was often the only way to keep initiative buoyant. This was as true of Bayreuth as it was of scholarly projects like the first Bach and Handel collected editions begun in the 1850s. Without the aid of non-commercial ventures like the German Bach and Handel Societies, founded in Leipzig in 1850 and 1856 respectively, these influential editions would not have materialized.

Between 1851 and 1885 the Leipzig firm of Breitkopf & Härtel, which printed and distributed the Bach and Handel editions, also relied on the good will and initiative of associations and individual scholars to embark on publication of the complete works of Palestrina, Beethoven, Mendelssohn, Mozart, Chopin, Schumann, Schubert and Schütz. Rightly described as 'the first serious and systematic attempt to establish the works of musical authors in a canonic way' that 'had the incidental effect . . . of canonizing the German tradition to which these composers belonged either in fact or by adoption',[28] the huge undertaking had obvious ideological implications. The fact that it valued archival precision less than it seemed to (many of the editions do not come up to the standards of even nineteenth-century methods of textual criticism) was a sign that it was not unaffected by the strong metaphysical element in nineteenth-century German historiography. Indeed, the rather abstract idea of a specifically 'German' music and the concept of a musical 'classicism' rooted in 'nature'[29] – two notions at the heart of nineteenth-century German writings on music that fuelled the immense editorial labour invested in the Breitkopf project – were not far removed in spirit from the traditional German ideology of the state common to, though differently expressed by, figures as diverse as Hegel and the much-misunderstood Leopold von Ranke.[30] This is not to say, of course, that the absolutism and the 'vulgarised Lutheran belief in authority'[31] at the core of the German state's ideology that claimed to be above parties and persons had the same pervasive influence on music as it did on politics. Nor is it possible to ignore the irony that in establishing German music as a part of this idealistic view it was the tenacious enterprise of individuals rather than the desultory and often non-existent support of state institutions that played the decisive role.

THE PRINCIPLE OF NATION AND THE NEW GERMAN SCHOOL

Not even the most tentative outline of a social history of German music in the second half of the nineteenth century can entirely avoid the labyrinthine subject of German idealism. Hegel's provocative speculation that with Romanticism art had come to an end to make way for a 'higher' form of awareness – philosophy – was certainly one reason for the marked decline of his influence on aesthetics that began even before the 1848–9 revolution. This is not to say that artists and philosophers stopped thinking in grandiose historical terms or that they simply brought Hegel down to earth by deflating his 'absolute philosophy' (to use Ludwig Feuerbach's mocking term) into something more human and immediate. Rather, the quasi-religious tradition of metaphysics was reclaimed, so to speak, for the physical realm – 'the purely human', as Wagner liked to call it – merely as if Hegelian dogma had unnaturally separated the two.[32] More important still, the rebellion against Hegel produced a variety of aesthetic and historiographical schemas which not only ensured the survival of art as a human activity without diminishing its philosophical significance, but also had a major impact (lasting to the present day) on the way the history of Western music as a whole was perceived.

None the less Hegel's spirit continued to haunt his critics. The invasion of the 'absolute' by empirical categories led to uneasy paradoxes which, to put it bluntly, were best resolved by an appeal to patriotic instinct. This accounts for the famous suggestive phrases in Wagner's sayings about German art and his own work that oddly mix the nebulous and the concrete (e.g. 'purely human', 'endless melody', 'musical deeds made visible', 'invisible theatre'). A greater identification of idealism in music with tangible objects (e.g. mass-produced busts of famous composers) and even cities or towns like Leipzig and Bayreuth, which became famous as centres of musical progress, also reflected the conflation of the abstract and the real. The empirical labours invested in the Breitkopf collected editions, for instance, served to build a huge monument to German idealism that was close in spirit to what have been called Germany's 'secular temples'.[33] Indeed, a comparison with landmarks like, say, the 'Walhalla' in Regensburg or Ernst von Bandel's Hermann Monument in the Teutoberg Forest, both of which idealize figures of the past (or rather allow them to step out of it) with an overdose of national pride that refuses to admit essential distinctions of historical importance, is not as absurd as it first appears. Nor of course is the parallel with the relatively long-standing notion among intellectuals of a 'national music' that mixed a quasi-religious worship of 'art' with high-minded ideas about the 'natural' affinity between the music of the people (in the form of Lutheran chorales) and the German masters of instrumental music.[34] At mid-century the idea even began to assume (as the resounding success of Wagner's *Die Meistersinger* was to prove) the status of a popular middle-class belief. The disparate icons in Germany's cultural temples could only be harmonized by the principle of nation that stood for growth as well as unity.

Yet an apocalyptic tone – nothing less than the spectre of Hegel's notion about the 'end' of art – was still noticeable in writings on music that seemed to exhort the German tradition to remain steadfast by conjuring up visions of its imminent demise as well. 'Our age is the end of music as we have known it in the past', Brendel proclaimed in 1850.[35] No less rhetorically A. B. Marx asked whether music had 'reached the boundary of progress – the end? or will creative genius reveal itself in a new form?'[36] (Views similar to those of Brendel and Marx still echo through the writings of modern cultural critics, including Brendel's negative remarks on the limitation of the concert repertory to a 'small group' of 'recognized classics' and the allegedly ever-shortening attention spans of audiences.[37]) A slogan like *Zukunfts-musik* or 'music of the future' – the invention of which is usually wrongly attributed to the conservative critic Ludwig Bischoff[38] – was tossed around in fiery controversies almost as if the existence of civilization itself was at stake. Hoping to reconcile the opposing factions by reaffirming the principle of nation, Brendel claimed that the counter-slogan *neudeutsche Schule*, or 'New German School', could act as a truce in the war of words – a polemical battle he found so unsettling that he even likened it to the religious fanaticism rife in Germany in earlier times.

Brendel's concept of the New German School is really a seductive paradox that offers what appears to be at first sight a generously broad view of history and nations while at the same time casually flinging together three essentially dissimilar figures – Berlioz, Liszt and Wagner – in the name of the 'German spirit'. Brendel explained the odd inclusion of two foreigners by arguing that the group represented the 'universal' side of German music: the fusion of the 'plain introspection' of the north with the 'passion' of the south. Thus the 'new' German music was the old mixture of the 'purely' German (Bach, Beethoven) and Franco-Italian influence on German music (Handel, Gluck, Mozart) raised to a higher power. Liszt and Berlioz had been 'nourished' and 'strengthened' by the German spirit. It was only logical, therefore, that their works should find a haven in Germany (among other things, Brendel was thinking of the success of Liszt's 'Berlioz Week' held in Weimar in November 1852) and that together with Wagner, the 'pure' German, they should be the standard-bearers of Germany's musical future.

Brendel launched his idea of the New German School at a significant moment in the history of musical modernity in a speech to a conference of musicians in Leipzig in 1859 to mark the 25th anniversary of the *Neue Zeitschrift für Musik*.[39] Leipzig, which Wagner once referred to as 'little Paris'[40] (as if to say that the focus of European culture was at last beginning to move into Teutonic realms), was certainly the right place for a disquisition on modern music and Germany's musical past. For other centres like Cologne, the home of Bischoff's implacably revisionist *Niederrheinische Musik-zeitung*, the speech must have looked like the misguided musings of a local patriot trimmed with touches of enlightened universalism. But in the context of Leipzig it was bound to make a mark. The city was regarded both as a focal point for musical progressives and a centre where the historicist image of German music was being forged – a reputation reflected by the policy of Breitkopf & Härtel, which launched not only its epoch-making series of collected editions in the 1850s and early 1860s but also *the* modernist work of the nineteenth century: Wagner's *Tristan*.

What is remarkable about the amiable sophistry of Brendel's speech, however, is that it proved to be so resilient. The label 'New German School' has never vanished from the history books (perhaps because historians have been understandably reluctant to discover exactly what Brendel meant by it). And even if it is by no means the only reason why we still tend to see late nineteenth-century music as so many satellite 'nationalisms' revolving round a large German Romantic planet, it has not been without influence in helping to establish the primacy of the German tradition in Western music as a powerful historiographical norm. The familiar critical defence of certain early nineteenth-century Italian operas, for instance, in terms of 'progress' and 'originality' that supposedly transcend the genres in which such composers as Rossini and Donizetti were obliged to write is to come to those operas with decidedly Germanic expectations.[41] With the evolution of the 'special path' theory, too, music and society in Germany in the second half of the nineteenth century have tended to become the Jekyll and Hyde of European history: the one a paragon of virtue and the other a burgeoning monster. This is nowhere more obvious than in the heated controversies about Wagner's role in Germany's alleged historical 'aberration' where, by taking either a morally naive view of Wagner or a simplistic one of German political history, the adversaries inevitably reinforce a dual mystique.

'REALISTIC CREATIVITY' AND THE BAYREUTH FESTIVAL THEATRE

No matter how one tries to unravel the contradictions of nineteenth-century German music and its reception, its almost ostentatious ambition to flee into a realm of 'pure' subjectivity and aestheticism on one hand and its undoubted success in the 'real' world on the other is a paradox that is less easy to explain than it looks. (The argument that the allure of the music simply offers a welcome 'utopian' escape from social discontent is consoling but ultimately facile.) Attempts to 'historicize' the turbulent intellectual façade of German music – the debate about the validity of 'programme' music for instance – usefully expose blatant contradictions in the arguments about aesthetics but none the less tend to reaffirm the bland and comforting notion of artistic 'autonomy' they set out to question. Indeed, one of the ironies of this attractive approach (which, in spite of ignoring the thorny question of the ideological role of music in German history, at least has a critical edge) is that it tends to distort the peculiarity of the tradition it idealizes. Even Carl Dahlhaus, who could hardly be accused of ignoring the elusive paradoxes of German idealism, accepted that there was a 'vast distance' between music in the second half of the nineteenth century and the social and technological developments that gained momentum in Europe after 1848–9.[42] It is hard to see, however, why music should have been so remote from reality at just that moment in history when leading musicians and writers on music – especially those in Germany – were more articulate about and critical of the world around them than they had probably ever been before.

In this context the word 'Romantic' has done more than its fair share in fostering the illusion that the gap exists. It is no coincidence that Schumann, who was more sensitive to social issues than he is usually given credit for, was sceptical of the label.[43] And after 1849 Wagner jettisoned it altogether. (By 1851 he doubted whether even *Lohengrin* could be described as 'Romantic' and withdrew the designation 'grand Romantic opera' from his later revisions of *Tannhäuser*.[44]) One has only to compare, say, the two versions of Schumann's Fourth Symphony (1841 and 1851), Liszt's early piano music with the Sonata in B minor (1852–3) or Wagner's early Romantic operas and the *Ring* to detect a significant change of outlook – greater objectivity and inevitability of design, for instance, and more unity between detail and large form. This was not so much a return to the spirit of the Classical style as a desire for a kind of 'pure' Romanticism that had something systematic and – unlikely as it sounds – even unromantic about it. Indeed, Shaw nearly said as much when he insisted that the political allegory of the *Ring* would have had more 'coherence' without the traces of Romanticism left over from its early conception in the 1840s.[45]

The obsession with (often abstruse) inner cohesion in Schumann's late music; the thematic transformations in Liszt's symphonic poems and their crushingly triumphant finales; Wagner's interlocking leitmotifs and philosophy of salvation: this represented a modern and selfconsciously affirmative aesthetic markedly different from the elusive world of the early Romantics and more in tune with the age of 'positivism' than it is usually taken to be. The career of Max Maria von Weber – the first son of Carl Maria (named after the hero of *Der Freischütz*) and an international expert on, and imaginative writer about, Germany's rapidly expanding railway system from the middle of the century to his death in 1881 – can almost be taken to symbolize the difference. It was even said that this extraordinary man, author of a posthumous collection of allegorical pieces called *Of the Rolling Winged Wheel* had discovered 'the poetry of rails'. Max Maria, in the words of a contemporary biographer, was 'typical of a phenomenon decisive in our culture: the transition from the sphere of fancy and thought to that of applied activity, realistic creativity'.[46]

To speak of 'distance' at all in late nineteenth-century art, including music, is to ignore, among other things, its passion for allegory that played a major role in reconciling the age of science with some highly ambivalent feelings about it. Among German musicians, Wagner was by far the most resourceful example of 'realistic creativity' who not only invented an inexhaustible store of allegory that translated the fears and hopes of a rapidly changing modern industrial society into art, but also set out to realize his ideals with an energetic and innovatory pragmatism that few artists have equalled before or since. He first had the idea of a special theatre for his works as early as 1850 in Zurich, where he envisaged a temporary building made of planks that could be pulled down as soon as the performances were over.[47] In the 1860s he had more concrete plans for Munich, where he planned to build not only a permanent theatre on the Gasteig, a promontory by the River Isar in full view from the city centre, but also a magnificent new street that would lead from the Briennerstrasse, where he lived, through the royal gardens and directly to the theatre on the other side of the river over a specially built bridge. The new road alone would have meant dismantling part of the central district of Lehel. Understandably, politicians and large sectors of the public were appalled at the disruption and expense the project would have caused, and the plan came to nothing.

True to Wagner's vision of a unified Germany, and to his patron King Ludwig II, he eventually chose to build his festival theatre in Bayreuth, a small town that was both in the middle of Germany and in Ludwig's domain of Bavaria. Partly rural in character, the town was quite unlike Munich, and even less like such large cities as Leipzig and Berlin, which had expanded rapidly under the impact of Germany's highly effective process of industrialization and growth of population. (Between 1850 and the early 1870s the population of Germany had increased by six million.[48]) Nor was the town a spa or a holiday resort that had to submit to pleasure-seeking crowds in summer – an audience for serious art that Wagner considered to be 'quite the wrong sort'.[49] In other words, Bayreuth symbolized the destiny of what Wagner hoped would eventually become a wholesome nation free from the deleterious effects of modern civilization. It also represented the fulfilment of an artistic dream on which that destiny supposedly depended. 'Now that we have saved the body of Germany', Wagner wrote grandly to Ludwig II after the Franco-Prussian War of 1870, hinting broadly at the proposed Bayreuth project, 'what we have to do next is to fortify the German soul.'[50]

With the onset of the economic depression in 1873, however, Wagner began to diagnose a fatal disease in German culture that darkened his philosophy to a point where, after Hitler, it has become

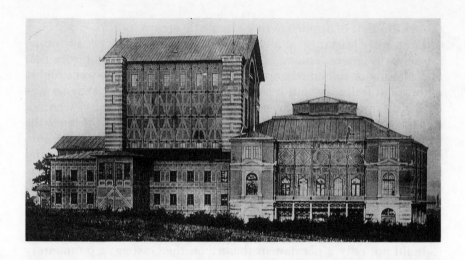

12.(b) Four tickets for the first performance of Wagner's 'Ring' cycle at the Bayreuth festival theatre in August 1876

all too easy simply to condemn him and his Bayreuth circle as harbingers of the Third Reich, and particularly its horrific anti-semitism. It is certainly sometimes hard to see Wagner's Bayreuth ideology apart from the racism that gathered pace in German domestic politics from the mid-1870s.[51] Yet at this time Wagner's public stance on the racist issue was exceedingly reticent, so much so that hard-liners like Eugen Dühring could accuse him of altering the 'antisemitic dissonances' in his earlier writings to 'softer chords' that were inaudible beneath the 'metallic sound' of the 'Jewish gold' that was helping to finance the 'very luxurious and expensive productions of the music of the future'.[52] The diaries of Wagner's wife Cosima prove beyond doubt, however, that the rancour of the Bayreuth Meister against the Jews continued unabated in private until his death in 1883. His unwillingness to show solidarity with the antisemitic movement in public was certainly pragmatic, as Dühring's visceral metaphor blatantly conveys. Wagner also felt that popular racism had turned the debate about the so-called Jewish question into something 'vulgar'. Still a believer in the old pre-1848–9 left-Hegelian stereo-type of the Jew as a symbol of market relations, he saw the movement – not without sardonic irony – in danger of becoming yet another victim of the commodity mass culture that the Jews themselves had allegedly created. Certainly, the 'softer' antisemitic 'chords' in Wagner's later writings could be explained as an attempt to protect his antisemitism, as it were, from popular consumption by subduing it to a point where only cultivated and 'enlightened' parts of the intelligentsia acquainted with his earlier writings could understand its implications.

Wagner's antisemitism was only part of a darkly orchestrated jeremiad on the fate of Germany that dominated his later thinking. Indeed, to keep himself intellectually buoyant the aging Wagner conjured up such a bizarrely intoxicating brew of perils for the Germans – from vivisection and the eating of meat to the established church and the identity (or rather misidentity) of the German state – that it is no wonder that even the astutest of his admirers were initially overcome by it. Nietzsche, who was Wagner's most trenchant propagandist until their famous estrangement in the late 1870s, expressed this particularly exotic brand of cultural paranoia in typically stark and startling terms. Our suspicion, he said, is that the famous 'nation of thinkers' has 'stopped thinking and exchanged thought for darkness'.[53]

Tempting as it is to see Wagner and Nietzsche's doom-mongering as a self-fulfilling prophecy that somehow contributed to the eventual downfall of Germany, the reality of Bayreuth turned out to be different. Outside Wagner's most intimate circle, from the first his ideological agenda was perceived by many admirers more moderately, and even sceptically, than is often realized. Nietzsche's 'Admonition to the Germans' quoted above was commissioned in 1873 by the Wagnerverein in Mannheim for a public appeal in aid of the Bayreuth project and then – much to Wagner's annoyance – rejected as too polemical. For Wagner and Nietzsche, of course, this pragmatic decision, even the eventual success of Bayreuth itself, was doubtless equivalent to a triumph for philistinism. Certainly on the issue of Bayreuth's disconcerting attraction for supposedly unenlightened visitors, sympathetic critics like Bernard Shaw were inclined to agree:

> European society was compelled to admit that Wagner was 'a success'. Royal personages, detesting his music, sat out the perform-ances in the row of boxes set apart for princes. They all complimented him on the astonishing 'push' with which, in the teeth of all obstacles, he had turned a fabulous and visionary project into a concrete commercial reality . . . these congratulations had no other effect upon Wagner than to open his eyes to the fact that the Bayreuth experiment, as an attempt to evade the ordinary social and commercial conditions of theatrical enterprise, was a failure . . . The money, supposed to be contributed by the faithful, was begged by energetic subscription-hunting ladies from people who must have had the most grotesque misconceptions of the composer's aims: among others, the Khedive of Egypt and the Sultan of Turkey.[54]

Wagner's ambition to fend off the reduction of his festival theatre to the status of a commodity went hand in hand with unpleasant nationalist rhetoric – an odd mixture of liberal idealism and backward xenophobia that explains some of the paradoxes of his Bayreuth 'success'. Even after his death visitors from abroad were not exactly received with open arms by Cosima who, in private at least, com-plained in a letter to Richard Strauss (7 January 1890) that 'the worthy Germans don't know any better than to rejoice that so many foreigners are coming here'.[55] Many Germans, of course, knew better than Cosima that with the passage of time Bayreuth looked less like a shrine that could allegedly purify the German soul than, quite simply, a monument of international significance where audiences from all over the world had a chance of experiencing the works of one of the most important composers of the century, performed as he supposedly intended. Wagner himself, who valued his artistic and intellectual independence above all else, would have almost certainly disagreed with the crude attempts of Cosima, and her acolytes Houston Stewart Chamberlain and Hans von Wolzogen, to turn the Bayreuth idea into populist dogma. In the event, Cosima's invective against the cultural distractions that were supposed to be deflecting Germany from its true course (she described the German people to Strauss as 'white-washed' with 'Brahmsianism' and having had 'Judaism clapped on' to them) was not as widely influential as she would have liked. Her almost military use of the German language certainly had its brutal moments. To Strauss she spoke of having 'occupied' and 'purged' the Rhineland and the area around the River Main with her favourite Bayreuth luminaries who held – or, she hoped, were about to hold – theatre posts in that part of Germany. Yet although Felix Mottl and Felix Weingartner already had important conducting positions in Karlsruhe and Mannheim, her attempts to entice Strauss to Frankfurt, and to find an influential place for Humperdinck in Düsseldorf, were conspicuously unsuccessful.

Even at the height of Wagner's fame towards the end of the century Cosima could hardly be described as the leader of a populist movement. Indeed, compared, say, to the enormous impact of Julius Langbehn's passionately anti-modernist book *Rembrandt the Educator*, first published in Leipzig in 1890,[56] Bayreuth looked decidedly élitist. That is not to say that Wagner had no effect at all on Germany's political mass movements. But the comparison does suggest that to turn him into a kind of Nazi paterfamilias, as some historians have tried to do, is to exaggerate the true extent of his popularity and influence. The striking international success of Bayreuth with the intelligentsia of Europe made it a suspect candidate for the robustly nationalist cause in any case, let alone a cause that had adamantly set its sights against the 'decadence' of modern society. Not only was Bayreuth visited by artists and critics from abroad who, blithely ignoring Cosima's sabre-rattling, still found Wagner worth talking about: the festival theatre was for many years by far the most important focal point for a new generation of musicians who regarded it as the Mecca of musical modernity.

NOTES

[1] The earliest proof of Wagner's preoccupation with the *Ring* is dated 1 April 1848. For details see *Wagner Werk-Verzeichnis*, ed. J. Deathridge, M. Geek and E. Voss (Mainz, 1986), 404.

[2] R. Pohl, *Gesammelte Schriften über Musik und Musiker* (Leipzig, 1883), i, 5.

[3] For convenience the term 'middle classes' is used in alternation with 'bourgeoisie' throughout this chapter to refer to social groups within the hierarchy between the nobility on one hand and the peasantry and proletariat on the other. This is not the place to discuss the problems arising from this oversimplified use of the terms, except to say that during the second half of the nineteenth century the distinctions between the heterogeneous groups that made up the middle classes grew much sharper – a process that requires a more differentiated range of terms, including 'Bürgertum', 'Mittelstand', 'petite bourgeoisie' and so on. Unless they are closely defined, however, these terms slide all too easily between different meanings according to the context in which they are used. I have therefore avoided them here. For a brief and useful discussion see S. Volkov, *The Rise of Popular Antimodernism in Germany* (Princeton, 1978), 123ff.

[4] See the appendix to *Louis Spohr: Lebenserinnerungen*, ed. F. Göthel, ii, 185. Also C. Brown, *Louis Spohr: a Critical Biography* (Cambridge, 1984), 309ff.

[5] *Robert Schumanns Briefe, Neue Folge*, ed. F. G. Jansen (Leipzig, 2/1904), 306, 461, 310. The title-page of the Four Marches is reproduced in K. Hofmann, *Die Erstdrucke der Werke von Robert Schumann* (Tutzing, 1979), 166. G. Abraham's statement that the larger type for the date 'was suppressed on more prudent reflection' is incorrect; see *Grove 6*, xvi, 844.

[6] J. J. McGann, *The Romantic Ideology: a Critical Investigation* (Chicago and London, 1983), 13.

[7] R. Wagner, 'Eine Mitteilung an meine Freunde' [1851], *Sämtliche Schriften und Dichtungen* (Leipzig, 1911–14), iv, 308f. (*Richard Wagner's Prose Works*, ed. and trans. W. A. Ellis (London, 1892–9/*R*1972), i, 355; the translation has been considerably modified.)

[8] A. J. P. Taylor, *The Course of German History* (London, 1985), 69 [first published in 1945].

[9] D. Blackbourn and G. Eley, *The Peculiarities of German History: Bourgeois Society and Politics in Nineteenth-Century Germany* (Oxford, 1984), 161. See also T. Nipperdey, 'Kritik oder Objektivität? Zur Beurteilung der Revolution von 1848', *Gesellschaft, Kultur, Theorie* (Göttingen, 1976), 259ff. For a view strongly influenced, like A. J. P. Taylor, by the idea of a 'special path', see H. U. Wehler, *The German Empire 1871–1918*, trans. K. Traynor (Leamington Spa and Dover, New Hampshire, 1985) [first published in German in 1973].

[10] Wagner, *Sämtliche Schriften*, ii, 233–73. An idiosyncratic English translation is in the seventh volume of *Richard Wagner's Prose Works*. For a useful though far from complete summary, see E. Newman, *The Life of Richard Wagner* (Cambridge, 1976), i, 495ff.

[11] Quoted in P. Bekker, *Das deutsche Musikleben* (Berlin, 1919), 125.

[12] Newman, *The Life of Richard Wagner*, i, 161.

[13] Ibid, 134.

[14] Ibid, 136. To perform *Lohengrin* with the forces Newman says Liszt used would have required a complete reworking of the score, for which there is no evidence.

[15] *Franz Liszt: Richard Wagner Briefwechsel*, ed. H. Kesting (Frankfurt, 1988), 120. Liszt found the resources too for other productions of contemporary or neglected operas (several also first performances) and to conduct innumerable concerts with new or unknown works. A selective list is given in *NZM*, l (1859), 70. Among the opera productions were Wagner's *Tannhäuser*, Berlioz's *Benvenuto Cellini*, Meyerbeer's *Les Huguenots*, Verdi's *Ernani*, *I due Foscari* and *Il trovatore*, and Schumann's *Genoveva*. Apart from *Lohengrin*, first performances included Schubert's *Alfonso und Estrella*, Heinrich Dorn's *Die Nibelungen* and Peter Cornelius's *Der Barbier von Bagdad*. Liszt conducted nine of his symphonic poems in his Weimar concerts, as well as works by Berlioz, Bülow, Gade, Glinka, Hiller, Joachim, A. B. Marx, Schumann, Sobolewski and Wagner.

[16] *NZM*, l (1859), 71; the words are quoted from a Viennese periodical.

[17] Ibid.

[18] T. Nipperdey, *Deutsche Geschichte 1800–1866* (Munich, 1983), 674.

[19] Bekker, *Das deutsche Musikleben*, 24.

[20] Nipperdey, *Gesellschaft, Kultur, Theorie*, 180f.

[21] Blackbourn and Eley, *The Peculiarities of German History*, 196.

[22] A. B. Marx, *The Music of the Nineteenth Century and its Culture*, trans. A. H. Wehrhan (London, 1855), 58 [the original German edition appeared the same year].

[23] Quoted from documents in the Deutsches Zentralarchiv, Merseberg, in G. Knepler, *Musikgeschichte des 19. Jahrhunderts* (Berlin, 1961), ii, 718.

[24] The first German music festival was founded by G. F. Bischoff in Frankenhausen (Thuringia) in 1810. The Lower Rhine festivals were begun in 1817 in Elberfeld and continued at regular intervals alternately in Aachen, Cologne and Düsseldorf. Distinguished conductors in the second half of the nineteenth century included Liszt (1857), Franz Lachner (1861, 1870), Anton Rubinstein (1872), Joachim (1875, 1878), Brahms (1883, 1884) and Hans Richter (1888, 1889, 1891, 1897). For more on the Lower Rhine Music Festivals up to the late 1860s see E. A. Hauchecorne, *Blätter der Erinnerung an die fünfzigjährige Dauer der Niederrheinischen Musikfeste* (Cologne, 1868); and C. H. Porter, 'The New Public and the Reordering of the Musical Establishment: the Lower Rhine Music Festivals, 1818–67', *19th-Century Music*, iii (1979–80), 211–24.

[25] Quoted in Newman, *The Life of Richard Wagner*, iv, 695 [original German text in C. F. Glasenapp, *Das Leben Richard Wagners* (Leipzig, 1911), vi, 695].

[26] See F. May, *The Life of Johannes Brahms* (London, 1905), i, 214f, 239f.

[27] R. Heuberger, *Erinnerungen an Johannes Brahms*, ed. K. Hofmann (Tutzing, 1971), 141.

[28] P. Brett, 'Text, Context, and the Early Music Editor', *Authenticity and Early Music*, ed. N. Kenyon (Oxford, 1988), 86. It is worth mentioning that two pioneering biographies – O. Jahn, *W. A. Mozart*, and F. Chrysander, *Georg Friedrich Händel* – were also published in Leipzig in the 1850s.

[29] See C. Dahlhaus, *Nineteenth-Century Music*, trans. J. Bradford Robinson (Berkeley and Los Angeles, 1989), 326.

[30] See G. G. Iggers, *The German Conception of History* (Middletown, Conn., rev. 2/1983), 64ff. Ranke's famous dictum that history is about 'what really happened' (*wie es eigentlich gewesen*) is

not synonymous with a 'scientific' approach to historiography, as many American and English historians have assumed. Iggers shows that the remark is in fact part of a philosophical view that has more to do with idealism and religion than empiricism.

[31] Wehler, *The German Empire*, 101.

[32] For an elaboration of this point, see C. Dahlhaus, *The Idea of Absolute Music*, trans. R. Lustig (Chicago and London, 1989), 21.

[33] D. Sternberger, *Panorama of the Nineteenth Century*, trans. J. Neugroschel with an introduction by E. Heller (Oxford, 1977), 120f.

[34] For an almost exemplary exposition of this idealist view see Wagner's essay 'German Music' [1840] in *Wagner Writes from Paris . . .*, ed. and trans. R. L. Jacobs and G. Skelton (London, 1973), 36ff ['Über deutsches Musikwesen', *Sämtliche Schriften*, i, 149ff]. Dahlhaus states that the ideology of a German 'national music' started gaining ground among the educated middle classes with the publication of Forkel's famous Bach biography in 1802. See Dahlhaus, 'Wagner und Bach', *Klassische und romantische Musikästhetik* (Laaber, 1988), 452.

[35] F. Brendel, *Geschichte der Musik in Italien, Deutschland und Frankreich: 22 Vorlesungen gehalten zu Leipzig im Jahre 1850* (Leipzig, 1852), 532.

[36] A. B. Marx, *The Music of the Nineteenth Century*, 79.

[37] Brendel, *Geschichte der Musik*, 518, 521.

[38] The myth that Bischoff coined the slogan was invented by Wagner. In fact, Bischoff, who wrote about 'Zukunftsmusik' in 1859 in the *Niederrheinische Musikzeitung* (no.41), which he edited, was far from the first to use the word. F. A. Riccius, a contributor to the *Rheinische Musikzeitung*, which Bischoff also edited, used it in 1853. There are other examples and variants even before this. As early as 1833, for instance, Schumann wrote positively (as one might expect) of 'zukünftige Musik'. See *Wörterbuch der Unhöflichkeit: Richard Wagner im Spiegel der Kritik*, ed. W. Tappert with a foreword by H. Friedrich (Munich, 1967), 128–33; and the entry 'Zukunfts-musik' in *Riemann Musiklexikon: Sachteil* (Mainz, 1967), 1082. The slogan, incidentally, had achieved notoriety abroad before 1859 as well. To cite one example: the London *Punch* referred disparagingly in 1858 to Wagner, Liszt 'and other crotchet-mongers of the *Music of the Future*' (20 Nov, p.211).

[39] For the whole of Brendel's speech, see 'Zur Anbahnung einer Verständigung', *NZM*, 1 (1859), 265–73.

[40] R. Wagner, *Sämtliche Schriften*, x, 3. *Prose Works*, ed. and trans. A. Ellis, vi, 5; Ellis's somewhat idiosyncratic translation is 'Paris minor'.

[41] This is one of J. A. Hepokoski's main points in his review of P. Gossett, '*Anna Bolena*' and the Artistic Maturity of Gaetano Donizetti (Oxford, 1985), in *19th-Century Music*, xii (1988–9), 75.

[42] C. Dahlhaus, *Nineteenth-Century Music*, 193.

[43] See L. B. Plantinga, *Schumann as Critic* (New Haven and London, 1967), 103ff.

[44] See Wagner, 'Eine Mitteilung', *Sämtliche Schriften*, iv, 298, and *Wagner Werk-Verzeichnis*, 257.

[45] B. Shaw, 'The Perfect Wagnerite', *The Bodley Head Bernard Shaw: Shaw's Music* (London, Sydney and Toronto, 1981), iii, 495; see also, 'Some Imperfect Wagnerites', ibid, 555ff.

[46] See Sternberger, *Panorama of the Nineteenth Century*, 20ff.

[47] See Wagner's letter from Zurich to E. B. Kietz of 14 Sept 1850 in *Selected Letters*, ed. B. Millington and S. Spencer (London, 1987), 216f.

[48] See Volkov, *The Rise of Popular Antimodernism*, 39.

[49] Letter of 1 Nov 1871 to the Bayreuth banker Friedrich Feustel in *Selected Letters*, 783.

[50] Letter of 1 March 1871 in *König Ludwig II. und Richard Wagner: Briefwechsel*, ed. O. Strobel (Karlsruhe, 1936), ii, 322.

[51] Wehler reports that no fewer than 500 publications 'on the Jewish question' appeared between 1873 and 1890; see *The German Empire 1871–1918*, 106.

[52] E. Dühring, *Die Judenfrage als Racen-, Sitten-, und Culturfrage. Mit einer weltgeschichtlichen Antwort* (Karlsruhe and Leipzig, 2/1881), 75–6.

[53] F. Nietzsche, 'Mahnruf an die Deutschen', *Werke*, ed. G. Colli and M. Montinari, 3rd ser., ii, Nachgelassene Schriften 1870–1873 (Berlin, 1973), 389–90.

[54] B. Shaw, 'The Perfect Wagnerite', 535f.

[55] C. Wagner, *Das zweite Leben*, ed. D. Mack (Munich and Zurich, 1980), 205; quotations in the next paragraph are from the same letter.

[56] For the best account of Langbehn and his famous book, see F. Stern, *The Politics of Cultural Despair* (Berkeley and Los Angeles, 1961), 97ff.

BIBLIOGRAPHICAL NOTE

Historical background

The years 1848–90 in the controversial history of Germany and its culture are so beset with problems of interpretation, and even basic information, that anything written on the subject (including this chapter) has to be treated critically not as a final word, but as a contribution to a continuing debate. In addition to studies referred to in the text and notes, two books that are engagingly written and informative are G. A. Craig's *The Germans* (New York, 1982) and H. James's *A German Identity 1770–1990* (London, 1989). Craig and James, however, include accounts of Wagner, Nietzsche and the Bayreuth circle that are not without problems; and I hope Craig's blanket remark that after 'the debacle of 1848 . . . the educated middle class . . . was relegated to the uninspiring occupation of making and spending money' will raise a few eyebrows.

Among the books I have mentioned my favourites are A. J. P. Taylor's basically wrong-headed but stimulating and sharply written *The Course of German History* (London, 1985; first published 1945) and D. Blackbourn and G. Eley's cogently argued *The Pecularities of German History* (Oxford, 1984). One of the best and most original studies of the nineteenth century that embraces German culture in a way that reaches beneath its surface is D. Sternberger's *Panorama of the Nineteenth Century*, trans. J. Neugroschel with an introduction by E. Heller (Oxford, 1977).

Music

One of the most stimulating and really critical accounts of German music in the second half of the nineteenth century can be found in W. Mellers's contribution to *Man and his Music: the Story of Musical Experience in the West* (London, 1962). C. Dahlhaus's famous *Nineteenth-Century Music*, trans. J. Bradford Robinson (Berkeley and Los Angeles, 1989), includes the most substantial attempt so far to see the subject from a wider historical angle, though it tends to lose its way too often in a ghost town of 'categories' and 'concepts' (important as these are); for all its efforts to take social context into account it is a curiously remote book. Less convoluted books that are worth reading are G. Abraham's *A Hundred Years of Music* (London, 3/1964); R. M. Longyear's *Nineteenth-Century Romanticism in Music* (Englewood Cliffs, 2/1973); L. Plantinga's *Romantic Music: a History of Musical Style in Nineteenth-Century Europe* (New York and London, 1984); and A. Whittall's *Romantic Music: a Concise History from Schubert to Sibelius* (London, 1987).

Although I have been critical of E. Newman's *The Life of Richard Wagner* (4 vols.; Cambridge, 1976), two chapters in the first volume, 'The State of Music in Germany' and 'The Economic and Social Status of the Musician', are still the most substantial accounts of these subjects in English. Indeed, the entire biography has such breadth and detail that it is essential reading for anyone interested in nineteenth-century German culture. Also broad in scope, though written with less perceptive critical zest, are R. W. Gutman's *Richard Wagner: the Man, his Mind, and his Music* (New York and London, 1968) and M. Gregor-Dellin's *Richard Wagner: sein Leben – sein Werk – sein Jahrhundert* (Munich and Zurich, 1980; abridged Eng. trans., by J. M. Brownjohn, London, 1983).

Books on Wagner, of course, are legion. The reader may find it convenient to start with the relatively concise surveys in *The New Grove Wagner* (London, 1984), by J. Deathridge and C. Dahlhaus, and B. Millington's *Wagner* (London, 1984), a thorough and up-to-date contribution to the Master Musicians series. A clear and cogent study of the stage works is Dahlhaus, *Richard Wagner's Music Dramas*, trans. M. Whittall (Cambridge, 1979), who has also contributed three important chapters to *The Wagner Handbook*, ed. J. Deathridge, P. Wapnewski and U. Müller (Cambridge, Mass., 1991).

Fine critical interpretations can be found in T. W. Adorno's *In Search of Wagner*, trans. R. Livingstone (London, 1981; for a gloss of this difficult book and the problematic rendering of its title in English, see J. Deathridge's review in *19th-Century Music*, vii, (1983–4), 81ff), the collection of writings on Wagner by Thomas Mann in *Pro and Contra Wagner*, trans. A. Blunden, with an introduction by E. Heller (London, 1985), E. Bloch's *Essays on the Philosophy of Music*, trans. P. Palmer with an introduction by D. Drew (Cambridge, 1985), and the chapter 'Opera as Symphonic Poem' in J. Kerman, *Opera as Drama* (London, rev. 2/1989).

Books on the influence of Wagner's Bayreuth circle strictly speaking belong to a later period than the one covered here. But as this influence began to gain momentum in the 1880s, it seems appropriate to mention two publications in English: *Wagnerism in European Culture and Politics*, ed. D. C. Large and W. Weber in collaboration with A. Dzamba Sessa (Ithaca, NY, and London, 1984), which contains much information, though the section on Wagner's Bayreuth disciples is a particularly unlucky victim of the 'special path' theory I have discussed; and G. C. Field's fascinating study of H. S. Chamberlain, *Evangelist of Race* (New York, 1981) – although also hardly immune from a somewhat demonized view of the history of Bayreuth, it has many fine qualities, not least an excellent annotated bibliography. A similarly well-researched study of Cosima Wagner, one of the most formidable, if elusive, influences on German culture after her husband's death, has yet to be written.

Wide-ranging studies in English of other major composers active in Germany in 1848–90 are surprisingly hard to find considering the popularity of their music. The most glaring example is Brahms. (Though he lived for much of his life in Vienna, he spent his formative years in Germany and initiated first performances of many of his major works there.) There is, however, no shortage of in-depth articles about aspects of his life and music. The reader could do worse than to start with K. Geiringer's old-fashioned and rather grandiose *Brahms: his Life and Work* (Boston and London, 3/1963). In addition, M. Macdonald's *Brahms* (London, 1990), a study of the life and works in the Master Musicians series, is to be warmly recommended. More adventurous readers should consult either of the biographical, documentary and analytical studies *Brahms* and *Brahms 2*, ed. R. Pascall and M. Musgrave respectively (Cambridge, 1983 and 1987). One of the best books on the music is W. Frisch's *Brahms and the Principle of Developing Variation* (Berkeley, Los Angeles and London, 1984), though it cannot be recommended to readers without advanced technical knowledge.

Again, there is no full-scale modern biography of Liszt, though one by A. Walker is in progress. If the highly readable first two volumes (New York and London, 1983 and 1989), covering Liszt's virtuoso and Weimar years, are anything to go by, this will be an indispensable work which will illuminate not only the composer's career in the second half of the nineteenth century, but also a great deal about Germany's musical and cultural life. The symposium *Franz Liszt: the Man and his Music*, ed. A. Walker (London, 1970, 2/1976), is uneven but can also be recommended. The same can be said of H. Searle's *The Music of Franz Liszt* (New York, rev. 2/1966) and D. Watson's very readable survey *Liszt* (London, 1989) in the Master Musicians series.

Schumann's final years just fall into the period under review, though it is precisely this part of his life and work that has generally been seriously misunderstood. The only (valiant) attempt to come to terms with it without prejudice in English is H. Truscott, 'The Evolution of Schumann's Last Period', *The Chesterian*, xxi (1957), 76ff, 103ff. For those who read German, a more sophisticated and by far the most illuminating study is R. Kapp, *Studien zum Spätwerk Robert Schumanns* (Tutzing, 1984).

Chapter III

Vienna:
Absolutism and Nostalgia

PAUL BANKS

On the eve of the year of revolutions Vienna, the imperial city, the sixth largest centre of population in Europe, presented the outward appearance of a quiescent capital, submitting to the authoritarian rule of Prince Metternich, the State Chancellor and upholder of the old order. Yet beneath the administrative and political stability maintained by Metternich and the Staatskonferenz on behalf of the mentally feeble Emperor Ferdinand (1793–1875, reigned 1835–48), the first stirrings of political and social unrest were making themselves manifest. The dark flame of nationalism had been ignited throughout the empire and burst with varying degrees of intensity, the slow march of industrialization imposed increasingly stressful social changes, the most severe of which was growing unemployment (culminating, though not ending, in the Prague machine-breaking riots of 1844), and a series of bad harvests and natural disasters in the late 1840s led to hunger and inflation.

Another striking Viennese paradox lay in its architectural and social geography. The imperial, bureaucratic, social and economic life of the city was concentrated within the ancient defensive walls, ditch and surrounding glacis: although Joseph II created parks on the glacis in the 1780s, the heart of Vienna was still a walled city. Yet as Ludwig von Förster observed in 1847,[1] within this medieval enclave there was not a single example of medieval domestic architecture; indeed the oldest such buildings dated from no earlier than the late seventeenth century. The creation of an essentially eighteenth-century administrative and aristocratic enclave within a medieval fortification reflects both the military insecurity of the Habsburgs and one of the most devastating pieces of pre-Nazi Austrian social engineering, the dynasty's thorough and entirely successful Counter-Reformation campaign to convert what in the early sixteenth century had been a major Lutheran city, with a substantial and powerful class of burghers, into a bastion of Catholicism. The commercially important merchant class was fragmented and dispersed, the most determined and resolute members choosing emigration rather than conversion or financial ruin.[2] (As late as 1837 a similar choice was imposed on a small enclave of Protestants living in the Tyrol as a result of the post-Josephinian rapprochement between the Vatican and Vienna.[3]) The result may have been a success for the Counter-Reformation, removing leading heretics and making available building land for the aristocratic newcomers attracted to the court, but it hampered the economy and may well have contributed to the development of the complacent and compliant character of the Viennese middle class.[4] As has been observed of the Vormärz period, 'we should be flattering the honest Viennese bourgeois if we represented them as in any way seething with unrest during these years: the vast majority remained as insouciantly apolitical as ever'.[5]

The cosiness now usually associated with the period – but which was only true for a limited number of the populace – is inevitably conjured up by its other historical label: Biedermeier. Yet even here there is a twofold aspect to the images evoked. One is a life founded on domestic virtues, Christmases spent round the newly introduced Christmas tree, music-making and conversation at home, as exemplified by Schubertiads. But the importance of public social activity cannot be overestimated. Encouraged by Metternich, the theatre had flourished as a politically acceptable form of mass entertainment, though it is significant that in spite of Franz Grillparzer's dramatic genius, it is the commercial theatre of Ferdinand Raimund (1790–1836) and Johann Nestroy (1801–1862) that most completely reflects and comments on the changing temper of the age. After the deaths of Beethoven (1827) and Schubert (1828) the most lasting and influential developments in instrumental music lay not in the realm of high art but in that of popular dance music, presided over by Josef Lanner (1801–43), Johann Strauss the elder (1804–49) and their lesser colleagues. After the death of Weber (1826), whose pathbreaking but flawed Romantic opera *Euryanthe* (1823) had been written for Vienna, Italian and French composers supplied the overwhelming majority of new operas for the city and it was only in the 1840s that German composers like Kreutzer and Lortzing gained access to the Viennese court stage in any number, culminating not in Nicolai's comic masterpiece *Die lustige Weiber von Windsor*, which was rejected by the Hofoper, but in the première of Flotow's *Martha* (1847). The true heirs to Weber's inheritance, Marschner and Wagner, were much less welcome: *Hans Heiling* waited thirteen years, *Der Templar und die Jüdin* 30 and *Der Vampyr* 56 for their Viennese premières, and the city first saw a work by Wagner only in 1857 (*Tannhäuser*).

The absolutist régime did nothing to discourage any inherent cultural resistances to the potentially disruptive influence of Romanticism,[6] and imposed a complex system of censorship in an attempt to exclude from the Habsburg lands any literature that might tend to subvert the status quo. Similar considerations also influenced the encouragement given to the 'positive sciences' and the discouragement of philosophy, with consequences that extended deep into the future of Austrian culture and academic life. The absolutism of the period 1815–48 worked in the sense that it maintained a veneer of stability, of contentment – faithfully recorded by such visitors as Mrs Frances Trollope and Peter Turnbull[7] – which was gradually formed into the myth of Old Vienna, an extraordinarily successful legend which retained its power well into the twentieth century, not least thanks to commercial exploitation.[8] All myths are founded on some truth, and for a section of the population Old Vienna did exist and, as was admitted many years later by Victor Adler (1852–1918), one of the founders of the Austrian Social Democrat Party, the harsher impositions of absolutism were tempered by slovenliness. Either because of such bureaucratic carelessness or, more likely, because the administration considered the commercial stage a useful safety-valve through which tensions and grievances could be aired and dissipated, Nestroy's social satires were tolerated; thanks (probably) to the rivalry between Kolowrat and Metternich – the two chief actors in the political arena – Eduard von Bauernfeld's comedy *Grossjährig*, a barely concealed attack on Metternich's system, was performed with great success at the Hofburgtheater in 1846–8.

When in March 1848 discontent finally quitted the realm of art and stepped into reality, its emigration was sparked off by revolution in France and rapidly spread from Vienna to the far corners of the monarchy, revealing class-conflict and bringing to the fore a relatively new phenomenon: nationalism. But two demands united many of those involved in the Vienna uprising: the removal of Metternich and the establishment of some sort of constitutional government. Both were met; on 13 March Metternich resigned and on 15 March the emperor announced he would summon representatives to discuss a constitution. This was followed by a draft (the Pillersdorf Constitution), published on 25 April, which proposed significant improvements of civil liberties, but a political structure for the state which found no favour with the Vienna populace. Further street demonstrations followed, and on 15 May the government agreed to changes, including an expansion of the proposed franchise and a unicameral parliament; on 17 May Ferdinand left Vienna for Innsbruck to return only in August. Proponents of absolutism within the court were beginning to reassert themselves behind the scenes, but the elections for the Reichstag were held and it was formally opened on 22 July.

Many in Germany saw events in Paris and Vienna as heralding the first step in the overthrow of the existing social order, including Richard Wagner whose poetic *Gruss aus Sachsen an die Wiener* was published in the *Allgemeine Österreichische Zeitung* on 1 June.[9] Later in the month Wagner obtained leave from his post as royal Kapellmeister at Dresden and travelled immediately to Vienna, where he probably hoped to arrange a production of *Rienzi* and to promote his ideas for the reorganizing of the Viennese theatres.[10] The times were hardly propitious for either enterprise, and Wagner had to content himself with drinking in the heady revolutionary brew and meeting a number of writers, including Grillparzer and Bauernfeld, and, among other musicians, the composer and distinguished music critic A. J. Becher, who was active in revolutionary politics and was summarily executed by the imperial forces when Vienna was finally subdued.

Other composers caught up in the atmosphere of the times were more fortunate. The activity of the Strauss family is particularly noteworthy because it reflects the complex and often contradictory responses of the Viennese bourgeoisie to the events of 1848. In the last years of the *Vormärz* the two Johann Strausses had been appointed Kapellmeister of the two regiments of Vienna's civic guard, essentially middle-class organizations which, since the Napoleonic wars, had become more or less ceremonial in significance. One of the first concessions wrung from the government on 13 March was the expansion of the civic guard into a large-scale national guard, large enough to take over policing of the troubled capital city from the army which, through its brutal attempt to suppress street demonstrations, had aroused great hostility. The new national guard was designed to defend the bourgeois revolution and Johann Strauss the younger immediately applied for the post of Kapellmeister in it; he was appointed. His revolutionary sympathies were made explicit by his compositions of the period (for example *Freiheits-und Barrikadenlieder*, *Spottpolka gegen die Ligourianer*, *Revolutionsmarsch*), his leadership of the band during fighting and his playing of the *Marseillaise* even after Vienna had been overrun by counter-revolutionary forces. As might be expected, the elder Strauss was more ambivalent about events, probably mirroring the feeling of most of the middle-class listeners and dancers who constituted his public. His *Österreichische National-Garde-Marsche* (first heard on 19 March 1848) and *Marsch der Studenten-Legion* (30 April) celebrate two of the leading defenders of the initial phase of the revolution and the *Marche des Einigen Deutschlands* (26 July) reflects the rise of German nationalism associated with the contemporary deliberations in Frankfurt; in May he had also been appointed Kapellmeister to one of the national guard bands.

Yet, like many Austrians, Strauss felt a profound loyalty to Austria and to Kaiser Ferdinand, and increasingly events in Vienna alienated many who had initially supported the uprising. Although the Reichstag had pushed through the emancipation of the peasants, the beneficiaries felt no sympathy for the revolution, and various disturbances in Vienna during August and September encouraged many of the bourgeoisie to leave; support for the revolution was narrowing to a group of Viennese intellectuals and their supporters among the proletariat, and the only (and in the event, fruitless) hope for its success would be support from the hard-pressed Hungarians who were waging their own struggle against the authority of the Habsburg government. For those who longed for a restoration of stability, hope lay chiefly in the army, which remained loyal to the crown. The first signs of the eventual success of the counter-revolutionary forces came from Italy where, in May and July, at St Lucia and Custozza, Field-Marshal Radetzky won victories that eliminated the Piedmontese threat to Austria's Italian provinces and released armed forces to reinforce the struggle against internal enemies in Hungary and Austria. Nevertheless for many the patriotic importance of these victories overshadowed their possible political significance, and in celebrating Radetzky both Grillparzer (*Feldmarschall Radetzky*) and Strauss (*Radetzky-Marsch*) were giving voice to a widespread sentiment.[11]

On 6 October the Vienna revolution entered its last phase. A regiment ordered to reinforce the forces fighting in Hungary refused to board their train; when troops sent to quell the mutiny opened fire on the crowd which had gathered, street fighting erupted. Latour, the minister of war, was hunted down and lynched, and Ferdinand and the court fled to Olmütz: the scene was now set for the *coup de grâce*. Imperial forces surrounded the capital, fighting began on 24 October and the city was overrun five days later. Many activists were rounded up and 25, including Becher, were executed. In spite of this defeat of the forces for reform in the western half of the empire (the Hungarian struggle continued well into the following year) the constitutionalist cause was not yet lost. The Reichstag had reassembled at Kremsier, near Olmütz, and the minister president of Ferdinand's new government, Prince Felix Schwarzenberg, encouraged the representatives to formulate a constitution. But while the vestige of a representative body deliberated, the imperial machine was preparing to reassert its complex authority.

On 2 December Ferdinand reluctantly abdicated in favour of his nephew, Franz Josef, and on 7 March the Reichstag was dissolved and an alternative constitution formulated by the minister of the interior, Count Stadion, was promulgated. This was by no means illiberal, guaranteeing important freedoms to the populace, but the crown retained sweeping powers, and the representative bodies, the parliament and Landtage (for individual provinces within the monarchy) were to be merely advisory. In the event elections were only ever held for the local councils (whose authority had been reduced from that envisaged by the March Constitution): those for the Landtage and

13. *Johann Strauss (the younger) leading his orchestra at the Volksgarten, Vienna; lithograph (1853) by F. Kaliwoda*

parliament scheduled to be convened in 1850 and 1851 never took place, and on 31 December 1851 Franz Josef issued the Sylvester Patent which cancelled the March Constitution, reserving to himself the responsibility for the administration of all public affairs and removing most of the fundamental rights of his subjects: the period of neo-absolutism was in full swing.

It was in this political climate that Viennese cultural life resumed, and within it Johann Strauss the younger (1825–99) occupied a prominent position. His father had died in 1849, and if in part his vigorous defiance of authority in 1848 was an extension of his personal struggle against his father, who attempted to block his artistic development, then the resolutions of these conflicts overlap and parallel one another in striking ways. Within a fortnight of his father's death, Johann had healed the breach with the older orchestra and appeared at its head in the Volksgarten, just as in 1863, his revolutionary past now overlooked if not forgiven, he accepted from the emperor the title created for his father: K. K. Hofballmusikdirektor.

As a composer of dance music Strauss achieved an unexpected degree of sophistication in melodic organization, manipulation of waltz rhythm and harmonic language, arousing the admiration of

14. 'Der Zigeunerbaron' ('The Gypsy Baron'): poster by J. Weiner for the first performance of Johann Strauss's operetta, first performed at the Theater an der Wien on 24 October 1885

many composers devoted to high art (including both Wagner and Brahms) while retaining his enormous popularity. However, another genre was growing in appeal during the 1860s and eventually diverted Strauss's attention. Since the 1820s Vienna had eagerly imported *opéra comique* from Paris, with Auber in particular enjoying considerable popularity. Such imports had co-existed beside the indigenous genres, notably that of the satirical dialect comedy, cultivated by Nestroy, and to some extent the parody and satire of Offenbach's operettas may well be features that encouraged their phenomenal success in the commercial theatres of Vienna from the late 1850s. It was inevitable that local composers would seek to capitalize on this, and the first to do so was Franz von Suppé with *Das Pensionat* (Theater an der Wien, 1860). Although he had earlier collaborated on various parodies, including *Der Tannenhäuser*, it was gaiety and élan that formed the most striking characteristics of his music. These features, along with a distinctive style by now firmly associated with Vienna, were also the basis of Strauss's own operetta idiom, though he turned to the medium with reluctance, all too aware of his lack of responsiveness to words and of theatrical experience; it was only with his third stage work, *Die Fledermaus* (Theater an der Wien, 1874), that he achieved a lasting success.

Viennese operetta, with its generalized references (if any) to the city and avoidance of any satirical features that might limit its appeal, was destined for international success, but it marked the end of the Viennese tradition of popular theatre, with its reliance on Viennese dialect and specific references to the city, its daily life, society and theatrical traditions. A few writers, notably Ludwig Anzengruber (1839–89), attempted to re-establish the genre in the early 1870s, but the dream was unobtainable. The society out of which popular theatre had grown was being transformed by Austria's belated but rapid industrialization.

Between 1868 and 1874, 682 joint stock companies were established and in the 1860s the annual growth rate of the economy was 8–10%.[12] The results were as much social as economic: a new stratification of society with the rapid creation of an aristocracy of capital. Peasants from the whole empire flooded into the city in search of employment, creating a huge working class that had no connection with Viennese theatrical tradition. Inflation, which followed industrial expansion, reduced the value of salaries and increased ticket prices: the lower middle class, the traditional audience for the popular stage, were excluded from regular attendance at the theatre. The new genre, which contributed so powerfully to the image of Vienna, cherished not only by outsiders but by the Viennese themselves, offered generalizations and sentiment in place of indigenous detail and wit. Characteristically, *Die Fledermaus*, the most famous and potent celebration of a carefree life of leisure which so powerfully contributed to the myth of Old Vienna, drew on a French play based on a German original, and the economic stability the libretto presupposed was severely shaken by a stock-market crash the year before the première.

Beyond the boundaries of popular music Vienna retained its status as one of Europe's great musical centres, but chiefly because of the variety and quality of its performing tradition. From the point of view of high art, its musical life did not encompass a significant body of indigenous creative achievement, but the foundations of an extraordinary flowering of compositional talent in the early twentieth century were laid by the revitalization inspired by the arrival in Vienna during the 1860s and 70s of composers of outstanding genius from Germany and the Habsburg lands: Wagner (1813–83), Bruckner (1824–96), Brahms (1833–97), Mahler (1860–1911) and Wolf (1860–1903).

The city they found was undergoing a process of physical and social transformation. On 20 December 1857 Franz Josef sent a letter-patent to Alexander Bach, the minister president, authorizing the removal of the fortifications surrounding the Innere Stadt, a move in part signifying a victory for the industrial and commercial interests which had been pressing for it since the revolution of 1848. The arguments of the militarists, who believed that such defences were necessary in case of another proletarian revolution, had been dominant during the years of absolutism which had followed the events of 1848–9; but because of the spread of industrialization and the state's reliance on loans to cover the regular budget deficits, financial interests were gaining ground and played an increasing role in the formation of policy.

By 1865 the Ringstrasse, a wide boulevard following the outline of the old ramparts, was partly ready for use and in 1869 the first of the public buildings that grew up along it was opened: The Hofoper. Further examples of the Ringstrasse style followed: the Votivkirche (1879; Gothic), the Art and Natural History Museums (1881), the parliament building (1883; Greek), the Rathaus (1883; northern Gothic), the university (1884; Italian Renaissance) and the Hofburgtheater (1888; early Baroque). Even before the building programme was completed, the absence of any consistent style had evoked critical comment, not least from one of Mahler's closest friends, the archaeologist Fritz Löhr: 'Who'll buy Classical – Gothic – German or Italian Renaissance? And all of it – what more could one ask – neatly displayed; for this is the architectural old-clothes market of the Imperial capital city of Vienna'.[13]

But the stylistic diversity (indeed incongruity) of the Ringstrasse's architecture was perhaps, in part, a reaction against years of aesthetic

15. The Ringstrasse, Vienna, soon after completion of (left to right), the parliament building, the Rathaus, the university and the Hofburgtheater, in front of which is the Volksgarten; photograph, c1890

conformity; it was only in the early twentieth century that distinctive modern architectural idioms began to crystallize in the work of Otto Wagner, Josef Hoffmann and Joseph Maria Olbrich. Moreover, as one commentator put it:

> the mixture of inventive drive and petrified pride, or real and imitation marble, in the Ringstrasse architecture was appropriate as the official face of New Vienna. It was a contrived mask, but so are all official faces. Because of its bogus elements, not in spite of them, it was genuine in its way.[14]

In view of Löhr's critique it is ironic that, more than any of his contemporaries, it was Mahler who, particularly in his early works, exploited creatively such stylistic heterogeneity, juxtaposing the most disparate idioms[15] and thus drawing on a new source of aesthetically significant contrasts and enlarging the expressive range of his music.

If the demolition of Vienna's fortifications was the result of capitalism's success in Austria, the motivation to complete most of the great public buildings was heightened by one of its failures. The absolutism of the 1850s had not halted industrialization in the empire, but by the end of the decade the Ministry of Finance, though successful in reducing the annual national deficit, was running out of assets and credit. It was therefore natural that when the 1857

83

financial crisis spread from New York, London and Paris to Vienna, there should be demands for constitutional control over government expenditure. This pressure became irresistible after the military defeats at Marengo and Solferino in 1859 and the inevitable rise in government spending incurred by the Italian war; the monarchy embarked on eight years of constitutional experiment which led ultimately to the Compromise of 1867 which created the Austro-Hungarian Monarchy/Empire. The final impetus was supplied by the Prussian defeat of the Austrian army at Königgrätz in 1866 and the ending of Austrian hopes of hegemony within Germany.

Since the early 1860s the dominant political force in the monarchy had been the German liberals, described as:

> heirs of the men who had carried through the bourgeois revolution of 1848 in Vienna, and they were 'constitutionalist' and 'left' in that they demanded limitation of the Monarch's authority, especially in financial matters . . . They also stood for the most complete liberty of the citizen *vis-à-vis* the state . . . In other respects they had indeed shed any revolutionary ardours which they ever possessed. They were at least as hostile as the feudalists to allowing any political power to the classes below them. Their economic philosophy was of pure Mancunian *laissez-faire* . . . and allowed and approved the most ruthless exploitation of the economically weak.[16]

The Compromise confirmed modest representative institutions in both halves of the Dual Monarchy, though the crown retained considerable autonomy. Even such relatively modest constitutional concessions proved to be powerful stimulus to the economy, and the resulting prosperity, though ephemeral, enabled the state to record surpluses in the national budgets for 1869–72. The bubble eventually burst on 7 May 1873, Black Friday; many small investors were ruined and the boom was brought to an abrupt end. The completion of most of the public Ringstrasse buildings conceived in times of plenty was hastened to provide employment for those thrown out of work by the slump. Bruckner's anxiety to ensure financial security for himself in Vienna, which clearly exasperated Herbeck during the negotiations in 1868 for Bruckner's appointment to the staff of the conservatory of the Gesellschaft der Musikfreunde and which may well have been founded on memories of 1857 and perhaps even folk-memories of the virtual state bankruptcy of 1811, proved to be all too justified.

Apart from the Hofoper, the first phase of rebuilding had concentrated largely on the erection of living accommodation for the bourgeoisie and aristocracy. Because of the rapidly expanding population, Vienna suffered from a chronic housing shortage (which persisted well into the 1920s) and consequently rents were high, nearly twice the comparable rates in London.[17] Yet such comparisons can be made only with difficulty because of the radically different patterns of accommodation, domestic architecture and resulting way of life. In London single-family living units had evolved from essentially medieval designs, but the Counter-Reformation and the establishment of Vienna as a Kaiserstadt had established the *Adelspalast* as the model to be imitated, even by the Miethauser, the large apartment blocks that formed the bulk of middle-class housing from the mid-eighteenth century. By the mid-nineteenth such structures (*Zinspaläste*: 'rent-palaces') offered façades no less deceptive than those of the public buildings on the Ringstrasse. Behind the opulent exteriors living conditions were often relatively cramped, with convenience being sacrificed to provide rooms for social display. Such facilities as running water and an adequate sewerage system were only slowly developed; even in 1910 only a few dwellings had a private water-closet or bathroom. Although the more substantial party walls of Viennese buildings offered residents greater privacy than those of Parisian apartments, they often lacked corridors and rooms were simply arranged in a line, one leading to another. This is exemplified by Bruckner's relatively spacious accommodation at 7 Hessgasse, just off the northern side of the Ringstrasse:

> From the anteroom, which in its darkness and with long-looped-wreaths hanging on the walls was rather reminiscent of a funeral-parlour, one passed through a domestic room to reach Bruckner's work-room ... Just in the middle stood an old yellowish-brown grand piano with open lid and music on the stand. Music and a considerable portion of Bruckner's wardrobe lay on the lid in mutual fellowship. Near the right-hand of the two windows placed opposite the door, stood the work-table ... The corner by the left-hand window was filled by a huge cubic box: the house-organ. A chest of drawers, an utterly simple iron bedstead and a wash-stand completed the modest furnishings.[18]

This was a good address, with large rooms, for which Bruckner was almost certainly paying less than the market rate thanks to the owner, Dr Anton Ölzelt-Newin, one of his admirers.[19] Brahms's apartment at Karlsgasse 4, just to the south-west of the Karlskirche, at the opposite side of the city, was broadly similar: the sitting-room could be reached only by passing the kitchen and through the bedroom.[20] Such arrangements were viewed by contemporary English writers as disgraceful breaches of decorum and privacy; even the *Allgemeine Bauzeitung* confessed in 1860 that 'we Viennese very seldom feel truly at home in our rented flats'. There is significant evidence that such domestic overcrowding reinforced other social factors which encouraged the Viennese to lead an existence even more public than that of the Parisians, and within this framework the luxurious cafés became a second home for many:

> The Ringstrasse cafés were as important monuments to Viennese culture as the museums and theatres and educational establishments. No longer the centres of ideological discussion they had been before 1848, cafés acquired social rather than political functions. The 'family café' became an important type in the 1870s, and special features were added to attract ladies.[21]

By the 1880s Brahms had established a pattern of life which exemplifies the Viennese milieu:

> Brahms was a very early riser, and liked to prepare his own breakfast . . . The morning was devoted to work. His lunch, and as a rule his evening meal, he took in his favourite restaurant *Zum roten Igel* which, thanks to Brahms, had become the rendezvous of the musical circles of the capital . . . After his lunch Brahms used to take a stroll in the lovely *Stadtpark* where he drank a cup of black coffee. The afternoon was devoted to further work or to social engagements; in the evenings he often returned to the *Igel*, drinking his last cup of Mocha, very late at night, in a café near his flat.[22]

In outline Bruckner's way of life differed only in that as a teacher and organist his timetable was more formally structured: indeed, although it was not his regular resort, he too patronized the *Roter Igel*.[23] Brahms and Bruckner also had in common their close links with another pillar of Viennese life, the Gesellschaft der Musikfreunde.

The contribution of this association to the cultural life of Vienna and the Habsburg lands as a whole is a remarkable tribute to the devotion and energy of its leading members, particularly after 1848. It began in 1812 as a group of music-lovers whose chief aim was the promotion of music through private concerts performed by the members themselves and through the musical training offered by a conservatory (opened in 1817). The revolution interrupted the concert-giving activity of the Gesellschaft and threatened the existence of the conservatory. The latter had been closed at the beginning of June 1848 because of shortage of funds, and the nationalization of the institution as a means of securing its future was considered. Initially in 1849 the government refused a full-scale take-over but hinted at the possibility of a grant, only to reject even that idea – a change of mind that needs to be viewed in the light of the authorities' awareness of the prominent role played by students in the revolution and the closure in September 1848 of Vienna University. Only when absolutism was confidently reasserting itself were the means provided for a resumption of the Gesellschaft's educational activity and in May 1851 the city council and the state provided grants for that purpose.

In the years which followed, the Gesellschaft's cultural importance was established. Its concerts (most now public) formed one of the most important series in the city; it founded as an associated organization the

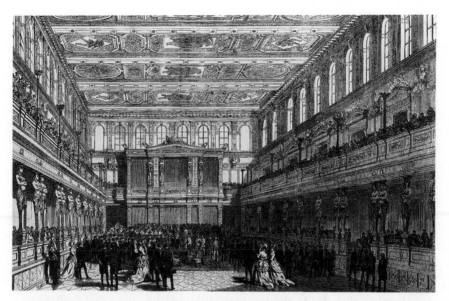

16. Ceremony for the laying of the final stone of the Grosser Musikvereinsaal, Vienna, designed by Theophil Hansen and opened in 1870; engraving after V. Katzler

Singverein, one of the capital's most important choral societies; the conservatory broadened its curriculum and offered an increasingly sophisticated professional training for young musicians; and thanks to gifts, bequests and the work of such outstanding scholars as G. Nottebohm, C. F. Pohl and E. Mandyczewski, the library became one of the world's greatest music collections. Such expansion placed great strain on the accommodation provided by the Gesellschaft's original building in the Tuchlauben and as soon as Franz Josef announced the removal of the fortifications around the Innere Stadt, the directors of the Gesellschaft recognized an opportunity to build more spacious accommodation and began planning to do so. At the Gesellschaft's 50th anniversary celebrations it was announced that a substantial site had been donated by the state and that part of the proceeds from two future state lotteries would be set aside to help finance the construction of a new building. Unfortunately the Austro-Prussian War of 1866 severely curtailed the lotteries' proceeds and it was only in 1869 that the conservatory was able to move and in 1870 that the official opening was held. The result, designed by Theophil Hansen, was one of the earliest public buildings to embody the new Ringstrasse style (pseudo-classical in this case) and it was much admired. The main concert hall, the Grosser Musikvereinsaal, had a warm, generous acoustic and its decorations created 'a harmonious relationship with Viennese society's cult of beauty . . . the Musik-verein became the centre of Vienna's rich concert life and a hospitable locale for the public display of Vienna's bourgeois circles'.[24]

Brahms's relationship to the Gesellschaft on a personal level was secured by his friendship with several members of the staff, such as the music historians Nottebohm and Pohl, the pianist and teacher Julius Epstein and the composers and theory teachers Robert Fuchs and Hermann Graedner, and with such directors as Nicholas Dumba. But on a professional level it was not entirely unclouded. When he first arrived in Vienna, in 1862, it was as a pianist that Brahms aroused the most wholehearted enthusiasm: Viennese audiences (and critics, including Eduard Hanslick, Brahms's strongest ally in later years) initially found some of the more sophisticated musical processes in the first two piano quartets and the serenades too austere and intimidating.[25] The problem was encapsulated a few years later by Theodor Billroth, the distinguished surgeon and admirer of Brahms's music, who wrote after the performance of three movements from the *German Requiem* at a Gesellschaft concert on 1 December 1867:

> Hanslick says, quite rightly, that [Brahms] has the same fault as Bach and Beethoven; he has too little of the sensuous in his art both as a composer and pianist. I think it is rather an intentional avoidance of everything sensuous as of a fault. His Requiem is so nobly spiritual and so Protestant-Bachish that it was difficult to make it go down here. The hissing and clapping became quite violent; it was a party conflict.[26]

Nevertheless Brahms's impact on musical life in the Austrian capital was such that in 1863 he was offered the conductorship of the Singakademie, a mixed choir established in 1858 by (among others) F. Stegmayer who had for some years been responsible for rehearsing the Gesellschaft's choral forces.[27] Frustrated by the institution's dilatoriness in establishing its own choral society, Stegmayer cooperated in the formation of an independent choir, and although the Singakademie was allowed to rehearse on Gesellschaft property, a considerable rivalry sprang up between it and the slightly younger Singverein; that rivalry did not encourage wholehearted enthusiasm when Brahms was invited in 1870 to succeed Herbeck as conductor of the Gesellschaft concerts. In any case Brahms rejected the terms and his counter-proposals were not acceptable to the society; but relations remained cordial and after Anton Rubinstein's departure in 1872 Brahms was again offered the post, which he held until 1875.[28] Whatever the artistic success of his concerts, it seems clear that he was not always concerned to fulfil the organizational demands of the job and was probably glad to be free of its responsibilities. Thereafter the Gesellschaft showed its estimation of his judgment by appointing him to the board of directors in 1881, a position he held until his death.

Brahms was ambivalent about accepting appointments, and in this he perhaps epitomizes the dilemma of the musician in the nineteenth century – whether to accept the security and artistic constraints of a formal post or the uncertainty and freedom of a freelance existence. For Brahms the latter was less fraught with uncertainties than it might have been: as an outstanding pianist he had a means of substantially supplementing the income from his creative work, and early in his career he had established close business contacts with distinguished publishers of international stature in Germany (for example, Breitkopf & Härtel and Simrock) and Switzerland (Rieter-Biedermann), relationships made easier by the fact that the over-whelming majority of Brahms's works were in saleable genres – piano, chamber and choral music and lieder.

Bruckner was in an entirely different position. He was one of the finest organists of the period, but recital opportunities were relatively rare (concert tours to France and England did at least bring inter-national recognition), so his performing talents were exploited pri-marily in ecclesiastical and educational posts. Such a career probably suited Bruckner's temperament in many ways, providing the security and social status he sought, even though it severely reduced the time he could devote to composition: state grants (1868, 1870, 1890–96) and private annuity (1889–96) did little until the composer's last years to allow for any alleviation of his teaching commitments. Ironically Bruckner's attempt to crown his pedagogic career, and at the same time achieve financial security and more time for creative work, through an appointment at the University of Vienna, backfired initially. Universities in Austria were undergoing a renaissance, with academic and administrative restructuring, rapidly growing student numbers (doubled between the early 1850s and 1880s) and significant contributions to scholarship in a number of fields, not least history, philology and art history. To be associated with such a flourishing intellectual environment must have been attractive to Bruckner, but his applications in 1867, 1874 and 1875 to be appointed teacher of composition (harmony and counterpoint) at the university reveals a dubious evaluation of pedagogic methodology and a curious insensi-tivity to the structure of Austrian higher education. The educational value of lectures about harmony and counterpoint (rather than more practically orientated teaching methods) was doubtful and, more important, the universities were concerned with scholarship, not practical tuition in the arts, which was the responsibility of such institutions as the conservatory of the Gesellschaft der Musikfreunde and (from 1868) the Kunstgewerbeschule. Perhaps because of the support of the Minister of Education, Karl Edler von Stremayer, Bruckner's third petition was partly successful: he was permitted to give the lectures but was unpaid; only in 1877 was he awarded a salary.[29]

If Bruckner's responsibilities as a teacher and court musician eroded the time he could devote to composition, his creative work never directly brought him any significant financial rewards. His liturgical and other choral works gained performances fairly readily, but securing a hearing for his symphonies proved difficult, and this, coupled with the fact that his contacts were for many years confined more or less to Austria and that most of his mature work lay in relatively unprofitable genres (large-scale liturgical music and the symphony), contributed to Bruckner's failure to secure greater international recognition through publications. There were no songs or piano works and only one chamber piece (the String Quintet, published in 1884) to appeal to the market for domestic music, and his publishers were exclusively Austrian. By the mid-century Vienna had lost its international status as a centre of serious music publication to Leipzig, Berlin and Hamburg: catalogues were overwhelmingly dominated by popular music, printing standards had fallen and Viennese firms failed to compete with the technological advances made in Germany. Not only were his publishers of little more than provincial status, they were (perhaps understandably) reluctant to publish his music without some form of subsidy (the Seventh, Fourth, Third (1889 version) and Eighth symphonies all first appeared under such conditions). Apparently the only fee Bruckner ever received from a publisher was 50 Gulden from Rättig for the *Te Deum*.

On the whole, Brahms seems to have accepted that his choice of independence meant his social status would largely depend on the public's assessment of his artistic achievement. Bruckner's perceptions seem to have been more complex, reflecting in part perhaps a pre-Romantic *Weltanschauung*: it should be remembered that Bruckner was brought up in the Austrian provinces during the *Vormärz*. His early attitude to music resembles that of a craftsman, his long period of study with Simon Sechter (1788–1867) being an apprenticeship, so the revelation of Wagner's music in 1862 must have offered not just new technical possibilities but the idea of the composer as genius. Bruckner's natural modesty must have made self-evaluation – was he craftsman or genius? – difficult: hence, perhaps, the importance to him of appointments whose sole advantage (at least initially) was the conferral of status. Thus he was willing to act as an unpaid organist *in Expektanz* at the Hofkapelle for ten years (1868–78) until he was eventually awarded a salary of 800 Gulden. The court musicians' function was by then largely reduced to providing liturgical music and occasional concerts of an undemanding, popular repertory (dance music was normally organized independently by the Hofballmusik-direktor). Apart from allowing Bruckner to retain a professional involvement with the musical tradition he knew best, it brought him into circles surrounding what for him was still the source and embodiment of secular authority. His devotion to the emperor (to whom the Eighth Symphony is dedicated) may have appeared absurdly anachronistic to some, but it seems his deference was appreciated at court as a reminder of a vanished age,[30] and, whatever status it may have conferred, it also bore more tangible fruit: Franz Josef decorated Bruckner with the Order of Franz Josef (coupled with a grant from his private purse) in 1886, subsidized the publication of the Third (1889 version) and Eighth symphonies, and when Bruckner could no longer climb the stairs to his apartment in Hessgasse, gave him the use of the *Kustodenstöckl* next to the Upper Belvedere Palace.

Even more than Bruckner, Wagner relied on subsidies, but in his case funds were drawn from all sources, including publishers, industrialists, royalty, friends and acquaintances. Wagner's expenditure was on a scale beyond Bruckner's wildest dreams – it encompassed the creation of the Bayreuth Festspielhaus – yet his financial reliance on others was never allowed to compromise his artistic independence: with typical virtuosity Wagner achieved the best of both worlds. Unsurprisingly his style of living was the subject of gossip, not least in Vienna during his periods of residence there, but it is regrettable to find Brahms playing a role in making such comment public.[31]

Wagner's most extended visits to Vienna were in the early 1860s (before Bruckner or Brahms had moved there permanently) for rehearsals for the planned première of *Tristan und Isolde* at the Hofoper. Although the opera house had not been at the forefront of theatres willing to perform his early stage works, it was in Vienna, in 1861, that Wagner first heard *Lohengrin* and that the planned *Tristan* gained support. However, the reliability of the proposed tenor, Aloys Ander, was soon in doubt (he seems to have become terrified by the role) and eventually the Isolde, Luise Dustmann, also lost her commitment to the project. So, in spite of the management's promises, the orchestra's enthusiasm and numerous rehearsals, the production was finally abandoned in March 1864; on the face of it a defeat almost as serious as the fiasco of *Tannhäuser* in Paris in 1861. Yet neither this setback nor the growing hostility of the Viennese press towards Wagner dampened the Hofoper management's enthusiasm for Wagner premières and they eagerly (but unsuccessfully) tried to secure the first performance of *Die Meistersinger* for the opening of the new opera house in 1869. The director, Jauner, resorted to out-and-out blackmail over singers Wagner wanted for the first Bayreuth Festival to secure his collaboration in productions of *Tannhäuser* and *Lohengrin* in 1875 and permission to perform *Die Walküre* in 1877.

By this time the Hofoper had on its staff one of Wagner's protégés, Hans Richter (appointed Kapellmeister in 1875), but although Wagner's stage works were included in the Viennese repertory they

17. *Interior of the Hofoper, Vienna, during the inaugural performance of Mozart's 'Don Giovanni' on 25 May 1869; engraving after L. E. Petrovits*

did not receive model performances: there was no unified approach to production, Richter was willing to accede to the local predilection for heavily cut versions and his interpretations lacked the agogic flexibility favoured by Wagner.[32] It was not until the late 1890s that the Hofoper was to pass into the hands of a director whose artistic approach was founded on Wagnerian ideals and who had the ability and determination to put such ideals into practice: Gustav Mahler. Nevertheless, and in spite of all the controversy encouraged (if not generated) by the Viennese press, Wagner's art was established as an important element of Viennese culture by the end of the 1870s. Wagner was perceived as a leading proponent of the 'new' in the arts and as such found enthusiastic supporters among the young, not least the three students, Felix Mottl, Guido Adler and Karl Wolff, who formed the Akademischer Wagner-Verein in 1872. But for many Wagner's significance went beyond the merely artistic and encompassed much wider social and political issues, a response encouraged by the recent history of the Dual Monarchy.

One of the characteristic activities of young bourgeois Austrians in the later nineteenth century was the formation of clubs, literary societies and discussion groups. The Wagner-Verein was an important focus for musicians including Hugo Wolf and Gustav Mahler who both arrived in Vienna in 1875 to begin courses at the Gesellschaft der Musikfreunde's conservatory. But there were others with related but wider interests, including a Pythagorean group headed by Friedrich

Eckstein (a Bruckner pupil) which numbered Wolf among its members. At the vegetarian restaurant on the corner of Wallnerstrasse and Fahnengasse and at the more famous Café Griensteidl this association came into contact with another centred on Engelbert Pernerstorfer which, as well as Mahler, included an extraordinary number of young men destined to play prominent roles in the political and cultural life of the state, ranging from Viktor Adler to Georg von Schönerer, later a pan-German nationalist and much admired by Adolf Hitler.

For most of these young men the bonds that linked them were a rejection of the newly established liberal society and a deep commitment to German nationalism. Another shared experience for many members of the Pernerstorfer group was that of assimilationist Jews who, having rejected both the faith of their fathers and many of the values of contemporary society, sought new, unifying values through a passionate participation in German culture. The group viewed the exclusion of Austria from the new Germany with disgust and grew to hate the Habsburg dynasty. Moreover, the fact that Austria's first liberal administration came to power as a by-product of the state's need to gain the assistance of Napoleon III, the occupant of what Viktor Adler described as 'the worm-eaten throne of despotism', filled them with distaste for the new government. The appeal of Wagner and (the youthful) Nietzsche to such groups was that in their writings they offered both a critique of cultural and political life and the prospect of regeneration through art, a vision that seems to have underpinned Mahler's subsequent career as both conductor and composer.

Wolf and Mahler were far more receptive to the non-musical ramifications of the Wagnerian phenomenon than Bruckner (one of the few supporters of Wagner on the teaching staff of the conservatory) but they too were deeply influenced by the Bayreuth master on a musical level. Wolf's well-publicized Wagnerian partisanship, his association with leading Wagnerian supporters, the role played by the Akademischer Wagner-Verein in promoting his music and his adoption as a significant disciple by Wagnerian commentators have ensured that Wolf's indebtedness to his model has remained predominant in perceptions of his work. The fact that his greatest achievements were in a genre that exploits words and music also encourages assumptions about the essentially Wagnerian basis of his aesthetics of song composition. But Wolf needs to be liberated from the restrictive implications of the label 'the Wagner of the lied': his treatment of the relationship between words and music and his musical resources are far more varied than such a sobriquet implies. In contrast, though Mahler's Wagnerian allegiances were hardly less pronounced, their changing significance for his musical development have yet to be fully appreciated. The overt references to Wagnerian models (usually relatively diatonic) in his early works are gradually replaced by more subtle creative explorations of the implications of Wagner's chromaticism.

The musical responses of Wolf, Mahler and Bruckner to Wagner are notable for their variety – unlike the contemporary French reaction to his influence. This diversity is particularly apparent if comparisons are made in the one genre common to Wolf and Mahler: lieder. For Wolf the basic musical material is almost always epigrammatic though capable of extension, growth and transformation; for Mahler it is a more extended unit. In Wolf the texture is often founded on four-part writing; in Mahler thinner, more linear writing predominates. Ironically, Bruckner, who devoted so much of his career to teaching, had little creative impact on the younger generation of Austrian composers. Apart from Hans Rott (1858–84), whose promising career was cut short by insanity and an early death, none of his pupils revealed any notable gifts, and for all their loyalty to him as a supporter of the Wagnerian cause in a hostile environment, Mahler and Wolf, the most talented of his younger supporters, have relatively few points of contact with his idiom. Their music occasionally invites comparison with Bruckner's work because of their shared musical heritage (Schubert being a musical ancestor of all three) and Mahler's symphonies sometimes allude to Bruckner's music and exploit types of material (for example the chorale) familiar from Bruckner's contribution to the genre. But the parallels are relatively few and superficial. Bruckner's style grew out of a provincial tradition of sacred music unfamiliar (perhaps even inaccessible) to Mahler and Wolf, and his grafting of Wagnerian elements on to this root was necessarily so idiosyncratic that its potential as a stylistic model for younger composers was limited. Brahms, on the other hand, taught little and had a knack of discouraging young admirers who sought his advice (Wolf and Rott among them), yet his richly woven idiom, combining a sense of contained powerful emotions and motivic and harmonic processes of great subtlety and complexity, proved to be a fruitful model for subsequent generations of Viennese composers, even those, like Alexander von Zemlinsky (1871–1942), whose creative standpoint was forward- rather than backward-looking.

With its familiar tendency to periodization, hindsight encourages us to see in the history of Viennese musical life at the end of the century a cluster of historically significant events centred on the mid-1890s. Some mark endings – the deaths of Bruckner (1896) and Brahms (1897) and the creative extinction of Wolf (a victim of syphilis); others mark new beginnings – the appointment of Mahler as director of the Hofoper (1897), of Guido Adler as Hanslick's successor at the University of Vienna (1898), and the appearance of a Viennese composer of multi-faceted genius, who not only exploited the resources opened up by Wagner but also offered the first distinctive creative response to Brahms's legacy. Schoenberg's early public career coincided with radical developments in a host of other fields of human activity, ranging from psychology and philosophy to the fine and applied arts. Vienna, still obsessed with a nostalgic view of its own culture, nurtured internationally influential transformations in the way people might think about themselves, their society and their art, beside which the architectural and political transformation of Vienna in the Ringstrasse period are of merely local significance.

NOTES

[1] Quoted in D. J. Olsen, *The City as a Work of Art: London, Paris, Vienna* (New Haven and London, 1986), 96.

[2] See I. Barea, *Vienna* (New York, 1966), 43ff.

[3] C. A. Macartney, *The Habsburg Empire 1790–1918* (London, 1969), 263.

[4] Barea, *Vienna*, 52.

[5] Macartney, *The Habsburg Empire*, 303.

[6] An indication of this tendency is the *Sammlung deutscher Beyspiele zur Bildung des Styls* which until 1848 was the only German reading-book used in Austrian Gymnasiums: it contained no examples of Romantic literature. See *Das Zeitalter Kaiser Franz Josefs*, i: *Teil: von der Revolution zur Gründerzeit 1848–1880* (Vienna, 1984), ii, no.25, 11.

[7] F. Trollope, *Vienna and the Austrians* (London, 1838); P. E. Turnbull, *Austria* (London, 1840).

[8] It is also maintained in books with some pretensions to scholarship, so we find H. E. Jacob writing that 'the gruesome juxtaposition of diamond-bedizened nobles and howling proletarians was to be found in the streets of Paris but never existed in Vienna' (*Johann Strauss: a Century of Light Music* (London, 1940), 23); a not dissimilar statement appears in M. Brion's *Daily Life in the Vienna of Mozart and Schubert* (London, 1959), 14.

[9] The opening chapters of E. Newman's *The Life of Richard Wagner* (London, 1933–47/R 1976), ii, remain the standard account of this period of Wagner's career.

[10] No copy of this plan has survived.

[11] Both were later to celebrate a much less worthy bastion of the imperial régime, the militarily incompetent General Jellacic.

[12] See Macartney, *The Habsburg Empire*, 608, and I. T. Berend and G. Ranki, *Economic Development in East-Central Europe in the 19th and 20th Centuries* (New York, 1974), 115.

[13] F. Löhr, 'Über einige Einflüsse der Antike auf unsere Kultur', *Deutsche Worte*, v/1 (1885), 184–5, quoted in K. Blaukopf, *Mahler: a Documentary Study* (London, 1976), 173. Mahler asked Löhr to send him a copy.

[14] Barea, *Vienna*, 224.

[15] The third movement of the First Symphony and the first movement of the Third are two striking examples.

[16] Macartney, *The Habsburg Empire*, 519–20.

[17] See Olsen, *The City as a Work of Art*, 125; this fascinating book is the source of much of the information in the following paragraphs.

[18] F. Klose, *Meine Lehrjahre bei Bruckner* (Regensburg, 1927), 10. Bruckner moved from Währingerstrasse into this apartment in 1876.

[19] See M. Wagner, *Anton Bruckner in Wien: eine kritische Studie zu seiner Persönlichkeit*, ed. F. Grasberger (Graz, 1980), 21.

[20] See K. Geiringer, *Brahms: his Life and Work* (London, 2/1963), 108; Brahms moved in at Christmas 1871 and a fourth room (for his library) was added later.

[21] Olsen, *The City as a Work of Art*, 243; chapter 14 as a whole offers a fascinating account and analysis of the interaction of architecture and social activity in Vienna.

[22] Geiringer, *Brahms*, 165.

[23] Bruckner met Brahms there on at least one occasion. See Klose, *Meine Lehrjahre*, 147.

[24] R. Hirschfeld, *Geschichte der k. k. Gesellschaft der Musikfreunde in Wien*, pt.2 (Vienna, 1912), 121.

[25] See, for example, Hanslick's comments on the G minor Piano Quartet in *Vienna's Golden Years of Music, 1850–1900*, ed. H. Pleasants (London, 1951), 81ff.

[26] Quoted in F. May, *The Life of Johannes Brahms*, ii, 396. The terms used by Billroth encourage one to wonder to what extent religious and political factors may have been responsible for the audience's reaction: the work would certainly have been understood as strongly Protestant and the Germans had just defeated Austria at Königgrätz.

[27] For a detailed account of the pre-history and history of the Singverein, and its relations with the Singakademie, see A. Böhm, *Geschichte des Singvereins der Gesellschaft der Musikfreunde in Wien* (Vienna, 1908). Brahms's rival for the Singakademie post was the deeply conservative chorus master of St Michael's, Franz Krenn. In 1875 he was appointed Dessoff's successor as composition teacher at the conservatory and there taught Mahler.

[28] It is notable that he was paid less than his predecessor (Rubinstein) and successor (Herbeck).

[29] See the important reassessment of this whole episode in Wagner, 'Bruckner in Wien'.

[30] See the letter of Princess Sayn-Wittgenstein-Berleburg quoted in A. Göllerich and M. Auer, *Anton Bruckner: ein Lebens- und Schaffensbild* (Regensburg, 1922–37), iv, pt.3, 506.

[31] See E. Newman, *The Life of Richard Wagner*, iii (London, 1945/R1976), 532ff.

[32] Newman, op cit, iv (1947), 425.

[33] This whole episode in Viennese cultural life is explored by W. J. McGrath in *Dionysian Art and Populist Politics in Austria* (New Haven and London, 1974).

BIBLIOGRAPHICAL NOTE

General background

From the death of Schubert (1828) to the arrival of Bruckner and Brahms in the 1860s the imperial capital of Austro-Hungary offered a permanent home to none of the period's major composers, and as a result the years immediately before and after the revolutionary year of 1848 is relatively sparsely covered by existing histories. Moreover the political, social and intellectual climate of the age is probably less familiar to music-lovers and students than those of, say Joseph II and Mozart or Freud and the Second Viennese School.

Although C.A. Macartney's extensive *The Habsburg Empire 1790–1918* (London, 1969) is primarily concerned with political and diplomatic history and is unremarkable in terms of style, it touches on many aspects of the empire's history and offers an extraordinarily rich and sustained narrative; Macartney makes detailed use of Hungarian sources. A. J. May's *The Hapsburg Monarchy 1867–1914* (Cambridge, Mass., 1951) is another study that sees political developments within a wider intellectual and cultural context. R. A. Kahn's *A History of the Habsburg Empire 1526–1918* (Berkeley, 1977) offers a valuable survey and an extensive bibliographical essay. Austrian history is viewed in the European context and in provocatively partisan light by E. J. Hobsbawm in *The Age of Revolution* (London, 1977) and *The Age of Capital: Europe 1848–1875* (London, 1975). A recent and ambitious collaborative two-part work, *Das Zeitalter Kaiser Franz Josefs* (Vienna, 1984–7), consists of extensive if somewhat frugally illustrated catalogues to two major exhibitions at Schloss Grafenegg, accompanied in each case by a wide-ranging volume of essays, the first covering the period 1848–80, the second the period 1880–1916. These essays are generally of high standard, combining valuable overviews which reflect recent developments in Austrian attitudes to the period and excellent bibliographies. The best-known English study of Vienna is Ilsa Barea's *Vienna: Legend and Reality* (London, 1966) which, chattily readable and organized on historical lines, gives generous coverage of the nineteenth century.

One aspect of the empire's development from the 1860s which had far-reaching (and ultimately devastating) effects on world history was the emancipation of the Jews, their migration to urban centres (particularly Vienna) and their increasing impact within the artistic, professional and economic life of the state. There has been a daunting amount written on this topic; W. O. McCagg's recent *A History of Habsburg Jews, 1670–1918* (Bloomington, 1989), though tending towards the anecdotal, offers a readable introduction with a good bibliography.

Theatres

The organization of the theatres in Vienna is comprehensively covered by F. Hadamowsky, *Wien: Theatergeschichte* (Vienna, 1988). Censorship in the first half of the nineteenth century is succinctly surveyed by J. Hüttner, 'Theatre Censorship in Metternich's Vienna', *Theatre Quarterly*, xxxvii (1980), 234–48. For an authoritative introduction to the popular theatre see two books by J. Hein, *Das Wiener Volkstheater* (Darmstadt, 1978) and *Johann Nestroy* (Stuttgart, 1990). These should be supplemented by the relevant chapters in H. Aust and others, *Volksstück* (Munich, 1989). All three of these books have good bibliographies. New productions of operas and operettas in Vienna are listed in A. Bauer, *Opern und Operetten in Wien* (Graz, 1955). The repertory of the Opera House is catalogued by F. Hadamowsky, *Die Wiener Hoftheater (Staatsoper)*, Part 2: *Die Wiener Hofoper (Staatsoper) 1811–1974* (Vienna, 1975). The fullest account of what was musically the most important of the commercial theatres is given by A. Bauer, *150 Jahre Theater an der Wien* (Vienna, 1952).

Music

There are few overviews in English of this period though *Heritage of Music*, iii, ed. M. Raeburn and A. Kendall (Oxford, 1989), offers good coverage; O. Biba's essay on music in the first of the Grafenegg volumes is an admirable and wide-ranging German summary. The major institutions and genres have been discussed only in German-language studies such as A. Böhm, *Geschichte des Singvereins der Gesellschaft der Musikfreunde in Wien* (Vienna, 1908); R. V. Perger and R. Hirschfeld, *Geschichte des k.k. Gesellschaft der Musikfreunde in Wien*, 2 vols. (Vienna, 1912); H. Kralik, *Die Wiener Philharmoniker und ihre Dirigenten* (Vienna, 1960); E. Tittel, *Österreichische Kirchenmusik* (Vienna, 1961); H. Herrmann-Schneider, *Status und Funktion des Hofkapellmeisters in Wien (1848–1918)* (Innsbruck, 1981); and M. Wagner, *Geschichte der österreichischen Musikkritik in Beispielen* (Tutzing, 1979).

There is no inevitable correlation between the achievement of composers and the extent and quality of the scholarly attention they attract. Nowhere is this clearer than in the case of English-language coverage of the leading creative figures of this period. There is as yet no substantial modern biography of either Brahms or Bruckner and on the whole the treatment of the Strauss family has been undistinguished; on the other hand, D. Mitchell's *Gustav Mahler: the Early Years* (London, 1958, rev. 2/1980) was a pathbreaking examination of the composer; and the biographies of Wagner and Hugo Wolf by E. Newman (London, 1933–47) and F. Walker (London, 2/1968) are major contributions to an understanding of their subjects.

One of the most useful books on any of the Strauss family is the documentary by M. Schönherr and K. Reinöhl, *Johann Strauss Vater* (Vienna, 1954), which has recently been joined by the multi-volume *Johann Strauss (Sohn): Leben und Werk in Briefen und Dokumenten*, ed. F. Mailer (Tutzing, 1983–). The Wagner bibliography is gigantic but as yet there is no broad-based study of Wagner's impact on Viennese culture to compliment W. J. McGrath's excellent but sharply focussed *Dionysian Art and Populist Politics in Austria* (New Haven and London, 1974).

The chief biographical studies of Brahms and Bruckner are venerable German treatments which have coloured perceptions of these composers for many years: M.

The Late Romantic Era

Kalbeck, *Johannes Brahms* (Berlin, 1904–14), and A. Göllerich, *Anton Bruckner: ein Lebens- und Schaffensbild*, ed. M. Auer (Regensburg, 1928–37); K. Geiringer, *Johannes Brahms: his Life and Work* (London, 1962); and H. H. Schönzeler, *Bruckner* (London, 1970), offer serviceable biographical primers. Much of the two composers' correspondence has been published in German, but only three volumes of Brahms's letters have appeared in English translation and none of Bruckner's. Similarly it is Brahms who has attracted a wealth of analytical attention; the results have appeared mainly in scholarly journals and symposia such as *Brahms: Biographical, Documentary and Analytical Studies*, ed. R. Pascall (Cambridge, 1983), and *Brahms 2*, ed. M. Musgrave (Cambridge, 1987). Musgrave has also published the best modern introduction to the music – *The Music of Brahms* (London, 1985). At present the analysis of Bruckner's music has not achieved a comparable level of sophistication, though the series *Anton Bruckner: Dokumente und Studien* and *Bruckner Symposium* published by the Anton Bruckner Institute of Linz have contributed to and reflected the resurgence of other approaches to the composer's output.

Access to literature on all aspects of Mahler's life and career is offered by two indispensable works: B. and E. Vondenhoff, *Gustav Mahler Dokumentation*, 2 vols. (Tutzing, 1978–83), and S. M. Namenwirth, *Gustav Mahler: a Critical Bibliography*, 3 vols. (Wiesbaden, 1987). The wealth of English-language publications concerned with Mahler's life and music reflects something of the pattern of the rediscovery of his music, which gathered force from the late 1950s. D. Mitchell's first volume has since grown into a magnificent, as yet unfinished four-part study, each component of which has adopted a different approach to the works under consideration: *Gustav Mahler: the Wunderhorn Years* (London, 1975); *Gustav Mahler: Songs and Symphonies of Life and Death* (London, 1985). The first volume of Henri-Louis de la Grange's magisterial biography originally appeared in English as *Mahler: a Biography* (London, 1974), but a revised and complete translation of the whole work (*Gustav Mahler: chronique d'une vie*, 3 vols. (Paris, 1979–84)) is in preparation. Several collections of Mahler's letters have been published, and most have appeared in translation. A great deal of the best analytical writing about his music has been in articles and theses.

On the whole, apart from F. Walker's marvellous biography, Wolf has received relatively little attention from English-speaking scholars. E. Sams's *The Lieder of Hugo Wolf* (London, 1981) and his article in *Grove 6* remain good introductions, and D.J. Stein's *Hugo Wolf's Lieder and Extension of Tonality* (Ann Arbor, 1985) offers a more analytical approach. Few of the published letters or Wolf's critical writings have been translated.

Chapter IV

Paris: Opera Reigns Supreme

JAMES HARDING

The France that Napoleon created has been with us for nearly two centuries. His influence remains pervasive and inescapable throughout every aspect of French life. He modelled the legal system and divided the country into administrative units, each named after a local river and with its prefect whose duty was to keep an eye on the provinces and report to central government in Paris any unrest or conspiracy. Education was reformed and new institutions were created to ensure *la carrière ouverte aux talents*. The constitution of the Comédie-Française was dictated by the busy emperor at a spare moment during the Moscow campaign, and he found time, between plotting battle positions, to reorganize the Paris Conservatoire. The system of *concierges* in Paris houses gave him a useful network of spies who kept the police in touch with what was going on. He even laid down the method by which houses in the streets of the capital were to be numbered. As a young man he had written a sentimental novel in the best – or perhaps the worst – tradition of the emergent Romantic movement. He is now known to have composed an opera; it probably followed the model of Paisiello, a composer said to be his favourite musician.

Napoleon died in 1821, a few months before his 52nd birthday, having in his will provided for a legacy to whomever should assassinate the Duke of Wellington. In 1840 his remains were brought back from exile in St Helena and buried with pomp at Les Invalides. By that time the restored monarchy had been established for 25 years. The throne was occupied by Louis-Philippe, now in the tenth year of his reign, a member of the Orleans family, a dumpy, undistinguished little man whose pear-shaped person delighted caricaturists. He was apt to carry an umbrella on his walks through Paris and he lived with his queen in a bourgeois domesticity far removed from the splendour of his predecessors. His very dullness emphasized the apparent stability of the régime. Under Louis-Philippe the country prospered. 'Enrichissez-vous!' was the message of his government, and although the poet Lamartine complained that 'la France s'ennuie', the fat king's subjects appeared content to make money and improve their

99

living standards. The hectic glamour of Napoleon's régime seemed to be forgotten. With the death of his son the danger of a Bonapartist revival no longer existed. The emperor's statue in the Place Vendôme was even restored and, thought the government, the ceremonial interment of his remains on French soil could safely be allowed. The Napoleonic legend, they decided, was dead. They were wrong.

In politics, as Disraeli observed, the unexpected always happens. Napoleon had a nephew, Charles Louis Napoleon Bonaparte, son of the brother whom he made King of Holland. The boy developed into a brooding politician who in 1840, the year of his uncle's reburial, landed at Boulogne and claimed France for 'la grande ombre de l'empereur Napoléon'. The comic-opera adventure ended with his capture, trial and condemnation to prison in a chilly fortress on the Somme. Six years later he escaped back to exile in England where, undeterred, he waited patiently. His hour sounded in 1848: there were revolutions throughout Europe when Paris abruptly rebelled and crowds marched through the streets roaring 'Vive l'empereur!' An astonished Louis-Philippe was obliged to abdicate and take refuge in England. A 'Mr and Mrs Smith' who arrived weary and dishevelled at Newhaven were revealed to be the king and queen en route for exile in Surrey.

At about the same time Louis-Napoleon was travelling in the opposite direction. There was fighting in the streets of Paris, the barricades went up and parliament only survived by courtesy of the army which crushed the uprising with bloody ferocity. Elections were held and Louis-Napoleon allowed himself, under a charming quirk of electoral law, to be voted in for no fewer than five constituencies. His maiden speech reassured those who feared a Napoleonic revival: the manner was ponderous, the voice had a thick Teutonic accent, the phrases were uninspired. His slogan now was 'il ne faut rien brusquer', and he proceeded with a bovine caution that encouraged most people to underestimate him.

Within months he was elected President of France under a new constitution. Three years later, by which time he had consolidated his position, a brilliantly executed *coup d'état* gave him absolute power. A plebiscite soon afterwards enabled him to declare himself Emperor of the French, Napoleon III, and a Second Empire, the sequel to his uncle's, now came into being. It lasted for eighteen years until the Franco-Prussian War of 1870, a débâcle in which Napoleon III's guile was outmatched by that of Bismarck. The Second Empire crashed amid humiliation and carnage in the streets of Paris. It was succeeded by the Third Republic, a much greyer régime and one that lacked the nostalgic undertones of Napoleonic grandeur. Yet the maligned Third Republic endured much longer than any of the other administrations that had succeeded the Bourbon monarchy, and it did not expire until

1940, when German troops marched once again into Paris as they had done in 1870.

*

Louis-Philippe, Napoleon III and successive presidents of the republic had something in common: none of them took much interest in the arts or literature. Louis-Philippe was tone-deaf. Louis-Napoleon allowed himself the indulgence of laughing at Offenbach's impudent satires but went no further in his appreciation of music. He did, admittedly, encourage his lieutenant Haussmann to modernize Paris by demolishing the medieval jumble of alleyways and crooked lanes and replacing them with broad, airy perspectives and grandiose modern buildings. His purpose was practical as much as aesthetic, for the wide new boulevards would allow the army uninterrupted lines of fire if the need arose to quell armed mobs or riots. In spite of the official philistinism of Louis-Philippe's reign, the literature written during the period was revolutionary.

In 1830, the year of Louis-Philippe's accession, Victor Hugo's flamboyant melodrama *Hernani* scandalized thinking people with its disregard for the conventions of the classical theatre. So riotous was the first night that it became known as 'la bataille d'*Hernani*'. The Romantic movement in literature, first glimpsed in the writings of Rousseau and Chateaubriand, burst out with violence. Hugo was its leader, a superb master of language like Tennyson, though, again like Tennyson, lacking the intellectual resource to match his wizardry in words. The historical novels of Walter Scott and the plays of Shakespeare were a revelation for Romantic writers struggling to throw off the traditions of centuries. Few Romantic authors were concerned with music. George Sand's involvement with Chopin was inspired by extra-musical reasons.[1] Balzac was a friend of Berlioz and used him as the basis for a character in one of his stories. The poet Alfred de Vigny had an affair with Augusta Holmès, a forgotten minor composer. His fellow poet Théophile Gautier wrote musical criticism, often, it is true, ghosted by other hands; but he did collaborate on the scenario of *Giselle*, the quintessential Romantic ballet by Adolphe Adam, composer of many operas now little remembered. The only contemporary writer with genuine musical tastes was Stendhal, a rather solitary figure who nourished a consuming passion for Rossini and Cimarosa and wrote of them with inaccuracy but enthusiasm.

Exciting things were happening in literature. Hugo was pouring out verse and gigantic novels like *Les misérables* and *Notre Dame de Paris* (always mistranslated as *The Hunchback of Notre Dame*: the hero of the novel is not the hunchback but the cathedral itself) and Balzac was creating that vast and enthralling fresco of society which he called *La comédie humaine*. While Hugo was still alive Flaubert produced his masterpiece *Madame Bovary* and Baudelaire published *Les fleurs du mal*, both to be persecuted for immorality under Louis-Napoleon.

The artistic ferment extended to painting. The Barbizon school borrowed inspiration from England, too, through the pictures of Constable. They were to be followed by the impressionists. In 1863, the year of Manet's *Le déjeuner sur l'herbe*, a picture that shocked, so many avant-garde painters were rejected by the Salon (the Paris equivalent of the Royal Academy Exhibition) that they banded together and organized what they defiantly called the 'Salon des Refusés'.

No such excitement pervaded the musical world. Ernest Reyer observed that the Italians and the Germans love music and the French do not hate it.[2] A faint echo of the Romantic taste for exoticism is to be heard in Félicien David's *Le désert*, a symphonic ode, and in his opera *Lalla-Rookh*; he had worked in Egypt and his inclination was personal rather than doctrinaire. The exotic is also evoked later in Saint-Saëns' *Samson et Dalila* and other lesser works. The composer most influenced by Romantic ideas was Berlioz. Shakespeare gave him both inspiration and a wife, Harriet Smithson, the Irish actress who bowled him over when she appeared in Paris as a member of the English troupe playing, among others, *Hamlet*. For Berlioz, Shakespeare was next to God as a creator. The impact of Shakespeare may be seen in the overture *Le roir Lear*, in *Roméo et Juliette*, in *La mort d'Ophélie*, in *Béatrice et Bénédict* and even in the great opera *Les troyens à Carthage*. Like all good Romantics, Berlioz paid tribute to Walter Scott, in the overture *Waverley*, and to Byron with *Harold en Italie*. But he was a lone voice in musical Paris – too original, too inventive for his time. Like Stendhal, he died long before his work achieved the recognition it deserved.

While Shakespeare had been a major influence on the Romantics, his place was taken, so far as the next generation of writers was concerned, paradoxically by the German composer Richard Wagner. When Baudelaire first heard *Tannhäuser* and *Lohengrin* in the early 1860s he was overwhelmed by the majesty and grandeur of the music. In a letter to Wagner he wrote: 'Above all I want to tell you that I owe you *the greatest musical enjoyment I have ever experienced*'.[3] Moreover, Wagner's theory of music drama as an amalgam of music, poetry and art tallied with Baudelaire's doctrine of 'correspondances', to quote the title of his famous poem ('La nature est un temple où de vivants piliers/Laissent parfois sortir de confuses paroles'), where he implied that everything around us is but a symbol of spiritual reality. At the same time, he continued, the universe is made up of innumerable *correspondances* or relationships: scent, colour and sound are closely linked. A scent can suggest a colour, a colour a sound, and so forth. The *Revue wagnérienne*, a literary and musical journal that flourished from 1885 to 1888, sought not only to propagate Wagner's music but also to make known his poetic and artistic innovations. Among its contributors was Stéphane Mallarmé, hermetic leader of the symbolist school which Baudelaire prefigured. In his sonnet *Hommage* and in *Rêverie d'un poète français* Mallarmé paid tribute to the composer whose example inspired the symbolists to emphasize the musical nature of poetry and to 'orchestrate' their poems by choosing words for their colour and evocative powers.[4] Poetry was to evoke rather than describe, to be fluid rather than fixed and to deal with moods, impressions and fleeting sensation rather than reality.

The most striking manifestation of Wagner's influence on French literature was the philosophical tragedy *Axël* by the flamboyant Villiers de l'Isle-Adam. This epic is set in a German medieval castle in the early nineteenth century and argues that if a dream comes true it can never equal the anticipation it has aroused. Renunciation is the only answer. The hero and heroine fall in love and passionately evoke the joy of their future life. They decide, however, that reality will be powerless to fulfil their high expectation so they drink poison from a jewelled cup and die together. *Axël* contains the famous line: 'Live? The servants will do that for us'.[5] Debussy was strongly attached to the play and even composed incidental music for one of the scenes.[6]

For the public music meant opera. This attitude sprang from a tradition reaching back many years and exemplified by Louis XIV. The Sun King was accompanied by music on his walks at Versailles, in church, at supper and at the card table. His favoured composers were Lully and Delalande, and he himself played the lute, the harpsichord and the guitar. Music, in his view, was a refinement of life to be appreciated and enjoyed in the same way as choice wines and gourmet food. It was not a medium of personal expression or philosophical inquiry. Music was best when accompanying spectacular scenes and gorgeous ballets. Most Parisians in the nineteenth century would have agreed.

Their needs were met mainly by two establishments. The more august was familiarly known as the Opéra, otherwise the Académie Royale de Musique, or 'Impériale' or 'Nationale', depending on the régime at the time. It dated back to the seventeenth century and, in its long life, had been housed in twelve different theatres. Towards the end of the Second Empire the Opéra found a permanent home off the Boulevard des Capucines in a building inspired by Napoleon III's *folie du bâtiment*. A vast and ornate edifice gradually arose, to be crowned by Millet's statue of Apollo and decorated with a façade of exuberant festoons, medallions and gilded corybants. This left only

18. Staircase of the Paris Opéra (designed by Charles Garnier) during the opening ceremony on 5 January 1875; painting by Edouard Detaille

enough room to depict eight of the Muses. Inside, the designer Charles Garnier, later responsible for a smaller version of his masterpiece in the opera house at Monte Carlo, continued imposing vistas of mirrors, ceremonial staircases and glittering chandeliers. Every variety of marble, porphyry and granite was used to create an impression of magnificence. There was even a suite of high-ceilinged rooms at the back approached by an inclined ramp so that the emperor could descend from his carriage and make an entry undisturbed by crowds and possible assassins. The Franco-Prussian War interrupted building operations, the Opéra served as a ration warehouse for the duration, and the 'Pavillon de l'Empereur', in the permanent absence of its occupant, was turned into a library and museum.

As much a declaration of political faith as an artistic phenomenon, the Opéra came second only to the Comédie-Française in the hierarchy of theatres laid down by Napoleon. Its function, said the decree of 1807, was to stage spectacles 'entirely in music' and ballets 'of the noble and graceful sort'. Next came the Opéra-Comique which had to perform comedies and dramas mingling spoken dialogue with songs, arias and concerted numbers. After the Opéra and Opéra-Comique were listed 'secondary theatres', no more than eight, which were not allowed to feature more than three performers on stage at the same time. This Napoleonic restriction was gradually eroded and at last swept away during the Second Empire, chiefly through the ingenious manoeuvres of the operetta composers Hervé and Offenbach. The Opéra-Comique was almost as old as the Opéra though much more rakish, for it had its origins in the ancient fairs of Paris. This accounts for the confusing difference between *opéra* and *opéra comique*. The latter, strictly speaking, used spoken dialogue; the former did not. Over the years, however, the distinction has become blurred, and one finds *Carmen*, than which nothing could be more tragic, in the repertory of the Opéra-Comique. Like the Opéra, the Opéra-Comique finally came to rest in a handsome building where it has remained ever since. This was in 1840, when it set up headquarters in a smaller but no less elaborate home than the Opéra's, known as the 'Salle Favart' after the famous playwright and librettist. The unusual situation of the Opéra-Comique, which faces in the opposite direction from the teeming boulevards, was dictated not by any consideration of primness but by the ground landlord's need to retain a profitable block of rented apartments nearby.

The Opéra and the Opéra-Comique were run during the nineteenth century by a mixture of public and private enterprise. Individual entrepreneurs took responsibility for the programmes under licence from the Ministry of the Interior, later from the Ministry of Education and Fine Arts. The risk was theirs – and a large part of the profits. One of the most colourful impresarios was Dr Véron, a Balzacian figure who built up a fortune out of patent medicines and showed an equal flair in running the Opéra.[7] There was money to be made from it. Such was the popularity of the genre that the rewards might be compared with those offered by films today. The singers, of course, earned much more than composers, and were as lavishly fêted and adored as pop stars. Yet even the humble individual who wrote the music could aspire to riches undreamt of had he limited himself to symphonies and chamber pieces. A successful opera paid large dividends and was the only way in which, short of a legacy, a composer could enjoy a comfortable living.

A visit to the opera was a social occasion. Whole families took out subscriptions, troths were plighted in *loges*, business deals concluded during the interval. On state occasions there were ceremonial performances for visiting notabilities. The opera was as much an instrument of government hospitality as the subsidized brothel which entertained foreign politicians in the rue Chabanais. For nineteenth-century Parisians the Opéra and the Opéra-Comique supplied all their entertainment needs. They wanted to be amused, moved and thrilled. They wanted to see beautiful singers, lovely scenery and exciting stage pictures. It helped if the music was pleasant and easy enough to be hummed or played on a parlour piano.

The man who could give them all these things was the cosmopolitan Giacomo Meyerbeer, otherwise Jakob Liebmann Beer, a German who had changed his name under the terms of a substantial legacy. After time in Italy, where he absorbed the lesson of Rossini and wrote operas in the Italian style, he settled in Paris. The city was ripe for him. To his musical gifts he added those of a brilliant entrepreneur. Large private means and the big sums his music earned enabled him to subsidize his projects with a lavishness no other composer rivalled. Each new opera was launched with much thought and meticulous planning. Everything in Meyerbeer's operas, including the music, was subordinated to glamorous spectacle. Audiences loved historical characters, glittering processions and luxurious clothes, so he provided them – and Pauline Viardot too. Meyerbeer's chief collaborator was Eugène Scribe, a dramatist whose productions eventually numbered some 400 plays and many librettos for, among others, Auber, Halévy, Bizet and Verdi. Scribe had a theatrical flair which ensured success for many nineteenth-century operas. So efficient was his stage technique that he could make a dramatic point merely by the skilful placing of a chair. With *Robert le diable*, *Les Huguenots*, *Le prophète* and *L'africaine* he and Meyerbeer captivated the public taste for medievalism, pageantry and tales of mystery. Audiences were charmed by parades of bathing beauties and graceful skaters, thrilled by coronations and explosions, fascinated by eerie

19. Meyerbeer's opera 'L'africaine': Act 4 scene i (designed by Cambon and Thierry) in the first production at the Paris Opéra on 28 April 1865; engraving from 'L'illustration' (6 May 1865)

visions of ghostly nuns. There were gypsy dances and awesome ceremonies to be admired, and witches' covens and towering temples.

'*Robert le diable* and *Les Huguenots* were spoken of in a voice of hushed awe', Saint-Saëns tartly recalled in his memoirs when he looked back on younger days. Meyerbeer was exalted as the equal of Beethoven and Michelangelo, the greatest composer of his time and one whose immortality seemed assured. Today he is largely overlooked. His operas do not succeed when they are revived because they were directed at a type of audience which no longer exists and because they depend on superb visual appeal which no modern theatre can afford. The patrons of his operas came from the businessmen and professionals who had gained prosperity under the reign of Louis-Philippe and were eager for diversion from the cares of making money. They would take to the opera especially powerful opera glasses designed to reveal in the sharpest detail every charm of the ballet dancers.

Yet for all the indifference with which Meyerbeer is now regarded, he was a considerable technician: within its limits his music is remarkably inventive. His melancholy fate is to have been the source of ideas which other, greater composers have taken up and developed. His influence can be detected in Berlioz and Verdi, and there is even a slight echo in Chopin. Wagner, too, shows traces of the contagion,

107

despite the antisemitic fury with which he assailed the composer of *Les Huguenots*. Meyerbeer's reign at the Opéra ended only long after his death in 1865. *Les Huguenots* even lingered on into the twentieth century and, by 1936, the year of its eleventh revival, had received well over a thousand performances.[8]

Berlioz, meanwhile, was vigorously excluded from Meyerbeer's fief, in spite of all his attempts to enter it. His opera *Benvenuto Cellini* was hissed at its Opéra première and only lasted for three performances. Paris did not want it, so Liszt, with his usual generosity, came to the rescue and staged it at Weimar. Neither of Berlioz's other operas, *Les troyens* or *Béatrice et Bénédict*, had first performances at the Opéra. Only in Germany did the struggling composer find the interest and support he sought for his work.

Indeed, there were not many other French composers who enjoyed the favours of the Opéra. The shadow of Meyerbeer lay heavily on the repertory which, apart from a handful of new works, chiefly comprised a stock of well-tried attractions, earning for the Opéra the derisive nickname 'le musée de la musique'. These works included *La juive*, dating back to 1835, by Fromenthal Halévy, an industrious imitator of Meyerbeer who wrote some twenty operas often with the aid of Scribe. Halévy is best remembered as father of the girl who became the model for Proust's Duchesse de Guermantes, as Bizet's father-in-law, as brother to the philosopher Léon Halévy and as uncle to the Ludovic who was Offenbach's collaborator. *La juive*, a melodrama about a fifteenth-century Jewess destined for martyrdom, enjoyed a long life, not least because it contained a splendid part, that of the heroine's father, which enabled stars like Caruso to shine with all the brilliance their admirers expected of them.

Another pillar of the repertory was *Hamlet* by Ambroise Thomas, a composer much decorated and bemedalled in his time, member of the Académie des Beaux Arts and influential head of the Conservatoire. Rossini's *Guillaume Tell* always proved a box-office draw and so too did Donizetti's *Lucia di Lammermoor* (based on Walter Scott's novel) and *La favorite* (with a libretto by Scribe). There were, however, occasional though hesitant signs of young talent coming to light. In 1851 the Opéra presented *Sapho*, Gounod's first stage work. It was not a success and vanished after seven performances, in spite of the singing of Pauline Viardot. None the less it sounded a new note and brought with it an air of Gluckian purity. The failure of *Sapho* may have been partly because it expressed dramatic conflict in strictly musical terms rather than through the lavish scenic effects demanded by patrons of the Opéra. Gounod's next attempt, *La nonne sanglante*, to a libretto by the omnipresent Scribe, had an equally disappointing reception, and so did the grandiose *Reine de Saba*. Only with *Faust* and *Roméo et Juliette* did he establish himself at the Opéra: by the end of the century they had become reliable crowd-pullers. The originality of *Faust* lay in Gounod's flexible handling of words, the way he varied rhythms and broke up cadences in a manner that prepares for the later experiments of Massenet and Debussy. That his work represented a dangerous novelty among the hidebound preserves of the Opéra was shown by an unusual incident after the première of *La nonne sanglante*. Meyerbeer, always sensitive to the latest developments, rushed up and overwhelmed Gounod with a torrent of compliments: here, Meyerbeer obviously thought, was a young rival who might well prove a threat and who must be won over from the start.

After the Franco-Prussian War of 1870, when the Opéra at last ensconced itself in Charles Garnier's impressive new building, fresh talents began to appear. Massenet's *Le roi de Lahore*, an exercise in oriental splendour *à la* Meyerbeer, dates from 1877. *Le Cid* and *Esclarmonde* confirmed his hold on the public and showed that, like his famous predecessor, he had the art of wooing audiences. His greatest success, however, was *Manon*, which belonged to the repertory of the Opéra-Comique, at the Salle Favart. Even there Meyerbeer kept up a substantial presence. He was represented by two works, *L'étoile du nord* and *Le pardon de Ploërmel* (otherwise known as *Dinorah*), and though he never felt wholly at ease in the very French genre of *opéra comique*, he could justifiably regard the Salle Favart as an outpost of his empire.

More typical of the composers who were prominent at the Opéra-Comique was Daniel-François-Esprit Auber. His name assured patrons of an evening's entertainment that would be elegant to the ear and liberally ornamented with showpieces for beautiful prima donnas. Auber was a typical boulevardier, lightly cynical, humorous and amused rather than outraged by the depravity of men and women. His industry was effortless. When he died at 79 he had written more than 70 stage works. Except for his grand opera *La muette de Portici*, also known as *Masaniello*, which, thanks to its political content, survives as a historical footnote to the Belgian revolution of 1830, his *opéras comiques* were the lightest of entertainments. Typical are *Fra Diavolo*, *Les diamants de la couronne* and others which are faintly remembered because their appealing overtures survive. His regular partner as librettist was Scribe, who fitted words to Auber's music and tailored round it a dramatic structure that was always immaculate and built with cunning stagecraft. Auber's work, though now out of fashion, still sparkles; *Manon Lescaut*, for example, overshadowed since by Massenet's famous adaptation of Prévost's novel, contains passages that engage the emotions. Wry, disillusioned, an inveterate bachelor who liked to be surrounded by pretty women, Auber looked back on his long and successful life and mused: 'I loved music until I was 30 with the true passion of a young man! I loved it so much that it became my mistress, but since then it has been my wife'.[9] He died in 1871, his world destroyed and his urbanity shattered by the horrors of the Franco-Prussian war.

Halévy, too, was a familiar name at the Opéra-Comique with *Les mousquetaires de la reine*. So was Adolphe Adam, composer of the ballet *Giselle*, whose *Le toréador* and *Si j'étais roi* diverted audiences for many an evening. Over the stage at the Opéra-Comique there trooped an endearing procession of Richard Lionhearts, Caliphs of Baghdad, Postillions of Longjumeau and Thieving Magpies who commanded a regular and loyal following. One of the most popular items in the repertory was Donizetti's *La fille du régiment* which had been specially written for the Salle Favart. By the end of the century it had received close on a thousand performances.

The 1860s, however, saw the beginnings of change at the Opéra-Comique. The first sign was Ambroise Thomas's *Mignon*. A pillar of the establishment, head of the Conservatoire, member of the Institut, he seems an unlikely herald of the new, especially when one recalls Chabrier's witty remark: 'There are three types of music, good, bad, and the music of Ambroise Thomas'.[10] *Mignon*, like Gounod's *Faust* (for which the Germans have not forgiven him), is only a shadow of the Goethe masterpiece on which it is based; yet it had an appealing grace of melody and a fluent line which introduced a more thoughtful climate than the one to which opera-goers brought up on the pleasing trifles of Auber and the craftsmanlike works of Hérold and Boieldieu were accustomed. The new atmosphere was confirmed in 1872 by a reasonably faithful performance of Mozart's *Le mariage de Figaro*, until then known only in mediocre adaptations which were travesties of the original.

An infusion of Gounod confirmed the rejuvenation of the Opéra-Comique. *Le médecin malgré lui*, given its première in the same year as *Le mariage de Figaro*, faithfully conveys the humour of Molière's play with skill and delicacy. Dyagilev much admired its Rossinian high spirits, and it comes as a pleasant surprise to those who associate Gounod with the more pompous attitudes of grand opera. *Roméo et Juliette* also figured for a time at the Salle Favart before going on to a permanent home at the Opéra. The Opéra-Comique could, however, claim as its own the delectable *Mireille*. First given there in 1874, it took time to establish itself; once audiences grew accustomed to its novel inspiration and the music's wistful naturalness, *Mireille* and its exquisite portrayal of tragic love in Provence became a major attraction at the Opéra-Comique.

By 1875 the seal was set on the new look at the Opéra-Comique by the première of *Carmen*. Bizet, like Berlioz, was influenced by the ideas of the Romantic literary movement. His *Pêcheurs de perles* was set in the exotic milieu beloved of Gautier and Nerval. *La jolie fille de Perth* drew

20. Scenes from Bizet's opera 'Carmen', first performed at the Opéra-Comique, Paris, on 3 March 1875; engraving from 'L'illustration' (13 March 1875)

on a novel by Walter Scott whose techniques were admired and assimilated by Victor Hugo. *Carmen* was based on a novel by Prosper Mérimée, who, though his cool style was far removed from the flamboyant excess of a Hugo or a Balzac, was none the less a thorough Romantic in his choice of colourful locales and his depiction of violent feeling. The first night of *Carmen* shocked the family audience at the Opéra-Comique, who were scandalized by this sordid tale of passion and murder among Spaniards of the lowest class. It was some time before Bizet's gorgeous melodies and superb orchestration made *Carmen* one of the most famous items in the repertory. One critic voicing his immediate reaction spoke for many: 'All this will not enable *Carmen* to hold the stage as long as the productions of Hérold, Boieldieu, Adam or Auber'. In fact, the opposite soon happened. By 1959, when *Carmen* transferred to the repertory of the Opéra, it had received nearly 3000 performances on the stage where once it dismayed respectable *pères de famille*.

Another notable event was the première of *Les contes d'Hoffmann* at the Opéra-Comique in 1881, a few months after the death of its composer Jacques Offenbach at the age of 61. For several years he had toiled over what he hoped would be his masterpiece. He was usually a fast worker – indeed, he once composed, orchestrated and produced an operetta within a week to win a bet. By birth a German Jew, who spoke his adopted language in a thick Teutonic accent, he composed music which, at least to foreigners, was the most characteristically Parisian in its lightness and spontaneity. At his own little theatre, the Bouffes Parisiens, he entertained the Second Empire with a string of operettas and became unofficial jester to Louis-Napoleon who, amused rather than discomfited by such impudent political satires as *Orphée aux enfers* and *La belle Hélène*, granted him the French nationality he craved.

Offenbach's hold on his public inevitably weakened after the Franco-Prussian war and the onset of a more serious Third Republic. It had been his ambition to write grand opera and he believed that *Les contes d'Hoffmann* would achieve his wish. The work at which he slaved throughout his dying days, however, proved to be a magnificent failure. His true genius is to be found in his hundred or so operettas; they are constantly revived throughout the world while the more 'serious' productions of his contemporaries, the Meyerbeers and the Halévys, lie neglected.

The world of Offenbach has an irresistible rhythm. It is impertinent and raffish. The men are fools or knaves, the women unsophisticated girls or ambitious harpies. There is room for sentiment, not too deep but poignant enough to acknowledge the existence of better things. This is the world of the boulevardier, amused, tolerant, shrewd and on occasion slightly surprised to meet with honesty or goodness.

Melody flows with a spontaneous lilt that recalls the airiness and simplicity of those earlier composers Monsigny and Grétry whom Offenbach admired. The current is free and lucid. Yet beneath the carefree surface there lurks a tinge of pessimism. However unbridled the waltz, however joyous the polka, the revels must end.

Saint-Saëns, not an indulgent critic, allowed him 'Great fertility. The gift of melody. A harmony that is sometimes refined. Much wit and inventiveness. Extreme theatrical skill. Which is more than what was necessary to succeed. He succeeded'.[11] Despite his occasionally patchy orchestration and often brutal handling of the French language, Offenbach evolved the exact style of saying what he wanted to say. The mood of the Second Empire was cynical, even fatalistic, and Offenbach expressed it admirably.

To the Opéra, the Opéra-Comique and the Bouffes Parisiens should be added the Théâtre-Lyrique which, like Offenbach's theatre, was wholly run by private enterprise. It was here that major operas by Gounod and Bizet had a first hearing before they were taken up by the Opéra and the Opéra-Comique. The Opéra, in particular, was closely linked with politics. A politician eager for publicity had only to ask a question about affairs at the Opéra to gain the satisfaction of seeing himself reported by the newspapers including, more especially, those read back in his constituency. (The more things change the more they remain the same: over a hundred years after Louis-Napoleon ordered the construction of a great new opera house as a statement of faith in the Second Empire, President Mitterrand commissioned the building of the Opéra de la Bastille as a symbol of his own régime's prestige.)

In a city where opera was regarded as the perfect form of musical expression it was inevitable that the main teaching institution should be ruled by composers for the theatre. When Cherubini resigned as head of the Conservatoire in 1842 his place was taken by Auber, who stayed until his death in 1871. Entry to the Conservatoire was regulated, according to French educational tradition, by a vigorously competitive system of examination. Among the composition teachers there during this period were Massenet, the leading opera composer of his time, and Delibes, whose ballets were much admired by Tchaikovsky. Organ classes were taken by César Franck. Auber was a reasonably efficient administrator who found time, amid his busy social life and ceaseless output for the theatre, to introduce new classes for training military bandsmen and to set up a committee which finally established the standard musical pitch. Auber was succeeded at his death by Ambroise Thomas who fought a stubborn and finally victorious battle with the Ministry of Fine Arts to move the Conservatoire from its cramped premises in the rue du Faubourg Poissonnière and to settle in more spacious accommodation elsewhere. Saint-Saëns, who studied there in the late 1840s, wrote:

I loved its decaying atmosphere, its total absence of modernity, its
air of olden days. I loved the absurd little courtyard where the
desperate squawks of sopranos and tenors, the trillings of pianos, the
honkings of trumpets and trombones and the arpeggios of clarinets
all mingled together to produce that ultra-polyphony which avant-
garde composers try to achieve without success. Above all, I love my
memories of the musical education which was imparted to me in
that ridiculous and venerable palace, long since too small to contain
the pupils who came from all corners of the world to overcrowd it.[12]

The most public function of the Conservatoire was to administer the
Prix de Rome. This was under the aegis of the Académie des Beaux
Arts, a constituent body of the Institut de France. Housed since 1806
in Le Vau's elegant seventeenth-century building on the bank of the
Seine, the Institut grouped together five academies. The most famous
is the Académie Française which consists of 40 writers, or 'immortels',
who are elected after campaigns of Byzantine complexity. By no
means all its members turn out to be immortal. Descartes never
belonged to it, and neither did Verlaine, Flaubert, Maupassant or
Molière; on the other hand Voltaire, Racine, Hugo and Valéry were
distinguished figures there. The Académie des Beaux Arts, which
works on the same system, covers music as well as painting, sculpture,
engraving and architecture.

Among the duties of the seven composer members was awarding
the Prix de Rome annually to final-year students from the Conservatoire. The successful candidate received a government scholarship
which enabled him to spend four years in Rome at the Villa Medici,
owned by the Institut, to undergo the civilizing influence of Italian
culture and to perfect his art by sending back to Paris for judgment by
a committee occasional *envois* of his works. The competition for the
Prix de Rome involved writing a cantata, usually to an execrable
libretto, under strict examination conditions. From 1840 to 1890 the
only prizewinners whose names have survived are Bizet, Massenet,
Debussy and Charpentier, the composer of *Louise*. That in itself is no
criticism of the Prix de Rome, but it may be argued that the failure of
Saint-Saëns and, later, of Ravel, to win it demonstrates a certain
short-sightedness on the part of the judging committee, who were
even disconcerted by the mild novelty of Debussy's youthful *envois*.
Finally, a significant aspect of the Prix de Rome, and yet another
indication of the theatre's hold, was a regulation that entitled the
prizewinner to have a one-act opera of his composition produced at
the Opéra-Comique.[13]

Another important duty of the Conservatoire was to run an
institution which, for many years, provided the only regular series of
public orchestral concerts in the capital. During the eighteenth
century all theatres were closed throughout Holy Week. Since Pari-

sians were deprived of the pleasures of opera-going they found an alternative in what became known as *concerts spirituels*. These consisted at first of severely religious works, though more secular music came to be included. By the beginning of the nineteenth century the *concerts spirituels* had faded. They were replaced in 1828 by the Société des Concerts du Conservatoire; its founder was an energetic violinist, François-Antoine Habeneck, former musical director of the Opéra and a teacher at the Conservatoire. When he tried to introduce Beethoven symphonies at the *concerts spirituels*, the frequent opposition, both of the audience and of his own players, inspired him to make other arrangements that would assure a more sympathetic hearing for this music.

With the approval of Cherubini, Habeneck set up the Société des Concerts du Conservatoire and directed it for some twenty years. The first concert in 1828 included the *Eroica*, which, thanks to Habeneck's persistence, was repeated at later concerts. So were other Beethoven symphonies, which he persuaded Parisian audiences to accept. There followed programmes in memory of Mozart and of Haydn and concerts of new music by Weber, though few did not include either a symphony or an important work by Beethoven. In spite of Berlioz's mockery of him, Habeneck was a valiant pioneer, but his efforts did not reach a large public. Audiences at the Société were exclusive and made up of wealthy subscribers. As a student anxious to hear Beethoven, Mozart and Haydn, the young Saint-Saëns was only able to snatch a few shreds of music by virtue of slipping past the doorkeeper and hiding in the corridor. 'How many people have cherished all their lives the dream of a stall at the Conservatoire', he wrote later, 'without being able to achieve it! How many composers have longed to see their name on that little yellow poster, no bigger than a man's hand, and have died bereft of the supreme consolation!'[14]

The task of bringing music to a wider public was left to three conductors whose names were to be perpetuated in the titles of great Paris orchestras. The first, Jules Pasdeloup, was a domineering man with a furious temper. His Société des Jeunes Artistes, which he founded in 1852, made him a powerful force in Parisian music-making over several decades. At the vast Cirque d'Hiver, which could seat 4000 people, he inaugurated his famous Concerts Populaires. Besides the German classics he bravely introduced the controversial Wagner, forcing audiences to accept a composer whose name on the programme inevitably brought protests and riots. He had little to do with contemporary French composers. 'Write masterpieces like Beethoven's', he would grumble, 'and I'll play them'. None the less he did, on occasion, play symphonies by Gounod and Saint-Saëns as a gracious nod to the younger generation. The organization he founded

21. *Programme of the first Concert National given at the Théâtre de l'Odéon on 2 March 1873, conducted by Edouard Colonne, after whom the series was later named*

eventually became the Association Artistique des Concerts Colonne, and after an initial period of competition with the Concerts Populaires it established itself firmly enough to fulfil his ambition and to give early performances of orchestral works by Massenet, Lalo and Franck. His renderings of Berlioz, who was very gradually beginning to win acceptance, were noted for their fire and colour, and his playing of *La damnation de Faust*, which had sunk into oblivion since its première 30 years before, so excited audiences that he was obliged to repeat it at half a dozen subsequent concerts. He also championed the cause of Wagner, and when he died in 1910 this enterprising musician had already conducted the first performance of Ravel's *Rapsodie espagnole* and helped to spread the fame of Debussy's *Prélude à L'après-midi d'un faune.*

The third member of this trinity of conductors who changed the face of French concert life was Charles Lamoureux. He had prudently married the heiress daughter of a rich toothpaste manufacturer and, financially independent, he was able to include in his programmes the music he himself liked even if his audiences did not. At rehearsal he terrified his players, and such was the vigorous language he used that the hall doors were kept closed to avoid shocking passers-by. If an audience did not approve of a new work, he calmly repeated it in later concerts until they did. He was particularly helpful in winning popularity for Chabrier, of whose music, unconventional and full of harmonic novelties, he was an excellent interpreter. When he staged *Lohengrin* there was uproar and fights in the street, all of which seemed only to increase his determination to impose Wagner on the French. With his Concerts Lamoureux, he also did much to foster the acceptance of new music by such compatriots as Lalo, Franck, Saint-Saëns and d'Indy.

Away from public concerts other enterprising tendencies could be noted. Lamoureux had founded the Séances Populaires de Musique de Chambre in 1859 and the Société de l'Harmonie Sacrée in 1873. Chamber music was also served by the Société des Derniers Quatuors de Beethoven which in 1851 began to encourage study of what had been regarded as a difficult period in Beethoven's music. The Société Alard-Franchomme, established in 1848, specialized in playing Classical quartets. One of its partners was the cellist Auguste Franchomme, a close friend of Chopin with whom he wrote a duet on airs from Meyerbeer's *Robert le diable*; his playing, according to the critic Fétis, was distinguished by its charm, graceful and expressive singing style and rare correctness of intonation. Another group was the Société Armingaud, formed by the violinist Jules Armingaud about 1856 to play string quartets; its members included Edouard Lalo, who, as well as composing, played the viola, violin and cello. The work of all these organizations, the public concert-giving bodies and the more modest chamber-music groups, however, was soon to receive a powerful stimulus from the Société Nationale de Musique. Formed exclusively of younger composers, it became the largest single influence on the development of contemporary French music.

In 1871 France was a prostrate and humiliated nation. The Franco-Prussian War shattered the Second Empire and led to the capitulation of Sedan. An uprising in Paris against the provisional government brought about the establishment of the Commune and a civil war characterized by atrocities and bitterness. When it was finally crushed the country faced the task of paying huge indemnities to the triumphant German victor who claimed, in addition, the province of Alsace and wide tracts of Lorraine. Social and political structures were crippled; trade and industry were halted. On the face of it, it did not seem a favourable time for artistic initiatives.

Yet, strangely, there were propitious factors. Napoleon III's grand opera house did not open until 1875 and other theatres took time to re-establish themselves. Opera needs substantial finance and long preparation. Now was the moment when other forms of music could begin to flourish. Although its sponsors probably did not realize this, the Société Nationale de Musique, which came into existence between the Armistice and the Commune, had taken root at just the right moment. Unlike the small chamber-music groups and the exclusive Société des Concerts du Conservatoire, the new organization was dedicated to propagating the work of French composers. It had no concert hall or permanent headquarters and depended on the Pleyel and Erard piano companies for the use of premises. Its defiant slogan was 'Ars Gallica'.

The founder-members of the Société Nationale de Musique were led by Saint-Saëns and by Romain Bussine, a singing teacher at the Conservatoire. Towards the end of his long life Saint-Saëns became a notorious reactionary and denounced many of his early enthusiasms, but as a young man he had seemed a dangerous revolutionary. He championed Wagner and Schumann at a time when both were regarded by *bien-pensants* as eccentrics. A superb virtuoso pianist, he reawakened his countrymen to the virtues of Rameau and of Mozart's piano concertos. As a close friend and admirer of Liszt, who staged his opera *Samson et Dalila* when no French theatre would so much as consider it, he followed his hero's example and wrote four symphonic poems, making the genre familiar in France where, apart from occasional modest pieces by such as Félicien David, it was little known. He also composed five piano concertos which served as models where few had existed. So did his three published symphonies. His restless curiosity made him an eloquent advocate of Handel, Bach and Gluck, then much neglected.

The Société Nationale gave its inaugural concert on 17 November 1871 at the Salle Pleyel. It was well received and quickly followed by others. Later in the season a programme of the most successful works was given. As Saint-Saëns recalled:

> The distinguished audience did not seek to hide its surprise. So it was possible, then, to make up an interesting programme with new compositions by French composers! . . . It is permissible to say that on that date the aim of the Société was achieved and from then onwards French names appeared on concert programmes to which no-one had hitherto dared admit them. The barriers were down.[15]

By 1914 the Société had given first performances of many important new works by Chabrier, Fauré, Ravel, Debussy and Dukas.

That historic concert included a trio by César Franck, a member of the Société's committee. This early piece gave little sign of the talent he developed, for his best music was not written until he had passed the age of 50. Born in Liège of German descent, he studied at the Paris Conservatoire and, in his maturity, brought to French music a rare warmth and solidity of construction. His piano quintet, dedicated to

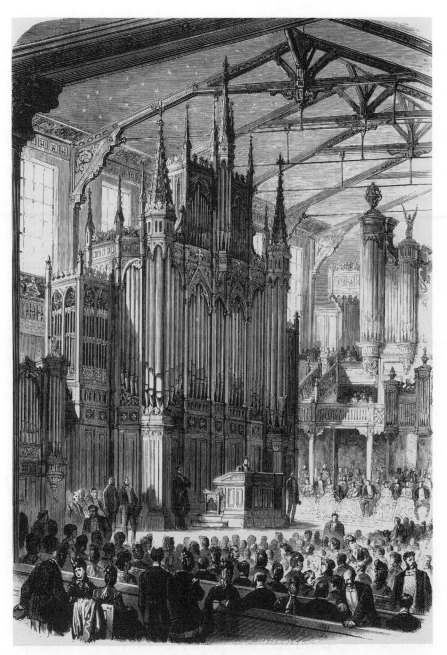

22. *The showroom of the organ builder Cavaillé-Coll, whose instruments played a crucial role in the revival of French organ music after 1850; engraving from 'L'illustration' (12 March 1870). César Franck, an 'artistic representative' of the firm, played on a particularly fine example at the church of Ste Clotilde where he was organist*

Saint-Saëns and first heard at a Société concert in 1880, is typical of his preference for expansive, long-breathed melodies, haunting chromaticism and frequent modulation. The four symphonic poems, inspired among others by poems of Victor Hugo and Leconte de Lisle, show his mastery of orchestral colour, as does the great Symphony in D minor which uses cyclical form in a uniquely personal way. That he could also write 'brilliant' virtuoso music is proved by the *Variations symphoniques* for piano and orchestra. He was typical of this new generation of French composers in that his genius was orientated more towards symphonic works than to opera, which he essayed on several occasions without success. Franck gathered round him, as a benevolent 'pater seraphicus', a group of admiring young disciples, including Duparc and Chausson, led by Vincent d'Indy.[16]

Franck considered Henri Duparc, a youthful member of the Société Nationale, to be his most gifted follower. Although Duparc left only a small amount of music, its quality would seem to bear out Franck's opinion. Stricken by an obscure nervous disease in his late 30s, he was obliged to give up composing. Yet the songs he produced, a mere dozen or so, entitle him to an honourable position in French music. *L'invitation au voyage*, his exquisite setting of Baudelaire, has an acute sense of poetry and an aching nostalgia that re-create in purely musical terms the verbal concepts expressed in the verse. Another Baudelaire song, *La vie antérieure*, on which he laboured for some eight years, represents the culmination of his art with its subtle, elusive evocation of the mysterious world conjured up by the poet. Even when he set the verse of minor poets like Jean Lahor and Armand Silvestre he added the touch of unmistakable genius which puts him in the first rank of French songwriters. He often orchestrated the accompaniments, and in these, as well as in his symphonic poem *Lénore*, he demonstrated an intuitive grasp of the orchestra.

So did his friend and fellow disciple Ernest Chausson, whose *Poème de l'amour et de la mer* delicately translates poetic metaphor into music. With his unerring sense of instrumental colour Chausson may be seen as the connecting link between Franck and Debussy. The work of Vincent d'Indy, Franck's most tenacious disciple, later a prominent member of the Société Nationale and founder in 1894 of the Schola Cantorum, an important training institution for young musicians, lies outside the period of this survey.

A composer for whom the Société Nationale de Musique catered ideally was Edouard Lalo. After playing for ten years or so in the Armingaud quartet he devoted himself entirely to composing. Many of his songs were first given by his wife, a professional contralto, at Société concerts, where his other works received a hearing. Even so, his music gained more favour initially in Germany than in his native land. That is not surprising as his G minor Symphony has a distinctly

Brahmsian flavour. Lalo is best known as composer of the *Symphonie espagnole* which the virtuoso Sarasate commissioned as a showpiece for himself. From the German classics he had learnt the importance of good construction, to which he added his personal gift for richness of colour and supple harmonies. These were underscored by a crisp sense of rhythm which he doubtless owed to his Spanish ancestry. In *Le roi d'Ys*, however, he was able to absorb the influence of Wagner and to write, in his adaptation of an old Breton legend, a movingly original opera.

Gabriel Fauré was among the youngest members of the Société Nationale. At the time of its foundation he had already composed a number of charming salon works: songs reflecting the style of Gounod and piano pieces recalling Mendelssohn and Schumann. He was one of the few French composers of the time who, while admiring Wagner, succeeded in avoiding his influence. Within a few years he had become a master of song in which the harmonies and the vocal lines are indissolubly wedded. Words and music come together in a union at once fluid and indivisible. It would be mistaken to see him merely as a forerunner of Debussy. The universe he created in the song cycle *La bonne chanson* and in such piano works as the nocturnes is self-contained and wholly his own.

An independent figure who should be mentioned is Emmanuel Chabrier. He began his career as a civil servant and all his life was an enlightened art collector. Since he never studied at the Conservatoire, relying on himself and on private lessons for his training, he was dismissed as an amateur by more conventional musicians when his work began to startle Paris audiences with its daring novelty. His *Menuet pompeux* was to influence Ravel and Satie and his exuberant *España* left its mark on Stravinsky's *Petrushka*. His flamboyant technique as a pianist inspired the *Dix pièces pittoresques* which are full of innovations considered reprehensible by academic opinion at the time. He, of all French composers, was perhaps the most passionately in love with Wagner's music, as he showed, sometimes to excess, in the opera *Gwendoline*. He was more himself, more natural, in the operas *L'étoile*, *Le roi malgré lui* and *Une education manquée*, where he displayed to full measure his irresistible and effervescent sense of humour. Yet even Chabrier, lone wolf though he was, owed a debt to the Société Nationale. His more substantial piano pieces were played there for the first time by, among others, Saint-Saëns. The Société Nationale continued its work into the twentieth century, and though by then it was rivalled by the Société Musicale Indépendante, which differed from it by including foreign works in programmes, its achievement in fostering the renewal of French music throughout the 1870s and 1880s cannot be denied. Native composers at last had a platform where they could be given a fair hearing. Although opera

23. *Madame Manet at the Piano; painting (c1867) by Edouard Manet. Chabrier (who owned 14 paintings by Manet) dedicated his Impromptu for piano (1873) to her*

continued to be a favourite relaxation for the general public, its tyranny over musical life was broken and composers were encouraged to write symphonic works that before the 1870s might never have had the chance of performance.

The musical revival in France after the Franco-Prussian War was not restricted to contemporary works. Composers from an earlier age were rediscovered and reinterpreted. Saint-Saëns, as has been noted, stimulated interest in Rameau, Mozart and Handel and even persuaded Berlioz, who had previously regarded Bach as an uninspiring manufacturer of fugues, that the master of Leipzig was a great composer. His evangelizing had been anticipated by Gounod, his mentor and senior. Though generally associated more with the theatre than with the organ-loft, Gounod was deeply religious and from his youth pleaded the cause of Bach and Palestrina. His enthusiasm helped to inspire Charles Bordes, a pupil of César Franck, who toured France with a choir that revealed the beauties of old music to audiences hitherto unaware of it. At the same time monks at the Abbey of Solesmes helped forward the renewal of church music by restoring the texts of Gregorian chant and purifying them of errors and misconceptions which had grown up over the centuries, obscuring their true spirit.

The slow but gradual work of the Société des Concerts du Conservatoire, of the smaller chamber music groups, of individual conductors and, most important, of the Société Nationale de Musique, prepared the ground for the activity which galvanized the French scene in the decades after 1870. To these must be added the powerful influence of Wagner. Although it was sometimes harmful and could bring unfortunate results (as in Chabrier's sadly uncharacteristic opera *Gwendoline*) Wagner's example had a tonic effect. It extended far beyond the period under discussion and even into the next century, when it inspired hostile reaction from Erik Satie and others who sought to purge French music of what they regarded as a cloying and unwelcome trend. In the meantime the way had been opened for younger composers like Fauré, Debussy and Ravel to reaffirm the supremacy of French art.

NOTES

[1] The liaison, inevitably, ended in tears and Sand revenged herself by making Chopin the model for the rootless and neurotic hero of her novel *Lucrezia Floriani* (1847).

[2] Ernest Reyer (1823–1909) is better known for his witticisms than for his operas, which include a Wagnerian *Sigurd* and a ballet, *Saccountala*, on which he collaborated with Théophile Gautier. He also fulfilled the crazy task of adapting Flaubert's epic *Salammbô* as a five-act opera.

[3] 'Lettre à Richard Wagner', in *Baudelaire: oeuvres complètes* (Paris, 1968), 1205; the same volume contains 'Richard Wagner et Tannhäuser à Paris' and 'Encore quelques mots', where Baudelaire champions Wagner against his French detractors and finds common artistic ground with him.

[4] S. Mallarmé, *Oeuvres complètes, poésie-prose* (Paris, 1961), 71, 541–6.

[5] A full discussion of *Axël* is in the standard biography, A. W. Raitt, *Villiers de l'Isle-Adam* (Oxford, 1981).

[6] The manuscript is now lost.

[7] As a newspaper magnate Véron founded the *Revue de Paris* and revitalized *Le constitutionnel* with the aid of sensational serials, turning it into a powerful supporter of Louis-Napoleon; his six-volume *Mémoires d'un bourgeois de Paris* (Paris, 1853–5) are fascinating.

[8] Meyerbeer's contribution to French music and the nature of his influence and achievement have been admirably summed up by M. Cooper, 'Giacomo Meyerbeer, 1791–1864', *PRMA*, xc (1963–4), 97–129 [special issue].

[9] Quoted in C. Malherbe, *Auber* (Paris, 1911), 23.

[10] Quoted in R. Myers, *Emmanuel Chabrier and his Circle* (London, 1969), 3.

[11] C. Saint-Saëns, *Harmonie et mélodie* (Paris, 1885), 224.

[12] C. Saint-Saëns, 'Le vieux Conservatoire', in *Ecole buissonnnière* (Paris, 1913), 39.

[13] There were, of course, other music schools in Paris. The Swiss composer Louis Niedermeyer, who founded in 1853 the school that bears his name, wrote works for the theatre before devoting himself to church music; one of the teachers was Saint-Saëns, who there struck up a lifelong friendship with his pupil Gabriel Fauré. It is a pleasing irony that the Ecole Niedermeyer, intended to train composers of religious music, should have produced so many graduates who found more distinction as writers of operetta and musical comedy, among them André Messager, Vasseur, Audran, Terrasse and Missa.

[14] C. Saint-Saëns: 'La Société des Concerts', in *Harmonie et mélodie* (Paris, 1885), 189.

[15] C. Saint-Saëns, 'La Société Nationale de Musique', in *Harmonie et mélodie*, 207–8.
[16] Franck and his disciples are exhaustively discussed and assessed in L. Davies, *César Franck and his Circle* (London, 1970).

BIBLIOGRAPHICAL NOTE

Historical and cultural background

The standard general history of France is E. Lavisse's multi-volume *Histoire de la France contemporaine* (Paris, 1920–22) in which the volume by C. Seignobos, *La révolution de 1848 et l'empire* (Paris, 1921), refers specifically to the period, as does the same author's *L'évolution de la troisième république, 1875–1914*. A reliable short history in English is A. Cobban's *A History of Modern France*, 3 vols. (London, 1965). Individual topics and personalities have been treated by the underestimated P. Guedalla, *The Second Empire* (London, 1922), and by F. A. Simpson, *The Rise of Louis Napoleon* (London, 1909). The most succinct and lapidary survey of French literature remains L. Strachey, *Landmarks in French Literature* (London, 1912), though G. L. Lanson, *Histoire de la littérature française* (Paris, 1902, and subsequent edns.) is not to be despised, especially when consulted with R. Lalou, *Histoire de la littérature française contemporaine*, of which the first volume (Paris, 1947) is helpful on the period from 1870.

Music

M. Cooper, *French Music from the Death of Berlioz to the Death of Fauré* (Oxford, 1951), covers part of the period with elegance and scholarship. A readable general history is P. Landormy's *La musique française de la Marseillaise à la mort de Berlioz* (Paris, 1944) and *La musique française de Franck à Debussy* (Paris, 1943). A more critical account is J. Gaudefroy-Demombynes, *Histoire de la musique française* (Paris, 1946), and the Pléiade *Histoire de la musique*, ed. R. Manuel, vol.ii (Paris, 1963). O. Sére's *Musiciens français d'aujourd'hui* (Paris, 1911, 1921) groups biographical articles on individual composers with useful bibliographies and work-lists. P. Lalo's *De Rameau à Ravel: portraits et souvenirs* (Paris, 1947) is especially valuable because, as the son of Edouard Lalo, he knew several of the composers about whom he wrote.

The history of musical institutions is well served by L. Rohozinski, *Cinquante ans de musique française de 1874 à 1925*, 2 vols. (Paris, 1925). The Opéra is covered, idiosyncratically, by Castil-Blaze in *L'Académie impériale de musique de 1645 à 1855*, 2 vols. (Paris, 1855). Later developments are chronicled in C. Dupêchez, *Histoire de l'Opéra de Paris, 1875–1980* (Paris, 1985). C. Nuitter, *Le nouvel Opéra* (Paris, 1875), is a painstaking account of Napoleon III's new building down to such details as the number of keys (7593) and of steps to the staircases (6319). S. Wolff, *L'Opéra au Palais Garnier de 1875 à 1962* (Paris, 1962), lists full casts and production details of every opera and ballet presented there during the relevant period. S. Wolff and A. Lejeune, *Les quinze salles de l'Opéra* (Paris, n.d.), gives a historical survey from early beginnings to the present day. F. Clément and P. Larousse, *Dictionnaire lyrique, ou Histoire des opéras* (Paris, 1869, 1881, 1897), deals extensively with long-lost operas but should be used with care. Opera as an artistic and especially a commercial enterprise is well documented in T. Walsh's *Second Empire Opera: the Théâtre Lyrique, Paris, 1851–1870* (London, 1981), K. Pendle, *Eugène Scribe and French Opera of the Nineteenth Century* (Ann Arbor, 1979), casts light on many dark places. The most reliable work on the Opéra-Comique is A. Soubies and C. Malherbe, *Histoire de l'Opéra-Comique, la seconde Salle Favart, 1840–1860* (Paris, 1892), while there is a broader history in J. Gourbet, *Histoire de l'Opéra-Comique* (Paris, 1978). The lighter stage is exhaustively surveyed by F.

Bruyas, *Histoire de l'opérette en France, 1855–1965* (Lyons, 1974), and is also treated in Rohozinski, *Cinquante ans de musique française.*

A great deal of information about contemporary musical activity may be gleaned from F. J. Fétis, *Biographie universelle des musiciens,* 8 vols. (Paris, 1835); 2 suppl. vols., ed. A. Pougin (Paris, 1878). Another important source is A. Elwart, *Histoire de la Société des Concerts du Conservatoire impériale de musique* (Paris, 1860), supplemented by A. Dandelot, *La Société des Concerts du Conservatoire* (Paris, 1923). Colonne, Lamoureux and their respective organizations are discussed in H. Imbert, *Portraits et études* (Paris, 1894), while their rival Pasdeloup figures in A. Elwart, *Histoire des concerts populaires* (Paris, 1864), and in A. Jullien, *Musique: mélanges d'histoire et de critique* (Paris, 1896).

Personal memoirs contain eye-witness accounts and recollections, though the prejudices of the memorialist should be allowed for, especially in the case of Berlioz and Saint-Saëns. A. Adam's *Souvenirs d'un musicien* (Paris, 1857, 1871) and *Derniers souvenirs d'un musicien* (Paris, 1857, 1859) are worth attention, as are Gounod's posthumous *Mémoires d'un artiste* (Paris, 1896). Berlioz's *Mémoires* (Paris, 1870) are a classic in their own right and furnish an often hilarious account of Parisian musical life and institutions; they have been translated into English, in a way that does justice to the wit and verve of the original, by D. Cairns (London, 1969, 2/1970), whose substantial biography of Berlioz is currently underway: vol.i (London, 1989). Saint-Saëns' *Harmonie et mélodie* (Paris, 1885), *Portraits et souvenirs* (Paris, 1899, 1909) and *Ecole buissonnière* (Paris, 1913) paint a vivid picture of musical conditions in Paris during the first four decades of the period.

Biographies and studies of individual composers abound. Meyerbeer is dispatched once and for all by M. Cooper's indispensable 'Giacomo Meyerbeer, 1791–1864', *PRMA,* xc (1963–4); 97–129. The following full-length studies are available: C. Malherbe, *Auber* (Paris, 1911); G. Faure, *Boieldieu, sa vie, son oeuvre,* 2 vols. (Paris, 1944–5); A. Cocquis, *Léo Delibes: sa vie et son oeuvre (1836–1891)* (Paris, 1957); A. Pougin, *Hérold* (Paris, 1906); H. de Curzon, *Ambroise Thomas* (Paris, 1921); V. d'Indy, *César Franck* (Paris, 1924), is an exercise in hagiography. More balanced is L. Vallas, *La véritable histoire de César Franck, 1822–1890* (Paris, 1955). L. Davies, *César Franck and his Circle* (London, 1970), is an enthusiastic collective study with lengthy sections on Chausson, Lekeu, Duparc and d'Indy.

Bizet is best served in English by W. Dean, *Bizet* (London, 1948, rev. and enlarged 3/1975), and M. Curtiss, *Bizet and his World* (New York and London, 1958). J. Desaymard, *E. Chabrier d'après ses lettres: l'homme et l'oeuvre* (Paris, 1934), is rewarding reading, while F. Poulenc's little book *Emmanuel Chabrier* (Paris, 1961) is worth its weight in gold since here we have one creative artist's appreciation of another. Other background details to the period may be found in J. Harding, *Saint-Saëns and his Circle* (London, 1965), *Massenet* (London, 1970), *Gounod* (London, 1975), *Folies de Paris: the Rise and Fall of French Operetta* (London, 1979) and *Offenbach* (London, 1980).

Chapter V

Italy: the Decline of a Tradition

JOHN ROSSELLI

In the winter of 1855–6 a young English student of singing could be found going for walks on top of the bastions that still hemmed in the city of Milan. He would have preferred to get clean away into the countryside, but that would have meant on his return facing a sort of customs examination from the officials who levied a municipal tax on incoming goods at each of the city gates. It was easier to take the air on top of the walls.[1]

Three years before the unification of Italy in 1859–60, Milan was still in many ways close to a Renaissance town, walled, gated, a place of narrow streets lined with plain ochre-washed houses as well as with churches and palaces, clearly marked off from the countryside where the overwhelming majority of the population lived; and so were most other Italian towns. Yet Milan was in many ways in the vanguard of progress. It had a railway connecting it with Venice, as well as an active commercial, intellectual and professional life. It had recently become the musical capital of Italy: that was why the young English singer, among many others, was studying there. A few years earlier, in 1848, Milan had risen against its Austrian rulers and, in the celebrated 'five days' of street fighting, had won its independence. Everything had then gone wrong, not least relations among groups of Italians with clashing views and ambitions. The Austrians were able to march back in; they fastened on Milan, and indirectly on all of Italy except independent Piedmont, a rule far more tyrannical than what had gone before.

It had to be more tyrannical because the 1848 revolutions had shaken old loyalties and assumptions beyond repair. From all the Italian states many members of local élites had gone into exile. Old beliefs in possible solutions to the problem of divided Italy (a federation that would leave the existing states intact, a republic spontaneously established by a people newly united in self-sacrificing righteousness) had turned out to be illusory; some of the exiles now accepted what looked like a realistic goal – absorption of north and central Italy by Piedmont, thanks to some fresh turn in European affairs. Few expected that as early as 1860 the whole of Italy except

Venetia and Rome would suddenly come under the Piedmontese crown. Venetia followed in 1866, Rome in 1870.

Even where the old walls were not torn down after unification (as they were in Milan), the commercial and administrative centres of the new kingdom now expanded greatly. In Turin, Milan, Genoa and Rome a building boom resulted in thousands of ponderous, often ornate blocks of flats along new wide avenues serviced by trams. Though modern industry on any scale did not come until the 1890s – even then mainly in the Turin–Milan–Genoa triangle – Italy was consciously joining the ranks of advanced nations. Like the new country's unity, its hold on modernity was as yet precarious. It therefore had to be asserted in overblown public buildings that even now startle the visitor, such as Milan Central station or the Victor Emmanuel monument in Rome. The reality around the turn of the century was, for many people, poverty, illiteracy, narrow local horizons; the pretension upheld by governments and by much élite opinion was that Italy should be acknowledged as one of the great powers, entitled to a colonial empire and a place in European councils.

Like the visual arts, musical life in the new Italy expressed a mixed assertiveness and unease. The musical world of pre-1848 Italy had scarcely needed to proclaim its own importance and value. It was far too busy turning out a stream of new operas for almost instant performance throughout a network of Italian and foreign theatres. Opera was the old Italy's musical business, in two senses: as the focus of urban social life within the peninsula, opera dominated the work of Italian musicians; as a triumphant art form, it had no serious rivals on the lyric stage of any 'civilized' country other than France.

This operatic activity culminated in Verdi's three great popular works of 1851–3, *Rigoletto*, *Il trovatore* and *La traviata*. Within a few years they were being performed (literally) from China to Peru. Scratch companies might bawl their way through them, satirists might guy them (as Gilbert and Sullivan did); but they were indestructible. In these three operas Verdi at once summed up 40 years' Italian musical experience and opened new paths. *Il trovatore* distilled all that was ardent and dynamic in the closed forms of Italian opera of the Romantic era: prodigious energy issuing from rapt contemplation, whether in the single aria with its twofold structure of meditative cantabile and fast cabaletta or in the ensemble or scene that embodied the same structure on a broader scale by building up to a largo – a moment of stasis – resolved by a headlong stretta. The most notorious example is Manrico's aria 'Ah si ben mio', followed, at the news that his mother is about to be burnt at the stake, by 'Di quella pira', with its unwritten high Cs (two if the second stanza is included, three if (as used to happen) an encore is given).

From the start the literal-minded have asked why the tenor trouba-
dour does not rush off to rescue his mother instead of singing about it;
but in Italian Romantic opera, a highly conventional form, what
counts is not realism but the discharge of feeling by the most powerful
musical means.

La traviata and especially *Rigoletto* opened up new ways of handling
subject matter and musico-dramatic structure. Opera could now find
heroism in the low-born and the disreputable; it could blend grotesque
or sardonic humour with tragic awe; it could accommodate a delicate
pathos once reserved for the 'semi-serious' genre – the pathos of
woman as victim – and raise it to a tragic dignity. It could also begin
to get away from the dominance of the aria: Verdi designed both
operas largely as a string of duets: in the last act of *Rigoletto* (as earlier
in Rigoletto's brooding monologue 'Pari siamo' and his encounter
with Sparafucile) he built up whole scenes from fragments of arioso
held together by the economical use of recurring themes. He had
found a new way to marry power and flexibility.

Verdi's triumph came just as the creative force of Italian opera
began to flag. Repertory opera (the repeated performance of a few
well-known works) began to creep in, both as a term and as a practice,
just ahead of the 1848 revolutions. It was confirmed by the prolonged
political and economic crisis of 1848–53. Leading theatres cut down
the number of new works they presented. The many new opera houses
built in Italy and elsewhere from about 1850 were often larger than
their predecessors and were designed for a largely middle-class
audience. A slightly later generation of theatres, often known as
politeama, some of which were originally built as circus-like structures
of wood, iron and canvas, held yet larger audiences: about 4000 in the
Teatro Politeama of Buenos Aires (1879), a city then heavily populated
by Italian immigrants, and still more in some North American
theatres. Such houses came into being with repertory opera, from
which they lived.

They also lived off the new genre of operetta, an immensely
successful import from Paris and Vienna, cheaper than opera in every
sense (one of its attractions was that it often hovered on the edge of
impropriety without going so far as to drive ladies from the theatre).
Italian comic opera had had a flickering Indian summer in the 1850s,
with innocuous, derivative, now-forgotten works such as the Ricci
brothers' *Crispino e la comare* (1850) or De Ferrari's *Pipelet* (1855).
Some of these had a long career, but operetta established itself as the
ruling popular form until the coming of the cinema – alongside low-
price performances of a few evergreen operas.

Opera seasons were still put on by impresarios but, except in the
Americas, they were now dominated by a few music publishers who
could at last enforce a composer's copyright. Publishers commissioned

24. Headquarters of the publishing firm Ricordi, next to La Scala, Milan, in the 'Casino Ricordi' which they occupied 1844–67; engraving (c1845)

operas and decided where they should be produced; they sent out stage directions as well as set and costume designs and they largely controlled casting. By 1888 a series of mergers had reduced the important music publishers to two, Ricordi and Sonzogno, who battled it out for a number of years. A musically sensitive publisher like Giulio Ricordi (1840–1912) could take a chance on the young Puccini, subsidizing him for nine years before seeing a dependable return – which was huge and lasting.

The chief reason why the young Puccini had to be carefully fostered (unlike composers in the old Italian system who had plunged almost at once into a busy theatrical career) was that successful new operas were now both rare and highly remunerative. An opera that stood out from the ruck, as a leading critic put it in 1882, represented capital: with performances and sales of vocal scores it could yield 'as much as a large farm'.[2] Such an opera could reach more people and more parts of the world than ever before. But somehow the creative springs that had produced a continual stream of new works in the days of Rossini, Bellini, Donizetti and the young Verdi were running low.

One reason for this was the coming of the new Italy, with its middle class eager for European standing in politics and culture. In the nationalistic Europe of the mid- and late nineteenth century, Italian opera had many foreign detractors. It was said to be absurd, crude and outrageously expensive. But that did not prevent audiences everywhere from flocking to Verdi's operas: a French comedy of 1861 in which two bourgeois families set out to dazzle each other with their alleged social graces has one of the fathers complain that this involves repeatedly attending performances of *Rigoletto*.[3] But members of the Italian élite now began to wonder whether there might not be something in the criticisms. They themselves were not as single-mindedly absorbed in opera as they had been before 1848. New concerns had arisen. There was now an active political life, freedom of discussion in newspapers and magazines, a greater interest in reading novels. Most important, Italians were no longer so confident of leading everyone else in the composition and performance of music.

*

While Italy had been taken up almost exclusively with opera, the rest of Europe had gradually come to give the Viennese Classical school of Haydn, Mozart and Beethoven a special place in the musical hierarchy. The greatest masterpieces were now held to be instrumental works, mainly symphonies, Beethoven's in particular. The best new music ought to be as profound in its insights as Beethoven's, and as titanic in its aspirations: such was the aim, even though in practice concert fare in the middle decades of the century still included a good deal of operatic selections, medleys and fantasias.

By the time of Italian unification a group of young artists in Milan known as the *scapigliati* ('dishevelled ones') shared these assumptions. A poem by one of them, Arrigo Boito (1842–1918), called for the cleansing of the altar of Italian musical art, 'now befouled like the walls of a brothel'. At almost the same time in a private house in Florence a concert was given consisting of Beethoven's Eroica Symphony (in Czerny's two-piano version), a string quintet by a local composer, Mendelssohn's D minor Piano Concerto and Hummel's *Rondo brillante* for piano. Florence had for some time been a self-conscious candidate for the intellectual leadership of Italy; it also had a high concentration of foreign residents. Beethoven's music had had performances there since the 1820s and there was a society for those interested in Classical music which in 1861, a little after the concert just described, was able to mount Beethoven's Second Symphony and Mozart's Requiem – with what forces is not clear; the society had previously given Haydn's First Symphony in a transcription by Clementi for piano quintet.[4]

The Viennese school had never been totally neglected in Italy, but even in Florence it had been the concern of a small minority. One of its promoters was Rossini. As a composer he was the object of monotonous complaints of 'Germanism', that is, over-elaborate instrumentation, supposedly contrary to the Italian spirit. As director (in effect) of the municipal music school at Bologna from 1839, he made pupils study Mozart and Weber, shortly joined by Haydn and Beethoven.[5] In this and other public music schools – which were established piecemeal throughout the century, on the model of the Paris Conservatoire – budding musicians were supposed to study ancient music and to attain some kind of literary culture; but the economic rewards and popular success of opera kept most of them eager for an operatic career. Nevertheless, an interest in instrumental music and symphonic development gradually spread. In the 1860s Italians began to found 'quartet societies' and to listen to orchestras directed by a modern type of conductor, some 40 years after such practices had become the norm in Leipzig and Paris.

These developments were closely linked. 'Quartet societies' did not lead Italian composers to start writing much chamber music, though some was composed, and Verdi wrote one delightful quartet on an idiosyncratic, non-Viennese scheme. But these societies led to a new interest in playing and listening to instrumental music, including chamber works; and as we have seen from the Florence concert mentioned above, programmes might include works that we think of as 'chamber' and 'orchestral'.

However, the first Italian conductor in the modern sense, Angelo Mariani (1822–73), built up an orchestra fit to cope with most kinds of nineteenth-century music. This was at Bologna, where the municipality maintained a permanent orchestra, chiefly to play in the leading opera house which it owned. Mariani had a number of successors, culminating in the world-renowned Arturo Toscanini (1867–1957). Of the others, the most significant was probably Giuseppe Martucci (1856–1909), who conducted notable symphonic concerts in his native city of Naples and gave the first Italian performance of Wagner's *Tristan und Isolde* (1888). That was at Bologna, where Mariani had conducted the first Italian production of a Wagner opera, *Lohengrin* (1871); thanks in part to Mariani, it was Bologna's turn to see itself as leader of advanced musical taste.

*

These Wagner performances, coming 23 and 21 years after the German premières, were significant. Italy was still so dominated by opera that for most people the possibilities of mid- and late nineteenth-century orchestration were demonstrated not by symphonies but by foreign operas. Martucci, for instance, wrote symphonies and other orchestral works some of which still impress listeners on the rare occasions when they are performed; but his conducting of *Tristan* was

25. *Scenes from the four acts of Ponchielli's opera 'La Gioconda', first performed at La Scala on 8 April 1876 (La Gioconda is in the centre, holding the knife with which she is about to commit suicide); engraving from 'L'illustrazione italiana' (1876)*

probably far more influential. The foreign operas that colonized Italy were first those of Meyerbeer (from about 1850 to 1880 held to be an encyclopedic genius), then the revolutionary later works of Wagner and, arriving at about the same time but much more speedily, the operas of French composers (Gounod, Massenet, Bizet). It was a token of a national inferiority complex that these foreigners were both widely resented and widely imitated.

Verdi, indisputably the leading Italian composer, went his own way and had no followers. The difficulties others faced, and did not resolve, are illustrated by the careers of Boito, Amilcare Ponchielli (1834–86) and Alfredo Catalani (1854–93). Boito was essentially a literary man; as a musician he was an amateur and behaved like one, reworking his second opera *Nerone* for half a century and even then leaving it unfinished. Both in this and in *Mefistofele* (1868; reduced and rewritten 1875), signs of a genuine artistic intelligence go together with an inability to organize an effective musico-dramatic structure. *Mefistofele* in its first, six-hour version (now lost but for the libretto) embodied the highest ambitions: to stage Goethe's *Faust* in its full intellectual and poetic scope and to revolutionize Italian opera. How far its resounding failure was deserved we cannot tell; the later version has many original touches – interesting sonorities and contrasts in the prologue, a good 'speaking' vocal line for the devil, a striking single woodwind line behind Gretchen's confession – juxtaposed again and again with banalities; the whole fails to cohere. *Nerone* is at least as ambitious and no less patchy; it adds a touch of hysteria, with much reliance on stentorian high notes.

Ponchielli started out as a bandmaster, an experience reflected in such instantly hummable, short-breathed tunes as those in the Dance of the Hours from his most popular opera, *La Gioconda* (1876, with a pseudonymous libretto by Boito). Like the new department stores starting up at about the time of its composition, *La Gioconda* has something for everybody – and plenty of it, in repeatable patterns: lots of villainy, romantic effusion, extras amid spectacular scenery and melodies (apt, however, to become invertebrate after a few bars).

Catalani was in some ways Ponchielli's opposite, a sensitive musician who (one suspects) might have done better in Paris writing instrumental works on the fanciful Nordic themes he preferred. In Italy he more or less had to write operas. They often show the vocal line remaining on one note or moving stepwise while the orchestra weaves delicate, interesting patterns round it. In his best work, *La Wally* (1892), Catalani was able to devise effective musical structures which, however, do not always work well dramatically, for example the intertwining choruses at the start of Act 2. This is partly because Catalani lacked stage sense – a feel for just how long a movement should last: the big rescue scene goes with a swing until Wally's long-winded solo dissipates the tension. Indeed a composer with stage sense would not have accepted the dire Tyrolean libretto (about a big mountain girl who has never been kissed). Its author, Luigi Illica, was to write better for the more acute and demanding Puccini.

As these younger composers floundered, Verdi was feeling his way towards his own highly individual late development. He took remarkably little from others apart from assimilating (and improving on) the epic-historical procedures of Parisian grand opera. The first task he undertook after his great trio of popular operas was indeed his first wholly new work for Paris, *Les vêpres siciliennes* (1855), in which he did not quite avoid letting his individual voice be swamped by the required paraphernalia of tableau and procession. A more notable experiment was *Simon Boccanegra* (first version, 1857). Here Verdi parted company with the long Italian tradition of decorative singing, even for the specific dramatic purposes to which he had confined it in his recent works (in *La traviata*, for instance, to express the heroine's febrile attempts at gaiety). The vocal setting was now largely syllabic; the vocal line in the finest parts of the opera, such as Fiesco's 'Il lacerato spirito', is at once craggy and of an austere nobility. For *Boccanegra* turns on the relationship between two fathers and their daughters, a theme close to Verdi's heart, and the conflict between implacability and forgiveness; the lovers and their music are less strongly characterized.

Boccanegra also marked an advance towards freer forward movement and away from the closed forms of the aria–cabaletta, largo–stretta, meditation–explosion convention. This was an aspect of a European movement throughout the arts, not only in opera: a broad shift from poetry to prose, from tragedy to the novel, ultimately from aristocracy to democracy. Though 'Wagnerism' was the label attached to it, Italian composers took part in this movement without necessarily sounding like Wagner: in Catalani's *La Wally*, for instance, miniature arias, themselves of irregular design, are integrated into a free-flowing orchestral development.

Verdi shared in this movement but worked it out in his highly individual way. The cabaletta gradually disappeared from his works, though there is a cabaletta-like resolution as late as *Aida* (1871), at the end of the duet between Radamès and Aida in the Nile scene. The big finale at the end of an act survived until *Otello* (1887), his penultimate opera. Only in *Falstaff* (1893) were all the conclusions drawn. Verdi's attitude was shown when he came to revise *Boccanegra* in 1880–81. Some existing numbers could be kept, he wrote, 'even though they contain cabalettas. Save the mark! However, I haven't such a horror of cabalettas'.[6]

What Verdi particularly sought, and imposed on his librettists, was the *parola scenica*, the 'stageworthy statement', in which vivid wording allied with a brief, potent musical phrase would unmistakably drive home a dramatic point. In his late works increasing numbers of *parole sceniche*, ever pithier, took up the space formerly given over to pattern-making. Scenes and whole operas were now held together by fragments of recurring themes or by skilful dovetailing. The new Council Chamber scene added to the revised *Boccanegra* is a good example. In this scene of high conflict, vocal and orchestral statements are extraordinarily rapid, a series of musical lightning flashes which none the less build up to two great climactic *parole sceniche*: the Doge's plea for peace and reconciliation and the final curse. The cumulative effect is hair-raising.

Before this late phase Verdi wrote his last opera intended for the ordinary traffic of the Italian stage, *Un ballo in maschera* (1859), a work of particular elegance and dash; in its irresistible middle act a driving, passionate love duet leads up to one of the master scenes in all musical theatre, which exhilaratingly combines sardonic comedy with emotional high tension. The king's friend tries to shield the king's mistress by pretending to have a moonlight tryst with her, then discovers her to be his own wife: his anger, her distress, the mocking conspirators' little tune with its staccato leaps and passing acciaccature and trills, make up a multi-layered effect of which only opera is capable.

After *Un ballo* Verdi could do as he pleased. In the remaining 42 years of his life he composed only five operas, the String Quartet, the Requiem and the *Quattro pezzi sacri* – a total break with the musical world in which he had been brought up. When he was offered lavish commissions abroad he took the opportunity of carrying Parisian grand opera as close to perfect realization as so unwieldy a form could be. Of *La forza del destino* (1862), *Don Carlos* (1867) and *Aida* (1871) only *Don Carlos* was written for Paris; but all three embodied and outdid Meyerbeerian grand opera with its epic structure and its spectacular illustration of clashing historical forces. *La forza del destino* and *Don Carlos* have had chequered careers, though both probably stand higher in public esteem now than ever before. Verdi himself reworked them – *Don Carlos* several times – probably because their sprawling length and ambitious aims got in the way of musico-dramatic coherence. In both, austere, self-sacrificing devotion is the theme most deeply explored; it runs through the nobly arching melodies of Leonora's 'Madre, pietosa vergine' as she seeks refuge from a world of war and hatred, and through the Queen's 'Tu che le vanità' set against the barren exigencies of power. In both, again, Verdi was at his most experimental: the cabaletta almost disappeared in favour of arias either briefer or on a looser, three-movement pattern; the scenes with the disreputable monk Fra Melitone in *La forza* used the free style of sung speech that was to blossom in the last

26. *Giuseppe Verdi and Napoleon III; caricature (c1867) from the time of the first performance of 'Don Carlos' in Paris*

operas; *Don Carlos*, especially in its 1884 reworking, was boldly innovatory in its dark, often unexpected harmonies and its fore-shortening of operatic forms – what in 1867 still called for a formal duet could now be resolved in a few bars. The defects of both works (apart from an unevenness of proportion which Verdi never quite remedied) were those of Parisian grand opera, which required picturesque and illustrative matter that did not advance the drama, like the scarf song in *Don Carlos* or the 'Rataplan' in *La forza* (the chorus imitating a corps of drummers, a piece of Second Empire frippery). But the genuine grandeur of both overwhelms all objections.

Aida holds a curious position. It is one of the handful of indestruct-ible works, like *Rigoletto*; in spite of *Aida*'s manifold demands, popular opera companies for many years would fling it on to the stage as their opening work, knowing it pulled in the crowds; the results must often have been dire, and yet the opera has survived. Today, though, commentators and producers are uneasy about a work they take to be bound up with late nineteenth-century colonialism, militarism, racialism and kitsch exoticism. Hence such oddities as *Aida* without a triumphal march, or set in a modern colonial Egypt run by nonentities in *sola topis*. This comes of a misreading. The opera's premise is indeed imperial conquest and resistance to it, but its burden, as in *Don Carlos*, is the plight of the loving, generous individual crushed by authority, whether the father's or the state's. Verdi took that authority seriously.

Aida, again, is better proportioned than its two predecessors (perhaps another point against it for those who prefer the experimental sketch to the finished masterpiece). Its harmonic language, innovatory in its unexpected changes and chromaticisms, is consistent, as is the layout of scenes – continuous and well balanced. For a work that sums up grand opera it is remarkably swift and economical. Processions and ballets are not dwelt on; when we witness a prolonged ritual it fulfils a strong dramatic function (the priests' unanswered challenge to Radamès offstage, three times repeated, with Amneris's anguished comments on stage). The finale to one act ('Ma tu re') builds up to a grand multi-layered climax, but the crucial scenes are mostly intimate exchanges and the ending is another operatic masterstroke, at once rapt and poignant: the entombed lovers' simple, wide-arched melody against Amneris's monotone plea for peace above and the priestess's chant offstage. Nothing could be more remote from kitsch exoticism than the magical opening of the Nile scene, a Mediterranean night evoked by faintly oriental-sounding flute against simple string figuration and harmonics.

The two Shakespearean works that closed Verdi's career as an opera composer, *Otello* (1887) and *Falstaff* (1893), have always stood high in critical esteem though *Falstaff* is too refined and idiosyncratic to have been really popular. Boito's treatment of Shakespeare in both librettos – transposing, paring down, dovetailing – is highly ingenious and crucial to the operas, but *Otello* suffers from his frigid conceits and late nineteenth-century diabolism, as in Iago's Credo; this would matter more if Verdi had not been able to absorb Boito's antiquarian language into the music. Of the serried beauties of *Otello*, the rarest is perhaps the duet between Othello and Desdemona that closes Act 1: Verdi now had the new mastery of flexible and spare orchestration, the old mastery of simple yet apt melody and the wisdom needed to express that least canvassed of operatic emotions, a love between husband and wife that is calm, happy and sexually fulfilled.

Alongside the new, irregular 'speaking' style of vocal setting (as in the narrative of Cassio's dream) there are remnants of old forms, cabaletta and act finale. No such remnants occur in *Falstaff*. Even when Falstaff has a miniaturized formal aria ('Quand'ero paggio', lasting half a minute), it is a tiny diamond in a fabric made up of musical fragments from which Verdi, by cunning transition and juxtaposition, weaves a ceaseless forward movement. Not even the young lovers' exchanges are allowed to do more than open up a gleaming parenthesis here and there, and the 'big' ensemble (with Falstaff gasping in the laundry basket as Ford and his men advance on the screen behind which they believe him to be hiding) is not large in the conventional sense of building up to a grand climax followed by a *stretta*; it is highly complex, mercurial and interrupted, and the climax when it comes (Falstaff's ducking in the Thames) is a sudden musical laugh.

There is something uncanny about *Falstaff*, one of the few clearly identifiable 'last works'. At nearly 80, Verdi – as we may hear in the final fugue – was at once ironically detached, indulgent to a world he must shortly leave, and ruthlessly capable of building an individual musical structure out of the lightest, briefest materials. This remarkable work led nowhere in particular but technically it influenced the lighter conversational exchanges in Puccini's *La bohème* and *Madama Butterfly*.

*

Verdi was the only Italian composer of this period to leave a mark on sacred music. Saverio Mercadante's masses and other religious music, which he wrote up to his death in 1870, once pleased James Joyce; they seem no longer to be performed. Rossini's *Petite messe solennelle* of 1864, an eccentric late work by a composer long settled in Paris, had international success but did not establish itself in Italian affections as his earlier *Stabat mater* had.

In the long history of Italian church music these years were the darkest. Many choirs disappeared or were steeped in mediocrity. The country was dominated by opera. The old patrons of religious music (other than the pope) had gone; many of those members of the new secular élite who took an interest in non-operatic music were anti-clerical and looked to science to light the path. There was some regard for the old Italian tradition of church music, thought to be epitomized by Palestrina. From the 1880s a revival of interest in medieval and Renaissance music was under way, stirred partly by Italian but rather more by German and French scholarship. About the turn of the century the priest-composer Lorenzo Perosi was writing oratorios and other ecclesiastical works highly regarded in their day and occasionally still heard in Italy; they suggest an eclectic mixture of medieval and Renaissance influences and *fin-de-siècle* wanness. Music of this kind led the Vatican, in 1903–4, to ordain a reform marking a sharp break from secular styles and a return to the traditions of plainchant and classical polyphony.

When Verdi wrote his Requiem (1874), these changes lay in the future. The dominant outlook was still the belief in scientific method and progress, in Italy summed up as positivism. Verdi was too profound an artist to accept this unreservedly; his own outlook was a kind of stoicism. The purpose of the Requiem was not liturgical; it

27. First performance of Verdi's Requiem in the Chiesa di S Marco, Milan, in 1874; engraving by Centenari after Pessina from 'L'illustrazione universale' (4 June 1874)

represented Verdi's desire to commemorate the great novelist and poet Alessandro Manzoni. (One movement, the 'Libera me', was left from an earlier, abandoned project for a commemorative mass for Rossini, to be written by several composers.) The Requiem used to be deprecated in Protestant countries as 'operatic', but it is one of the most frequently performed sacred works – an odd fate for a work intended for a special occasion.

Rather than operatic, the Requiem is highly dramatic. With his piercing imagination Verdi dramatizes the terror of the individual faced with the 'stupefaction' of death and judgment. Any cause for unease is theological. There is in Verdi no transcendence – not even the mild transcendence attained by Fauré in his Requiem a few years later – no sense of an otherness in the universe of which the human soul may be part. Not only in the storm of the 'Dies irae', with its blows on the bass drum opening up the end of all things, but also in the meditativeness of the 'Lux aeterna', the individual soul is in the world, like Leonora in *La forza* or the Queen at the end of *Don Carlos*, and whatever power confronts it is somewhere else. There is no transfiguration; the work ends (against liturgical usage) with the still

139

troubled 'Libera me'. The work is far removed from the dulcet piety of the church music most popular at the time – that of Gounod. Besides bringing forward one strikingly imaginative idea after another, the scoring is spare, translucent, as in the seraphic athleticism of the 'Sanctus' or the inwardness of the 'Agnus Dei', where soprano and mezzo in octaves trace a line suggestive of plainchant yet in no way antiquarian, garlanded at the third variation by three flutes in converse. Like *Falstaff*, though in a different way, the Requiem is unique; it draws its power from the maturing of Verdi's artistic personality. This was not an example that other Italian composers were equipped to follow.

*

When Italian musicians again scored worldwide success it was yet again in opera, but opera marked off from the tradition of Rossini and Verdi. In 1890 the one-act *Cavalleria rusticana*, by the unknown Pietro Mascagni (1863–1945), became the most immediate hit since *Il trovatore*. Within a few years a 'young school' of composers had grown up, turning out operas few of which have lasted. This 'young school' was the product of the new Italy with its European pretensions covering serious inadequacies. Unlike the older school, which had grown up as heir to a long, craftsmanlike musical tradition, the leading members of the 'young school' were selfconsciously modern and literary-minded. They began by identifying themselves with the naturalistic school of Zola (in Italy dubbed *verismo*) which professed documentary realism while gloating over sordid and violent aspects of life; but they later took on the aesthetic or decadent movement with its interest in the stylized, the exotic and the bizarre (in Italy dominated by the flawed great poet Gabriele D'Annunzio) – elements with which, unlike Richard Strauss or Debussy, they were ill equipped to cope. At the same time the composers of the 'young school' excelled at using music for theatrical effect; they knew much better than Boito or Catalani how long an episode should last or where a high note should be placed for maximum applause. Their music tended to work best when it was most utilitarian and was advancing the action and to sound tawdry or empty when striving for beauty or significance (like the Ballatella in Ruggero Leoncavallo's *Pagliacci* of 1892).

Such characteristic products as *Andrea Chenier* (1896) and *Fedora* (1898), both by Umberto Giordano (1867–1948), work as a succession of theatrical coups while offering little more musical substance than does a typical film score of the 1940s (with which they have a good deal in common). Much the same may be said of the more languid *Adriana Lecouvreur* (1902) by Francesco Cilea (1866–1950). Like Mascagni and Giordano in their later phase, the younger Riccardo

28. Scenes from Leoncavallo's opera 'Pagliacci', first performed at the Teatro Del Verme, Milan, on 21 May 1892; engraving from 'Il teatro illustrato' (1892)

Zandonai (1883–1944) came under the influence of D'Annunzio and his followers; his *Francesca da Rimini* (1914, with a libretto based on D'Annunzio's play) has sumptuous, often inventive orchestration but succumbs to the overblown text. In the end, the first fruit of the 'new school' still seems the most genuine: *Cavalleria rusticana* with its poster-like harmonic simplicity and folklike tunes comes across as spontaneous people's theatre, free from the smell of contrivance that mars the rest.[7]

The vogue for these and similar works called into being a new type of opera singer, with a gift for intense and violent dramatic expression; the best, such as Gemma Bellincioni, were remarkable artists, but too many bawled or broke up the legato line on which such older works as Verdi's depend. By the early years of this century the repertory of Italian opera houses had come down to a small number of works endlessly repeated. Nothing of Rossini's survived except *Il barbiere di Siviglia* (and nothing earlier than Rossini but for an occasional, reverential Gluck *Orfeo* to show off a contralto). Donizetti's vast output was represented almost exclusively by *Lucia di Lammermoor* (with *La favorite* again as a contralto warhorse), Bellini by an occasional *Norma* or *La sonnambula*. The staples were Verdi's operas from *Rigoletto* on (plus *Nabucco* and *Ernani* from the early phase), *Les Huguenots*, *Lohengrin*, *Faust*, *Carmen*, one or two more modern French operas, the more successful works of the Italian 'young school' and, of course, Puccini.

*

Giacomo Puccini (1858–1924) was at one time grouped with the 'young school'; he was also denounced as trivial, garish, insincere, a commercial exploiter of sentiment carried to the point of sentimentality. But we can now see Puccini as a musician at once individual and eclectic, who learnt from most of his immediate predecessors and contemporaries (not just from Italians but also from Wagner, Massenet, Debussy, Stravinsky) and was still breaking new ground at the time of his death. At least four of Puccini's works stand at the heart of the repertory no opera house can be without.

Nevertheless, Puccini's musico-dramatic personality still poses a problem. On the one hand he belonged to the new Euro-American world of music in which styles could spread rapidly from one country to another; he was at home in Berlin and New York, he wrote one of his later operas for performance in New York and on an American subject (*La fanciulla del West*, 1910) and originally intended another (*La rondine*, 1917) for Vienna. On the other hand, as a fourth-generation member of a family of Lucca composers and organists he stood heir to the tradition of Italian musical craftsmanship and remained to a great extent a Tuscan provincial in outlook.

After his early experience of failure Puccini developed a keen sense of what would work on the operatic stage; he became no less demanding than Verdi about the texts he set and avoided being engulfed by the D'Annunzio cult. Yet his literary taste and emotional make-up were immature; they drew him again and again to stories that exploited the frail, suffering woman and the appeal of 'little things'. In his treatment of a subject like *Tosca*, with a public, political dimension (which Verdi, who at one time thought of setting it, would surely have brought out), Puccini dwelt on erotic relationships at their most ardent, stressing the element of sado-masochism; that Cavaradossi is a 'Voltairean' democrat is barely noticeable. It is easy to show Puccini as a typical petty bourgeois who fed a like-minded

29. Poster (1899) by A. Hohenstein for Puccini's 'Tosca', first performed at the Teatro Costanzi, Rome, on 14 January 1900, and at La Scala, Milan, later the same year

143

audience with skilful versions of their erotic and exotic fantasies; yet that is largely beside the point. Puccini's weaknesses are swallowed up in the quality of his achievement as a musical dramatist, the result of high skill and discrimination as well as of melodic inventiveness.

Puccini stands or falls by those works that have most often been attacked as melodramatic or sentimental – *Tosca* (1900) and *Madama Butterfly* (1904): only by giving pride of place to the libretto can we treat them as fundamentally unlike *La bohème* (1896), whose charm most people acknowledge. Putting the words first was in fact quite contrary to Puccini's mode of composition. For the sake of the musical structure he sometimes distorted the word-setting, as in Tosca's 'Vissi d'arte', where the word 'tabernacoli' is stressed on the first and last syllables rather than, as in ordinary speech, on the third. The first act of *Tosca*, like that of *Butterfly* and of *Manon Lescaut* (1893), Puccini's first mature opera, is organized symphonically in the sense that it is cunningly woven out of themes of which some are associated with individual characters: Tosca's theme in falling triplets, which we hear just ahead of her entrance, suggesting loving kindness at odds with her mood; the scherzo-like theme of the lovers' hideaway ('Non la sospiri la nostra casetta'); Scarpia's menace as chief oppressor of Rome. These themes are used more formally and less systematically than Wagner's leitmotifs: they are at times 'tags' to be developed according to the circumstances of the moment, but more often they are a means of knitting a whole scene or act together.

In these first acts – as, later, in those of *La fanciulla del West* and *Turandot* (1926; finished by Franco Alfano) – Puccini depicted a whole milieu by deploying minor characters and chorus and, where appropriate, by using musical local colour, such as the oriental pentatonic scale in *Butterfly*; the heroine is introduced late, her voice typically heard offstage at first, so that her musical personality can be insinuated into the audience's mind. In later acts the dramatic action focusses on the principal characters caught up in 'strong' situations, but even here their vocal outbursts are as a rule calibrated so that what seems overwhelming is in fact brief: Tosca's outcry when she can no longer bear to hear her lover being tortured, Cavaradossi's 'Vittoria', Butterfly's 'Un bel dì'.

A great deal of the work of urging the action forward is done by the interplay between voices and an orchestral texture at once striking and distinguished – sometimes, indeed, by the orchestra alone. A supreme example is the passage for muted violins as Scarpia writes out the safe conduct and Tosca desperately wonders what to do next. With its syncopations, its double-dotted notes and its hypnotic turning within a small compass this music conveys both an infinity of desolation and an extreme of expectancy and tension. Much the same could be said of the weird little march before and after the execution (ostinato bass figure, unexpected inner chromaticisms and gradual crescendo and decrescendo) or, in gentler vein, of the lullaby with humming chorus and flute and pizzicato accompaniment as Butterfly, Suzuki and the child settle down to await Pinkerton's arrival. These and many more are the work of a master musical dramatist, and they are achieved with the most thought-out economy of means.

Butterfly abounds in examples of Puccini's 'conversational style', which enables him to play the action along lightly without falling into a shapeless, continuous arioso; he had already deployed it in the young people's horseplay in *La bohème* and was to bring it to an intricate consummation in *Gianni Schicchi*, his crackling one-act farce of 1918 – the last successful work in the long history of Italian comic opera.

The core of Puccini's appeal, however, is erotic. Audiences are won over, often unawares, by the musicianly skills just described, but what they consciously come back to is the expression of full-hearted romantic love with an unabashed sexual promise (the Act 1 duet in *Butterfly*) or reminiscence ('E lucevan le stelle' in Act 3 of *Tosca*). Unmistakably though not blatantly, such passages draw on the pattern of mounting climax characteristic of sexual orgasm. (So, by more long-range methods, does the Prelude to Wagner's *Tristan und Isolde*). The encounters between Mimì and Rodolfo in *La bohème* stay on the plane of romantic boy-girl love, but here too Puccini's characteristic progressions and his moments of brief expansiveness have seldom if ever been matched in conveying the total absorption of two people in one another.

Puccini's crowning achievement in this line was surely to have been the final duet of *Turandot* in which the princess melts into human love. It had to balance the work after the notable cruelty of what goes before: we need to feel that the 'princess of ice and death' has been transformed to the roots of her being. A Freudian-inspired theory has been put forward according to which Puccini was unable to compose the duet because the opera's subject came too close to his own immature and unresolved relation to women, whom he could experience only as mother-tyrant or as child-victim.[8] Puccini's immaturity does have something to do with his subjects and the way he treated them, but it seems extremely doubtful whether artists' neuroses govern their work in such a literal way. It is at least as likely that Puccini did not write the final duet because he fell ill and died. Alfano's setting (whether in the cut form usually sung or in the full version recently given currency) does not do the job. That he based it on Puccini's sketches proves nothing: Puccini might well have had new ideas.

This is a great pity, for *Turandot* is otherwise an extraordinary and compelling work, the culmination of Puccini's long career as a musical experimenter. Its harmony is far bolder than anything he had ventured before, with fierce dissonances and departures from tonality (foreshadowed in the organ-grinder episode in *Il tabarro*, one of the three one-acters making up the *Trittico* of 1918, and even in the remarkable passage in *Tosca* where Scarpia's interrogation of Cavaradossi onstage clashes with Tosca singing the cantata across the courtyard). Its range of instrumental colour is great, from convincingly barbaric ferocity to the utmost delicacy in Liù's arias; its vocal writing is highly characterized, from the asperity of Turandot's part to the angular yet gentle grotesquerie of the three masks Ping, Pang and Pong. Its first act (again 'symphonic' and dominated by the chorus) is masterly in its musical organization.

*

By the early years of this century Puccini was beginning to feel the draught of intellectual reaction against his work. Some of this came of jealousy – it seems to have lain behind the notorious demonstration on the failed first night of *Butterfly*; but at a deeper level more of the élite were turning against the whole tradition of nineteenth-century Italian opera. The young radicals who called themselves Futurists denounced bourgeois art and with it, as a 1910 manifesto by the composer Francesco Balilla Pratella put it, the 'heavy and suffocating crop' of opera with which the Italian musical establishment had blotted out more vital musical initiatives; about the future Pratella was vague, but for a general call to repudiate the past and trust to nature and modern man. Others equally critical of the condition of Italian music had, on the contrary, revivalist aims: in 1911 the young musicologist Fausto Torrefranca denounced Puccini's works in *La voce*, an influential magazine whose writers combined nationalism with a summons to spiritual and intellectual renewal; a year later he published a book, in effect an anti-Puccini manifesto and a call for Italian music to modernize itself by going back to its roots.[9]

This was not a new idea. A famous Verdi saying was 'Let's go back to the old – it will be a step forward'. By this Verdi seems to have meant little more than that Italian composers should learn from their earlier tradition rather than from foreign contemporaries (though he himself was willing to pick up ideas from Meyerbeer and, in a small way, from the Wagner of *Die Meistersinger*; in his late works he was also more obviously an innovator than a traditionalist).

A more fundamental influence was D'Annunzio. In his 1894 novel *Il trionfo della morte* (with its significant title) he recognized in *Tristan und Isolde* the wellspring both of the aesthetic sensibility he spoke for and of the modernist movement in the arts. D'Annunzio was musically untrained and most of his knowledge of Wagner was secondhand, through modern French culture (which he did know well). Nevertheless he was uncommonly sensitive to music, in his own verse and elsewhere; and he raised genuine issues. German music, that of Beethoven and Wagner above all, in its profundity and daring towered above that of nineteenth-century Italians who had lost their way in the tinsel world of opera (he once dismissed Mascagni as a 'bandmaster', though the two later collaborated – disastrously). At the same time D'Annunzio and his followers were nationalists, not the kind of liberal, outward-looking nationalists – concerned with popular revolt or with institutional change – who had led the Risorgimento, but late Romantic nationalists with their minds fixed on the physical as well as the spiritual roots of the Italian people and on its need to express itself in heroic, preferably warlike action. This made for a love-hate relationship with German music and a search for Italian musical roots going well beyond the traditional reverence for Palestrina.[10]

Revivalists now moved on several fronts. Some Italian musicians started collecting 'authentic' folk music – something that had gone on in north European countries since the eighteenth century but that had been largely neglected in Italy, except by visiting foreigners like Berlioz. Nineteenth-century Italian composers used folkish turns of melody, as Donizetti and Verdi did in their occasional songs, and there was a thriving industry turning out Neapolitan and related songs that were vastly popular though not 'sprung from the people', those of Paolo Tosti (1846–1916) being the most famous. 'O sole mio', 'Santa Lucia', 'Funiculì funiculà' and many others belonged to this tradition. Peasants' harvest songs or Calabrian bagpipe music were another matter, harmonically much less familiar. In the accepted art music of the time they could inspire only an occasional touch of strangeness; the best-known example is the shepherd boy's song during the dawn music in Act 3 of *Tosca*. Used more systematically, sources of this kind would inspire a departure from opera as a form.

Much the same was true of the new interest in medieval plainchant and Renaissance polyphony. D'Annunzio led a revival of everything medieval and Italian, whether in literature, the visual arts or music. Italian concern with drama carried by the solo voice was not, however, to be readily set aside. Young composers still wished to write for vivid singers. Those who repudiated Italian opera as it had developed in the nineteenth century could turn back to its origins – to the early Florentine works of about 1600, but especially to Monteverdi. He had set the Italian language in a way that was dramatic yet natural, free from what were seen as the intolerable artifice and excess of later conventions. D'Annunzio again led the way in proclaiming 'back to Monteverdi', and there were performances of *L'Orfeo* in

Milan and Bologna in 1909–10; even these came nearly 30 years after a first exhumation in Germany.

What 'back to Monteverdi' meant in practice is bound up with the story of the 'generation of 1880' – the young Italian composers who now came forward but whose main work was done after 1914. Their hostility meant that opera could no longer be the unquestioned central expression of Italian music. It would at best need to develop into a kind of music drama much barer than anything offered by the 'young school' or Puccini.

The crisis that overtook Italian opera about the time of World War I was in part artistic; it was also financial and institutional. With the extension of suffrage and the coming of democratic politics, municipalities were less willing to spend local tax revenue on subsidizing the pleasures of the rich. In 1897 the Milan city council refused, though only temporarily, to pay anything towards the La Scala season. There followed a long period of wrangles and attempted compromises until in 1920, under the impact of wartime and postwar inflation and disruption, the box-holders agreed in effect to surrender their property rights and join with the city and the leaders of Milan business in setting up La Scala as a non-profit-making body. The new institution won a state subsidy and legal framework and became the model for the gradual reorganization of Italian operatic life.

These new arrangements made opera houses more respectable, but also brought them closer to the condition of museums. Even in the land of Verdi and Puccini, opera as a creative art was, by 1914, at a low ebb. As the leading popular art it was about to be displaced by the cinema, which in Italy as elsewhere spread rapidly during the war and especially in the early 1920s. There would still be audiences in Italy for *Rigoletto* and *Tosca*, but fewer and irretrievably divided from the concerns of the musical élite.

NOTES

[1] C. Santley, *Student and Singer* (London, 1892), 68–9.

[2] A. Biaggi, preface to G. Vaccaj, *Vita di Nicola Vaccaj* (Bologna, 1882), pp.viii–ix, xvii–xviii.

[3] E. Labiche, *La poudre aux yeux* (1861).

[4] C. Sartori, *L'avventura del violino: l'Italia musicale dell'ottocento nella biografia e nei carteggi di Antonio Bazzini* (Turin, 1978), 86–7; for earlier Florentine interest in Viennese Classical music, see M. De Angelis, *La musica del Granduca* (Florence, 1978).

[5] C. Sartori, *Il R. Conservatorio di Musica G. B. Martini di Bologna* (Florence, 1942), 136–40.

[6] Verdi to Giulio Ricordi, 20 Nov 1880, quoted in J. Budden, *The Operas of Verdi* (London, 1973–81), ii, 255.

[7] Even after the first performance of *Pagliacci*, *Cavalleria rusticana* was not necessarily paired with it. For some years Mascagni's opera was given in all sorts of combinations; some popular theatres gave it with an act of *Il barbiere di Siviglia* or two acts of *Lucia di Lammermoor*. It now needs a better match – perhaps a good Donizetti comic one-acter or *Gianni Schicchi*.

[8] M. Carner, *Puccini: a Critical Biography* (London, 1958), 256–65, 468–9.

[9] C. Tisdall and A. Bozzolla, *Futurism* (London, 1977), 111–13; F. Torrefranca, *Giacomo Puccini e l'opera internazionale* (Turin, 1912). See also Torrefranca's article 'Problemi del dopoguerra musicale', *Critica musicale*, i (1918), 33–9, 57–66, 88–92, in which he reviews his earlier career.

[10] R. Tedeschi, *D'Annunzio e la musica* (Florence, 1988) is a full, ruthlessly unsympathetic account.

BIBLIOGRAPHICAL NOTE

General background

English-language general histories of manageable length are D. Mack Smith's *Italy: a Modern History* (Ann Arbor, 1959) and M. Clark's *Modern Italy 1871–1982* (London, 1984). Famous alternative interpretations of this still controversial period are those of B. Croce, *A History of Italy 1871–1915*, trans. C. M. Ady (Oxford, 1929; originally published Bari, 1928), and A. Gramsci, found chiefly in his *Letteratura e vita nazionale* (Turin, 1950) and *Selections from Cultural Writings*, ed. D. Forgacs and G. Nowell-Smith, trans. W. Boelhower (London, 1985). *Storia d'Italia*, ed. R. Romano and C. Vivanti (6 vols. in 9 parts, Turin, 1973–6), includes (iv/2) a stimulating essay by A. Asor Rosa on the cultural history of the period; it points out the neglect of music by Italian intellectuals and has something to say about Verdi but not about Puccini.

A great deal has been published in Italian on intellectual and artistic life, perhaps most notably by W. Binni, *La poetica del decadentismo* (Florence, 3/1961). Much less has appeared in English, but see (on D'Annunzio) A. Rhodes, *The Poet as Superman* (London, 1959), and, on the noisiest radical movement, C. Tisdall and A. Bozzolla, *Futurism* (London, 1977). A. Andreoli's *Gabriele d'Annunzio* (Florence, 1988), in its lavish illustrations, covers a good deal more than the poet's life and tastes. Many theatre posters survive and give a good notion of changing taste; they are reproduced in several illustrated works on La Scala, Milan, none of them otherwise satisfactory as a history of the theatre.

The musical world

Two penetrating essays on the problems facing Italian composers in the latter half of the nineteenth century are the chapters 'The Collapse of a Tradition' and 'A Problem of Identity' in volumes ii and iii of J. Budden's *The Operas of Verdi*, 3 vols. (London, 1973–81). He has a further chapter on Verdi and his fellow composers in *A Verdi Companion*, ed. W. Weaver and M. Chusid (London, 1979). A dense but worthwhile essay on the aesthetics of late nineteenth-century opera is G. Morelli's 'Suicidio e pazza gioia: Ponchielli e la poetica nell'opera italiana neo-nazional-popolare', in *Amilcare Ponchielli 1834–1886* (Casalmorano, 1986). Morelli is the author of another pregnant essay on musical education in *Il Conservatorio Benedetto Marcello di Venezia 1876–1976*, ed..P. Verado (Venice, 1977).

There is much interesting information on the growth of instrumental music (as well as musical education) in C. Sartori's *L'avventura del violino: l'Italia musicale dell'ottocento nella biografia e nei carteggi di Antonio Bazzini* (Turin, 1978), a 'life and letters' study of the violinist-composer-teacher Antonio Bazzini, and on the beginnings of concert-giving on a large scale in G. Depanis's *I concerti popolari ed il Teatro Regio di Torino*, 2 vols. (Turin, 1914–15); the early chapters of H. Sachs's *Toscanini* (London, 1978) are also useful. There is unfortunately no thorough study of the central institution of the Italian musical world in this period, the publishing house of Ricordi.

On opera, the six-volume *Storia dell'opera italiana*, ed. L. Bianconi and G. Pestelli (Turin, 1984–), of which vols.iv, v and vi have appeared, is designed to set opera in its social context and to discuss it according to its creative and productive aspects, where the earlier *Storia dell'opera*, ed. G. Barblan and A. Basso, 6 vols. (Turin, 1977) is organized more according to schools and individual composers. Extraordinarily detailed dossiers of the creation of Verdi's last three operas are H. Busch, *Verdi's Aida: the History of an Opera in Letters and Documents* (Minneapolis, 1978), and *Carteggio Verdi–Boito*, ed. M. Medici and M. Conati (Parma, 1978). Busch has now (1989) covered *Otello* in the same way. *Wagner in Italia*, ed. G. Rostirolla (Turin, 1982), brings together essays on Wagner's influence; there is nothing comparable on the influence, at least as important, of French composers. The business and organization of opera is dealt with in J. Rosselli, *The Opera Industry in Italy from Cimarosa to Verdi: the Role of the Impresario* (Cambridge, 1984), and in L. Trezzini and A. Curtolo, *Oltre le quinte: idee, cultura e organizzazione del teatro musicale in Italia* (Venice, 1983); visual aspects are splendidly illustrated in vol.iii (by M.V. Ferrero) of *Storia del Teatro Regio di Torino*, ed. A. Basso, 4 vols. (Turin, 1976–80).

Composers

The finest study of Verdi's operas is J. Budden's, already mentioned; he has also written a one-volume account of Verdi's life and works (including a detailed study of the Requiem) in the Master Musicians series (London, 1985; best read in the corrected paperback edition, 1986). The challenging G. Baldini, *Abitare la battaglia*, ed. F. D'Amico (Milan, 1970), trans. R. Parker as *The Story of Giuseppe Verdi* (Cambridge, 1980), is, in spite of the English title, largely a study of the operas; it was left uncompleted at the author's death and does not deal fully with anything later than *Un ballo in maschera* (1859). There are distinguished critical studies by J. Hepokoski of *Otello* and *Falstaff* (Cambridge, 1983 and 1987).

On Puccini the fullest study in English is M. Carner, *Puccini: a Critical Biography* (London, 1958), whose psychoanalytical interpretations are however disputable; there is at least as much to be gained from the briefer E. Greenfield, *Puccini: Keeper of the Seal* (London, 1958), and from W. Ashbrook, *The Complete Operas of Puccini* (Oxford, 1967, rev. 2/1985). The most revealing source for Puccini the man is the collection of letters to his family, *Puccini com'era*, ed. A. Marchetti (Milan, 1973). Other Italian composers of the period fare less well: their works (apart from *Cavalleria rusticana* and *Pagliacci*) are seldom heard, their reputations uncertain. Probably the best study, P. Nardi's *Arrigo Boito* (Milan, 1942), suffers from having appeared at a time when Boito's importance could still be taken for granted.

Chapter VI

Spain: a Nation in Turbulence

LIONEL SALTER

Throughout the nineteenth century, save for a couple of decades from the mid-1870s, Spain was riven by political and social turmoil. The War of Independence (the Peninsular War) that had driven Joseph Bonaparte from the throne was followed by the 1812 Constitution of Cádiz; but its attempts to establish a more liberal system of centralized government by a monarch acting through responsible ministers, and to reduce the feudal stranglehold of the church and nobility, were nullified two years later on the return from exile of Ferdinand VII, a harshly repressive absolutist who ruthlessly persecuted his opponents and plunged the country into instability and bankruptcy. From then on, Spain, complicated as were the convolutions of its history, could basically be likened by the essayist Larra to 'a new Penelope alternately weaving and unpicking her tapestry'. There was a constant seesaw between reactionary forces and reformist, anti-clerical elements, accompanied by revolutions, invasions, conspiracies, civil wars provoked by Ferdinand's brother Don Carlos (not to be confused with Verdi's hero), military uprisings, extremist factions and political assassinations.

Under Ferdinand's daughter Isabella and in the preceding years of her mother Maria Cristina's regency, thousands of the intellectuals banished by Ferdinand returned from exile, bringing with them radical ideas born of the Romantic movement which gave a powerful stimulus to regional aspirations. A decree of 1837 closing convents and monasteries and confiscating and selling church lands (to pay for the wars and rescue the country from its huge debts) led to a stormy off-and-on relationship with the Vatican and the rise of a moneyed middle class that was strengthened by the development of industry and the railways.

Increasing radicalism (fed by the revolutionary ardour then sweeping Europe), widespread rioting and court scandals eventually, in 1868, led to Isabella being forced out. In the ensuing chaos (which sparked off the Franco-Prussian war) the Duke of Aosta accepted the crown but abdicated only two years later, and after a second Carlist rising a federal republic was declared in 1873, though Catalonia maintained its autonomy and anarchy ruled in Andalucía. Within a year the new republic had four presidents, and to bring some calm to the country's increasing disorder Isabella's son Alfonso was invited to become king. A new constitution on British lines was drawn up and lasted for about half a century; but corruption was rife, violent anarchy erupted in Barcelona (and was as violently suppressed) and agricultural areas like Murcia suffered great poverty.

The loss of Cuba, Puerto Rico and the Philippines in 1898, after a war with the USA, was a humiliation and a serious blow to Spain's economic stability as well as to its morale; and under the next king, Alfonso XIII, the political system disintegrated still further, with trouble in Morocco, bloody riots in Catalonia and renewed anti-clericalism caused by an again dominant and intolerant church, whose religious orders were swollen by expulsions from France. At the outbreak of World War I, Spain had little option but to remain neutral, since the conservatives, the church and the army were sympathetic to Germany, while the liberals, and especially the Catalan and Basque nationalists, sided with the Allies.

The latter half of the nineteenth century and the start of the twentieth were rich in all genres of literature – novels, essays, poetry, drama – but the constant turbulence of the period proved inimical to the production of creative work of real distinction in the abstract arts. In painting, after Goya's death in 1828 there were only minor figures such as Fortuny, Sorolla and Zuloaga until the appearance, at the turn of the century, of Picasso, with Juan Gris in his wake; no notable architects arose until the advent of Gaudí and Domènech; and in music few composers aroused much more than local interest or won recognition outside Spain until, again at the turn of the century, the arrival of Albéniz (1860–1909) and Enrique Granados (1867–1916).

In the early 1800s Spain, in any case, had musically been a virtual fiefdom of Italy. After the dominance of Italian *opera seria* in the previous century, not only had the works of Mercadante (who spent two years in the Iberian peninsula) and, more particularly, Bellini, Donizetti and Rossini taken the country (along with the rest of Europe) by storm, but their influence had also filtered into non-operatic spheres. Italian music was favoured at court by Maria Cristina (a Neapolitan); and when she founded a royal conservatory in 1831 it was with an Italian singer as director: moreover, all tuition was conducted in Italian (though by this she may have wished to help Spanish singers compete successfully with foreigners), and to her credit she also appointed as the first professor of composition a Catalan, Ramón Carnicer, who had written operas on such national figures as Don Juan and Christopher Columbus (but in italianate style and to Italian librettos).

CHURCH MUSIC, REGIONALISM, THE CHORAL MOVEMENT

Carnicer had also composed funeral music for Ferdinand VII's death in 1833, besides two requiems and other pieces of church music; but apart from his works and those of the prolific Ignacio Ovejero, religious music, which once had been the glory of Spain's golden age, was at an extremely low ebb. The works of the early masters lay largely forgotten and unavailable, and though great quantities of music were being written, an arid academicism prevailed. The severe blow dealt by the *desarmortazición* of 1837 was followed up in 1851 by a Concordat limiting the musical personnel of churches to a director and an organist (both of whom had to be clerics), one tenor (plus one alto in the case of metropolitan chapels) and choirboys.

The first significant efforts to improve the quality of church music were made by Hilarión Eslava (*maestro de capilla* of the royal chapel and in 1866 director of the conservatory). A florid *Miserere* by him – written for the tenor Gayarre, who made an international reputation[1] – was for long performed annually in Seville during Holy Week: more important, he published a history of Spanish religious music and, in 1869, a ten-volume anthology of sacred vocal music, *Lira sacro-hispana*. Others whose contributions should not be overlooked were Julián Calvo (organist of Murcia Cathedral for 30 years, with eighteen masses to his credit) and the enormously prolific Salvador Giner, who wrote a fine requiem for Alfonso XII's queen in 1878 and became director of the Valencia Conservatory. The major figure, however, in this as in other spheres was Felipe Pedrell, not so much as a composer (though he wrote eight masses and other sacred works) as the greatest of nineteenth-century Spanish musical scholars: he exercised an enduring influence on succeeding generations, particularly by echoing the eighteenth-century Padre Feijóo's enthusiasm for the golden-age masters and condemnation of showy italianate styles that secularized and theatricalized religious music. Pedrell edited several musical periodicals (including *Salterio sacro-hispano*, *Notas musicales y literarias*, *La música religiosa en España*) and published valuable collections of organ and church music, besides the complete works of Victoria.

His friend Vicente Ripollés, a pupil of Giner and for a time *maestro de capilla* in Seville before returning to Valencia, became a focal point for a number of musicians who shared his enthusiasm for Gregorian plainchant: these included Federico Olmeda (who had been studying twelfth-century music in Santiago de Compostela), Vicente Goicoechea (*maestro de capilla* at Valladolid Cathedral) and the latter's pupil José Otaño (who founded the *Revista sacra hispana* and edited it for fifteen years). In 1896 a congress in Bilbao, urging stylistic purification, recommended the publication of early Spanish masterpieces; and this aim received powerful backing when the 1903 *Motu proprio* papal bull urged the adoption of plainchant and a return to the ideals of the classical polyphonists. Goicoechea, who set an example by his own compositions, together with Otaño organized a Congress of Sacred Music in 1907; and almost regardless of vigorous anti-clericalism, further congresses at two- or three-year intervals continued to help in raising standards.

Great as was Pedrell's achievement in concentrating attention on the works of his country's sixteenth-century musicians and on the wealth of its national folksong, he had not been entirely without predecessors in these aims. Foremost among earlier scholars had been Carnicer's pupil Asenjo Barbieri, a cultivated musician of remarkable and diverse talents whose extensive collection of documents and musical material he bequeathed to the National Library: most valuably, he transcribed and published 459 works from the library of the royal palace in his *Cancionero musical de los siglos XV y XVI*. In 1846 he had founded the periodical *La España musical*, though this had been preceded four years earlier by Spain's first musical magazine, *La Iberia musical*, established by Espín y Guillén (whose opera *Padilla* had been warmly praised by both Rossini and Verdi). This earlier magazine had included music supplements; and to intensify its impact, monthly subscription concerts had been organized. Interest in the national heritage was also fanned by Baltasar Saldoni (the conservatory's first professor of singing) who, despite initially being entirely Italian in his musical sympathies, urged the younger generation to give their works a national character, and after some 40 years of preparation (not as thorough, unfortunately, as modern scholarship would have wished) produced a massive four-volume dictionary of Spanish musicians.

Inspired by the rising tide of regionalism after the death of Ferdinand VII, the most active area of research, however, was that of provincial folk music, enormously vital and rich in its diversity. Apart from an early (1826) collection of Basque dances, interest had at first centred on folk texts. Agustín Durán had begun a monumental collection of *romances* (ballads) in 1828 and Fernán Caballero, after writing her colourful novel of Andalusian life, *La gaviota*, published a volume of Andalusian folk poetry in 1859. Later anthologists added music as an appendix, as in Rodriguez Marín's huge collection of 8000 *coplas*, but from the 1870s primarily musical publications (often by cathedral organists) appeared at an ever-quickening pace. Eduardo Ocón's *Cantos españoles* and José Inzenga's *Cantos y bailes populares de España* (for which they both cast their nets wide) were followed by more specialized studies of the songs and dances of Murcia (by Calvo), Catalonia (in a number of collections, including one by Pedrell), Castile and Burgos (both by Olmeda), Montaña, Santander, Valencia and Salamanca (by Dámaso Ledesma, organist at its cathedral for 32 years).

*

This activity was paralleled in the literary world by the spread of the regional novel, which at the same period was expanding the scope of the earlier *costumbristas* (writers of picturesque essays, on the lines of Addison and Steele, on local customs, characters and scenes, such as Serafín's *Escenas andaluzas*). In 1874 appeared two Andalusian novels – Juan Valera's *Pepita Jiménez* (adapted twenty years later for an opera by Albéniz) and Pedro Alarcón's *Sombrero de tres picos* (on which Falla was to base his most popular ballet). Pereda wrote short stories and novels about the Montaña district, Pardo Bazán about Galicia, the Dickensian-style Pérez Galdos about almost every province in Spain and about Madrid. Equally, poets hymned their own regions – Antonio Machado's passionate love of Castile is the counterpart of Joaquín Turina's musical obsession with Seville – and some wrote in local dialects such as Extremaduran or Galician. Predictably, Catalan novelists and poets furthered the cause of their native tongue, and Verdaguer (writer of *L'Atlàntida*, set by Falla) has been called 'the greatest nineteenth-century Spanish epic poet as well as a notable lyricist'.

It would be hard to over-estimate the influence of folk music – very much a living force almost to the present day – on Spanish composers: its rhythms, harmonies and melodic contours have been so omnipresent as to have amounted to clichés that even now have not been outgrown and have to some extent hindered Spanish concert music from being taken *au grand sérieux* by the musical world at large. Nevertheless, in the nineteenth century the fascinating exuberance of Spain's folk music cast an irresistible spell on many visitors and onlookers from other countries – the composers apart from Liszt being, curiously, mostly Russian (Glinka, Balakirev, Rimsky-Korsakov, Glazunov) or French (Lalo, Bizet, Chabrier, Debussy, Ravel).

Besides being collected, transcribed and published, Spanish folk music, hitherto transmitted only orally, also acquired a new dimension in the folksong arrangements created for the choral societies that sprang up in the second half of the century. These originally came into being less from purely musical motives than as an experiment in education and social reform. A young radical, Anselmo Clavé, had viewed with concern the decline into boredom, mental apathy and even vice of the low-paid working men who had flocked into northern towns as a result of industrial expansion. Although of limited musical education, he wrote songs and simple arrangements for small groups to sing at home: surprised and encouraged by their success, in 1859 he formed, in the maritime quarter of Barcelona, a choir of 40 voices: this was the first Spanish choral society. It gave concerts that included dancing: an orchestra was added to the organization, which in 1857 took the name Euterpe, and soon it was imitated by new societies all over Catalonia. These came together in 1860 for a massed festival, at which Clavé conducted 200 singers and 150 instrumentalists: in successive annual festivals these numbers steadily increased, so that by the fourth festival, in 1864 (which lasted for three days), 2000 choralists and an orchestra of 300 were assembled from 57 societies.

The Euterpe society closed down in 1868 and Clavé went into politics, but the seeds he had sown took root in other northern provinces (Galicia, Navarra and the Basque country) and, most significantly, eventually came to full flower in 1891 with the formation of the Orfeo Catalá (for its first six years composed of male voices only). The co-founders of this celebrated choir, Luis Millet and Amadeo Vives, composed extensively and arranged folksongs for it, besides introducing new works and fostering the performance of sixteenth-century polyphony and other choral classics. In 1908 it built its own concert hall in Barcelona, the elaborately ornate Palau de la Música Catalana. Further encouragement had been given specifically to Catalan folk music in 1896, when Enric Morera (a Pedrell pupil) founded the Catalunya Nova choir.

CONCERT LIFE

Town and village bands, café ensembles and theatre orchestras, mostly of modest standard, had always been abundant throughout Spain, and in these many of the country's leading musicians gained early experience; but more sophisticated concert life lagged badly behind the rest of Europe – not until 1866, for example, was a Beethoven symphony heard in Madrid. In Barcelona a Philharmonic Society had indeed been founded in 1844 and had survived for thirteen years, but its repertory was confined mainly to excerpts from Italian operas, for which audiences had an insatiable appetite. The absence of professional orchestras until after the middle of the century presented composers with little incentive to write symphonic works, even had they possessed the technique to do so – which was rarely the case.

Advances towards higher instrumental goals were due largely to the work of three outstanding musicians. Barbieri, who made his mark in so many different spheres of musical life, founded a Madrid orchestra in 1859: seven years later it was amalgamated with the orchestra of the Madrid Conservatory, directed by Joaquín Gaztambide – another Carnicer pupil, who had been a ballet and opera conductor – to become the Sociedad de Conciertos, which did valuable work until the end of the century. During its first decade its conductors were, successively, Barbieri, Gaztambide and the violinist Jesús Monasterio, who had meanwhile also enriched musical life in Madrid by forming, in 1863, a Quartet Society concentrating on the German classics.

After studying in Brussels with de Bériot, Monasterio had appeared as a soloist in various European countries, and on de Bériot's retirement had been offered his post; but he preferred to remain in Spain. For many years he taught at the conservatory (becoming its director in 1894); and he was also appointed conductor of Barcelona's first symphonic concert society when it was founded in 1880.

The success of such initiatives encouraged other parts of the country to emulate their example. In 1870 Ocón, on returning from Paris, where he had been befriended by Gounod and had taught singing, founded a Philharmonic Society in his birthplace, Málaga; and from 1878 the violin virtuoso Sarasate, who had won international acclaim and to whom Saint-Saëns, Lalo, Bruch and others dedicated concertos, organized annual summer festivals in his native Pamplona, in which he could indulge his enthusiasm for chamber music, including the recently composed string quartets of Brahms. In general, however, the public was still catching up with the Classical repertory; and it was as a correction to its antipathy to new music that Tomás Bretón, for two years, ran his Unión Artística-Musical concerts which introduced a large number of contemporary works. In 1886 Antonio Nicolau, who was to become director of the Municipal School of Music in Barcelona, founded and conducted the Catalan Concert Society, which gave first performances of compositions by Pedrell and other contemporaries, besides offering works still barely known in Spain (including Berlioz's Requiem).

It makes melancholy reading to contemplate a list of concert works written in the last quarter of the century by Spanish composers who had awakened to symphonic possibilities, since practically all have sunk without trace. Who has ever heard Gabriel Balart's five symphonies, the nine by Nicolau Manent or the five by Berlioz's friend and pupil Miguel Marqués, the symphonic poems of Giner, Ruperto Chapí or Nicolau, the string quartets of Chapí or Bretón? In the great majority of cases these suffered from an inability to develop material (a failing that continued to bedevil Spanish musicians well into the twentieth century) and a poverty of texture arising from lack of contrapuntal resource: a further weakness lay in well-intentioned but excessive reliance on folk themes, some too short-winded to lend themselves to effective symphonic treatment.

These faults were basically attributable to the dearth of composition teachers experienced in purely orchestral or chamber music writing. Of those through whose hands many had passed, Emilio Arrieta and Carnicer were essentially stage composers, Eslava was primarily interested in church music and opera, and Pedrell, for all his importance in other fields, was not a symphonic writer of any weight. Not until the arrival of Humperdinck, who taught composition in Barcelona from 1885 to 1887 (and who contributed to the wave of

30. Palau de la Música, Barcelona, designed by Luis Domenech y Montaner in 1908: interior of the concert hall (note the proscenium arch representing the Ride of the Valkyries, and the reliefs of damsels playing musical instruments at the back of the stage)

Wagnerism that engulfed Catalonia – to the extent that the proscenium arch of the Palau de la Música is a striking *haut-relief* representing the Ride of the Valkyries), Gabriel Balart (who succeeded him as professor of composition there) and Emilio Serrano (teacher of Conrado del Campo and many others) was an adequate level of tuition reached. Serrano himself (director of the Royal Opera for three years and founder of the Círculo de Bellas Artes concerts) wrote a not inconsiderable symphony (1887) and a tone poem on a Quixote subject (1908); Jaime Pahissa had some success with a string symphony (1900) and the symphonic poem *El camí* (1909); and Conrado del Campo won a prize offered by the Sociedad de Conciertos for his symphonic poem *Ante las ruinas* (1899) and several other prizes for later works of a similar kind – his Straussian *Divina comedia* (1908) was indeed praised by Debussy for 'the potency of its construction'.

If Spanish composers in the nineteenth century failed to make an impact on the musical world at large, national prestige was upheld by the country's interpretative artists, many of whom rose to international fame. In the vocal sphere the remarkable García family was of the first importance: its progenitor Manuel (Rossini's original Almaviva in *Il barbiere di Siviglia*) and his daughter Maria Malibran had both died in the 1830s, but the triumphal operatic career of another daughter, Pauline Viardot-García (equally gifted as a painter and a linguist) continued until the early 1860s, and even after that she was the soloist in the first performance of Brahms's *Alto Rhapsody*; and her elder brother Manuel, who lived to the age of 101, invented the laryngoscope, taught Jenny Lind and Charles Santley, and was a professor at the Royal Academy of Music in London for 45 years. Notable singers who appeared on the scene after the turn of the century were the soprano Lucrezia Bori and the mezzo Conchita Supervia (who made her début in Bretón's opera *Los amantes de Teruel*).

There was no violinist to match Sarasate's fame, but Monasterio's pupil Fernández Arbós, who later went on to study with Vieuxtemps and Joachim, held the posts of leader of the Berlin Philharmonic Orchestra, professor at the Hamburg Conservatory and leader of the Glasgow Orchestra before teaching at the Royal College of Music in London for over twenty years from 1894, later combining with this the post of conductor of the Sinfónica de Madrid when it supplanted the earlier Sociedad de Conciertos (whose last director had been Bretón). Pau Casals, who restored Bach's cello suites to the repertory and became a living legend, had also, in his youth, been a pupil of Monasterio for chamber music. Not surprisingly, Spain produced Europe's leading guitarists: Francisco Tárrega, who raised the status of his instrument by the virtuosity with which he astonished France, England, Belgium, Switzerland and Italy; his pupils Miguel Lobet and, particularly, Emilio Pujol; and above all Andrés Segovia, whose unrivalled career began in 1909. A pianist of the greatest distinction was Ricardo Viñes, who spent much of his life in Paris (where he had completed his studies) and was a notable protagonist of new music.

MUSIC FOR THE STAGE
The area of music in which Spain's vitality was concentrated in the second half of the nineteenth century was that of the lyric theatre. The heightened consciousness of a national past, nurtured by the Romantic movement, had led to a sense of frustration at Italian domination; and in 1847 half a dozen composers, under Eslava's chairmanship, formed the España Musical society to promote Spanish opera. A few tentative efforts followed, ranging from an opera on a Spanish subject (but in Italian) by the Milan-trained Arrieta, and some parodies of Italian opera, to a revival of the zarzuela tradition, whose simpler musical level, despised by some serious-minded musicians, made a stronger appeal to unsophisticated audiences. These new zarzuelas, far more akin to the humorous eighteenth-century scenic *tonadillas* than to the early courtly zarzuelas based on classical mythology, dealt predominantly with lower-class life in all its variety, from farce to tragedy, with spoken dialogue and abundant use of folk music and dancing.

The success of Rafael Hernando's *La duende*, which ran for 126 consecutive nights, fired six composers to form a Sociedad Artística to take over the Teatro del Circo and present three zarzuelas a year there. The opening, with Gaztambide's ominously titled *Tribulaciones*, was very nearly a disaster, but the situation was transformed by the substitution of Barbieri's three-act *Jugar con fuego*, which was greeted with enthusiasm and taken as a model. It was followed with other successes; and for a time it was common for composers to work together as a team. Barcelona, Seville and Valencia were quick to imitate Madrid. Not the least significant feature of the zarzuela's rapid rise in popularity was that it began to attract playwrights and librettists of quality (though some librettos were adapted from those of the Opéra-Comique in Paris – Gaztambide's *Catalina*, for example, was based on Scribe's *L'étoile du nord*).

In 1856 the Sociedad Artística (whose membership had somewhat changed) built its own Teatro de la Zarzuela, which seated 2500. This was not achieved without protests from a number of disgruntled singers and composers (mostly with no experience of opera) who looked down on the zarzuela and petitioned the government (in vain) for assistance in setting 'real' Spanish opera on its feet. Barbieri, however, argued that all that was needed to attain this 'much desired' goal was to replace the zarzuela's spoken dialogue with recitative – a course Arrieta later followed in revising his *Marina*, the most successful of his 50 zarzuelas. One of the great hits of the new theatre's first decade was Gaztambide's *Los magyares* which was exceptional in having four acts and a non-Spanish setting; but almost the only piece of this period to have survived is Barbieri's *Pan y toros* (in which Goya appears). Zarzuela companies toured to enthusiastic audiences and Catalonia followed Madrid's creative lead with works (by Clavé and others) in Catalan, though by a government decree (abolished only in 1868) all Catalan stage works had to include at least one Castilian-speaking character: Balart more prudently wrote all his zarzuelas in Spanish.

For a few years the zarzuela underwent a divagation when the astute impresario Arderius, noting the craze for Offenbach's satirical parodies in Paris, formed a company of 'Bufos Madrileños', for which José Rogel wrote *El joven Telémaco* and other comedies. One result of this innovation was that, after the 1868 revolution, political elements infiltrated zarzuelas – allusively in Josep Vilar's *L'ultima rei de Magnòlia* or under the guise of history in Cristóbal Oudrid's *El molinero de Subiza* (performed 300 times in one year) and Barbieri's *El barberillo de Lavapies* (the most celebrated work in the entire repertory). But owing to the political upheaval, the cost of living (exacerbated by a change of currency) had risen sharply and theatre attendances dropped until managers hit on a scheme of mounting four different hour-long spectacles every evening, charging lower prices for each performance separately.

31. Title-page of the zarzuela 'Gigantes y cabezudos' (1898) by Fernández Caballero

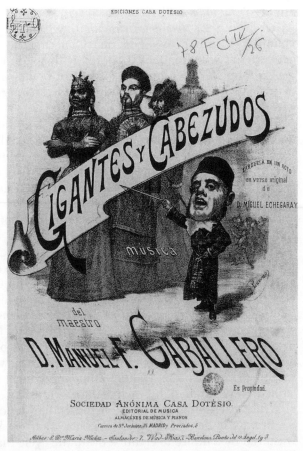

This marked the appearance of the *género chico*, the short, usually realistic form which for 30 years or so was all the rage – more than 1500 were written, mostly ephemeral and many trivial; in the century's final decade eleven Madrid theatres were devoted to this genre. The *zarzuela grande* dwindled: the Teatro Apolo, opened in 1873 for that form of entertainment, was forced to surrender to the new fashion, of which it became known as the 'cathedral'. The greater freedom of expression allowed under the restoration of the monarchy made it possible for Fernández Caballero to score a popular success in 1876 with a piece celebrating the *Marseillaise* (followed by another in Catalan on the same subject by Manent) though Caballero prudently covered his tracks two years later with a monarchic work, *El salto del pasiego*. The output of the new wave of zarzuela composers was staggering: Caballero wrote some 200 works (including *La viejecita*[2] and *Gigantes y cabezudos*), Gómez Calleja over 280, the vivacious Ruperto Chapí about 160 (among them *El tambor de granaderos* and *La Revoltosa*, but also the three-act *La tempestad*, which Saint-Saëns greatly

161

admired, *La bruja* and *El rey que rabió*), Jerónimo Giménez, a stylish writer whose *La tempranica* ran for three years, about 100. Another voluminous writer was Federico Chueca, 'the barrel-organ of his generation', who frequently worked with Joaquín Valverde (their *La gran vía*, on the opening of the Madrid boulevard in 1886, received nearly 1000 performances, though their *Agua, azucarillos y aguardiente* was musically superior).

The high-water mark of the *género chico* flood was Bretón's *La verbena de la Paloma* (still popular a century later), though Bretón, like Chapí (his junior by only three months) had set his sights on serious Spanish opera. The first breakthrough in this field had come when Valenti Zubiaurre (a pupil of Eslava who eventually succeeded him in the royal chapel) had won a national prize in 1871 with his *Fernando el emplezado* and six years later gained appreciation with *Ledia*. Chapí won a government grant with his one-act opera *Las naves de Cortés* to study in Rome, and on his return his three-act *Roger de Flor* was produced in 1878; the first one-acter by Bretón, who had also received a scholarship to study in Italy, had appeared three years earlier, but it was not until 1889 that he enjoyed the recognition of the serious-minded, when his *Los amantes de Teruel*, after being staged in Madrid, was taken up in Barcelona, Vienna and Prague. It nevertheless must have been especially galling for him that it had been sung in Italian, as all his life he had fought for opera in the vernacular and had inveighed against the Italian influence which had, in his words, 'stifled and degraded' his own country's music.

While attempting to shake off the Italian hold, however, Spanish opera was under threat from another quarter: Wagnerism. Pedrell was fired by a desire to create a dramatic cycle that would not merely borrow Spanish outward trappings but express the quintessence of the national spirit – in reality the Catalan spirit – as he felt that Wagner had done with his epic Germanic legends. He embarked on a trilogy, the first part entitled *Els Pirineus*, and expounded his theories in an accompanying manifesto, *Por nuestra música*, which was to have a profound effect on the next generation; but his high-minded purpose was not matched by a corresponding musical inspiration, and only in the trilogy's second part, *La Celestina*, did he more nearly approach his ideal. Wagnerian influence was to be strengthened when Antonio Ribera, the young manager of the Liceo opera house, went to study with Mottl, conducted at Bayreuth and returned to Barcelona to found a Wagnerian Association and present his hero's works in Spanish translation. After initial hesitance, Barcelona audiences unreceptive to Wagner came to favour a new development in 1901, the Teatre Líric Català: its chief representatives were Enric Morera (with *El comte Arnau*, the same subject as the last part of Pedrell's trilogy, and *Emporium*), the violin virtuoso Juan Manén (with *Juana de*

Nápoles) and Urbà Fando, whose *El somni de la Innocència* was performed well over 1000 times.

Thanks to improved musical education, the level of compositional technique was rising. Naively tuneful zarzuelas continued to pour out from writers like the facile José Serrano, but the works of the cultivated Vives, while equally numerous, were constructed with more art and orchestrated with greater finesse. Reflecting the 'Generation of 1898' literary figures' quest for broader horizons and the sloughing off of over-restrictive *españolismo*, Vives's *Bohemios* (1904) took Paris as its scene and signalled a move away from zarzuela, with its traditionally Spanish settings, towards operetta – a move soon followed by other composers with works set in (to cite only three examples) Holland, Venice or ancient Egypt and including non-Spanish dance rhythms. Vives showed that he had not, however, abandoned local colour by introducing the Galician bagpipe into his 'lyric eclogue' *Maruxa*. In 1898 he had written an opera on the Arthurian legend, a subject then much in vogue (Albéniz, fettered to an unhappy contract with a wealthy English amateur librettist, was soon to spend his time unprofitably on a flat-footed Arthurian cycle). Another composer of refinement was José Usandizaga, who had been a pupil of Vincent d'Indy in Paris and who, in his short life of only 28 years, created a sensation with a 'lyric pastoral' in the Basque tongue and won acclaim for *Las golondrinas*, an opera (originally a zarzuela) about circus folk.

Shortly before the triumph of his comedy *La verbena de la Paloma*, Bretón had aroused wild enthusiasm at the Liceo with his opera *Garín* (in which a sardana is danced on stage) – so much so that he was presented with a box of cigars each wrapped in a 1000-peseta note; in 1895 he reached the zenith of his operatic career with the veristic *La Dolores*, set in Aragón. Chapí also had further operatic successes with *Circe* and *Margarita la Tornera* (produced the day before his death in 1909). But new opera composers were coming to the fore. Emilio Serrano (not to be confused with José), although he had for long been an ardent protagonist of national opera, had had his first real breakthrough in 1898 with *Gonzalo de Córdoba*; in 1904, the year of Pedrell's *La Celestina*, his pupil Falla, who had so far written only zarzuelas (two in collaboration with Vives), won a prize with *La vida breve*, but nine years were to pass before it was staged (and then not in Spain but in France). Pahissa (later to be his biographer) achieved 100 performances of his romantic *La presó de Lleida* (1906), based on a Catalan folksong; it was expanded twenty years later under a new title and he went on to create a stir with his abrasive *Gala Placidia*, set during the Visigoth invasion of Roman Spain. Usandizaga's contemporary and friend Jesús Guridi, who did much for the folk music of the Basque country, attracted notice with his 'lyric idyll' *Mirentxu*; and

Conrado del Campo began a distinguished theatrical career in 1910 with the passionate one-act *El final de Don Alvaro*.

A new renaissance seemed to be dawning at the turn of the century, when for almost the first time a few Spanish composers, very diverse in personality, made a distinct impact on the world at large: in each case their vision had been enlarged by studies or residence outside their native country. Albéniz, a Catalan, led a spectacularly picaresque existence, repeatedly running away from home and travelling widely as a piano prodigy, until the age of 13, when he went to study in Leipzig, then Brussels, and finally with Liszt; at 23 he met and was powerfully influenced by Pedrell. He was then writing vast quantities of salon piano pieces, but at 30 decided to go to Paris to consolidate his compositional technique. There he worked with d'Indy and Dukas and taught the piano at the Schola Cantorum. His comic opera, *The Magic Opal*, was produced in London, but a series of operas to highflown but feeble librettos by a rich patron proved an aberration except for *Pepita Jiménez* (1896), which made its way in Europe. By far his most important achievement was *Iberia*, a suite of twelve evocations of various parts of Spain (mostly Andalusian), clothing idealized folk rhythms, harmonies and turns of phrase in an extremely complex and virtuoso pianistic texture that owed much to Liszt.

His fellow Catalan Granados was a quiet, diffident character whose music exudes a delicate poetic Romanticism that has been likened to that of Grieg. At sixteen he had become a pupil of Pedrell's and four years later went to Paris (sharing a room with the pianist Ricardo Viñes, a doughty interpreter of Debussy and Ravel as well as of his compatriots). Granados's *Danzas españolas*, begun in 1892, had nothing of Albéniz's extrovert brilliance but presented native idioms in a form playable by pianists of more modest attainments: they proved highly attractive, as did his Murcian zarzuela *María del Carmen* (1898), which won him a decoration from the king. Another five stage works, however, met with far less response. What fascinated Granados was not his native Catalonia nor the heady colours of Andalucía, but classical Castile: he set, in quasi-eighteenth-century style, a number of *tonadillas* dealing with the emotions of the Madrid dandies and belles pictured by Goya (of whom he was a fervent admirer), and in 1911 wrote a series of *Goyescas*, extended piano vignettes making considerable technical demands but more Chopinesque in style than Lisztian. In spite of awkwardnesses in construction, these were hailed as establishing, along with Albéniz's *Iberia*, a new peak in Spanish instrumental music: they were cobbled into an opera that was given its première in 1916 in New York (on returning from which Granados was drowned when his ship was torpedoed).

Of greater significance, eventually, than either of these was their junior, Falla (born in Cádiz, but Catalan on his mother's side).

Spain's undisputed leading composer of modern times, possessed of literary leanings and, technically, an unusual mastery of form, he was given valuable guidance by Pedrell, who inspired him to espouse the cause of a purified national music. After winning an opera competition with *La vida breve* (as well as a big piano competition), Falla made his way in 1907 to Paris, where he lived for seven years, was befriended by Dukas, Albéniz and Viñes, and became an admirer of Debussy and Ravel. His Seven Spanish Folksongs, imaginative re-creations breathing new life into the originals, were an instant hit and have since been performed almost to excess. In 1915 he wrote an entertainment for the dancer Pastora Imperia, later recast as the passionate gypsy ballet *El amor brujo*, and sketched some piano *Nocturnes* which, on the advice of Viñes, he reshaped for piano and orchestra to become the haunting, impressionistic *Noches en los jardines de España*. These works were to be the foundation-stones of his great international reputation: he was to create several more fine works in a basically Andalusian idiom before radically changing his style in the 1920s.

Joaquín Turina, who had had the same Madrid piano teacher as Falla, like him spent a number of years studying with d'Indy in Paris (where Albéniz, Falla and Turina once took a collective vow to 'fight for our national music'). Less original in thought and less technically accomplished than Falla, more rhapsodic in his construction and more overtly 'picturesque', he nevertheless gained a triumph, after writing a few piano pieces and chamber works, with his orchestral *Procesión del Rocío* in 1913.

By the outbreak of World War I, Spain was beginning to make its mark in the international musical world; and this was to continue for the next couple of decades until, in 1936, the country was again plunged into chaos by civil war.

NOTES

[1] Besides appearing in Italy, South America, Paris, Vienna and St Petersburg, he sang in the Covent Garden seasons of 1877–81 and 1886–7.

[2] Its plot resembles that of Brandon Thomas's farce *Charley's Aunt*, written five years earlier.

BIBLIOGRAPHICAL NOTE

Political and social background

The fullest account of the political and social background to this troubled period in Spain is the admirably written *The History of Spain* by L. Bertrand and C. Petrie (London, 1934); somewhat more compact, but well balanced and clear-minded, is H. V. Livermore's *A History of Spain* (London, 2/1966). R. Carr's *Spain 1808–1939* (Oxford, 1966), supplemented by his *Modern Spain 1875–1980* (Oxford, 1980), considers political, economic and social factors in detail and deals particularly well with Spanish liberalism. For artistic matters R. Altamira y Crevea, *A History of Spanish Civilisation* (London, 1930), is warmly recommended, as is *Spain: a Companion to Spanish Studies*, ed. P. E. Russell (London, 1973), which contains sections on literature, the visual arts and music; a short but perceptive book in the same sphere is J. B. Trend, *The Civilisation of Spain* (Oxford, 1944). On literature, G. Brenan's *The Literature of the Spanish People* (Cambridge, 1965) is excellent and very readable: for those not requiring so much detail G. T. Northup's *An Introduction to Spanish Literature* (Chicago, 1925) would be useful.

Music

On specifically musical matters in Spain the *Diccionario de la música Labor* (Barcelona, 1954) is the nearest approach to a comprehensive encyclopedia in the Spanish language: the only general studies in English are G. Chase's *The Music of Spain* (New York, 2/1959) and A. Livermore's *A Short History of Spanish Music* (London, 1972), the latter, in spite of being written in a confused, macaronic literary style and being unreliable on dates, offering some unusual insights. For those who can read Spanish, however, the most thorough study of all aspects of music in Spain throughout the centuries is J. Subirá's *Historia de la música española e hispanoamericana* (Barcelona, 1953); it contains sections on the religious and secular music of the period under discussion here. There is a short but informative account (in Spanish) of religious music in A. Araiz Martinez's *Historia de la música religiosa en España* (Barcelona, 1942) in the Colección Labor series of handbooks.

Not surprisingly it is the theatre which has attracted the greatest attention from critics and writers. Nearly all recommendable books on this subject, however, are in Spanish. A. Fernandez-Cid's *Cien años de teatro musical en España* (Madrid, 1975) takes the widest conspectus; very detailed, though available in handy pocket-size, is A. Peña y Goñi's *España desde la ópera a la zarzuela* (Madrid, 1967) though it covers the period only up to the 1890s; J. Subirá's *Historia de la música teatral en España* (Barcelona, 1945), again in the Colección Labor series, is brief and succinct. The most authoritative study of the evolution of the zarzuela, which also (most valuably) considers over 100 works in detail, is R. and C. Alier's *Libro de la zarzuela* (Barcelona, 1982); other histories of the form are Cotarelo y Mori's *Historia de la zarzuela* (Madrid, 1934) and, in German, R. Mindlin's *Die Zarzuela* (Zürich, 1965). Discursive and chattily anecdotal as it is, M. Muñoz's *Historia del teatro en España*, iii: *La zarzuela y el género chico* (Madrid, 1965) contains material of incidental interest.

Chapter VII

Russia: East Meets West

DAVID FANNING

Music and society is a topic nineteenth-century Russian composers would have warmed to and which would have had special meaning for them. The notion that music and the arts could take their subject matter from life and in return have some influence on it was embraced more wholeheartedly in Russia than anywhere else, to the extent that art that neglected those principles was viewed as at best irrelevant, at worst immoral. For composers these precepts could take the form of 'progressive' social viewpoints allied to non-traditional musical idioms, as with Musorgsky (1839–81), or of spontaneous lyricism, based on solid musical professionalism and more or less indifferent to social issues, as with Tchaikovsky (1840–93) and Rakhmaninov (1873–1943). In either case rejection of 'art for art's sake' was a prerequisite of artistic 'truthfulness'.

The best Russian music has conveyed those values worldwide to the present day. But there are less obvious reasons why Russian music of this period is historically significant. Musorgsky's innovations opened the way both for the quiet revolution of Debussy and for new attitudes to musical continuity handed down via Stravinsky (1882–1971) to composers of our own time. Thus the antidote to Wagner was prepared and administered. On the other hand, twentieth-century film and entertainment music owes an incalculable debt to Tchaikovsky and Rakhmaninov, quite apart from their influence on Mahler, Sibelius, Shostakovich, Gershwin and others.

With the sole exception of Glinka (1804–57), Russian music from before 1848 plays little part in today's cultural life. Yet from that date its significance is profound. How did this transformation come about? Were the same forces at work as produced the novels of Dostoyevsky and Tolstoy, and later the dramas and short stories of Chekhov? Certainly there are developments in all the arts, and in art, politics and Russian society, which look invitingly similar, and these can offer the newcomer a means of orientation. But closer consideration reveals dynamic forces – individual triumphs and failures, self-doubts, changes of heart, shifting alliances and so on – which suggest the limited value of such parallels. The issues that divided Russian musicians and that produced the intense rivalries of the 1860s and 70s were only partly the same as those so fiercely debated by the intelligentsia. They crystallized around the issue of professionalism – how a composer should learn and refine his craft, which indigenous and which foreign elements were adaptable and which positively dangerous in that process.

One obvious reason why Russian influence on twentieth-century European culture has been so pervasive is that among composers Prokofiev (1891–1953), Rakhmaninov and Stravinsky, among performers Heifetz, Auer and Horowitz, among painters and sculptors Kandinsky, Chagall and the brothers Gabo, along with the entire entourage of Dyagilev's Ballets Russes, decided to settle in the West at the time of the 1917 Bolshevik Revolution or shortly afterwards. Coupled with the deaths about that time of Rimsky-Korsakov (1844–1908), Balakirev (1837–1910), Lyadov (1855–1914), Taneyev (1856–1915), Skryabin (1872–1915) and Cui (1835–1918), and the chaos of the early Soviet years, it also explains why this is an exceptionally clear cut-off point in Russia's own musical history.

In 1848 the situation was different. This was indeed the year Anton Rubinstein (1829–94) returned from tours and studies abroad and began to plan the transformation of Russia's musical institutions. It was also the year Glinka composed his orchestral fantasy *Kamarinskaya*, described by Tchaikovsky as the seed for the entire Russian symphonic tradition: 'just as the whole oak is in the acorn'. But the acorn was dormant for a number of years. Rubinstein's First Symphony of 1851 had its roots firmly in the German Romantic tradition and was of no real consequence so far as Russian music is concerned; the up-and-coming Dargomïzhsky (1813–69) produced nothing of lasting significance before his opera *Rusalka* of 1856; and the other potential heirs to Glinka's mantle did not come to maturity until the 1860s.

However, 1848 remains an important watershed so far as political and intellectual history is concerned, albeit in ways rather different in Russia from the rest of Europe. Russia, along with Britain, escaped the widespread revolutionary flare-ups of that year; but where other régimes responded with concessionary measures, to a large extent defusing liberal discontent, the tsarist autocracy, still flushed with its new-found international role in the aftermath of the Napoleonic wars, actually issued warnings to revolutionaries in Europe and backed them up with troops in support of Austrian and Hungarian counter-revolutions. An already repressive domestic policy was further tightened, and from 1848 until the accession of Alexander II in 1855 Russian intellectuals and writers were in retreat.

Nicholas I had come to power on the death of his brother Alexander

I in December 1825 and had immediately been confronted with the Decembrist Revolt. This was an attempt by a loose alliance of disaffected servicemen, gentry and intellectuals to take advantage of the confusion following Alexander's unexpected death and to instal a more liberal régime. Its organization was deficient and it was easily put down, but it scared Nicholas. Whatever moderately progressive policies he continued to favour in the late 1820s were set aside after the French revolution of 1830 and the Polish rebellion of the following year, and 1848 set the seal on official repression. Russia increasingly resembled a police state, much given to suppressing fictive conspiracies. A famous incident was the Petrashevsky affair of 1849, in which fifteen 'subversives' (whose discussion groups seem wholly innocuous by modern standards) were condemned to death and only reprieved at the gallows. Among them was the 28-year-old Dostoyevsky who was subsequently sent to prison in Siberia, where he gathered material for his novel *From the House of the Dead*.

Even more revealing had been the case of Pyotr Chaadayev's 'Philosophical Letter' published in 1836. Chaadayev, a former guardsman in the Napoleonic campaigns, wrote scathingly about the barbarism of Russia past and present and thereby created a furore. The Moscow *Teleskop* which had published the 'Letter' was suppressed, its editor exiled and the censor who had passed it dismissed. Chaadayev was declared insane by order of the tsar and for a year received daily visits from a physician and a policeman. General Benckendorff, head of the Third Section (the official political police) responded, apparently in all seriousness, in terms that also set the tone for future literary censorship: 'Russia's past has been admirable; her present is more than magnificent: as to her future, it is beyond the power of the boldest imagination to portray'.[1] It is indicative that this view should have been propounded by a Baltic German writing in French.

In the second half of the century intellectuals watched with mounting frustration as the autocracy's attempts at reform stumbled forward while their own increasingly radical proposals ran up against total apathy among the people whose lot they were devoted to improving. Alexander II, 'The Liberator', came to the throne in 1855 and instigated numerous reforms, most dramatically the Emancipation of the Serfs in 1861. But an attempt on his life in 1866 threw his liberalizing instincts into reverse. He was eventually assassinated in 1881. With that experience in mind his successor Alexander III presided over another era of repression and stagnation until 1894. The amiable, but old-fashioned and ineffectual Nicholas II then came to the throne. Defeat in war with Japan (1904–5) and the brutal suppression of demonstrations at the tsar's Winter Palace in 1905 led to a revolutionary situation and a major concession in the form of a representative assembly called the Duma (1905 is sometimes referred to as the Russian 1848). Belated industrialization had been dragging the country painfully into the modern world, but dire misfortune in the war with Germany produced disaffection in the armed forces and the general population, clearing the way for the 1917 revolution.

Alexander II's long rule coincides with the formation of the Mighty Handful under the guidance of Balakirev (1837–1910), the establishment of conservatories in St Petersburg and Moscow and the rise of Tchaikovsky, as well as the golden age of literature, and his assassination roughly coincides with the deaths of Musorgsky, Dostoyevsky and Turgenev. Under Alexander III there was a period of artistic as well as social retrenchment: Balakirev's influence waned, old rivalries became blurred and there was a fresh alliance of old and new faces around the rich patron Mitrofan Belyayev. Finally in the reign of Nicholas II the intellectual community was split between hardline political agitators and anti-realist factions, while in the musical world Tchaikovsky was dead and alongside his epigones a new generation turned from realism towards unashamed emotionalism, mysticism and modernism; it was the age of Rakhmaninov and Skryabin, closely to be followed by Stravinsky and Prokofiev.

The evolution of individual and collective musical trends blurs those apparent parallels at all points and it might be best to regard them as no more than an aide-mémoire. But under a rigidly autocratic system with a tiny bourgeoisie it is only natural that the intellectual climate should be partly defined by the personality and policies of the head of state. So long as it is borne in mind that artists tend to define themselves against rather than in alignment with the political establishment, the approach should prove useful.

BEFORE 1855

The uniqueness of Russia can be more readily understood with reference to her weaknesses than to her strengths. They are not difficult to identify. In 1682 Peter the Great had inherited what was already the largest country in the world. Its further expansion was conditioned by the push towards well-defined, easily defended frontiers and the need for maritime outlets for commerce. During the nineteenth century, wars and treaties led to the annexation of Finland and parts of Poland (including Warsaw) in the west, of Moldavia, Kazakhstan and neighbouring provinces in the south, and of the Amur province in the east, the last leading to the foundation of Vladivostok in 1860. The population grew from some 60 million in 1835 to 166 million in 1913, numerically inferior only to China and India. But it was a land mass of predominantly poor soil and harsh climate with a population mainly of peasantry living in medieval conditions, with diverse racial backgrounds and little or no sense of unified nationhood. To secure Russia's territorial integrity and harness her scattered resources an autocratic system had evolved in which the sovereign and the state played a greater role than in any other European nation, directly administering many economic enterprises, the Academy of Sciences and even the Holy Synod. Its achievements were considerable, notably in the opening up of communications by railway networks in the nineteenth century. But the cost in terms of social alienation was high and the system became locked into an alternation between attempts at reform to correct its own grosser injustices, and periodic bouts of repression in response to 'conspiracies', real or imaginary.[2]

A notable distinction from the rest of Europe was the absence of effective means for registering political dissent. With no semblance of a parliament until 1905 and no political parties or effective pressure groups (ineffective ones abounded) opposition tended to be expressed by the peasantry in minimal cooperation and flight to sparsely inhabited areas, by the intellectuals in covert revolutionary activity. The amount of human energy wasted in these ways, and in employing agents to suppress opposition, is incalculable. The Orthodox Church must be accounted among Russia's weak institutions too. Arguments have raged over to what extent the Russian people are inherently devout or atheistic; the significance of the church for the ordinary Russian was probably as much a case of release from the oppression of day-to-day life as of spontaneous piety. What is undeniable is the contempt the church provoked among intellectuals for allowing itself to be administered by the state and among the peasantry for the fleshly weaknesses of many of its priests. Even the censorship, designed to protect autocracy, orthodoxy and nationality (the three articles of patriotism known as 'Official Nationality') and whose officials in Nicholas I's reign were reckoned to exceed the number of books published in a year, could be notoriously inept.[3]

No-one interested in Russian culture can fail to notice the apparent preponderance of titled gentry (nobility and gentry are synonymous in Russian history) in its novels and dramas. The landed aristocracy itself traced its ancestry to the earliest days of Russia; the title of prince passed to every child (thus nobility by no means always implied great wealth), close relatives of the tsar being styled 'grand prince'. It was the born aristocrats who, following Catherine the Great's lead in the late eighteenth century, set the fashion for French speech and manners, soon taken up by the middle gentry. However, those entering the official service as soldiers or administrators could have nobility, land and a quota of serfs (tied peasants) conferred on them. Peter the Great had built on this process with his celebrated Table of Ranks; designed to make the civil service as attractive as a military career, it involved eight hereditary and six non-hereditary

171

ranks. To these Alexander I added the title of 'honoured citizen' as a reward for achievement in commerce, education and the arts; the stratification persisted with only minor amendments until 1917.

The tsarist administration recruited its members from an educated, largely self-perpetuating élite attracted by the privileged status offered by the Ranks: freedom from direct taxes and corporal punishment and freedom to travel through the country without restriction. Before the nineteenth century there had been an erratic approach to state education and in 1800 the only real schools were the private ones of the nobility, which taught such 'accomplishments' as French and dancing. By 1825 Alexander's educational reforms had taken effect, but there were still fewer than 300,000 pupils (barely two per cent of the school-age population) and only 70,000 of those under the aegis of the Education Ministry (there were about 100,000 in military schools, 50,000 in church schools and 40,000 in 'specialized' schools). Landowners and industrialists financed a few schools but mostly had their own children educated privately, usually by German tutors, often abroad. 'By 1850 . . . about two-fifths of the bureaucrats were sons of nobles, and about one-third sons of junior officers or of junior bureaucrats. Sons of priests, especially evident in the provinces, accounted for about one-fifth.'[4]

The bureaucracy, massive though it was, made up no more than two per cent of the population. Priests and a slowly rising middle class of merchants, teachers and other professional people accounted for a further two per cent. But the vast majority of Russians worked on the land, either as state peasants or as serfs, tied to estates whose bosses ranged in their attitudes from enlightened paternalism to unspeakable cruelty (one was known to have 30 full-time torturers, with assistants, on his staff). The peasantry was also subject to a poll tax – the principal source of finance for the armed services and the court – from which the gentry and clergy were exempt. Discontent increased in the late eighteenth century when serf-owning gentry were relieved of the obligation to serve the state, while the serfs remained bound to their masters (this was a prime reason for the Pugachov rebellion of 1773–5).

Social mobility before the emancipation of 1861 largely took the form of serfs emigrating southwards to escape intolerable conditions of service; and although exceptions can be cited – the eighteenth-century poet and polymath Lomonosov was a fisherman's son, Chekhov came from a provincial grocer's family – on the whole the social order remained rigidly stratified. The outward sign of the privileged in uniform (civil servants, schoolboys, students and professors, as well as the services) and of unshaven, sheepskin-clad peasants, was repeatedly remarked on by foreign visitors. It was not until the end of the nineteenth century that the process of industrialization called forth a substantial bourgeoisie. Having been the only country effectively to enslave its own population, Russia faced appalling difficulties in liberating it; for her intellectuals nineteenth-century nationalism was about liberation not from an external oppressor but from herself.

The concentration of privilege and culture in the two main cities of Moscow and St Petersburg, containing barely four per cent of the population, must also be borne in mind (it continues and is one reason why internal exile is a far more effective punishment than non-Russians might think). Having been the capital city in the sixteenth and seventeenth centuries Moscow had entered a period of decline when Peter the Great moved the capital to the newly built St Petersburg in 1693. That decline was arrested to some extent under Catherine when Moscow provided a cultural haven for those opposed to the Frenchification emanating from St Petersburg; but it deepened when whole districts were burnt during the Napoleonic invasion of 1812 and the city only returned to prosperity later in the century. St Petersburg was dubbed (by Francesco Algarotti, an Italian visitor in 1739) 'Russia's window on the West'. That was partly for obvious geographical reasons and partly because it had become the focal point for Peter's many imported Western customs. For many years the St Petersburgers regarded Muscovites as unsophisticated, and in return the citizens of Moscow looked on their northern counterparts as not fully Russian. Not that this had much, if any, bearing on musical rivalries, as will be seen.

In terms of cultural activity Russia's remaining cities were never in contention; and outside the cities the cultivation of art music was restricted to noble households and various groups organized by them (for instance the serf orchestra on Glinka's uncle's estate, which gave him some of his earliest musical experiences). But if the masses played no direct part in the evolution of Russian musical culture, their inner life – at least as imagined by those in a position to reflect on it and draw on it for artistic ends – certainly did. Those experiences, particularly of mass suffering, were deeply ingrained in the national psyche. Experiences such as *strada* (literally 'suffering'), the brief frenzied toil on the land before the enforced idleness of autumn and winter, and *razmakh*, the manic 'letting-go' of peasant festivity associated with sometimes fatal drinking bouts, were no less deeply absorbed. They contribute to the alternating passion and apathy, hysteria and brooding, archetypally present in Russian music from Tchaikovsky to Shostakovich and beyond.[5] In addition, various categories of 'outsider' have supplied the Russian artist with rich material, notably the *yurodivïy* (not a village idiot but a 'holy fool', who in exchange for a life of abject misery gained the privilege of voicing uncomfortable truths) and various orders of wandering monk.[6]

The artists who were to draw on these experiences did so not with a view to satisfying, much less rejecting, bourgeois or aristocratic tastes but from a conviction that they could contribute to internal reform and the greater glory of their people. They were sustained, cajoled and assailed by the all-important intelligentsia. Drawn at first primarily from the nobility, especially ex-guards officers, but soon including citizens from a variety of occupations, the intelligentsia can trace its ancestry to the largely imported officialdom of Peter the Great's time. Catherine the Great's Francophilia introduced many new progressive ideas, which left this educated minority stirred up but with no vent for its interests, and it shared in the general disillusionment of European thinkers in the aftermath of the French Revolution. The question of who belonged to the intelligentsia – whether or not such writers as Ostrovsky, Tolstoy and Dostoyevsky should be included – has been a matter of dispute. In the Soviet Union today the term is the rough equivalent of 'white-collar worker'; in nineteenth-century Russia it is more usefully definable as 'that [class] which is intensely and actively interested in political and social issues'.[7] Within the intelligentsia views were fluid and dynamic; but for the generation before 1848, Russia's new statesmanlike role in post-Napoleonic Europe focussed attention on a single burning issue: her relationship with the West.

The defeat of Napoleon had instilled in many Russian thinkers an idealized notion of national unity, coupled with the intense awareness, brought back by officers who had served in France, of internal disorder and injustice. They found themselves confronted with the 'accursed questions' of how the lives of the Russian people were to be improved, and the answers, provisional, subject to revision and changes of heart as they were, crystallized round whether Russia had more to learn from the West (the Westernizer view) or the West more to learn from Russia (the Slavophile view). There was a sharp division of attitudes to the Westernization undertaken by Peter the Great (Slavophiles tended to regard it as an aberration) and to the church (Westernizers tended to be atheists). The sentimental belief in the virtues of the peasant village community (*mir*) was more or less shared by both factions; for the Slavophile it was a token of moral superiority over the West, for the Westernizer the model for a future socialist order. Historians' proof in the 1850s that the *mir* was not of Slavic origin and had only been introduced to facilitate tax collection, did little to dislodge those views.[8]

In the 1830s discussions were fertilized by philosophical ideas from Germany (principally Hegel and Schelling) and political ones from France (principally Rousseau on culture, Fourier on utopian socialism). Hegel's notion of dialectic (thesis-antithesis-synthesis), embracing a justification of atrocity if it contributed to a desired historical outcome, was a great morale-booster. Initial agreement on opposition to the autocracy gave place to factionalism in the 1850s and a growing identity of Slavophile thought with the status quo. Finding themselves incapable of action within the system to ameliorate conditions, increasing numbers of intellectuals were drawn to solutions outside it.[9]

The crucial personalities so far as the arts are concerned were the literary critic Belinsky (1811–48) and the publicist, critic and novelist Chernïshevsky (1828–89). The fact that one was the grandson, the other the son, of a priest, is suggestive of the quasi-religious fervour, the secularly formulated messianism, which characterized so much of the intelligentsia's thought.[10]

'After him [Belinsky] no Russian writer was wholly free from the belief that to write was, first and foremost, to bear witness to the truth.'[11] Indeed this belief was brought to bear on the past and present in ways that sometimes surprised its targets: Pushkin was no doubt gratified to be described as the founder of Russian literature, but he was taken aback when held up as a champion of a new social order; Gogol, who expressed support for the establishment of church and monarchy, found himself subject to a virulent attack (see n.10). But it was to be some years before the new attitude bore fruit. In the 1840s, following a long period of comparative stability since the Decembrist revolt, censorship had been slackening and subversive ideas were more or less openly discussed; but the 1848 revolutions in Europe, and Nicholas's repressive measures in response, changed all that, contributing to a hardening of attitudes and the introspective leanings of the intelligentsia, as indeed of most writers: 'For seven years after the death of Belinsky in 1848, all literary development ceased. This period was the darkest hour before the dawn of the second great renascence of Russian literature'.[12]

Musicians could scarcely avoid the influence of these ideas. But finding the means of engaging with them was another matter. Russia came into the nineteenth century with a rich heritage of folk and church music, albeit that the former was not available in published form until Trutovsky's collections of 1776, 1778 and 1779 and that the latter was subject to bowdlerized updating by the well-meaning activities of the imperial chapel.[13] But its art music was only in its infancy, its institutions and practice dominated by foreigners and aristocratic amateurs. The foreign influence was principally Italian, deriving from the enthusiasms of Empress Anna in the 1730s, and French, deriving from those of Catherine in the 1760s (though only indirectly – Catherine herself was tone deaf). The Italian Opera Company in St Petersburg, established by Anna, was lavishly subsidized until the 1880s. Its productions, using illustrious foreign singers, were internationally acclaimed. Beside it was maintained, with much lower subsidy, a Russian opera troupe, with salaries barely a tenth of those paid to foreign stars; it performed in a converted circus hall, which, rebuilt after fire in 1859, became the Mariinsky Theatre (now the Kirov). Concerts took place mainly in the Lenten season when theatrical performances were banned; they were largely sponsored by aristocratic societies – the Philharmonic Society from 1802, the Concert Society from 1850 – and drew on the foreign players from the opera and wealthy amateurs.[14]

Germans had always formed a sizable proportion of the gentry and they supplied the first commercial music publishers in St Petersburg from 1773. A large number of instrumental and theory teachers settled in Russia, notably the Irishman Field, the German Henselt, the Langer family and Villoing (who taught the Rubinstein brothers). From the gentry came such dilettante writers as Ulïbïshev (author of an enthusiastic book on Mozart), Odoyevsky (adviser to Glinka) and von Lenz (influential proponent of Fétis's three-period approach to Beethoven).

Among the educated classes it was accepted that cultivation of music was desirable but not on a professional level (unless by world-renowned foreign virtuosos). The government did not extend the privileges of 'free artist', conferrable on painters, sculptors and actors, to musicians, and a member of the gentry who became a musician in the Imperial Theatre had to renounce the privileges of nobility. Later generations were to be divided over whether amateurism or the foreign influence was the more detrimental to the development of Russian music.

Glinka stood at the end of an old line as much as at the beginning of the new, and, like Pushkin's, his achievement was interpreted by his successors in ways that would have startled him. Because of his aristocratic background he did not need to work for a living until his fondness for the good life led him to be grateful for the appointment as Kapellmeister to the imperial chapel later in life. Before that he rejected the option of a career in the foreign service for the life of a musical dilettante in the salons of St Petersburg, improving his talents as composer, singer and pianist by means of private lessons with foreign visitors and during tours abroad. In this he was no different from his now obscure predecessors and contemporaries like Berezovsky (1745–77), Bortnyansky (1751–1825), Alyab'yev (1787–1851) and Verstovsky (1799–1862). But it was on a trip to Italy in 1832–3 that a combination of self-disgust and nostalgia led to a decisive resolution: 'A longing for my own country led me gradually to the idea of writing in a Russian manner'; and when an author friend at one of St Petersburg's cultural gatherings suggested the patriotic story of *Ivan Susanin*, the peasant who misdirects a Polish army and saves the life of the tsar at the cost of his own, Glinka embarked on what was to be an epoch-making opera.

If the story of *A Life for the Tsar*, as it was named at final rehearsals, captured the patriotic imagination of Russians in the post-Napoleon era (or rather, of that tiny portion of Russians who followed cultural developments), its elevation of folksong to something fit for principal as well as minor characters, and its inauguration of Russian recitative where previous Russian operas had contained spoken dialogue, were decisive musical breakthroughs. But it must not be assumed that Glinka thereby established a totally new way of composing on which his compatriots then seized; rather he showed that it was possible for a Russian to achieve something like the level of competence of a Weber or a Rossini and to give his music a recognizably Russian accent, even if the language was still essentially foreign.

It was Glinka's second opera *Ruslan and Lyudmila*, a setting of a Pushkin fairy tale completed and produced in 1842, which contributed more to a specifically Russian musical vernacular, in particular with its devices for conveying the supernatural and the grotesque. The descending whole-tone scale associated with the wicked dwarf Chernomor became a symbol for supernatural authority. It also opened the door to experiments with other non-major/minor scale patterns (modes) that offered richness and colour without the emotional yearning of chromaticism. Such modes, especially those built on semi-symmetrical interval patterns, were to become something of a fetish for Rimsky-Korsakov and a vital enabling force for Stravinsky, in whose neo-classicism they became emancipated from their representational origins. For the abduction of Lyudmila, Glinka borrowed from Berlioz a spine-tingling and disorientating harmony, which was to be taken up so avidly that it is sometimes known as the 'Russian 6th'. It is perhaps best understood as a 'coloration' of the tonic, and as such it is associated with the more general technique of pivoting traditionally unrelated chords round a shared note or notes.

These innovations were symptomatic of an attitude to harmony as far-reaching and subversive as Wagner's. For while extreme chromaticism undermined the functions of tonality by threatening to escape from the gravitational pull of the tonic (the logical extension being Schoenberg's anguished atonality), the Russians undermined it by a tendency to disregard functions altogether (the logical extension being the ecstatic-contemplative states of Debussy, Skryabin and Messiaen).

With *Kamarinskaya*, an orchestral fantasy on two folktunes, Glinka patented another startling innovation, showing that a melody could remain unvaried (through some 70 repetitions in this case) while its background changed.[15] This shifting of initiative away from melodic

177

to rhythmic and textural invention was a radical shake-up of the elements of musical language. It suggested that composition could also be a game, and the resourcefulness with which Glinka played it gave Russian composers a new repertory of devices – hence Tchaikovsky's reference to the acorn and the oak. In this sense the inconsequential 'chopsticks' variations published in 1878 as *Paraphrases* by Rimsky-Korsakov, Cui, Lyadov (1855–1914) and Borodin (1833–87) are a quintessential Russian work.

For Glinka's successors the issues raised by his operas offered plenty to be grappled with. There was the heroic, romantic vein of *A Life for the Tsar*, which particularly appealed to Tchaikovsky, and the fantastic, modernistic vein of *Ruslan*, taken up by Balakirev and his circle. The one inspired an infatuation with dramatic 'truth', the other with the 'marvellous'. Both showed how folksong might play a significant part in shaping a distinctive musical language. Both were characterized by a bright, open orchestral texture also evident in Glinka's Spanish orchestral fantasies (which in turn showed that specifically Russian nationalism was less important to him than the idea of national colour in general).[16]

Glinka also bequeathed some unsolved problems, such as how to compose a Russian symphony and how to handle counterpoint. It is not difficult to see these as manifestations of more general Russian characteristics:

> In the Russian soul there is a sort of immensity, a vagueness, a predilection for the infinite, such as is suggested by the great plain of Russia. For this reason the Russian people have found difficulty in achieving mastery over these vast expanses and in reducing them to orderly shape. There has been a vast elemental strength in the Russian people combined with a comparatively weak sense of form.[17]

The Russian instinct for 'enriched consonance', such as the 'coloured tonic', is as ancient as its famous church bells (Glinka's home region of Smolensk was well known for its strident campanology), but counterpoint, and with it the engendering of dynamic motion of the kind perfected in the Viennese Classical symphony, was not part of that instinct. Above all Glinka gave his successors ideals to live up to and the confidence that it was possible to do so. His dictum, 'the people are the composers; we are only the arrangers', provided a banner as inspiring as any in intellectual and literary circles.

1855–81
The similarities between pre- and post-revolutionary Russia are numerous. They have to be viewed as a preliminary to understanding rather than its end product, however. It is tempting, for example,

to see the accession of Alexander II in 1855 as engendering a 'thaw' comparable to that brought about by Khrushchev from 1953. But if the equation of those two rulers is already somewhat shaky, any comparison between the preceding suppressions under Nicholas I and the systematic exterminations under Stalin is absurd; nor are the cultural situations any more than superficially comparable.

Alexander II's achievements are unquestionable. The emancipation of the serfs in 1861 and reforms of the judiciary, the local government, the military and education, earned him the nickname 'the Liberator'. Censorship became punitive rather than preventative: where proposed publications had previously to be submitted for approval (often to several different offices) they now merely faced punishment for infringements. Without any fundamental change in regulations much of the self-censorship undertaken under Nicholas evaporated. Book publication, which stood at 1020 new titles in 1855, was 10,691 in 1894, roughly equal to the combined output of Britain and the USA.[18]

Many of Alexander's reforms proceeded out of dire necessity and self-interest. The Crimean War of 1854–7 had shown how inefficient the armed forces were, and officials were becoming ever more conscious of the growing economic gap between Russia and the industrialized Western world. Even so, such things did not prevent later Russian and Soviet leaders embarking on murderous, self-defeating policies, and credit for avoiding similar paths must be given to the personality of Alexander himself. The relatively broad and liberal education, the travels to Europe and Siberia, the contact with prisoners and exiles, the experience on various state committees, all of which helped to form that personality, arose from Nicholas's wish that his son would be better prepared for the throne than he had been. They were arguably a greater service to Russia than any of Nicholas's policies as tsar.

Nevertheless Alexander's liberalism was relative. It did not exclude the traditional love of pomp and ceremony. At his coronation the national anthem, composed by Count L'vov (see n.13) in 1833 to replace the British anthem used until then, was performed three times during the firework display, first by 1000 voices, then with the addition of massed choirs and military bands, and finally accompanied by cannon-fire 'by means of an electro-galvanic apparatus'. The words were perhaps less than innovatory – 'God, save the Tsar! / Mighty and strong reign for our glory; / Reign for the dread of our enemies, / O Tsar of the Orthodox faith! / God, save the Tsar!'[19]

Not all the reforms had the desired effect. The liberated serfs were grouped compulsorily into communes and felt that their allocations of land were inadequate, though this probably had much to do with the inadequacy of farming methods. Many landowners found the transition to capitalist methods, providing machinery and hiring labour, just as difficult. (Musorgsky's was among the many land-owning families which suffered drastic changes in fortune, though he whole-heartedly approved of the emancipation.) Thus, in common with most totalitarian régimes, Russia found that cautious liberalization released as much pent-up discontent as creative energy, and official qualms were stirring even before 1866 when a former university student aimed a bullet at the tsar and missed. Military and judicial reforms continued, but educational institutions lost a degree of their new-found autonomy and the atmosphere of relative tolerance changed overnight. Renewed international tensions with the rise of Bismarck and a unified Germany in the 1870s contributed to official unease.

In the meantime political agitation had been taking on a steadily more uncompromising tone, fed by the expansion of the universities and aggravated there by poor teaching and antiquated institutional practices. Again the experience of the Crimean War played its part, in the sense that 'the emergence of naked force killed a great deal of tender-minded idealism'.[20] Here the tempting parallels are very much with America and Europe a hundred years on, complete with long-haired men and close-cropped women. Old-style liberalism was largely abandoned in favour of the hard line, with its concomitant atheism, feminism and revolutionary commitment. In his last essay Herzen wrote, 'One must open men's eyes, not tear them out'. To the 'new men' of the 1860s this was no longer self-evident. When an 1840s idealist turned to novels it was Herzen's *Who is to Blame?* (1848), dealing with weak-willed representatives of diverse literary trends; the realism of the 1860s is enshrined in Chernïshevsky's more actively titled *What is to be Done?* (1863), set in a seamstresses' cooperative, with strong-willed characters and a didactic, moralistic thrust. Among the principal radical voices were Bakunin ('The passion for destruction is a creative passion'), Pisarev ('What can be smashed, must be smashed') and Tkachov. Nechayev reached a pinnacle of unscrupulousness in his attempt to get friends and acquaintances arrested so that they would convert from liberals to revolutionaries. Such extremism, which paid so little respect to religiosity or liberal-ism, tended to dissolve the old Slavophile-Westernizer dichotomy, the one transmogrifying into conservative Pan-Slavism (the movement for the union of the Slavic peoples under the leadership of the tsar), the other fusing with elements of Slavophilism to produce populism.

A turning-point came in 1874 and 1875 when the *Narodniki* (popu-lists) who modelled their hopes for the future on the *mir* and the *artel* (traditional cooperative workshops) decided to follow Herzen's injunc-tion and 'go to the people'. They encountered widespread indifference, if not outright hostility – 'Socialism bounced off people like peas from a wall'.[21] Although the populist movement did not vanish, this failure prompted a split between various kinds of disillusioned soul, notably those who backed off from political involvement into the kind of aestheticism which had been anathema since the advent of Belinsky and those who concluded that the people had to be dragged willy-nilly into revolution. For the latter, any means justified that end. One of their sub-groupings, the 'People's Will', eventually contrived the assassination of Alexander II after a succession of failed attempts.

The 1860s and 70s were the golden age of Russian literature. The term does not customarily embrace the most overtly political and prescriptive fiction, such as *What is to be Done?* (often described as the worst work of fiction ever written), but it does encompass, indeed it is almost synonymous with, the adoption of realism as opposed to idealism of the 1840s, and it is associated with the elevation of truth above beauty, both highly congenial to the intelligentsia. Realism was an international phenomenon in the second half of the nineteenth century, but its moral-political commitment and its centre-stage placing distinguished the Russian brand from all others. In literature the chief representatives are Dostoyevsky, the most uncompromising chronicler of Russia's woes, and Turgenev, who in the character of Barazov from *Fathers and Sons* (1862) created the archetypal nihilist, with his claims that 'A decent chemist is twenty times more useful than any poet' or that the entire works of Pushkin were not worth a single well-made pair of boots. The lesser-known Goncharov created Oblomov (in the novel of that name, 1859), the incarnation of the 'superfluous man' who takes 100 pages to get out of bed and spends most of his life in dressing-gown and slippers. The playwright Ostrovsky was notable for his delineations of domestic tyrants and the introduction of folksongs into his plays.

The influence of the intelligentsia is still more evident in the work of Tolstoy, who turned his back on much of his earlier work and embraced the essential tenets of Chernïshevsky, among them that 'the function of art was to help men to satisfy their wants more rationally, to disseminate knowledge, to combat ignorance, prejudice, and the anti-social passions, to improve life in the most literal and narrow sense of these words',[22] with the corollary that all other art was useless. For Tolstoy, as he was to write in *What is Art?* (1898), a peasant choir was more uplifting than a late Beethoven sonata. Such radical doubts about culture had been voiced before, most famously by Rousseau, but never had they been so central or so influential as in nineteenth-century Russia. Tolstoy extended his contempt to thinkers, dismissing Hegel, the idol of the previous generation, as so much incomprehensible gibberish. The fact that Dostoyevsky and Tolstoy remained Christian, albeit as non-church-goers, is one factor distancing them from the radical intellectuals.

It is Russia's painters, among whom Repin (1844–1930) is the best known, who offer still closer parallels to the development of the intelligentsia. Their rebellion against old-fashioned academicism led many of them to form their own *artel*s and to the association of *peredvizhniki* ('travelling art exhibits') which, like the populists' efforts, signally failed to stir the peasantry to new consciousness. This brand of realism continued to flourish, thanks in part to vigorous publicizing by Stasov between 1856 and his death in 1906, side by side with the impressionist and modernist movements that entered Russia in the 1890s and early 1900s.[23]

Among the intelligentsia's less endearing features was its capacity for misrepresentation. This faculty was shared by commentators on music. Initially it involved the canonization of Glinka and the subtle slanting of his ideas (*A Life for the Tsar* was as much royalist as folkist in its message, and in the last decade of his life Glinka confessed his waning interest in composition *à la Russe*). Associated with the Glinka personality cult was a reluctance to see any virtue in contemporary Western music. Later misrepresentations take on an increasingly aggressive political tone, particularly on the part of Stasov; and since a number of them have been handed down both by Soviet commentators with axes to grind and by Western ones with deadlines to meet, we have to proceed with caution.

The man considered by the fledgling nationalists as the antichrist to Glinka was Anton Rubinstein. Born in Russia but trained in Germany, this pianist-composer had concluded that Russian music's main needs were for professional concert organization and training of the kind from which he himself had benefited. With aristocratic and state patronage he established the Russian Musical Society (1859) and the St Petersburg Conservatory (officially opened in 1862). His brother Nicholas was soon dispatched to found a conservatory in Moscow (1866), taking with him a composer from the first class of St Petersburg graduates – Tchaikovsky.

This direction – élitist, professional, administered by foreigners and funded by aristocrats and the state – was the opposite of Balakirev's vision. To his mind it threatened to turn Russian music into an outpost of Germany rather than a flourishing centre in its own right. Accordingly in 1862, in collaboration with the distinguished choral conductor Lomakin and taking the example of the flourishing Sunday school movement with basic literacy taught by volunteer teachers, he set up a Free Music School in St Petersburg. The educational programme was to be aimed at beginners and based on singing and rudiments. In the meantime he had been gathering a group of like-minded amateur talents, first the Lithuanian-born military engineer César Cui (from 1855), then the ex-cadet and future civil servant Musorgsky (1857), the naval officer Rimsky-Korsakov

32. Portrait of Tolstoy as Ploughman; painting (1887) by Ilya Repin

(1861) and the distinguished chemist Borodin (1862). The fortunes of the circle reached a highpoint in 1867 when Balakirev was invited to conduct the Russian Musical Society concerts, Rubinstein having resigned his posts after prolonged internal disagreements.

Balakirev is generally referred to as the only professional in the group. Certainly he made a living from piano playing and conducting (not a reliable one, for in 1872 he was forced to take a job in the goods department of the Warsaw railway), but his compositional training had hardly been professional, involving merely study of the classics (courtesy of Ulïbïshev, whose library he inherited) and trial-and-error composition; it was these methods he recommended to members of his circle, as well as supplying ideas for subject matter and musical themes and 'correcting' their work bar-by-bar.

In 1867, on hearing that delegates to the Pan-Slavic Congress were to visit St Petersburg, Balakirev mounted a concert in their honour, conducting works by Glinka, Dargomïzhsky, Rimsky-Korsakov and himself. Stasov's review was ecstatic: 'May God grant that our Slavic guests never forget today's concert, may He grant that they preserve forever the memory of how much poetry, feeling, talent, and ability there is in the small but already mighty handful [*moguchaya kuchka*, literally 'mighty little heap'] of Russian musicians'. The description stuck, and the group even engaged in communal projects such as the opera-ballet *Mlada* (1872, unfinished). But collaboration was mainly a case of Balakirev prompting and advising, and of Rimsky-Korsakov posthumously (re)orchestrating, revising and completing.

The members of the Handful had differing and unequal talents and gradually lost all cohesion in the 1870s. Cui, musically the weakest, turned out a succession of operatic failures and is remembered chiefly as a critic.[24] Balakirev himself passed through various psychological and religious crises and seemed to expend more creative energy goading others than producing his own music; his gradual inclining towards the Pan-Slav movement made inevitable a rift with Stasov, at heart a Westernizer, and the progressively more radical Musorgsky.[25] Borodin was constantly distracted by his non-musical activities and frequently could only compose when illness confined him to his bed. Musorgsky drank himself to death. Rimsky-Korsakov survived, but at the cost of increasing creative sterility and academic guilt-feelings. The rift with Rubinstein was never as absolute as the Handful's propaganda might suggest. That ideas passed to and fro is demonstrated by Balakirev in 1861 finding himself 'strongly attracted' to Rubinstein's *Ocean* Symphony and reporting his enthusiasm to Stasov, who proposed a 'more Russian' work based on the legend of the Novgorod merchant Sadko, an idea passed on by Balakirev to Rimsky-Korsakov who proceeded to compose the piece.

Initially close to the Handful, but gradually distanced from it, was Aleksandr Serov (1820–71). Like Cui he divided his time between caustic criticism and unsuccessful operatic composition. It was his (less than enlightened) embracing of Wagnerism from about 1858 which really set him apart from former allies like Stasov, though in due course the Handful did all it could to invent other grounds for marginalizing him as 'opera's "superfluous man"'.[26]

Thus 'In the 1860s the Balakirev circle and Serov mounted separate campaigns against Rubinstein, often from different directions and with different weapons, while skirmishing simultaneously with each other'.[27] Rubinstein maintained a dignified silence; indeed he forbade his associates to polemicize in print, although he gained an ally of sorts in the journalism of Hermann Laroche (1845–1904), a fellow student of Tchaikovsky and disciple of Hanslick (a rare phenomenon indeed in Russia).

Balakirev's circle had no monopoly on nationalist sentiment. Modernism and anti-academicism were its prime distinguishing features, manifested among other things in Balakirev's attitude to folksong. Where most previous folksong collections had relied on town-dwellers' reminiscences, the 23-year-old Balakirev 'bombarded ... [by Stasov] with radical reading matter'[28] and mindful of Chernïshevsky's prescription of folksong as an artefact not of art but of nature, 'went to the people'. The resulting publication was hardly scientific – the very act of supplying piano accompaniments ensured that – and previous collections had been equally respectful of the metrical freedoms of folksong. But Balakirev's modal diatonic accompaniments at least established an approach to harmonization that did not force the tunes into conformity with Western practice and that looked beyond old-fashioned textbook formulae. For most Russian composers folksong was to some extent a mediating force between life and art; Balakirev showed how it could also be a mediating force between nationalism and modernism.

The Handful was obsessed with the future of the Russian opera. Indeed Balakirev was so caught up with the desiderata of opera that he never managed to compose one himself. His colleagues were united in their contempt for frivolity or second-hand idioms, such as they claimed to find in Offenbach, Meyerbeer, Rossini, Verdi, Hérold and others. Rubinstein, with some justification, was scarcely considered.[29] Some attempts excited great interest at the time but did not establish a place in the repertory – notably Serov's *Judith* (1861–3), *Rogneda* (1865) and *The Power of the Fiend* (1871), Cui's *William Ratcliff* (1861–8), which provided a prototype for the semi-hero semi-villain protagonist, and Dargomïzhsky's *Rusalka*.[30] All these apparent failures are significant at least in that they provided models to work against; and some specific ideas were salvaged – both *Rogneda* and *William Ratcliff* contain the pivoting harmonies later to be immortalized in the Coronation Scene of *Boris Godunov*.

The most significant project, however, was Dargomïzhsky's *The Stone Guest* (incomplete at his death in 1869) which is occasionally revived today. Perhaps inspired by Serov's praise for his 'performance' of the words in *Rusalka*, Dargomïzhsky embarked upon a word-for-word setting of Pushkin's version of the Don Giovanni story, using an unbroken arioso: 'I want sound directly to express the word. I want truth' (an interesting equation). Others have followed such a course – Debussy in *Pelléas et Mélisande*, Schoenberg in *Erwartung*, Shostakovich in his unfinished *The Gamblers*. But it was Musorgsky who first took up the idea, embarking on his own word-for-word setting of Pushkin's *The Marriage* (1868). This was even more uncompromising and modernist, partly because Pushkin's prose (as opposed to the iambic pentameters of *The Stone Guest*) lent itself naturally to continuous recitative rather than arioso. Musorgsky's experiment went no further than one unorchestrated act. But in this context *Boris Godunov* (first version 1868–9) represents something of a compromise rather than the radical departure it seems to be from the vantage point of mainstream European opera. *Boris* also signalled the end of word-music experiments and inaugurated a vogue for historical opera, taken up by Rimsky-Korsakov in *The Maid of Pskov* (see n.18) and Tchaikovsky in *The Oprichnik* (1870–72).

Musorgsky was the closest in spirit of all the musicians to the intelligentsia. For a while from 1863 he lived in a commune along the lines suggested by Chernïshevsky. But the label of populist (see n.25) should be handled with care. You can take political ideas out to the people, you can mount travelling art exhibitions; taking *Boris Godunov* to the cornfields is more problematic and getting peasants into an opera house almost more so, even if they themselves are supposed to be the heroes. In fact the 'people-as-hero' in *Boris* is something of an over-statement, justified only by the scene in the Kromy woods added in the 1874 revision. There for the first time the crowd appears as a rebellious force. Without this scene, the historian Kostomarov's famous reported description, 'no opera, but a page of history', rings only half-true.

The decline of a personality racked by guilt and afflicted by

33. Ivan Mel'nikov as Boris Godunov, the role he created at the première of the revised version of Musorgsky's opera at the Mariinsky Theatre, St Petersburg, on 8 February 1874

circumstances beyond control is undoubtedly Musorgsky's prime concern. So obsessed is he with Boris's self-doubt at his coronation that he gives him a monologue which by any criteria of realism is absurd. In *Boris* and in his songs, Musorgsky is the finest musical portrayer of desolation and death between Schubert and Mahler, while Prokofiev's grotesquerie is scarcely conceivable without his example.

Empathy, it has been said, is Musorgsky's greatest gift. Selective empathy, with characters embodying something of his own psychological makeup, is one of Tchaikovsky's. It is also one reason why *Eugene Onegin* and to a lesser extent *The Queen of Spades* are the most successful of his dozen surviving operas. *Onegin* hinges on the Letter Scene in which Tatyana declares her love for Onegin (by the time he discovers his feeling for her she is married and rejects him, in spite of her continuing infatuation). Her mixed emotions are hauntingly conveyed in a recurring four-bar phrase – a 'Russian 6th' with its frisson of strangeness in the second bar and yearning Germanic appoggiaturas in the horn's rejoinder. Mixture of emotion is arguably as crucial to Tchaikovsky's symphonic music as is his gift for memorable melody.

It is indicative of Tchaikovsky's priorities that this essentially rhapsodic scene is more classically shaped than anything in *Boris*; and that when he set about an opera on the *Boris* story, he started with the love scene between Marina and Dmitry. But more noteworthy is the fact that *Boris* and *Onegin* both favour tableau, narrative and self-examining monologues over ensemble and confrontation. Both also ignore the Aristotelian unities of dramatic action: *Boris* is a chronicle on Shakespearian lines, *Onegin* a collection of lyric scenes which Tchaikovsky himself feared did not satisfy the 'requirements of opera'. In fact most Russian operas avoid the usual Western assumptions about dramatic action, and the instinct arguably persists as far as Stravinsky's *Oedipus rex* (1926–7). The widespread view that *Onegin* is somehow 'less Russian' was countered by both Prokofiev and Stravinsky, who agreed that *Onegin* was more 'Russian' than *Boris*. Stravinsky put the conviction into practice when he drew on similar musical idioms for his comic opera *Mavra* (1921–2).

The symphony question was scarcely less problematic. In a projected Ukrainian Symphony, Glinka had stumbled on the 'impossibility of getting out of the German rut in the development', perhaps not realizing that the problem almost certainly lay more with the exposition – that is, in the nature of the themes – than with the development section itself. Although Balakirev had gone some way towards expanding and symphonicizing Glinka's legacy, it was still not clear how a fully fledged Russian symphony might come about (this period between Schumann and Brahms/Bruckner saw some-

34. *Mariya Klimentova as Tatyana in the Letter Scene from Tchaikovsky's opera 'Eugene Onegin'; she created the role at the first performance, by students of the Moscow Conservatory, on 29 March 1879*

thing of a crisis of confidence in the European symphony too, dominated as it was by the Lisztian symphonic poem). Stasov's prescription, 'The symphony must cease to be composed of four movements as Haydn and Mozart thought it up . . . the future form of music is formlessness', was one of his less helpful suggestions. Musorgsky summed up his reservations: '*Symphonic development in the technical sense* is just like German philosophy – all worked out and systematized . . . When a German thinks, he *reasons* his way to a *conclusion*. Our Russian brother, on the other hand, starts with the conclusion and then might amuse himself with reasoning'.

Balakirev prompted various more or less successful 'national dialect' symphonies – Rimsky's First (1861–2),[31] Borodin's First (1862–7), Tchaikovsky's first three (original versions 1866, 1872, 1875). But Musorgsky's apprentice-piece Symphony in D (1861–2) was put aside, and Balakirev's own First Symphony was left unfinished in 1866 and only completed in 1897. Even more productive was Balakirev's idea of orchestral music as 'theatre without a stage', embodied in his music for *King Lear* (1858–61). This had an immediate influence on Tchaikovsky's fantasy overture *Romeo and Juliet* (1869) and his symphonic fantasy *The Tempest* (1873), and together with Rubinstein's techniques of sequential spinning-out and the emotionalism of Liszt's symphonic poems it was to be a catalyst for his mature last three symphonies.

The Fourth Symphony dates from the same crisis period in Tchaikovsky's life as *Onegin* (1877–8) and the obsession with fate is avowedly crucial. Here it is enshrined in the opening theme (recurring Fs and A♭s harmonized with a succession of non-functional 'coloured tonics') which casts a shadow over even the most apparently innocent ideas. The process of psychological ebb and flow, building on the example of Berlioz's *Symphonie fantastique*, established the subjective symphony (one that externalizes the personality of its creator) as a force to be reckoned with. Mahler and Shostakovich were to be deeply in its debt.

Not that there is any weakening of structural awareness. Tchaikovsky radically rethinks the tonal basis of the sonata first movement, constructing it on rising tiers of minor 3rds so that the recapitulation may be fused with the mounting hysteria of the development and the traditional sense of resolution implied by the returning tonic made ambivalent. There is even a convincing, if unusual, solution to the symphonic integration of folksong in that the finale makes the 'Birch Tree' song the object of escapism ('To the people!'), desperately showing that any attempt to escape from fate is doomed to failure.

To construct a detailed psychological programme for Tchaikovsky's Fourth Symphony, based on the composer's hints in a famous letter to his patroness Nadezhda von Meck, would not be a difficult or pointless undertaking. Nor would it be uninteresting to construct a detailed cinematic scenario for Borodin's Second (1869–76), which incorporates material from his temporarily shelved opera *Prince Igor*. Whereas to discuss either piece in the opposite terms would be ludicrous. Borodin's achievement, a happy, well-balanced work independent of classical models with a scherzo in the extraordinary metre of 1/1, is in many ways as great as Tchaikovsky's. There is none of Tchaikovsky's pain in Borodin's lyricism, none of Tchaikovsky's desperation in his energy; Borodin seems to have found and can cheerfully exult in what Tchaikovsky strives for.

Tchaikovsky justly complained of his symphonic compositions that the 'seams showed'; but music-lovers have forgiven that more easily than the seamless, but soulless perfection of many of his followers. The other side to the hyper-emotionalism of the late symphonies was a growing interest in Mozart (*Mozartiana*, 1887), calm neo-classicism

(Rococo Variations, 1876) and ballet. While remaining hostile to Brahms and Wagner he confessed a weakness for such congenial melodists as Bizet, Delibes, Massenet and Grieg.[32]

It is clear that the political setback of 1866 had no immediate impact on music; Rubinstein's problems and Balakirev's ascendancy meant that 'radical' nationalism had tremendous momentum. In the 1870s, however, the musical battle-lines became increasingly blurred. Serov died unexpectedly in 1871; that year the St Petersburg Conservatory, having recently undergone a change of management, engaged Rimsky-Korsakov as composition teacher, and his appointment changed the orientation both of the conservatory and of the Balakirev circle. Balakirev's domination had already been weakening and now he was overwhelmed by depression, disappointment and ill-health. With his retreat, internal differences in the Handful came to the surface: Cui, for instance, came out with a vociferous attack on *Boris Godunov*. The old rivalries were effectively dead by 1873, in spite of the attempts of Stasov to pretend otherwise. But though Rubinstein and Balakirev both gave the appearance of defeated men, they had in large measure achieved their aims of professionalization and nationalization respectively. The banners were now to be carried by others.

1881–94

With the deaths of Dostoyevsky and Musorgsky in 1881 and Turgenev in 1883, the golden age of Russian realism was effectively over. A new tsar, as mindful of his predecessor's fate as Nicholas had been of the Decembrists, instigated a new clampdown, the intelligentsia was still in disarray after the failure of populism, and the arts had lost the strongest personalities who might have swum against the tide of disillusionment. The period about 1870, when Musorgsky, Rimsky-Korsakov and Tchaikovsky viewed themselves 'not as "mere" musicians but as participants [in] and contributors to their country's seething intellectual life'[33] would not return, except in the very different guise of Skryabin's theosophical apocalypticism. If Alexander II's reign is simplistically characterized, along with Khrushchev's, as a thaw, that of Alexander III equally merits the now fashionable label for Brezhnev's stagnation.

In fact the economy was in the unusually capable hands of the imperial economic advisers Bunge and Witte. They had presided over a doubling in industrial production between 1860 and 1880 and there was to be a further doubling under Alexander III. Pre-revolutionary Russia was set on a course towards genuine modernization, with a degree of compulsion and hardship that was very real for the many peasants forced into the industrial system but infinitesimal beside that to be inflicted under Stalin. It was in constitutional and cultural

35. *Title-page of the first edition of the vocal score (Moscow: Jürgenson, 1876) of Tchaikovsky's opera 'Vakula the Smith', based on Gogol's fairy tale 'Christmas Eve'*

matters that Russia stagnated, thanks in large measure to the influence over the tsar of the reactionary Pobedonostsev, who as tutor and adviser to both Alexander III and Nicholas II was in no small measure responsible for the autocracy's eventual failure to ward off revolution.

Rumours were spread that Alexander II had been murdered by Jews, and a series of well-organized pogroms followed, apparently sponsored by the Holy League, an extremist band of nationalists and antisemites, and tacitly supported by Pobedonostsev. The partitions of Poland in 1772, 1793 and 1795 had brought many Jews into the population for the first time and they were allocated areas in Lithuania, Poland, White Russia and Ukraine, known collectively as the Pale, beyond which they were forbidden to work. After some relaxation of restrictions in the first part of Alexander II's reign the Polish Rebellion of 1863, blamed by some on the Jews, led to mounting antisemitism. Those Jews who then decided to emigrate (principally to the Americas) avoided the even worse persecutions that were to follow under the actively antisemitic Nicholas II and especially in World War I when Cossacks murdered large numbers of Jews under pretext of uncovering German spies. Antisemitism had never been far from the surface of Russian life; even such supposedly enlightened musicians as Balakirev and Cui were prone to it as part of their more general ideological xenophobia. The Rubinstein family had converted to Christianity, but like Mahler they found that this was no guarantee against invective and discrimination.

Alexander II had finally set aside the Third Section, the political police, in 1880, but after his death it reappeared in the guise of the *Okhrana* (literally, 'guard'), bolstered by thousands of informers and actually viewed as a necessary evil by the many Russians who were shocked by the assassination and who (justifiably) regarded the revolutionaries as enemies of peaceful change.

While this may have had a debilitating effect on an intelligentsia already reeling from the failure of populism, the rest of the country was being shaken up by industrialization. This created the beginnings of a proletariat, which in classic Marxist theory was the precondition for revolution – yet another blow to the old-style utopian socialists who had been advocating gradual change for the better, bypassing the capitalist phase altogether. Marx and his Communist manifesto of 1848 had argued that socialist railing against the injustices of capitalism was beside the point because the latter was in any case foredoomed. The growing number of socialists who embraced this doctrine did so with a kind of religious conviction that they were predestined to triumph. For a while a curious situation obtained in which Marxists supported capitalism because of its prospects for long-term revolution and the authorities tolerated Marxists because they did not advocate terrorism and might weaken the populists. Thus in 1872 the first volume of *Das Kapital* in Russian translation passed the censor and the beginnings of a Marxist movement were seen, although its main influence was to be felt only in Nicholas II's reign.

As new political ideas formed which seemed to have little place for any kind of art (the superstructure in Marxist theory) so new generations of artists began to dissociate themselves from politics. A resurgence of art for art's sake and mysticism was in sight. Old-style realism continued to be championed by Stasov and Tolstoy, but they gradually came to be seen as anachronisms; and since the new literary figures of Chekhov and Gorky were not in the public eye until the 1890s this was a stagnant time for literature. The truces between musical factions were paralleled in conciliatory moves between the Academy of Fine Arts and the Association for Travelling Art Exhibits about 1886.

One undoubted growth area was science, which had been flourishing since the 1830s, irrespective of vacillations in educational policy. In the second half of the century the surgeon Pirogov, the mathematician (and first woman professor in the world) Sof'ya Kovalevskaya, the physiologist Pavlov (conditioned reflex) and chemist Mendeleyev (periodic table) all came to the fore.

The spirit of scientific positivism had an interesting musical consequence in the attitude to folksong. Mel'gunov's collections appeared in 1879 and 1885, in transcriptions which acknowledged the fact that 'authentic' folksong was performed heterophonically – that is with several different descants (*podgolosoki*) sung simultaneously – and therefore could not be furnished with piano accompaniment without falsifying its nature. This news came too late to have much impact on the nationalist composers, however, and it is a sign of Rimsky-Korsakov's newly developed academicism that he denounced these versions as barbarous, the same terms in which fusty German professors had previously denounced Balakirev's modal accompaniments.

The years 1881–7 were barren for Rimsky-Korsakov, who spent much of his time completing and orchestrating Musorgsky's and Borodin's unfinished works. But he sprang to life with his *Spanish Capriccio* (1887), *Sheherazade* (1888) and the *Russian Easter Festival Overture* (1888), consolidating his acknowledged gift for musical exoticism. The 'sleeping, contemplative East', to which Russians often ascribe their native tendency to inertia, had long exerted a compelling fascination. This did not usually involve research in the field, however; Rimsky-Korsakov picked up a Persian theme for *Mlada* (1889–90) in a northern summer resort. Balakirev heard the Armenian theme used in *Islamey* (1869) in Moscow and the quasi-oriental theme for the finale of his first symphony in a third-class railway compartment on the Finnish railway. It was Rimsky-Korsakov who, taking the hint from Liszt, devised a systematic musical language for exoticism, with one of its main elements an alternating tone–semitone scale which was to become a vital tool for Stravinsky and Messiaen.[34]

In 1889, after performances of *Der Ring des Nibelungen* in St Petersburg (*Die Meistersinger* and *Tristan* did not follow until 1898), the mature Wagner's influence was finally felt in Russia, at first on Rimsky-Korsakov's orchestration (see his posthumously published *Principles of Orchestration*, 1913) and his new series of operas. The objections to Wagner had long been founded on ignorance or ideological preconception.[35] Tchaikovsky voiced another aspect of the Wagner rejection: 'So that the feeling should be warm and vital, I've always tried to choose subjects in which the characters are real living people, feeling as I do. That's why I find Wagnerian subjects, in which there's nothing human, intolerable'.

Tchaikovsky had consolidated his position and become a colossal influence on the new generation, not least on his pupil (and addressee

36. Sheherazade: costumes designed by Léon Bakst for the ballet on Rimsky-Korsakov's symphonic suite (1888), danced by the Ballets Russes at the Paris Opéra on 4 June 1910; from the supplement to 'Comoedia illustré' (15 June 1910)

of the above-quoted remarks) Taneyev. It was Taneyev who introduced into Russian music the influence of Brahms, together with an obsession with counterpoint which found few other takers at the turn of the century. These were the two leading figures of the 1880s who were to set the stage for Glazunov (1865–1936) and Skryabin.

Glazunov had already burst on to the scene with his First Symphony, composed at the age of 16. The rich timber-merchant Belyayev (1836–1904) heard its first performance in 1885 and determined to publish it, thus inaugurating a new circle centred on Rimsky-Korsakov, who by now greatly preferred Belyayev's practical to Balakirev's ideological despotism. He also founded the Russian Symphony Concerts in 1885 and a series of Quartet Evenings in 1891. Compared with Balakirev, Belyayev's tastes were cooler to opera and warmer to chamber music, comparatively indifferent to folksong and positively allergic to church music; this did not stop him from publishing works of many different complexions, but it did have some influence on the general direction taken.

Glazunov was taught by Rimsky-Korsakov to deplore the 'clumsiness' and 'amateurishness' of the folklorists and to appropriate only their superficial qualities. That was the kind of impulse which led to Rimsky-Korsakov's revisions of his friends' works, to his own crippling self-doubts and to the general unadventurous solidity of Glazunov, Lyadov, Arensky (1861–1906), Grechaninov (1864–1956) and others of the Belyayev circle who have been accused of 'emotional anaemia'.[36]

1894–1917

Russia at the turn of the century gives the impression of a crazy machine: the engine of its tardy industrial revolution making mighty strides (there was a further doubling of output between 1892 and 1900 and yet another by 1914) but the clutch of its social cohesion showing alarming signs of wear, and the steering and brake mechanisms of its institutional control increasingly unable to cope. With hindsight the 1917 revolution seems an inevitable nemesis.

The accession of Nicholas II in 1894 brought no such change of direction as had been seen in 1855 or 1881. Nicholas was in many ways a kindlier man than his father, but the instincts of autocracy, antisemitism and militarism were too deeply ingrained for him to be able to influence events for the better. Although the early years of his reign were blessed by the good advice of such ministers as Witte, in later years Nicholas tended to appoint and listen to yes-men. His superstitious, interfering wife, his haemophiliac son and heir, and the bizarre figure of Rasputin, made the imperial family a sorry spectacle.

There were two developments in this period which sealed the autocracy's fate. The first was a missed opportunity. Popular dis-

37. *Lenin (seated, centre), with members of the League of Struggle for the Emancipation of the Working Class, in St Petersburg, 1897*

content was at a peak following defeat in war with Japan (1904–5), and the shooting of peaceful protesters outside the Winter Palace in January dealt a decisive blow to the view of the tsar as the 'Little Father' who could be turned to in times of great suffering. There were widespread strikes and localized peasant revolts and a famous mutiny on the battleship *Potyomkin* (immortalized in Eisenstein's film of 1925).[37] The potentially revolutionary situation led Nicholas to concede a form of representative assembly, the Duma (mainly a talking-shop, since legislative power was retained by a council of ministers).

After two false starts the Third Duma of 1907–12 produced useful reforms, but the hesitant steps towards democracy foundered on the clumsy diplomacy of Prime Minister Stolïpin, and the Fourth Duma lacked the unity of purpose and trust of imperial authority which might have steered Russia past the second critical point, World War I. Incompetently managed and aggravated by chronic short-comings of distribution, the war sapped the morale of the population and, crucially, the army. Soldiers refused to implement the re-pressions which had been the time-honoured solution to discontent, and in February 1917 Nicholas was finally forced to abdicate. The provisional government which took over was hijacked in October (November by the Western calendar) by the Bolsheviks (so called because they were in the majority in 1903 when Lenin had provoked a split in the Marxist social democrats). Before 1917 few would have predicted their coming to power, but they prevailed largely by virtue of their ruthlessness (a lesson learnt from the relative tolerance of the autocracy that had permitted them to function).

It is as convenient to set the apocalyptic tone of Skryabin's music and Russian symbolist poetry alongside the end of the Romanovs as it is to associate Mahler's valedictory late works with the death-throes of the Habsburgs. But in the Russian case this has to be understood in the context of a widening gulf between politics and the arts. If the decadents, as many turn-of-the-century artists were happy to be known, took up prophetic stances, it was no longer with a view to political involvement but as a token of quasi-religious, grandiose oblivion: the cult of ecstasy.

Until a septic tumour on the lip rudely negated Skryabin's claims to immortality, he had been ascending in a giddy spiral towards and past megalomania to the point where his last project, the *Mysterium*, was to involve a seven-day performance in the Himalayas ending in the general enlightenment of mankind. The path to this ambitious goal had led from virtuoso pianism in a feverish Chopinesque style, through devout Wagnerianism (but expressed in symphony rather than opera) crossed with influences from Debussyan impressionism. A prime technical means, evident in a stream of keyboard works from the Fourth Sonata, was the 'mystic chord', another species of 'coloured tonic', which could be shifted round by symmetrically patterned transpositions and decked out with impressionistic flurries. The basic technique was not sophisticated but the improvisatory overlay was capable of near-delirious or trance-like evocations.[38]

Like Musorgsky, Skryabin was in many ways closer in spirit to contemporary writers than to his composer colleagues – and to painters as well, since Russian impressionism had arrived with Vrubel, to be followed by Kandinsky, whose move towards abstraction strikingly parallels Skryabin's towards non-tonality. Among poets the apocalyptic note was struck by Bal'mont, Blok, Bryusov, Vyacheslav Ivanov and Sologub. Since Pushkin and Lermontov, poetry had been on the retreat, unable to match the claims of the realist novel as an agent of social transformation.[39] After an interlude of pale Parnassianism, Russian poets finally discovered a voice as clamorous and passionate as the novelists before them. The under-pinning philosophy was that of Vladimir Solovyov, who took up Boehme's view of the universe in terms of Sophia, a cosmic version of the eternal feminine, which one might either dismiss in four words or drool over in four thousand. Like the philosopher Rozanov, Skryabin saw creativity as quasi-sexual: 'The creative act is inextricably linked to the sexual. The creative impulse has all the signs of sexual stimulation in my own case ... and maximum creative power is inseparable from maximum eroticism'. This stood on its head Pisarev's contemptuous nihilist equation of aesthetic pleasure with sexual gratification.

Collectively these artists make up what is often referred to as the Russian renaissance (or sometimes the third renaissance, after those of the 1820s and 1860s). But they by no means had a monopoly on artistic trends – Maksim Gorky's novel *The Mother* of 1906, for instance, set the tone for what was to become the official doctrine of socialist realism in the 1930s.

Skryabin was in many ways atypical of Russian composers and he had no significant followers (Lourié, Rebikov and Roslavets were pale shadows; a number of experimenters in post-Skryabin musical systems were active between 1915 and 1930 but little of their music survives). The representative figures of the era are Lyadov, Arensky, Grechaninov, Glier (1875–1956), Metner (1880–1951), Myaskovsky (1881–1950) and Ippolitov-Ivanov (1859–1935), inheritors of the emotionalism of Tchaikovsky[40] and the craftsmanship of Rimsky-Korsakov. From 1909 much of their work was published by Kusevitsky, a conductor and double bass player who, having married into money, took over the role of Maecenas from Belyayev. None could match the easy fluency of the prolific Glazunov, who, almost by the law of averages, occasionally hit on real inspiration (the Bacchanale from *The Seasons* of 1899, for instance) and who as head of the St Petersburg Conservatory from 1905 exerted enormous influence. He was undoubtedly a force for the general welfare of Russian music and musicians,[41] but the more interesting figures were the less well-balanced ones like Rakhmaninov, Stravinsky and Prokofiev, all from rich families, all highly gifted pianists, all destined to leave Russia at the time of the revolution and, so far as aesthetics are concerned, all heading in totally different directions.

There is a popular view of Rakhmaninov as the musical poet of pathos, yearning for the homeland, striving to preserve moments of emotional intensity which in real life evaporate all too quickly. And there is a professional view of a shallow composer of limited means. Both opinions are probably truer than revisionist counter-proposals, but which carries more weight is debatable. His ability to create a musical catharsis out of individual vulnerability and suffering has ensured his immortality and it defines a crucial dimension of Russian music. Stravinsky brought very different kinds of Russianness to the West – the kind it loved in *The Firebird* (1909–10) and *Petrushka* (1910–11), the kind it loved to hate in *The Rite of Spring* (1911–13), the kind it was fascinated by in *The Wedding* (1914–17) and the kind it did not care about in *Mavra* (1921–2).[42] Prokofiev arrived like a bolt from the blue, scandalizing his St Petersburg professors by climbing on Musorgsky's shoulders for his grotesquerie, on Tchaikovsky's for his wide-intervalled lyricism and neo-classicism, on Skryabin's for his mysticism and on Stravinsky's for his mechanical excitement.

It would be forcing a point to detect in Chekhov's gently melancholic plays (and Stanislavsky's Moscow Art Theatre, which did so much to promote them) the literary counterpart to Rakhmaninov; though Skryabin had no scruples about lumping them together with Tchaikovsky, juxtaposing his own 'uplift' with their 'depression'. But there is some point in drawing attention to the reaction against them in the work of Meyerkhold and the parallel anti-Romantic reaction in Stravinsky and Prokofiev. Circusization, one of the watchwords of the more adventurous dramatists and cinematographers, is a shared phenomenon. But the source of the parallel is in the avant-garde circles of the turn of the century, especially *Mir iskusstva* ('The World of Art'), a journal published by Dyagilev between 1899 and 1904. Dyagilev was initially an organizer of art exhibitions and as such his aestheticism brought him into conflict with the aging Stasov, a full decade before his historic opera and ballet season in Paris. The Evenings of Contemporary Music (1901–12), run on a shoestring budget by the musicologist and scientist Karatïgin, brought the newest music of Debussy, Reger and Schoenberg to St Petersburg, as well as promoting Stravinsky and Prokofiev.

*

Surveying the social background of the composers named in this chapter, the preponderance of 'privileged' families is remarkable, notwithstanding the tribulations many had to go through; and the élitism of Dyagilev's circle may be judged from the average circulation of *Mir iskusstva* – just over a thousand in a country of some 180 million. When Lunacharsky was appointed to oversee cultural education under the Bolshevik régime, he was determined that the arts should be available to peasant and (ex-)prince alike, to province as well as capital. The price in terms of freedom of expression was high and it drove many artists into exile, where they have fertilized Western intellectual and cultural life ever since.

Rakhmaninov, Prokofiev, Metner, Grechaninov, Nikolay and Aleksandr Cherepnin and Stravinsky settled abroad. The West, which had been enthusiastically embracing Russian music from Borodin and Tchaikovsky in the 1870s onwards, inherited a significant portion of its hard-won gains. In broadest terms these were the rediscovery of the essential, primordial qualities of music as sound, as play, as gesture, and as magic (whether rhythmic-incantatory or harmonic-ecstatic), emphasizing sensitivity and instinct, moving away from memory and the conscious intellect – an alternative to Wagner and post-Wagnerianism. So far as realism and political engagement go, any relevance to Weill, Henze, Nono and the like seems tenuous; but the legacy was reclaimed in the most unexpected way by Shostakovich, the first important composer to spend all his formative years under the Soviet régime. Drawing on the long Russian tradition of crypto-statement (*vran'yo*: roughly speaking 'blarney') he found an extraordinarily effective means for confronting the unspeakable. In all these respects Russian music in the long run achieved what its most far-fetched propaganda said it would (if not in precisely the ways the propagandists had in mind) – a radical counterblast to the German mainstream and an infusion of Slavic values into the West.

NOTES

[1] S. Monas, *The Third Section: Police and Society under Nicholas I* (Cambridge, Mass., 1961), 169.

[2] The first ruler to style himself 'tsar' (i.e. Caesar) was Ivan (III) the Great (1462–1505) and the title was formally adopted by his grandson Ivan the Terrible (1533–84). Both belonged to the Rurik dynasty, reputed to descend from the Scandinavian warrior of that name who came to rule the Slav people of Novgorod in 862 (the date traditionally taken for the establishment of ancient Russia).

[3] See Monas, *The Third Section*, chap.4. Censorship had been a familiar force in Russia since the religious schism of the mid-seventeenth century, but it only became institutionalized at the time of the French Revolution. From then on it was intended to suppress all opinions that might challenge the legitimacy of the autocracy, and incidentally any which might offend 'accepted morality'.

[4] J. Westwood, *Endurance and Endeavour: Russian History 1812–1986* (Oxford, 3/1987), 49.

[5] In one attractive theory this is traceable to the practice of tightly swaddling babies: 'Constricted and enshrouded during most of the day, when he can move only his eyes and must bottle up emotions of rage or joy, the mummified infant is periodically unwrapped for a delicious romp during which he can kick his legs about and relish a brief ecstasy or tantrum'; R. Hingley, *The Russian Mind* (London, 1977), 35.

[6] Among the many bizarre religious sects were the 'Khlysty ("whips") who liked to flog each other; the "gapers" who prayed with open mouths so that the Holy Spirit might enter into them; the "wanderers" who were always on the move in search of God's truth; and the "jumpers", who prayed while jumping so that their prayers would be closer to God'; Westwood, *Endurance and Endeavour*, 18.

[7] D. Mirsky, *A History of Russian Literature* (London, 1964), 322. The term 'intelligentsia' may have been first coined by Johann Georg Schwarz, lecturer on philosophy at Moscow University; J. Carmichael, *A Cultural History of Russia* (London, 1968), 129. But it only gained wide currency and its accepted modern connotations in the 1860s.

[8] The best-known Slavophiles were Khomyakov (1804–60), Kireyevsky (1808–56), the Aksakov family (1817–60) and Samarin (1819–76). At its most extreme, Slavophilism was expressed in the adoption of the *murmolka* and *zipun*, the cap and homespun coat of native Russian dress. Belinsky and, initially, Herzen were regarded as the most important Westernizers of the 1830s generation (see nn. 9 and 10).

[9] 'Both sides loved Russia. The Slavophiles loved her as a mother, the Westernizers as a child'; N. Berdyayev, *The Russian Idea* (London, 1947), 39. As Herzen wrote: 'We, like Janus . . . looked in opposite directions, while *one heart beat in us all'*. Herzen, of aristocratic, albeit illegitimate birth, was one of the first of the 'conscience-stricken gentry'. He was exiled in 1847 and eventually settled in London, from where he edited the influential magazine *Kolokol* ('The Bell'). He eventually reached a kind of synthesis of Slavophile and Westernizer views, which came to be known as 'populism'. In 1851 he produced the remarkably prescient warning, 'Communism is the Russian autocracy turned upside down'.

10 Belinsky has been canonized in the Soviet Union as a forerunner of Marxism/Leninism. He is famous for his passionate reproof of Gogol: 'The Russian people is right. It sees in writers of Russia its only leaders, defenders, and saviours from the darkness of Russian autocracy, orthodoxy, and nationalism. It can forgive a bad book but not a harmful one'. The presumption to speak on behalf of the Russian people (who, as the intelligentsia came to realize, were wholly indifferent in such matters) is as remarkable as the insistence on (morally correct) content as opposed to aesthetic values. Chernïshevsky belongs to the next generation. His main precepts were the rejection of idealism and art for art's sake, his major contribution to literary theory being his master's essay, *The Aesthetic Relations of Art to Reality* (1855).

11 I. Berlin, *Russian Thinkers* (London, 1978), 266.

12 M. Baring, *An Outline of Russian Literature* (Westport, Conn., 1971 [original edn. 1915]), 159.

13 For details see A. Swan, *Russian Music and its Sources in Chant and Folk-song* (London, 1973), especially pp.19–21, 115–20. Imitation folksongs enjoyed a vogue in the early nineteenth century, alongside the *romans*, in imitation of the French *romance*. The imperial choir and chapel, like the Imperial Theatre, had been dominated by Italians and Italian taste until the complete cycle of court chant was assembled in 1846 by Count Alexey L'vov (1798–1870), a general, adjutant to Nicholas I, violinist and composer, who supplied the chant melodies with harmonizations in Germanic style.

14 Beethoven's symphonies received their first public performances in St Petersburg between 1833 (the *Pastoral*) and 1869 (no.1); B. Asaf'yev, *Russian Music from the Beginning of the Nineteenth Century*, trans. A. Swan (Ann Arbor, 1953), 305.

15 The same theme had been given similar but less extensive treatment in John Field's *Air russe favori varié pour le piano* published in Moscow in 1809; see G. Abraham, *The Concise Oxford History of Music* (London, 1979), 633.

16 For a detailed account of reactions to Glinka's operas, see R. Taruskin, *Opera and Drama in Russia: as Preached and Practiced in the 1860s* (Ann Arbor, 1981), 1–32.

17 Berdyayev, *The Russian Idea*, 2.

18 Music occasionally encountered the censor, as when Rimsky-Korsakov's first opera *The Maid of Pskov* (1868–72) had to be altered because the original libretto referred to medieval Pskov's republican form of government.

19 Westwood, *Endurance and Endeavour*, 59.

20 Berlin, *Russian Thinkers*, 63.

21 Ibid, 232.

22 Ibid, 229.

23 See Y. Olkhovsky, *Vladimir Stasov and Russian National Culture* (Ann Arbor, 1983). Historian of art and music, staunch nationalist, follower of Belinsky and close associate of the Balakirev circle, Stasov was to become the acknowledged head of the Handful with Balakirev's decline in the 1870s. He suggested the subjects of Balakirev's *King Lear*, Borodin's *Prince Igor*, Musorgsky's *Khovanshchina*, Rimsky-Korsakov's *Sheherazade*, Serov's *Rogneda*, Tchaikovsky's *The Tempest* – and he received a gratifying number of dedications in return.

24 Cui was a very unpleasant critic on the whole: 'Rubinstein is not a Russian composer. He is only a Russian who composes', was one of his milder (and more revealing) sallies. His diatribe following the première of Rakhmaninov's First Symphony in 1897 nearly stopped the latter composing altogether.

25 '[In the early 1870s] Musorgsky developed into a musical "populist" and "realist" – the only member of Balakirev's circle to whom these terms can be applied legitimately'; R. Ridenour, *Nationalism, Modernism, and Personal Rivalry in Nineteenth-Century Russian Music* (Ann Arbor, 1981), 218.

26 For detailed musical assessments of this important composer see Taruskin, *Opera and Drama*, chaps.2, 3 and 4; this book also contains the most detailed commentaries in English on Dargomïzhsky and Cui.

27 Ridenour, *Nationalism*, 97.

28 R. Taruskin, 'How the Acorn Took Root: a Tale of Russia', *19th-Century Music*, vi (1982–3), 205.

29 'Stage *Elijah* and you have a Rubinsteinian opera; take the staging away from [Rubenstein's] *The Tower of Babel* or *The Macabees* and you have a Mendelssohnian oratorio'; Taruskin, *Opera and Drama*, xiii.

30 It is a measure of the seriousness with which the issue of Russian opera was regarded that Serov's critique of *Rusalka* appeared in ten instalments of the *Muzïkal'nïy i teatral'nïy vestnik*

('Musical and Theatrical Herald'); Taruskin, *Opera and Drama*, 49.

[31] Rimsky-Korsakov's Symphony no.1 was partly composed while his ship was at anchor on the Thames, and tried out on a Thames-side pub piano; Abraham, *Studies in Russian Music*, 279.

[32] 'I played over the music of that scoundrel Brahms. What a giftless bastard! It annoys me that this self-inflated mediocrity is hailed as a genius. Why, in comparison with him, Raff is a giant, not to speak of Rubinstein, who is after all a live and important human being, while Brahms is chaotic and absolutely empty dried-up stuff.'; diary entry, 9 Oct 1886, quoted in N. Slonimsky, *Lexicon of Musical Invective* (New York, 1953), 73. Brahms's supporter Hanslick may not have contributed to Tchaikovsky's critical neutrality: 'Tchaikovsky's Violin Concerto gives us for the first time the hideous notion that there can be music that stinks to the ear'; *Neue freie presse* (5 Dec 1881), quoted in Slonimsky, *A Lexicon of Musical Invective*, 207.

[33] Taruskin, '"The Present in the Past": Russian Opera and Russian Historiography, ca. 1870', in *Russian and Soviet Music: Essays for Boris Schwarz*, ed. M. Brown (Ann Arbor, 1984) 136.

[34] R. Taruskin, 'Chernomor to Kashchei: Harmonic Sorcery; or, Stravinsky's "Angle"', *JAMS*, xxxviii (1985), 72–142.

[35] '*Zukunftsmusik* is not Wagner, but Dargomïzhsky and Musorgsky', as Stasov wrote in 1870; Taruskin, *Opera and Drama*, 324; see also ibid., 292–3.

[36] Asaf'yev, *Russian Music*, 186.

[37] Even Rimsky-Korsakov became involved in support of student demonstrations. The censors, seeing a caricature of the autocracy in his last opera *The Golden Cockerel*, took revenge by preventing its performance during his lifetime.

[38] See J. Reise, 'Late Skriabin: some Principles Behind the Style', *19th-Century Music*, vi (1982–3), 220–31.

[39] Mirsky, *A History of Russian Literature*, includes sections on the 'Decline of poetry' (1830s) and 'The utter decline of poetry' (1860s and 70s). M. Cooper, 'Alexander Skriabin and the Russian Renaissance', in *Slavonic and Western Music: Essays for Gerald Abraham*, ed. M. Brown and R. Wiley (Ann Arbor, 1985), is a useful brief summary of the aesthetic issues of the day.

[40] Rumours that Tchaikovsky committed suicide to prevent a homosexual affair being made public are probably groundless; A. Poznansky, 'Tchaikovsky's Suicide: Myth and Reality', *19th-Century Music*, xi (1987–8), 199–220.

[41] See S. Volkov, *Testimony: the Memoirs of Shostakovich as Related to and Edited by Solomon Volkov*, (London, 1979), especially 123–30.

[42] Sources for the dramatic content of all but the last-named are given in S. Karlinsky, 'Stravinsky and Russian Pre-Literate Theater', *19th-Century Music*, vi (1982–3), 232–40.

BIBLIOGRAPHICAL NOTE

General background

J. Westwood's *Endurance and Endeavour: Russian History 1812–1986* (Oxford, 1987) is a scholarly and up-to-date but also readable and entertaining general history. For an understanding of the intellectual climate, anthologies of source readings such as *Russian Intellectual History*, ed. M. Raeff (New York, 1966), and *Readings in Russian Civilization*, ed. T. Riha (London, 1969), are indispensable; penetrating commentary on the same subject may be found in I. Berlin's *Russian Thinkers* (London, 1978). D. Mirsky's *A History of Russian Literature* (London, 1964) is still a standard work, which may be supplemented by *A Handbook of Russian Literature*, ed. V. Terras (London and New Haven, 1985). Mirsky's *Russia: a Social History* (London, 1931) remains valuable; R. Hingley's *The Russian Mind* (London, 1977) is more selective but also more up-to-date and energetically (even provocatively) written.

Music

General histories of Russian music have faced difficulties in the language barrier and undependable access to scores. Reliance on early secondary sources in Western languages has been problematic since these have tended to mirror the propagandist viewpoints of Cui (*La musique en Russie*, Paris, 1880) and Stasov. R.A. Leonard's *A History of Russian Music* (London, 1957) and J. Bakst's *A History of Russian-Soviet Music* (New York, 1966) have been criticized from this point of view but they remain the only recent book-length studies of their kind in English. A. Swan's *Russian Music and its Sources in Chant and Folk-Song* (London, 1973) is a useful study from the viewpoint of its title but it was incomplete on the author's death and remains sketchy and inaccurate. Coverage of Russian sacred and folk music is more thorough in the respective articles in *Grove 6*.

B. Asaf'yev's *Russian Music from the Beginning of the Nineteenth Century*, trans. Swan (Ann Arbor, 1953), offers the most comprehensive coverage of the subject in English and is valuable for its extensive discussion of minor figures. However it is hard to come by and it suffers from the slanting of ideas towards the approved ideology of Soviet Russia (the original dates from 1930). To some extent that is true of most Soviet studies, but A. Gozenpud's work on opera must be singled out as a monumental and scholarly achievement: *Russkiy opernïy teatr XIX veka*, 3 vols. (Leningrad, 1969–73). In addition, Soviet scholars have been assiduous, and for the most part scrupulous, in editing letters and memoirs, some of which are available in translation, notably Rimsky-Korsakov's *My Musical Life* (London, 1974) and parts of Tchaikovsky's correspondence, *Piotr Ilyich Tchaikovsky, Letters to his Family: an Autobiography*, ed. G. von Meck (London, 1981).

Among single-composer studies, D. Brown's of Glinka (London, 1974) and Tchaikovsky, 3 vols. of 4 (London, 1978–86), are recommendable, and the two volumes of *The New Grove Russian Masters* offer convenient life-and-works summaries of the most significant figures (London, 1986). For lively, expert, occasionally idiosyncratic insights, covering general and specialized topics, G. Abraham's many essays are all useful: *Studies in Russian Music* (London, 1969), *On Russian Music* (New York, 1970), *Slavonic and Romantic Music* (London, 1968).

The groundwork for a new level of understanding is being laid by the scholarly series 'Russian Music Studies' published by UMI Research Press. Perhaps the most valuable volumes to date are R. Ridenour's *Nationalism, Modernism, and Personal Rivalry in Nineteenth-Century Russian Music* (Ann Arbor, 1981), R. Taruskin's *Opera and Drama in Russia as Preached and Practiced in the 1860s* (Ann Arbor, 1981) and *Musorgsky: in Memoriam 1881–1981*, ed. M. Brown (Ann Arbor, 1982). Further seminal articles and chapters by Taruskin are cited in the notes to this chapter.

Two powerful and densely argued studies by C. Dahlhaus, *Realism in Nineteenth-Century Music* (Cambridge, 1985) and *Between Romanticism and Modernism* (London, 1980), place Russian musical nationalism and realism in an international context.

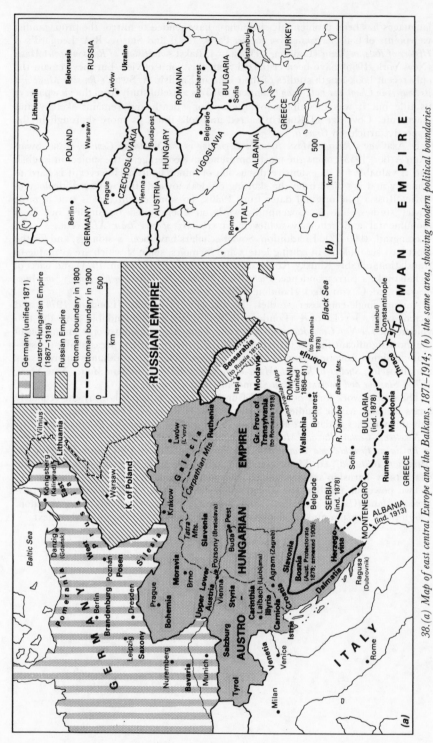

38. (*a*) Map of east central Europe and the Balkans, 1871–1914; (*b*) the same area, showing modern political boundaries

Chapter VIII

East Central Europe: the Struggle for National Identity

JIM SAMSON

PRELUDE: BEFORE THE REVOLUTIONS

The revolutions of 1848 had no single underlying meaning. Even within the Habsburg Empire quite separate discontents were interleaved. There was a struggle for social justice, as powerful in Vienna as it was in Paris. There was a struggle for constitutional rights, exercising the liberal intelligentsia in Prague as it did in the German cities. And there was a struggle for national self-determination, impelling Hungary, as it did northern Italy, towards a wholesale war of liberation. Primary causes are difficult to disentangle, but in the eastern empire at least the political issues acquired a particular immediacy, ultimately absorbing the social issues into all-embracing nationalist programmes. It was national rather than class interests which were most obviously at stake in risings against the Habsburgs, not least in their eastern territories.

Admittedly there was little agreement about the 'nations', which is hardly surprising given the many ethnic groups that had settled in east central Europe over the centuries. Some, like the Poles, the Czechs, the Bulgars and the Magyars, could look back to historic kingdoms to validate their claims to autonomy. Others, like the Slovaks, Lachs, Slovenes and Ukrainians, lacked any such political roots, but their sense of ethnic identity, sustained by language, tradition and custom, was no less strong and their desire for political independence no less real. For the most part these lands were outposts of empire, Ottoman as well as Habsburg[1] and there is little sense in which they formed part of any larger socio-political entity which corresponds to the 'eastern Europe' created by Yalta.

In fact it remains a controversial question whether east central Europe may be said to have any real identity as a historical unit. It has been argued that the region which, roughly speaking, separates Russia and Germany had coherence and distinctiveness on cultural, religious and political grounds, with roots in medieval kingdoms which were 'Western' by most criteria of their age.[2] By this reasoning

205

the region's collective profile in later years was a result of the constant political frustration of its orientation towards Western rather than Eastern culture. That profile, in short, is defined in relation to Western norms which are absent but desired. Yet it may also be argued that the division of Europe runs deeper, that it is not to be explained solely in terms of political interventions but that it has a basis in long-standing social, cultural and even spiritual divergence. From this perspective the collective identity of central Europe might be located (even to this day) precisely in its mediation of two opposing systems.[3]

The divided church was an important root of later social and political divisions, but in due course these later divisions generated their own momentum which diverged radically from the geography of the religious divide.[4] From the sixteenth century western Europe (or much of it) gradually abandoned feudalism in favour of a developing national consciousness and urban modernity. No such development took place in the lands east of the River Elbe. We would scarcely expect it in the Ottoman-ruled areas of modern Romania, Bulgaria and Yugoslavia, but even in the more Westernized Habsburg territories feudalism remained strongly entrenched, with an unusually large and powerful noble class compared with western Europe. Under Habsburg rule, the estates of east central Europe gained steady but decisive victory over the towns, which were mostly excluded from the polity and which remained isolated from, rather than becoming centres for, surrounding rural districts. Often indeed there was an ethnic distinction between town and country, with a German-Jewish urban community typically surrounded by a Slav or Magyar rural population. In essence these societies remained agrarian right through to the late nineteenth century, with an urban middle class emerging only tentatively in all but the Bohemian lands.

Inevitably social modernization advanced furthest in those areas which had closest political ties with the West, notably the Czech lands, Hungary, Poland and the Habsburg territories of modern Yugoslavia and Romania. It was here, too, that the cultural traditions developed in western Europe were best able to flourish. Bohemia and Moravia in particular had been closely associated with Austro-German culture since the momentous Habsburg victory of 1620, and they were subject in varying degrees to policies of Germanization. Among other things native languages were suppressed and many of the estates were colonized by an Austrian 'aristocracy'. There were of course benefits as well as penalties. Moravia remained relatively backward until the late nineteenth century, but Bohemia under the Habsburgs shared many features of modernized Western societies, including the beginnings of a politically aware and culturally active urban bourgeoisie. It is hardly surprising then that the dynasty was viewed ambivalently by the Czechs. They had their modest rising in 1848, but they opposed the Viennese radicals and at the Slavonic Congress in Prague later that year they made clear their preference for partial autonomy within the empire rather than absorption into an expanded German Confederation, as proposed by the Frankfurt Parliament.

Similarly in Hungary (which included Transylvania and Slovakia) attitudes to the Habsburgs were by no means uniformly hostile, at least before the War of Independence (1848–9). The Magyars had traditionally been allowed a measure of autonomy within the empire and their main political thrust was to dominate the other ethnic groups in Hungary rather than to remove the Habsburgs. In essence early nineteenth-century Magyar nationalism was itself a form of imperialism. And in social-historical terms the estates remained much more powerful in Hungary than in neighbouring Bohemia, with the higher gentry more firmly established and the society in consequence more conservative. Even with the gradual rise of industrialism in the nineteenth century, manufacture took on something of a feudal character, sponsored and controlled by the wealthy landlords and ultimately responding to Austrian demands rather than Hungarian needs.

In Poland the situation was uniquely complex politically owing to the tripartition of the late eighteenth century, involving the Hohenzollerns and Romanovs as well as the Habsburgs. The nationality question loomed especially large, and it was a swelling tide of nationalist feeling, fomented in political clubs and secret societies, that led to the unsuccessful rising of 1830. Ironically that rising put an end to a promising period of social, economic and cultural modernization, at least in the so-called 'Congress Kingdom',[5] and even to some measures of democratization. The repression that followed 1830 reduced Polish society once more to a stratified neo-feudalism in which the 'political nation' was confined to an upper stratum of nobility whose attitude to the partitioning powers was often ambivalent. The voice of radical Poland could be raised only in exile.

In all three territories, as also in Habsburg Slovenia and Croatia, a feudal structure survived in some form and degree well into the nineteenth century, and its disintegration under the pressure of west European example and influence was not answered by any adequately matured alternative structures. The social modernization and cultural renewal that characterized these lands in the late eighteenth and early nineteenth centuries were less the product of an organic internal evolution of society than the response to 'enlightened' ideas and practices from the West which stimulated, and then fused with, a slowly developing nationalist commitment. Nationalism was to dominate the politics and culture of east central Europe in the second half of the nineteenth century. Yet precisely because of its later success we may overstate its importance in explaining the 'awakenings' earlier in the century. Those awakenings were facilitated rather than obstructed by the dynastic presence.

Musical life was an integral part of the gradual transition in much of central Europe from an essentially cosmopolitan artistic and intellectual rebirth in the late eighteenth century to the distinctive national cultures of the early twentieth. The familiar career of Haydn affords a glimpse into the aristocratic musical world typical of much of the region before the nineteenth century. In both Poland and Hungary most of that small, select group of families making up the higher nobility maintained some sort of musical establishment, though seldom as lavish and prestigious as the one provided by the Esterházy princes. In Hungary there were the Batthgánys and the Scéchenyis, the latter playing an important part in political as well as cultural life. In Poland there were the Radziwiłłs, Potockis and Czartoryskis, whose estates (especially that of the Czartoryskis at Pulawy) were major cultural centres, albeit less well endowed after than before the partitions. Bohemia, too, had its aristocratic music-making, though it was hampered by the tendency for a 'foreign' gentry to spend much of its time in absentia. Musical life at these courts was provided mainly by imported musicians. It was not so different from, and was often modelled on, that of the more prestigious German courts, and its fate was the same.

The pattern of music-making began to change in the early nineteenth century, as processes and policies of social modernization in western Europe gradually spread eastwards. The familiar features of middle-class musical life inevitably followed, transplanted to the eastern Habsburg lands even when the social conditions which had made them possible in the West did not yet obtain. In particular the musical centre of gravity shifted from court to city, as commercially run theatres, concert-giving music societies, voluntary singing 'associations' and newly founded conservatories began to take precedence over the subsidized operatic and concert life characteristic of an earlier age. Along with the explosion of publishing and instrument manufacture taking place all over Europe, these changes added up to a slow but insistent professionalization of musical life – in effect creating a new type of musician as well as a new type of concert. Naturally the transformation was gradual. It was also a more fragile process than in western Europe, not least because of political volatility.

Nowhere did politics impinge more directly than in Poland. Warsaw in the early years of the century had seen a major revitalization of its musical life. Opera, mainly Italian, was given at the National Theatre and concerts were organized by the Society for National and Religious

Music and the Society for Amateur Music. There was a School of Singing and Declamation, and in 1821 the conservatory was established, just three years before Chopin enrolled. This was part of a more general cultural and intellectual rebirth, epitomized above all in the foundation of Warsaw University in 1818. It all seemed promising, but cultural life was quite unable to survive the 1830 rising and its punitive aftermath. Chopin left Poland a week before the fighting broke out. Had he returned in later life he would scarcely have recognized the musical world of Warsaw: its profile was provincial and insular, its activities were hampered by censorship, and its organization lacked all but the vestiges of that institutional framework which had been built up in the first quarter of the century. Polish musical life had been drained dry.

There was much greater continuity in Prague and Budapest.[6] These cities had quite different profiles and traditions, the one with a fine medieval heritage, the other still awaiting its most impressive development as an imperial capital, but they also had much in common. Until the mid-century both were thoroughly German in all but name, with their administrative structures, their artistic organizations and their social mores modelled in large part on those of Vienna. This had implications for music-making at all levels. As in post-Congress Vienna, fashionable 'society' in the eastern capitals was rapidly extending beyond the titled aristocracy, and its entertainments – balls, banquets, salons and café concerts – promoted a new and distinctive repertory of professional popular music.

The staple fare was the waltz and the quadrille, but enlivened by such local varieties as the polka (developed from a Bohemian peasant round dance) and the *csárdás* (an outgrowth of the 'verbunkos' style of Hungarian gypsy and popular music), both well established in their homelands by 1848 and about to spread rapidly throughout Europe. Indeed the triumph of the *csárdás* was itself a part of the national independence movement in Hungary.[7] The popularity of this repertory was enormous. Not only was it taken up by the 'low-status' public of the promenade concert, dance hall and domestic drawing-room; it also fed the serious composer and was thus absorbed into the élitist world of classical music concerts.

Such concerts flourished in both cities in the early nineteenth century, with Prague in particular maintaining a reputation for music that originated well before then; Burney and Mozart, among others, had been eloquent in its praise. As in western cities, the most popular and flamboyant occasions were ad hoc benefit concerts featuring touring virtuosos, but music societies that organized regular chamber and orchestral concerts were also established. One of the first was founded in Prague in 1803, but by 1840 there were several in both cities, including the enterprising Society of Musicians in Pest. Such societies were among the early institutional responses to underlying changes in the patronage of music and music-making, as a strengthening middle class increasingly shaped and directed the formal culture of Europe as a whole. The new teaching institutions were a further response. The conservatory in Prague was founded in 1811, pre-dating the Vienna Conservatory by six years, while the Singing School of the Society of Musicians, prototype of the Budapest Academy, opened in 1840, under the leadership of Gábor Mátray.

Opera was popular in both capitals, though it was more often given in German than in Czech or Hungarian. In Budapest native-language productions were promoted early in the century by the Hungarian Theatre Company of Buda, founded in 1807 (a particular favourite was József Ruzitska's Singspiel *Béla futása* ('Bela's Flight') of 1822), but this rapidly lost ground to the rival German company, performing at the newly founded and prestigious Town Theatre from 1812. Opera in Hungarian was re-established in the capital only with the opening of the National Theatre in Pest in 1837. In Prague, too, there was a tug-of-war between the languages. The main venue in the early nineteenth century was the German-dominated Estates Theatre, but at Stoger's New Theatre, founded in 1842, Czech-language productions began to make headway.[8] By then operas by Czech composers had already proved popular, following pioneering efforts by František Škroup, notably his Singspiel *Drátenik* ('The Tinker') of 1826.

Naturally these cities can hardly be taken as representative of east central Europe as a whole. But the gradual transformation of the infrastructure of musical life in Prague and Budapest (as also in Warsaw before 1830) formed part of a larger pattern. On a more modest scale, similar transformations were taking place in other cities throughout the empire and elsewhere in the eastern lands. Kraków and Lwów (L'vov) both established music societies in the early nineteenth century, with the Kraków Society maintaining its own choir and small orchestra. There were also opera companies in both cities, though their repertories were predominantly foreign. Brno had its philharmonic society (founded 1808) and Pozsony (Bratislava) its opera house (founded 1776). In Laibach (Ljubljana) there was a philharmonic society active since the 1790s, while in Zagreb the Musikverein (later the Croatian Musical Institute) was formed in 1827. In Bucharest a philharmonic society was established in 1833, and in Iaşi, the Moldavian capital, a philharmonic school was formed in 1836, to become a state conservatory in 1860. Thus, the cities of east central Europe were slowly establishing the institutional base from which a nationally orientated music, to which patronal conditions had not been conducive, might be developed. A nationalist aesthetic was in turn encouraged by the political conditions of the post-revolutionary era.

THE DUAL MONARCHY

The aftermath of revolution was a period of neo-absolutism in the eastern Habsburg lands. Until 1859 the 'Bach system'[9] ensured that the administrative structure of the empire remained centralized, highly bureaucratic and German-dominated. The effect of this return to centralist and repressive policies was to sharpen a sense of periphery and thus of national identity among the subject peoples of the empire, not only in the Czech lands and Hungary but in northern Italy and the Balkans. In the long term the dynastic tradition was unable to withstand the steadily growing pressure of these national-isms. But even in the short term the Habsburgs were obliged to make constitutional concessions throughout the empire because of a series of crushing and humiliating military defeats.

These concessions began in the early 1860s. With the Habsburg defeat in the Sardinian war of 1859 and the consequent loss of Italian provinces, Austria was reluctantly accorded some constitutional measures and these were extended in turn to the eastern Empire. A degree of self-government was achieved in the Czech lands and Hungary in the 1860s, and also in Galicia, the Austrian province of Poland. Unhappily the rest of Poland remained isolated from such promising developments. The failure of the largely uncoordinated risings in 1863 inaugurated one of the darkest periods in Poland's troubled history, not only in the Russian province where the risings occurred but also in Prussian Poland where Bismarck's policies of 'de-nationalization' became increasingly repressive and ruthless.

Bismarck's principal concern was not Poland, of course, but a struggle for German domination which culminated in the Austro-Prussian War of 1866. And it was the Habsburg defeat in that war which occasioned further concessions to the growing nationalist clamour of northern Italy and the eastern empire. The historic 'Compromise' of 1867 was a turning-point – a general readjustment of positions. Hungary virtually achieved independence under the so-called 'Dual Monarchy', and with the unification of both Italy and Germany a few years later other problems in the empire were reduced (for a time at least) to the status of 'local' difficulties. There was greater stability in the empire in the closing decades of the century. But it was a deceptive calm. Hungary and Italy may have benefited, but the new establishment served if anything only to strengthen the political nationalisms of the many other groups that remained dis-advantaged, most notably the Czechs.

Those nationalisms were increasingly underpinned by social change, as the eastern territories responded to Germany's rapid economic growth in the decades after 1848. In Bohemia a mercantile middle class had already emerged, consolidating its power and influence in a climate of steadily growing industrialism, and as the century drew to a

211

close there were signs of similar developments in Poland and Hungary. Yet this issue is far from simple. The growth of the towns, as well as the emancipation of the peasantry, did indeed weaken the position of the land-owning aristocracy in east central Europe. But the powerful and influential bourgeois society which created and consolidated nationalism in the West never fully emerged in the Habsburg lands.

To some extent this was true even of Austria itself, poised as it was between its imperial and its German identities. Here, as elsewhere in the empire, liberal capitalism failed to develop into a circulating, expanding economic system and remained confined to the German and German-Jewish milieu of the towns. Unrefreshed by the national-isms of the eastern territories and increasingly distanced from the surface glitter of a decaying imperial society, 'progressive' artistic circles in Vienna began to assume an introverted, even inbred character, culminating at the turn of the century in the emergence of a radical, alienated avant garde among the Jewish intelligentsia of the city. By contrast the bourgeoisie of the eastern empire mustered their artistic and intellectual energies in support of the nationalist cause. There was an ethnic as well as a nationalist dimension. The gathering strength of Slavonic nationalisms, at times articulated in Pan-Slavonic movements, became an ever-greater challenge not only to the Austrian Germans but to the Germans generally.

This was reflected in growing divisions in the organization of musical life throughout the region. In the second half of the century formal musical culture increasingly reflected the growing rivalry between native and foreign (usually German) communities. At the same time it proclaimed through its institutions a strengthening commitment to nationalism. In several towns the main performing forces, especially for opera, were segregated fairly strictly along national lines. Even where separate venues were not available there would often be two companies, German and native, as in Lwów, Zagreb and Budapest. In Prague the division was cleaner still. The Estates Theatre (and in summer the New Town Theatre) continued to offer German-language opera throughout the century, though its leading position was usurped by the establishment of the Neues Deutsches Theater in 1888. The Czech community, meanwhile, was served by the Provisional Theatre, opened in 1861 and designed exclusively for Czech-language productions (drama as well as opera). It was for the tiny Provisional Theatre that many of the masterpieces by Smetana and Dvořák were composed and it remained the home of the Czech opera for some twenty years before the opening of the long-awaited National Theatre in 1882.

The proliferation of so-called 'national theatres' throughout east central Europe was in itself an indication of the gradual focussing of the nationalist cause and the increasing association of that cause with

39. Interior of the Provisional Theatre, Prague, opened in 1861 as a home for Czech-language opera and drama; engraving

an emerging bourgeoisie. The example of Prague was followed some two years later by Brno. 'National theatres' had already been established in Pest (1837), Bucharest (1852) and Belgrade (1869), and they would soon appear in Zagreb (1870) and Pozsony (1886). In each case the enterprise, often involving a lengthy building programme, came to take on powerfully symbolic values.

One of the earliest was in Warsaw, appropriately enough, since the issue of a national style was thrashed out in Poland rather earlier than in other parts of central Europe. From the late eighteenth century Warsaw's National Theatre not only presented regular Polish-language productions: the most popular operas in its repertory were by Polish composers, with pride of place going to Jan Stefani's *Cud Mniemany* ('The Supposed Miracle', 1794), a Singspiel comparable in its significance for Polish music with Ruzitska's *Béla futása* in Hungary or Škroup's *Drátenik* in the Czech lands. All this changed after the uprising, of course, when the theatre lost both its title 'National' and much of its characteristic repertory. There were improvements in the 1850s, but in the aftermath of the 1863 risings, with the consequent diaspora, much of the city's musical life again came to a standstill. The opera continued but it was as much for the benefit of Russian officials as for the native population, and it was maintained under a strict régime of censorship.

Not surprisingly, operatic repertories throughout east central Europe were dominated for most of the century by the mainstreams of west European music. Even in Prague, where national opera of the highest musical quality was established by the 1860s, it was Italian and especially French opera that was most frequently performed at the Provisional and (subsequently) the National Theatres in the late nineteenth century. Only in the early twentieth did the balance change in favour of Czech opera. Of the four most frequently performed works at the National Theatre from 1900 to 1920, for instance, three were by Smetana and the fourth by Dvořák.[10]

There was a similar preference for French and Italian opera at the National Theatre in Pest, at least during Ferenc Erkel's lengthy spell as director. With the opening of the Royal Hungarian Opera House in 1884 a more adventurous and catholic repertory (including Wagner) was promoted, especially under the batons of Mahler and Nikisch, but operas by native Hungarian composers like Erkel himself achieved neither the immediate nor the lasting success of their counterparts in Bohemia. This was also true of Poland. Stanisław Moniuszko was a more considerable creative figure than Erkel and his operas were given frequent productions at the Grand Theatre in Warsaw. But in purely statistical terms they made little impression alongside the theatre's predominantly Italian repertory.

As with opera, the concert life of east central Europe was often segregated along national lines. In Brno, for example, concerts were organized for the German population at the Deutsches Hags and for a native audience at the Besedni Dom. In Laibach there was a comparable division between the Philharmonische Gesellschaft and the Glasbena Matica. In both towns the segregation was far from water-tight and was indeed treated rather casually. Yet elsewhere it could amount almost to a cultural war. In Poznań, for instance (especially after 1870), Poles would avoid the German concerts at all costs, attending only the Polish concerts at the Hotel Bazar. It is noteworthy that in all three cases the German concerts had much the higher standards, not least because it proved difficult to find adequate funding for the others.

Funding was indeed a common problem, especially in the smaller towns and cities. As a result the majority of orchestral concerts would be ad hoc affairs, given either by the opera orchestra or by amateur ensembles, with eclectic programmes rather in the manner of early nineteenth-century benefit concerts. Typically there would be numerous attempts to found a regular orchestra, but financial backing was hard to come by and in many cases (including Warsaw, Zagreb and Pozsony) a philharmonic society, complete with professional performers and a permanent musical director, was established only in the early twentieth century. Prague and Budapest aside, a middle-class concert life was still struggling to reach maturity in the region as a whole in the late nineteenth century.

Again it was Prague and Budapest that adopted the most progressive and ambitious programmes. The Žofín Academy concerts in Prague and Erkel's Philharmonic Concerts in Budapest gave ample space to 'modern' music, notably the programme symphonies of Berlioz and the symphonic poems of Liszt and his circle. Nor was Wagner neglected. Indeed his music was more widely disseminated in the concert hall and in the home (through piano transcriptions) than in the theatre. Native composers fared less well. They were represented in concerts throughout east central Europe, but as with opera it was only in the Czech lands that they made a significant and lasting contribution to chamber and orchestral repertories.

Given that art music programmes were dominated by foreign composers, it seemed to many that the best hope for an authentic native voice lay not in the theatre or the concert hall but in more popular communal and domestic music-making. The choral societies and wind bands that sprang up in the Czech lands, Hungary and Austrian Poland played only a minor role and often drew their membership from both native and German communities. Yet even here the status of folksong arrangements and of such popular genres as the *verbunkos*, polka and *krakowiak* began to change in the second half of the century, taking on something of a nationalist and at times an anti-German character. This was even more explicit in the popular music played by gypsy orchestras in Hungary and Romania, which came to be viewed as a national idiom in direct antithesis to German art. Home music-making was also important in this respect, especially songs to native texts – 'for home use', as Moniuszko labelled his songbooks. At a time when native languages were often under threat, such songs had an important social and political role, fostering and cementing a spirit of national identity.

In east central Europe, then, the division between popular music-making and high art music often acquired an additional layer of meaning, to the extent that the latter was identified by many with an imported, 'foreign' culture. It was partly the mission of such composers as Smetana, Moniuszko and Erkel to break down this perception of art music. We need only compare their lives and careers with those of an earlier generation of composers to register something of this ambition. In an earlier age the central European lands were unable to provide a sufficient livelihood for all but a few of their native musicians and the more gifted would inevitably drift abroad – to the German courts, to Italy and above all to Paris and Vienna: witness the careers of Dušek, Voříšek, Chopin and Liszt. By contrast the later composer would typically settle in his homeland and involve himself actively with its institutions as he set about the conscious task of building a repertory of modern national music. The real change came after the mid-century, partly because the transformation of a court tradition into one based on municipal institutions and commercial enterprise was by then largely complete, but also because an ideological commitment to nationalism had by then fully matured.

THE SPIRIT OF THE NATION

The Slavic renaissance of the late eighteenth century was in part a response to, and in part promoted, the eastward flow of that whole complex of ideas associated with the Enlightenment and early Romanticism, including the political doctrine of liberalism. Yet as these ideas were transmitted from western Europe they were also transformed. We may express it over-simply as follows. 'Liberalism' in France meant liberation from oppressive government (revolution); in Germany it meant liberation from too many oppressive governments (unification); in east central Europe it meant liberation from foreign oppression (independence). Indeed Germany played a crucial mediating role (because of its historical and geographical position) in the transformation of ideological currents as they passed from west to east.[11] What had started as political liberalism in France was translated into cultural-linguistic nationalism in Germany and then into political nationalism in east central Europe.

Herder was a key figure in this process of mediation. His writings on the importance of cultural heritage and especially of language as embodying the heart of a nation and the spirit of its people were used, or abused, by the prophets of nationalism to define political programmes far from Herder's own imaginings. His few words on the future of the Slavonic peoples were to become slogans of political nationalism in the eastern territories as they sought to forge independent national states modelled on the bourgeois national states of the West. Yet because the societies of east central Europe were so different, nationalism was promoted there not only by the emerging bourgeoisie (as in the West) but also by the established class-conscious middle gentry, who claimed – largely in their own interests – to speak on behalf of the *Volkswille*. Because of this obvious divorce between ideology and social realities, nationalism in these lands tended to thrive on myth and dream – the myth of a glorious past, the dream of a glorious future.

Political nationalism was not of course confined to the Czechs, the Magyars and the Poles. It flourished no less among the Slovenes, Serbs, Croats, Bulgars, Slovaks, Romanians and Ruthenians.[12] And since all could not be successful, nationalism in practice involved a form of imperialism. The success of the Magyars was achieved at the expense of the Slovaks, just as the success of the Germans had been at the expense of the Poles and the (limited) success of the Poles at the expense of the Ruthenians. In this spirit of almost Darwinian competition and mutual distrust, constant recourse was taken to 'historic rights', which in turn motivated a wave of 'heritage gathering', the manufacture of political and cultural roots, however specious. The historicism common to Europe as a whole in the later nineteenth century thus took on a very special significance in east central Europe. It was reflected not only in the rapid growth of self-justifying national histories but in the nationalist programmes adopted by artists in every sphere.

Cultural and political nationalism took much of its stand on the issue of language, which was widely regarded – following Herder – as a leading criterion of nationhood. The political struggle for language rights in education and the public domain was hard and bitter, but it was ultimately successful in Hungary, the Czech lands (less so Slovakia), Serbia, Croatia and even Poland, in spite of Bismarck's best efforts. These successes entailed extensive linguistic renovation and literary revival, as a plethora of dictionaries, grammars and translations transformed often casual vernaculars into sophisticated vehicles for nationally orientated literatures.

The groundwork was done in the early nineteenth century. František Pallacký, so-called 'father of the nation', was a key figure in the Czech lands. His *History of the Czech Nation in Bohemia and Moravia* laid the foundations not only for later Czech historiography but for a literary renaissance too. Other leading 'enlighteners' were František Celakovský, whose lyric poetry was inspired by Czech folklore, Karel Erben, whose folk ballads *A Garland of National Tales* were plundered by Smetana and his successors, and Jan Kollár, who turned to the remote Slavonic past for his epic poem *The Daughter of Slava*. The epic poem was favoured not only in the Czech lands but in Hungary and Poland too. Those of János Arany and Mikály Vörösmarty, in particular the latter's *Zalan's Flight*, were characteristic, but the genre reached its zenith in *Pan Tadeusz* by Adam Mickiewicz. Mickiewicz also gave consummate expression to that quasi-religious messianic strain commonly found in central European nationalism, notably in the third part of his *Ancestors* and in his *Book of the Polish Nations*.[13]

To some extent there was a change of tone following the mid-century, as the 'Romantic' nationalism of these authors, given its main outlet in lyric or epic poetry, made room for a 'realist' nationalism, more attuned to the medium of prose. In the Czech lands stories and novels of peasant life (inspired partly by Russian prototypes) became popular, with Božena Němcová a pioneering figure, while the realist novel, often explicitly critical of the status quo, was developed in Hungary by Mór Jókai and in Poland by Sinkiewicz. But

40. *Bedřich Smetana's 'Má vlast'; title-page of the fourth ('From Bohemian fields and groves') in the cycle of tone poems known as 'My fatherland' (first edition of the arrangement for piano duet, 1880)*

underlying both the 'Romantic' and the 'realist' varieties of literary nationalism was a belief that the individual creative achievement was at the same time a national achievement which could also stand confidently alongside the highest pinnacles of west European culture. Increasingly this belief informed the work of composers too.

No less than the poet, the composer rummaged the history, mythology and folklore of his country to render his nationalist statement, with major initiatives taken by Moniuszko in Poland, by Erkel in Hungary and by Smetana in Bohemia. We might compare, for instance, the themes and treatments of Moniuszko's *Halka* and *Straszny dwór* ('The Haunted Manor') with Erkel's *Brankovics György* and *Sarolta* and for that matter with Smetana's *Braniboři v Čechách* ('The Brandenburgers in Bohemia') and *Prodaná nevěsta* ('The Bartered Bride'). In each case the complementary genres – roughly speaking, serious and comic opera – were aligned with complementary dimensions of popular nationalism, heroic and rustic respectively. For all three composers the formula was an immediate, though not in every case a lasting, success in local contexts.

Opera may have been the obvious genre for the nationalist composer, but programmatic instrumental music ran it a close second. Indeed the flowering of the symphonic poem in Russia and central Europe must be understood at least in part as a response to the nationalist imperative. The high-flown, poetic or loosely philosophical subject matter that characterized some (by no means all) of Liszt's pioneering symphonic poems gave way to more 'narrative' programmes based on national history, geography and folklore, as the genre became popular in Russia and the Czech lands. Smetana, Fibich and Dvořák all celebrated Bohemia in this way and in the process made important contributions to the brief history of the symphonic poem.

All in all a body of music from east central Europe gathered round national images and symbols, the elusive category 'national style' gradually taking on a clearer definition, as it had already done to some extent in Russia. In essence a category determined by reception, it increasingly influenced musical material in a determinate way, with both generalized stylistic properties and highly specific musical gestures beginning to acquire connotative values through recurrence. Such qualities and gestures (for late nineteenth-century Czech music they might include harmonic movement outlining triads a major 3rd apart, two-part writing involving parallel 3rds and 6ths, use of melodic cells which repeat a 5th above and so forth) are not of themselves defining features of a national style.[14] They occur often enough in other contexts. It is their recurrent association with extra-musical symbols of national culture which enables them to stand – in appropriate contexts – for the nation.

Such correspondences can of course prove an easy prey to wishful thinking. Yet there are symbols of a more specifically musical character too. In particular musical gestures which traditionally generated a powerful historical resonance had obvious value for the national composer. We might think here of the role played by the Hussite chorale in Czech music, from its appearance in Smetana's *Má vlast*, through Dvořák's *Hussite Overture* to Janáček's *Mr Brouček's Excursion* and Novák's *South Bohemian Suite*. In Hungary the Rákóczi song and march was used in much the same way, from early variations by Erkel to Liszt's Fifteenth Hungarian Rhapsody and *Hungarian Coronation Mass*.

The importance of language as a factor and criterion of nationality also influenced the practice of composers in east central Europe. The nature of a spoken language will inevitably affect the music that sets it, but under a nationalist imperative language may well become a more powerfully originating element, through the renewed respect it commands. Ultimately, if indirectly, it may leave its mark on instrumental music too. It has been suggested that in both Czech and Hungarian peasant song musical beauties are a 'triumph over the language' and that for the same reason there is a paucity of art songs by Czech and Hungarian composers.[15] Whatever the truth of that, the pinched vowel sounds and first syllable stresses of both languages (which are of course unrelated philologically) made specific demands of the composer, encouraging a small compass, short note values and specific (often 'scotch snap') rhythmic configurations. Such demands were especially insistent on those later composers who abandoned the *lingua franca* represented by German late Romanticism. For Janáček and Bartók fidelity to the rhythms and inflections of the spoken language was an article of nationalist, as well as realist, faith.

But the most powerful symbol of nationalism in central Europe was the music of the 'folk'. Folk art, including music, had a special richness and vitality in the as yet unmodernized rural communities of east central Europe, where it was still clearly rooted in specific social functions. It is even arguable that the major contribution of these lands to music history – at least until the late nineteenth century – lay precisely in these richly diversified oral traditions, as impressive in their own way as the astonishing flowering of an autonomous art music in the West. The nationalist movements of the nineteenth century made substantial capital out of folklore, which they viewed – somewhat spuriously – as a collective expression of national (as opposed to social or regional) identities.

The association of folklore with the spirit of the nation, analogous in a way to Herder's views on the significance of language and resting partly on ill-defined notions of the peasant as the bearer of an unpolluted national culture, was not of course unique to the Slavonic lands. It played a prominent role in the early Romantic movement in Germany, for instance, resulting in such works as Weber's *Der Freischütz* and Marschner's *Der Vampyr* and contributing in no small measure to the creation of that most quintessentially Romantic of all musical genres, the lied. But it was in eastern and central Europe that the equation of folk culture and nationalism was given its most

41. Hungarian gypsy band with cimbalom (centre), two fiddles and bass; oil painting (nineteenth century) by an unknown artist

persuasive publicity. It was already a debating point in early nineteenth-century Poland and it became a compositional reality in the polonaises and mazurkas of Chopin. By the mid-century it had gained a solid footing in Russia and it quickly spread to the rest of central Europe and beyond.

Folksong and dance, then, assumed considerable privilege in the nineteenth century and the activity of collecting gathered momentum, providing the composer with easily accessible, if less than authentic, sources. In the early years of the century there was already pioneering, if problematical, work by Anton Pann in Romania, Jan Rittersberk in the Czech lands and Ádám Pálóczi Horváth in Hungary, but it was above all Oscar Kolberg's monumental publications in Poland, amounting to some 30 volumes, which helped to place folksong collection on a more rigorous footing, preparing the way for the scholarly methods adopted in the late nineteenth and early twentieth centuries, initially in German scholarship, but most famously in the work of Bartók and Kodály.

In addition to the collection of traditional layers of folk music, moreover, there was an upsurge of creativity in popular song in the nineteenth century, especially associated with the gypsy bands of Hungary and Romania. The popular dance tunes of János Bihari in Hungary, based mainly on a *verbunkos* style which can be traced to the late eighteenth century, are a case in point. They amounted to what

Kodály later described as a 'Hungarian musical vernacular', and as such they could serve the committed nationalist composer no less than traditional peasant music. In some celebrated cases the peasant music was actually viewed as a corruption of the 'folk music' played by gypsy orchestras.[16]

There was nothing new in the composer turning to folk or popular music, and in the early nineteenth century the practice was especially common as a means of creating lively local colour. But what was new from around the mid-century was the spirit in which this music was deployed, as it came increasingly under the sway of a nationalist commitment. No longer a decorative elaboration of existing musical language (and as such available to all) it became a means of reshaping it (supposedly revealing its full depth and significance only to natives of the country). Even when presented in the form of simple transcriptions by native composers, folk and popular material now carried the burden of a nationalist ideology.

Liberalism and nationalism were the two major political ideologies of the nineteenth century, both stemming from the same intellectual and social roots and ultimately converging in the triumph of the bourgeois nation state. It is perhaps not too simplistic to suggest that where western Europe led the liberal cause, culminating in the rise to power of the bourgeoisie, east central Europe focussed its major attentions on nationalism. This is reflected in the manipulation of two 'innocent' musics for ideological purposes. On one hand the music of Viennese Classicism was allowed to serve the interests of a dominant social class, a development associated in particular with the consolidation of a standard concert repertory in western Europe; on the other, rural folk music was pressed into the service of a political ideology, a theme we associate above all with the rise of national schools in eastern and central Europe.

NATIONAL SCHOOLS

A national perspective does not especially illuminate the stylistic history of central European music before 1848, the year in which this survey begins. There is little sense, for instance, in which the music of Dušek, Tomášek or Voříšek embodies qualities of 'Czechness'. Even the Hungarian elements in Liszt's early music need to be interpreted with some care: they were as much a response to the vogue for *chansons populaires* of foreign origin (especially strong in Paris) as a nationalist statement. And this is also broadly true of the Polish elements in early, Warsaw-period Chopin, which are little different in manner or intention from Polish elements in Hummel or Weber.

Yet for all that, Poland was an early exception to the 'cosmopolitanism' of music in east central Europe in the early nineteenth century. The issue of a national art was much in the air in the newly partitioned country and composers were strongly urged to infuse their music – especially their operas – with national (meaning folkloristic) elements. There is some irony in the fact that these ideas came to their fullest fruition in the music Chopin composed after he left Poland in 1830, when his attitude to the polonaise and mazurka changed profoundly. No longer a conventional means of creating Polish colour, the dances became for Chopin an expression, in turn defiant and tender, of national identity. The nationalist point was the more potent, moreover, in that folk material was integrated with the most advanced achievements and techniques of contemporary European art music. Here indeed was the foundation upon which a viable national tradition might have been built.

That such a tradition failed to develop was due above all to the repressive aftermath of the 1830 rising. Musical life in Poland after the rising was uneducated and conservative, with little sustained institutional development in any of its major centres, Warsaw, Kraków, Lwów or Poznań. The music that responded most directly to the country's needs during these years was not Chopin's, which so obviously transcended those needs, but that of Stanisław Moniuszko (1819–72) in his twelve *Śpiewniki domowe* ('Songbooks for Home Use') and in his operas. In the provincial setting of Vilnius and later in Warsaw he fathered a national operatic style of conservative bent, colouring the European styles of an earlier generation with the rhythms of Polish national dances in a blend that was to dictate the musical formulation of 'Polishness' to later composers.

Halka, first performed in Warsaw in its present version in 1858, was really the first Polish 'grand opera'. Heavily indebted to Italian composers in its vocal lyricism, to French models in its design and to Weber in its orchestral style, it won Polish hearts through its colourful use of national dances as the basis of arias, choruses and orchestral movements, through Halka's affecting Krakovian folksong in Act 1 and through the Highlanders' dances in Act 3. Moniuszko followed *Halka* with three operas – *Flis* ('The Raftsman'), with a libretto not unlike the plot of *The Bartered Bride*, *Hrabina* ('The Countess') and *Verbum nobile* – before composing his masterpiece *Straszny dwór* ('The Haunted Manor') between 1863 and 1865.

The Haunted Manor was written during a troubled period for Warsaw and for Moniuszko personally. At the time of the insurrection in 1863 the Grand Theatre was converted into a barracks: Moniuszko's post as director of Polish operas (the main director of the opera was the Italian Jan Quattrini) was lost and his only source of income was from his position (from December 1863) as professor of choral conducting at Apolinary Kątski's newly founded Musical Institute (later transformed into a reconstituted Warsaw Conservatory).[17] The survival of that institute and the later establishment (1870) of

42. *Stanisław Moniuszko conducting at the Warsaw Musical Society; engraving from 'Biesiada literacka' (1892)*

Wislicki's Warsaw Music Society, which provided one of the few forums in Warsaw for chamber and orchestral music at rooms in the Grand Theatre, are testament to the determination of a handful of musicians and music-lovers to preserve some semblance of institutional musical life in the Russian territories during what amounted to a reign of terror. *The Haunted Manor* was itself an early victim of the ruthless censorship which followed 1863; after three productions, all received with popular enthusiasm, it was banned by the censor and not performed again in Warsaw until 1914.

It was Moniuszko rather than Chopin who formed the model for later Polish composers in their conscious search for a national idiom at a time of political repression. Władyslaw Żelenski (1837–1921) and Zygmunt Noskowski (1846–1909) were the leading composers and teachers during the last quarter of the century. Like Moniuszko, Żelenski was happiest in vocal music, but Noskowski was one of the few nineteenth-century Polish composers to turn his attention to orchestral music. In addition to his three symphonies and Symphonic Variations he composed the symphonic poems *Morskie Oko* (1875) and *Step* ('The Steppe', 1896). Both composers consolidated Moniuszko's achievements, but by contemporary European standards their musical languages were anachronistic in the extreme, broadly comparable in idiom though not in quality to the music of such early

Romantic masters as Mendelssohn and Schumann.

Several younger composers, however, tried to come to terms with the legacy of Chopin and indeed with the innovations of Wagner. Some of the music of Juliusz Zarębski (1854–85), in particular his Piano Quintet and his piano piece *Les roses et les épines*, applies harmonic techniques derived from Wagner to a piano style influenced by both Chopin and Liszt. Wagner was also the inspiration for the opera *Mindowe* by Henryk Jarecki (1846–1918), both in its general musico-dramatic conception and to an extent in more detailed phraseology. Such works tell us much about Polish attitudes in the later nineteenth century. Quite apart from the hostility of audiences to any attempt at innovation (*Mindowe* was Jarecki's least successful opera), the innovatory qualities of the works themselves amount to little more than a dressing on basically conservative fare. The inconsistencies of style are at times extreme and they serve to emphasize that only a composer of truly remarkable gifts would have been capable of breaking through the barrier of conservatism which isolated Polish music from European mainstreams. Indeed to the outside world Polish music at the turn of the century was represented almost exclusively by virtuoso performer-composers such as Wieniawski and Paderewski.

Much more than Poland, and for obvious historical reasons, Hungary in the nineteenth century was dominated by Austro-German culture, so that attempts to forge an independent national style in music were bound to encounter formidable difficulties. The musical capitals were Budapest and Poszony (now Bratislava in Czechoslovakia but until 1918 a Hungarian-Slovakian city much influenced by nearby Vienna) and the major creative figures in the second half of the century were Liszt and Ferenc Erkel (1810–93). We might compare their respective roles in Hungarian culture with those of Chopin and Moniuszko in Poland. Where Erkel spoke to native Hungarians about Hungary in a language accessible to all, Liszt spoke to the world at large about Hungary, and in the language of contemporary European art music.

Erkel played a dominant role in the musical life of Budapest, as conductor at the National Theatre, as a leading pianist, as founder and conductor of the Philharmonic Concerts and in his later years as director of the Academy of Music, whose establishment in 1875 (with Liszt as its president) was an event of the utmost importance to the future of music in Hungary. His early operatic output is similar to Moniuszko's in its fusion of early nineteenth-century Italian and French styles with popular national elements – melodic and rhythmic formulae derived from the *verbunkos* and *csárdás*. This is the idiom of *Báthori Mária* of 1840 and *Hunyadi László* of 1844, both to librettos by Béni Egressy, and also of the more mature and successful *Bánk bán*, composed (like most of Erkel's later music) in collaboration with his two sons and given its first performance in 1861.

In later years Erkel was interested increasingly in the music of Wagner and Liszt. This interest betrayed itself only in modest ways in his musical language generally, but it encouraged him to explore the possibilities of a Hungarian national music drama. Of the two works which might (by stretching a point) be so described, *Brankovics György*, first performed in 1874, has been widely regarded as Erkel's masterpiece. Like Moniuszko's *The Haunted Manor*, it ran into difficulties with the authorities and was withdrawn after its first two years at the National Theatre; also like the Moniuszko work, it has a secure place in the native repertory today but has seldom crossed the national frontier.

Erkel's counterpart in the field of instrumental music was Mihály Mosonyi (1815–70), whose piano and orchestral music represents a kind of fusion of popular *verbunkos* traditions and the idiom of German late Romanticism. But Mosonyi's achievements in instrumental music were easily overshadowed by those of Liszt, the most celebrated of all nineteenth-century Hungarian composers. Hungarian nationalism was certainly an ingredient, though only one of many, in Liszt's music. By the late 1830s he was writing works in *verbunkos* style, using gypsy-like pianistic techniques (notably cimbalom effects), the 'Hungarian' scale, with its two augmented 2nds, and the so-called 'Magyar cadence'. This popular idiom, based largely on the dance music of such composers as János Bihari and Antal Csermák, was just as capable of serving as a musical symbol of nationalism as the traditional Magyar peasant music whose significance Liszt so notoriously misunderstood. But it was only following the mid-century, when he rethought so many aspects of his art, that Liszt turned to Hungarian features in a spirit of nationalism rather than exoticism.

Liszt had almost certainly completed the first fifteen *Rhapsodies hongroises* in their definitive form by 1847. There followed a gap of some 30 years before he turned to the genre again. In the intervening period he wrote a great many 'Hungarian' works, including *Hungaria* (1856), *Die heilige Elisabeth* (1865) and the *Coronation Mass* (1867), together with such piano pieces as *Sunt lacrymae rerum* from the third book of *Années de pèlerinage* (1869–72). All these works draw on Hungarian features to underline a nationalist commitment rather than to cultivate a typically Romantic exoticism. And the change of aesthetic is clear even in the four late *Rhapsodies hongroises*, where we might reasonably have expected a more popular idiom. These are markedly more advanced in harmonic language and much less overtly virtuoso than the first fifteen rhapsodies. Most remarkable is the seventeenth, a curiously brief, elliptical piece which welds together the seemingly incompatible worlds of Hungarian scales and 'modern'

43. *Franz Liszt giving a piano recital before Franz Josef in the small room of the Concert Hall, Pest, on 18 March 1872; painting by Schams and Lafite*

symmetrical harmonies based on augmented triads and superimposed 4ths.

Liszt himself always declared that he was a part of Hungarian culture, despite his deficiency in the language. He kept in close touch with his homeland throughout his life, giving regular recitals at Pest, Pozsony and Estergom, and from 1869 onwards – in the new political context of the Dual Monarchy – he visited Budapest every year for several months.[18] With Rome and Weimar, it formed one corner of his latterday *vie trifurquée*. During these years he regarded the revitalization of Hungarian music as a priority, and it is clear that he hoped to establish in Budapest – notably through the Academy of Music – a centre of progressive ideas every bit the equal of his circle at Weimar.

Budapest seemed in many ways ripe for the challenge. With its two halves formally merged and its status greatly enhanced in a new Austro-Hungarian empire, the city witnessed a genuine rebirth towards the end of the century. There were massive building pro-grammes, whose monumental character was an obvious expression of pride in the nation and confidence in its future, and there was an explosion of intellectual and artistic energy which spilt over into the musical world. In addition to the all-important Academy of Music and the thriving and improving concert life at the Philharmonic Society, the Royal Hungarian Opera House was formally established in 1884. It looked promising on every level. Yet there were irreconcilables in the search for Hungarian cultural identity and the urge to belong to the modern (Western) world.[19] In some ways the political framework since the Compromise encouraged a renewed cosmopolitanism in Hungarian culture and specifically a further wave of Austro-German influence. The effects were noticeable in musical life, and especially at the Budapest Academy.

The Academy did a great deal to bring the highest standards of performance to Budapest, which became in particular an important centre of piano pedagogy. Composition teaching was also enlightened and professional, but since many of the teachers were of German origin or culture, their approach was unlikely to promote national styles among the new generation of Hungarian composers. These included Mor Vavrinecz, Henrik Gobbi and János Végh, but the most talented was Ernö Dohnányi (1877–1960), a composer of genuine distinction, but whose late Romantic idiom was given only surface Hungarian colouring, even in ostensibly 'Hungarian' works. As the gulf between composed music in the German manner and improvised popular music in Hungarian style widened in the early twentieth century, two of Dohnányi's contemporaries and close friends among the younger generation of composers sought with some urgency a new synthesis. Their achievements amounted to a radical renewal of Hungarian music, a new wave of nationalism which had its counterparts in all the arts.[20]

Of the Polish and Hungarian composers considered above only Chopin and Liszt achieved international success in their lifetimes and subsequently. Both cultivated images of their native lands and used musical symbols (folkloric or popular) to convey those images, albeit only in selected works. At the same time they combined national material with the most advanced contemporary techniques of European music, fusing, as it were, nationalism and modernism. Their music derived energy from national material but was not confined by it nor indeed by a nationalist aesthetic. Unlike Moniuszko and Erkel, they worked in the world at large. Theirs were individual achievements, standing well clear of the surrounding lowlands of nineteenth-century Polish and Hungarian music as a whole.

It was above all in Russia – in the music of Glinka and the Balakirev circle – that the fusion of nationalism and modernism produced the first substantial and highly valued collective repertory infused by Slavonic nationalism; and significantly it was a repertory that owed a good deal stylistically to both Chopin and Liszt. Because of their cultural distance from the West, moreover, Russian composers succeeded in establishing an independence of European techniques which was later to prove of seminal importance for the history of musical language generally. In central Europe it was only the Czech lands that could match these achievements, at least before the turn of the century. There are useful parallels to be drawn here, but there are also crucial differences. Above all the historical and geographical proximity of German culture ensured that the Czech masters maintained a much closer dialogue with west European traditions than their Russian counterparts.

It was the aim of Bedřich Smetana (1824–84) to create a modern Czech music – and both adjectives here are of equal importance. Significantly it was in the 1860s, when he finally settled in Prague following extended exposure to the radical ideas of the Liszt circle in Weimar, that this aim was fully realized. Like Chopin, Liszt and Balakirev, Smetana committed himself to an alliance between national images and symbols on the one hand and progressive European music on the other. His return to Prague (after five years as director of the Göteborg Philharmonic Society, coincided with the opening of the Provisional Theatre amid a general resurgence of Czech culture in response to the constitutional changes of the early 1860s. Smetana played an energetic, though often controversial, part in this resurgence, as director of the major choral society Hlahol and later as conductor at the Provisional Theatre, before his deafness confined him exclusively to composition.

Smetana has been described as the father of modern Czech music, and it is true that, like Glinka a generation earlier, he created a store of devices and associations (including, but by no means predominantly, folkloric characteristics) on which his later compatriots would draw. *Braniboři v Čechách* ('The Brandenburgers in Bohemia'), composed in 1862–3 for an opera competition on Czech national themes, laid the foundations for the later development of Czech national opera. Its account of German oppression in Bohemia was in tune with the rising swell of nationalism there at the time, and when it was finally staged in 1866 it was an enormous popular success. It was followed by *Prodaná nevěsta* ('The Bartered Bride'), whose village setting and folkdance rhythms tapped a quite different wellspring of nationalism. Smetana went on to compose another six major operas, culminating in the national epic *Libuše*, first performed at the opening of the National Theatre in 1881 though completed some nine years earlier, and *Dve vdovy* ('The Two Widows', 1874), which pioneered a melodrama technique later to be developed by Zdeněk Fibich. His crowning achievement was the well-known set of tone poems *Má vlast* (1874–9), which triumphantly celebrate the geography, history and mythology of Bohemia.

Smetana's successor, complement and to some extent rival in late nineteenth-century Czech music was Antonín Dvořák (1841–1904). Admittedly Dvořák's success was more with orchestral and chamber music than with opera, but that was by no means his own evaluation. His last years were devoted to opera, revising his second opera *Jacobin* in 1897, ten years after it was composed, and going on to write *Čert a Káča* ('The Devil and Kate', 1899) and *Rusalka* (1900). All three deal with Czech themes, the latter two based on folktales. Dvořák's love of Czech legend had already been celebrated in a series of tone poems (1896) based on well-known ballads by Erben, but not all his music is overtly Czech in this manner. His nationalist commitment is never in doubt, but in some ways it was a position at least as close to Tchaikovsky's as to Balakirev's if we are to resume the parallel with Russia. His first and last operas, *Dimitrij* (1882) and *Armida* (1904), have little obvious link with Bohemia, and his symphonic and chamber music, indebted variously to Schubert, Wagner and in particular Brahms, sets out to 'place' its national characteristics within the framework of a predominantly cosmopolitan idiom.

More than any Czech composer of the later nineteenth century, Dvořák achieved international recognition – in Germany, England and Russia, and also in America, where he became director of the New York Conservatory in 1892. By comparison, such composers as Zdeněk Fibich (1850–1900) and Josef Bohuslav Foerster (1859–1951) appear as relatively minor figures, though Fibich did make a genuinely original contribution to the Czech school. His tone poems and melodramas are in a broadly late Romantic style, using Lisztian cyclic devices and – in the tone poems – remarkable narrative detail and realism. But in some works, notably the later opera *Šárka*, he took over and made creative use of several aspects of Smetana's musical language, in due course passing them on to his pupil Otakar Ostrčil (1879–1935), one of the more original figures from the second generation of Czech composers.

Janáček apart, there was relatively little in the music of that generation which added significantly to the achievements of Czech nationalism. At the end of his life Dvořák was professor of composition at the Prague Conservatory, and several of these composers were his pupils. The best known were Vitezslav Novák (1870–1949) and Josef Suk (1874–1935), who both followed the line of Romantic nationalism associated with Dvořák. This was also the path taken at first by Leoš Janáček (1854–1928) before he established a special contact with the folk music of his homeland (significantly Moravia rather than Bohemia) and in the process rejuvenated the whole of Czech music. His contribution to his country's music might be compared broadly with that of Musorgsky in Russia.

National schools have a limited lifespan, tending as they do to develop from the (provincial) particular towards the (significant) universal. They have vitality only when the two are held in balance, as they were for a period in nineteenth-century Russia and in the Czech lands. In Russia, where the main features of Slavonic nationalism first took shape, the wave was already on the decline in the 1870s. In the Czech lands it was beginning to dip in the 1890s, before a second wave (qualitatively different from the first) briefly but influentially surged in the early twentieth century. In Poland and Hungary the provincial and the significant coexisted for brief periods without really converging creatively. Each country produced a 'school' of provincial figures and each produced a leading composer, in whose music nationalist features played an important but not a predominant role. In both cases the central drive of nationalism came only with the twentieth century. As it did also in Romania.

The development of musical institutions in Romania proceeded rapidly in the later nineteenth century, coinciding with major political changes, notably the Union of Wallachia and Moldavia (1859), giving *de facto* independence from the Turks, though formal independence came only in 1878 (Transylvania was ceded much later in 1918). The Ottoman presence was indeed a restriction on the development of an organized musical life in Romania, but it was unable to counteract the close links with the West of an essentially 'Latinate' culture, links greatly strengthened by Napoleon III's interest in the region. National theatres were established in Bucharest, Iaşi and Craiova, state conservatories in Iaşi (1860) and Bucharest (1864), a philharmonic society in Bucharest (1868) and above all the Romanian Opera in 1877. There was even a specialist music journal *Musicul român* ('The Romanian Musician') established in 1861.

The stage was being set for a healthier future, but there was little of any real value produced by Romanian composers during the nineteenth century. A few operas became popular, notably the vaudeville *Baba Hirca* ('The Harridan', 1848) by Alexandru Flechtenmacher (1823–98) and the grand opera *Mihai în ajunul bătăliei de la Călugăreni* ('Michael the Bold on the Eve of the Calugareni Battle', 1848) by Ion Andrei Wachmann (1907–63). There was some promise, too, in the composers of the next generation, among them Eduard Caudella (1841–1924) and Ciprian Porombescu (1853–83). But it is symptomatic that Caudella should be remembered today almost exclusively as the teacher of George Enescu, the first Romanian composer of real international standing.

Of the three provinces making up modern Romania, two were under Ottoman rule for most of the century, while one was part of the Habsburg Empire until 1918. There was a similar division among the Balkan states and their neighbours. Serbia, like Greece, gained its independence from the Turks in 1830 and the tentative beginnings of Western musical traditions can be traced in both Belgrade and Athens from that date. In Bosnia and Hercegovina, on the other hand, as in Montenegro and Bulgaria, organized musical life began only after the expulsion of the Turks in 1878, while in Macedonia it awaited the early twentieth century.

In none of these Ottoman-ruled territories were there the long-standing cultural links with the West which had been established in Romania. There were liberation movements, of course, and they were given cultural expression in part through the beginnings of a Western-influenced popular urban music, especially patriotic and revolutionary songs (some using Western notation). But this was a small beginning. In most respects the societies of Bosnia and Hercegovina, of Bulgaria, of Montenegro and of Macedonia were still in the mould of medieval fiefdoms within which music played a distinctly minor role, apart from Eastern Orthodox chant in some quarters and folk music in all. Indeed the place of music was formally constrained by the traditions of the Ottoman Empire in which musicians were considered of low caste and public music-making was confined to the gypsy, Jewish and Greek communities.

By contrast Slovenia, Croatia and Dalmatia, on the periphery of the Habsburg Empire, were closely linked to west European culture. Dubrovnik, capital of Habsburg Dalmatia, never developed a thriving formal culture, but the other capitals, Laibach and Zagreb, followed the pattern of Habsburg cities elsewhere in the institutionalization of their musical life in the nineteenth century. By the end of the century, both cities had their music societies (notably Zagreb's National Illyrian Music Society), their opera companies and in the case of Laibach a fully-fledged philharmonic society.

Little of the music composed in these provinces has remained in the repertory. Slovenian composers on the whole developed a cosmopolitan late Romantic idiom influenced by Brahms and Dvořák and occasionally, as in Risto Savin's opera *Lepa Vida* ('Lovely Vida', 1907), by Wagner. At times, too, they responded to modern French harmonic techniques, as in some of the music of Anton Lajovic (1878–1960).[21] In Croatia, on the other hand, there was a lively nationalist (Illyrian) movement which paralleled rather closely the Hungarian experience in its diffusion into more cosmopolitan tendencies towards the end of the century. Much of this was associated with the arrival in Zagreb in 1870 of the immensely prolific Ivan Zajc. Zajc played an important part in encouraging professional standards in Croatian musical life, notably at the Croatian National Theatre in Zagreb, but his musical language was conservative and derivative and he offered little of promise to a later generation of composers.[22]

The new century intensified the nationalist ferment in the Balkans. That ferment was given cultural expression within literary traditions that were already highly developed in several of the states, and in this respect the harmonization of Serbian and Croatian was clearly seminal. The achievements were considerable, ranging from the Slovenian writings of Josip Jurčić, Josip Stritar and Janez Trdina to Serbian novels by Bora Stanković and modernist Croatian poetry by

Silvije Strahímire Kranjčević. Yet for reasons which are difficult to explicate fully – though an underdeveloped institutional (especially pedagogical) life must surely be part of the explanation – little of this creative vitality found a parallel in music. There was no Janáček or Bartók in the Balkan states; nor was there a Szymanowski or an Enescu.

NEW PATHS

The Balkan peninsula was to provide the spark that set off Europe's conflagration in 1914, when this survey ends. At the turn of the century the 'foreground' politics of the region were confused, to say the least, as Ottoman and Habsburg dynasties came into collision, while the Russian empire and the Western powers watched, waited and occasionally intervened. There was confusion, too, about the aims of individual provinces as cultural separatism increasingly took over from an earlier more generalized (Illyrian) pan-Slavism. Slovenia aspired to freedom from the Habsburgs; Croatia was menaced by the Hungarians; Bosnia and Hercegovina were annexed by Austria; Serbia and Bulgaria wrangled over Macedonia. The history is involved, but in the end the Balkan wars provided the foundation for a modern Yugoslavia, though it could never have become a reality without the Great War.

There is a 'middleground' structure underpinning the foreground events that led to war. It rests above all in an inexorably mounting tension between the strengthening racial identities of the Germans and the Slavs. This was a problem in the Balkans, as also in Prussian Poland. But the front line of the battle was in the Czech lands. Since 1848 the Czechs were widely perceived as the leaders in liberation movements against the Habsburgs, and their resistance increased following the Compromise of 1867. That resistance was expressed through popular movements like the 'Sokols' as well as through the successive political manoeuvrings of the Young Czech Party, the Czech National Party and the Realist Party (under Masaryk), all articulating the hopes of a strong bourgeoisie for Czech rights and ultimately independence. The war brought a temporary resolution to the struggle between Germans and Slavs, but significantly it was achieved at the expense of the Magyars. Hungary's aspirations were drastically thwarted following 1918, as Croatia joined Serbia, Transylvania became part of Romania and Slovakia moved to the Czechs.

The 'background' reality which ultimately made war inevitable was the irreconcilability of the dynastic principle and nationalism. In the end the nation state prevailed, as the Ottoman, Habsburg, Hohenzollern and Romanov dynasties crumbled one by one. Poland was the most obvious beneficiary. For all the best efforts of her secret

National League, her Socialist Party and her National Democratic Party, she remained a pawn on the European chessboard, and her independence in 1918 would have been inconceivable without a European war. Elsewhere the new 'nations' had an arbitrary enough character, formed as much from expedient alliances as from any genuine ethnic or geographical rationalization. It was, all the same, a resolution of sorts, albeit a temporary one.

We may identify, then, two kinds of nationalism in the first two decades of the century. In the years immediately preceding the war the apparent intractability of the old political structures lent a note of renewed urgency and fervour to independence movements throughout the region. Immediately after it, on the other hand, there was a quite different celebratory nationalism in some, newly independent, parts of the region. Either way the early twentieth century witnessed a rapid intensification of nationalist energy in east central Europe, and something of that energy was captured in the vitality of new musical movements in the Czech lands, Hungary, Poland and Romania.

These later nationalisms were expressed above all through an enhanced respect for peasant music, assisted by more scientific collecting methods, including the phonograph. There was a new realism in the approach to folk traditions, qualitatively different from the revivalist idealism and largely unscientific attitudes of the nineteenth century. The timing was appropriate, moreover, since the renewed interest in folksong, with its capacity to renovate existing methods, coincided with a widespread breakdown of established norms of musical language. It was partly his rediscovery of the richness of Moravian folk music from 1888 onwards which led to Janáček's change of direction from a Romantic nationalism akin to Dvořák to a radical new language close in essentials to Musorgsky, though probably achieved independently. The first fruit of this change was the opera *Její Pastorkyňa* ('Her Foster-Daughter'), usually known today as *Jenůfa*. It was completed in 1903, but it was only with the Prague performance in 1916 that Janáček emerged from the relative obscurity of his life in Brno to become an internationally recognized composer.

The striking originality of *Jenůfa*, and of Janáček's music generally, is not just a matter of folk music and nationalism. That may have been the initial impulse which enabled him to shake off an earlier idiom, but it was soon absorbed by a much larger commitment to realism, expressed not just in subject matter but in the faithful adherence of melodic shapes to the inflections of speech, as also to the sounds of nature. From these shapes Janáček welded a unique musical language which essentially departs from the formal and harmonic conventions of eighteenth- and nineteenth-century music. In some ways he took Musorgsky's achievement a stage further. The phrase is

44. Béla Bartók collecting songs from Slovak peasants in the village of Darázs in 1907

no longer shaped and directed by harmonic progression but takes its life from ostinato patterns supporting short-breathed, speech-related motifs, often of an underlying modal character. The larger movement is determined in turn by a mosaic-like juxtaposition of these motifs, quite different in dynamic from traditional phrase-building methods. In his rejection of orthodox tonality and in his exploratory approach to the resources and materials of his art, Janáček was a pioneer of musical modernism.

In Hungary, too, a new approach to folk music was instrumental in creating a national resurgence. Early in the century Bartók and Kodály engaged in the collection, classification and analysis of indigenous peasant music, and they allowed this music – with help from modern French harmonic methods – to prise them free of the Austro-German styles which dominated Hungarian music (including their own early work) at the time. Of the two, Bartók was the more radical. In a number of short pieces dating from 1908 (*Ten Easy Piano Pieces, Fourteen Bagatelles*) he signalled an even more decisive break with the past than Janáček's, though in other major works from the period (First Violin Concerto, First String Quartet) the world of German late Romanticism lingered. The opera *Bluebeard's Castle* of 1911 was the first major achievement not just of Bartók's musical development but of modern Hungarian music generally. Yet even here the spirit of Wagner has not been fully exorcised.

It was only in the postwar years that Bartók finally achieved the closely integrated and self-consistent musical language of his maturity. As with Janáček, however, it would be too constricting to confine that musical language within a nationalist aesthetic, though Bartók remained a committed Hungarian patriot throughout his life. By drawing upon the folk music of Romania, Turkey and north Africa as well as that of Hungary, he indicated that his project had become a much greater, essentially universal one. He sought above all a genuine integration and synthesis – at the deepest levels of structure – of two musical worlds, the melodic-linear pentatonic cultures of Eastern and folk music on the one hand and the harmonic-spatial diatonic culture of west European art music on the other. In the process he forged a style of uncompromising modernism, and it was as a modernist, rather than a nationalist, that he came to the attention of a wider public in the years after 1918.

In Poland and Romania the path taken by Bartók was followed by two leading, largely underrated composers of the early twentieth century. Like Bartók, both Karol Szymanowski and Enescu adhered initially to nineteenth-century late Romantic idioms, German in Szymanowski's case, German and French in Enescu's. Also like Bartók they turned to modern French music as a source of liberation from these influences, before finally drawing their main inspiration from indigenous traditions. We might take the second symphonies of both composers as representative of the first stage of the journey, and their third symphonies as representative of the second stage. That journey was still incomplete in 1914, reaching its goal only in the music they composed during the 1920s. In such works as their second string quartets, Szymanowski and Enescu drew on folk music from the Polish highlands and Romania respectively, integrating it with an 'advanced' harmonic language as Bartók had done, and in a manner that owed something directly to him. In their finest works, notably the operas *Król Roger* ('King Roger') and *Oedipe*, Polish and Romanian music came of age.

Following the achievements of these four seminal figures in early twentieth-century music, a national perspective again becomes of limited value as a means of understanding the music of east central Europe. Nationalism was indeed the essential agent of a musical 'awakening' throughout the region, but once awakened these musical cultures entered the world at large. The next generation of composers did not in every case abandon the nationalist element, but it ceased to be the central motivating impulse of their musical language. If anything music in Europe as a whole moved towards an international neo-classical idiom between the wars, with Stravinsky and Schoenberg offering different models of a common process. The younger generation of central European composers followed that path too. In Poland they were actively encouraged to do so by Szymanowski himself. It was only much later, in the radically changed political climate which followed Yalta, that nationalism became once more a vital issue in east central Europe.

NOTES

[1] There were Turkish administrations in Wallachia and Moldavia, in Bulgaria, in Bosnia and in Montenegro until the expulsion of the Turks after 1878. Serbia had already won its independence in 1830, as had Greece, while in Macedonia the Turks remained until 1903 following the rebellion of Saint Elias.

[2] O. Halecki, *The Limits and Divisions of European History* (New York, 1950); see also *Borderlands of Western Civilization* (New York, 1952).

[3] In this chapter I shall use the term 'east central Europe' or occasionally 'central Europe' rather than 'eastern Europe', which projects today's political division rather too cleanly on to the nineteenth-century map. There are anomalies here, however, and it should be noted in particular that this chapter will include a discussion on the Balkans.

[4] See A. P. Vlasto, *The Entry of the Slavs into Christendom* (Cambridge, 1970).

[5] The 'Congress Kingdom', perhaps more justifiably described as the 'Compromise Kingdom', was created after 1815 with Tsar Alexander I as 'King'; it was given its own liberal constitution and a measure of autonomy within the Russian sector but was disbanded after the insurrection in 1831.

[6] Strictly speaking Buda and Pest; the two towns on either side of the Danube were only formally united in 1873.

[7] For a fuller account see B. Sárosi, *Folk Music: Hungarian Musical Idiom*, trans. M. Steiner (Budapest, 1986); also B. Szabolsci, *A Concise History of Hungarian Music* (Budapest and London, 1964).

[8] See J. Tyrrell, *Czech Opera* (Cambridge, 1988).

[9] Alexander Bach (1806–67) was Minister of the Interior in the restored Habsburg monarchy.

[10] Tyrrell, op cit.

[11] P. F. Sugar, 'External and Domestic Roots of East European Nationalism', in *Nationalism in Eastern Europe*, ed. P. F. Sugar and I. J. Lederer (Seattle and London, 1969).

[12] On the latter, see K.-P. Himka, *Galician Villagers and the Ukrainian National Movement in the Nineteenth Century* (New York, 1988).

[13] See A. Walicki, *Philosophy and Romantic Nationalism: the Case of Poland* (Oxford, 1982).

[14] M. Beckerman, 'In Search of Czechness in Music', *19th-Century Music*, x (1986–7), 61–73.

[15] G. Abraham, 'The Factor of Language', in *The Tradition of Western Music* (London, 1974).

[16] See B. Sárosi, *Gypsy Music*, trans. F. Macnicol (Budapest, 1971).

[17] Elsner's earlier conservatory was closed in 1831 after the uprising.

[18] See D. Legány, *Liszt and his Country (1869–1873)*, trans. G. Gulyas (Budapest, 1976).

[19] J. Lucacs, *Budapest 1900: a Historical Portrait of a City and its Culture* (London, 1989).

[20] For an interesting account of new movements in Hungarian literature see 'The Early Twentieth-Century Hungarian Avant-Garde', a special issue of *Hungarian Studies Review*, xv (spring 1988).

[21] For an outline see the early parts of N. O'Loughlin, *Slovenian Composition since the First World War* (diss., U. of Leicester, 1978).

[22] See I. Županović, *Centuries of Croatian Music*, trans. V. Ivír (Zagreb, 1984).

BIBLIOGRAPHICAL NOTE

Historical background

As I have indicated in the early stages of this chapter, the status of the region as a historical and cultural unit is open to debate. 'A kingdom of the spirit' or a region cemented by common elements in its political, socio-economic and cultural past? The debate continues and has been given special significance by major political changes in the Communist world of eastern and central Europe during the 1980s. Some of the main positions have been articulated in issues of *The Times Literary Supplement* in 1989 (see especially nos.4480 and 4512) and the arguments are rehearsed thoughtfully in T. G. Ash's *The Uses of Adversity: Essays on the Fate of Central Europe* (London, 1989).

Much of the general literature on the region is informed by strongly held interpretative positions and needs to be read critically. A good idea is to balance the position of O. Halecki (*The Limits and Divisions of European History*, New York, 1950, and *Borderlands of Western Civilisation*, New York, 1952) against that of R. Portal (*The Slavs*, trans. P. Evans, London, 1965). More 'neutral' accounts may be found in books by F. Dvornik, including *The Making of Central Europe* (London, 1949) and *The Slavs in European History and Civilisation* (New Brunswick, 1962), and in *Nationalism in Eastern Europe*, ed. P. F. Sugar and I. Lederer (Seattle and London, 1969). Also useful, though more specialized, is H. Kohn's *Pan-Slavism: its History and Ideology* (Indiana, 1953).

Music

A central difficulty is that most of the historiography of any value is not in English. G. Abraham's *Slavonic and Romantic Music* (London, 1968) and *Essays on Russian and East European Music* (Oxford, 1985) contain interesting studies of miscellaneous topics, mainly Polish and Czech, but offer no overall view. For the rest, the rather pedestrian (at best) nature of the general studies which are available in English should not be taken as a fair measure of the state of historical musicology in the field. Of books dealing with particular countries, R. Newmarch's *The Music of Czechoslovakia* (London, New York and Toronto, 1942) still provides a useful reference point, more recommendable on the whole than the later study by V. Stepanek and B. Karasek, *An Outline of Czech and Slovak Music* (Prague, 1964). A more specialized account of a central aspect of Czech music, and a breakthrough in Slavonic music studies generally, is J. Tyrrell's admirably thorough and penetrating study *Czech Opera* (Cambridge, 1988).

Hungary is best served by B. Szabolski's *A Concise History of Hungarian Music*, trans. S. Karig (Budapest and London, 1964), and Poland by *Polish Music*, ed. S. Jarociński (Warsaw, 1965). The latter pinpoints a problem common to many of the books in this area: translations tend to be hopelessly inadequate and can give a distorted view of the quality of the scholarship. For basic information, however, the English reader often has no choice but to turn to such material. For Romania it would be V. Cosma's *A Concise History of Romanian Music* (Bucharest, 1982); for Croatia J. Andreis's *Music in Croatia*, trans. V. Ivír (Zagreb, 1974) or I. Županović's *Centuries of Croatian Music*, trans. V. Ivír (Zagreb, 1984); and for Serbia S. Djurić-Klajn's *A Survey of Serbian Music through the Ages*, trans. N. Ćurčija-Prodanović (Belgrade, 1972).

On individual nineteenth-century composers the Czech lands have, unsurprisingly, come out best. B. Large's *Smetana* (London, 1970) is still the best introduction but it has been admirably supplemented by J. Clapham's *Smetana* (London, 1972) in the Master Musicians series. Clapham's two studies of Dvořák, *Antonin Dvořák: Musician and Craftsman* (London, 1966) and *Dvořák* (Newton Abbot and London, 1979), are the major commentaries on the other leading figure in late nineteenth-century Czech music. The Liszt bibliography is of course immense. A good general introduction is D. Watson's *Liszt* (London, 1983), but a study which usefully concentrates on his connections with Hungary in later years is D. Legány, *Liszt and his Country (1869–1873)*, trans. G. Gulyas (Budapest, 1976). There are no recommendable books in English on Moniuszko or Erkel.

With later composers there is a rather better spread. Two general books on Janáček, both of value but in some respects a little outdated, are J. Vogel's *Leoš*

Janáček (London, 1962) and H. Hollander's monograph *Janáček* (London, 1963). General studies of the operas by E. Chisolm (*The Operas of Leoš Janáček*, London, 1971) and M. Ewens (*Janáček's Tragic Operas*, London, 1977) are distinctly uneven, but J. Tyrrell's account of *Kát'a Kabanová* (Cambridge, 1982) is excellent. Bartók has generated a vast reading-list, of which we might mention two recommendable general studies: H. Stevens's *The Life and Music of Bela Bartók* (New York, 1953, 2/1964) has worn surprisingly well; a more recent, well-balanced account is P. Griffiths's *Bartók* (London, 1984). For Szymanowski there is a general study by J. Samson, *The Music of Szymanowski* (London and New York, 1980), but for Enescu the material in English is confined to a short booklet by G. Constantinescu, *George Enescu: his Life and Work* (Bucharest, 1981), together with a special Enescu issue of the English-language *Romanian Review*, viii (1981).

Chapter IX

Scandinavia: Unity in Diversity

JOHN BERGSAGEL

Though in common usage, the term 'Scandinavia' is not well defined – or rather, it is variously defined. The Scandinavian peninsula consists only of Norway and Sweden; it stretches down from the Arctic with the Atlantic Ocean to the west and the Gulf of Bothnia to the east and at its southern tip divides, Norway to the west, Sweden to the east, as if to make room for Denmark, projecting up from the northern edge of the mainland of Europe. The three countries were once connected when the Baltic Sea was enclosed as an inland sea, and they are populated by related peoples who speak related languages and whose cultures and histories have always been closely interrelated. Norway, Sweden and Denmark, then, make a natural group and for most people comprise the essential Scandinavia. By all other criteria than geographical proximity, however, the islands that for more than a thousand years have been Scandinavian outposts stretching across the North Atlantic must also be included: no longer the Shetland and Orkneys, now counted among the British Isles, but the Faroes and Greenland, which are still in union with Denmark, and Iceland, an independent republic since 1944. On the eastern side, though separated from the Scandinavian peninsula for most of its length by water, Finland has boundaries with Norway and Sweden in the north. It is thus geographically more a part of Scandinavia than is Iceland, but Finland is also separated from its Scandinavian neighbours by its very different language and mythology. However, after centuries of association with Sweden, testified to by the retention of Swedish as a second official language, it too belongs historically and culturally within the concept of the Scandinavian family of nations, represented in the symbol of the present day Scandinavian (or Nordic) Council by five white swans in flight.

At the beginning of the nineteenth century the situation was rather different from now: Finland was a province of Sweden, as it had been for some 600 years, and Norway, with its North Atlantic islands, the Faroes and Iceland, was (since 1380) at least nominally a twin kingdom with Denmark, which then (until 1864) also included the dukedoms of Schleswig and Holstein under the Danish sovereign.

As the century opened, the shadow of Napoleon fell across the Scandinavian countries, as it did over the rest of Europe, and soon brought about radical change.

Denmark was a relatively large, prosperous and powerful nation at the beginning of the nineteenth century, but as the century progressed she became poorer, smaller and weaker. Her situation was thus different from that of the other Scandinavian countries: a revival of national feeling was necessary to restore a measure of pride and self-confidence and was therefore primarily for home consumption. Norwegians, on the other hand, after their success in 1814, had an abundance of self-confidence; their need was to project their national identity on to the consciousness of the outside world. They were remarkably successful and in 1905 they succeeded by peaceful and democratic means in convincing Sweden of their right to stand alone and to choose their own king. Sweden was not under such pressures and its nationalism therefore seems neither as desperate as Denmark's nor as aggressive as Norway's. Perhaps because they lacked urgency, Swedish national expressions, while developing in keeping with the spirit of the times and enriching Swedish cultural life, failed to attract international attention equal to that accorded Danish and Norwegian achievements until August Strindberg appeared at the end of the century. After some 25 years of separation from Sweden, the Finnish people began in the 1830s to cultivate the Finnish language at the expense of Swedish and as a defence against Russian. A new nation was formed which declared its independence of Russia in 1917 and, relieving its linguistic isolation by retaining Swedish as an official language, rejoined the Scandinavian community. Iceland too began in the 1830s to assert its national identity. In 1874 she was granted her own constitution and in 1918 her independence as a state in union with Denmark, a union finally dissolved in 1944.

It is hardly surprising that in such circumstances the spark of nationalism, so characteristic of the Romantic movement, should have been kindled in every part of Scandinavia and that it should burn as the various fires were fanned until after World War I. Romantic influences were already at work in Scandinavia in the latter part of the eighteenth century, as may be seen in the revival of interest in the ancient sagas and medieval ballads. If Scandinavian music at this time was in debt to Germany, the transmission of the Scandinavian literary heritage into German letters, by way of F. G. Klopstock, court poet to Frederick V in Denmark (1751–70), among others, may be seen as redressing the balance somewhat.

The philosophy of German Romanticism as propounded by Schelling, asserting the mystical union of nature and spirit and the revelation of the divine through religion and history, struck a responsive note in the young poet Adam Oehlenschläger (1779–1850),

241

whose national feelings had already been aroused by Nelson's attack on the Danish fleet the year before and had been expressed in a poem which included the line 'the ancient spirit has awakened from its slumber'. In such poems as *Guldhornene* (1803) and dramas on such Old Norse subjects as *Hakon Jarl, Palnatoke* and *Axel og Valborg*, Oehlenschläger became the most important spokesman for the ancient spirit revived in a new Scandinavian national Romanticism. But his achievement was surpassed by that of Nicolai Frederik Severin Grundtvig (1783–1872), whose contributions as clergyman, theologian, historian, philologist, translator, hymnwriter, teacher and politician pervaded every aspect of Danish life, making him the most outstanding figure in nineteenth-century Denmark.

In Sweden the 'Gothic League' was founded in 1811 to stimulate national feeling and stiffen moral fibre through the study of the 'Gothic' past, the history and heroic deeds of the Scandinavian sagas and mythology. Among its members were such leaders of Swedish intellectual and cultural life as Esaias Tegnér (1782–1846), whose *Frithiofs Saga* (1825), a retelling of an old Norse tale inspired by

45. *'Lemminkäinen's Mother' (1897), one of a series of paintings by Akseli Gallen-Kallela on subjects from the Finnish national epic the 'Kalevala'; in this episode the hero Lemminkäinen lies wounded beside the River Tuonela, attended by his mother*

Oehlenschläger's *Helge* (1814), is considered a classic of national Romanticism.[1]

After the separation of Finland from Sweden in 1809 a national Finnish literature written in Swedish manifested itself in the poetry of Johan Ludvig Runeberg (1804–77) and the historical novels of Zacharias Topelius (1818–98). Literature in Finnish received a strong impulse from the publication of orally transmitted folksongs and legends, the systematic collection of which had been started in the latter part of the eighteenth century, especially in editions by the philologist Elias Lönnrot (1802–84). Lönnrot concluded that many of the epic poems he collected were disconnected parts of one great epic which he reassembled, with lines of his own joining the fragments in an order with a narrative coherence. The result was the *Kalevala*; he published the first version in 1835 and a much enlarged final one in 1849. It was accepted as a national epic and came to play an important part in shaping national consciousness and encouraging the struggle for independence. Its scenes and characters (such as the shepherd Lemminkäinen) have been the inspiration for many Finnish artists (among them Gallen-Kallela) and composers (including Sibelius).[2]

The cultural life of Norway's educated classes had long been under Danish influence (there was also an important exchange in the other direction) and even after she had her own university in Christiania in 1811 and her own constitution in 1814, in spite of being forced to accept a political union with Sweden, her cultural orientation remained towards Denmark.[3] How, or if, this could be reconciled with the ambition to develop an independent Norwegian culture became a matter of contention between two factions: the 'patriots', who believed in breaking all ties with Denmark, and the 'intelligentsia', who feared the development of a culture fostered in nationalist isolation. Henrik Ibsen (1828–1906) and Bjørnstjerne Bjørnson (1832–1910), the two writers who were to dominate Norwegian literature for the rest of the century, began their work in the spirit of national Romanticism.

The Finnish language was accorded equal official status with Swedish in 1863 and with Aleksis Kivi (1834–72), whose *Seven Brothers* (1870) was the first Finnish novel, Finland had a national writer. In 1872 Kaarlo Bergbom (1843–1906) founded a Finnish National Theatre. A growing national Romanticism is revealed in the work of the group Nuori Suomi ('Young Finland').

Iceland, where the old Norse language has changed least over the centuries, occupies a special position as guardian of the ancient Scandinavian literary heritage. Most of the manuscripts containing the written record were collected in the seventeenth and eighteenth centuries, chiefly by Arni Magnússon (1663–1730), who deposited them with the university library in Copenhagen.[4] When the movement for independence from Denmark began to gather strength in the

1830s, a national Romantic literature was represented by Jónas Hallgrimsson (1807–45), whose poetry is especially admired, and Jón Thorodsson (1819–68), who published the first novel in Icelandic in 1850. Literature in Iceland served an extremely small language group and understandably some continued to be written in Danish.

Iceland, with a population of *c*47,000 in 1800, growing to *c*78,000 by 1900, was by far the smallest of the Scandinavian countries, but the other countries also had small populations: Denmark, 930,000 in 1800, 2,450,000 in 1900; Norway, 883,000 in 1800, 2,240,000 in 1900; Sweden, 2,347,000 in 1800, 5,136,000 in 1900; and Finland, 833,000 in 1800, 2,656,000 in 1900. In each of these nations cultural life was concentrated in a few small cities.

It was inevitable that within these small groups creative spirits should know each other and understandable that they should take advantage of the relationship of language and culture to establish a larger community and reach a wider public. Indeed, relationships were often so intertwined, often through marriage, that one can almost regard Scandinavia's cultural figures as a separate class of society.

Musicians have always tended to be thrown together in a rather exclusive fraternity. Musical talent often manifests itself in musical dynasties, of which nineteenth-century Scandinavia had its notable examples: the Hartmanns in Denmark, the Lindemans in Norway, the Berwalds in Sweden. To these families other musical ones were connected. The Hartmanns, Hornemans, Hammmerichs, August Winding, Niels Gade and Emil Erslev occupied many of the commanding positions in Danish musical life (and to a lesser extent abroad) as composers, conductors, performers, teachers, administrators, publishers, critics and, in one case, even, as musicologist, for several decades. However, from having been artisans, musicians now came to enjoy the prestige accorded to artists, who in the Romantic view were recipients of an enviable divine gift. Being better educated than in former times, they moved socially out of their professional isolation and met on equal and intimate footing with other artistic, intellectual and cultural figures and shared their interests and attitudes.

Copenhagen and Stockholm were, of course, royal residences and thus enjoyed the advantages of royal theatres and court orchestras of long tradition, which until the middle of the century provided the chief professional employment and performance. For the rest, the musical interests of a growing educated middle class found outlet in numerous clubs and societies of varying degrees of activity and ambition in which music was cultivated largely by amateurs and dilettantes. Besides keeping the discriminating public in touch with the current European repertory by performing a representative selection of operas and giving occasional concerts, which included

46. *Musical evening in the home of the Copenhagen wine merchant and music-lover Christian Waagepetersen; painting (1834) by Wilhelm Marstrand. C. E. F. Weyse is at the piano, and round him stand (left to right) the composers J. F. Frøhlich, an unknown person, I. F. Bredal, H. Matthison-Hansen and J. P. E. Hartmann; D. F. Kuhlau (who had died in 1832) is present as a portrait by Christian Horneman*

providing a forum for visits by distinguished composers and performers, the royal theatres, in which drama, music and dance lived under one roof and administration, were also the temples of native artistic effort. Here musicians became associated with the flourishing school of poets and playwrights which, as we have seen, took the lead in introducing Romanticism in Scandinavia, being called on to provide music for the cantatas commissioned for official occasions and, in varying amounts, for plays, *syngespil*, operas and ballets.

In Denmark, musical life at the beginning of the century was dominated by two composers of stature: Christoph Ernst Friedrich Weyse (1774–1842) and Daniel Friedrich Kuhlau (1786–1832). Weyse was above all a church musician; he composed cantatas and oratorios and provided musical settings of many of Grundtvig's hymns and of Ingemann's *Morning and Evening Songs*, which are among his best music. However, it is as a composer of songs and *romancer* that he is especially admired; most were written for his Singspiels and secular cantatas, for example *Sovedrikken* ('The Sleeping Draught', 1809) and *Ludlams Hule* ('Ludlam's Cave', 1816), both with texts by

Oehlenschläger, *Eventyr i Rosenborg Have* ('An Adventure in Rosenborg Gardens', 1827) and the *Reformation Cantata* (1836), both with texts by J. L. Heiberg, and *Festen på Kenilworth* ('The Feast at Kenilworth', 1836) with a text by H. C. Andersen. A devoted admirer of Mozart, Weyse found Beethoven too modern, yet he responded to the current of national Romanticism and published as nearly his last work a collection of folksongs. *Halviresindstyve gamle kaempeviser* ('Fifty Old Heroic Ballads', 1840–42); based in part on the pioneer work of W.H.F. Abrahamson R. Nyerup and K.L. Rahbek, *Udvalgte danske viser fra middelalderen* ('Selected Danish Ballads of the Middle Ages', 1812–14), which had included a number of tunes. His settings had piano accompaniments in the style of his romances, as had those of the more comprehensive collection *Folke-sange og melodier, faedrelandske og fremmede* ('Folk Songs and Melodies, Danish and Foreign', 1842–55, enlarged 1861–71), published by his pupil A. P. Berggreen (1801–80).

Kuhlau, who had met and been befriended by Beethoven in Vienna in 1825, was less conservative than Weyse. His piano music, which besides the popular sonatas and sonatinas includes fantasias and variations on Danish, Norwegian and Swedish folksongs, and his chamber music (perhaps especially the works for flute) are still well known. Nevertheless, it was as a dramatic composer that he was outstanding in his day, for instance with the Singspiel to a text by Oehlenschläger, *Røverborgen* ('The Robbers' Castle', 1814), and the operas *Trylleharpen* ('The Magic Harp', 1817), *Elisa* (1820) and, above all, *Lulu* (1824), which draws on the same story as Mozart's *Die Zauberflöte*. However, Kuhlau's most enduring dramatic work is his incidental music to *Elverhøj* ('The Elves' Hill', 1828), a festive play by J. L. Heiberg of richly national feeling for a royal wedding, in which Kuhlau incorporated Danish and Swedish folksongs. The brilliant overture uses several of these melodies and culminates with the definitive version of what has become one of Denmark's national anthems, *Kong Christian stod ved højen mast.*

The full expression of Danish musical Romanticism is realized in the music of Johan Peter Emilius Hartmann (1805–1900). Through-out his long life he occupied an honoured and influential position in Copenhagen's – which is to say Denmark's – musical life; but it was perhaps with his music for the stage that he made his most personal contribution. His operas *Ravnen* ('The Raven', 1832) and *Liden Kirsten* ('Little Kirsten', 1846), both to librettos by H. C. Andersen, attracted attention to Danish national Romantic music outside Denmark (the former was the subject of a lengthy review by Robert Schumann in *Neue Zeitschrift für Musik*, the latter was produced by Liszt at Weimar in 1854) but full appreciation of his genius seems to have been reserved for Scandinavians. That may be partly because of his apparent identification with subjects from Scandinavian history and mythology, especially as presented by Oehlenschläger. His sympathy with the Old Norse appears in *Guldhornene* (1832), a melodrama, interpreting Oehlenschläger's poem of 1803 as a recitation to an orchestral accompaniment; later he composed overtures and incidental music to his plays *Olaf den hellige* (1838), *Hakon Jarl* (1844 and 1857), *Axel og Valborg* (1856), *Correggio* (1858) and *Yrsa* (1883). It is evident also in the music he composed for the ballets (*Et folkesagn*, 1854; *Valkyrien*; 1861, and *Thrymskviden*, 1868) of his childhood friend, the choreographer and ballet master August Bournonville (1805–79), who created a Danish ballet tradition still lovingly maintained by the Royal Danish Ballet. In this collaboration Hartmann followed the example of his friend Johannes Frederik Frøhlich (1806–60), who had composed the music (incorporating folksong melodies) to Bournonville's historical ballets *Waldemar* (1835) and *Erik Menveds Barndom* ('The Childhood of Erik Menved', 1843), based on Ingemann's historical novels from medieval Denmark.

In Sweden, too, an interest in folksongs developed alongside literary Romanticism. Two members of the Gothic League, the historian, poet and amateur composer E. G. Geijer and pastor Arvid August Afzelius (1785–1871), published a three-volume collection *Swenska folkvisor* in 1814–17, and Afzelius contributed melodies to the anthology *Traditioner af swenska folk-dansar* published in 1814–15 by Olof Åhlström (1756–1835), a composer and pioneer music publisher. In this atmosphere of literature and folksong, especially as cultivated at Uppsala University, the solo song flourished: in addition to Geijer's songs, the settings of Tegnér's *Frithjofs saga* by the Finnish-born clarinet virtuoso and composer Bernhard Crusell (1775–1838) enjoyed lasting popularity. The greatest early songwriter was Adolf Fredrik Lindblad (1801–78), who wrote some 215, about a third of them to his own poems, in which the influence of Swedish folksong is often evident. Many were in the repertory of the phenomenally popular Swedish singer Jenny Lind (1820–87), who sang them all over the world. Lindblad came under the influence of the poet-composers Atterbom and Geijer at Uppsala 1822–5 and during a study trip with Geijer (1825–7) he met leading figures of German Romanticism and studied with Zelter in Berlin. There he began a lifelong friendship with another of Zelter's pupils, the young Felix Mendelssohn, in whose home he lived for a time, establishing a connection between Swedish musical life and the Leipzig circle round Mendelssohn and Schumann. Lindblad founded a music school in Stockholm in 1827 and, unlike most of his contemporaries, made his living as a professional musician. He wrote a Symphony in C, performed with success by Mendelssohn in Leipzig and reviewed

47. 'Midsummer Dance'; painting (1897) by Anders Zorn that expresses the deep concern felt by many Scandinavian artists, composers and writers for the preservation of national peasant traditions

by Schumann. He also wrote one of the first operas attempted by a Swedish composer, *Frondörerna* ('The Rebels', 1835), but it met with less success and this fiasco, as he regarded it, together with other disappointments, caused Lindblad to withdraw from composition in the larger forms (though a second symphony in D exists in manuscript) and devote himself primarily to songwriting. Foreign opera dominated at the Royal Theatre until well into the second half of the century, and even so original a composer as Franz Adolf Berwald (1796–1868) had to wait until 1862 for a performance of his *Estrella de Soria* (1841–8) while his *Drottning av Golconda* (1864) was not performed until a hundred years after his death. *Vaïmlänningarne* ('The People from Varmland', 1846), by Andreas Randel (1806–64), in which many of the songs are arrangements of folksongs, had a great success, however, and is still performed.

A special branch of song composition is represented by the music written for the male choruses and quartets which have always been among the most popular and long-lived of the amateur musical societies throughout Scandinavia. Not surprisingly, the tradition of (male) student song societies seems to have begun at Uppsala

University under the director of music, J. F. Haeffner (1759–1833), whence it spread to Lund (1831), where it achieved a high standard under the direction of Otto Lindblad (1809–64), and further to Copenhagen (1839) and Christiania (1845).

The classic edition of Norwegian folk music is the monumental collection, *Aeldre og nyere norske fjeldmelodier* ('Older and Newer Norwegian Mountain Melodies', 1853–67; posthumous supplement 1907), collected and edited by Ludvig Mathias Lindeman (1812–87); but a strong folksong element is already apparent in the first Norwegian Singspiel, *Fjeldeventyret* ('The Adventure in the Mountains', 1825), by Waldemar Thrane (1790–1828), and is in no small part responsible for the popularity it has always enjoyed and which keeps it in the Norwegian State Opera repertory. As Christiania had no professional theatre before 1827, it was written for and performed by an amateur society, Det musikalske Lyceum, of which Thrane, an excellent violinist, was musical director. When the eighteen-year-old Ole Bull (1810–80), who came to Christiania from Bergen in 1828, failed his Latin entrance examination to read theology at the university, he succeeded Thrane in his post. Bull learnt folk music from the country fiddlers (of whom Torgeir Augundson, called 'Myllarguten' ('The Miller's Boy'), was the most famous) and his compositions and improvisations on Norwegian folksongs and dances, which he often played on the special Hardanger fiddle (a folk instrument with an extra set of strings which vibrate sympathetically), were a feature of his concerts as he travelled around the world. In 1852 he even published a little collection of folk melodies in arrangements for piano as an appendix to a book on Norwegian regional folk costumes. Grieg dedicated his first set of folksong arrangements (op.17, 1869) to him.

As one of the foremost virtuosos of his time, Bull was the first Norwegian to become an international celebrity and he devoted himself tirelessly to making Norway and Norwegian music known. He was not entirely alone: in Paris in the late 1840s he often played chamber music with another Norwegian, Thomas Dyke Acland Tellefsen (1823–74), a pupil and disciple of Chopin who enjoyed a considerable reputation as pianist and teacher, especially in France and England. His compositions, though strongly under his master's influence, nevertheless include many nationalistic traits. The last movement of his Piano Concerto no.1 (1852) uses a folk melody which is also included in Lindeman's collection, while numerous other pieces, in particular his mazurkas, are reminiscent of Norwegian folk music.

In Scandinavia, however, the musician's life was not so glamorous. Opportunities for proper training were inadequate, as were facilities for performing orchestral music and operas. Halfdan Kjerulf (1815–

48. 'The Bridal Procession in Hardanger'; the painting (1848) by A. Tidemand and H. Gude which inspired one of Halfdan Kjerulf's most popular pieces for male chorus, a setting of a poem by A. Munch

68), the most important Norwegian composer before Grieg, though trained as a pianist, regarded himself as a dilettante when he was asked to become conductor of the newly founded Norwegian Students' Choir in 1845. He was 34 before he got a chance to go abroad for two years of serious study in Copenhagen and Leipzig; on his return to Christiania he established himself as a piano teacher and composer. His works are all in smaller forms – piano pieces, including interesting folksong arrangements, some 130 *romanser* and 40 pieces for male choir and male quartet. His songs and choruses, in which he showed a cultivated literary taste that favoured Bjørnson, Welhaven and his brother Theodor, are still regarded as among the treasures of Norwegian vocal music and important in the creation of an independent Norwegian musical language.

Franz Berwald (1796–1868) was from a family which for generations had produced professional musicians, so he lacked not so much musical education as opportunities to show the Stockholm of his day that he was the most original Swedish composer of the nineteenth century. He spent 1829–42 and 1846–9 abroad, mostly in Berlin, where he ran an orthopaedic institute, in Vienna where his success led to his election to honorary membership of the Mozarteum in Salzburg, and in Paris. Most of the compositions for which he is admired today date from the 1840s, in particular his four remarkable symphonies: no.1, *Sérieuse*; no.2, *Capricieuse*; no.3, *Singulière*; and no.4 in E♭. Yet he met no appreciation when he returned to Sweden, where a dilettantism still favoured the melodic appeal of smaller forms of vocal music. His attempts to gain appointments as music director at Uppsala University and as conductor of the court orchestra were unsuccessful and in the 1850s he was manager of a glass works in northern Sweden. Not until 1864 was he elected to the Swedish Musical Academy and only in 1867, the year before his death, was he appointed professor of composition there. In spite of the advocacy of admirers like Ludvig Norman (1831–85), who, as teacher at the conservatory and conductor of the court orchestra, came to occupy the position in Swedish musical life which had been denied Berwald, recognition of his genius has had to wait until the twentieth century.

Ludvig Norman and August Söderman (1832–76) were two other leading Scandinavian musicians whose training in Leipzig was decisive in shaping their development. But whereas Norman followed Berwald's lead and made his greatest contribution as a composer of instrumental music (three symphonies and much chamber music), Söderman's career developed in the theatre (made possible when the Royal Theatre's monopoly was abandoned in 1842) and his position as the most original nineteenth-century Swedish composer after Berwald was earned primarily with his vocal music (for example *Ett bondbröllop* ('A Peasant Wedding') for male chorus, 1868), with which he satisfied the impatiently felt need for Swedish national Romantic expression.

The attention paid to the symphonic repertory by Scandinavian composers after *c*1840 stands in marked contrast to the opinion held in some quarters that as a form the symphony was 'dead' between about 1850 and 1870 – between Mendelssohn and Schumann, and Brahms and Bruckner.[5] Other Swedish composers of symphonies in the 1860s and 70s include Oscar Byström and J.A. Hägg, while in Norway symphonies were written by O. Winther-Hjelm and Johan Svendsen. If Berwald was the most original symphonist, the Dane Niels Wilhelm Gade (1817–1890) was the most influential; he was responsible, directly or indirectly, for the loyalty to the conservative Romanticism of the Leipzig tradition which dominated most symphonic writing in Scandinavia until the powerful renewal of the form around the turn of the century by Carl Nielsen in Denmark and Jean Sibelius in Finland. The unusual example of Frøhlich's youthful Symphony in E♭ (1830), a form scarcely cultivated in Denmark in the early years of the century, may have been the inspiration for J. P. E. Hartmann to write a Symphony in G minor (1835), followed by a second in E major (1848); but it remained for Gade, with eight symphonies written between 1842 and 1871, to make this his chief form of expression.

Gade made his bow on the musical scene with a Romantic overture, *Efterklange af Ossian* ('Echoes of Ossian', 1840), which won a competition announced by Musikforeningen, a society founded in honour of Weyse in 1836 to publish Danish music, encourage Danish composers with prize competitions and give concert performances. The first two objectives had a short life but Musikforeningen for most of the nineteenth century was the principal forum for music in Copenhagen. It performed Gade's overture in 1841 and recommended it for publication to Breitkopf & Härtel in Leipzig, where it was printed under the Romantic motto (from Uhland) 'Formel hält uns nicht gebunden, unsre Kunst heisst Poesi'. In 1842 he wrote his First Symphony, basing the first movement on his own folksong-like setting of a poem by Ingemann in praise of Danish nature. This he sent to Mendelssohn who gave it its first performance at a Gewandhaus concert in 1843. That year Gade went to Leipzig, where he was warmly welcomed by both Mendelssohn and Schumann, and where he was engaged as a teacher at the newly founded academy and joint conductor with Mendelssohn of the Gewandhaus concerts. After Mendelssohn's death in 1847 he continued as sole conductor, but with the outbreak of Denmark's war with Germany in 1848 he returned to Denmark and remained for the rest of his life in Copenhagen, where he came to occupy a position comparable to Mendelssohn's, in Leipzig. In 1850 he assumed leadership of Musikforeningen's concerts, which he directed for 40 years and brought to a high standard.

The reorganization of the Royal Theatre in 1849, the establishment of private theatres and the development of a second professional orchestra in connection with the Tivoli Gardens (opened in 1843) under the direction of Hans Christian Lumbye (1810–74), who conducted not only his own popular marches, waltzes and polkas but also the symphonic repertory, including new Danish and Scandinavian works, created a musical environment in Copenhagen envied by the rest of Scandinavia. Kjerulf spent six months there (1849–50) during which time he attended 44 opera performances (of which he particularly admired the 'genuine Danish music' of J. P. E. Hartmann's *Liden Kirsten*) and heard 20 concerts.

Of Gade's large output in all forms (except opera), he is best remembered (in addition to the two early works mentioned above) for his Fourth, Sixth and Eighth symphonies, the Bournonville ballets *Napoli* (1842), of which he wrote Act 2 (the rest is by Paulli and others), and *Et folkesagn* ('A Legend', 1853–4), of which he wrote Acts 1 and 3 while his father-in-law wrote Act 2, the cantatas *Elverskud* ('The Elf-King's Daughter', 1853) and *Psyche* (written for the Birmingham Festival, 1882). These are perhaps the works in which he most successfully combines his early national Romanticism with the more neutral stylistic influence of Mendelssohn to achieve a convincing, individual result. He was Denmark's first composer of international rank and the leading representative of Scandinavian music until superseded by the Norwegian Grieg.

Edvard Grieg (1843–1907) was another of Ole Bull's discoveries; thanks to Bull, the talented boy was sent in 1858 to the Leipzig Conservatory, where he remained for four years. (30 years later the now famous Grieg similarly used·his influence to intercede with a reluctant father on behalf of Frederick Delius's musical career.) After Leipzig, still unsure of himself, Grieg stayed for most of 1863–6 in Copenhagen, where he was affected by the Nordic tone he recognized in the music of Hartmann and Gade, and where meeting H. C. Andersen inspired him to compose the four songs op.5 in which a personal style begins to take form (no.3, *Jeg elsker dig* ('I love you') remains one of his best loved). Grieg felt at home in Copenhagen, 'the capital of Scandinavia', and took an active part in its musical life. Thus in 1865 he joined his friend and fellow student from Leipzig, Christian Frederik Emil Horneman (1840–1906), one of the most original and progressive Danish composers of the second half of the nineteenth century, as well as the talented, intensely patriotic, but tragically short-lived Norwegian Rikard Nordraak (1842–66) and the Danish organist and advocate of Liszt and Wagner, Gottfred Matthison-Hansen (1832–1909), in founding the Euterpe Society. It was a concert society 'with Nordic purpose and in Nordic spirit' for the performance of modern, especially Scandinavian, music which Gade could not or would not include in the programmes of Musikforeningen – the first instance was Horneman's own brilliant, colourful *Aladdin Overture* (1864), inspired by Oehlenschläger's play, which was also the subject of his most ambitious opera (1888).[6]

It was at this time that Grieg's style began to become more specifically Norwegian. It is natural that this should coincide with his return to Norway, but it is surely not an accident that it also coincided with the completion of Lindeman's great edition of Norwegian folk music in 1867. In this 'previously undiscovered expression of the soul of the Norwegian people' Grieg not surprisingly found elements of melody and rhythm on which to build a national art; but less expected, perhaps, was that he also found in it the means to an original harmonic language which became a most important aspect of his style. Late in life he wrote: 'I have found that the mysterious profundity of our folk music is due to its undreamt of harmonic possibilities. In my treatment of them I have tried to express my sense of the hidden harmonies of our folk melodies'. His harmonic originality, seen at its most adventurous in the three sets of pieces for piano in which he harmonizes folk melodies, opp.17, 66 and 72, came to exert an influence on the 'impressionist' style of such composers as

49. Poster by Edvard Munch for a performance of Ibsen's 'Peer Gynt', with Grieg's music, in Paris in 1896

Delius, Debussy and Ravel. Important too was his association with the great men of Norwegian letters, especially Bjørnson and Ibsen, with whom he collaborated on the stage works *Sigurd Jorsalfar* op.22 and *Peer Gynt* op.23, respectively, but also A. O. Vinje, A. Garborg, V. Krag, J. Paulsen and others, as well as Danish poets like H. C. Andersen and H. Drachmann, to whose texts he wrote some 140 *romanser* which are, perhaps, his finest achievements.

Grieg's lyrical vein also came to expression in numerous piano pieces, ten volumes of which he published under the general title 'Lyric Pieces'. When they met in 1863, Gade naturally told him to 'go home and write a symphony'. He did, but in 1867 he withdrew it and wrote on the score that it should never be played again, an injunction respected until 1981 when, under sensational circumstances, it was performed from photocopies brought to Moscow, after which it was thought futile to maintain the ban in the rest of the world. Grieg wrote few pieces for orchestra or in cyclic sonata form, but among them are such successful works at the Piano Concerto in A minor op.16, three violin sonatas (opp.8, 13 and 45) and the G minor String Quartet op.27.

Grieg fulfilled the ambition of all national movements: to produce an artist great enough to make what is loved and admired at home seem important and influential internationally. His music brought Norway into the homes and concert halls of the rest of the world, but the maturing of Norway's national aspirations were also represented in the concert hall by Johan Svendsen (1840–1908). The two were close friends and profoundly admired each other, especially, perhaps, because they found complementary rather than competitive forms of expression. Whereas Grieg was at his best with voice and piano, Svendsen's medium was the orchestra, as may be seen in such brilliant pieces as *Carnival in Paris, Norwegian Artists' Carnival, Zorahayda, Romeo and Juliet* and his four Norwegian Rhapsodies. But while these scores reveal Svendsen's cosmopolitan experience, they also show that he shared Grieg's feeling for the folk music of his homeland. His thematic material makes ample reference to Norwegian folk melodies and some of his settings rival Grieg's in sheer loveliness. He did not have Grieg's great harmonic originality but he had other qualities of which the generous Grieg professed envy: in addition to his easy mastery of the orchestra he had the true symphonist's command of form and, indeed, he is reckoned as the initiator of the Norwegian symphonic tradition. He was not the first Norwegian to write a symphony (Winther-Hjelm preceded him by a few years), but his Symphony no.1 in D, op.4, (written while he was still a student at Leipzig), and especially his no.2 in B♭, are the first to retain a place in the repertory. He also wrote a violin concerto and a cello concerto, as well as a quartet, a quintet and an octet for strings – not to mention a popular Romance for violin and orchestra. Svendsen was a conductor of international standing, from 1883 conductor of the Royal Theatre in Copenhagen. After this he composed little, but he exerted a progressive influence on Danish musical life (not least on Carl Nielsen) in the last years of Gade's régime.

Emil Hartmann (1836–98) continued in the tradition of his father, J. P. E. Hartmann, and of his brother-in-law Gade, with a Bournonville ballet *Fjeldstuen* ('The Mountain Hut', 1859), written in collaboration with his other brother-in-law, August Winding, and much other theatre and orchestral music, including seven symphonies and three concertos. He too studied in Leipzig and he achieved recognition in Germany, particularly with his music on Scandinavian subjects – an overture to Ibsen's *Haermaendene paa Helgeland* ('Soldiers on Helgeland'), the symphonic poem *Hakon Jarl*, and his orchestral suites on Scandinavian folk melodies. Peter Heise (1830–79), too, was faithful to the tradition of Gade but he occupies a special place as perhaps the most important song composer in Danish musical history. He was in close contact with the literary figures of his time and with a rare poetic sensibility he provided over 200 musical settings of poems by most of Denmark's best Romantic poets from Oehlenschläger to

255

Drachmann (for example his last song cycle, *Dyvekes Sange*, 1879) as well as by other Scandinavian and some German and English poets. He wrote a symphony and chamber music, but his chief monument, in addition to his songs, is his national historical opera *Drot og Marsk* ('King and Marshal', 1878), the most important Danish nineteenth-century opera.

C. F. E. Horneman was respectful of, but often in opposition to, the increasingly conservative Hartmann-Gade tradition. His temperament and restless energy were against both his consistent development as a composer and the unprejudiced acceptance of his compositions. He mostly met disappointment during his lifetime, but after his death Carl Nielson recognized him as 'a refining fire who melted down the false and burnt away the spurious' in Danish music. Before he was twenty he had written two precocious string quartets which, with the mastery of the orchestra revealed in the *Aladdin Overture*, could have raised expectations of a symphonic production. But most of his effort went into music for the theatre, of which, in addition to *Aladdin*, he is now remembered especially for his music to Drachmann's plays: the Renaissance *Esther* (1889) and medieval Danish *Gurre* (1901).

Drachmann was also a source of inspiration for P. E. Lange-Müller (1850–1926) who wrote incidental music to several of his plays, among which *Der var engang* ('Once upon a Time', 1887)[7] has achieved a position as a national entertainment comparable in public favour to *Elverhøy* by Heiberg and Kuhlau. From his large and varied output, which includes two symphonies, a violin concerto, two suites for orchestra and a piano trio, Lange-Müller's enduring reputation rests on his vocal music. His *romancer* are the best Danish songs after Hense's: sensitive and subtle settings of a wide range of authors including Drachmann, Ingemann, J. P. Jacobsen and, above all, his friend Thor Lange, resident for many years in Russia, who also wrote the texts of his lovely *Three Madonna Songs* for *a cappella* chorus (1900).

By the end of the nineteenth century, national Romanticism in Scandinavia had run its course and the way was clear for new developments – or should have been. Furthermore, in the 1860s Sweden and Denmark acquired their own conservatories, as did Finland and Norway before the end of the century, and this should have loosened, if not entirely dissolved, the ties that bound Scandinavian musicians to the German tradition, especially that of the Mendelssohn-Schumann school at Leipzig. But with Gade as the founder-director (with J. P. E. Hartmann and H. Paulli) of the Copenhagen Conservatory (1867), and Ludvig Norman as teacher of composition at the Stockholm Conservatory (which grew out of the Musical Academy in 1866), radical change was not to be expected. It was the same in Finland, where the dominant musical figure throughout most of the century, Fredrik Pacius (1809–91), was born and trained in Germany, and Martin Wegelius (1846–1906), who founded the Helsinki Music Institute in 1882 and was its director until his death, was yet another graduate of the Leipzig Conservatory. The conservatory in Christiania was created in 1892 on the basis of a school for organists founded by L. M. Lindeman in 1883, but until then (and also after) Norwegian composers, such as Johan Selmer (1844–1910), Johannes Haarklou (1847–1925), Christian Sinding (1856–1941), Hjalmar Borgstrøm (1864–1925) and Johan Halvorsen (1864–1935), had at least part of their training at Leipzig, Sinding during at least three periods;[8] and some, such as Sinding, Borgstrøm and G. Schjelderup (1859–1933), lived much of their lives in Germany.

So powerful was the dominance of Grieg and Svendsen that at the beginning of the twentieth century it was difficult for other impulses to penetrate Norwegian music. Selmer, who for health reasons travelled a great deal, came under the influence of French music, especially Berlioz, in Paris about 1870 and attempted to develop a less narrowly national style, earning thereby a reputation for being a radical in his musical as well as his social views. But it was Sinding, whose excellent Piano Quintet op.5 seemed to promise a new departure in 1885 (it shocked Tchaikovsky) but whose style failed to progress significantly, who came to represent Norwegian music rather traditionally in the aftermath of the golden age. One might have thought that Sweden, without a figure of international stature comparable to Gade in Denmark or Grieg in Norway, would have been receptive to what was going on outside the country. To a certain extent it was, in the person of Emil Sjögren (1853–1918), who was internationally orientated, not least to what was happening in Paris, where he was a frequent visitor. He was also a warm Scandinavian, responsive to what he encountered in Norway and Denmark, both in music and literature. He was a friend of Lange-Müller and like him made his greatest contribution as a composer of songs, for which he chose texts by Bjørnson and Ibsen, Drachmann and J. P. Jacobsen,[9] as well as by the newer Swedish poets like E. Josephson, W. von Heidenstam and G. Fröding.

But Sweden had not yet fully realized its ambition of a full-blooded national Romantic music, building on the foundation laid by Söderman and Andreas Hallén (1846–1925): this want was supplied by two talented and long-lived composers, Wilhelm Peterson-Berger (1867–1942) and Hugo Alfvén (1872–1960), who effectively delayed the progress of newer tendencies in Swedish music until well into the twentieth century. Peterson-Berger was a Wagner enthusiast who wrote music dramas (for example *Arnljot*, 1907–9) and five symphonies, but whose lyrical gift was most successfully expressed in his numerous songs, choral works and piano pieces. Alfvén also wrote five symphonies and, in his capacity as music director at Uppsala, a large number of pieces for male chorus, songs and other works; but his most memorable legacy is his brilliantly written orchestral programme music, of which his Swedish Rhapsody no.1, *Midsommarvaka* ('Midsummer Vigil', 1903), is the most famous. His symphonies are still performed in Sweden but they could not in the long run bear the comparison with Sibelius's to which the continuing cultural ties between Sweden and Finland inevitably subjected them.

Less influenced by folksong and more alert to what was going on outside Sweden, in particular in Denmark and Finland at the turn of the century, was Wilhelm Stenhammar (1871–1927), who must be credited with attempting to lead Swedish music beyond the national Romanticism in which he himself began, and providing a basis for the development of modern Swedish music. He wrote an opera, two symphonies and two piano concertos, songs and cantatas and a series of six string quartets which show his rapid development in a period of stylistic change (1894–1916) and which are among the most important contributions to Scandinavian chamber music. His Serenade in F for orchestra (1911–13, revised 1919) is a fine work that reveals a composer of real character and skill who was unfortunately overshadowed by Carl Nielsen in Denmark and Jean Sibelius in Finland.

Carl Nielsen (1865–1931) and Jean Sibelius (1865–1957) are unquestionably the greatest Scandinavian composers of modern times and, as Gade and Grieg did in the nineteenth century, they earn for Scandinavian music a central place in European music in the twentieth. It is consistent with the pattern of development we have been tracing to recognize that, though they were born in the same year, such was the situation in Scandinavia that the two composers started from different positions in relation to the European mainstream, the one looking forward, the other looking backward, so to speak. Nevertheless, they in fact complement each other in their musical achievements.

The two countries on the outer fringes, whose need was perhaps greatest, had not yet established their national identities in music. The lack of an adequate urban community in Iceland throughout the nineteenth century was not conducive to the development of institutions for the cultivation of music in its fullest potential. As a consequence, Iceland's first professional pianist-composer, Sveinbjörn Sveinbjörnsson (1847–1927), after training in Copenhagen and Leipzig, settled in Edinburgh, where he lived as a pianist and teacher. He composed mainly songs (including the Icelandic national anthem) and choruses, but also some chamber music and two Icelandic Rhapsodies for orchestra. Of great importance, however, was that the collecting and publishing of the ancient Nordic island people's remarkable folksong heritage was undertaken before it became too late, even in so isolated a place. Bjarni Thorsteinsson (1861–1938) published a large, important collection, *Islenzk thjódhlög* (1903–6) which, though it may not now satisfy the strictest scientific standards, provided a basis for further study. The Dane, Angul Hammerich (1848–1931), awarded the first doctoral degree in music history from a Danish university (1892), devoted a study to Icelandic music in 1899.

In Finland, too, the development of a creative musical environment was delayed by the political and cultural upheavals of the early years of the century. Pacius and Wegelius laid the foundations in the new capital of Helsinki, and in the same year as Wegelius founded the Music Institute (1882), Robert Kajanus (1856–1933) founded the Helsinki Orchestral Society. He too had studied in Leipzig, then for a year with Johan Svendsen in Paris. As a composer he often found his inspiration in national subjects – *Kullervo* (1881), two Finnish Rhapsodies (1882, 1889) and *Aino* (1885), a symphonic poem with final chorus drawing (as did *Kullervo*) on the *Kalevala*. It was hearing a performance of *Aino* conducted by Kajanus in Berlin in 1890 that inspired Sibelius, who had been Wegelius's pupil and Busoni's friend at the Helsinki Institute, to turn to the Finnish national epic for his own *Kullervo Symphony* (1892). After the successful performance by

50. *'Symposium' ('The Problem'); group portrait (1894) by Akseli Gallen-Kallela, with (right to left) Jean Sibelius, Robert Kajanus, Oskar Merikanto and the artist (the 'problem' seems to be symbolized by the winged creature on the left)*

Kajanus of this, his first major orchestral work (with chorus), Sibelius's position in Finnish musical life was assured and Kajanus became his champion. The works that followed show Sibelius having espoused the cause of national Romanticism: *En saga* (1892, revised 1902), the *Karelia* Suite (1893), the *Lemminkäinen* Suite (or *Four Legends*, of which the third is *The Swan of Tuonela*, 1895) and the first set of *Scènes historiques* (1899), of which the last, as *Finlandia*, became the expression of the suppressed Russian province's nationalism and was heard around Europe, though banned in Finland.

However, by this time he had written his First Symphony (1899) and, though the struggle for national independence was not yet won, Sibelius's vision began to reach beyond the limits of region and nation. So did his reputation: he became a sought-after guest in the musical centres of the Continent, England and, eventually (1914), the USA, which enabled him to hear a great deal of music and to acquaint himself with the newest trends. What he encountered did not attract him to post-Wagnerian complexity and opulence or distract him from the symphony as a viable form. His development and achievement is best seen in the series of seven that he wrote from 1899 to 1924 (the legendary Eighth, said to have existed in 1929, has never been seen or heard by others).[10] These show a progress away from national Romanticism in the direction of neo-classicism (or 'European classicism', as Erik Tawaststjerna prefers to call it); after the overtly Romantic Second Symphony (1901–2), the Violin Concerto (1903) and the tone poem *Pohjola's Daughter* (1906), based on yet another scene in the *Kalevala*, this stylistic change is seen in the increasing austerity of the Third Symphony (1907).

The new style did not go unnoticed: whereas in his *Die Musik Skandinaviens* (1906) Walter Niemann had written 'Sibelius' Musik ist reine Heimatkunst', the following year the critic Karl Flodin could write 'Sibelius is a classic master. Never have I so fully realized that Jean Sibelius belongs to all five continents as when I had the good fortune to make the acquaintance of his Third Symphony'. The Fourth (1911), which perfectly illustrates the 'severity and style, and the profound logic that created an inner connection between all the motifs' that Sibelius said (in a conversation with Mahler in 1907) were the qualities that attracted him to the form, was found difficult by its first audiences but has come to be regarded by many as perhaps Sibelius's finest solution of the symphonic problem. The heroic and exciting Fifth (1915) is probably the most popular, but behind its immediate appeal lies the same intense concern with concision and concentration, as revealed by the composer's two revisions (in 1916 and 1919) which reduced the four movements to three.

Sibelius felt strongly the isolation imposed on him by World War I and, after the war, that his way was a lonely path diverging from the mainstream of modern music in the rest of Europe. He remained true to his convictions, however, and after a period of silent withdrawal sent out from the northern forests and lakes of a now independent Finland his serene and contemplative Sixth Symphony (1923), which he characterized as a glass of 'pure cold water', into a world now used to sipping cocktails. This was followed immediately by the monumental Seventh (1924), a symphony in one movement (originally entitled 'Symphonic Fantasia') which represents the ultimate realization of Sibelius's conception of symphonic – indeed, musical – form as the continuous, integrated flow of ideas which finds its inevitable, peculiar, not pre-ordained, order. Only two more works of importance were to come from his pen, both in 1926: incidental music to Shakespeare's *The Tempest*, commissioned by the Royal Theatre in Copenhagen, and a final evocation of the *Kalevala* in the tone poem *Tapiola* (named after Tapio, god of the forest), which, in Robert Layton's simile, is to the forest what 'Debussy's *La mer* is to the sea. Both display his remarkable mastery of the orchestra and his ability to represent in sounds the scenes and sensations of his inspiration.

There seems to be no simple explanation of Sibelius's silence during his last 30 years, but that he should conclude his career with a national epic reminds one of the special nature of his nationalism which was not based on an interest in or study of folksong but on ancient literature and mythology and on the nature it describes and inhabits. His position as a national composer was absolute, he became the embodiment of Finnish music, a standard against which the 'Finnishness' of other music was measured.

Perhaps because of the influence of Mendelssohn on Gade, or simply through the moderation of the Scandinavian temperament, Romanticism in Denmark was contained within more or less classical limits. National Romanticism came to Denmark first of the Scandinavian countries and had run its course before the passing of Gade and J. P. E. Hartmann. With the exception of the precocious but anachronistic Rued Langgaard (1893–1952), late Romanticism never reached any more extreme expression than the songs of Lange-Müller and the symphonies of Victor Bendix (1851–1926), in particular no. 2 (of four), *Sommerklange fra Sydrusland* ('Summer Sounds from Southern Russia', 1888), and Louis Glass (1864–1936), especially no.5 (of six), with the innocent, but, in the light of later events, unfortunate title *Svastica* (1919). Asger Hamerik (1843–1923), who lived most of his active musical life outside Denmark, first in Paris, then as director (1871–98) of the Peabody Institute in Baltimore, Maryland, prided himself on having been Berlioz's only pupil; and August Enna (1859–1939) admitted the influence of both Wagner and Verdi in making him the most successful opera composer in Denmark around the turn of the century – whose works were also performed abroad. However, the powerful, classically inclined musical personality of Carl Nielsen effectively discouraged the further development of late Romantic style along post-Wagnerian lines and led Danish music into new paths.

Carl Nielsen was born in humble circumstances on the island of Funen. With local assistance, he went to Copenhagen in 1883 and on the strength of a string quartet was accepted by Gade to the conservatory, where he also studied with J. P. E. Hartmann. He was then appointed second violinist in the Royal Orchestra under Johan Svendsen, who in 1894 conducted the first performance of his First Symphony (1892). Already in this remarkably assured first work his distinctive personality is evident – not only in its melody and rhythm but also in an unusual treatment of tonality which proceeds from G minor to an ending in C, which is described as 'progressive tonality'. Nielsen's six symphonies, no.2, *The Four Temperaments* (1902), no.3 *Sinfonia espansiva* (1911) no.4, *The Inextinguishable* (1916), no.5 (1922) and no.6, *Sinfonia semplice* (1925), chart the development of a powerful creative mind which, like Sibelius's, was largely shaped independently of contemporary trends in the rest of Europe. But though Nielsen's quality was apparent from the start, neither at home nor abroad was he immediately accorded the recognition Sibelius enjoyed. One reason may have been that he was not seen as the voice of a nation not previously heard but now asking for recognition of her individuality and independence. Not until his Third Symphony did Nielsen win acceptance as Denmark's leading composer, and then it was not only for his symphonies and the four string quartets he had written by that time. He had also written two operas, *Saul og David* (1901), a monumental work with some of the qualities of an oratorio, and the very different *Maskarade* (1906), a charming piece based on a comedy by the Norwegian-Danish Ludvig Holberg (the eighteenth-century father of Danish theatre) which has acquired the status of a national opera. More important, he had begun the series of songs and hymns which he wrote to provide new and worthy, but simple, settings of Danish poetry for the people to sing; in this he collaborated with the organist, composer and music historian Thomas Laub (1852–1927), who exercised a profound influence on the reform of Danish church music.

In an interview for a Norwegian paper, Nielsen said of his Third Symphony: 'I am – or better – I was often a bone of contention . . . but that was because I wanted to protest against the typical Danish smoothing over. I want stronger rhythms and more advanced harmony'. His wish was recognized: a Danish critic wrote, 'It is the new dominant element in twentieth-century music, rhythm, that now makes its entry into the Danish symphony'. The Third Symphony was hailed as the new voice of Scandinavia when Nielson conducted it in Holland and Germany and elsewhere in 1912, and together with Sibelius's Fourth Symphony of the same year it represents Scandinavian musical achievement at the beginning of World War I. During and after the war, while Sibelius in his isolation was cultivating his inner experience with an intensity that eventually made further communication impossible, Nielsen was reaching out to humanity and developing in his own way the elements of 'stronger rhythms and more advanced harmony', not to mention new formal structures, which enabled him to speak to a world of changing values. 'Music is life, and like it, inextinguishable', was the motto of his Fourth Symphony; and for many his Fourth, the two-movement Fifth and at least the first movement of the problematic Sixth represent the culmination of this development. Others would reserve this accolade for the remarkable one-movement Clarinet Concerto (1928) and the difficult *Commotio* for organ (1931), his final work.

It was no doubt the discovery of so individual a 'modern' composer, unaligned with other trends, which belatedly brought him international recognition after World War II and established the fact that, having contributed richly to all aspects of European culture in the nineteenth century, Scandinavia continued proudly in the twentieth with at least two composers of international stature.

NOTES

[1] This poem provided Max Bruch with the texts of two choral works written in the 1860s: *Frithjof: Szenen aus der Frithjof Sage* op.23 and *Frithjof aus seines Vaters Grabhügel* op.27.

[2] The first issue of the English-language *Finnish Musical Quarterly* (May 1985) had as its main theme 'The *Kalevala* . . . and the impact that the national epic has had on Finnish music'.

[3] 'The smallest and poorest of the Scandinavian states, she was ruled politically from Stockholm and culturally from Copenhagen'; M. C. Bradbrook, *Ibsen the Norwegian: a Revaluation* (London, 1966), 21.

[4] An institute bearing Magnússon's name was later established round this priceless collection. In the 1970s Denmark agreed to restore to Iceland the manuscripts of the greatest national interest.

[5] See, for example, C. Dahlhaus, *Die Musik des 19. Jahrhunderts* (Wiesbaden and Laaber, 1980), 65, 220.

[6] Oehlenschläger wrote *Aladdin* in German too, in which form it provided the text for the chorale finale of Busoni's monumental Piano Concerto op.39 (1903–4).

[7] In German translation, as *Es war einmal*, it was also set by Zemlinsky (1899).

[8] The last of these (1887–9) coincided with the period when Halvorsen and the English composer Frederick Delius (1862–1934) were there and when Grieg made a visit to Leipzig. Lifelong friendships were established which, taken together with his earlier passion for the Scandinavian countries and their cultures, served to attach Delius as an active participant to developments in Scandinavian Romanticism.

[9] See J. Bergsagel, 'J. P. Jacobsen and Music', in *J. P. Jacobsens Spor, 1885–1985* (Copenhagen, 1985), 283–313.

[10] See E. Tawaststjerna, 'Sibelius's Eighth Symphony: an Insoluble Mystery', *Finnish Musical Quarterly* (1985), 61.

The Late Romantic Era

BIBLIOGRAPHICAL NOTE

Historical and cultural background

Whereas the geographical, linguistic and cultural community of the Scandinavian peoples is obvious to foreigners and is generally taken for granted, the differences between them, which define them as five independent nations, are often subtle and to some extent subjective and difficult to appreciate without a knowledge of Scandinavian languages. However, there is a useful annotated list of books and articles in English compiled by S. P. Oakley, *Scandinavian History 1520–1970*, 'Helps for Students of History Series, 91' (Historical Association, 59a Kennington Park Road, London SE11 4JH, 1984).

Of those works which attempt to treat Scandinavia as a whole, the most comprehensive is *Scandinavia Past and Present*, ed. J. Bukdahl and others, 3 vols., ([Odense], 1959), which provides in translation a series of studies of all aspects of the history, cultural as well as political, of the Scandinavian countries as seen by Scandinavian specialists. Relevant to this period is vol.ii, *Through Revolutions to Liberty*, which alone runs to 652 pages and is richly illustrated. Of more modest proportions, T. K. Derry, *A History of Scandinavia: Norway, Sweden, Denmark, Finland and Iceland* (London, 1979), can be recommended as offering the unified view of a single, knowledgeable, outside observer.

E. Bredsdorff, B. Mortensen and R. Popperwell, *An Introduction to Scandinavian Literature* (Cambridge and Copenhagen, 1951/R1970), provides a good, short survey, though 'Scandinavia' is limited here to Denmark, Norway and Sweden. C. Laurin, E. Hannover and J. Thiis, *Scandinavian Art* (New York, 1922), by now a venerable standard guide, can be supplemented by such exhibition catalogues as *C.W. Eckersberg og hans elever* [Statens Museum for Kunst] (Copenhagen, 1983); *Eckersberg i Rom* [Thorvaldsens Museum] (Copenhagen, 1987); *Danish Painting: the Golden Age* [National Gallery] (London, 1984); *J.C. Dahl i Italien 1820–1821* [Thorvaldsens Museum] (Copenhagen, 1987); *1880-erne i nordisk maleri* [Statens Museum for Kunst] (Copenhagen, 1986); K. Varnedoe, *Northern Light: Realism and Symbolism in Scandinavian Painting, 1880–1910* [Brooklyn Museum] (New York, 1982); R. Nesgaard, *The Mystic North* [Art Gallery of Ontario] (Toronto, 1984) and *Dreams of a Summer Night: Scandinavian Painting at the Turn of the Century* [Arts Council of Great Britain] (London, 1986). To these may be added R. Rosenblum, *Modern Painting and the Northern Romantic Tradition: Friedrich to Rothko* (New York, 1975); K. Voss, *Skagensmalerne og denes billeder på Skagens Museum* (Copenhagen, 1975); W. Vaughan, *Romantic Art* (London, 1978); and the revised version of the 1982 catalogue by K. Varnedoe published in book form as *Northern Light: Nordic Art at the Turn of the Century* (New Haven and London, 1988).

Music

An interesting work in German with no counterpart in English is W. Niemann, *Das Nordlandbuch: eine Einführung in die gesamte nordische Natur und Kultur* (Berlin, 1909), a document of the period under consideration. The author, an enthusiastic admirer of Scandinavia, was an excellent musician who also wrote *Die Musik Skandinaviens* (Leipzig, 1906), one of the very few attempts to provide a comprehensive survey of the music of the area (including Finland) as a cultural whole, and *Die nordische Klavier-Musik* (Leipzig, 1918), as well as the studies *Grieg* (with G. Schjelderup) (Leipzig, 1908) and *Sibelius* (Leipzig, 1917). Of peculiar interest for the immediacy of its first-hand observations is H. von Bülow, *Skandinavische Concertreiseskizzen (April und Mai 1882)* (Charlottenburg and Berlin, 1882–; repr. in *H. von Bülow: Briefe und Schriften*, iii (Leipzig, 1896), 408–37).

The only general survey in English is J. Horton, *Scandinavian Music: a Short History* (London, 1963). Such brief English-language introductions to the music of the individual nations as *Music in Denmark*, ed. K. Ketting (Copenhagen, 1987), K. Lange and A. Östvedt, *Norwegian Music: a Brief Survey* (London, 1958), B. Alander, *Swedish Music* (Stockholm, 1956) and T. Mäkinen and S. Nummi, *Musica fennica* (Helsinki, 1965), are no substitutes for the national histories by N. Schiørring, *Musikkens historie i Danmark*, 3 vols. (Copenhagen, 1977–8), N. Grinde, *Norsk Musikkhistorie* (Oslo, Bergen and Tromsø, 1971, rev. 3/1981), A. Aulin and H. Connor, *Svensk musik*, 2 vols. (Stockholm, 1974–7), and T. Haapanen, *Finlands musikhistoria* [in Swedish] (Helsinki, 1956), which have not been translated.

Some assistance in understanding the musical environment in Scandinavia can nevertheless be obtained from the individual studies of some of its leading composers. R. Layton, *Franz Berwald* (London, 1959), contributed significantly to the twentieth-century recognition of Berwald outside Sweden. Similarly, R. Simpson, *Carl Nielsen, Symphonist* (London, 1952, rev. 2/1979), which includes a biographical essay by Nielsen's Danish biographer T. Meyer, provided a qualified examination of the music which was influential in consolidating the largely postwar international interest in the great Danish composer. A collection of studies by specialists was published on the centenary of his birth in two parallel editions, the English version being *Carl Nielsen, 1865–1965: Centenary Essays*, ed. J. Balzer (Copenhagen, 1965). Observing the fact that Nielsen's centenary was also Sibelius's, R. Simpson published *Sibelius and Nielsen: a Centenary Essay* (London, 1965).

Ole Bull is a key figure in the creation of Norwegian national consciousness, both at home and abroad; but M. Smith, *The Life of Ole Bull* (Princeton, 1943/R1973), perhaps represents Bull's American second family too much to be entirely satisfactory from a Norwegian point of view. W. Behrend, *Niels W. Gade* (German edn., Leipzig, 1918), remains the only book in a non-Scandinavian language on this central figure in nineteenth-century Scandinavian music, though this situation may be improved now that the centenary of his death has been reached.

Grieg, on the other hand, has been the subject of many studies in a variety of languages; they are all now superseded (but not necessarily invalidated – for example, *Grieg: a Symposium*, ed. G. Abraham (London, 1948), and J. Horton, *Grieg* (London, 1974), by the splendidly thorough and lavishly produced book by F. Benestad and D. Schjelderup-Ebbe, *Edvard Grieg: the Man and the Artist* (Gloucester, 1988), an excellent translation by W. L. Halverson and L. B. Sateren of the original Norwegian *Edvard Grieg: mennesket og kunstner* (Oslo, 1980). Berestad and Schjelderup-Ebbe have recently completed a corresponding *Johan Svendsen: mennesket og kunstner* (Oslo, 1990), the long-awaited, first full-scale study of this important figure in Scandinavian musical life.

Sibelius too has not lacked international attention but all earlier treatments pale beside the monumental achievement of E. Tawaststjerna. Originally written in Swedish, it was published first in a Finnish translation (5 vols.) prepared under the author's guidance. This was reworked for the Swedish edition (3 vols.), and the English edition is yet another revision resulting from the close collaboration of the author with the translator, R. Layton, himself a noted Sibelius authority – *Sibelius* (London, 1965, rev. 2/1978) and *Sibelius and his World* (London, 1970, rev. 3/1983); the superb result, of which two volumes of the projected three have appeared, is E. Tawaststjerna, *Sibelius* (London, 1976–).

Chapter X

Victorian England: an Age of Expansion

DONALD BURROWS

With the Royal Jubilees of 1887 and 1897 in Britain came the selfconsciousness of a 'Victorian Age': prosperous, successful, confident, innovatory and leading the world in many areas of human endeavour. Apart from the continuity provided by the monarch herself, there was some substance to this image, for British society had pursued its own path largely untrammelled by the effects of violent divisions of revolutionary fervour or the fervid attempts to create a unified national consciousness that were characteristic of other major European societies. Such an outcome could hardly have been foreseen in 1848, however, when suffrage and corn laws were still perceived as potentially destabilizing national issues. Many people, including musicians, fled to Britain from the consequences of the 1848 revolutions elsewhere and, as had been the case with the famous French Revolution half a century before, there was little confidence that London would not see a similar turbulence. Even the Great Exhibition of 1851, which symbolizes the prosperity and stability of mid-Victorian society, was darkened by official fears (unrealized in practice) that the gathering of the people might be the excuse for some threatening disturbance. Stability and confidence were achievements, not inborn characteristics, of Victorian Britain, and they were accompanied by realistic recognition of limitations and doubts. Strong religious and ethical pressures were at work, but these divided as well as unified: the authority of the Church of Rome and the challenge provided by *The Origin of Species* were subjects of controversy that absorbed as much energy among articulate people as social and political issues. And against the powers of self-improvement provided by economic expansion and the inventive harnessing of new technology there was the constant reminder of the mockery of human mortality, probably never more forcefully expressed than in Tennyson's *In Memoriam*. No European society had more elaborate funerary rituals; had the Protestant culture not been so strongly engrained, it might have been a golden age for the requiem and *Stabat mater*.

1848 is a convenient symbolic starting date for one phase of British musical history. Felix Mendelssohn died in Leipzig on 4 November 1847 at the age of 38. His influence on English musical life had been considerable – and direct. He had been a frequent and welcome visitor and had conducted the first performance of *Elijah* at Birmingham in 1846: as late as April 1847 he had returned for four performances of *Elijah* in London and for visits to Manchester and Birmingham. Of equal importance to the influence of his music was the status Mendelssohn gained for the musical profession. Among sections of English society, particularly that part of the middle class in which the nonconformist influence was strong, there was a suspicion of musicians and actors and of the places where they worked. It was not unknown for a young musical enthusiast who wanted to attend a concert to have to deceive his parents into believing that he was going to a football match.[1] In Mendelssohn musicians could point to one of their profession whose private life was beyond reproach, whose choice of texts for musical setting was acceptable and who was received as an honoured guest by the royal family.

There seems to have been a genuine rapport between Mendelssohn and the Prince Consort, perhaps because they had grown up within similar German intellectual backgrounds. To Prince Albert, who had received a training in music as an accepted part of an all-round 'scientific' education,[2] attitudes to music and musicians in Britain must have seemed strange. To judge from his later actions, it also seems probable that he fairly quickly became dissatisfied with the level of musical patronage (using the word in its broadest sense) that he found in England. Until his death in 1861 he was in the forefront of those encouraging public schemes for musical training and performance. In the next generation this encouragement was taken up by the Duke of Edinburgh, Queen Victoria's second son;[3] he too brought welcome respectability to the musical profession, counterbalancing his elder brother's less respectable enthusiasm for the stage.

It is not possible to review the course of music in Victorian England, particularly in London, without considering a few strong and determined individuals. They were not in the main creative musicians, nor even primarily performers, but a group that might be described as 'enablers' – Prince Albert himself, Henry Cole, George Grove and Richard Bowley – who wanted to promote a growth in the quantity and quality of professional and amateur music-making. The phrase 'the land without music' was not coined until 1914, by which time it was inappropriate. It could have been used with a little more justice in 1848, if narrowly applied to the nationality of composers and performers in London. Certainly there was a demand for music: Weber, Chopin, Liszt and Paganini had all profited from it.[4] The 1830s had seen the first chamber-music concerts in London, the first one-man piano recital and the launching of the first weekly music journal.[5] But the native musical profession was insecure; apart from a limited number of jobs in church music and the theatre, there were few opportunities for continuous, long-term employment. The instinct of the 'enablers' was sound: what was needed was the establishment of an institutional base that would channel and educate such demand for music as existed or could be created.

As the quality and range of music-making developed after 1848, two significant tensions came to the surface more strongly. More predictable, though perhaps less significant, was that between native and imported talent. Except in church music, the musical profession in 1848 was dominated by Italians and Germans in vocal and instrumental music respectively. Good foreign musicians were fairly continuously welcomed by British audiences: British singers who adopted Italian names showed good business sense. While training for British musicians remained limited and performance opportunities continued to expand, this situation caused no difficulties, but towards the turn of the century, as the effects of improvements in British professional training began to be felt, the increased number of would-be performers created circumstances of potential conflict.

More subtle was the tension between the acceptance of a highly regarded 'classical' repertory and the encouragement of new composition. There came a point, again towards the end of the century, when a country of imperial glory felt a selfconscious need to identify its own living composers. Yet there was also apparently a need among Victorian musicians for 'authority' figures. The veneration of Handel was well established before the end of the eighteenth century, accompanied by an only slightly lesser veneration of Haydn. To the pantheon were added in succession Beethoven and Mendelssohn, and with Mendelssohn came J. S. Bach: the London Bach Society was founded in 1849. The music of these composers remained well regarded and new names were added – Schubert, Mozart and, eventually, Wagner. It has sometimes been contended that the admitted mediocrity of much music composed in Victorian Britain can be attributed to the overbearing shadows of these figures, Handel and Mendelssohn in particular. No doubt performers complained if their new music was not like the repertory from which they normally gained satisfaction; professional critics, on the other hand, usually complained when the new music was too much like Handel or Mendelssohn. However, there seems little evidence that genuine originality was stifled; if anything, new works were more technically accomplished because their composers had good models to work from, and there were more of them because of the opportunities created on the back of the regular repertory. A further interpretation of this situation is suggested below.

CONCERT LIFE

The existence of a large potential audience in London was demonstrated – and perhaps partly created – by the successful series of concerts managed and conducted by Louis Jullien between 1842 and 1859.[6] His programmes were spectacular and miscellaneous, but his activities were described sympathetically even by George Grove:

> His aim was always to popularize music, and the means he adopted for so doing were the largest band, the very best performers, both solo and orchestral, and the most attractive pieces. His programmes contained a certain amount of classical music, and later on in his career he gave whole symphonies, and even two on one evening. But the characteristic features of Jullien's concerts were, first, his Monster Quadrille, and secondly himself. He provided a fresh quadrille for each season, and it was usually in close connection with the event of the day. In some of them as many as six military bands were added to the immense permanent orchestra. With coat thrown widely open, white waistcoat, elaborately embroidered shirt-front, wristbands of extravagant length turned back over his cuffs, a wealth of black hair and a black moustache he wielded his baton, encouraged his forces, repressed the turbulence of his audience with indescribable gravity and magnificence, seized a violin or piccolo at the moment of climax and at last sank exhausted into his gorgeous velvet chair. All pieces of Beethoven's were conducted with a jewelled baton and in a pair of clean kid gloves, handed him on a silver salver. After his month at Drury Lane, Covent Garden or Her Majesty's, Jullien carried off his whole company of players and singers through the provinces, including Scotland and even Ireland.
>
> With much obvious charlatanism, what Jullien aimed at was good, and what he aimed at he did thoroughly well. He was a public amuser, but he was also a public reformer.

Jullien's concerts took place in theatres, for in 1850 there was no concert hall in London adequate to modern needs in accommodating either the growing symphony orchestra or the size of audience that was economically necessary for that orchestra's support. The principal venue was the largest of the Hanover Square Rooms which had been built to meet eighteenth-century conditions. The new St James's Hall, which opened in 1858 with a concert attended by the Prince Consort, had a floor area of 139′ × 60′ (as against 95′ × 35′ at Hanover Square) and could seat more than 2000 people. As at Hanover Square, the new hall was part of a larger suite including a smaller hall and banqueting rooms, but to London music-lovers 'St James's Hall' meant the large hall. The smaller one was sometimes known as the 'Christy Minstrels' Hall' after the troupe that regularly performed there; when St James's Hall in its turn became outmoded, one of the complaints against it was that concerts were interrupted by the sound of the minstrels and the smell of cooking.

51. Opening concert at St James's Hall, London, 1858; engraving from the 'Illustrated London News' (10 April 1858)

The music publishers Chappell had a strong financial interest in St James's Hall. Promotion by publishers was an important feature of London concert life: Novello supported a series of oratorio performances conducted by Joseph Barnby, and Boosey & Co. gave concerts to promote their latest ballads. Chappell's interest in St James's Hall was perhaps more disinterested: they supported the project as patrons though they no doubt hoped to see a return through commercial lettings. Unfortunately the site of the hall, between Piccadilly and Regent Street, proved to be on quicksand and building costs were about £70,000 instead of the expected £23,000, so finances were difficult from the start. It was doubly unfortunate that, for orchestral concerts, the hall soon found itself in unexpected competition with the successful Crystal Palace, so its most famous resident series was not of orchestral music: the Popular Concerts, at first held on Mondays but from 1865 on Mondays and Saturdays, featured vocal and instrumental soloists, and a resident string quartet. The title 'popular' was well justified by audience figures and by 1887 the 1000th concert had been given. The composers most frequently represented in the programmes were Beethoven, Schumann, Mozart and Mendelssohn, with Chopin, Haydn and J. S. Bach not far behind. Bach's organ music had been played in some of the first concerts, and it was with a Bach fugue subject that Sullivan characterized the Popular Concerts when they were mentioned in *The Mikado*.[7] An important feature of the series was the programme booklets, which contained descriptive-analytical notes on the music. They cost 6*d.*; admission charges were 5*s.* (stalls), 3*s.* (balcony) and 6*d.* (gallery).

Yet St James's Hall was not completely devoid of performances of orchestral music, and a significant development was the transference of the Philharmonic Society concerts there from Hanover Square in 1869. The Philharmonic Society, founded in 1813 and managed by professional musicians, was London's most influential concert society, organizing eight performances each season. It commissioned orchestral works from leading composers of the day and, where possible, lured them to London to conduct their pieces: they had negotiated honourably with both Beethoven and Mendelssohn.

The appointment of Michael Costa as director-conductor of the Philharmonic Society's performances between 1848 and 1854 improved the orchestra's technical standard but the programmes were unadventurous and little new music was introduced to capitalize on this improvement. The society's dominance was challenged by the formation in 1852 of a New Philharmonic Society (partly promoted by Cramer the music publishers) to present concerts with less conventional programmes; it lasted until 1879 but did not effect any startling change. One of its most interesting seasons was in 1855 when Berlioz took part; but it coincided with one of the Philharmonic Society's more adventurous years, involving a visit from Richard Wagner. The Philharmonic Society seems to have re-established its leading position after its move to St James's Hall in 1869, when it also introduced programme notes comparable to those of the Popular Concerts.

By the time St James's Hall opened in 1858, the Crystal Palace concerts were well under way. Though geographically not so central, the Crystal Palace was served by an easy rail link to Sydenham and it became an important concert venue. There was also the attraction of the building itself, created originally for the Great Exhibition at Kensington in 1851. After the building had been re-erected on its new site, the orchestral concerts there fairly quickly became an established institution, but such concerts had not been part of the original policy of the Crystal Palace Company and much of the credit for this innovation must go to George Grove.

Grove, born in 1820 the son of a London fishmonger, originally followed a career as a civil engineer. While serving his apprenticeship he seems to have spent most of his spare time attending concerts or studying and copying music at the British Museum. His work took him to Jamaica and Bermuda in connection with the construction of lighthouses and he was subsequently engaged in various railway projects, including Chester Station and the Britannia Bridge. His musical copybooks accompanied him round the world. After the completion of the Britannia Bridge his career changed direction and in 1850 he succeeded John Scott Russell (another engineer) as secretary of the Society of Arts. He was thus at the centre of the activity around the Great Exhibition, and it was a logical move when in May 1852 he became secretary to the Crystal Palace Company which had purchased the Exhibition building. He retained this post for two decades, during which time he was responsible for overseeing the palace's diverse activities – exhibitions, lectures, religious gatherings, animal shows and much more. His energies went well beyond the call of duty and he retained his association with the concert series there after he had resigned the general secretaryship. For more than 40 years he was the organizing power behind the Crystal Palace concerts and the author of the programme notes.

The official opening of the Crystal Palace in its new location at Sydenham was on 10 April 1854 in the presence of the Queen and Prince Consort. Grove had been sent to visit Tennyson to negotiate an ode for the occasion, to be set to music by Berlioz, but the project fell through – apparently to everyone's relief. Before the opening the prince had summoned Costa and informed him that he expected something better than the musical performance that had taken place at the opening of the Great Exhibition, which the prince described as 'below criticism'. Even so, the 'Hallelujah' chorus at the opening of the palace was not an unqualified success:

> the new brass band of foreigners, conducted by Herr Schallehn, a foreigner, was seldom in time and always out of tune with the choir; and the parts for all sort of brass instruments, added to the score by some bold and uncompromising hand, helped rather to mystify than augment the effect of Handel's tremendous paean, which, had an English musician been appointed conductor, could have been left alone in its glory.[8]

Schallehn and his wind band had been taken on as part of the palace's permanent amenities. It was not strictly a brass band but a military one comprising woodwind and brass instruments played by some of the best practitioners in London (though that was clearly not apparent in the opening concert); in the routine programmes of marches, galops and quadrilles it compared favourably with famous visiting bands. Schallehn's leadership was short-lived: after a quarrel within the band, he was replaced in 1855 by August Manns, a clarinettist and conductor and Schallehn's former deputy. It was the combination of the talents of Manns as conductor and Grove as organizer that generated the Crystal Palace concerts. Many of the band players were 'double-handed' – they played string instruments as well as wind – and soon after his appointment Manns gave a concert of music for string orchestra. It was but a short step to turning the band into a symphony orchestra, and on 1 December 1855 Manns conducted two movements of Beethoven's Seventh Symphony with a full orchestra. Over the next couple of months he gave regular Saturday performances, the programmes including four of Beethoven's symphonies and Mozart's 40th. This was followed by an ambitious programme on 26 January 1856 to mark the centenary of Mozart's birth.

The problem of a suitable venue for orchestral concerts within the palace became acute. The band's early performances had been in the central transept, and Manns had performed his string orchestra concert in the more intimate surroundings of the Bohemian Glass Court. For the Mozart concert a music room was created in the north wing, with room for an audience of 900 at most. 1500 people turned up. Eventually a new performing area was created in the centre transept; there Manns conducted weekly Saturday concerts, following an annual season between October and April. Before the first season was out, the programmes had included the first English performances of Schubert's 'Great' C major Symphony and Schumann's Fourth. Programmes usually contained two overtures, a symphony, a concerto or some other piece of orchestral music and four songs. With the orchestra's nucleus drawn from the permanent Crystal Palace band, Manns had the good fortune of regular rehearsal with the same group, something virtually unknown for an orchestra of this size in London, even at the opera house.

The combination of good performing standards and interesting programmes mixing novelties with the staple diet made these concerts very successful. They were no less appreciated by the musicians for whom they signalled regular and congenial employment. The orchestra was however kept at a moderate size to maintain financial security: works involving larger orchestras with triple woodwind and extensive batteries of brass and strings were more likely to be included in the Philharmonic Society's programmes.

The quality of ensemble achieved at the Crystal Palace was favourably commented on by the young music critic George Bernard Shaw:

> The second Crystal Palace concert of this year took place on Saturday afternoon, the 17th. The program included Cherubini's earnest and refined overture to Medea, Haydn's Oxford symphony, and an overture to Alfieri's tragedy of Saul, the latter being heard for

the first – and possibly the last – time in England. . . . Signor Bazzini's overture, if not strikingly original, is sufficiently entertaining to justify its introduction by Mr Manns. Mlle Marie Krebs played Beethoven's fourth concerto in her characteristic style, crisply and steadily. Throughout the concert the orchestra acquitted themselves most satisfactorily. The performances to which we are accustomed in London seem to move in a narrow circle from weak incompetence or coarse violence to the perfection of lifeless finish, according to the incapacity, the misdirected energy, or the cold autocracy which distinguished the conductors. At Sydenham, thanks to Mr Manns, we can hear an orchestra capable of interpreting with refinement and expression the greatest instrumental compositions, more especially those of Beethoven.[9]

The Crystal Palace concerts had wide appeal: in addition to the 'musical' audience of informed connoisseurs they took over the more popular audience that had been discovered and developed in London by Jullien. There was also a more casual audience:

Saturday was the day when the largest crowds were to be expected, for it was the workers' half-holiday. Not all the workers spending Saturday evening at the Crystal Palace would be likely to go there for the music alone, but they would sample it along with the other entertainments just as the visitors to the Great Exhibition had done. The workers, too, were people of a wide variety of types, for besides heavy manual workers, the innumerable clerical workers with whom London abounded were all equally free on Saturday evenings, and, although the taverns still drew a good proportion of the people, there were great numbers of wage-earners whose religious principles led them to avoid such evils, and to seek sources of entertainment for themselves and their families where liquor was not in evidence. These people had perforce to avoid the theatres, and chose musical performances as the best type of entertainment available in the social environment they knew.[10]

In addition to a wide social catchment, the Crystal Palace concerts were probably the first to attract regularly the geographically dispersed audience that the railway brought within reach of London. Musical enthusiasts from the provinces were willing to make considerable sacrifices to attend the concerts. Edward Elgar remembered coming from Worcester in the 1870s:

The greatest thing in my strenuous life was to hear orchestral music. I lived 120 miles from London. To hear a novelty at the Crystal Palace, then the real home of orchestral music in England, many times I have left home at 6.30, arrived at Paddington about 11, travelled by underground to Victoria, thence to the Crystal Palace; where, if the train was not late I might hear a few minutes of the rehearsal. Concert at 3, then a reversal of the journey described,

ending at midnight; and after all these exertions and privations –
(lunch and dinner were generally omitted) – I heard my symphony
once only.[11]

In many respects 1885–95 was the golden decade for the London concert-goer. The Crystal Palace orchestra was at its peak,
and elsewhere you could have heard performances conducted by
Dvořák, Saint-Saëns, Tchaikovsky and Grieg: all these appeared in
the Philharmonic Society's concerts (for which Dvořák and Saint-
Saëns expressly composed symphonies), and their visits included
other engagements in London and the provinces. Of the outstanding
contemporary European symphonic composers only Brahms resisted
the society's invitations, though his music appeared in their programmes from 1873 onwards; Joseph Joachim, a violinist closely
associated with Brahms's music, appeared frequently in London as a
soloist and quartet leader. With the advent of these new eminent
musicians, London's musical taste had decisively come out of the
'Mendelssohn shadow', a spectre that had already partly been broken
– though not very satisfactorily – by Gounod's success in London in
the 1870s.

The Crystal Palace concerts continued to flourish but there were
changes elsewhere. St James's Hall closed in 1905 (the Hanover
Square Rooms had already closed, in 1874) but new halls were
opened: the Royal Albert Hall in 1871, Alexandra Palace in 1873
(both containing outstanding organs built by Henry Willis), the
Steinway Hall in 1875, the Wigmore Hall in 1901 and the Aeolian
Hall in 1904, the last three under the patronage of piano manufac-
turers. For orchestral concerts the most significant new building was
the Queen's Hall, opened in 1893: the Philharmonic Society transferred its concerts there in 1894 and a year later the hall saw the
beginning of the Promenade Concerts promoted by Robert Newman
and conducted by Henry Wood. (The 'promenade' idea had hitherto
been a feature of theatre concerts such as Jullien's.) While the 'piano'
halls became successful central venues for chamber music, no less
significant was the formation of the People's Concert Society in 1878
to bring music to the poorer parts of London: the Finsbury branch
was outstandingly successful and developed a reputation for performances of chamber music at the South Place Sunday Popular Concerts.

CHORAL MUSIC

Few images of Victorian music-making are more powerful than the
spectacular contemporary engravings of the monster-sized Crystal
Palace Handel Festivals; they have also gained a place in the history
of musical aesthetics and criticism by virtue of the controversy
surrounding the rearrangement of Handel's music with 'additional

52. Scene outside the Queen's Hall, London, with sandwich-men advertising a Promenade Concert in the 1895 season, to be conducted by Henry Wood

accompaniments' that was characteristic of their style. The Crystal Palace Handel Festivals, like the orchestral concerts, began very soon after the reopening of the building on its new site.

On 1 September 1856 the Crystal Palace Company addressed a letter to the Sacred Harmonic Society[12] suggesting a rehearsal of several oratorios at the Crystal Palace in preparation for a commemoration in 1859 of the centenary of Handel's death. The assumption seems to have been that the commemoration should be celebrated on the largest possible scale. Much of the credit for seeing it and subsequent festivities into existence goes to Richard Bowley, the Sacred Harmonic Society's librarian from 1837 and treasurer from 1853. There were two 'trial runs', in 1857 and 1858. In 1857 three oratorios, *Messiah, Judas Maccabaeus* and *Israel in Egypt*, were performed by a choir of 2000 and an orchestra of 500, attracting an audience of over 48,000. During one performance the royal dignitaries were observed beating time, the queen with a fan and Prince Albert with a roll of paper (it is not clear whether this was in response to the music or to the heat of a crowded performance in mid-June).

In 1858 Bowley became general manager of the Crystal Palace Company. One of his first acts was to redesign the area used for orchestral music at the Saturday Concerts: he then adapted the central transept to the demands of the 1859 Handel Commemoration. In its final form the auditorium measured 360' by 216' exclusive of side galleries. The orchestral platform was provided with resonators to throw the sound forward, and over the whole area was erected a *volarium*, or false roof, in an effort to control reflections of sound from the ceiling. The three performances in 1859 consisted of *Messiah, Israel in Egypt* and a programme of selections from Handel's music. At each the choir exceeded 2700 and the orchestra 450; the audience totalled 81,319. The performances were complemented by an exhibition of Handel's autograph music (from the Royal Music Library) and relics. The chorus included 'renowned singers from the continent', but participation from the provinces was probably more important: there was a strong contingent, for example, from Bradford. A large body of performers usually brings a large audience: through their financial success and the enthusiasm of performers and audience to relive these performances (and their outing to London) the Handel festivals became a triennial event. There was a two-year gap after 1883, to accommodate the bicentenary of Handel's birth in 1885. Costa conducted until 1880, Manns from 1883 to 1900 and Frederic Cowen from 1903. Numerically, the peak of the festivals' success was reached in the 1880s with a chorus of 4000, an orchestra of 500 and, one year, an audience reaching 87,769.

The Crystal Palace Handel Festivals can obviously be related to the Handel Commemorations of 1784 (with subsequent festivals between 1785 and 1791) and 1834 at Westminster Abbey, but there was an important difference. In 1834 Sir George Smart, conductor of the Handel Commemoration, had rebuffed attempts by amateur choral singers to take part, claiming that this would have deprived cathedral lay-clerks of work. The 1834 commemoration, like its predecessors, was a professional occasion for the performers and a 'society' one for the audience. The Crystal Palace Handel Festivals, by contrast, were dominated by amateur singers and the audience they brought. A chorus of 4000 voices was remarkable in itself and was a measure of the achievement for the various systems of singing teaching that had been developed and promoted from the 1840s by Kay, Hullah, Mainzer and Curwen. By the 1860s the effects of their methods had worked their way into British musical life – and not only in London: the Crystal Palace performances may be regarded as 'super-festivals' that only repeated on a bigger scale what was to be found in the larger provincial cities.

With the building of the great Victorian town halls went the establishment of large provincial music festivals. The original Free Trade Hall in Manchester (1843) had been closely associated in its early days with the singing classes of Mainzer and Hullah. Sometimes, as at Birmingham, the festival grew out of an older charitable event

53. (a) The 1859 Crystal Palace Handel Festival; engraving from the 'Illustrated London News' (2 July 1859)

previously celebrated by semi-professional performers in a large local church but now absorbing the energies of amateur singers and moving into the town hall with the full achievement of civic dignity. In one remarkable case, that of the Three Choirs Festival, there was even no need for a hall: the participating cathedrals were modified with tiered staging for the large oratorio performances. At Leeds the opening of the town hall in 1858 by the queen was an important factor behind the foundation not only of the Leeds Festival but also of the Leeds Philharmonic Society in 1871. As a musical institution the Leeds Philharmonic Society did not hold the field for long: the Leeds Choral Union followed in 1896 and the New Leeds Choral Society in 1902. The completion of a town hall was usually accompanied by the provision of a large organ and the appointment of a borough organist who, in addition to giving recitals, could accompany choral societies in their less spectacular programmes when an orchestra was not available. In Leeds the organist Herbert Fricker even extended his duties to the creation of weekly municipal concerts involving a regular orchestra of local professional musicians. Such opportunities were

53.(b) Some of the events at Crystal Palace during June/July 1875 as listed in the programme for 7 June that year

rare, however, and the late date is significant: the foundation of a professional orchestra by Charles Hallé (a French emigré driven to Britain by the 1848 revolution) in Manchester in 1858 was unique within earlier Victorian England.[13] For most provincial choral festivals the accompanying orchestra might contain a few local professional instrumentalists, who would be supplemented by far more brought in from London.[14]

London was still the centre of professional music-making. A provincial festival gained more fame and status from engaging London musicians (a famous conductor, solo singers and sufficient players to make up a large orchestra) than from encouraging local talent. In return, metropolitan professional musicians relied on provincial jobs and the 'festival circuit': even an established conductor like Costa apparently considered it worthwhile to maintain an active interest in provincial festivals. They increased the demand for professional singers as oratorio soloists, and the newly developing business of professional management found a nationwide function. There was even a semi-professional element among the amateur choral singers. At the Three Choirs Festival in 1886 the 'home' cathedrals provided 134 singers who were supplemented by 90 from elsewhere, of which 24 came from Bradford and twenty each from Bristol and Cardiff. A contingent from Leeds sang Sullivan's *Golden Legend* as a separate item at the next festival, and the presence of 50 singers from Leeds was commented on again in 1888.

The festival performances of large, complex works accompanied by a large orchestra were only the top of a pyramid of provincial music-making. The second half of the nineteenth century saw the creation of many amateur provincial choral associations; some remained modest in size and repertory while others grew towards greater ambitions. It was not unknown for new choirs to be created by binary fission, as local arguments over personalities or the choice of repertory produced unreconciled conflicts. Some choirs remained sol-fa bound; others found the greatest satisfaction in taking part in the fast-developing local competitive music festivals. Much depended on the tastes of the leading choral enthusiasts of a particular locality. In Hanley, Staffordshire, for example, Swinnerton Heap conducted a 'festival' type choir, while James Garner maintained a Glee and Madrigal Society whose programmes ranged from partsongs to Handel's lesser-known oratorios, but not beyond.[15] Social factors, some class-based and some reflecting prevailing religious groupings, also contributed to the maintenance of apparently parallel choral societies in the same place. The dedication of organizers and rank and file members was often intense. In Lincoln, for example, Thomas Cooper's previously diverse interests pursued through the Mechanics' Institute were immediately set aside on the foundation of a choral society, whereupon 'all resolves about study, and purposes of intellectual progress, and interests however important, were sacrificed for my new passion': he became the first secretary of the Lincoln Choral Society.[16]

OTHER MUSICAL ACTIVITIES

While the expansion of London's concert life and the nationwide flowering of choral performance may justifiably be regarded as two of the most spectacular developments in Victorian music-making, progress in other activities was far from negligible. Nearly as startling as the growth of choral music was that of brass bands, and the two had many features in common. Brass bands were provincial and localized, but again had a national focus: the regular performing venue might be the local park on a Sunday afternoon, but the highest accolade was a prize at a Crystal Palace Brass Band Festival. There was often a close association between bands and industrial patrons who provided instruments and a rehearsal room, but that was not the only pattern of patronage, nor did the industrial north of England have a preponderance of bands. While dances and character-pieces formed a considerable part of the repertory, another important part consisted of arrangements from the repertory of 'high art', drawing both on such 'classics' as Handel and 'moderns' as Verdi. The band world, though expansive, was enclosed with its own culture and publications; it is perhaps unfortunate that the virtuosity of many bandsmen was not transferable to the orchestral world, just as many talented choral singers were limited by their discomfort with staff notation.

Developments in church music relied on native British talent. The Anglican tradition, moribund but still formally existent in the early years of Victoria's reign, later showed signs of revival, both in a renewed seriousness concerning standards of performance and in the new music provided by such cathedral musicians as S. S. Wesley, John Stainer and John Goss. At cathedral and parish level the mid-century reforming zeal of Thomas Helmore and his 'High' Anglican associates contributed to the raising of standards in choral services. The influence of the nonconformists was felt outside their churches as well as within: they formed the dedicated core of many choral societies, regarding the oratorio tradition as an acceptable artistic outlet for a temperate society.

The prevailing social and religious forces within the middle classes seem to have encouraged music-making in the home, which played an important part in Victorian life. In 1850 the piano was still something of a luxury item, but by 1871 it was estimated that there were 400,000 in Britain and a million pianists. The next twenty years saw the real boom in piano sales: good-quality German pianos invaded the upper end of the market; but far greater expansion was at the lower end, as cheaper instruments and the 'three-year' hire-purchase system

54. Domestic music-making; engraving (1890s)

brought a piano within the means of those with modest incomes. Pianos and music were sold in cities and large towns. Music publishers produced a flood of simplified classics and 'effective' piano pieces so that the daughter of the household could make a decent showing on the instrument; and the piano was the essential accompanying instrument for the sentimental ballads and comic songs that achieved unprecedented sales in the last quarter of the century. A popular ballad like *The Holy City* was selling 50,000 copies a year by the 1890s; Sullivan's *The Lost Chord* sold 500,000 between 1877 and 1902. These figures reflect musical needs that are now difficult to recapture in the age of electricity: voice, violin, piano and harmonium were ready to hand when the family was assembled. It would have been rare for anyone in the provinces to have heard orchestral performances of all Beethoven's symphonies in a lifetime, hence the arrangements of orchestral music that appeared in the programmes of brass bands or organists, or played by the ingenious mechanical instruments that preceded the invention of the gramophone.

Although provincial musical theatre existed and London companies undertook provincial tours, the greatest range of theatrical enterprise was inevitably in the capital. The most constant and secure institutions were at the highest and lowest levels, the 'Italian' opera and the popular theatre. In 1846 Covent Garden Theatre became a permanent opera house, the home of the 'Royal Italian Opera'. Conducted initially by Costa and attracting singers of the calibre of

Grisi and Patti, England's leading opera house flourished throughout the period under discussion, surviving destruction by fire in 1856 (it was quickly rebuilt) and a financial setback in the mid-1880s. In 1892 Wagner's complete *Ring* was given, conducted by Mahler, and later also under Mottl and Richter. The Carl Rosa Opera Company, founded in Manchester in 1873, moved to London in 1875, giving performances in English: it had considerable success in the first few years but thereafter suffered as Covent Garden's fortunes revived. There was still an insufficient economic base for more than one grand opera company in London, as Handel had discovered a century and a half before.

There was considerable growth during the second half of the nineteenth century in popular theatre with an incidental musical element. The development of music halls is symbolized by the change from public-house-type table seating to full theatrical interiors in these buildings. Music-hall programmes interspersed humorous or sentimental sketches with ballads, community songs or instrumental solos. By an Act of Parliament of 1843, music halls were not allowed to perform 'dramatic representations', but the dividing line between music-hall entertainments and 'theatre' was in practice non-existent. The accompaniment of the melodramas and dramatic sketches that were the staple fare of popular theatres and music halls usually required the employment of at least a small musical ensemble.

The most exciting creative developments in the theatre, however, were somewhere between the extremes just described, in the success-ful establishment of Richard D'Oyly Carte's operetta enterprises. The famous collaboration of W. S. Gilbert and Arthur Sullivan brought together elements that had already enjoyed some success with London audiences: burlesque theatre and French operetta, the latter hitherto represented mainly by the works of Jacques Offenbach. Between *HMS Pinafore* (1878) and *The Gondoliers* (1889) Gilbert and Sullivan produced masterpieces nearly every year in their characteristic genre, and Carte built the Savoy Theatre to accommodate them. Such success did not attend Carte's other operatic venture, the Royal English Opera House. The Covent Garden audience was apparently not transferable to a 'serious' original English opera: Sullivan's *Ivanhoe*, intended as the initiating showpiece in 1891, failed to make its mark and Carte quickly sold his theatre to become a home for music hall. Here, history seems to have repeated itself, for twenty years earlier Sullivan had been a conductor of a shortlived Royal National Opera at St James's Theatre, which had similarly failed to dent London's musical consciousness with Michael Balfe's *The Rose of Castile*. It is perhaps ironic that, while the 'Savoy' operas may be seen in terms of an English development of French models of operetta, the parodies of musical styles and operatic situations within them refer largely to

55. *Title-page of P. Bucalossi's waltz arranged from airs from 'The Gondoliers' by Gilbert and Sullivan, published by Chappell & Co. (c1890)*

Italian opera: opera audiences in London would rather see parodies of their favourite style than a new attempt at English grand opera. One of Sullivan's first professional musical posts in London had been as organist to the Royal Italian Opera under Costa.

CULTURE AND EDUCATION

There were distinct changes in the acceptance and status of 'serious' music-making in England during the second half of the nineteenth century, but the causes and even the mechanisms of change are difficult to identify. In the 1850s the attitudes of Prince Albert and George Grove reflect a crusading spirit: they consciously attempted to educate an 'unmusical' public into better ways. To a large extent their ambitions were fulfilled in the long term, because the direction of their leadership was matched by various accommodating forces with Victorian society. The economic aspect, though important, cannot have been decisive: while real incomes rose during the period, generating considerable wealth, the direction of that wealth towards musical ends was the result of choices governed by many other complex factors. Except in choral singing, there was no sudden spectacular numerical 'success': it was a matter of steady growth in many areas. While London's population doubled in the half-century from 1848, newspaper advertisements indicate that the provision of concerts increased five-fold.[17]

Changed attitudes towards the acceptance of a place for music in Victorian life and towards the status of British musicians within society accompanied this growth. Elementary education, initially through singing-classes and then through the effects of the 1870 Education Act, played its part in attracting more people to music, and an increasing number seemed ready to pursue musical interests further. George Grove's first *Dictionary of Music and Musicians* appeared in four volumes between 1879 and 1890; it was a dual monument to the availability of competent musical scholarship in Britain and to the number of 'intelligent enquirers' at whom the dictionary was aimed. (Its size and consequent cost put it beyond the range of many of the 'enquirers', but the growth in 'public' libraries and reading rooms counterbalanced this.) Scholarly organizations were not new in the 1870s but, in contrast to their predecessors, they attained some degree of permanence. A London-based Handel Society had published sixteen volumes of that composer's work between 1843 and 1858, but then faded away; more enduring was the Purcell Society, which began publishing a complete edition of Purcell's music in 1876.[18]

The Musical Institute of London, whose aims included 'the culti-vation of the art and science of music, the holding of conversazioni for the reading of papers on musical subjects and the publication of transactions', attracted 200 members but only survived for two years after its foundation in 1851; another similar organization, the Musical Society of London, lasted from 1858 to 1867. By contrast, the 'Musical Association for the Investigation and Discussion of subjects connected with the Art and Science of Music' passed the test of survival: it was founded in the 1870s by John Stainer, organist of St Paul's Cathedral, and by William Pole, a civil engineer, and flourishes today as the Royal Musical Association.

The development of facilities for professional musical training was both a symptom and an agent of change. With it came the gradual recognition of an established British musical profession. The image of a professional musician in 1850 (except in church music) would almost certainly have been that of a foreigner, though a few British musicians (for example the pianist and composer Sterndale Bennett) had achieved recognition both in Britain and Europe. The Royal Academy of Music, founded in 1822, had by 1848 made only a tentative contribution towards establishing a music profession; in the rare event of a young person wishing to follow a musical career, the best advice would still have been to study abroad. Sullivan's early career was typical: in 1856 he won the first Mendelssohn Scholarship, enabling him (after an initial year at the Royal Academy of Music) to study in Leipzig in the company of the young Edvard Grieg and Katharina Bach, a distant relation of Johann Sebastian. Sullivan, however, was of the last generation that needed to find its principal musical education abroad, though a brief continental spell remained desirable for some time. The foundation (and survival) rate of musical training and examining institutions, mainly based in London, in mid-Victorian Britain was remarkable: they include the Royal Military School, Kneller Hall (1856), the London Academy of Music (1861), the Royal College of Organists (1864), the National College of Music (1864), the London Organ School (1865) and the College of Church Music (1872) (later renamed Trinity College of Music).

The developments leading to the foundation of the Royal College of Music merit separate attention. It had been part of the vision of Prince Albert's circle that the area around the original Great Exhibition site in South Kensington, purchased with the profits from the Exhibition and the sale of the building, should become the site of training centres for the nation's scientific and cultural expertise. In 1854 the Prince Consort had expressed interest in the foundation of a new music college in London and the idea was strongly supported by the Society of Arts, which set up an independent committee in 1865 to inquire into the state of musical education at home and abroad. Protracted negotiations with the Royal Academy of Music began, one of the options under consideration being the transference of a revivified academy to the South Kensington site. By the early 1870s these negotiations had broken down and Henry Cole went ahead to promote a 'Scheme of Musical Scholarship' to raise funds for a new institution. The Duke of Edinburgh joined the music committee of the Society of Arts, a Kensington builder donated the £20,000 required for a building[19] and the 'National Training School for Music', with Sullivan as principal, opened in 1876.[20] The Training School's scholarships were only endowed for five years, but that gave time for the organization of a more ambitious permanent institution. The Prince of Wales laid a draft charter for the Royal College of Music before the Privy Council in June 1879. In 1881 George Grove joined the committee whose task was to see the college into tangible existence, and took an active role in the work. The college was conceived as a national focus for advanced musical training, and for the next two years Grove's attentions were divided between work on his musical dictionary and nationwide tours to persuade the provinces to support the college with donations now and students later. On one occasion the cause of the college was promoted in Manchester in the presence of the Duke of Albany, the Duke of Edinburgh and Prince Christian; in Liverpool the Duke of Edinburgh conducted his *Galatea* waltz in a fund-raising programme.

The college, with Grove as its first principal, opened in 1883, and in 1890 moved into a larger building at South Kensington provided by a substantial donation from the Yorkshire industrialist Samson Fox. The college's aspirations and the nature of its student population are apparent from this report of the opening ceremony in 1883:

> At the conclusion of the ceremony the Royal party visited in turn all the class-rooms in the building, where the students and pupils were already in their places, with the professors of the various depart-ments of instruction. So that the mechanism of the new conserva-torium was set to work at once, and has already been busy for at least three weeks in a mission of a more than usually comprehensive nature; designed ultimately to collect and promote the latent musical talent not only of London and the home counties, and of the United Kingdom, but of India and the colonies and even of the United States and all English-speaking countries and nations. With these more than national and even more than Imperial objects the College commences with a subscribed fund amounting to £110,000; by the aid of which, and as a bold but wise beginning, fifty scholarships have been established. Of these, thirty-five confer a free education in music, and fifteen provide not only a free education, but also a maintenance for the scholars. Half the scholarships are held by boys and half by girls. 'London, with its vast population', said the Prince of Wales in his inaugural speech, 'sends only twelve out of the fifty. The remaining thirty-eight come as follows: twenty-eight from fourteen different counties in England, two from Scotland, six from Ireland, one from Wales and one from Jersey.' The scholars were selected from 1,588 candidates examined by local boards. Subsequently 480 were sent up for a final examination conducted by the various professors at the College in Kensington. The result was the unanimous election of seventeen scholars for the pianoforte, thirteen for singing, eight for the violin, six for composition, two for

the violoncello, one for the organ, one for the clarinet, one for the flute and one for the harp. In addition to the fifty scholars, forty-two persons have entered their names as paying students in the College.[21]

Yet the editor of the *Musical Times* still perceived a 'national intellectual bias' opposed to music:

There is no object in pandering to our national failing – hypocrisy – and slurring over the fact that the £110,000 subscribed, equal to a twelve-thousandth part of the national income, or to about one-third of a farthing per head of the population, is by no means munificent or encouraging. The subscription is the result of fourteen months' whipping of the country, since the bishops, ministers, clergy of all denominations, the nobles and municipal dignitaries of the kingdom assembled in the banqueting room of St. James's Palace, and swore fealty to the designs of the Prince of Wales and his Royal brothers in regard to the establishment of a College of Music. Boxes for voluntary contributions in the streets and lanes would have produced more. There are, of course, abundant reasons for this apparent niggardliness. Some of these reasons are political, some religious, and others are only moral and even musical. But the main reason is that whilst the heart of the country is true to the project and to the Prince, the national intellectual bias is opposed to what it is pleased to consider non-essentials. We are all honourable men and lovers of music; but, to the ordinary educated Englishman, music is an abstraction until united with some essential, such as sectarian opinion, or utilised for charitable purposes, or made incarnate in a brass band ministering to the works of the flesh and of fashion.

This complaint is perhaps a reflection of the higher expectations in 1883, when provision and standards for professional education in music were much higher than they had been in 1848. And the Royal College proved to be neither a national monopolist in music education nor the last of the important foundations. In London the Guildhall School of Music was founded in 1880, and it was not long before provincial centres set up their own conservatories, the most important being at Birmingham (1886), Glasgow (1890) and Manchester (1893). Suburban centres developed their own music schools: the London area saw the foundation of the Watford School of Music (1880), the Croydon Conservatoire (1883) and the Blackheath Conservatoire (1883). During the last twenty years of the century the proliferation of music schools, varying in size, quality and teaching level, fulfilled a demand among interested amateurs as well as would-be professional musicians and thereby encouraged an expansion of amateur music-making. The larger colleges produced teachers whose influence spread back to the suburban or provincial areas where they secured posts or practices. The examinations of the Associated Board of the Royal Schools of Music, begun in 1880, quickly reflected the burgeoning of instrumental tuition. It seems likely that amateur orchestras experienced a major growth around the turn of the century as the effects of new educational opportunities dispersed throughout the country (in much the same way that choral societies had mushroomed a generation after the establishment of the first singing classes).

It is against this background that we can put into perspective the appearance of significant British composers. Again Sullivan is an interesting transitional figure. Trained in the old Kapellmeister tradition as a performer-composer, he returned from his continental training to find openings that would not have been available to a British composer of the previous generation: several established and regular concert series in London (for both chamber and orchestral music) and provincial festivals that performed and commissioned new works. Later Sullivan found a rich response from a new educated audience for English operetta, ('rich' in both senses: the partnership earned Gilbert and Sullivan £90,000 between 1879 and 1890). The next generation of composers could take these opportunities for granted and could benefit from structured technical training in Britain.

The foundation staff of the Royal College of Music included 'for counterpoint and composition, Dr. Bridge, Mr. Villiers Stanford and Dr. Hubert Parry'. Henceforth composition was a 'subject' fit for systematic study. It is perhaps only slightly unjust to suggest that such study is apparent in the generally fluent and workmanlike music of Parry, Stanford and Mackenzie. Their choral and orchestral pieces, operas, songs and chamber music have proved worthy of revival though few survive the test of repeated hearings; many display technical prowess that their musical inspiration cannot match. There are few more tantalizing musical passages than the beginning of Parry's *Blest Pair of Sirens* (1887): the grand Wagnerian opening is extraordinary in its sweep and forward movement and its promise is continued by the first choral paragraph, but inspiration gives out – unfortunately coinciding with the words 'And to our high-raised phantasy present that undisturbed song'.

To be able to describe the opening as 'Wagnerian' is itself significant, not only in relating Parry to the dominant musical influences of his age but also in reflecting an easy and positive relationship between British composers and European stimuli. It was not so later: the generation that matured after 1914 developed an obsession, in part creative and in part stultifying, with 'Englishness', the backwash of an uncertain empire. Nevertheless a vein of English musical selfconsciousness in the previous period led to some valuable rescue archaeology for English folksong just before the advent of modern media threatened old aural cultures. The antiquarian cast

56. *Title-page of the score of Elgar's overture 'Cockaigne' op.40, published by Boosey & Company (1901)*

of folksong studies is reflected in the title of William Chappell's *Popular Music of Olden Time* (published 1855–9); 1898 saw the foundation of the English Folk Song Society.

It is convenient, and not entirely accidental, that the period under review comes to a climax with the music of Edward Elgar. Elgar did not receive the formal training in composition provided by the new conservatories, but his career followed a path that had been laid by the expansion of musical activity and the changing attitude to English music and musicians during the preceding half-century. Brought up in a provincial musical environment, thanks to the local demand that supported his father's piano-tuning practice and music shop in Worcester, Elgar initially wanted to follow a career as a violin soloist. When this failed there were other outlets to sustain him while he dreamt of better things: these outlets included teaching and playing the violin (including participation in the orchestra for the Three Choirs Festival), conducting the local Worcester orchestra and glee club, and appointments as an asylum band-master and church organist. Elgar's output includes many pieces in the typical lighter Victorian genres – songs, partsongs and character-pieces such as *Chanson de matin*. As a 'serious' composer he was a late developer; he was 42 when the 'Enigma' Variations were first performed in 1899. But recognition came swiftly and he received his knighthood only five years later. Like Sullivan he rose from relatively modest origins to dine with kings and princes, yet Elgar retained vestiges of an earlier Victorian attitude in feeling that his wife, by throwing in her lot with a mere musician, had married 'beneath herself'.

In two productive decades after the 'Enigma' Variations Elgar showed himself, like Purcell two centuries before, to be 'an Englishman equal with the best abroad', in a series of works displaying originality, invention and a mastery of orchestration. *The Dream of Gerontius*, *The Apostles* and *The Kingdom* are worthy contributions to the oratorio tradition and the two symphonies and two concertos made significant contributions to the orchestral repertory. Like that of Parry, Elgar's music stands in a positive relation to European musical traditions; his individuality does not disguise his indebtedness to significant forebears, in particular Schumann. But, unlike Parry, Elgar was a 'second-generation composer' and by 1899 the cultural soil in Britain was sufficiently deep to allow his potential talents to be realized. It appears, indeed, that in Victorian Britain the construction of the institutional base for audiences and for a native music profession was necessary before a major composer could flourish.

NOTES

[1] See the footnote to 'Popular Concerts' in *Grove 5*.

[2] The prince's musical talents included organ playing, singing and composition; his compositions included hymn-tunes and anthems.

[3] Alfred Ernest (1843–1900), married to the daughter of Tsar Alexander II of Russia.

[4] Their visits included tours to provincial cities, but it was the London audiences that provided the principal financial security.

[5] For a more comprehensive list, see *The Romantic Age, 1800–1914*, ed. N. Temperley, Athlone History of Music in Britain, v (London, 1981), 5.

⁶ For a typical Jullien programme, given in Bradford in 1848, see E. D. Mackerness, *A Social History of English Music* (London, 1966), 182.

⁷ The subject of the fugue in G minor (BWV 542), introduced in the woodwind to accompany the lines: The music-hall singer attends a series/ Of masses and fugues and 'ops'/ By Bach, interwoven/ With Spohr and Beethoven/ At classical Monday Pops.

⁸ *Musical World* (17 June 1854); quoted in P. M. Young, *George Grove, 1820–1900* (London, 1980), 63.

⁹ *The Hornet* (28 Feb 1877).

¹⁰ R. Nettel, *The Orchestra in England: a Social History* (London, 1946, 3/1956), 211–12.

¹¹ Quoted in J. N. Moore, *Elgar on Record* (London, 1974), 78; by 'my symphony' Elgar meant 'the symphony that I wanted to hear', not one of his own composition.

¹² The Sacred Harmonic Society was a London choral society that had grown quickly since its foundation in 1832: by 1854, when it took part in the reopening of the Crystal Palace, the ubiquitous Costa had been appointed conductor and about 700 performers took part in the regular concerts.

¹³ The first full-time professional municipal orchestra was the Bournemouth Symphony Orchestra, founded in the 1890s; direct municipal support was less forthcoming for the Hallé Orchestra which relied principally on subscription concert series in the cities and large towns of northern England.

¹⁴ In addition to the major choral and orchestral events, festival schedules usually included concerts by vocal and instrumental soloists and chamber ensembles, normally using some of the individual talent imported for the larger performances.

¹⁵ For a detailed treatment of this subject, see R. Nettel, *Music in the Five Towns, 1840–1914* (Oxford, 1944). Hanley was the largest of the 'five towns' and Staffordshire was one of the six most industrialized counties in Britain; the opening in 1888 of the Victoria Hall in Hanley, seating 3000, was significant to the development of Heap's choir.

¹⁶ See Mackerness, *A Social History*, 150–51.

¹⁷ See A. Jacobs, *Arthur Sullivan: a Victorian Musician* (Oxford, 1984), 3.

¹⁸ The task approached completion a century later.

¹⁹ This building housed the Royal College of Organists until 1990.

²⁰ Even then it was still believed that the academy might eventually agree to merge with the training school, but negotiations were finally abandoned in 1878.

²¹ *MT*, xxiv (1883), 309–10.

BIBLIOGRAPHICAL NOTE

General background

Basic modern narrative histories are G. Best's *Mid-Victorian Britain, 1851–1875* (London, 1979), D. E. D. Beales's *From Castlereagh to Gladstone* (London, 1980) and H. Pelling's *Modern Britain* (London, 1980). The two relevant volumes of the Oxford History of England, E. L. Woodward, *The Age of Reform, 1815–70* (Oxford, 2/1960), and R. C. K. Ensor, *England, 1870–1914* (Oxford, 1936), are more detailed but nevertheless heavily weighted towards political history. Studies of economic history include R. S. Sayers's *A History of Economic Change in England, 1880–1939* (Oxford, 1967), W. Ashworth's *An Economic History of England, 1870–1939* (London, 1960) and W. H. B. Court's *British Economic History, 1870–1914* (Cambridge, 1965); recent 'social' histories include F. Bédarida's *A Social History of England, 1851–1975* (London, 1979) and A. Briggs's *Social History of England* (London, 1983). Music and musical culture receive only superficial treatment in the general histories.

The musical world

The need for a rounded and wide-ranging treatment of music during the period has been filled by *The Romantic Age, 1800–1914*, ed. N. Temperley, Athlone History of Music in Britain, v (London, 1981). In addition to covering a broad field of music-making in a series of essays of high quality, this volume provides a wealth of bibliographical references. Though largely superseded by this volume, the relevant sections of two older books, E. Walker, rev. J. Westrup, *A History of Music in England* (Oxford, 1952), and P. M. Young, *A History of British Music* (London, 1967), contain interesting insights; the same is true of the specialist study by F. Howes, *The English Musical Renaissance* (London, 1966). Similarly, useful attention can still be given to the relevant section of E. D. Mackerness, *A Social History of English Music* (London, 1966). Music as a 'popular' cultural activity is the subject of a careful survey in D. Russell, *Popular Music in England, 1880–1914* (Manchester, 1984): this book gives impressive coverage of such areas as musical education, brass bands, choral societies and the extent to which music (of various sorts) penetrated 'the masses', supported by good statistical and analytical material. R. Pearsall's *Victorian Popular Music* (Newton Abbot, 1973), more anecdotal in approach, remains a valuable complement to Russell's book.

On specific topics first recourse can be taken to individual articles in *Grove 6*; in addition to biographical entries, those dealing with music in leading cities and such general topics as tonic sol-fa education contain a wealth of useful and well-balanced information. Nor should earlier editions of *Grove* be ignored: apart from the contemporary perspective of some of the writing, their articles devoted relatively more space to the music and musical activities of their own or immediately preceding periods.

Any references to contemporary critical literature must be idiosyncratic, but a couple of writers cannot be ignored: the Rev. H. R. Haweis, whose *Music and Morals* ran through seemingly endless editions from 1871; and the lively musical criticism of the young George Bernard Shaw as a newspaper correspondent in London from 1876. His work has been collected in *The Complete Musical Criticism of Bernard Shaw*, ed. D. H. Laurence (London, 1989). For the interaction of industrial, commercial and social factors, two musical case studies are of particular interest: C. Ehrlich's *The Piano: a History* (Oxford, 2/1990) and M. Hurd's *Vincent Novello and Company* (London, 1981), the latter supplemented by the anonymous *A Century and a Half in Soho* (London, 1961). W. Pole's *Musical Instruments in the Great Exhibition of 1851* (London, 1851) is an interesting starting-point for the technological background to instrumental music. For the development of the musical profession, and for many insights into the social context, C. Ehrlich's *The Music Profession in Britain since the Eighteenth Century* (Oxford, 1985) is invaluable.

For provincial music-making, in addition to the articles on individual cities in *Grove 6*, two substantial local studies are R. Nettel's *Music in the Five Towns, 1840–1914* (Oxford, 1944) and Watkins Shaw's *The Three Choirs Festival* (Worcester and London, 1954), the latter summarizing and analysing much of the detailed narrative to be found in D. Lysons, J. Amott, C. L. Williams and H. G. Chance, *Origin and Progress of the Meeting of the Three Choirs of Gloucester, Worcester and Hereford* (Gloucester, 1895). The musical progress of women in a period when the musical profession was largely male-dominated is charted in D. Hyde, *New-Found Voices* (Liskeard, 1984), and the less exalted (though often attractive) musical cultures are the subject of R. Pearsall's *Victorian Popular Music* (London, 1973). Of relevance to the whole country is the appropriate section of N. Temperley's *The Music of the English Parish Church* (Cambridge, 1979).

Individual musicians

The leading creative musicians of the period are well served by two recent biographies, A. Jacobs, *Arthur Sullivan: a Victorian Musician* (Oxford, 1984) (which includes an extensive bibliography) and J. N. Moore, *Elgar: a Creative Life* (Oxford, 1984), the latter perhaps best taken in conjunction with the same author's *Elgar: a Life in Photographs* (London, 1972). They largely, but not completely, supersede biographies of Sullivan by P. M. Young (London, 1971, rev. 2/1973) and of Elgar by P. M. Young (London, 1955), M. Kennedy (London, 1982) and D. McVeagh (London, 1955). Other single-composer biographies are C. L. Graves, *Hubert Parry*, 2 vols. (London, 1926), J. F. Porte, *Sir Charles Villiers Stanford* (London, 1921), and M. Hurd, *Immortal Hour: the Life and Period of Rutland Boughton* (London, 1962).

There are no comparable biographical studies of Sterndale Bennett, Macfarren, Mackenzie or Costa, though Mackenzie's autobiographical reminiscences were published (London, 1927), as were those of Macfarren's brother Walter, who was himself a musician (London, 1905). However, two other important figures in the musical life of the period are well served. Although there is no modern biography of Hallé as such, *The Autobiography of Charles Hallé, with Correspondence and Diaries*, ed. M. Kennedy (London, 1972), supplements C. E. and M. Hallé, *Life and Letters of Sir Charles Hallé* (London, 1896). The leading musical 'enabler' is magnificently portrayed in P. M. Young, *George Grove, 1820–1900* (London, 1980).

Chapter XI

The USA: Classical, Industrial and Invisible Music

CHARLES HAMM

The events of 1848 and immediately afterwards which were to change the course of European life had little immediate impact on the USA. Largely isolated from the rest of the world, and as yet playing virtually no role in Europe's political and cultural affairs, America was absorbed by internal matters: geographical expansion, mostly westwards; the evolution of a political system grounded in European models yet inexorably taking on a character of its own; growing regional friction between the agrarian south and the more urban and industrial north; the confrontation of moral issues inherent in the institution of slavery and the slow development of a capitalist mode of production. Though most Americans were of European descent, and European immigration continued and accelerated in the middle decades of the nineteenth century, the most important measure of American life and culture at this critical moment in the nation's history must lie in the growing departure from European patterns, not in retention of older ways.

*

On the evening of 6 February 1843, at the Bowery Amphitheatre, New York, a 'novel, grotesque, original and surpassingly melodious ethiopian band' billed as the Virginia Minstrels offered a 'Negro Concert' as part of a circus evening. According to advertisements for the event, the troupe performed 'songs, refrains, and ditties as sung by the southern slaves at all their merry meetings such as the gathering in of the cotton and sugar crops, corn huskings, slave weddings and junketings', accompanying their singing and dancing with banjo, fiddle, tambourine and 'bone castanetts'. But the four participants – William M. Whitlock, Frank Brower, Dick Pelham, Dan Emmett – were not black slaves, or even ex-slaves: they were white professional entertainers, who had lived and worked chiefly in the northern, slave-free states of the Union, performing with blackened faces. After successful performances in New York and Boston, the Virginia Minstrels sailed for England on 21 April, performing at Liverpool, Manchester and then London, where a journalist explained that their repertory consisted of 'some of the aboriginal airs of the interior of Africa, modernized if not humanized in the slave states of the Union, and adapted to ears polite'.[1] The troupe disbanded on 14 July, with two of the performers returning to the USA and the other two performing with local musicians in England, Ireland and Scotland, helping to establish a taste for 'negro minstrelsy' on both sides of the Atlantic.

The Virginia Minstrels were not the first to impersonate blacks on the musical stage, either in the United States or the British Isles. From the late 1820s, George Washington Dixon, George Nichols, J. W. Sweeney, Bob Farrell and particularly Thomas Dartmouth Rice had entertained theatre audiences in America with comic portrayals of southern plantation slaves, and also free blacks with a propensity for outlandish clothing and language. Rice, in 1836, took his one-character 'Ethiopian opera' to England; his song *Jim Crow* became 'the first great international song hit of American popular music'.[2] The success of the Virginia Minstrels brought emulation by the Christy Minstrels (though E. P. Christy claimed that his company had performed such entertainments as early as 1842), the Ethiopian Serenaders, White's Minstrels, Buckley's New Orleans Serenaders and countless other troupes. Within a decade the minstrel show became the most popular genre of musical theatre in the USA, a popularity that was to continue throughout the nineteenth century and well into the twentieth. Originally an entr'acte in a circus or part of an evening of mixed theatre, it soon developed into a full evening's entertainment with a large cast, distinctive music and a stylized structure of its own. To understand why such a genre came into being, and what role it played in shaping American culture, one must first examine the structure of American life in the second quarter of the century.

*

It has been said that the American Revolution was not a true revolution, merely a change in government. The political, religious, educational, social and legal institutions of the new nation were founded on English models and at first firmly controlled by men of British descent. The Declaration of Independence, the Constitution and the Bill of Rights laid the theoretical and legal basis for what in time was to become a distinctively American form of democracy, but in practice the USA began its history as a form of government, and a society, little different from the one from which it had fought to free

57.(a) *'Music of the Original Christy Minstrels': cover of a collection of songs published by Oliver Ditson (Boston, c1848)*

(b) *Poster (by Strobridge, 1894) for Primrose & West's Big Minstrel Festival*

itself. Public office could be held only by landed white males, who were also the only people to hold the franchise; Amerindians were excluded from participation in social and political processes, slavery was legal and women and ethnic minorities had virtually no opportunity to be involved in the governing of nation, state or even community.

But by the presidential election of 1828, most white males had the franchise, whether or not they owned property, and more than twice as many people voted than ever before. A large proportion of the new voters favoured Andrew Jackson, a 'land speculator, merchant, slave trader, and the most aggressive enemy of the Indians in early American history',[3] who had won popular fame by defeating the British in the Battle of New Orleans and then subduing the Creek and Seminole Indians in the southern states. He became the first American president from a background other than southern aristocracy or old New England family.

It was no coincidence that the minstrel show emerged during the era of 'Jacksonian democracy'. The first mass political party in America's history was built round a leader who, like most of his supporters, had little formal education. The modern mass press and mass transportation originated in this era and the minstrel show represented the beginning of mass entertainment in the USA. Even more to the point, the ideology of the minstrel show reinforced that of Jacksonian democracy:

> For the Jacksonian party the three basic principles of its period of ascendancy were: expansion (nationalism), antimonopoly (egalitarianism) and white supremacy ... Before the Civil War, the Democratic Party was dominant nationally, having controlled the Federal government without major interruption since the first election of Jackson in 1828. Continuance of such control depended upon unity among the party's regional branches. But the price of unity, as set by Southern Democrats, was that the national party must defend the institution of slavery ... Minstrelsy's political stance was a defense of slavery ... [It] faithfully reproduced the white slaveowners' viewpoint, because its main content stemmed from the myth of the benign plantation.[4]

On the minstrel stage, putative slaves sang of enjoying their work in the fields, of dancing and singing at night and on Sunday, of being devoted to kindly masters: 'Gib me de place called Dixie Land, wid hoe and shubble in my hand; Whar fiddles ring and banjos play, I'de dance all night and work all day' (Dan Emmett, 1860).

The tunes of minstrel songs and dances were mostly appropriated from, or modelled on, Anglo-Celtic music preserved in the New World by descendants of non-literate immigrants from the British Isles.[5] The characteristic instruments of the minstrel stage were the banjo and the bones, both of African origin, and the fiddle, the European violin played in the style used to accompany popular dancing among both whites and blacks. Thus what was taken at the time to be a new popular style was actually pieced together from elements of white and black oral musical cultures, a pattern that was to repeat itself in American music many times in the nineteenth and twentieth centuries. Just as the political ideology of Jacksonian democracy spread to urban and middle-class America, undergoing modification and refinement in the process, so the minstrel show and its music began to appeal to an ever-widening range of Americans. Stephen Foster did not publish his first minstrel songs under his own name since this sort of music was originally identified with a social status lower than his own. But in 1852 he decided to 'reinstate [his] name on [his] songs and to pursue the Ethiopian business without fear or shame', since these songs had 'done a great deal to build up a taste for the Ethiopian songs among refined people by making the words suitable to their taste, instead of the trashy and really offensive words which belong to some songs of that order'.[6]

Foster's 'plantation songs', as his later minstrel songs were called, had indeed changed the style of music of the minstrel stage. In place of pentatonic tunes involving Anglo-Celtic idioms, he wrote melodies in the style of his more 'refined' parlour songs. Written in verse-chorus form, with four-part vocal harmony in the chorus, these songs suited both the minstrel stage, with the entire company joining in the chorus, and the genteel home circle, with family and friends singing to the accompaniment of piano or guitar. And Foster's texts were indeed less 'trashy and offensive' than those of earlier minstrel songs, including his own. Blacks were now portrayed as experiencing the universal human emotions of love, the loneliness of old age, sorrow at the death of loved ones:

> When I saw Nelly in de morning,
>   Smile till she open'd up her eyes,
> Seem'd like de light ob day a dawning,
>   Jist 'fore de sun begin to rise.

> Now I'm unhappy and I'm weeping,
>   Can't tote de cotton-wood no more,
> Last night while Nelly was a sleeping,
>   Death came a knockin' at de door.[7]

But they were still slaves; they still loved their masters; they still longed for plantation life if they were separated from it. The pro-slavery ideology of the minstrel show was merely refined by Foster and his emulators to speak to more 'cultured' levels of the American population.

There was popular music in the 1840s and 50s other than minstrel songs. Some looked to America's British past, to the tradition of Thomas Moore's *Irish Melodies* and the simpler songs of Henry Bishop, Henry Russell and their peers. Stephen Foster, John Hill Hewitt and a host of other American songwriters turned out their own 'parlour' songs – genteel in sentiment and technically suitable for home performance by musically literate amateurs, many of them women from the privileged classes. Other popular songs, including those of the Hutchinsons, a touring family group from New Hampshire, opposed the Jacksonian ideology. Though their early repertory had consisted mostly of sentimental and melodramatic pieces, they made their greatest impact with songs addressing the issues of temperance, universal suffrage, the threatened genocide of the American Indian, child labour and, above all, abolition. In the words of one of their members, they were 'more social reformers than musicians', and William Lloyd Garrison praised them for making music 'directly and purposely subservient to the freedom, welfare, happiness, and moral elevation of the people'. Travelling to Britain in 1845, they sang chiefly to working-class audiences in provincial towns and at labour meetings and formed a friendship with Charles Dickens.

But whatever its political agenda, America's new popular music, disseminated to a rapidly growing number of people through the medium of printed sheet music and text-only songsters, was seen to be in harmony with the involvement of an ever-wider range of Americans in the affairs of their country. As the classically trained musician George F. Root put it:

> I should be wasting my time in trying to supply the wants of a few people, who are already abundantly supplied by the best writers of Europe . . . I saw that mine must be the 'people's song', still, I am ashamed to say, I shared the feeling that was around me in regard to that grade of music. But when Stephen C. Foster's wonderful melodies (as I now see them) began to appear, and the famous Christy's Minstrels began to make them known, I 'took a hand in' and wrote a few . . . It is easy to write *correctly* a simple song, but so to use the material of which such a song must be made that it will be received and live in the hearts of the people is quite another matter.[8]

Other forms of American music at mid-century reflected the trend towards greater democratization. A rapid increase in musical literacy was at the heart of much of this new activity. Earlier, the skill of reading music could be learnt only through private instruction, affordable chiefly by the privileged classes through attendance at singing schools and private academies. But in the 1840s the growing network of public grammar schools began including instruction in music in the curriculum, through the efforts of Lowell Mason,

Thomas Hastings, George Root, William Bradbury and others. By the middle of the century schools in Boston, Buffalo, Pittsburgh, New Orleans, Louisville and many other cities and towns were teaching basic musical literacy and elementary performing skills. Pupils learnt to sing simple choral music – arrangements of popular and light classical pieces and new compositions written for this purpose. They performed in class for their own pleasure and for other students and families. Some schools were able to mount productions of entire cantatas and children's operettas, such as George F. Root's *The Flower Queen, or The Coronation of the Rose* (1851) and *The Haymakers* (1857).[9]

The impact of proliferating musical literacy extended beyond schools themselves. The size, number and musical sophistication of church choirs constantly increased as a result of the growing number of competent singers, as did the repertory of sacred pieces written by American composers. Home performance of songs and instrumental pieces, a pastime formerly restricted to the most privileged classes, spread to the parlours of the increasingly complex network of America's middle classes.

There were also village bands, which had existed in New England since the early nineteenth century. Drawing their membership from the community, performing military, dance and concert music for civic and social occasions, they had spread from the Atlantic seaboard to the south and west by the 1840s and 50s. Their repertory consisted of marches (some European and some American), a variety of social dances written or arranged for concert performance, arrangements of popular songs and operatic arias, and a scattering of concert pieces written specifically for such bands. Players of modest ability and musical training could join, the repertory was accessible in style to audiences with little or no background in music, and these bands functioned socially in the context of village and town life.

*

The music discussed so far was that of America's 'democratic middle', encompassing the professional and merchant classes, skilled crafts-men and workers in both urban and rural America, German immi-grants who brought with them a tradition of amateur music-making, and various other newly literate and enfranchised individuals and groups in the country's proto-capitalist society. They were the most rapidly growing segments of the American population, and their involvement in the political and cultural life of the USA was creating a society increasingly different from that of any nation of western Europe. But there was other music in America.

Concert and operatic life in colonial and federal America had been modelled on that of England. The musical stage was dominated by the ballad and comic operas of Charles Dibdin, William Shield, Samuel Arnold and Henry Bishop and by 'Englished' versions of Italian operas: Rophino Lacy's version of Rossini's *La Cenerentola*, for instance, was the single most popular stage work in the country for several decades. Subscription and benefit concerts by visiting and immigrant European musicians, recruited from Drury Lane, Haymarket and Covent Garden, included pieces by composers most favoured in London and the provinces: Haydn, Pleyél, Sammartini, Mozart, an occasional piece by Beethoven. Concerts and operas were performed in theatres, which also offered legitimate and comic theatre and even outright amusement. An evening's programme would often combine what we would now consider art and entertainment, and the appeal of British comic opera cut across social classes. Audiences were socially segregated, though, with the privileged classes occupying the boxes and the public in the pit and gallery.

Jacksonian democracy resulted in even more social mixing in the theatre, to the displeasure of the élite. In the words of one New York matron, 'unfortunately, we of ourselves are not sufficiently numerous to support an Opera so we have been forced to admit the people'.[10] But by mid-century the élite, beginning to recapture some of its privileged status in American life, had devised the threefold strategy of 'separating opera from theater by establishing a special place for its performance', 'sharpen[ing] and objectify[ing] a code of behavior' and 'increasing[ly] insisting that only foreign-language opera could meet their standards of excellence'.[11] The first theatre built specifically for Italian opera in New York opened in 1833, followed by Palmo's Opera House in 1844, the Astor Place Opera House in 1847 and the New York Academy of Music in 1853–4. Walt Whitman described an evening at the Academy of Music in the 1850s:

> What a gay show! The lookers on – the crowds of pedestrians – the numerous private carriages dashing up to the great porch – the splendid and shiny horses – the footmen jumping down and opening the carriage doors – the beautiful and richly dresst women alighting, and passing up the steps under the full blaze of the lights. Inside, hundreds upon hundreds of gas-lights, softened with globes of ground glass, shed their brilliancy upon the scene. Seated in the red velvet arm-chairs of the parquette, and on the sofas of the dress-circle, are groups of gentlemen, and of the most superbly dressed women, some of them with that high bred air, and self-possession, obtained by mixing much with the 'best society'.[12]

William Henry Fry, the first native-born American to write grand operas, made no secret of his admiration for the Italian style and the evolving social role of opera. *Aurelia the Vestal* (1841) was cast in the mould of Spontini's *La vestale* and Bellini's *Norma*. His *Leonora*, given its première in Philadelphia in 1845, was no less Italianate and was performed in Italian as *Giulio e Leonora* when revived at the Academy of Music in New York in 1858.

Some Americans were put off by the 'aristocratic distinction' of these new opera houses and the apparent folly of attending a dramatic performance in a foreign language:

> We cannot endure to sit by and see the performers splitting their sides with laughter, and we not to take the joke; dissolving in 'briny tears', and we not permitted to sympathize with them; or running each other through the body, and we devoid of the means of condemning or justifying the act.[13]

But it was precisely this mystifying ritual of dress, behaviour and repertory which was prized by the élite as setting attendance at such events above entertainment enjoyed by the less privileged.

Concert attendance, involving the same strategies of ritualized dress and behaviour and dependence on a foreign repertory, was another form of 'ritual mystification serv[ing] the function of helping to unify the [American élite]'.[14] Pieces by Beethoven, Mendelssohn, Spohr, Schubert, Schumann and other composers of the modern German school dominated programmes of the Boston Handel and Haydn Society, the Musical Fund Society of Philadelphia, the Sacred Music Society of New York and the Philharmonic Society of New York, which gave its first concert in 1842. The performers and conductors of these organizations were mostly Germans. Many had come to America expressly in search of such employment, while others were part of the politically inspired exodus of the middle decades of the century, when German immigrants made up more than a third of all people admitted to the USA. George Bristow, one of the few American violinists in the New York Philharmonic, resented this growing German monopoly:

> [Does] the Philharmonic Society exist . . . to play exclusively the works of German masters, especially if they be dead, in order that our critics may translate their ready-made praises from German? . . . Let them pack back to Germany and enjoy the police and bayonets and aristocratic kicks and cuffs of that land, where an artist is a serf to a nobleman, as the history of all their great composers shows. America has made the political revolution which illuminates the world, while Germany is still beshrouded with a pall of feudal darkness. While America has been thus far able to do the chief things for the dignity of man, forsooth she must be denied the brains for original Art, and must stand like a beggar, deferentially cap in hand, when she comes to compete with the ability of any dirty German village.[15]

But when Bristow and other Americans set out to write classical music, they could think of nothing else but to follow German models. As a critic said of Bristow's Symphony no.2, 'its chief fault is a pretty serious one: a decided want of originality. It is full of reminiscences of other composers, Weber, Mendelssohn, Spohr, Haydn, Mozart, I know not what'.[16] The same could be said of his *Rip Van Winkle* which was equally Germanic in musical style in spite of being based on a famous piece of American literature. In time, as the large German populations of Cincinnati, St Louis, Louisville, New Orleans and Milwaukee moved into the mainstream of American urban life, German dominance of America's concert life was to prove a magnet drawing large numbers of America's urban middle classes into active involvement with classical music, as performers and audiences.

Another group of Americans for whom the mystification surrounding opera and symphony was impenetrable and uninteresting, but whose social and musical ambitions were not satisfied by the minstrel show and other popular repertories, turned to the 'music of democratic sociability'.[17] This stratum of American musical life revolved round the careers and repertory of a succession of touring European virtuosos, beginning with three violinists (Alexander Artôt, Ole Bull and Henri Vieuxtemps) and continuing with the pianists Leopold de Mayer, Henri Herz, Richard Hoffman, Charles Grobe and Maurice Strakosch. There were also instrumental groups, the Germania Musical Society from Berlin and the orchestra of Louis Antoine Jullien, and, most notably, the singer Jenny Lind. These were classically trained musicians; but as touring artists whose financial rewards depended on audience size, they emphasized an easily accessible repertory, virtuosity for its own sake and stage personality. Their programmes included variations on familiar tunes, programmatic pieces usually of their own composition, concert waltzes, polkas, galops and other dances, and an occasional movement from a classical piece. Travelling the length and breadth of the country, they offered American audiences a concert experience in a 'democratic' social environment, stripped of mystification, with their foreign origin serving as attractive and charming exoticism, not as a signal of their remoteness from American life and culture.

The American pianist Louis Moreau Gottschalk offered audiences this same mixture of showmanship and exoticism. A native of New Orleans, he studied and gave concerts successfully in France before returning to the USA in 1853 for several extended concert tours featuring his own piano compositions, ranging from the extravagantly virtuoso (*Le carnaval de Venise, grand caprice et variations*) to the sentimentally programmatic (*The Last Hope, The Dying Poet*) to pieces tinged with melodic and rhythmic references to the exotic music of New Orleans and the Caribbean (*Bamboula, Ojos criollos*).

The USA: Classical, Industrial and Invisible Music

*

Jacksonian democracy by no means extended to the entire population of the USA. Slaves were of course excluded from political and social participation in American life, as were Amerindians, many non-literate immigrants from the British Isles who had gravitated to remote and thinly populated regions, and other immigrant groups who had established ethnic enclaves in America's cities and country-side. Each group had brought its own musical tradition to the New World. In some cases these were preserved with remarkable faithful-ness; in others they mingled with musical styles from other cultures.

Amerindians, who had migrated from north-eastern Asia to the Americas tens of thousands of years before European exploration and colonization, retained Asian elements in their culture and music, though over the centuries these had developed in distinctive ways. Non-literate British immigrants brought narrative ballads, lyric songs and dance music from England, Scotland and Ireland, and this repertory gradually took on a distinctively American flavour through modification of texts, the addition of the banjo and fiddle to both instrumental and vocal forms, and the creation of new songs and dances. Black slaves, assimilating the European-based music of their masters into African performance styles, created the new genre of the 'shout' or spiritual, as well as new forms of recreational dance music combining African and European instruments. Cajuns, making their way from France to Acadia to Louisiana, and Hispanics in the south and west, in regions not yet part of the USA, developed syncretic genres unique to these areas.

Performed and preserved orally within each ethnic tradition, this music was of no more interest to the participants in Jacksonian democracy, or to America's old and new aristocracy who would eventually contest again for political power, than were the people who played and sang it. It was literally invisible, almost never recorded or disseminated in musical notation, rarely mentioned in contemporary scholarly or journalistic writing. Much of it has been irrevocably lost; but in recent decades scholars using techniques learnt from anthro-pology and oral history have reconstructed some of its history. Ironically, this 'invisible' music is considered by many contemporary scholars to be the most distinctively American music of the entire nineteenth century and to be the foundation for many important American styles of the twentieth century.

*

The first bombardment of Fort Sumter, off the coast of South Carolina, on 12 April 1861, marked the beginning of armed conflict between the USA and the thirteen southern and western states which seceded to form the Confederate States of America, a struggle lasting until the surrender of Lee's Army of Northern Virginia at Appomatox on 9 April 1865. The Civil War shaped American life and culture more than any other event of the entire century:

> For four years the nation was wracked by a seemingly endless blood letting. When the guns finally fell silent in the spring of 1865, more than 630,000 Americans had died. Americans had inflicted upon one another more casualties than had ever been sustained in a previous, or subsequent, foreign war. In the course of the struggle, a war of limited objectives had been translated into total war. The enemy was no longer armies, but entire civilian populations. When final defeat engulfed the South, its economy was in shambles; vast stretches of its territory were ruined; and its social institutions rooted in slavery had been smashed.[18]

The Civil War was truly a people's war, involving the entire population of the country, including many groups excluded from political participation in Jacksonian democracy. Though the fighting was carried out largely by white males, 200,000 blacks – freedmen and runaway slaves – served in the Union army and navy, and tens of thousands of recent immigrants from Germany and Ireland fought too, often in ethnically organized regiments. Many women were involved as nurses and other volunteer workers. Children in their early teens enlisted as drummer-boys. Black slaves in the south followed events as well as they could, and as the war neared its conclusion, more and more refused to work or attempted to escape, to join the ranks of the Union armies as they penetrated into the south. Battles were often fought in populated areas and harsh retributive tactics were carried out against the civilian population, particularly by Union armies in the deep south.

The most important short-term impact of the war on American music was to spark the creation of a large number of popular songs, which penetrated deeply into the nation's consciousness, and to give an important boost to the music-publishing industry. American songwriters wrote great rallying songs, sentimental ballads reflecting the pain and sorrow of separation and death, lively and often humorous songs of camp and field, and dramatic songs detailing heroic and tragic happenings on the battlefield. Mostly in the verse-chorus form popularized in the previous decade by Stephen Foster, these songs were disseminated both as sheet music, for the musically literate, and in songsters containing only texts, for those who could not read music. They were 'people's songs': they were sung by virtually the entire population in both north and south, by combatants while marching or round campfires in the evening and at home in the parlour; they were frequently based on familiar tunes, such as traditional Anglo-Celtic melodies (*The Girl I Left Behind Me* and *When Johnny Comes Marching Home*) or popular minstrel songs (*Dixie*); and they were accepted into oral tradition by non-literate people.

Ironically, though the war was a grim battle to the death between north and south, the two regions were nevertheless united by this common repertory 'voic[ing] the pleasure and pain, the love and longing, the despair and delight, the sorrow and resignation, and the consolation of the plain people – who felt in these an utterance for emotions which they felt but could not express'.[19] When the Chapple Publishing Company of Boston published a collection of 'heart songs, dear to the American people' in 1909, a 'Top Four Hundred' anthology of the nineteenth century, fully a quarter of the selections dated from the five-year period of the Civil War and the anthology enjoyed equal circulation in north and south.

The long-term effects of the Civil War on American music must be mapped on a much larger terrain. Though all southern states had been readmitted to the Union by 1870, differences and tensions between north and south persisted to such a degree that significant cultural interchange between the two regions did not resume until well into the twentieth century. Thus American music in the second half of the nineteenth century must be studied as two quite different histories: one centred in the north – visible, public and disseminated throughout most of the country; the other mostly southern and largely invisible.

Some historians have suggested that the Civil War was fought chiefly over slavery, but others have insisted on a much broader view:

> The clash was not over slavery as a moral institution – most northerners did not care enough about slavery to make sacrifices for it, certainly not the sacrifice of war. It was not a clash of peoples (most northern whites were not economically favored, not politically powerful; most southern whites were poor farmers, not decision-makers) but of elites. The northern elite wanted economic expansion – free land, free labor, a free market, a bank of the United States. The slave interests opposed all that; they saw Lincoln and the Republicans as making continuation of their pleasant and prosperous way of life impossible in the future.[20]

Northern victory resulted in large part from superior industrial production and logistics, and afterwards:

> Northern economy expanded with unprecedented speed . . . With millions of dollars at their command for investment, captains of industry leaped forward to build more factories and railways, open up and develop additional resources, and enlarge the output of

machine industries in every direction. At their disposal inventors, besides improving old machines, placed new machines, materials, and processes, on which new industries of gigantic proportions were constructed.[21]

Modern American capitalism was taking shape, bringing sweeping changes to American life in the east and mid-west. There was intensified migration from rural to urban areas. European immigration was allowed to increase manyfold, to augment the urban labour force, to help consume the goods resulting from increased production and to help raise agricultural production to the level necessary to support the country's growing population. Capital was increasingly centralized and the country's social structures began shifting to patterns related to but significantly different from the class structures of industrial Europe.

Popular music responded to, and was part of, these changing patterns. A handful of music publishers had managed a marginal financial existence in the decades before the Civil War, but in the second half of the century, building on the profits of the war years, the publishing firms of Oliver Ditson in Boston, William Hall in New York, Root & Cady and Lyon & Healy in Chicago, Lee & Walker in Philadelphia, Willig in Baltimore and John Church & Company in Cincinnati expanded their catalogues and sales by concentrating on those types of music most attractive to the complex network of middle classes benefiting from expanding industrialism. There were sentimental parlour ballads; easy piano pieces in the continuing genteel tradition; comic and melodramatic songs popularized in vaudeville, a new form of popular theatre aimed at the middle and urban working classes; simple choral pieces for school and community chorus; instrumental dances written or arranged for amateur performers; instruction books for guitar, flute, parlour organ and other instruments, complete with simple compositions and arrangements of well-known pieces.[22]

Some composers benefited from this expansion of the market. Stephen Foster had been the first American songwriter to support himself from fees and royalties, albeit precariously and for only a few years. In the 1870s and 80s, though, more and more songwriters – Henry Tucker, Septimus Winner, Hart Pease Danks, Will Hays, Charles A. White – were able to make a substantial part of their living from their music. Their compositions were designed for a population emotionally exhausted by the war, willing to settle for a repertory easy to perform and remote from any of the painful issues of the near past or present.

Minstrel songs, written for the still-popular minstrel show as well as the new vaudeville stage, continued to make up a substantial part of

58. *Cover of 'A Requiem in Memory of Ellsworth', by George William Warren, published by Firth Pond & Co. (New York, 1861)*

59. Poster (c1890) by the Estey Organ Company, Brattleboro, Vermont, advertising their 'cottage organ' and 'organ method'

this song repertory. The reasons for this are not difficult to find. The myth that blacks were unsuited for anything other than the most menial work persisted, even in the industrial north, which developed a strategy of encouraging European immigration to satisfy its need for unskilled and semi-skilled labour. Black Americans were not accepted socially in the north, where it was thought that their place was still in the south. The ideology of postwar minstrel songs continued to be pro-slavery, even though slavery no longer existed legally – and even if some of the performers on the minstrel stage were now black, sometimes singing songs written by blacks, like this one by James Bland (1878):

> Carry me back to old Virginny,
> That's where the cotton and the corn and tatoes grow,
> There's where the birds warble sweet in the springtime,
> There's where the old darkey's heart am long'd to go.
> There's where I labored so hard for old Massa,
> Day after day in the field of yellow corn,
> No place on earth do I love more sincerely,
> Than old Virginny, the state where I was born.

*

As the nineteenth century neared an end, America's economic growth became even more oligarchial. A small group of industrialists and bankers, based mostly in New York and including Andrew Carnegie, J. P. Morgan and John D. Rockefeller, gained power over most of the major areas of business in the USA. These men:

> could often exercise a decisive influence over the cost of raw materials, the prices of finished products, and the fortunes of independent competitors. Besides wielding control over their particular areas of the national economy such as oil or steel, corporation promoters built up a wider domination over economy in general, over politics, and over public opinion by creating inter-locking directorates among corporations and other forms of affiliation with business interests.[23]

So too with the popular-music industry. Aggressive music publishers, beginning in the 1880s with the companies of T. B. Harms, Willis Woodward and M. Witmark & Sons, developed techniques designed to maximize sales and profits of sheet music while centralizing control of the industry. By the end of the century the vast majority of America's popular music was produced by a small number of companies, most of them on 'Tin Pan Alley' in New York, all following similar policies and turning out similar products. The economic potential of this industry was most dramatically demonstrated when Charles K. Harris's song *After the Ball* (1892) sold five million copies in only a few years.

All Tin Pan Alley songs were cast in the same mould, as though turned out on an assembly line. They were written in verse-chorus form, drawing on the rhythms of fashionable social dances (waltz, quickstep, ragtime) and using melodic and textual 'hooks' to ensure immediate familiarity. The blandness of the texts of Tin Pan Alley songs and their persistent refusal to touch on issues of substance can be explained at least in part on economic grounds. These songs were consumed chiefly by the growing millions of Americans situated somewhere between the extremes of capital and labour – entre-preneurs, tradesmen, professional people, teachers, clerical workers and the like – who did not share directly in the profits of industrial capitalism, but whose economic and social status was linked to the industrial economy. Though some of these people were aware of the exploitation of the working force and attempted to address these problems through liberal activism, the vast majority were content to focus on their own lives and to ignore America's social problems. Tin Pan Alley songs, with their concentration on romantic love and nostalgia for America's agrarian past, encouraged such benign neglect.[24]

For several decades from the 1880s, millions of new immigrants from central Europe and the Mediterranean came to the USA fleeing political persecution and structural poverty, encouraged to settle in America by liberal immigration policies growing out of industry's need for cheap labour. Many settled in cities, as industrial workers, tradesmen and craftsmen. Old tension between north and south began to be replaced by new ones between urban centres populated largely by recent immigrants, the majority Catholics and Jews, and the more rural areas, peopled chiefly by Protestants of western European and Scandinavian origin.

Political and cultural power remained very much in the hands of the 'older' Americans, who became increasingly alarmed by the country's shifting demography. A Congressional Committee on Immigration released a 42-volume report in 1910 detailing the 'alarming effects of immigration'. Suggestions were put forward for controlling the flow of 'undesirable' aliens into the country and minimizing the impact on American life of those already there. By the early 1920s the climate in America could only be described as proto-fascist. The Immigration Act of 1924 put a virtual end to immigration from Mediterranean, central European and Third World countries. The Ku Klux Klan had a membership of almost five million 'white male persons, native-born Gentile citizens of the United States of America', determined to use all possible means to keep political power in the hands of the British-descended population. The pianist-composer John Powell used the threat of 'the annihilation of white civilization' to justify the establishment of Anglo Saxon Clubs attempting to find 'fundamental and final solutions to our racial problems'.[25]

Even though some 85% of the population of New York City in the early twentieth century was made up of immigrants, first-generation Americans and blacks recently arrived from the south, its cultural products revealed little of this cultural heritage. Jewish elements have been traced in a few tunes by Irving Berlin and George Gershwin and simplified rhythmic patterns derived from black music flavoured 'coon songs', ragtime songs and the syncopated music of the 1910s. But apart from these scattered exceptions, Tin Pan Alley songs used a generalized, common-practice harmonic, melodic and rhythmic vocabulary. And while lyrics of the 1890s and 1900s had sometimes referred to specific ethnic groups, texts became generalized by the 1910s, dealing chiefly with personal emotions. This avoidance of musical or textual ethnic references coincided with a strong backlash against the country's black and new immigrant population.

A new concept of popular music had thus been forged by Tin Pan Alley: an urban, industrial product made possible by the inexpensive mass production of sheet music, deliberately generalized in musical and textual content so as to be accessible to millions and politically

60. Cover of Irving Berlin's rag 'That Society Bear', published by Waterson, Berlin & Snyder (New York, 1912)

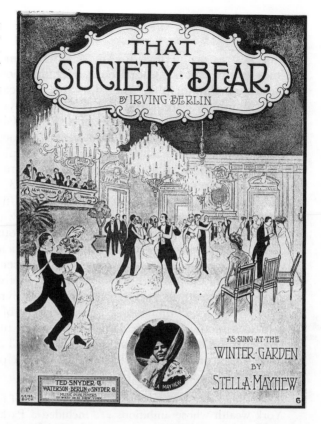

and socially noncommittal. Thus the products of Tin Pan Alley can be understood as manifestations of the new industrial age, contributing to the centralization of capital and the continuing disparity between the privileged and the dispossessed working classes. But they were more than that. A parallel between Tin Pan Alley and the new automobile industry has been suggested.[26] Henry Ford accumulated capital, certainly, and his assembly lines became models for a new mode of industrial production which exacerbated relations between capital and labour. But the products themselves, making private transport affordable by a large segment of the population for the first time, changed the nature of American life, bringing mobility, a new daily rhythm, a new relationship between place of residence and place of business and changing patterns of leisure activity. While all Tin Pan Alley songs may have been out of the same mould, they were attractive to the millions of Americans who consumed them, they helped shape the patterns of social and leisure life and they contributed to the social identity of middle- and upper-class Americans in the first decade of the new century.

*

New orchestras proliferated in American cities in the second half of the nineteenth century: the Brooklyn Philharmonic, the Germania Orchestra in Philadelphia, the Harvard Musical Association, the Boston Symphony Orchestra, the New York Symphony Orchestra and later the symphony orchestras of St Louis, Chicago, Cincinnati, Pittsburgh and Philadelphia. There were also societies and festivals for the performance of large choral-orchestral pieces, such as Cincinnati's biennial May Festival, and new opera companies, most notably the Metropolitan Opera, founded in 1883.

Classical music continued to serve as a mystifying focus for the social life of America's privileged classes. This was the Gilded Age, with a new élite centred on the leaders of the country's oligarchical industrial expansion, eager to assume the political and social roles played by aristocracies at other times and in other countries, including patronage of the arts. Andrew Carnegie contributed large sums to the New York Oratorio Society, the New York Symphony Orchestra and the New York Philharmonic and gave most of the money for the construction of the Carnegie Hall, which from its opening in 1891 ranked with the best concert halls in the world. Lesser figures of the capitalist élite contributed their share and participated in the public ritual of concert and opera attendance:

> The Gilded Age had produced a new stratum of fashionable New York wealth whose ambitions ... included a Park Avenue apartment, a Newport villa, and – copying Old World prerogatives – a box at the opera. Henry James called opera 'the only approach to the implication of the tiara known in American law' and 'the great vessel of social salvation'.[27]

Full-length operas and entire evenings of symphonic music at the Philharmonic were difficult going for many members of America's new social élite, however, and the conductor Theodore Thomas was the architect of an alternative strategy: more accessible programmes, still within the social context of a formal concert. A series of matinée concerts by his New York Symphony Orchestra in 1863 featured such popular artists as Gottschalk and a repertory mixing showy display works and the most familiar classical pieces, for instance a single movement of a symphony by Beethoven or Haydn with a handful of more 'serious' complete pieces. His later soirée concerts, on the same model, competed successfully with the New York Philharmonic, and in 1869 he took his orchestra on the first of a series of annual tours to the Atlantic seaboard and the mid-west. He began introducing pieces by the 'New German School' of Liszt and Wagner, a repertory still shunned by the Philharmonic, to great popular response. In 1865 he inaugurated a series of summer 'Garden Concerts', open-air events with the audience seated at tables or on the lawn, with refreshments available, reminiscent of the pleasure-garden entertainments of the late eighteenth and early nineteenth centuries and anticipating the 'pops' concerts of the twentieth.

In repertory, and in their reaching out to an audience of lesser pretensions, Thomas's concerts were a step towards the demystification of serious music. It would be too much to suggest that they represented a real move towards the democratization of this music; the vast majority of Americans were still not interested in such events and would have been socially uncomfortable if they had chosen to attend. Yet many people who would not have thought of going to the Metropolitan Opera or the New York Philharmonic derived pleasure from Thomas's concerts and those of his emulators. As was the case with so many aspects of America's musical life at the turn of the century, seeds were planted that were to have a dramatic impact on the later twentieth century.

German dominance of classical music continued and intensified. In 1892, for instance, only three of the hundred-odd members of the New York Philharmonic were not of German birth or origin. Repertories were dominated by German composers from Bach to Wagner and Brahms, and by pieces influenced by these men. This had a decisive impact on music written by American composers. Beginning with William Mason, virtually every American composer of the second half of the nineteenth century pursued a career marked by early study with German or German-trained teachers in the USA, further study abroad, usually in Germany, and a return to the USA to a career as a teacher or performer, while turning out compositions saturated with the techniques and spirit of the German school. John Knowles Paine, Dudley Buck, William Gilchrist, Silas Pratt, Frederic Grant Gleason, Arthur Foote, George Chadwick, Horatio Parker and Edward MacDowell were among those who trod this path.

The best of the symphonies, string quartets, oratorios, concertos and art songs written by these men were comparable in quality to most European music of the time. Paine's Mass in D (1865) and Symphony no.1 (1875), both modelled on pieces by Beethoven, are impressively crafted and at times moving, and his oratorio *St Peter* (1872) and the incidental music to *Oedipus rex* (1881) were often performed to appreciative audiences. Buck was most successful with his organ compositions, the Grand Sonata in E♭ (1866), for instance, and his pieces for chorus and orchestra, including *The Golden Legend* (1880). Foote was best at chamber music (Violin Sonata in G minor, 1889), which often betrays the influence of Brahms. Chadwick and Parker wrote prolifically in every medium, producing such excellent pieces as Chadwick's Symphony no.2 (1886) and Parker's oratorio

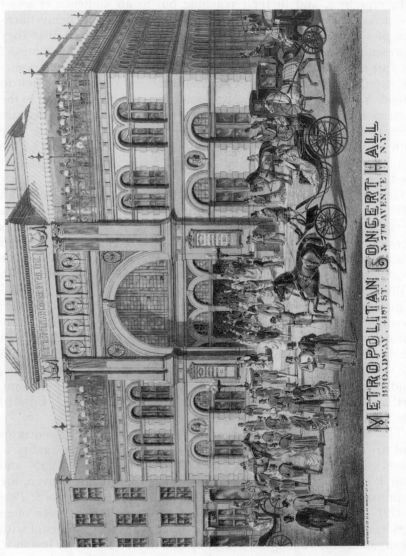

61. Poster (by Hopcraft & Co., c1880) advertising the Metropolitan Concert Hall, New York, where Rudolph Aronson initiated a series of promenade concerts in May 1880

Hora novissima (1893). And though MacDowell's rhetoric, particularly in his later years, suggests that he was seeking to break out of the Germanic mould, his two piano concertos and his symphonic poems continue along Teutonic paths. A contemporary evaluation of Chadwick sums up not only his work but that of his entire generation of American composers:

> Chadwick has imbibed the traditions of Germany through direct contact with the teachers of Leipzig and Munich. His facility and strength in the handling of the factors of composition are most admirable. A critical mind and sincere admiration for logic and symmetry save him from the excess radicalism into which young composers are so prone to fall.[28]

These men also shaped the academic study of music. Paine taught undergraduate and graduate courses at Harvard for 43 years; Parker taught at Yale; Chadwick was a teacher and then director of the New England Conservatory of Music; MacDowell was the first professor of music at Columbia University. Under their guidance, a conservative Germanic approach to music theory and history was imprinted on these prestigious eastern institutions and on schools in other parts of the country modelled on them. As Paine summed up: 'The only hope for the present and future is the adherence to the historical forms, as developed by Bach, Handel, Mozart and Beethoven, in church music, the oratorio, opera and instrumental music'.[29]

There was some concern with this dominance of America's music by European music and musicians, though. Spurred by Antonín Dvořák's suggestion that 'inspiration for truly national music might be derived from the negro melodies or Indian chants',[30] Rubin Goldmark, Harry Thacker Burleigh, Henry F. Gilbert, John Powell and above all Arthur Farwell set out to create a 'national musical art ... in which the German idiom is not the dominant factor'.[31] The Wa-Wan Press, established by Farwell in 1901, brought out several hundred pieces by 37 composers, most of them drawing on Amerindian, Afro-American or Anglo-American 'folk' melodies.

It is against this backdrop that the life and music of Charles Ives must be measured. At Yale, under Horatio Parker, Ives wrote student works cast generally in the approved Germanic model, though with idiosyncratic features: Symphony no.1 (1895–8), String Quartet no.1 (1896). His life and career has been shaped by historians into one of the great legends of American music: the genius who, forsaking a musical career in favour of the insurance business, was able to give free rein to his creative spirit and become 'the first great American composer of concert music, and unarguably the most original and significant one of the late 19th and early 20th centuries'.[32] His compositions abound in harmonic, rhythmic and tonal devices perhaps anticipating some of the innovations of Stravinsky and Schoenberg, in melodic paraphrases of popular songs, marches, hymns and classical pieces (often in dissonant collage), and in contrasts of dramatically varied textures, dynamic levels and harmonic constructs. His music has been seen as quintessentially American because of its iconoclastic nature, its obsessive quotation from earlier American music and its programmatic invocation of American history, landscape and literature. Dozens of his compositions have been hailed as works of unparalleled genius in the history of American music.

This may all be true, but the Ives mythology must be modified by other factors. First, virtually none of his major works was performed or published until the 1930s and 40s. Thus his impact on American musical life, and on other composers, belongs not to the early twentieth century but to a later era. Second, his chosen image was of the nineteenth-century Romantic, isolated by his genius, disdainful of lesser talents and of contemporary audiences. This ideological stance placed him at odds with Aaron Copland, George Gershwin and other slightly younger composers who attempted to redefine the role of classical music in American democracy. Third, musically and otherwise, he rejected the growing urban, industrialized, ethnically varied America of the early twentieth century in favour of the memory of the New England village of an earlier time. He was one of a group of 'Yankee composers' who:

> conducted an errand into the wilderness of the twentieth century to manifest New England's right to speak for America. They elided their Yankee and Victorian callings into a prophetic religious ideology, believing that a nation scuttling pell-mell into the twentieth century needed to affirm a unique consciousness. They hoped to herald America's glorious future by sublimating in music the spiritual heritage of New England . . . they believed that their Anglo-Saxon heritage had sired a neighborly sense of moral community peculiar to old New England, and they worried that theirs was the last generation of composers to retain a semblance of ethnic unity.[33]

*

As nineteenth-century America moved towards greater industrialization and urbanization, and the last pretences of Jacksonian democracy crumbled in the face of the centralized political and economic power structures of industrial capitalism, the music of America's working classes and ethnic subcultures became even less visible. To the European-born Frédéric Louis Ritter, attempting the first extended history of music in America,

The people's song is not to be found among the American people. The American farmer, mechanic, journeyman, stage-driver, shepherd, etc., does not sing . . . The serious, industrious inhabitant of this beautiful land does not express his joys and sorrows in sound; but for – the bleating of sheep, the crowing of cock, the singing of birds, – the woods, the pastures, the farmyard, would be silent and gloomy.[34]

Contrary to this dismissal of 'people's song' by Ritter and other scholars of the time, though, repertories of increasingly distinctive oral music were flourishing among America's ethnic and other subcultures. Rural descendants of Anglo-Celtic peoples, particularly in the south, were creating a rich store of oral narrative ballads, lyric songs and instrumental dances growing out of music brought from the British Isles. Professor F. J. Child of Harvard University collected and annotated a five-volume collection of the texts of English and Scottish ballads that survived in the USA,[35] but neither he nor other early folksong collectors had much interest in ballads created in America, nor in the musical innovations taking place in their performance, such as the addition of fiddle, banjo or guitar accompaniment. Direct evidence of this repertory, which was to develop into 'hillbilly' or country-western music, comes first with recordings by commercial phonograph companies in the early 1920s. The Cajuns, French-speaking refugees who had settled in rural Louisiana after their expulsion from Acadia by the British in 1755, developed their own musical dialect featuring Scottish fiddling styles and the accordion, which also went unremarked until recorded in the 1920s. It was the same for other pockets of ethnic music, even those in urban areas.

Most distinctive of all, and equally invisible, was the music of the former slave population of the south. The history of this music, reconstructed only in recent decades, tells us a great deal about larger issues in the USA in the early twentieth century. The Fourteenth and Fifteenth Amendments to the Constitution had granted citizenship to 'all persons born or naturalized in the United States', including former slaves; it had enjoined the individual states from 'mak[ing] or enforc[ing] any law which shall abridge the privileges or immunities of citizens of the United States'; and had stated unequivocally that the right to vote 'shall not be denied or abridged . . . on account of race, color, or previous condition of servitude'. At the conclusion of the Civil War, attempts were made to bring American blacks into the mainstream of American life. The Freedman's Bureau was established to assist them in becoming part of the political process, with the resultant election of many blacks to state legislatures in southern states. The American Missionary Association established seventeen schools in the south for the general education of former slaves and chartered seven colleges for general and theological education. Attempts were made to bring rudimentary health care to former slaves. But these gains had been eroded by the end of the century. White vigilante groups such as the Ku Klux Klan used terrorist tactics to discourage black political participation. Southern states enacted legislation making it difficult for ex-slaves to vote, and the federal government was increasingly unwilling to interfere, particularly after the Compromise of 1877 gave the presidency to Rutherford Hayes in return for the removal of the last troops from the south and assurances that the federal government would follow a policy of non-intervention in domestic affairs of the southern states, including racial policies. Black Americans found themselves abandoned by both major political parties and all but a handful of white liberals, and effectively denied the political and social equality promised them by constitutional amendment. They were unwanted in the north, despite a plea by Booker T. Washington that industrialists should employ blacks rather than European immigrants of 'strange tongues and habits'.

There had been a ripple of interest in the music of southern blacks during and immediately after the Civil War. Lewis Lockwood and Lucy McKim, northern abolitionists visiting the south, brought back word of a unique slave musical culture and a few notated samples of 'deliverance melodies'. *Slave Songs of the United States* (1867), compiled by William Francis Allen, Charles Pickard Ware and Lucy McKim Garrison, contained the text and music of 136 songs and a description of black performing style, making it clear that call-and-response patterns, rhythmic accompaniment of choral music and other African survivals were part of this tradition.

As political interest in the southern blacks waned, less attention was paid to their music. However, the realization that certain aspects of black music could be made attractive to white Americans, with proper mediation, began to penetrate the commercial music world. The Hutchinson Family performed and published their own arrangements of several slave songs. George L. White, a white staff member at Fisk University in Nashville, arranged a number of black religious songs for the school's Jubilee Singers; their performances for white audiences in the north and in Europe in the 1870s raised hundreds of thousands of dollars for the school and encouraged other black colleges to form similar groups, singing arrangements of spirituals by white (and eventually black) musicians. Published commercially as *Jubilee Songs*, this repertory proved to be a successful commodity, encouraging professional songwriters to turn out similar 'minstrel-spirituals' for the minstrel stage and home performance. In each case, call-and-response patterns and improvised polyphony in the black tradition were replaced by four-part triadic, homorhythmic arrangements drawing on traditional black melodies and texts but dramatic-

62. The Fisk Jubilee Singers; photograph, c1875

ally altering the mode of performance to suit the musical taste of white audiences.

The 1880s was also the decade of *New Coon in Town* by J. S. Putnam and hundreds of other 'coon songs' depicting black characters in essentially the same light as had the most flagrant pre-war minstrel songs. Popularized on the minstrel and vaudeville stages and widely sung in American parlours, these songs used simplified syncopated rhythmic patterns to suggest (at least to white audiences) something of the nature of black music, though they were indistinguishable in general musical style from other early Tin Pan Alley songs.

Ragtime had a somewhat more complicated history. The impetus for the genre came from a style of piano playing developed by black pianists in the lower mid-west, and a handful of black composers, including Scott Joplin, Thomas Turpin and James Scott, wrote and published pieces now accepted as masterpieces of American music. But the first published piece of this genre (*Mississippi Rag*, 1897) was by a white man, William Krell, as were the majority of subsequent piano rags. A succession of Tin Pan Alley 'ragtime' songs, from Joe Howard's *Hello! Ma Baby* (1899) through Irving Berlin's *Alexander's Ragtime Band* (1911), represented the most successful commercial application of ragtime rhythms; almost all these pieces were written by white composers, were aimed at white audiences and performers and made only passing and simplistic reference to the rhythms of black ragtime.

A pattern emerged that was to endure for many decades: white composers, performers, publishers and impresarios would skim off the superficial elements of a musical style originating among blacks for use in commercial music designed for white consumption. The same happened with early jazz, which furnished the rhythmic impulse for syncopated social dance styles popular among the urban white population of the 1910s, and with early blues. Black musicians might be involved in this process, for instance Jim Europe and W. C. Handy, but the end result would be no different: a product mediated for white taste, performed and marketed chiefly for whites. If this music represented black culture at all, it was that of the small black middle class, which had little choice but to share the taste of white America.

Black musicians performing for black audiences were under no pressure to cater for the taste of any other group, however, and it was in this setting that the music most representative of America's distinctive Afro-American culture flourished. Black pianists, particularly in the lower mid-west, developed playing styles to accompany social dancing in bars and other places of black entertainment, marked by syncopated and asymmetrical rhythmic patterns, considerable independence of the two hands and traces of call-and-response patterns. Commercial ragtime was a simplification of this performance style, which survives in recorded music from the 1920s and through its penetration into jazz and boogie-woogie. Black groups in New Orleans and elsewhere, with the instruments of white culture now available to them, began performing for dances, funerals and other social and ceremonial occasions. New ways of playing these instruments and new concepts of ensemble playing rooted in Afro-American styles led in time to the genre of jazz. Black congregations in urban churches began modifying the style of their religious singing. Piano, organ, drums and eventually guitars and saxophones were sometimes used as accompaniment, and new texts appropriate to urban life were devised. Call-and-response patterns, improvised polyphony and rhythmic movement by singers and congregation alike were retained in what would in time be called gospel music. Black solo songs, addressing the travails of the individual and perhaps originating as 'field hollers', became systematized in textual and musical structure and began to use accompanying instruments – fiddle, banjo, guitar, piano. In the 1920s and 30s this genre, now known as the blues, not only became an important form of black music, but also served as a structural basis for much jazz and other black instrumental music.

These and other styles and genres were musical expressions of black culture in the USA, created and performed by black musicians for black audiences. They had in common the retention of African performance styles and the assimilation of instruments from white culture. This music was almost unknown to white Americans of the time and went unmentioned in the scholarly and journalistic writing on American music dating from before World War I.

*

In the decades leading up to World War I, then, American musical culture moved along several quite different tracks. There was classical music, still firmly rooted in European tradition in its repertory, in the musical style of pieces written by American composers and, most of all, in the role it played in articulating and defining class structures. There was what might be called industrial music: mass-produced, stereotyped in content and musical structure, designed for the rapidly growing part of the population able to purchase and consume commodities produced by American capitalism. And there was the invisible music of those peoples still not sharing equally in the economic, social, political and educational benefits of American democracy. Some contributed their labour but were not rewarded enough to be able to use the products they helped turn out; some still pursued a pre-capitalist way of life in geographical and cultural isolation. Historians of the period praised the first, condemned the second out of hand and ignored the third. Today this judgment has been reversed: America's 'invisible' music has been reconstructed and highly prized; less attention is paid to classical music of the time; and the 'industrial' music of Tin Pan Alley has been increasingly studied.

NOTES

[1] *The Times* (26 June 1843).

[2] G. Chase, *America's Music: from the Pilgrims to the Present* (New York, rev. 2/1966), 264.

[3] H. Zinn, *A People's History of the United States* (New York, 1980), 125.

[4] A. Saxton, 'Blackface Minstrelsy and Jacksonian Ideology', *American Quarterly*, xxix (March 1975).

[5] For details see H. Nathan, *Dan Emmett and the Rise of Early Negro Minstrelsy* (Norman, 1962/R 1977).

[6] Letter from Foster to E. P. Christy, 25 May 1852.

[7] S. Foster, *Nelly Was a Lady* (1849).

[8] G. F. Root, *The Story of a Musical Life* (Cincinnati, 1891), 83.

[9] See D. L. Root, *American Popular Stage Music: 1860–1880* (Ann Arbor, 1981).

[10] Quoted in D. Grimstead, *Melodrama Unveiled: American Theatre and Culture, 1800–1850* (Chicago, 1968), 56.

[11] B. A. McConachie, 'New York Operagoing, 1825–50: Creating an Elite Social Ritual', *American Music*, vi (1988), 182.

[12] E. Holloway, *The Uncollected Poetry and Prose of Walt Whitman* (New York, 1932), 132.

[13] P. Hone, as quoted in J. Mattfeld, *A Hundred Years of Grand Opera in New York, 1825–1925* (New York, 1927), 34.

[14] McConachie, 'New York Operagoing', 181.

[15] Letter to *Dwight's Journal of Music* (11 March 1854).

[16] *Dwight's Journal* (8 March 1856).

[17] R. Offergeld, 'Gottschalk and Company: the Music of Democratic Sociability', disc notes to New World Record 257 (1976).

[18] J. P. Shenton, in preface to W. Barney, *Flawed Victory: a New Perspective on the Civil War* (New York, 1975), p.vii.

[19] *Heart Songs* (Boston, 1909), p.vi.

[20] Zinn, *A People's History*, 184.

[21] C. A. and M. R. Beard, *A Basic History of the United States* (New York, 1944), 292–3.

[22] For a detailed history of this period, see R. Sanjek, *American Popular Music and its Business* (Oxford and New York, 1988), ii, 225–420.

[23] C. A. and M. R. Beard, *A Basic History*, 309–10.

[24] Many European studies of American society have failed because of their uncritical application of Marxist-based theories of class structure and conflict.

[25] R. B. Sherman, 'The Last Stand: the Fight for Racial Integrity in Virginia in the 1920s', *Journal of Southern History*, liv/1 (Feb 1988), 69–92.

[26] D. Harker, *One for the Money: Politics and Popular Song* (London, 1980), pp.38–50.

[27] J. Horowitz, *Understanding Toscanini* (New York, 1987), 37.

[28] H. E. Krehbiel, *Music in America* (New York, 1901), vi, 951–2.

[29] M. A. DeWolfe Howe, 'John Knowles Paine', *MQ*, xxv (1939), 265.

[30] *Harper's New Monthly Magazine*, xc (Feb 1894), 432.

[31] A. Farwell, introduction to Wa-Wan Press (Sept 1903).

[32] J. Kirkpatrick, 'Ives, Charles', *Grove A*.

[33] M. S. Moore, *Yankee Blues: Musical Culture and American Identity* (Bloomington, 1985), 3–4.

[34] F. L. Ritter, *Music in America* (New York, 1883), 385.

[35] F. J. Child, *The English and Scottish Popular Ballads* (Boston and New York, 1882–98).

BIBLIOGRAPHICAL NOTE

General

Important studies of social and political issues in the USA during this period include R. J. Wilson, *In Quest of Community: Social Philosophy in the United States, 1860–1920* (New York, 1968), and, for the final two-thirds of the era, R. H. Wiebe, *The Search for Order, 1877–1920* (New York, 1967). R. A. Bartlett, *The New Country: a Social History of the American Frontier* (New York and Oxford, 1974), is a useful analysis of the country's westward expansion and the impact of the frontier experience on the developing nation. Useful essays on developing industrialization and urbanization are T. C. Cochran and W. Miller, *The Age of Enterprise: a Social History of Industrial America* (New York, 1961); P. S. Boyer, *Urban Masses and Moral Order in America, 1820–1920* (Cambridge, Mass., 1978); and S. P. Hays, *The Response to Industrialism, 1885–1914* (Chicago, 1957). A. Trachtenberg, *The Incorporation of America: Culture and Society in the Gilded Age* (New York, 1982), analyses the culture which nurtured classical music in turn-of-the-century America, while H. Zinn, *A People's History of the United States* (New York, 1980), is an iconoclastic reading of the country's history from the perspective of the underclasses and the dispossessed – those people who were creating the most distinctively American forms of folk and popular music. *Harvard Encyclopedia of American Ethnic Groups*, ed. S. Thernstrom (Cambridge, Mass., and London, 1980), is a superb reference source for the history of the national and ethnic groups settling in the USA.

Music

G. Chase's *America's Music: from the Pilgrims to the Present* (New York, 1955, rev. 3/ 1988) is a landmark in the historiography of music in the USA. Citing Charles Seeger's dictum that 'when the history of music in the New World is written, it will be found that the main concern has been with folk and popular music' in his introduction, Chase discusses folk and popular as well as classical genres, devoting the middle nine chapters to the historical era discussed in this chapter, though without developing a sense of historical interconnectedness. W. Mellers's estimable and imaginative *Music in a New Found Land: Themes and Developments in the History of American Music* (London, 1964, rev. 2/1987) unfortunately devotes only a single chapter to the nineteenth century but it contains useful observations on the roots of blues, jazz and other popular genres. H. W. Hitchcock, *Music in the United States: a Historical Introduction* (Englewood Cliffs, 1969, rev. 3/1988), devotes a middle section, 'The Romantic Century (1820–1920)', to equal consideration of the 'cultivated' and the 'vernacular' traditions. C. Hamm, in *Music in the New World* (New York and London, 1983), starts with the assumption that 'a historical study of the music of the United States must be concerned with both written and unwritten music and that popular and vernacular genres must be considered at least as carefully as the various forms of classical music', and focusses on the styles and genres of the period 1840–1920 for the entire middle of the book. The only book-length attempt to deal with the music of this era is the second volume (*The Gilded Years: 1865–1920*) of R. L. Davis's sweeping, unfocussed, derivative *A History of Music in American Life* (Malabar, Florida, 1982), which makes no attempt to analyse the era as shaping or reflecting a coherent historical whole.

The vast majority of the relevant literature is concerned with specific periods, genres and individual composers. C. Hamm, *Yesterdays: Popular Song in America* (New York and London, 1979), starting with the assumption that popular song in the USA has 'a continuous, unbroken, and coherent history', offers a detailed chronological and analytical map of the genre for the entire period in question. The most useful books dealing with blackface minstrelsy remain Hans Nathan, *Dan Emmett and the Rise of Early Negro Minstrelsy* (Norman, Oklahoma, 1962/R 1977), and R. C. Toll, *Blacking Up: the Minstrel Show in Nineteenth-Century America* (New York, 1974). D. Cockerell's *Excelsior: Journals of the Hutchinson Family Singers, 1842–1846* (Stuyvesant, NY, 1989) gives the most vivid and accurate picture of the early career and music of this important singing group and its impact on both the USA and Britain, and W. W. Austin, *'Susanna', 'Jeanie', and 'The Old Folks at Home': the Songs of Stephen C. Foster from his Time to Ours* (New York and London, 1975) is a startlingly original attempt to place Foster's music in the context of American culture and history. D. L. Root, *American Popular Stage Music: 1860–1880* (Ann Arbor, 1981), surveys both didactic and commercial musical theatre.

The first volume of V. B. Lawrence, *Strong on Music: the New York Music Scene in the Days of George Templeton Strong* (New York and Oxford, 1987), gives a detailed account of the emergence of a socially demarcated audience for classical music in New York at mid-century. W. T. Upton, *William Henry Fry* (New York, 1954), remains the best study of Fry and the era during which American composers first struggled with the issue of how a national identity might be shaped within the European-dominated genre of classical music; the first section of B.A. Zuck's *A History of Musical Americanism* (Ann Arbor, 1980) tackles the same issues. L. M. Gottschalk's *Notes of a Pianist*, originally published in 1881 and newly edited by J. Behrend (New York, 1964), gives an excellent view of the life, audience and repertory of the touring virtuoso.

B. C. Malone's *Southern Music, American Music* (Lexington, Kentucky, 1979) is concerned with the emergence of a distinctively southern regional style in the nineteenth and early twentieth centuries. The second volume of R. Sanjek's magisterial *American Popular Music and its Business* (Oxford and New York, 1988) gives the best available account of the development of commercial music publishing in the second half of the nineteenth century.

The most telling descriptions of German domination of musical life in the USA in the late nineteenth and early twentieth centuries and the struggles of American composers to find a niche in this environment are contemporary writings: T. Thomas, *A Musical Autobiography* (Chicago, 1905); W. Mason, *Memories of a Musical Life* (New

York, 1902); L. Gillman, *Edward MacDowell: a Study* (New York, 1908); and such early histories of music as L. C. Elson, *The History of American Music* (New York, 1904), and H. E. Krehbiel, *Music in America* (New York, 1901). There are more recent biographies of individual composers: G. W. Chadwick, *Horatio Parker* (New Haven, 1921); V. Yellin, *The Life and Operatic Works of George Whitefield Chadwick* (diss., Harvard U., 1957); and J. C. Schmidt, *The Life and Works of John Knowles Paine* (Ann Arbor, 1980).

The only attempt at a general history of the musical life of immigrants is N. Tawa's *A Sound of Strangers: Musical Culture, Acculturation, and the Post-Civil War Ethnic American* (Metuchen, NY, 1982). The cultural implications of the growing antagonism in the early twentieth century between older (chiefly Anglo-American) layers of American society and the country's new immigrants are analysed in M. S. Moore, *Yankee Blues: Musical Culture and American Identity* (Bloomington, 1985).

V. B. Lawrence, *The Wa-Wan Press, 1901–1910* (New York, 1970), is the best guide to the efforts of Arthur Farwell and his fellow 'Americanists'. As for Ives, the literature is vast and growing, beginning with H. and S. Cowell's landmark *Charles Ives and his Music* (New York, 1955) and *Essays Before a Sonata and Other Writings*, ed. H. Boatwright (New York, 1962), through V. Perlis, *Charles Ives Remembered: an Oral History* (New Haven, 1974), and H. W. Hitchcock, *Ives* (London, 1977), to J. P. Burkholder, *Charles Ives: the Ideas Behind the Music* (New Haven, 1985).

E. Southern, *The Music of Black Americans* (New York, 1971), is a brave attempt to collect historical information on African-American musicians active in all genres. Among the most useful writings on ragtime are the pioneering R. Blesh and H. Janis, *They All Played Ragtime* (New York, 1950), and E. Berlin, *Ragtime: a Musical and Cultural History* (Berkeley, 1980). Only a few items can be cited from the literature on pre-jazz and early jazz: G. Schuller, *Early Jazz: its Roots and Musical Development* (New York, 1968); S. B. Charters, *Jazz New Orleans: 1885–1957* (New York, 1958); D. Marquis, *In Search of Buddy Bolden* (Baton Rouge, 1978); and S. B. Charters, *Jazz: a History of the New York Scene* (New York, 1962). Most of the immense literature on the blues can only speculate on the genre before 1914, given the virtual absence of hard evidence; the best are S. Charters, *The Country Blues* (New York, 1959); J. T. Titon, *Early Downhome Blues: a Musical and Cultural Analysis* (Urbana, 1977); and R. Palmer, *Deep Blues* (New York, 1981).

The best general reference for specific information on composers, genres and the musical life of this (and any other) period in the history of the USA is *Grove A*.

Chapter XII

Latin America: Reflections and Reactions

GERARD BÉHAGUE

The period from about 1850 to about 1914 in Latin America saw the continued development of art-music activities initiated in the first half of the century; it also saw the beginnings of musical professionalism, with closer attention to education institutions on the part of central governments, the fuller development of opera seasons and, by the end of the century, the gradual establishment of symphony orchestras, resulting in a more or less regular concert life and a corresponding attention to orchestral music by local composers. The abolition of official slavery in the 1880s facilitated the interpenetration of rural and urban areas, so urban popular musical genres developed at that time, providing immediate sources for the first nationalist composers. The expansion of the middle classes in all the major cities of the continent encouraged an increase in successful salon-music composers and music publishers. The incipient national characterization of composition, both among art-music and popular composers, helped to create a democratic sense of the function and purpose of music in society; by the end of the nineteenth century one could find associations of popular concerts in some of the major Latin American cities, and the theatre, especially with its lighter genres, attracted a much larger proportion of the urban population.

One should stress that each Latin American country developed its musical life and institutions according to its own historical and socio-political conditions. This was also a period of little or no artistic and intellectual communication between the majority of Latin American nations, so no one country appeared as the major musical representative of the area. Western Europe continued therefore to be the musical model and main influence as well as the meeting-place of composers from different Latin nations.

MEXICO AND THE SPANISH CARIBBEAN
Under the dictatorship of Porfirio Díaz, who ruled from 1876 to 1910, Mexico underwent important social and cultural change. Assimila-

tion continued rapidly, transforming the country into a pre-dominantly mestizo population, with the Indian communities remaining isolated, however. Urban and industrial growth brought a small but increasingly important middle class of businessmen, bureaucrats and professionals, widening the socio-cultural gap between city and countryside. These new middle and upper classes continued to hold educational and artistic values that emulated the Romantic Europe of the mid-nineteenth century. Thus the production and consumption of salon music was enormous between about 1870 and 1910. The latter part of the century also saw the rise of virtuoso pianist-composers who cultivated salon genres and European-style Romantic piano music. The fact that the most popular salon composer, Juventino Rosas (1868–94), was a full-blooded Otomí Indian is significant in that there was no contradiction between his ethnic heritage and the fashionable type of music he produced. His set of waltzes *Sobre las olas*, in the purest French or Viennese salon-music tradition, acquired a resounding fame throughout the world.[1]

In spite of the popularity of European salon dances (polka, mazurka, schottish, waltz) among Mexican middle and upper classes, reflecting their cultural dependence, the piano virtuosos of the period, such as Tomás León (1826–93), Julio Ituarte (1845–1905), Ernesto Elorduy (1853–1912) and Felipe Villanueva (1862–93), began to pay attention to vernacular elements. As the very concept of nationalism in the arts derived from European Romanticism it was natural that these composers would be the first to turn their attention to their country's music. Ituarte's *Ecos de México* (c1880) uses and stylizes well-known national tunes, including *El Palomo*, *El Perico*, *Los Enanos* and *Las Mañanitas*, attempting at the same time to retain the character of each original song. Ituarte also wrote *Bouquet de flores*, a collection of a hundred habanera dances.

Elorduy and Villanueva cultivated the *danza* (or *contradanza*) *mexicana*, following the model of the Cuban *contradanzas* of Manuel Saumell and Ignacio Cervantes. The Cuban *contradanza*, which developed in the late eighteenth and early nineteenth centuries, was the source of many other Cuban popular dances (such as the *danza*, the habanera and the *danzón*) that were extremely influential throughout Latin America. The *contradanza* emphasized typical Afro-Cuban (as well as Dominican, Haitian and Puerto Rican) syncopations and had a typical dotted-figure accompaniment, characteristic of the later habanera; this distinctive figure, however, was also the rhythmic foundation of the *tango andaluz* and had been present in Mexican dances of the colonial period. Whatever the historical precedence, with Elorduy's and Villanueva's piano pieces the *danza mexicana* became a type of stylized popular music. Villanueva's *Danzas humorísticas* illustrate cross-metre combinations and syncopated patterns.

The use of polymetre (2/4 or 4/4 against 3/4) is significant, for it reveals the composer's awareness of the 'national' quality of the resulting hemiola.[2]

Ricardo Castro (1864–1907), the most successful of the Mexican piano virtuosos, had two of his works (a piano concerto and the opera *La légende de Rudel*) published in Germany. In 1903, under a grant from the Díaz government, he went to Europe for study and immediately had his Cello Concerto performed in Paris. A concert by him at the Salle Erard won the praise of *Le figaro* and *Le monde musical*. His Piano Concerto, given in Brussels in 1904, was described by a local critic as 'a dashing and effective work', indicating his full mastery of the conventions of European concert music of the time. *La légende de Rudel* (1906), however, with a libretto translated into Italian from the French original for its Mexican première, got an uneven reception, though Gustavo Campa (1863–1934), another official composer of the period, praised it as Castro's best work. Campa, a strong admirer of French music in the Massenet and Saint-Saëns vein, wrote the opera *Le roi poète* (1901), about a fifteenth-century Aztec king, Nezahualcoyotl, to a French libretto. The growing alienation from Mexican culture that this art music represented by the end of the Porfirian era led to further antagonism from Mexican audiences. Campa attributed it to the Mexican public's ignorance of great masterpieces and its preference for bullfights over operas.[3] He could not, of course, realize that barren operas, above all, symbolized a capitalist, foreign ideology, diametrically opposed to the cultural and political aspirations of the Mexican people on the eve of the revolution.

When the Mexican revolution started, Manuel M. Ponce (1882–1948), then 28, was a piano teacher at the Mexico City Conservatory. The pioneer of Romantic musical nationalism in Mexico, he cultivated both a Romantic salon-music style, as his internationally famous song *Estrellita* (1912) bears witness, and a national style (as in the piano pieces *Canciones mexicanas*). He studied mestizo folk music and his nationalist position was later consolidated.

In Cuba the latter part of the nineteenth century saw the appearance of remarkable Afro-Cuban musicians, foremost among which was Claudio Brindis de Salas (1852–1911), a virtuoso violinist. He studied at the Paris Conservatoire and for some time was an official musician at the court in Berlin where he had settled and married. Acclaimed throughout Europe and in South America for his extraordinary talent, he earned the title of the Cuban Paganini; but he died poor and forgotten in Buenos Aires. The other great Cuban virtuoso violinist was the mulatto José White (1836–1918) who was the Allard professor at the Paris Conservatoire. The most successful Cuban opera composers included Laureano Fuentes Matons (1825–98), author of *La hija de Jefté* (1875) and four zarzuelas, and Gaspar Villate (1851–1912), who had three of his operas first performed in Europe with considerable success (*Zilia*, 1877, Paris; *La czarine*, 1880, The Hague; and *Baltazar*, 1885, Madrid). Villate cultivated salon-music genres, writing many 'criolla' *contradanzas*, for which he is better remembered in Cuba than for his operas.

The two major figures representing Classical and Romantic styles were Antonio Raffelin (1796–1882) and Nicolas Ruiz Espadero (1832–90). Raffelin wrote symphonic and chamber music and, later in his life, technically accomplished sacred music. Espadero, many of whose works were performed in Europe by his friend Louis-Moreau Gottschalk, developed a typically Romantic piano style in an output that included fashionable fantasies on operatic themes. Occasionally he turned to the vernacular, as in his piece *Chant du guagiro* (the Guajiro is the predominantly white or mestizo peasant in Cuba), published in Paris with the sub-title 'grande scène caractéristique cubaine'. Cuban traits are conveyed in this piece through an interesting repetition of cross-rhythms, but they finally yield to the vapid virtuoso figuration of so many of his other piano works.

In the music of Ignacio Cervantes (1847–1905), the most significant nineteenth-century Cuban composer, the first decisive steps towards musical nationalism were taken. His solid training, acquired under Espadero in Havana, then Marmontel and Alkan in Paris, prevented him from succumbing to the current fashion for virtuosity. He had a successful career as a concert pianist in Cuba, in Europe and in the USA. Among his numerous piano works the 21 *Danzas cubanas* (1875–95), many of which are real *contradanzas*, constitute his best achievement within the early nationalist trend, with the incorporation of both Afro-Cuban and Guajiro musical elements into a Romantic piano style. The Cuban 'dances' use rhythmic patterns associated with the tango and habanera and the *cinquillo*, one of the most characteristic figures of Cuban folk and popular music which appears in Afro-Caribbean dances and is the basis for much Afro-Cuban ritual drumming. Cervantes's music foreshadowed a new awareness after World War I of a Cuban musical nationalism based on the country's deepest cultural roots.

The period following the Spanish-American War (1898) and the resulting proclamation of the Republic of Cuba (1901) represented a transition in the arts typified by an aspiration to be recognized as an independent modern nation in tune with the most up-to-date trends. In spite of independence, nationalist ideology was not compatible with this aspiration. Thus artistic expression rooted in folk or popular sources that could have been interpreted as provincial or colonialist was avoided. Rather the cosmopolitan current was based on assimilating the best that the civilized European nations had to offer. France and Germany were such nations. Besides the composer and band director Guillermo Tomás, the most representative figure of this era was Eduardo Sánchez de Fuentes (1874–1944). Though primarily remembered for his very popular *contradanza*/habanera called *Tú*, Sánchez de Fuentes was an opera composer who cultivated a *verismo* approach based on pseudo-Caribbean Indian music.

In Puerto Rico, Juan Morel Campos (1857–96) was the most creative composer of *danza puertorriqueña* during the second half of the century. Of some 550 works attributed to him, about half are *danzas* for the piano that reveal a diversified treatment of the popular form; but the two dominant varieties are the stylized, highly Romantic *danza* and the popular *danza criolla*. The political change experienced by Puerto Rico in 1898, when it came under the sovereignty of the USA, did not affect its prevailing Hispanic cultural character but it apparently changed the traditional governmental patronage of musical activities. Earlier, art-promoting organizations such as the Ateneo Puertorriqueño continued to sponsor composition and performance through contests and special presentations. The first two decades of the twentieth century saw the activities of a number of musicians of talent, among them Casimiro Duchesne (1860–1906), Julio Carlos de Arteaga (1865–1923) and Julián Andino (1845–1926), well known for his piece *El seis* for violin solo and as leader of the orchestra of the Municipal Theatre, and Fernando Callejo Ferrer (1862–1926).

VENEZUELA AND THE ANDEAN NATIONS
During the late nineteenth century the city of Caracas attempted to consolidate its theatrical and concert activities. The Teatro Municipal (first called Guzmán Blanco) was inaugurated in 1881 and the Teatro Caracas was reconstructed in 1885. These and other theatres supported intensive but irregular opera seasons with mostly Italian companies. The most successful Venezuelan virtuoso of the period was the pianist Teresa Carreño (1857–1917) who spent most of her career in Europe but who is viewed as a national idol.

In the Colombian capital, José María Ponce de León (1846–1882) wrote the only two Colombian operas produced in Bogotá in the nineteenth century (*Ester*, 1874, and *Florinda*, 1880). These and his sacred works followed European models. But some, such as *La hermosa sabana* and *Sinfonía sobre temas colombianos* (1881), show an early concern for national music within a predominantly Romantic vocabulary. Several of his compositions are based on typical Colombian folkdances like the *bambuco*, *pasillo* and *torbellino*. But his music was considered incomprehensible in his own country, which indicates that even standard nineteenth-century European styles had not been absorbed into Colombia's musical life. In the early twentieth century, that was compensated for and remedied by a preoccupation with

331

music education. Composers associated with the Conservatorio Nacional included Andrés Martinez Montoya (1869–1933), Santos Cifuentes Rodriguez (1870–1932), the first to write theoretical works (*Tratado de armonía*, London, 1892; *Teoría de la música*, Bogotá, 1907), and especially Guillermo Uribe-Holguín (1880–1971), the most influential composer of his generation and director of the conservatory from 1910.

In Peru, Romantic nationalism was expressed in the works of such late nineteenth-century composers as Claudio Rebagliati (1847–1909), whose piano album of folkdance tunes and songs entitled *Album Sud Americano* (1870) included 22 short pieces stylizing *zamacuecas*, *yaravíes*, *tonadas chilenas*, a *cashua* and a 'baile arequipeño'. The same Romantic approach to nationalism was followed by José María Valle Riestra (1859–1925), the first truly professional Peruvian composer, educated in Europe. His opera *Ollanta* (given its première in 1900), based on a well-known, half-historical and half-legendary story, acquired resounding fame as the first major work by a Peruvian composer. His technical competence in handling larger forms made a strong impression on his Peruvian contemporaries. *Ollanta* was in fact an ambitious attempt to create a national opera. Perhaps ineffective because so closely imitative of Italian models, it nevertheless at the time stood as a symbol of truly Peruvian art music – essentially music made in Peru, with Peruvian motifs. Less ambitious but in some ways a more impressive composer, Luis Duncker Lavalle (1874–1922) wrote attractive piano pieces in a semi-popular style inspired by mestizo folk-music genres. His *Quenas*, 'vals característico indígena', and *Vals cholito* re-create the most typical criolla musical expression of the urban areas of the early twentieth century. However, it would be in the 1920s and later that the Indianist ('indigenismo') trend would bring to Peruvian music its full identity.

La Paz, the effective capital of Bolivia (the nominal one is Sucre), began organizing its musical life around the mid-nineteenth century, but not until the early twentieth were musical organizations with any degree of continuity established. The foundation of the Military School of Music (1904) and the National Conservatory of Music (1908), the Circle of Fine Arts (1910) and other such institutions contributed to musical life, but professional art-music composers in Bolivia flourished only after World War I. In Santiago de Chile musical organizations were generally shortlived during the latter part of the century. The Sociedad Orquestal (1912), for example, under the direction of Nino Marcelli, sponsored the first performance in Chile of Beethoven's symphonies in 1913 but ceased its activities in 1914 after its conductor's departure for Europe. The first composer in Chile who showed an early interest in Chilean folk and indigenous music was Pedro Humberto Allende (1885–1959) who cultivated a national style based on mestizo folk-music references in a context of French impressionist techniques. In 1913–14 he wrote the symphonic suite *Escenas campesinas chilenas*, the first Chilean nationalist symphonic work with both harmonic and orchestral modernist overtones. But Chilean art music entered its most productive phase in the 1920s.

ARGENTINA AND URUGUAY

In Argentina the development of art-music activities and supporting institutions in the nineteenth century was almost exclusively confined to the capital of Buenos Aires. Opera flourished there in a number of theatres. The original Teatro Colón opened in 1857, followed by the Teatro de la Opera (1872), the Teatro Politeama (1879) and the Teatro Nacional (1882). Thereafter, major European and local companies ensured Buenos Aires's status as a major opera centre of the world. The new Teatro Colón, which would become internationally renowned, opened in 1908.

During the latter part of the century, Argentine opera and piano music began to be extensively produced, mostly in Buenos Aires. Two representative composers were Francisco A. Hargreaves (1849–1900) and Juan Gutiérrez (1840–1906). Hargreaves, an opera composer, was one of the first Argentine musicians to draw on folk-music sources. His lyric work *La gatta bianca*, given its première in Italy in 1875, was at the time considered the first truly Argentine opera. He wrote numerous piano pieces in a virtuoso salon style but also paid attention to criolla or 'native' music: he stylized such typical folksongs and dances as the *gato*, *vidalita*, *décima* and *cielito* in his *Aires nacionales* (*c*1880) for piano; one of the most popular was the caprice *El gato* ('Baile nacional del gaucho argentino') which became known in Europe, Peru and Chile. In spite of its Romantic style, it maintains some of the traits of its folk model, for example the prevailing 6/8 metre and the major mode. Hargreaves's 'danzas habaneras' *Chinita*, *Negrita* and *Catita* were written in a pianistic style somewhat similar to Gottschalk's.

The period after about 1880 was decisive in the professional musical life of Argentina. Some 30 important musical societies promoting symphonic, choral, chamber and stage music were established in Buenos Aires alone during the second half of the century. This encouraged appearances by such famous virtuosos as Thalberg, Napoleão, Gottschalk, Ritter and Sarasate. A series of 'National Concerts' organized in Buenos Aires between 1874 and 1882 introduced a large number of local professional musicians and gained them initial recognition. By the end of the century several symphonic works with some national character had been produced and performed. The band director and composer Saturnino F. Berón (1847–98), for

63. The Teatro Colón, Buenos Aires, opened in 1908

example, included national dances (such as the *pericón*) in his symphonic poem *La pampa*, first performed at the old Colón with considerable success in 1878. Similarly, Arturo Berutti (1862–1938) composed a *Sinfonía argentina* in 1890, having written several piano works tinged with national elements, such as the *Seis danzas americanas* (1887). Although he lived half his life in the twentieth century, Berutti belonged aesthetically and stylistically to the nineteenth, as did many of his contemporaries; he also followed a Romantic nationalist trend in his operas, among which *Pampa* (1897) and *Yupanki* (1899) draw on folk themes from the Gaucho and Andean Indian folk traditions.

The real thrust towards musical nationalism in Argentina came with Alberto Williams (1862–1952). During his long and productive life, Williams exerted a fundamental influence. He was a student at the Paris Conservatoire in the 1880s and of César Franck for composition, and his first piano works (published in Paris in 1887) reveal a clear Franckian influence. First-hand acquaintance with Argentine folk music, however, changed his outlook. His earliest work inspired by Gaucho folk music, *El rancho abandonado* (1890), achieved wide popularity. From that time he strove to find and develop what has been called 'the union of accent between the country *payador* [folk singer-poet] and the cultured musician; one, the natural voice, the other, the intellectualized voice of the same land'.[4] Williams's piano works reveal the extent to which he was able to synthesize distinctive modes of expression. The first album of the *Aires de la pampa* (*Tres hueyas*) appeared in 1893, followed by many others to a total of over 50 pieces, including *vidalitas*, *gatos*, *cielitos*, *marotes*, *zambas* and an especially large number of *milongas* (in both danced and sung forms).

It is significant that Williams chose to focus his attention on Gaucho music, for the nationalist trend in the other arts of Argentina also emphasized the 'gauchesco' tradition. It is pertinent to recall the dictum of Ricardo Rojas concerning the essence of Argentine nationalism, or *argentinidad*: it 'is constituted by a territory, by a people, by a state, by a language, and by an ideal that tends to define itself better every day'. In Argentine literature this ideal came to be embodied in the 'gauchesco' tradition, of which the masterpiece is the epic poem *Martín Fierro* (1872) by José Hernández. Rojas (1882–1957) wrote the bible of that tradition in his *History of Argentine Literature* (1917–22), particularly the two volumes entitled *Los gauchescos* in which he pays much attention to the folk music and dances of the pampa, with numerous music examples. Musical composition was the last art to identify itself with this tradition; when it did so, literature often served as the connecting link. Besides his *Aires de la pampa*, Williams evoked the various types of folksongs and dances associated with the pampa in many other works, for example the *Primera sonata argentina* op.74 (1917), whose scherzo movement, 'Malambo', inspired later similar treatment of that folkdance among nationalist composers.

Montevideo developed somewhat parallel musical activities to Buenos Aires during the nineteenth century, particularly in music for the theatre and salon. The major theatre, the Teatro Solís, inaugurated in 1856, presented some of the leading European opera stars and instrumental virtuosos and staged well-known works. There the Uruguayan composer Tomás Giribaldi (1847–1930) had two of his operas produced, *La parisina* (1878) and *Manfredi di Svevia* (1882), and the première of his First Symphony (1885). Orchestral associations appeared in Montevideo in the last years of the century, particularly the Orchestra of the 'Sociedad Beethoven' (1897), at first under the Spanish conductor Manuel Pérez Badía, then the Uruguayan Luis Sambucetti (1860–1926), who also conducted the Orquesta Nacional (1908–10 and 1912–14). Sambucetti had founded the Instituto Verdi (1890) from which several chamber music groups were formed. Sambucetti's and other Uruguayan composers' works of the beginning of the twentieth century revealed the close adherence to European Romantic and post-Romantic styles.

BRAZIL

In Brazil a movement toward the creation of a national lyric theatre began in 1857 with the promotion by Francisco Manuel da Silva (1795–1865) of the use of the vernacular in opera. Under government auspices the Imperial Academy of Music and National Opera was founded that year, with the additional goal of producing at least one new opera a year by a Brazilian composer. The Spaniard D. José Zapata y Amat, an active participant in this movement, was entrusted with the management of the new institution. In 1860 a new organization, the Opera Lírica Nacional, replaced the academy and produced the first opera to deal with a local subject, written (both score and libretto) by Brazilians: Elias Alvares Lôbo's *A noite de São João*, with a libretto based on poems by the Indianist writer José de Alencar.

During the next opera season, the Teatro Lírico Fluminense staged *A noite do castelo* by Antônio Carlos Gomes (1836–96), the most successful opera composer of the Americas in the nineteenth century. A student of the Italian Giannini at the Rio Imperial Conservatory, then of Lauro Rossi at the Milan Conservatory, Gomes spent most of his life in Italy. His fame there began with two musical comedies in a *bel-canto*-like popular style. But it was the triumph in Milan of *Il Guarany* at the Teatro alla Scala in 1870 that brought him international renown. The opera was produced in Rio on the emperor's birthday that same year and in almost all European capitals in the next few years. Its spectacular success was due to its effective melodies, its dramatic construction and, not least, to its libretto, based on the celebrated novel of the same title by José de Alencar. This picturesque story, with its Indian heroes and its Romantic stylization of Indian dances, made the opera all the more appealing for European audiences, and, within the limits of its style, it exhibits imaginative traits. The final version of the overture, written in 1871, became virtually a second national anthem in Brazil.

While Gomes was staying briefly in Brazil in 1880, his writer friend the Viscount of Taunay suggested the subject of another 'Brazilian' opera, *Lo schiavo* ('The Slave'). At that time the movement toward the abolition of slavery was gathering force in Brazil, and Taunay wrote a drama whose main characters were black slaves. However, the librettist, Paravicini, decided to make fundamental changes to submit to the standard 'scenic necessities' of Italian opera. Black slaves were replaced by Indians and the action was transposed to the sixteenth century instead of the eighteenth. Nevertheless, the première in Rio in 1889 was a success. Although Gomes tried several times to instil a Brazilian feeling into his works, his nationalist feelings were not highly developed and he did not consider opera a genre conducive to a national musical expression.

Concert life also began to expand in Rio de Janeiro, especially during the last 20 years of the century. Newly founded concert societies and clubs stimulated the appearance in Brazil of some of the most celebrated performing artists of the time. 1869 saw Gottschalk's triumphs (and death) in Rio de Janeiro. His example may have impressed young composers, for the introduction of popular elements to art music was not common at that time. The first Brazilian nationalist composition was published in 1869 by Brasílio Itiberê da Cunha (1846–1913), an amateur composer and remarkable pianist; his piano piece *A sertaneja* attempts to re-create melodically and rhythmically the character of urban popular music of the time, even quoting a characteristic melody. Romantic musical nationalism in Brazil in its early phase is best represented, however, by the music of Alexandre Levy (1864–92), a native of São Paulo. His awareness of urban popular music rather than rural folk music is seen in his most characteristic piece, the *Tango brasileiro* (1890) for piano, and the *Suite brésilienne* (1890) for orchestra. The suite is the forerunner of many Brazilian nationalist suites. Although conceived with some programmatic intention, it was planned as a series of dances, as indicated by the titles of two of its four movements: *Prelúdio, Dança rústica-Canção triste, À Beira do regato* and *Samba*. The prelude is based on a popular tune, 'Vem cá Bitú' and the samba on two traditional ones, 'Balaio, meu bem, Balaio' and 'Se eu te amei', the last very popular in São Paulo at the time; the movement's rhythmic foundation is related to the Brazilian tango-habanera of the 1880s, rather than to the samba.

The decisive step towards the creation of national music in Brazil was achieved in the 1890s and early 1900s through the works of Alberto Nepomuceno (1864–1920) and through his influence. As early as 1887 he showed an interest in popular music; as well as mazurkas, romances and berceuses, his early piano works include a *Dança de negros*, the first 'Negro dance' of the Brazilian repertory which he later used in the last movement of his *Série brasileira*. In Berlin in the early 1890s he wrote a string quartet with the designation 'Brasileiro', though the work shows only slight national characterization. His piano piece *Galhofeira* (1894), however, reveals his familiarity with urban popular dance music. The entire piece is based on a syncopated accompaniment pattern found in most urban popular forms, especially the tango and the *maxixe*; above it are reiterations and variants of a descending broken-chord figure alternating with a characteristic melodic theme, all reflecting the popular idiom. With the *Série brasileira* for orchestra, first performed in 1897, he went beyond the mere use or adaptation of popular melodies and rhythms. The last movement, '*Batuque*', explores the rhythmic elements of the Afro-Brazilian dance known generically as *batuque* and samba, with its stereotyped description of the frenzy of dance that relies on rhythmic ostinatos, crescendos and acceleration. The piece is indeed symptomatic of the discovery of the rhythmic primacy of popular music, prefiguring similar accomplishments in twentieth-century works.

The Late Romantic Era

NOTES

[1] In the early 1950s film *The Great Caruso* Rosas's waltz was arranged as the sentimental song *The Loveliest Night of the Year*, proof of its international, popular style.

[2] A representative collection of these pieces is found in R. M. Campos, *El folklore musical de las ciudades* (Mexico, 1930).

[3] See R. Stevenson, *Music in Mexico: a Historical Survey* (New York, 1952), 226–7.

[4] From V. Gesualdo, *Historia de la música en la Argentina* (Buenos Aires, 1961), i, 527.

BIBLIOGRAPHICAL NOTE

Historical background

Various histories of Latin America deal with the important socio-cultural developments during the period under consideration. Particularly useful, though not recent, are H. Herring, *A History of Latin America from the Beginnings to the Present* (London and New York, 3/1968); G. Arciniegas, *Latin America: a Cultural History* (New York, 1966); and L. Zea, *Dos etapas en el pensamiento en Hispanoamérica* (Mexico, 1949). Access to excellent sources on historical and sociological topics in English is provided in the second volume of L. Hanke's anthology *History of Latin American Civilization, Sources and Interpretations* (London and Boston, 1967) and in *Readings in Latin American History*, ii: *The Modern Experience*, ed. J. J. Johnson, P. J. Bakewell and M. D. Dodge (Durham, N. Carolina, 1985). The first part of L. Manigat's *L'Amérique latine au XXe siècle, 1889–1929* (Paris, 1973) provides relevant explanations of the socio-political transformations of Latin America at the turn of the twentieth century.

Music

A proper social theory of music has not been developed for Latin America and the Caribbean. The general approach of available studies is therefore bio-bibliographical and stylistic. The most up-to-date biographical information on the composers mentioned in this chapter is available in *Grove 6*. Important studies of nineteenth-century music in various countries by some of the best-known Latin American musicologists appear in *Die Musikkulturen Lateinamerikas im 19. Jahrhundert* (Regensburg, 1982), ed. R. Günther, with English summaries. Various national histories of music present good overviews of the period. For Mexico, R. Stevenson's *Music in Mexico* (New York, 1952), and vol.iii by G. Carmona of *La música en México*, ed. J. Estrada (Mexico, 1984), detail the music history from 1850 to the 1910 revolution.

The music of Cuba and Puerto Rico is treated respectively in A. Carpentier's *La música en Cuba* (Mexico, 1946) and in H. Campos-Parsi, *La música*, Gran Enciclopedia de Puerto Rico, vii (Madrid, 1976). Another good historical survey of Puerto Rican music is M. L. Muñoz, *La música en Puerto Rico: panorama histórico-cultural* (Sharon, Conn., 1966). Cuban popular music is thoroughly discussed by A. León in *Del canto y el tiempo* (Havana, 1984), while C. Dower provides a wealth of information on Puerto Rican music and musicians at the turn of the century in her *Puerto Rican Music following the Spanish American War* (Landham, Maryland, New York and London, 1983).

Musical activities and institutions in Caracas, Venezuela, are reviewed in J. A. Calcaño, *La ciudad y su música* (Caracas, 1958), while C. Salas and E. F. Calcaño give a historical account of 150 years of opera activity in *Sesquicentenario de la ópera en Caracas* (Caracas, 1960). J. I. Perdomo Escobar dedicates several chapters to musical developments in Colombia in the latter part of the nineteenth century in *Historia de la música en Colombia* (Bogota, 3/1963) and S. L. Moreno surveys music in Ecuador, including data on late nineteenth-century composers, in his monograph *La música en el Ecuador* in El Ecuador en Cien años de Independencia, ed. J. G. Orellana (Quito,

1930). The multi-author volume *La música en el Perú* (Lima, 1985) includes a very informative chapter on nineteenth-century Peruvian music by E. Iturriaga and J. C. Estenssoro.

The Chilean music historian E. Pereira Salas reconstructs in great detail the diverse music-making of his country in the period 1850–1900, from primary documents, in his *Historia de la música en Chile* (Santiago, 1957), brought up to date by S. Claro-Valdés and J. Urrutia Blondel in their *Historia de la música en Chile* (Santiago, 1974). Musical life in Bolivia was the subject of two publications: N. F. Naranjo, *La vida musical en La Paz*, in La Paz en su Cuarto Centenario (La Paz, 1948), and J. de Mesa, *La música en Bolivia*, in La Iglesia y el Patrimonio Cultural (La Paz, 1969).

Late nineteenth-century Argentine music is studied in great detail by V. Gesualdo in the second volume of his *Historia de la música en la Argentina* (Buenos Aires, 1961); L. Ayestarán's *La música en el Uruguay* (Montevideo, 1953) provides an excellent account of music in that country up to 1860. S. Salgado updates that history in her *Breve historia de la música culta en el Uruguay* (Montevideo, 1971).

The most informative sources for Brazilian music history of this period are L. H. Corrêa de Azevedo, *150 anos de música no Brasil, 1800–1950* (Rio de Janeiro, 1956); his *Relação das óperas de autores brasileiros* (Rio de Janeiro, 1938); F. C. Lange, 'A música erudita na regência e no império', in *História da civilização brasileira*, ii/3, ed. S. Buarque de Holanda (São Paulo, 1967); G. Béhague, *The Beginnings of Musical Nationalism in Brazil* (Detroit, 1971); B. Kiefer, *História da música brasileira, dos primórdios ao início do século XX* (Porto Alegre, 2/1977); and V. Mariz, *Historia da música no Brasil* (Rio de Janeiro, 2/1983).

Chapter XIII

Germany:
Cross-Currents and Contradictions

ARNOLD WHITTALL

In his novella *Death in Venice*, published in 1911, Thomas Mann tells
the story of how a writer who, in his art, prizes Apollonian restraint
above all, succumbs to the intoxicating spirit of Dionysus. This
portrait of an artist can also be read as a metaphor for an age, one that
was not simply 'decadent' – in thrall to the spirit of the *fin de siècle* –
but dominated by particularly strong cross-currents in intellectual
and artistic affairs, as well as in the 'real world' of politics and
economics that served, in combination, to generate the cultural
catastrophe of World War I.

Nowhere were these cross-currents stronger than in Germany:
'from 1890 to 1914 . . . we can detect in Germany two complementary
and contradictory processes – a cultural revival and the beginnings of
a "secession of the intellectuals." The tension between the two was to
give a character of painful self-searching to German intellectual life in
its most critical quarter-century'.[1] That intellectual life was dominated by academic historians and social scientists, many of whom
'found something repellent about the social atmosphere of Wilhelm-
inian Germany – its bragging, its parvenu vulgarity'. Yet just as
academics 'were frequently state functionaries of a government –
like that of Prussia – of whose constitution they thoroughly dis-
approved', so most artists, however painful their own self-searchings,
were obliged to achieve some accommodation with employers and
administrators in what was, after all, an expanding economy.
Whether or not, like Mann, they reached 1914 without having learnt
how to bring their 'contradictions into harmony', composers and
performing musicians had little choice (beyond dependence on private means and personal patronage) but to live and work within an
artistic environment the predominant characteristic of which was not
an all-pervading philistinism but an increasingly strong conservatism.

Certain aspects of that living and working will be the main concern
of this chapter, but the broader cultural context will be outlined first.
While historians of German literature of this period can discuss

developments in terms of modernism and expressionism, and historians of painting can link the radical Secessionist activities of the 1890s to the eventual flowering of expressionism after 1910, historians of German music are more likely to identify a persistent late Romanticism, a rejection of expressionism (save for the music the Austrian Schoenberg wrote in Berlin between 1911 and 1915) and even an early adumbration of the spirit of neo-classicism in the wry nostalgia of Richard Strauss, after *Elektra*, and the closely worked counterpoint of Max Reger. The main initiatives for the decisive transformation of the musical language of late Romanticism, and the exploration of new formal possibilities that went with that transformation, were taken in Paris (by Debussy) and Vienna (by Schoenberg), not in Germany. It is more than likely that Strauss's encounter with Schoenberg's Five Orchestral Pieces op.16 in 1909 played a part in his decision that modernism or expressionism were not for him. And even if Strauss's rejection of progressiveness did not become decisive until after the completion of *Die Frau ohne Schatten* in 1917[2] it is understandable that historians should not shrink from the obvious conclusions when comparing creative developments in France and Austria before 1914 with those in Germany.

Contemporary theorists, historians and critics were aware of the difficulties of living in the post-Wagnerian age when Wagner's own music was still of central significance. As the compositional avatars of progress and retrenchment alike sought to give their work the only qualities that would ensure its life – coherent structure and strong expression – there was a commendable willingness on the part of German theorists, notably Hugo Riemann, to focus on what they regarded as the prime source of that expression, chromatic harmony. For the present-day historian of theory, the value of this up-to-dateness seems tarnished by the evident contradiction between the sheer scale and strength of late Romantic music and the excessively dogmatic, obsessively 'vertical' approach of theorists who lacked much sense of the larger linear forces at work, even in Wagner, since they were unable to distinguish between structural harmonies and their prolongations. Present-day historians are therefore more likely to identify worthwhile up-to-dateness in the curiosity about new structural possibilities found in such writers as Hermann Schröder and Georg Capellen before 1914, not to mention the Berlin-based Busoni, all of whom in some ways anticipated postwar developments in the theory and practice of atonal and serial composition.[3]

Nevertheless, German music theorists made a significant contribution to the new discipline of musicology and to the increasing awareness of the tension between old and new that typified the late Romantic period. Tension was also evident in German writers on music whose material was more aesthetic than technical, between

those who argued that it was valuable to provide verbal interpretations of the 'affections' present in music[4] and those who cautioned
that 'music obeys its own inherent laws and does not refer to models
in nature or the human spirit'.[5] This latter emphasis on the self-
referentiality of music fitted particularly well with the views of
historians like Paul Bekker and Walter Niemann who argued that the
degree of closeness and sympathy between composer and audience,
believed to have existed in the days of Bach or Beethoven, no longer
obtained. Just as music referred primarily to itself and was therefore
best elucidated in terms of technical theories like Riemann's functional harmony, so composers were primarily independent individuals
rather than social beings. If Wagner had failed to create a new sense
of community between society and the artist, it was argued, it was
hardly likely that his (lesser) successors would – or should –
succeed.[6]

German writers on music stressed the individuality and independence of the composer within society, but it was natural they should
express a complementary anxiety about the ease with which that
individuality and independence might be eroded by foreign influences. Debussy, Mascagni and Puccini were the principal dangers:
and yet the defensiveness of critics and historians was scarcely
necessary. The leading German composer of the time, Richard
Strauss, was no more seriously tempted by impressionism or *verismo*
than he was by Viennese expressionism and its attendant atonality,
though he was well aware of Puccini's commercial success and
acknowledged the great Italian as his principal rival for the attention
of opera-house managements. Lesser composers, if anything, benefited rather than suffered from contact with outside influences. Even
so, the operas of Eugen d'Albert, especially *Tiefland* (1903), might well
have been less successful, artistically and commercially, had not their
debts to German traditions ultimately been more important than
those associations with *verismo* so widely noted at the time.[7] More
significant than the possibly damaging influence of foreign tendencies
on German composers was the enlightened interest of certain conductors and performers in radically inclined foreign composers (one
interesting example, the advocacy of Delius by Julius Buths in
Düsseldorf and Hans Haym in Elberfeld, will be discussed below).
Germany was by no means unwelcoming to foreign composers, from
Schoenberg to Ethel Smyth, and Strauss set a good example of
support for those whose music he no doubt regarded as too radical or
too inferior to pose a serious threat.

*

If the tension between old and new was the principal technical and aesthetic factor confronting composers, musicians generally were having to adapt to a similarly Janus-faced society in which long-established courts co-existed with newly expanded, increasingly wealthy cities. Between 1890 and 1914 Germany was the dominant industrial power in Europe.[8] It was an increasingly urbanized society; during the period under discussion the proportion of the population working on the land fell from well over 50 per cent to about 35 per cent. 'The German cities grew very fast indeed in the generation after 1870. They were also very ugly'; the economy flourished, yet the state, 'despite its large middle class and the growing prosperity of its working class', was more a 'managed autocracy' than a 'bourgeois democracy'. The resulting tension affected all aspects of life, even the management of opera houses, especially when administrators in thrall to the still-prominent aristocracy – or to the Prussian or Bavarian monarchies – clashed with artists determined to assert a degree of independence.

The German economic boom had the side-effect of boosting spending on the arts. There were new opera houses and concert halls, and expansion in that crucial service industry, music publishing. Opportunities for talented practical musicians increased and demands for the services of the exceptionally gifted, in an age when rail and sea travel had greatly improved, were correspondingly intense. The foundations of twentieth-century patterns of professional music-making were being laid, not least in the way new compositions were ceasing to be central to musical life. The 'museum culture' was being born.

The establishment of the German empire in 1871 had not led to any rapid loss of local cultural identity in the state capitals and cities, and many opportunities remained for musicians in centres smaller than Berlin, Hamburg or Munich. It was to the relatively small city of Weimar that Strauss moved in 1889, at the age of 25, to take up the post of Kapellmeister. In flight from the stresses of his native Munich, Strauss immediately thought the seat of the Grand Duke of Saxe Weimar a 'delightfully situated town'.[9] In spite of – or because of – its size, Weimar was a cultured city, with residents like the Baroness von Meyendorff, who had befriended Liszt during his years there. The Grand Duke himself dispensed patronage in a manner that would have been familiar a century earlier. On his master's golden wedding, in 1892, Strauss was the recipient of the Knight's Cross (second class) of the Grand Ducal Order of Vigilance.

Yet it was in the nature of a Kapellmeister's work – at least when that officer was an ambitious, talented and increasingly successful composer – that initial enthusiasm for both place and people would wane, sooner rather than later. After all, Strauss had already completed *Don Juan* and *Tod und Verklärung* before moving to Weimar: his principal creative project there was his first opera, *Guntram*. He was not even the senior conductor (there was a Hofkapellmeister) and the experience of conducting such works as *Fidelio*, *Tannhäuser* and *Lohengrin* with so small an orchestra led to disillusionment. Even so, the results were far from negative: Strauss's uncut performance of *Tristan und Isolde* in 1892 was a notable achievement for that time and there was a burst of Straussian pride when after a concert in Berlin in 1891 he wrote that 'my handful of string players [in Weimar] cut more of a dash than Bülow's fourteen violins'. With his particular enthusiasm for conducting the music of Liszt and Wagner, Strauss was able to continue the bias towards the (relatively) new, evident in Weimar since Liszt's time. (By the early 1890s *Lohengrin*, which had been given its first performance in Weimar by Liszt in 1850, had been performed a hundred times there.)

As Strauss became more widely known as both composer and conductor, and more frequently in demand, he was increasingly in conflict with officials and artists in Weimar itself. As he later admitted, 'I alienated the sympathies of many with my youthful impetuosity and extravagances'; but not even his worst enemies in the city could accuse him of indolence. As well as conducting operas and subscription concerts he was in demand as a pianist for chamber concerts and recitals. When possible he travelled to other, more prestigious centres like Berlin, Leipzig and Dresden, whose orchestra, in 1890, he declared the best at that time. In one week, in March 1892, he provided evidence, in a letter to his father, of the exhausting days he had spent:

> Tuesday evening *Tristan*, then left for here [Leipzig, some 60 miles] at 11.30 at night, Wednesday took the first rehearsal for the Liszt-Verein concert from 10 to 2.30, back to Weimar in the evening. Yesterday, Thursday, evening conducted *Lohengrin* in Eisenach, returned here at 1 a.m., today the second rehearsal from 10 till 1 and from 3 to 6, tomorrow principal rehearsal at 10, concert in the evening, programme: Liszt, *Die Ideale*, Schubert-Liszt: Wanderer Fantasy (Siloti), *Mazeppa*, piano solos, *Tod und Verklärung*.

A few days later, Strauss reported in a further letter that 'the whole affair in Leipzig was a sensational success'. On his departure 'young enthusiasts accompanied me to the station and cheered as the train pulled out, one even kissed my hand. In short, my fame is advancing by leaps and bounds'.

With this rate of activity, coupled with such heady success, it is scarcely surprising that Strauss's health suffered and he grew ever more restive in Weimar. By autumn 1893, when he returned from a prolonged journey of convalescence to Egypt and had completed *Guntram*, he was referring to 'dreary little Weimar', and to 'the miserable state of art that prevails here in Germany'. What was to be his final season there was notable for the world première of that least radical yet most attractive of post-Wagnerian operas, Humperdinck's *Hänsel und Gretel* (23 December 1893). After lengthy negotiations, further complicated by the fact that at this time such an appointment still needed Bavarian royal approval, Strauss signed a contract as Kapellmeister in Munich, from October 1894.

As Strauss well knew, Munich offered a very different environment from Weimar. He had worked in his birthplace before, as third conductor of the Hofoper (1886–9), and must have cherished the hope that the larger resources available in the Bavarian capital would compensate for the loss of some of the freedom he had enjoyed in Weimar. Yet the four years (1894–8) Strauss now spent in Munich soon developed the familiar pattern of tensions and disagreements with colleagues and administrators: of undoubted artistic achievements and rewards – these were the years of *Till Eulenspiegel, Also sprach Zarathustra, Don Quixote* and *Ein Heldenleben* – offset to no small extent by the demands of a system, and an audience, that required a richly varied diet in both opera house and concert hall. Munich in the 1890s was a centre of increasing activity and experiment in the arts, and though Strauss himself 'had no very close relationship with the writers, painters and others who were in the vanguard of the modern movement' he was soon at odds with a musical establishment suspicious of the new. 'It was not primarily Strauss's subjective, and what were felt to be "modern", interpretations of the classics which were unacceptable to the conservative majority in the orchestra and the public at large, but rather the programmes in which he obstinately persisted along the path he had set out upon in Weimar.' Strauss's reputation as a conductor therefore prospered more outside Munich than within it. Nor was his local position helped by the failure of his ambitious but in certain ways inept first opera *Guntram* on its première at the Hoftheater in November 1895. He was soon plotting his escape from the city that he felt persistently undervalued him, and though in 1896 he succeeded Hermann Levi as Hofkapellmeister he continued to look for another post. Finally, in 1898, he was appointed first Kapellmeister to the Prussian Court in Berlin, sharing the chief conductorship with Karl Muck. Elated at the prospect, Strauss hailed Berlin as 'a delightful city', a phrase similar to the one he had applied to Weimar nine years before. Nevertheless he would at last find in the German capital the sympathy with his own artistic ideals that had eluded him so far, and that sympathy, with the vital and varied cultural life that made Berlin special, was in turn to enrich his own creative work. While in Berlin he would compose in remarkably rapid succession his most innovatory – and most popular – operas, *Salome*, *Elektra* and *Der Rosenkavalier*.

*

The frustrations and rewards experienced by Strauss in Weimar and Munich during the 1890s were matched by Mahler in Hamburg. Mahler was not German by birth, but his impact on German musical life was considerable, and the story of his years as a conductor in Hamburg, from 1891 to 1897, reveals much about the forces at work in the cultural life of a large German city in the last decade of the nineteenth century.

Hamburg was a free city: there was no court to dominate and interfere. It was, moreover, a 'beautiful and animated city, with a magnificent harbour, and an admirable climate, where Mahler felt able to settle in what was for him unprecedented comfort'.[10] But the mere absence of a court did not result in the promotion of an uninhibited delight in experiment and innovation. What Mahler found at the Hamburg Opera on his arrival in 1891 was 'an audience of bourgeois and financiers who were interested mainly in beautiful voices and vocal fireworks'. Since 1874 the two theatres of Germany's second city had been run by the impresario Bernhard Baruch Pollini, a skilled manager and talent-scout who had a shrewd, well-developed sense of what the public wanted and who might therefore be regarded as more representative of the tastes and preferences of the time than Mahler himself.

In circumstances dominated by the laws of supply and demand, artistic values were scarcely pre-eminent, audiences undiscriminating. The number of performances and the variety of works were fearsome: no wonder the orchestra was often exhausted. In 1894–5, probably Mahler's most hectic Hamburg season, he conducted 134 performances at the opera, in a repertory ranging from Mozart and Weber to Verdi and Smetana (not forgetting large amounts of Wagner), as well as a variety of concerts, including two in celebration of Bismarck's birthday. The price for such constant and unremittingly varied musical activity in Hamburg was evidently a standard of performance that, given the demands on the permanent musicians, must have been vulnerable both to fatigue and boredom; and Mahler himself had all too little time or energy in which to nurture his gifts as a composer.

> Mahler's frustrations in Hamburg were many; the works that made up the vast repertoire were hardly ever rehearsed, and while he dreamed of uniting the opera's visual, dramatic and musical elements, so that the spectators could 'live' the drama and penetrate its inner meaning, Pollini paid attention only to the voices, caring

nothing for staging, dramatic truth or scenery. Consequently, in Hamburg, Mahler was never to conduct an 'ensemble' such as the one he had created, in spite of all obstacles, in Budapest, but only a group of admirable soloists. As a result, he never experienced complete artistic joy in all the time he was there.

The prestige of Hamburg was nevertheless such that, in spite of lack of rehearsal, Mahler could count on some of the best opera singers of the time, especially in the Wagner repertory. It seems likely, therefore, that artistic satisfaction, if not 'complete', was not negligible, at least until 1896, when Pollini's desire to be rid of Mahler began to make all aspects of life in Hamburg unpleasant. An indication of the power wielded by Pollini is that in 1892, when Mahler was absent from Hamburg for a while after the opening of the opera season, 'Pollini accused him of having broken his contract and tried to impose a fine of 12,000 marks, almost a year's salary'. Arbitration by a mutual friend resolved the matter, but trust between Mahler and Pollini was never fully restored. Such an experience left Mahler convinced that Hamburg was not a place where he could ever be completely himself. And yet Pollini's régime was not so draconian that Mahler was not able to travel widely and consolidate his reputation to the extent that he was soon being sought out by the most prestigious of all European opera houses, the Vienna Hofoper.

Mahler's Hamburg years greatly enhanced his reputation as a conductor. More important, perhaps, it seems likely that his success there helped to create the confidence with which he was able to embark on his first mature compositions. And though Mahler was considered more successful as an operatic than a symphonic conductor – he directed only one season of subscription concerts with the Hamburg Philharmonic (1894–5) – it was an orchestral concert in October 1893 that marked a significant step towards his eventual recognition as a composer. That concert included some of the *Wunderhorn* songs and the work that was to become the First Symphony, then described as '*Titan*: tone poem in symphonic form'.

Mahler's increasing creative confidence also owed much to the support of the most prominent and respected German performing musician of the time, Hans von Bülow, then nearing the end of his career (he died in 1894) but a formidable character with widespread influence. All the evidence is that Mahler, like Bülow, was a highly professional conductor well able to achieve the best possible results in difficult circumstances, though at the inevitable cost of tensions and hostility from musicians who were suffering no less than their conductor from the strains the system imposed.

It is not easy to establish to what extent that 'best' matches what would be found excellent, or even adequate, today. It was a time when conductors learnt primarily by experience and had no scruples about taking liberties with the scores they interpreted: Mahler himself was criticized for wayward tempos and doubling of instrumental parts in a performance of Beethoven's Ninth Symphony in Hamburg in 1895, and his 'improvements' of Schumann's symphonies are particularly well known. Only when the 'museum culture' of the later twentieth century came into its stride would such 'creative' behaviour by conductors be virtually outlawed. It should not be forgotten that, by the time he left Hamburg for Vienna Mahler, at 37, was still relatively young. There was a strong feeling in Hamburg that after his departure the city's musical life went into decline. Only when Otto Klemperer took over as chief conductor of the Opera in 1910 did it regain something of its earlier distinction. Mahler, 'relatively young' when he went but with only thirteen years of life left, sustained his German connections after 1897 mainly through the premières of most of his later symphonies: no.4 (1901, Munich), no.3 (1902, Krefeld), no.5 (1904, Cologne), no.6 (1906, Essen) and no.8 (1910, Munich).

*

An account of the experiences and attitudes of Richard Strauss and Mahler in the 1890s may prompt speculation about the extent to which the musical interests of any community are best served by talented performers whose principal ambition (and ability) is creative, not re-creative. After 1890 conductors came to be increasingly valued for the conviction they brought to what we now think of as the 'standard' repertory. They were not expected to spend much time on new works, still less to write them themselves, but to cultivate the familiar and well tried. Not that all interest in the new – provided it was not too radical – was suddenly eliminated. One of the most widely admired opera conductors, Ernst von Schuch, who worked in Dresden from 1872 to 1914 (the last 25 years of that long period as general music director), gave 51 world premières during his tenure and added over a hundred operas to the repertory. Moreover, von Schuch was able to benefit from a situation in which at least one leading contemporary composer – Richard Strauss – was 'good box office'. Strauss's admiration for the Dresden orchestra in 1890 has already been cited; after 1870, when its first concert hall was built, Dresden was one of the best musical centres in Germany. Strauss's *Feuersnot* (1901), *Salome* (1905), *Elektra* (1909) and *Der Rosenkavalier* (1911) had their premières there: one of the most remarkable, sustained examples of enlightened promotion of genius in the early twentieth century. Dresden had a rich musical life at all levels, in church and concert hall as well as in the opera house.

The one German centre in which musical life was not dominated by opera was Leipzig, though the degree of enterprise that led to the first performance there of Ethel Smyth's *The Wreckers* in 1906 is an indication that operatic life in the city should not be completely overlooked.[11] Nevertheless the Gewandhaus Orchestra is generally regarded as the city's leading musical institution, and under the long directorship of Carl Reinecke, from 1860 to 1895, it adopted an increasingly conservative stance, to such a degree that in 1884 the opening of a new Gewandhaus building was marked by three concerts in which the most recent music heard was by Schumann and Spohr. This hall had a capacity of just over 1500 and the orchestra in 1890 had a membership of 98, more than double that of the mid-1840s.[12] With the appointment in 1895 of Arthur Nikisch as Reinecke's successor the size of the orchestra increased still further and its repertory was extended to include all the major Romantic and late Romantic masters as well as such moderns as Delius and Schoenberg.

Nikisch is celebrated as one of the first 'modern' conductors with regard to technique: among accounts of his activities in Leipzig before 1914 is that of the young Englishman Adrian Boult, a lifelong admirer of his undemonstrative proficiency. Boult was one of the many foreign students attracted by the high reputation of the Leipzig Conservatory, of which Reinecke was director for a time. But the most significant composer-teacher in the city during this period was Max Reger, who worked not at the conservatory but at Leipzig University, where he was director of music (1907–11). Reger had no great geniuses among his pupils (though he did teach Othmar Schoeck and George Szell), yet he found the city congenial and composed some of his most imposing chamber and orchestral works there before moving on to Meiningen as conductor of the Court Orchestra. Here, although the orchestra (founded by von Bülow in 1880) was small, Reger introduced an adventurous repertory, encouraged by Duke Georg II of Saxe-Meiningen, ranging from Beethoven and Berlioz to Strauss and Debussy. Throughout this period Leipzig maintained its reputation as a city in which the publishing of compositions and music journals, notably the long-lived *Neue Zeitschrift für Musik*, flourished. Not only did church and choral music continue to prosper, but the city was even able to accommodate a second orchestra, the Philharmonic, founded towards the end of the nineteenth century.

The conservatory in Frankfurt was even more prestigious at this time than that in Leipzig. It was in Frankfurt in the 1890s that a young English music student, Henry Balfour Gardiner, was able to hear 'a wealth of modern music he had never previously encountered'.[13] The new opera house, opened in 1880, was notably well equipped. But it was for orchestral music – the premières of Strauss's *Also Sprach Zarathustra* and *Ein Heldenleben* both took place there, in 1896 and 1899 – that Frankfurt was most celebrated. The Hoch Conservatory was founded in 1877 and named after its benefactor, a

64.(a) *Richard Strauss (seated, centre) with leading members of the Dresden Opera in 1910:
(seated, left to right) Count Seebach (director-general), Strauss, Ernst von Schuch (conductor);
(standing, left to right) Max Hasait (technical director), Otto Altenkirch (scenic artist), Max
Reinhardt, Hugo von Hofmannsthal (librettist), Alfred Roller (set designer), Leonhard Fanto
(costume designer) and Georg Toller (producer)*

(b) *'Elektra' by Richard
Strauss: title-page of the
first edition of the vocal
score, designed by Louis
Corinth, published by
Adolph Fürstner (Berlin,
1908)*

wealthy Frankfurt citizen. The first director was Joachim Raff; after his death in 1882 his successor was Bernhard Scholz, a much less enlightened figure. The result was schism: the Hoch Conservatory favoured the apparent traditionalism propounded by the supporters of the notorious attack by Brahms and Joachim on the so-called 'New Germans', the adherents of Liszt and Wagner.

The radical teachers, encouraged by Hans von Bülow, formed a breakaway Raff Conservatory in 1883. During the 1890s the person who did most to enhance the reputation of the Hoch Conservatory was not Engelbert Humperdinck, whose teaching from 1890 to 1897 appears to have been confined to choral singing and solfeggio, but Iwan Knorr. Knorr had studied in Leipzig with Moscheles and Reinecke and joined the Frankfurt staff in 1883 on Brahms's recommendation. From 1888 he taught only composition and was eventually named 'royal professor' in 1895, succeeding Scholz as director in 1908 and continuing in the post until his death in 1916.

In the 1890s there were about 250 students each year at the conservatory, of whom more than half were women – an unusually high proportion and probably the result of Clara Schumann's association with the establishment from 1878 (she retired in 1892 but continued to teach privately until her death in 1896). By the time one of the most gifted foreign students, Percy Grainger, entered the conservatory in 1895, nearly a fifth of the students were from overseas: of the 257 enrolled for the 1895–6 session, 31 were from Great Britain, fourteen from America, three from Australia and two from New Zealand.[14] In England 'it was a generally held opinion at the time that musical education on the continent was superior to that available at home'.[15] In various ways, all the members of the so-called 'Frankfurt Group' – Balfour Gardiner, Percy Grainger, Norman O'Neill, Roger Quilter and Cyril Scott – benefited from their studies there: even the adolescent Grainger, though he was soon at odds with Knorr and ceased attending his counterpoint classes. Scott was more appreciative of Knorr, declaring in his memoirs that 'one of the secrets of Knorr's excellence as a teacher was that he never discouraged originality if it was in good taste'.[16] And Knorr himself, in a letter of 1907, observed that 'I have trained pupils, I might say, in all "price ranges", from the dyed-in-the-wool Philistine to people like Hans Pfitzner and the brilliant, revolutionary Cyril Scott. I have endeavoured to respect the individual and taken care not to impose my taste or my tendency on him'.

The only centre to outdo Frankfurt as a place of pilgrimage did so for rather different reasons. The Festspielhaus at Bayreuth had soon become a shrine to the vision and persistence of its creator, who had had the foresight to found a dynasty whose determination and persistence would match his own. There were fifteen Bayreuth

65. *Concert conducted by Carl Reinecke in the new Leipzig Gewandhaus; engraving after E. Limmer from the 'Illustrirte Zeitung' (Leipzig, 1891)*

Festivals between 1891 and 1914; the most crucial point of change came in 1907, when Siegfried Wagner, at 38, took over from his mother as director. Before 1907 the widespread respect for Cosima's position as the Master's widow did not eliminate a predictable diversity of opinion about the dramatic and musical quality of the productions for which she was responsible. In 1891, when *Tannhäuser* was performed in the Festspielhaus for the first time, under Felix Mottl, there was lavish praise from Richard Strauss for both con-ductor and orchestra. Three years later, George Bernard Shaw, starting from the entrenched belief that German orchestras were inferior to English ones, declared a performance of *Parsifal* to be an 'abomination' from the musical point of view.[17]

Cosima's greatest challenge was the revival of the *Ring* in 1896, the first staging at Bayreuth since its 1876 première. There were severe criticisms of Cosima from such (biassed) sources as Lilli Lehmann, whose memories of the Master himself were still vivid. It was generally acknowledged that the costumes were more successful than the settings. Nevertheless, the production, like all those directed by Cosima, was 'characterized by a strict subservience to dramatic form, and this disciplined approach led to the evolution of a method which eventually became known as the "Bayreuth style"'.[18] Cosima, like Richard before her, was the sworn enemy of conventional operatic 'acting'. It was vital that the singers reacted to each other rather than simply playing to the audience. Yet it seems that in practice she tended to inhibit spontaneity, stressing details at the expense of larger concerns.

The main problem faced by Cosima was the one that has always dominated Wagner performance: where are the singers adequate to these demanding works to come from, and should they be specially trained for the Wagner repertory? Cosima's attempt, in 1892, to fulfil Richard's wish and establish a special music school in Bayreuth itself soon foundered, but she did build up a reliable group of singers, among them Marie Brema, Pauline de Ahna (Richard Strauss's wife) and Rosa Sucher, around whom the relatively regular festivals of these two decades could be constructed.

No less vital for the survival of Bayreuth was the presence of able conductors. Wagner's own associate Hans Richter remained the principal source of continuity with the festival's origins (he was otherwise more active in Vienna and England than in Germany), while the most prominent of the younger recruits was Karl Muck, whose appearances at the festival spanned three decades (1901–30). It was nevertheless 'the son', Siegfried Wagner, who did most to mould the Bayreuth style in the early years of the twentieth century.

By the time he took over the festival directorship in 1907, Siegfried had been assisting his mother for sixteen years. He had become a successful opera composer in his own right – *Der Bärenhäuter* (1895) is no worse than many operas of the second rank performed at that time – and he was well schooled in the qualities needed to achieve his aims without futile attempts to imitate, still less to outdo, his parents. For this reason, however, it was only gradually that he took a firm grip, and his most important innovations, modernizing the theatre itself and encouraging new styles of production, came in the 1920s. Though changes could be discerned, in the 1908 production of *Lohengrin*, for example, the period of Siegfried's directorship from 1907 to 1914 has been described as 'an almost imperceptible continuation of Cosima Wagner's régime'.[19] By 1912 one foreign observer had a strong impression of decadence and decay,[20] and Bayreuth's uniqueness was further undermined by the failure to confine performances of *Parsifal* to the festival city when its copyright expired in 1913. Perhaps the most extraordinary consequence was the young Otto Klemperer's record: 23 performances of *Parsifal* in Barmen and 25 in Elberfeld, all in the 1913–14 season.[21]

*

In 1889 the 23-year-old Busoni called Berlin 'that odious, dreary, lazy, ostentatious, *parvenu* and expressionless town of Jews'.[22] Three years later he nevertheless decided to make his home there. Berlin was much more than a convenient base for reaching Europe's principal musical centres. Its sheer size, and the consequent diversity of its musical life, meant that however strong the prevailing conservatism of audiences and promoters, there was ample room for experiment. Challenges of all kinds to accepted institutions and ideas were possible, and while Busoni's challenge was at first more evident in his recital programmes and writings (his *Sketch of a New Aesthetic of Music* was first published, in German, in 1907) than in his compositions, he was only one of a number of creative musicians who found the city increasingly congenial as a place in which to live and work, and who in turn enriched its artistic life.

Of all the musicians resident in Berlin throughout this period, none was less sympathetic to progressive ideas than Max Bruch. Born in 1838, he had achieved early success with his First Violin Concerto (1864–6) and had devoted much time to music for Germany's flourishing choral societies. His career as a conductor had taken him to various centres, including a three-year spell in Liverpool (1880–83), but in 1890, at 53, he decided to return to the German capital (he had lived there between 1870 and 1873) without a conducting post. From 1891 to 1911 Bruch directed a composition masterclass at the Royal Academy of Arts, whose director was the great violinist Joachim. This not only brought Bruch the occasional talented pupil from overseas (Respighi, Vaughan Williams) but also enabled him to continue his activities as composer and conductor.

Bruch had never been sympathetic to the 'New Germans', and his disenchantment with the general state of music, performance as well as composition, intensified in his later years. In 1896 after a performance of his Third Violin Concerto conducted by Richard Strauss, Bruch referred to the young Bavarian as a rogue; in 1907 he described Mahler's music as 'destructive rubbish',[23] and he held equally unflattering views about Max Reger, among others. His works continued to be performed with reasonable regularity, not least because they were so carefully crafted, but critical reaction was increasingly negative. It is not necessarily that Berlin critics responded more positively to radical composers, but that we now see in their progressiveness the principal source of the city's musical vitality.

In spite of its increasingly cosmopolitan air, Berlin remained a city with a strong tradition of amateur and privately sponsored music-making. Since the early nineteenth century 'the court's role as the main stimulus of Berlin's musical life was increasingly taken over by churches, schools and dilettante families'.[24] Church choirs and choral societies flourished and the tradition of house concerts, begun by such wealthy families as the Mendelssohns, continued. The Berlin Philharmonic Orchestra, regarded for much of the twentieth century as the city's principal musical asset, grew not from the Court Orchestra but from another body founded by Benjamin Bilse in 1867. The Philharmonic began to consolidate its reputation as the city's best orchestra after 1895, when Arthur Nikisch became its chief conductor. The imperial court remained active in the city's musical life, especially in the administration of the royal opera, up to 1914; it was here that Richard Strauss served as general music director, in succession to Felix Weingartner, from 1898 to 1918.

When Strauss arrived in Berlin, he found that 'the repertory was unadventurous, aimed primarily at pleasing the court, flattering its dignity and respecting its politics'.[25] The administration kept the musicians in their place, to such a degree that 'conductors had no influence: their names did not appear on posters or programmes'. Nevertheless, the emperor, while not caring for Strauss's compositions, allowed him generous terms of service, and Strauss's early reactions were favourable. As he wrote to his father: 'I'm happy and very highly satisfied. I like Berlin with its splendid transport facilities ... The orchestra has excellent discipline. I am treated with the greatest respect. A real blessing after Munich'.

Strauss soon plunged into a typically hectic round of activities. 'Besides composing, he was conducting in the opera house – sometimes five times a week – and conscientiously coaching singers and orchestra in a large number of new additions to the repertory'. Since Weingartner was still in charge of concerts by the opera orchestra, and Nikisch was well ensconced with the Philharmonic, Strauss took on a third band, the Berliner Tonkünstler, and devised programmes dominated by new and recent compositions. He kept up this punishing routine until 1907, when illness forced him to reduce his work. In 1911 he gave up his permanent post at the Hofoper but remained in Berlin as guest conductor. By 1911, of course, he had begun to achieve worldwide renown as an opera composer.

Strauss's reputation as a champion of contemporary music was the main reason why Arnold Schoenberg sought his help during his first period of residence in Berlin (1901–3). Schoenberg was musical director of the Überbrettl, a small, cabaret-style theatre; it was a post scarcely likely to satisfy his deeper artistic ambitions, though the theatre itself was a significant part of the 'alternative' culture that would become even more prominent in Berlin in the 1920s. Strauss was sympathetic to Schoenberg, and helped him to obtain a teaching post at the Stern Conservatory in Berlin as well as a Liszt Prize, awarded by the Allgemeiner Deutscher Musikverein in 1902. Strauss is also credited with drawing Schoenberg's attention to the play by Maeterlinck that inspired his great orchestral tone poem *Pelleas und Melisande* (1902–3).

In 1909 Strauss diplomatically told Schoenberg that his Five

66.(a) *Arthur Nikisch with the Berlin Philharmonic Orchestra; photograph, c1900*

✳ PHILHARMONIE. ✳

Montag den 14. October 1895, Abends 7¹/₂ Uhr sehr präcise

I. Philharmonisches Concert.

Dirigent:

Arthur Nikisch.

Solist: **Josef Hofmann** (Klavier).

PROGRAMM.

1. Ouverture zu: „Leonore" No. 3, C-dur *L. v. Beethoven.*

2. Symphonie No. 5, E-moll, op. 64 (zum
   1. Mal) . . . . *P. Tschaïkowsky.*
   Andante. Allegro con anima. — Andante
   cantabile, con alcuna licenza. — Valse. Allegro
   moderato. — Finale. Andante maëstoso.

3. Klavier-Concert E-moll . . . . . . *F. Chopin.*
   (Instrumentirt von Adam Müncheimer aus Warschau).
   Allegro maëstoso. — Romanze. — Rondo.

4. Ouverture zu: „Tannhäuser" . . . . *R. Wagner.*

Concertflügel: BECHSTEIN.

II. Philharmon. Concert: Montag den 28. October 1895.
Dirigent: **Arthur Nikisch.**
Solist: **Raimund von Zur-Mühlen.**

Goldmark: Ouverture zu „Sakuntala". — **Wagner:** Preislieder aus den
Meistersingern. — **Bach:** Präludium, Adagio und Gavotte für Streichorchester
(z. 1. Mal). — Lieder. — **Brahms:** Symphonie No. 2, D-dur.

66.(b) *Programme of the
Philharmonic Concert,
conducted by Arthur
Nikisch, at the Berlin
Philharmonie on 14 Oct-
ober 1895*

67. Cover, designed by Wassily Kandinsky, for the almanac of the 'Blaue Reiter' (Munich, 1912), which included music by Schoenberg, Berg and Webern, as well as pictures, and articles on the visual arts, music and the theatre, by artists associated with the group

ALMA=
NACH
DER
BLAUE
REITER

R.PIPER & Cᵒ MÜNCHEN VERLAG

Orchestral Pieces op.16 'are such daring experiments in both content and sound that for the time being I cannot take the risk of presenting them to my ultra-conservative Berlin public'. No doubt Strauss would have taken the risk had he felt the music warranted it. Even so, he continued to do all he could to enable awards and bursaries to go Schoenberg's way, and in 1911 Schoenberg returned to Berlin, and another post at the Stern Conservatory. His arrival had been prepared by the successful performance of his *Pelleas und Melisande* by yet another Berlin orchestra (the Blüthner) in October 1910, but his reappearance in the city, and his sponsorship by such radicals as Busoni, provoked hostility as well as enthusiasm. (Schoenberg also became known to Kandinsky and his circle after a concert of his music in Munich in January 1911.)[26] Whatever the public and critical reaction, Schoenberg's second period of residence in Berlin, from 1911 to 1915, was one of considerable creative achievement. In particular, *Pierrot lunaire*, written between March and May 1912 and first performed in Berlin that October, divided the press, who disliked it, from the public, who approved. It was also a Berlin periodical, *Die*

357

Musik, that in 1912 produced one of the first extended studies of Schoenberg's work, by Arno Nadel, an associate of Busoni's.

In 1909 the 26-year-old Edgard Varèse moved from Paris to Berlin as director of the Symphonic Choir and remained a resident in or frequent visitor to the city until 1913. Like Schoenberg, he benefited from the advocacy of Strauss, who helped to ensure that his orchestral tone poem *Bourgogne* was given a hearing in Berlin in December 1910 (the work had a hostile reception and Varèse later destroyed it). Varèse did not lack for distinguished patrons, from the wealthy banker Fritz Andreae to Busoni, Karl Muck and Hugo von Hofmannsthal. In a letter to the wife of his publisher, Hofmannsthal wrote of a young musician 'struggling like a drowning person, running from one publisher, one agent to another . . . In addition to all this he has to support his wife and his grandfather in France'.[27] Yet Varèse was apparently reluctant to accept financial help from the poet, even though his time in Berlin was marked by health problems and family crises.

Only in Berlin, of all German cultural centres, could there be such striking conjunctions – Strauss and Schoenberg, Busoni and Varèse – not simply between Germans and non-Germans but between composers of different generations and remarkably different styles. There were other places where the predispositions and enthusiasms of individual musicians could produce unexpected examples of enlightened patronage, and none was more remarkable than Hans Haym's promotion, in Elberfeld, of Frederick Delius.

The association between Haym and Delius is one aspect of the extensive German interest in British music at this time, the best-known example probably being Julius Buths's performance of Elgar's *The Dream of Gerontius* (in his own German translation) at the Lower Rhine Music Festival in December 1901, which in turn helped to create the friendship between Elgar and Strauss (Buths had performed the 'Enigma' Variations earlier the same year). Buths conducted other English music, including that of Delius and Stanford, giving the German première of the latter's opera *Much Ado About Nothing* in Leipzig in 1902. But it was Haym who did most to further Delius's cause in Germany. He succeeded Buths as music director at Elberfeld (later, with Barmen, made part of the Rhineland conurbation of Wuppertal) and remained in the post until 1920, the year before his death. His most impressive achievement was the first complete performances in Germany of *A Mass of Life*, in 1909 and 1911. Reactions to Delius's music were not uniformly enthusiastic, and Haym's belief that he was a more worthy successor to Wagner than Strauss or anyone else may seem extravagant. But the fact that Haym was able to give a 'difficult' living composer such a prominent place in his programming is remarkable.[28]

Strasbourg was another centre of particular interest because of the important musicians active there. Alsace had become part of the German empire in 1871, and the government in Berlin, anxious to promote painless integration, made a special grant to the city's opera house.[29] It was nevertheless not until 1907 that Strasbourg attracted a musician of outstanding gifts: Hans Pfitzner. Pfitzner was born in 1869 and after studies in Frankfurt he taught and conducted in Berlin and Munich. He arrived in Strasbourg as director of the conservatory and conductor of the symphony orchestra, but it was as director of the opera, from 1910, that he made his greatest mark. His policy was to stage a limited number of exemplary productions which he himself produced as well as conducted. Although he had his limitations as a producer, slavishly adhering to stage directions, which must have created as many problems as it solved, the artistic results may well have been superior to those achieved in larger centres with greater resources, where the emphasis was on constant variety. Pfitzner's strong nationalist bias was evident in the repertory he favoured, though he did conduct a complete performance of a non-German rarity, Berlioz's *Roméo et Juliette*, in 1910. There were the usual small-theatre crises: in January 1913 Pfitzner took to the stage at short notice to sing the role of Beckmesser. By that time he had begun his opera *Palestrina* (1912–15) which has done more than any of his other works to ensure that he is taken seriously as a composer. And this composition was one reason (another was tensions with the Strasbourg establishment) why Pfitzner went on leave in 1914, to be replaced by Otto Klemperer.

Klemperer was then in his late twenties. His first conducting post, in Hamburg in 1910, had set the pattern for the mixture of high artistic achievement and personal, physical crises that was to recur throughout his long career. Even more than in Mahler's time, Hamburg by 1910 was a 'city governed by merchants who sought to keep public spending low'. Klemperer was worked hard – it was nothing to conduct *Lohengrin, Faust* and *Carmen* on consecutive nights – and in spite of his own successes he was depressed by the low standards of performance. He was absent on sick leave from spring 1911 to summer 1912, and on his return new artistic successes (including a *Ring*) were offset by the scandal of his affair with the young soprano Elisabeth Schumann. Klemperer resigned, and after an interlude in Barmen (all those performances of *Parsifal*) he arrived in Strasbourg in April 1914. The next significant stage of his career would begin after the war in a radically different cultural environment.

The Late Romantic Era

NOTES

1 H. S. Hughes, *Consciousness and Society: the Reorientation of European Social Thought, 1890–1930* (Brighton, 1979), 51; see also pp.50, 368.

2 C. Dahlhaus, trans. J. B. Robinson, *Nineteenth-Century Music* (Berkeley, 1989), 337.

3 A. Forte, 'Theory', *Dictionary of Twentieth-Century Music*, ed. J. Vinton (London, 1974).

4 See extracts from H. Kretzschmar, 'A Stimulus to Promote a Hermeneutics of Music' [1903], in *Music in European Thought 1851–1912*, ed. B. Bujić (Cambridge, 1988), 114.

5 See extracts from M. Dessoir, 'Aesthetics and General Theory of Art' [1907], in *Music in European Thought*, 383.

6 See P. Bekker, *Das Musikdrama der Gegenwart* (Stuttgart, 1909); R. Louis, *Die deutsche Musik der Gegenwart* (Munich and Leipzig, 1909); and W. Niemann, *Die Musik seit Richard Wagner* (Berlin, 1913). A useful discussion of these writers in historical context is in C. Hailey, *Between Vienna and Weimar: Franz Schreker and the Musical Cultures of his Time* (diss., Yale U., 1988), i, 94f.

7 See J. Williamson, 'Eugen d'Albert: Wagner and *Verismo*', *Music Review*, xlv/1 (1984), 26–46.

8 N. Stone, *Europe Transformed, 1878–1919* (London, 1983), 179; see also pp.136, 165, 174.

9 W. Schuh, trans. M. Whittall, *Richard Strauss: a Chronicle of the Early Years* (Cambridge, 1982), 177; see also pp.255, 253, 256–7, 327, 497, 379, 477.

10 H. L. de la Grange, *Mahler*, i (London, 1976), 231; see also pp.228, 318, 308, 261, 251.

11 E. Smyth, *What Happened Next* (London, 1940), 261–72.

12 D. Koury, *Orchestral Performing Practices in the Nineteenth Century: Size, Proportions, and Seating* (Ann Arbor, 1986), 206f.

13 S. Lloyd, *H. Balfour Gardiner* (Cambridge, 1984), 18.

14 P. Cahn, 'Percy Grainger's Frankfurt Years', *Studies in Music*, no.12 (1978), 112.

15 S. Lloyd, *H. Balfour Gardiner*, 6.

16 C. Scott, *Bone of Contention* (New York, 1969), 65; cited in Cahn, 'Percy Grainger's Frankfurt Years', 113 (see also p.108).

17 *The Bodley Head Bernard Shaw: Shaw's Music 3*, ed. D. H. Laurence (London, 1981), 304.

18 G. Skelton, *Wagner at Bayreuth* (London, 1965), 81.

19 Ibid, 115.

20 A. Boult, *My Own Trumpet* (London, 1973), 31.

21 M. Heuft-Hubscher, 'Wuppertal', *Grove 6*.

22 E. J. Dent, *Ferruccio Busoni* (London, 2/1974), 89.

23 C. Fifield, *Max Bruch: his Life and Works* (London, 1988), 260, 288.

24 H. Becker and R. D. Green, 'Berlin', *Grove 6*.

25 K. Wilhelm, trans. M. Whittall, *Richard Strauss: an Intimate Portrait* (London, 1989), 77; see also pp.82, 143.

26 See *Arnold Schoenberg and Wassily Kandinsky: Letters, Pictures and Documents*, ed. J. Hahl-Koch, trans. J. C. Crawford (London, 1984).

27 L. Varèse, *Varèse: a Looking-Glass Diary* (London, 1975), 89.

28 See L. Carley, 'Hans Haym: Delius's Prophet and Pioneer', *ML*, liv (1973), 1–24; in *A Delius Companion*, ed. C. Redwood, repr. (London, 1976).

29 P. Heyworth, *Otto Klemperer: his Life and Times*, i (Cambridge, 1983), 88; see also pp.90, 49.

BIBLIOGRAPHICAL NOTE

Cultural-historical background

In addition to the studies referred to in the notes above, there are useful accounts of developments in literature and the visual arts. R. Pascal's *From Naturalism to Expressionism: German Literature and Society, 1880–1918* (London, 1973) is particularly illuminating on the literary cultures of the cities, especially Berlin and Munich, while *Modernism, 1890–1930* (Harmondsworth, 1976), ed. M. Bradbury and J. McFarlane, places topics like 'Berlin and the Rise of Modernism (1886–96)' and 'German Expressionist Poetry' in a comprehensive international perspective. In painting, W.-D. Dube, *The Expressionists* (London, 1972), emphasizes the role of various German centres in the movement's evolution, and D. E. Gordon, *Expressionism in Art and Idea* (New Haven, 1987), explores expressionism as a cultural phenomenon.

Music

It is the more progressive music of the period 1890–1930 that has received by far the greatest attention from writers of historical and technical studies, so the bibliographies for France and Austria for these years are likely to be much richer than this one. Probably the most stimulating recent study dealing with the phenomenon of imperial German late Romanticism in the context of a general history of Romantic music is C. Dahlhaus's *Nineteenth-Century Music* (Berkeley, 1989). Valuable material may also be found in G. Abraham, *A Hundred Years of Music* (London, 4/1974), and in Abraham's contribution to vol.x of The New Oxford History of Music, *The Modern Age (1890–1960)* (London, 1974); see also A. Whittall, *Romantic Music: a Concise History from Schubert to Sibelius* (London, 1987).

Significant studies of composers not already referred to are N. Del Mar, *Richard Strauss: a Critical Commentary on his Life and Works*, 3 vols. (London, 1972/R1986), which is still the most rewarding as well as the largest comprehensive exploration of the composer. On a much smaller scale M. Kennedy, *Richard Strauss* (London, 1976), can also be recommended. D. Mitchell's *Gustav Mahler: the Wunderhorn Years* (London, 1975) deals in part with Mahler's Hamburg period. A. Beaumont's *Busoni the Composer* (London, 1985) and his translated edition of *Ferruccio Busoni: Selected Letters* (London, 1987) form the first significant attempt to supplement, if not replace, Dent's famous biography.

Of all the composers mentioned in this chapter, Schoenberg probably has the largest bibliography. Among the many studies that shed light on his Berlin years I recommend W. Reich, *Schoenberg: a Critical Biography* (London, 1971); M. Macdonald, *Schoenberg* (London, 1976); and C. Rosen, *Schoenberg* (London, 1976).

Chapter XIV

Fin-de-siècle Vienna: Politics and Modernism

PAUL BANKS

In 1873 the International Exhibition in Vienna had turned into a cultural and economic disaster: ravaged by stock-market collapse and cholera, it had offered a blow to Habsburg prestige to be set alongside the military defeats of 1859 and 1866. Nearly twenty years later another major exhibition proved more successful in promoting the Dual Monarchy's achievements. The political and economic conditions outwardly offered a welcome stability, and the subject matter of the Internationale Ausstellung für Musik- und Theaterwesen ensured that the host country's most significant contributions to European culture could be prominently displayed.

In spite of the liberal 'December Constitution' of 1867 – the constitutional instrument for the Cis-Leithanian (non-Hungarian) lands of the empire which had followed in the wake of the Ausgleich and its creation of the Dual Monarchy – the governments that resulted operated within a peculiarly Austrian type of parliamentary democracy. An irony of the situation was that the system's basis had been formulated by German-speaking liberals, but under it they rarely wielded the political power they expected.

> Yet this did not mean that the political power had passed to the non-Germans; it had passed away from the people's representatives altogether, back into the hands of the Emperor and his civil servants . . . [Franz Josef] still left the representatives of the people considerable elbow room, so long as they did not touch fundamentals, and, within those limits, the rules of genuine Parliamentary government were applied: votes were taken, and a Minister President regarded himself as bound (under normal conditions) to get for his decisions the affirmative support of a Parliamentary majority. Where, however, fundamentals were at issue, the Monarch's will was enforced, if necessary, over Parliament's head.[1]

The situation was summed up by one of the most compelling of the commentators on the empire's last years, Robert Musil:

By its constitution [Austria] was liberal, but its system of government was clerical. The system of government was clerical, but the
general attitude to life was liberal. Before the law all citizens were
equal: not everyone, of course, was a citizen. There was a parliament
which made such vigorous use of its liberty that it was usually kept
shut; but there was also an Emergency Powers Act, by means of
which it was possible to manage without Parliament. And, each time
that everyone was just beginning to rejoice in absolutism, the Crown
decreed that there must now be a return to parliamentary government.[2]

Under such conditions franchise reform was relatively less significant in gradually opening up the male population's ability to influence the decision-making process than would otherwise have been the
case. Nevertheless important shifts in the balance of power within the
Reichsrat resulted. In 1885, after a broadening of suffrage in 1883
which significantly increased the number of peasants and *petits
bourgeois* able to vote, the move was to the right: a further widening of
eligibility in 1896 to all literate males over the age of 24 who had been
resident in their constituency for six months resulted the following
year in a Reichsrat with greater prominence for nationalist and
socialist radicals. Finally, after years of political pressure on its behalf
from the social democrats, universal male suffrage was introduced in
1907 and the constitution of the Reichsrat elected later that year
showed a distinct swing to the left. Led by Viktor Adler, the social
democrats had begun to mobilize not only masses but also the support
of leading figures in both generations of the musical avant garde:
Mahler (a friend from Adler's youth)[3] and Schoenberg.[4]

In 1892 a period of relative stability in Cis-Leithanian politics was
about to end. Count Taaffe had been Minister President since 1879
but his longevity as the longest-serving head of government in
Austria's parliamentary history was more the result of the absence of
genuine parliamentary democracy than of any far-reaching grappling
with the monarchy's fundamental problems. A relatively strong
economy which by the early 1890s was allowing the state regularly to
record budget surpluses offered a cushion and important reform laws
relating to working conditions and sickness benefit were passed,[5] but
nationalism, the cancer at the heart of the monarchy's structure, was
more or less ignored. The predominant issue was the struggle between
the Czechs and Germans in Bohemia, which in the 1890s thrust itself
to the forefront of political life and led to serious street violence,
but that was merely a foretaste of conflicts that were to develop
throughout the Habsburg lands and lead to the monarchy's collapse
in 1918.

One of the strategies increasingly adopted by nationalist representatives was to obstruct parliamentary business, thus heightening

the sense that political involvement was pointless, particularly among the German bourgeoisie. 'Indeed, as civic action proved increasingly futile, art became almost a religion, the source of meaning and the food of the soul.'[6] The German liberals who in the 1860s and 70s had devoted themselves to accumulating wealth now saw their sons investing their time in cultivating the arts. For some – an important minority – the heightened valuation of art sprang from a belief in its engagement with the social and psychological forces undermining the foundations of Austria's (and particularly Vienna's) image of itself. Within the increasingly uncertain and alienating conditions of late nineteenth-century Vienna, the idea that art could play a role in helping modern man enter the garden of lost unities had a powerful appeal, and the advocacy by Nietzsche and Wagner of a programme for social and political regeneration through art found many supporters from Mahler's generation. Indeed, on the broadest level his symphonies can be understood as the outstanding creative response to Wagner's cultural programme, their innovations in musical content and structural organization helping to project more powerfully a sense of anxiety, despair and conflict and also the belief in the possibility of transcending such disruptive forces. Hence Mahler's comments in a revealing letter written during the rehearsals in Prague for the première of his Seventh Symphony, which indicates how far he had travelled from a simple aesthetic of the beautiful:

> One of the trumpets asked Bodanzky in despair: 'I'd like to know what is beautiful about blowing away at a trumpet stopped up to high C sharp'. This gave me an insight at once into the lot of man, who likewise, cannot understand why he must endure being stopped to the piercing agony of his own existence, cannot see what it's all for, and how his screech is to be attuned to the great harmony of the universal symphony of all creation.[7]

But such an optimistic vision of the role of art could not be long maintained. Though they might admire such works, artists of the next generation found it increasingly difficult to believe that any resolution of the conflicts their work so powerfully articulated was possible: expressionist art could no longer proffer quasi-religious hope, rather it refined its vocabulary for articulating existential Angst.

In both its phases this sophisticated view of art did not prove comfortable or enticing to the middle-class audience. Initially the Viennese obsession with the arts (particularly the performing arts) was fuelled by the *haute bourgeoisie*'s desire to confront the monarchy's aristocracy: having failed either to overcome its political power or to be assimilated into it directly the *nouveaux riches* could at least meet the aristocrats on equal terms in the patronage of the arts. However, by the end of the century, the function of art for Viennese middle-class society had altered, and in this change politics played a crucial part. If the Viennese burghers had begun by supporting the temple of art as a surrogate form of assimilation into the aristocracy, they ended by finding in it an escape, a refuge from the unpleasant world of increasingly threatening political reality.[8]

If the role of art was for many of its consumers in *fin-de-siècle* Vienna an escapist embellishment of life, it was one that was ardently cultivated and which answered a profound psychological need: this may help to account for the sophistication and evocative power of the products, particularly evident in the operettas of Franz Léhar, Oscar Straus, Leo Fall and the other successors to the tradition initiated by Johann Strauss the younger. For the cultural commentator Karl Kraus such works represented a debasement of an authentic genre as represented by Offenbach, but contemporary Viennese composers of art music were more ambivalent in their response: for Mahler, typically, the popular idioms of the day, particularly the ländler and the waltz, were objects of affection, to be evoked with relish, even if in his hands they could also appear corrosively banal.[9] It was in the work of younger composers (and not just Viennese), such as Berg (Three Orchestral Pieces, 1914), Bartók (*Two Portraits*, 1907–11) and Ravel (*La valse*, 1919–20) that sinister, grotesque and decadent elements were most strikingly and consistently associated wth the imperial city's most famous dance.

Just as the choice of subject matter for the 1892 Exhibition reflected the new priorities of *fin-de-siècle* Austria, the process of organizing it seems also to have embodied the 'politicization' of artistic life so typical of Vienna. Deprived of any significant political influence and the opportunities for second-hand involvement in intrigue and gossip afforded by political life, the Viennese middle class turned for such activity to the arts. The internal politics of the Burgtheater, Hofoper, Akademie der bildenden Künste and the Künstlerhaus attracted almost as much public attention as their artistic products, a situation not ameliorated by the coverage by the Viennese press. So it is typical of the age not only that there should have been significant disagreements between the organizer of the music history section of the Exhibition and the Gesellschaft der Musikfreunde (who initially refused to allow any of their rich collections to be used except in their own display), but also that it should have been alluded to in the preface to the section's catalogue[10] by one of the leading organizers of the event, the young professor of music history at the University of Prague, Guido Adler (1855–1941).

As Adler pointed out in the preface, the very fact that such a huge undertaking (over 7000 exhibits) was practicable reflected recent advances in sorting and cataloguing the monarchy's immense treasury of documents and other material in public and private collections. That there was an audience for such a project reflects changes in attitude towards music and its history, and the fact that it was organized in the Habsburg Empire says much for the importance of Austrian scholarship in the newly and rapidly developing field of musicology. Scholars from the German states had played a crucial role in the developing discipline in the late eighteenth and early nineteenth centuries, but the Habsburg lands had also made distinguished contributions and it was at Vienna in 1870 that the first *Professor ordinarius* in music history and aesthetics, Eduard Hanslick, was appointed.

Adler's contribution to the growth and organization of musicology can hardly be overestimated. In his youth it had only a modest foothold in academic life: like many of his distinguished predecessors, including R. G. Kieswetter (1773–1850), A. W. Ambros (1816–76) and Hanslick (1825–1904), Adler had taken a law degree before studying with Hanslick. By the time of his death it was a respected and fully fledged discipline with clearly defined aims and methods. In spite of his interest in Wagner[11] Adler's academic approach was far removed from the master's metaphysical speculations and was founded on an application of quasi-scientific techniques and procedures to the study of music and its history, a strategy in tune with the positivistic attitudes prevailing in Vienna. The collection and identification of works, and their subsequent classification (according to such categories as genre, style and period), occupied much of the new profession's activities and bear a striking resemblance to the approach adopted in the natural sciences (not least botany, zoology and geology).[12] The results appeared in such publications as the *Vierteljahrsschrift für Musikwissenschaft* (founded by Adler, Philip Spitta and Friedrich Chrysander in 1885) and the *Denkmäler der Tonkunst in Österreich* (edited by Adler from 1894 until 1938).

The analysis of music also occupied an important place in Adler's conception of musicology, but primarily as style analysis, as one of the tools of historical research:[13] he seems to have been much less interested in its potential significance as a sub-discipline that might contribute to an understanding of the musical processes embodied in particular works. His relegation of such studies to the field of 'systematic musicology' had far-reaching consequences:

> There seems to be no doubt in Adler's mind about the primacy of history in the system of musicology, and his description of its field, as well as the tabular summary, offer a clear illustration of this. The division of the entire field into historical and systematic musicology prevents him from realizing fully the implications of the term *Kunstwissenschaft* . . . [B]y overstressing the division he weakened the chances of an interaction between historical studies and the areas

covered by the disciplines forming his 'systematic musicology' and it could be argued that the legacy of this is noticeable in the entire subsequent history of musicology.[14]

It is therefore not surprising that Adler's Musikwissenschaftliches Institut produced few scholars whose main contributions might be described as analytical.

One exception, in more senses than one, was Ernst Kurth (1886–1946). Adler appointed him librarian at the institute in 1907 and the following year he took his doctorate with a thesis on Gluck,[15] but, although Kurth's subsequent writings evince an interest in style history which may be traced back to Adler, their main thrust is analytical and (perhaps more surprisingly) their underlying assumptions owe more to Schopenhauer and Gestalt psychology than to the positivism that fuelled and moulded Adler's research.

> Kurth was rejecting the prevailing tendency to apply the then common methods of natural science to human behaviour and activities, as if they were objects of the natural world rather than products of the mind. In this regard, Kurth follows the philosopher Wilhelm Dilthey, who taught that the investigatory methods of the natural sciences were inappropriate for the study of art.[16]

Kurth's approach, founded on a psycho-auditive interpretation of listener responses and a belief in the primacy of linear factors in most Western art music, and his apparent success in offering a strategy for understanding stylistically innovatory post-Wagnerian music, contributed to a considerable success at the time. In the longer term, though, his work has been overshadowed by the different analytical techniques fostered by two older musicians teaching in Vienna, Heinrich Schenker (1868–1935) and Arnold Schoenberg (1874–1951), who encouraged new and in some respects more sophisticated ways of listening to eighteenth- and nineteenth-century music.

Unlike Kurth, both Schoenberg and Schenker – in their different ways the two most outstandingly gifted music pedagogues Vienna had produced for many years – pursued their careers (more or less) outside institutions; indeed, Schoenberg was almost entirely self-taught. The talents of both were multi-faceted: Schenker was a pianist and a scholar notable for a profound awareness of the importance of manuscript and early printed sources both editorially and analytically; Schoenberg not only composed but also conducted, painted and wrote texts for some of his works. As analysts both were concerned to demonstrate the coherence of great music, but in other respects, particularly that of analytical technique, the differences are striking. Schenker's great contribution was to formulate a theory that concentrated on the interaction of linear and harmonic elements in tonal music as a means of accounting for the long-range unity of masterpieces composed between Bach and Brahms. Schoenberg, on the other hand, reflected his own compositional concerns, offering his most provocative insights in discussions of the ways in which the handling of themes and motifs conferred a logic on musical discourse.[17]

Not only were their analytical approaches different; so, to some extent, were the repertories they addressed. For Schenker, Wagnerian and post-Brahmsian innovation undermined the central tonal tradition, was of little aesthetic significance and did not figure significantly among his analytical preoccupations; but for Schoenberg, who was so conscious of the relationship of his own radical innovations to the continuing and developing tradition he respected, an analytical approach could serve as an effective vehicle for revealing that relationship. If the range of Schenker's analysis was circumscribed by essentially conservative aesthetic responses, the breadth of Schoenberg's was encouraged by a modernist outlook on music history which saw the radical transformation of tradition as the only plausible artistic standpoint. Nevertheless the two shared some preoccupations, not least the music of Bach, Beethoven and Brahms, and an adherence to the Austro-German tradition which precluded any great involvement with other repertories. Yet by a grim twist of fate the influence of their insights was stifled in Germany after 1933, and until well into the second half of the century it was in America and Britain that their main impact was felt. Both their Germanophile attitudes and the political forces that fractured the cultural life of Germany and, later, central Europe, were fuelled by social processes whose origins lay deep in the nineteenth century.

As the diverse nationalities which made up the polyglot Austrian Empire gradually acquired a sense of national identity, forged vigorous cultures and played a less docile political role, Jews were faced with bewildering choices:[18] whether to unite linguistically and culturally with the surrounding (usually non-German) population or with the ruling Germans who still held political and commercial power; whether to convert, or from the mid-1890s to join the Zionist movement. Patterns of response differed from land to land, often influenced by the attitudes of the gentile population. In Hungary from the mid-century there was a significant Magyarization within the large Jewish community; but in Galicia, Bohemia and Moravia more affluent Jews continued to offer allegiance to Teutonic ideals and more specifically to their bastion, the Kaiserstadt, Vienna. A fervent commitment to German culture offered not merely access to a rich tradition of European importance, but also a sense of belonging: from such roots flowered the deeply held, passionate Germanophile beliefs of a whole generation of Austrian Jews from Mahler, Schenker and Schoenberg to Siegmund Freud, Arthur Schnitzler and Ludwig

Wittgenstein. Yet the very success of assimilationist Jews contributed to the impending tragedy.

After 1848, and particularly after 1859, as the economy of the monarchy grew and modernized and the construction of the Ring-strasse began, financial incentives encouraged spectacular expansion of the capital. In the year of the revolution it had housed about 419,413; by 1869, 601,576 and by 1910, 2,031,498. Inevitably the percentage of the population born in Vienna declined, from 62.5% in 1840 to 34.4% in 1890, and a significant number of the immigrants were Jews from the provinces. From 6000–7000 in 1848, the community had risen to 175,318 in 1910; but this spectacular increase masks the fact that since 1880 there had been a decline in the rate of increase.[19] The causes were no doubt complex, but one was almost certainly the rise in Vienna of a new and more virulent form of anti-semitism, drawing its strength from economic, politico-religious and racial sources.

Some wealthy Jews in Vienna had played a crucial role in the life of the empire since the eighteenth century, but it was only in the 1860s that the legal constraints on Jews in Austria were removed and they were able to enter the professions. During the financial boom of the early Ringstrasse period Jewish financiers played a prominent part in the aggressive advance of liberal capitalism which, though it promoted growth in the Monarchy's economy, also entailed radical social and industrial change. Among the groups in Vienna that suffered most were the gentile *Kleinbürger*, the lower middle classes and artisans, pressed by economic changes wrought by laissez-faire capitalism and the influx of cheap labour from the provinces, an immigration that included a significant number of Jews. Similar economic factors impinged on the professional classes as young, ambitious Jewish men seized the opportunities offered by newly granted access to higher education and formed an increasing proportion of students, particularly in the law and medicine. Another growing concern in many circles was a perception that Catholicism was declining in the face of a rationalistic, technocratic liberalism. For Jews the disaster was that they were increasingly associated with liberalism by the mounting extremist forces, a decisive event being the 1873 crash.

Inevitably politicians, with greater or lesser degrees of cynicism, were willing to heighten and exploit the fears and prejudices of the social groups most unsettled by the impact of liberalism. Georg von Schönerer (1842–1921) was one of the first to incorporate explicit antisemitism in his political platform (from 1879), but the over-aggressiveness and anti-clericalism of this 'curious compound of gangster, philistine and aristocrat'[20] prevented him from creating an effective mass movement. Nevertheless he revealed a politically useful policy and an electorally successful brand of extra-parliamentary demagoguery which was exploited with spectacular success by the Christian Democrats; they formed a dominating mass movement round the figure of Karl Lueger (1844–1910), though Lueger's goals were rather different:

> Schönerer's central positive accomplishment was to metamorphose a tradition of the Old Left into an ideology of the New Right: he transformed democratic, *grossdeutsch* nationalism into racist Pan-Germanism. Lueger did the opposite: he transformed an ideology of the Old Right – Austrian political Catholicism – into an ideology of a New Left.[21]

Lueger's immediate goal was to take over the running of the municipal government of Vienna, so as to be in a position to end the corruption and waste which in his view pervaded the liberal administration. His commitment to non-Marxist socialism as a means of raising the proletariat's standard of living was genuine and the results – major improvements in infrastructure, education, health care and social policy – were tangible; but he was willing to adopt an antisemitic stance to achieve such ends. Whether or not his public pronouncements reflected his personal prejudices, they created an atmosphere in which such prejudices could proliferate. The court abhorred his demagoguery and antisemitism and the emperor refused to ratify Lueger's appointment as mayor of Vienna, following his success in the election of 1895; the electorate repeated their choice, however, and Franz Josef had to give in two years later: *der schöne Karl* was triumphantly installed in one of liberalism's monuments, the Rathaus.

Such was the climate Mahler found in 1897 when he finally achieved his ambition as a performing musician and returned to Vienna as Kapellmeister (soon to be promoted to director) at the Hofoper, the most important state-run musical institution in the empire. Not only was Lueger's antisemitic stance about to cast a shadow over his otherwise humane municipal policies, but Mahler immediately encountered the last vestiges of the once-common legal restrictions on Jews and public expressions of its widespread social correlate. None of this was a surprise, as a letter Mahler wrote to Ödön von Mihalovich during the negotiations for the post shows:

> My informants tell me there would be no doubt at all about my appointment – if I were not a Jew. But this is probably what will settle it . . . Still, a remark of Liechtenstein's [the Comptroller of the Court Theatre Directorate] . . . does leave me some ground for hope . . . [H]e said: 'Things are not so bad as that yet in Austria, for antisemitism to decide on matters of this kind'.[22]

In spite of Liechtenstein's attitude, which reflected that of Franz Josef, Mahler's Jewishness was an issue that probably would have barred him from the post had he not been willing to accept baptism as a Catholic (23 February 1897). That opportunistic factors determined the timing of this event is likely, but it certainly had a deeper significance as well. Mahler's whole outlook was that of an assimilated Jew, his cultural background was overwhelming German, and since his childhood he had been attracted to Catholic ritual: as the content of his works makes clear, Christian symbols and ideas held a powerful appeal. Though such a conversion might get round the legal barrier to a court appointment, a new racial component had been added to the traditional religious motivation of antisemitism. In the eyes of many, baptism could in no way mitigate an individual's ethnic origins and from the outset Mahler faced virulent attacks of which the following is an example, typical of the tactics of the antisemitic press against all prominent Jews:

> In our edition of 10 April we printed a note on the person of the newly appointed Opera Conductor, Mahler. At the time we already had an inkling of the origin of this celebrity and we therefore avoided publishing anything other than the bare facts about this unadulterated – Jew. The fact that he was acclaimed by the press in Budapest [which had a very substantial Jewish community] of course confirms our suspicion. We shall refrain completely from any over hasty judgment. The Jews' press will see whether the panegyrics with which they plaster their idol at present do not become washed away by the rain of reality as soon as Herr Mahler starts his Jew-boy antics on the podium.[23]

Time did nothing to alter or diminish this type of attack – the cancer of antisemitism was deeply embedded in Viennese life – and the prominence of Mahler's position made him an easy target.

The Hofoper's social and cultural importance was such that it was one of the first of the Ringstrasse buildings to be completed (1869) and from the outset it aspired to the highest standards of performance. Under the directorships of Johann Herbeck (1870–75) and Franz Jauner (1875–80) it had also been anxious to include the newest of Wagner's stage works in its repertory. However, under Mahler's immediate predecessor, Wilhelm Jahn (1881–97), there was some emphasis on French and Italian opera, bringing the institution 'to its peak as a place of aristocratic luxury and highly civilized entertainment';[24] during his directorship important new works were added to the repertory, notably *Tristan und Isolde* (1883), Verdi's *Otello* (1888), and *The Bartered Bride* (1896), and an exceptionally talented company of star singers was moulded, including Marie Renard, Edith Walker, Ernest van Dyck, Theodor Reichmann and Emil Scaria.

By the time Mahler assumed responsibility he had a distinctive approach to mounting operas: while assuming the highest musical standards, he sought to emphasize the 'unity of acting and singing, the intelligibility of plot, subordination of the stage action (and as a consequence the stage design) to dramatic logic ... [and the] maintenance of the superiority of musico-dramatic truth over *bel canto* grace'.[25] Undertaking a heavy schedule as a conductor and producer in his first three full seasons (in which he conducted 313 performances), Mahler gradually transformed the repertory, giving much greater prominence to Wagner and, later, Mozart, moulding a new ensemble of singers who could realize his musical and dramatic goals and attempting to move the ethos of the house away from the routine of repertory towards an ideal (but ultimately unrealizable) artistic organization in which every performance had the character of a festival.

One aspect of staging opera that Mahler was not in a position to transform initially was design. He was not a sophisticated connoisseur of the visual arts and he relied on Hofoper staff like Anton Brioschi (1855–1920, scene painter 1886–1920); however, at the turn of the century he appointed Heinrich Lefler (1863–1919) as chief stage designer. In November 1900, three months after his appointment, Lefler left the Künstlerhaus (the principal exhibiting organization of Vienna's conservative art establishment) and became one of the founder-members of what later coalesced as the independent Hagenbund, an important and long-lived group with innovatory ideas.[26] Although little is known about the circumstances of his appointment, it seems likely that Mahler saw Lefler as a forward-looking artist who would revitalize design at the Hofoper; whether Lefler was capable of achieving such a transformation is far from clear,[27] but in 1901, by a circuitous route, Mahler was introduced to members of one of Vienna's most important artistic groups, the Secession, and early the following year he married the stepdaughter of one of its leaders, Karl Moll. He now moved in the empire's most important avant-garde artistic circles.

The Vereinigung bildender Künstler Österreichs (Secession) had been formed in April 1897, largely by young artists dissatisfied with the artistic policies of the Künstlerhaus. The new group expanded rapidly and soon included the city's most important painters and architects, such as Gustav Klimt, Kolo Moser, Karl Moll, Max Kurzweil, Alfred Roller, Josef Hoffmann, Joseph Olbrich and Otto Wagner. There was no unified aesthetic programme to which they subscribed but there was at least a shared commitment to 'freedom of thought and feeling', and the leading members were consciously concerned with establishing a contemporary visual language. The declaration of independence was in itself not innovatory (the Munich Secession had earlier taken a similar step), but the rapid financial and political success that followed was unexpected. 57,000 visitors attended the association's first exhibition in March 1898; critics were generally favourable, a significant number of exhibits was sold and the whole event was given unmistakable official approval: Rudolf Bacher's iconographic celebration of Franz Josef's visit symbolizes what was to be a brief but astonishing period during which the political establishment and artistic avant garde cooperated.

In 1899 the Ministry of Culture established an advisory arts council urged to 'sustain . . . the fresh breeze that is blowing in domestic art, and to bring new resources to it',[28] a role well suited to a body numbering Otto Wagner, Karl Moll and Alfred Roller among its members. The thinking behind the government's promotion of cultural matters was articulated by the minister responsible: 'Although every development is rooted in national soil, yet works of art speak a common language, and entering into noble competition, lead to mutual understanding and reciprocal respect'.[29] The policy of supporting the modern movement was continued and (at least initially) extended by the non-democratic, bureaucratic administration of Dr Ernest von Koerber who took office in 1900. Faced with a Reichsrat virtually unable to function because of national rivalries, Koerber administered by decree, focussing his attention on the economy, modernization of the civil service and culture. In the first two areas he was remarkably successful, but his policies towards the arts were ultimately less influential. They were administered by the Minister of Culture, an outstandingly able scholar, Wilhelm von Hartel (1839–1907), who, as a devoted admirer of Wagner (who nevertheless rejected antisemitism), was fully conversant with the Wagnerian notion of art's potential for rejuvenating a fragmented society: the Secessionist view of its own character, as 'a form of art that would weld together all the characteristics of our multitide of constituent peoples into a new and proud unity',[30] was entirely consonant with his and the administration's policies. It is against this extraordinary background, of cooperation between artistic modernism and a bureaucracy battling to maintain an anachronistic state system in the face of destructive forces, that Klimt's commission to provide paintings for the new university building, the appointment of figures like Otto Wagner, Josef Hoffmann, Koloman Moser and Alfred Roller to important teaching posts, and masterpieces like Klimt's Beethoven Frieze, Wagner's Kirche am Steinhof and Post Office Savings Bank and Mahler's Eighth Symphony – his 'gift to the nation' composed in 1906 – are most aptly viewed.

Roller's appointment as chief stage designer at the Hofoper in 1903 was clearly consistent with the prevailing politico-cultural climate, but it was entirely the result of a communality of thought between Mahler and his collaborator. They shared a view that the stage design

68.(a) The Secession Building, Vienna, designed by Joseph Maria Olbrich and opened in 1898

68.(b) Gustav Klimt: detail of the Beethoven Frieze created for the Fourteenth Secession Exhibition (1902) of which Max Klinger's Beethoven Memorial was the centrepiece

69. Alfred Roller's design for the beginning of Act 2 of Wagner's 'Tristan und Isolde' in the production directed by Mahler at the Hofoper, Vienna, in 1903

was servant of the work performed, that its main role was to offer a space necessary for the presentation of the work and to contribute to its atmosphere. This involved a rejection of the prevalent naturalistic approach to staging in favour of a much more stylized and symbolic conception, and their approach at least paralleled and was perhaps influenced by the ideas of the most innovatory contemporary theorist in the field, Adolphe Appia (1862–1928). The result was often a radically simplified stage picture in which lighting effects played a crucial role. The nature of Roller's achievement was recognized from the first by one of the most important Wagnerian critics, Gustav Schönaich, who in reviewing *Tristan und Isolde*, the first Mahler-Roller production, offers insight into the character of the design (see fig.69):

> The idea of having the ship come on to the stage diagonally proved to be entirely felicitous. It made possible a splendid play of light on the sea, which was now visible to the audience over the side of the ship. The raising and lowering of the curtain and the sail produced extremely felicitous colour-contrasts. The overall coloration, determined by the richly nuanced orange of the dominant sail, satisfied the eye without distracting from events on the stage. The intentions which underlie the décor of the second act are extremely ingenious and derive from an intimate understanding of the mysterious interplay of allusions within the text: 'In darkness you – but I in light.' The poetic opposition of Day and Night which dominates this scene is reflected by the setting. The bare wall of the royal castle reflects white moonlight, while the bench on which the two lovers sink is plunged in darkness.[31]

375

The concern for the handling of light on stage was one of the factors which later in 1903 encouraged Mahler to have the orchestra pit lowered:

> Putting the pit lower is important for a discreet orchestral sound and important for the purposes of discreet lighting. I purposely avoid the words 'lighting effects'. We do not need crude effects, we want to make the *light* serve the theatre in *all* its grades, nuances and degrees of strength. To be always out for powerful effects is inartistic. But the matter does not end with the lighting: the whole of modern art has a part to play on the stage. Modern art, I say, not the Secession. What matters is the conjunction of all the arts.[32]

This is a highly revealing document for it shows concern not to ally the Hofoper approach exclusively with the Secession, probably because Mahler considered the Secession to be solely concerned with the visual arts, but this distancing may also embody a response to some of the unfavourable *Tristan* reviews which used the Secessionist label as part of their negative critical vocabulary;[33] it also shows the extent to which Wagnerian notions continued to underpin a self-proclaimed manifestation of modernism in art.

Mahler's achievement at the Hofoper was immense: a brief period when considerable financial resources and state support were allied to artistic aims of the utmost integrity, imagination and forward-looking vision. Yet it was an achievement not without ambiguities. The Hofoper's repertory had been overhauled, to some extent by the inclusion of new works, perhaps most notably Zemlinksy's *Es war einmal* (1900), Strauss's *Feuersnot* (1902) and Pfitzner's *Die Rose vom Liebesgarten* (1905), but even at the time Mahler was criticized for not offering more new works.[34] To some extent it was largely external circumstances that robbed him of the world or Vienna premières of Dvořák's *Rusalka*, Janáček's *Jenůfa* and Strauss's *Salome*, and he had accepted both Zemlinsky's *Der Traumgörge* and Debussy's *Pelléas et Mélisande* just before his departure. Nevertheless it is striking that all but one of his great collaborations with Roller were works of the past, that his lasting contribution to the Viennese opera repertory was the importance he placed on Wagner and the broadening of the Mozartian element.

Even Mahler's celebration of the past was deeply complex. Beethoven was viewed almost entirely through Wagnerian eyes, yet in Mozart that sort of perception was tempered by a form of nascent historicism. He might be willing to compose a new scene for Mozart's *Le nozze di Figaro*[35] (in spite of the tradition of such intervention in opera houses this can hardly be viewed as the act of an authenticist) but equally he insisted on using reduced orchestral forces, and a cembalo for recitatives, reflecting historical awareness. How ironic that these early manifestations of one of the symptoms of that increasing taste for the new which finds little to engage its interest in contemporary art and therefore finds an outlet by transforming the tradition by an appeal to 'authenticity' should appear in the re-creative work of an artist deeply committed to the notion of artistic 'progress' – one whose own compositions, while responding to so many earlier works and traditions, do so within an entirely contemporary context.

Mahler's engagement with the music of the past in no way compromised his commitment to modernism, but it may have helped to make some of his other theatrical innovations more acceptable to his audiences. Whatever the hopes of cultural and political regeneration that may have been entertained by Mahler and his establishment sponsors, that audience was an élite, perhaps more an artistic aristocracy than had been the case, but an élite nevertheless. The extent to which Mahler's status was conferred from above is revealed by his relationship with the Vienna Philharmonic Orchestra. Made up of members of the Hofoper orchestra, this brilliant ensemble was a self-governing concert-giving organization which elected its conductor. Mahler's predecessor had been the genial Hans Richter (1875–98); Mahler had none of his ability to collaborate with the players, seeking rather to impose his artistic will. In 1901, after a serious illness and all too aware of the orchestra's antipathy towards him, he resigned: his struggle to achieve the highest artistic results, fuelled by a passionate belief in the importance of art, failed to find widespread support even among musicians.

Vienna's concert life might have been expected to offer Mahler a more congenial environment since it presented none of the pressures of the Hofoper's repertory system. At the time there were few symphonic concerts. The long-established Philharmonic and Gesellschaft series (the latter consisting largely of choral works) offered between them fewer than twenty a year; in 1900 the Wiener Konzertvereinorchester was formed with Ferdinand Löwe as conductor, followed in 1907 by the Verein Wiener Tonkünstler under Oskar Nedbal. But the concert schedules remained modest and the professionalization of such public concerts was complete: Mahler should have found in Vienna the resources and conditions for ideal performances, but he had to wait until his last years in America, where the players were perhaps less able, to find a relatively favourable environment as a conductor of orchestral music.

It is one of Vienna's paradoxes that in spite of the relatively small number of orchestral concerts given there before the early years of the twentieth century it was the spiritual home for the three greatest post-Beethovenian symphonists the Austro-German tradition produced in the nineteenth century, and its symphonic tradition – though it failed to produce another master remotely comparable to Brahms, Bruckner or Mahler – was continued directly by further works of considerable stature by Franz Schmidt, Alexander von Zemlinsky and Egon Wellesz, and more tangentially by Schoenberg, Berg and Webern. The tradition flourished in spite of (or perhaps because of) the relatively limited opportunities for hearing major symphonic works in the concert hall. Primitive recording techniques and public taste discouraged record companies from extending their repertory from vocal and instrumental soloists to orchestral music until just before World War I,[36] so, as in the nineteenth century, the interested music-lover had to rely on piano transcriptions.

It was in such arrangements that Berg and Webern first came into contact with Mahler's symphonies, and Arthur Schnitzler's diaries reveal how important duet playing was in the life of a cultivated and capable amateur musician, though as a domestic activity rather than as part of the private social event typical of the early nineteenth century. Not only was the 'musikalischer Salon' less common, it was

70. Title-page of Mahler's Eighth Symphony, arranged for piano duet and published by Universal Edition (Vienna, 1912); the arrangement, by Alfred Neufeld, was revised by Alban Berg

now not unusual for the performers to be paid professionals rather than able members of the gathering, a trend related to the increasing technical difficulty of instrumental and vocal chamber music. The important new works in such genres were no longer intended for amateur performance but for chamber and lieder recitals by professionals; the talented dilettante had to rely increasingly on the more tractable works of the established repertory, arrangements or second-rate novelties. Such players, however accomplished, had also been excluded from the orchestras of societies like the Gesellschaft der Musikfreunde. Developments of this kind need to be viewed as part of a larger and paradoxical trend identified by Otto Biba: although music was increasingly available to consumers, it was beginning to lose ground as a spare-time activity.[37]

During the later nineteenth century, Viennese composers of serious art music had been faced with additional difficulties in making their work accessible because of the drastic decline in the standards of Viennese music publishing, which focussed increasingly on issuing popular music.[36] Brahms was lucky enough to have secured contacts with the leading German publishers, but the dissemination of Bruckner's music was not aided by the fact that almost all of it was issued by minor Viennese houses of little international standing. At the outset of his career, Mahler faced the same problem: his Second Symphony was published in the mid-1890s as a private venture financed by friends and admirers, and it was only taken over and reissued, together with first editions of the First and Third Symphonies, under the imprint of one Viennese publisher who did have significant outlets in Germany, Josef Weinberger,[39] after Guido Adler had intervened and secured a grant towards publication costs from the Gesellschaft zur Förderung deutscher Wissenschaft, Kunst und Literatur in Böhmen.[40] External financial support continued to play a role in the publication of works by Mahler's successors: Schoenberg, Berg and Webern all resorted to publishing their own works in a few instances and the initial publication of the vocal score of Berg's *Wozzeck* was subsidized by funds raised by Alma Mahler;[41] but for them (and to a lesser extent, for Mahler) the situation was transformed by the establishment in 1901 of a new publishing house, Universal Edition.

The foundation of the firm was of immense significance in Vienna and internationally, but regrettably the history of its origins is still not without mysteries. The initial planning was almost certainly undertaken in 1900, led by Josef Weinberger in collaboration with fellow publishers Bernhard Herzmansky and Adolf Robitschek, with financial backing by the banker Josef Simon (Johann Strauss's brother-in-law) and the participation of the printing company Josef Eberle. From the outset this was to be a project founded on a solid base of well-prepared modern editions of popular classics, practical arrangements and educational material (by July 1901 prescribed for use in music schools and conservatories by a government happy to reduce the import of such music from Germany) – but with a commitment to publishing new music. The success of the venture was spectacular: by the outbreak of World War I the catalogue contained over 4000 items and included works by some of the most distinguished European composers – Mahler, Schoenberg, Franz Schreker, Richard Strauss, Szymanowski and Delius. The importance of Universal Edition in disseminating the most innovatory music of the time can hardly be overestimated, though at first members of Schoenberg's circle seemed more aware of the company's failings than its heroic efforts in what initially might have appeared an almost hopeless task.

Having worked on some of Universal Edition's ubiquitous piano-duet arrangements (including Rossini's *Il barbiere di Siviglia*), Schoenberg signed a contract for the publication of his own compositions in 1909 (the year Mahler and Franz Schreker entered into similar agreements). Since 1903 his earlier works had appeared under the imprint of the Berlin firm Dreililienverlag, whose head was Max Marschalk, but sales had been anything but encouraging: up to 1911 the total sales of Schoenberg's opp.1–4, 6 and 7 (including those of single songs) had been 372 copies. The extent to which publishers now catered for an audience that studied such music rather than performed it is conveyed by the figures for two chamber works, *Verklärte Nacht* and the First String Quartet, which sold 57 and 52 copies of the scores but only nine and twelve copies of the parts respectively.[42] By joining Universal Edition Schoenberg gained the advantage of a relatively large publisher with an astonishingly active policy of furthering new music and a thorough approach to its promotion through effective publicity. It is difficult to estimate what impact on Schoenberg's finances (never healthy) the association had; by 1913 Universal was giving him advances and that year his royalties amounted to 860 out of a total income of 7040 marks.[43] It was only after the world war that the firm took on Berg and Webern, but both had been involved with the company on Schoenberg's behalf and had undertaken other tasks including the preparation of arrangements.

Unlike Berg, and to a lesser extent Webern, Schoenberg had no capital on which to call, and for most of his life teaching was his most regular source of income, but one that demanded an enormous amount of time and mental energy: viewed against this background Schoenberg's output appears prodigous. However, although Schoenberg's pedagogic gifts were widely recognized, the financial rewards were modest and for many years his survival depended on subsidy by admirers and rich patrons of the arts. One of the most important and devoted was Mahler. The two men had been introduced through

71. Gustav Mahler; portrait (1910) by Arnold Schoenberg

Mahler's young wife who, like Schoenberg, had studied with Alexander Zemlinsky. The relationship between such strong-willed and independently minded artists could not be without its turbulences, but deep mutual respect developed and Mahler offered Schoenberg moral and practical support; the latter included attempts to promote performances of the younger man's music, public defence of it in some of the more riotous concerts of new music and financial assistance both overt and surreptitious (at an exhibition in 1910 Mahler secretly purchased three of Schoenberg's paintings). As he lay dying, Mahler worried about his successor: 'If I go, he will have nobody left'.[44] In fact a Mahler Fund was established after his death; administered by Richard Strauss, Ferruccio Busoni and Bruno Walter, it provided grants to young musicians including Schoenberg.

However touching, Mahler's support of Schoenberg would not be particularly noteworthy but for the fact that he, like many members of the audiences who booed the new idiom, could not understand Schoenberg's music as it moved towards the emancipation of the dissonance and elimination of functional tonality. *Pelleas und Melisande* and the First Quartet obviously made a deep impression, but after hearing the First Chamber Symphony in 1907 Mahler commented 'I don't understand his music, but he's young and perhaps he's right. I am old and I dare say my ear is not sensitive enough'.[45] Personal esteem and an unswerving belief in artistic 'progress' and hence in the claims of modernism as the rightful inheritor of the tradition were powerful enough to override Mahler's aesthetic response, and modernism so dominated perceptions of Viennese musical history, particularly after World War II, that the achievements of composers who chose to follow paths other than that pioneered by Schoenberg and his pupils scarcely received a balanced assessment. If Schoenberg, Berg and Webern produced the greatest Viennese music of the period, the individuality and inventiveness of such composers as Franz Schmidt, Franz Schreker and Zemlinsky cannot be overlooked simply because of their 'conservatism'. There was indeed a sustained resistance to modernism and experiment in Vienna, shown not least in the rise of the Volksoper out of the racialist Kaiser-Jubiläums-Stadttheater and in the boom in operetta theatres. And this resistance was not simply a matter of conservative taste, as epitomized in Hanslick's criticism of Bruckner: it also found directly political expression, most clearly in the virulent and widespread antisemitic press commmentaries that pervaded the Viennese cultural climate. The historiographical model – to which Schoenberg automatically appealed when justifying his technical innovations – helped to polarize the debate at the time and subsequently to distort evaluations of this complex period in cultural history. As Carl Dahlhaus argued:

> The attempt to explain in terms of the philosophy of history Schoenberg's power to take decisions, that is, to interpret the diktat of the individual as that of history, is questionable inasmuch as the concept of the 'one' history which the philosophy of history assumes to exist is doubtful and may be suspected of being a myth. What really happens are histories – in the plural ... 'History' in the singular is a fiction.[46]

One of the fascinations of the pre-war years in Vienna, as in Paris, is the extent to which the typically twentieth-century plurality of 'histories' and cultures within high art becomes apparent.

Although 1914 might seem to represent an obvious turning-point in the history of the Habsburg monarchy, 1918 was probably more decisive in many respects: it was the end of the dynasty's reign and it saw the disintegration of the empire, which irrevocably transformed the political and social life of Vienna. On the other hand, the years leading up to World War I had already seen cultural transformations which revealed ever more clearly the marginalization of modernism in a capital which only a few years earlier had offered such a remarkably fertile environment for its growth.

The changing conditions had first been hinted at in the acerbic debate over Klimt's university paintings, which were greeted by a chorus of disapproval from the academic establishment. The matter became a political embarrassment even for a non-representative administration, and Klimt, sensing this, succeeded in repurchasing the three completed paintings in 1905 and withdrew into an increasingly private artistic world.[47] Although Hartel was still the minister concerned, the Koerber government had resigned in 1904 and the political conditions were changing. After 1907 Austria had a Reichsrat elected by universal male suffrage and the new governments were much less concerned to support an essentially élitist modernist art than their predecessors. Further symptoms of the new climate in Vienna can be seen in the failure of Otto Wagner to gain significant state commissions after the Post Office Savings Bank (the first stage was completed in 1905–6) and Mahler's departure from the Hofoper in 1907. As the train carrying Mahler on his journey to the New World pulled out of the Westbahnhof, Klimt muttered 'Vorbei' – 'finished'.

Klimt's pessimism must have seemed justified after the Kunstschau exhibitions of 1908 and 1909. The organization was the result of a second secession, this time from the Secession itself, and the exhibitions, held in temporary halls designed by Josef Hoffmann, were of immense historical importance, offering both established artists and architects like Klimt, Roller, Wagner and Hofmann, as well as the younger generation, particularly Kokoschka, Egon Schiele and Franz Schreker (with the ballet *Der Geburtstag der Infantin*), an important opportunity to make their work known in Vienna. But unlike the early exhibitions of the Secession, the Kunstschau events were a financial

72. Main hall (1905–6) of the Post Office Savings Bank, Vienna, designed by Otto Wagner

disaster: modernism was no longer salable.

Outwardly the social life of the Habsburg capital continued much as before, but as the subterranean political forces for dissolution gained strength it was the modernist movement in Viennese culture which was fragmenting. Crucial figures like Joseph Olbrich, Gustav Mahler, Richard Gerstl, Otto Weininger and Ludwig Hevesi were dead before the catastrophe of war descended, the last three by suicide. As Hermann Bahr wrote: 'Our epoch is shot through with a wild torment, and the pain has become no longer bearable. The cry for salvation is universal; the crucified are everywhere'.[48] Other leading creative artists left Vienna, including Webern, who departed for an unsettled life as a conductor in provincial theatres, and Kokoschka and Schoenberg who moved to Berlin, the city which in the postwar years was to supplant Vienna as the cultural capital of central Europe. Many of the most powerful and impressive creations of Viennese art in the period leading to 1914 articulated a sense of foreboding and uncertainty:

> I'm like a flag surrounded by distance.
> Divining the coming winds, I must share their existence,
> whereof things below reveal as yet no traces:
> doors are still closing softly and quiet are the fireplaces;
> windows are not yet shaking, and dust lies heavily.
>
> But I can already sense the storm, and surge like the sea.
> And spread myself out and into myself downfall
> and hurtle away and am all alone
> In the great storm.[49]

Rilke's vision in 1902 was prophetic, Schoenberg's setting of the text in 1916, as op.22 no.4, a grim product of hindsight.

NOTES

[1] C. A. Macartney, *The Habsburg Empire 1790–1918* (London, 1969), 604.

[2] R. Musil, *The Man without Qualities*, trans. E. Wilkins and E. Kaiser, 3 vols. (London, 1953–60), i, 32–3.

[3] Although it is not known how Mahler voted in 1907, in 1901 he had openly supported his old friend in the parliamentary elections (see the unpublished biography of Adler by Emma Adler, quoted in H.-L. de La Grange, *Mahler: l'âge d'or de Vienne (1900–07)* (Paris, 1983), 639; according to Hermann Bahr, Adler was an equally avid supporter of Mahler's performances at the Hofoper (Bahr, *Selbstbildnis* (Berlin, 1923), 213, and *Tagebuch 1918* (Innsbruck, 1919), 284.

[4] Schoenberg's support was probably only temporary (A. Schoenberg, 'My Attitude towards Politics', *Style and Idea* (London, 1975), 505–6; however the account offered in this note may well have been influenced by the atmosphere of Macarthyism prevalent in America when it was drafted) but he retained a lifelong friendship with David Joseph Bach (1874–1947), a distinguished music critic and fervent supporter of social democracy, who in 1906 founded the Workers' Symphony Concerts in Vienna and in the 1920s encouraged Webern's work with the organization.

[5] For a useful overview, see H. Hofmeister, 'Staatshilfe und Selbsthilfe', *Das Zeitalter Kaiser Franz Josephs*, ii: *1880–1916: Glanz und Elend: Beiträge* (Vienna, 1987), 83–106.

[6] C. E. Schorske, *Fin-de-siècle Vienna: Politics and Culture* (Cambridge, 1981), 9.

[7] A. Mahler, *Gustav Mahler: Memories and Letters*, trans. B. Creighton, ed. D. Mitchell (London, 1973), 304.

[8] Schorske, *Fin-de-siècle Vienna*, 8.

[9] An anecdote recounted by Alma Mahler (*Gustav Mahler*, 120) adds a sociological dimension: having heard *Die lustige Witwe* neither she nor Mahler could quite remember one passage and, being 'too highbrow to face buying the music', they went to Doblinger's music shop where Mahler distracted the assistant while Alma found the passage in a piano arrangement of the work.

[10] *Internationale Ausstellung für Musik- und Theaterwesen Wien 1892: Fach-Katalog der Musik-historischen Abtheilung von Deutschland und Oesterreich-Ungarn* (Vienna, 1892), pp.vii–viii.

[11] See p.92 above.

[12] Thus the fact that another of Adler's great predecessors, Ludwig von Köchel (1800–77), graduated in law but was also a keen student of botany and mineralogy aptly draws attention to the twin roots of musicological practice.

[13] It does not appear as such in Adler's classic schematic diagram illustrating his conception of musicology but figures prominently in his accompanying description of how a scholar might respond when confronted by an individual work of art. See 'Umfang, Methode und Ziel der Musikwissenschaft', *Vierteljahrsschrift für Musikwissenschaft*, i (1885), 5–20; a partial translation appears in B. Bujić, *Music in European Thought 1851–1912* (Cambridge, 1988), 348–55.

[14] B. Bujić, *Music in European Thought*, 342.

[15] See L. A. Rothfarb, *Ernst Kurth as Theorist and Analyst* (Philadelphia, 1988), 4ff (this volume is the most extensive introduction to Kurth's work available in English). Thanks to Adler, Kurth also met Mahler, who advised the young musician to take up conducting (perhaps surprising in view of the composer's approval of Berg's rejection of such a career).

[16] Ibid, 7.

[17] For a useful comparison, see C. Dahlhaus, 'Schoenberg and Schenker', in *Schoenberg and the New Music*, trans. D. Puffett and A. Clayton (Cambridge, 1987), 134–40.

[18] W. O. McCagg, *A History of Habsburg Jews, 1670–1918* (Bloomington, 1989), offers a useful modern account of such issues.

[19] Figures from McCagg, *A History of Habsburg Jews*, but see also M. Rozenblit, *The Jews of Vienna: Assimilation and Identity, 1867–1914* (Albany, 1983), for further quantitative details.

[20] Schorske, *Fin-de-siècle Vienna*, 120.

[21] Ibid, 133.

[22] Quoted in *Mahler: a Documentary Study*, ed. K. Blaukopf (London, 1976), 208.

[23] Ibid, 210, quoting from *Reichspost* (14 April 1897).

[24] R. Specht, *Das Wiener Operntheater, Erinnerung aus 50 Jahren* (Vienna, 1919), 28; translation from *Mahler*, ed. Blaukopf, 208.

[25] F. Willnauer, *Gustav Mahler und die Wiener Oper* (Vienna, 1979), 23.

[26] See *Vienna 1890–1920*, ed. R. Waissenberger (Secaucus, c1984).

[27] For an assessment of his work with Mahler, see de La Grange, *Mahler*.

[28] Quoted in Schorske, *Fin-de-siècle Vienna*, 237.

[29] Loc cit.

[30] See B. Szeps-Zuckerlandl, *My Life and History* (London, 1938), 142–3.

[31] *Wiener Allgemeine Zeitung* (25 Feb 1903); quoted in *Mahler*, ed. Blaukopf, 233–4.

[32] Interview in *Illustriertes Extrablatt* (9 Sept 1903); quoted in *Mahler*, ed. Blaukopf, 235.

[33] See, for example, H. Liebestöckl's review quoted in *Mahler*, ed. Blaukopf, 234.

[34] See P. Stefan, *Gustav Mahlers Erbe* (Munich, 1908), 9.

[35] See D. Mitchell, *Gustav Mahler: the Wunderhorn Years* (London, 1975), 419–22.

[36] A number of the most distinguished singers in Mahler's Hofoper ensemble made recordings during the period, but regrettably he made none (except some piano rolls); the first (acoustic!) recording of one of his symphonies was that of the Second, made by Oskar Fried in 1924.

[37] O. Biba, 'Musik', in *Das Zeitalter Kaiser Franz Josephs*, ii: *1880–1916: Glanz und Elend: Beiträge* (Vienna, 1987), 222.

[38] Austrian authors faced not dissimilar problems: see M. G. Hall, *Österreichische Verlags-geschichte 1918–1938* (Vienna, 1985). One of the root causes was Austrio-Hungary's failure to

sign the Berne Convention on copyright; unfortunately the history of this fascinating period in music publishing in Vienna has not yet been explored in depth.

[39] Weinberger had already published Mahler's first orchestral song cycle, the *Lieder eines fahrenden Gesellen* in 1897, but his main publishing interest lay in operetta, and in the case of Mahler's symphonies he seems to have acted rather as the agent for the printing firm of Josef Eberle & Co.

[40] The society had been formed as a response to the resurgence of Czech culture, but paradoxically both Mahler and Adler, German-speaking Jews from the same area on the border between Bohemia and Moravia, made significant contributions to the dissemination of Czech culture.

[41] See G. Perle, *The Operas of Alban Berg: . . . Wozzeck* (Berkeley, 1980), 193.

[42] See H. H. Stuckenschmidt, *Schoenberg: his Life, World and Work*, trans. H. Searle (London, 1977), 139.

[43] Ibid, 539–40.

[44] A. Mahler, *Gustav Mahler*, 198.

[45] Ibid, 112.

[46] C. Dahlhaus, *Schoenberg and the New Music*, 89.

[47] It is an indication of how circumscribed a world was occupied by the intellectual élite of Vienna at the time that when Webern defended his doctoral thesis in 1904, apart from Guido Adler the other examiners were two of the leading combatants in the academic debate over the university paintings, Friedrich Jodl (1849–1914) and Franz Wickhoff (1853–1909); Webern himself was a great admirer of Klimt's work.

[48] H. Bahr, *Essays* (Vienna, 1962), 129.

[49] *Buch der Bilder* (1902); this translation is by Stephen Spender and J. B. Leishman, from a CBS recording (79349).

BIBLIOGRAPHICAL NOTE

Cultural background

Glibness is an ever-present danger when attempts are made to draw parallels between different creative figures, but it is striking how, on the one hand, the three dominating presences in Viennese music, painting and architecture and forerunners of modernism, Gustav Mahler (1860–1911), Gustav Klimt (1862–1918) and Otto Wagner (1841–1918), had their artistic roots deep in Viennese traditions, and second the extent to which the scholarly attention devoted to their work has mushroomed since the early 1960s. Such studies as C. Nebehay, *Gustav Klimt Dokumentation* (Vienna, 1969), W. Hofmann, *Gustav Klimt und die Wiener Jahrhundertwende* (Salzburg, 1970), and H. Geretsegger and M. Peintner, *Otto Wagner 1841–1918* (Salzburg, 1978), and the works on Mahler cited in the bibliographical note to Chapter III represent highpoints in this literature.

In English it has been the more general treatments of the visual arts which have been most notable, particularly N. Powell, *The Sacred Spring: the Arts in Vienna 1898–1918* (London, 1974); P. Vergo, *Art in Vienna 1898–1918* (London, 1975); W. J. Schweiger, *Wiener Werkstaette: Design in Vienna, 1903–1932* (London, 1984); *Vienna 1890–1920*, ed. R. Waissenberger (Secaucus, 1984); J. Kallir, *Viennese Design and the Wiener Werkstätte* (London, 1986). The two most distinguished attempts to understand the interweaving of culture and politics on the broadest scale have been A. Janik and S. Toulmin, *Wittgenstein's Vienna* (New York, 1973), revised by R. Merkel as *Wittgensteins Wien* (Munich, 1985), and C. E. Schorske's magisterial *Fin-de-siècle Vienna: Politics and Culture* (Cambridge, 1981); recently E. Timms has cast light on such matters from a different angle in *Karl Kraus, Apocalyptic Satirist: Culture and Catastrophe in Habsburg Vienna* (New Haven and London, 1986). On the rampant antisemitism that coloured the political and cultural life of the period, see P. Pulzer, *The Rise of Political Anti-Semitism in Germany and Austria* (Oxford, rev. 2/1988); on the cultural background to it see S. Beller, *Vienna and the Jews 1867–1938: a Cultural History* (Cambridge, 1989).

The period has also been illuminated by impressive and (in some cases) hugely successful exhibitions which, fortunately, were accompanied by distinguished catalogues containing scholarly material of the utmost importance: L. Greve and W. Volke, *Jugend in Wien: Literatur um 1900* (Marbach, 1974); J. Kallir, *Arnold Schoenberg's Vienna* (New York, 1984); *Traum und Wirklichkeit: Wien 1870–1930* (Vienna, 1985); *Gustav Mahler: un homme, une oeuvre, une époque* (Paris, 1985); *Vienne 1880–1938: L'apocalypse joyeuse* (Paris, 1986); and *Das Zeitalter Kaiser Franz Josephs*, ii: *1880–1916: Glanz und Elend* (Vienna, 1987). In addition, an invaluable compilation of contemporary material is available in G. Wunberg's anthology *Die Wiener Moderne: Literatur, Kunst und Musik zwischen 1890 und 1910* (Stuttgart, 1981).

Music

Adler left an autobiography (*Wollen und Wirken: aus dem Leben eines Musikhistorikers* (Vienna, 1935)) recently supplemented by E. Reilly's *Gustav Mahler and Guido Adler* (Cambridge, 1982); but regrettably there is no adequate biographical study of Schenker's varied life and career. Among the numerous expositions of his analytical ideas, that by A. Forte, *Introduction to Schenkerian Analysis* (New York, 1982), is essential reading and I. Bent's concise but comprehensive *Analysis* (London, 1987) helps to locate Schenker's contribution in a historical perspective.

To those studies of Vienna's musical history and institutions referred to in the bibliographical note to Chapter III may be added some important sources. The history of the Hofoper has been well covered; essential reading are E. Pirchan, A. Witeschnik and O. Fritz, *300 Jahre Wiener Operntheater: Werk und Werden* (Vienna, 1953); A. J. Weltner, A. Przistaupinsky and F. Graf, *Das kaiser-königliche Hof-Operntheater in Wien: statistischer Rückblick auf die Personal-Verhältnisse und die künstlerische Thätigkeit während des Zeitraumes vom 25. Mai 1869 bis 30. April 1894* (Vienna, 1894); and A. Przistanpinksy, *50 Jahre Wiener Operntheater: eine Chronik des Hauses unde seiner Künstler in Wort und Bild* (Vienna, 1919). P. Stefan, *Gustav Mahlers Erbe* (Munich, 1908), and P. Stauber, *Das wahre Erbe Mahlers* (Vienna, 1909), offer the two sides of the controversy over Mahler's reign at the Hofoper. The reference works on the theatre listed in the Bibliographical Note to Chapter III may be supplemented by F. Willnauer, *Gustav Mahler und die Wiener Oper* (Vienna, 1979).

The best account of concert life in mid-nineteenth-century Vienna remains Hanslick's *Geschichte des Concertwesens in Wien* (Vienna, 1869) and his later volumes of collected reviews at least chart the course of its subsequent history. H. Kralik's *Die Wiener Philharmoniker und ihre Dirigenten* contains useful information, and *Das Rosé-Quartett: Fünfzig Jahre Kammermusik in Wien* (Vienna, [1932]) gives the repertory of one of the city's leading chamber music ensembles. There is no adequate history of Viennese music publishing around the turn of the century.

The scholarly reactions to the leading members of the Second Viennese School have been enormous. Schoenberg's multi-faceted genius has naturally provoked the most substantial responses, founded on J. Rufer's indispensable *The Works of Arnold Schoenberg: a Catalogue of his Compositions, Writings and Paintings* (London, 1962) and the Collected Edition (Mainz, 1966–); the *Journal of the Arnold Schoenberg Institute* (1976–) provides a forum for Schoenberg research. Bibliographical and analytical strategies have proved fruitful but regrettably the only attempt at a substantial Schoenberg biography is deeply flawed, marred by a lack of intellectual and aesthetic perception, a dour handling of the genre, and carelessness (H. H. Stuckenschmidt, *Schoenberg: his Life, World and Work* (London, 1977)). Fortunately an appreciation of Schoenberg's extraordinary personality can be reconstructed from the wide range of his writings and letters, published in English, most notably *Theory of Harmony* (London, 1978), *Style and Idea: Selected Writings* (London, 1975), *Structural Functions of Harmony* (London, 1954), *Letters* (London, 1964) and the magnificent *Berg-Schoenberg Correspondence: Selected Letters* (London, 1987).

For a time in the 1950s and 60s it was Webern, Schoenberg's pupil who offered so much creative stimulus to the postwar avant garde, who seemed to attract most scholarly attention, but precisely because of the nature of that interest the resulting articles and books tended to focus on technical and analytical aspects to the neglect of source and biographical studies. Even now no complete edition has begun, and no adequate catalogue of Webern's music and comparatively little of his correspondence is published. However H. Moldenhauer's massive *Anton Webern: Chronicle of his Life and Works* (New York and London, 1978) offers a comprehensive account of his life.

Unexpectedly it has been Berg who, of the school, has inspired some of the most distinguished scholarship: D. Jarman, *The Music of Alban Berg* (London, 1979); G. Perle, *The Operas of Alban Berg*, 2 vols. (Berkeley, 1980, 1985); J. Schmalfeldt, *Berg's Wozzeck: Harmonic Language and Dramatic Design* (New Haven and London, 1983). These, and the rich crop of articles, have transformed and immeasurably deepened the ways in which Berg's music is understood; paradoxically, in spite of the fact that it has become ever clearer that his art embodies references to his life, there is no reliable modern biography available. The *Berg-Schoenberg Correspondence* and *Alban Berg: Letters to his Wife* (London, 1971) offer partial insights; work on a collected edition is under way.

Chapter XV

Paris:
Conflicting Notions of Progress

JANN PASLER

One of the most critical issues underlying the passionate advocacy of this style or that, the conflicting expectations and desires, the power struggles and the increase in private support for music in France from 1890 to World War I was the debate about change: whether it was desirable; what it could mean to society; whether musical change could motivate or at least symbolize social change; whether it could change people – that is, imbue values.[1]

For the republicans celebrating twenty years of political stability (as long as any government since before the Revolution), change of any kind was risky: it could subvert their grip on the country. General Boulanger's attempted *coup d'état* in 1889, supported by hopeful *ancien régime* followers, numerous Catholics and some working-class idealists, had stirred up anxiety about the future, France being the only republic in Europe at the time. Fear increased in the 1890s as growing numbers of socialists penetrated the parliament, anarchists protested through random acts of violence, and the Dreyfus Affair caused internal divisions in every part of society.

Others outside the establishment, either completely or only marginally, did not necessarily value stability and preservation of the status quo. Too much was at stake for both the socialists and the old-world aristocrats. Both had hopes for a better world and believed music could help them realize their aspirations. The former wanted music to 'incite those who listen to act well, to live well'. But the wind-band music of the people was hardly uplifting, and to find the 'human grandeur' and 'moral truth' they sought in music, the *Revue socialiste* had to look to works like *Fervaal*, written by the aristocrat Vincent d'Indy.[2] Many aristocrats similarly turned to music as a way of asserting and returning to traditional values. For them, it provided a means of escaping the present, perhaps indulging their nostalgia for earlier times; and it often served as an analogue to religion. Some hoped their musical activities and support would help them recapture and transform the influence their class was losing rapidly and

389

inevitably in the socio-political realm.[3]

To explain more fully the struggles in the musical world of Paris before World War I, one must examine how these groups understood the nature of change. 'Progress' was the buzzword of the day: what kind of structure, when superimposed on past human endeavour, would motivate meaningful change in the future?[4] As various sections of society idealized different periods in France's past and held contradictory hopes for its future, there was wide disagreement as to the kind of progress desired. Some even denied the value of such a notion, especially when it came to the arts.

PROGRESS AS BOUNDLESS EXPANSION

'Progress' was a term originally used at the French Academy in the seventeenth century to argue for the superiority of modern thinkers over their predecessors, particularly in the area of acquired knowledge. Comte and the positivists later saw such a notion as the key to advancing from superstition to reason. In the late eighteenth and nineteenth centuries progress became an idea used by the bourgeois to validate and contextualize their successes in industrial development. The seemingly unlimited capacity for improvement in industrial production, particularly after the mid-1890s, the stabilization of France's money during this period and the growth of its gross national product into one of the best in Europe bolstered the idea of progress as a potent material and economic force. The concurrent rise of imperialist régimes and the colonialization of more and more land further contributed to the notion of progress as the accumulation of national power and therefore prestige.

Paralleling this expansion beyond previously defined limits in the technological, economic and political domains was a similar kind of musical progress. Throughout the nineteenth century, work on the design of instruments resulted in expanded chromatic and dynamic ranges and more variety in their timbral possibilities. Charles-Marie Widor discussed many of these in his *Technique de l'orchestre moderne* (1904). One of his largest chapters explains the chromatic glissandos and multiple harmonics that can easily be achieved on the harp since the development of the double-action mechanism. Successive improvements in the harp's mechanical precision, size and chromatic range led composers to write increasingly for it and, at the turn of the century, instigated extended debate at the Conservatoire over whether it had not become sufficiently important to merit a class of its own.[5]

The size of the orchestra had also increased dramatically by the end of the nineteenth century, eventually involving four woodwind instruments to a part and colossal brass, percussion and string sections. The public followed such development with great interest, so it would seem, for in magazine advertisements for concerts and on the covers of orchestral music programmes there appeared almost invariably the number of performers in the concert, especially when it surpassed a hundred. The 1891 production by the Société des Grandes Auditions de France of Handel's *Israel in Egypt*, for example, boasted 300 performers, while the French-English Festival organized by Gabriel Astruc at Trocadéro in 1909 advertised 1000 singers and orchestral players. So taken was the French poet Paul Valéry with this 'large-scale music' that he compared its power in the aesthetic realm with that of the new machines in the material one. In an essay he wrote after attending one of the Lamoureux orchestral concerts in 1893 Valéry explained:

> In the hierarchy of the arts, music on the grand scale as created by modern masters provides a real parallel with the powerful, the almost superabundant, resources which other moderns have been able to create in the realm of material enterprise. In a way, this large-scale music can draw upon almost unlimited reserves of aesthetic power. It plays with life's depths, the extremes of passion, simulates the complexities of thought, and seems to stir nature itself ... Just as our machines can perform our labours for us, giving us the benefit of speeds which far exceed our natural capacity, so music on the grand scale – with its ecstasies and rages always in wait to seize upon us, its limitless imaginings, its almost total powers of possession – offers and inspires us with states of feeling that are half unreal yet more powerful than most of our real ones. Not one of the other arts can claim such sovereignty.[6]

Composers at the turn of the century continued their 'progressive conquest of chords that were always more and more complex, always further away from that perfect consonance that is the ideal unison'.[7] But unlike their German and Austrian counterparts Richard Wagner, Hugo Wolf and Richard Strauss, who kept extended chromaticism tonally functional, French composers like Debussy and Ravel used 'uncatalogued' harmonies as unusual sounds for their own sake. They had little desire to add appendices to the harmony books. Harmonic complexity in their music more often results from chordal resonance than tonal ambiguity. They stacked intervals in increasing numbers, without necessarily resolving them, to colour a unison, a melodic line or a harmonic succession. By 1911, in Ravel's *Valses nobles et senti-mentales*, for example, one finds virtually an entire scale in his eleventh chords, as well as thirteenth and fifteenth chords that function as dominant sevenths. That same year Ravel's friend the critic M.-D. Calvocoressi proposed a concept of music based on sounds and their perception – indeed on psycho-physiology. With such a concept he challenged the German music theorist Hugo

73.(a) Universal Exhibition, 1889: a group of Vietnamese musicians

Riemann and hoped to debunk the traditional notion of music as metaphysics.

Much more than their German and Austrian neighbours, French composers also considered progress in music the result of increasing exposure to and potential assimilation of foreign idioms. The Conservatoire scholar, composer and folklorist Bourgault-Ducoudray, convinced by the need to 'extend the boundaries of musical expression', sought to 'rejuvenate' music through the use of all modes, not just the major and minor, still present in the folksongs of different countries. In a lecture at the Universal Exhibition of 1878, he proclaimed: 'All modes, old or new, European or exotic, insofar as they are capable of serving an expressive purpose, must be admitted by us and used by composers'.[8] In the 1880s the French Ministry began supporting research trips into the provinces and abroad. Julien Tiersot eventually published volumes of folksongs and had his own harmonizations of them performed in Parisian salons and concert halls. At the Universal Exhibitions of 1889 and 1900 French composers could actually hear music from places as far away as Vietnam and Java. Debussy borrowed ideas from both these traditions.[9] This interest in modality, the language of pre-tonal music in the West, suggests reactionary forces at work; but the way Bourgault-Ducoudray put it, potent musical resources were left behind when the West adopted tonal harmony as the *modus vivendi* of its music. Composers should return to modality as a means of taking off in new directions – and many did.

But by 1900, as nationalist sentiment grew in France, massive foreign influence on culture was no longer seen as an unambiguously progressive force. Intellectuals like Anatole France found that industrial progress had given rise 'to rivalries from one country to the next', and that it was 'the current modes of production' that created 'imperialism, colonial expansion, and armed peace'. From his perspective, capitalism, as 'responsible for the workers' internationalism and the cosmopolitanism of financiers', was 'essentially destructive of the patriotic and national spirit'.[10] Similarly, borrowing the newest musical ideas from one's neighbours caused composers to compromise the national identity of their music, to drift even further from that essence otherwise preserved in their folksongs.[11]

Composers sympathetic to the nationalists and officials responsible for protecting the interests of French artists began to question the contribution of foreign music to the future of French music. Debussy exploited the ambiguities of the 'Tristan' chord throughout his *Pelléas et Mélisande*,[12] but by the time it was first performed in 1902 he advised his French contemporaries to look past Wagner (*après Wagner*) rather than following him (*d'après Wagner*), and to reconsider their own musical roots. When complaints about the overwhelming presence of Wagner at the Opéra grew louder, the Minister of Public Education and Fine Arts reacted strongly. In 1901 he changed Article 11 of the

73.(b) Universal Exhibition, 1900: the pavilion of Siam

Cahiers de charges, the contract that stipulated what the Opéra must do in return for its 800,000-franc annual subsidy. Instead of requiring the Opéra director to produce two world premières by French composers, one of which must have three to five acts (as was the case in the 1890s), he exacted six premières by French composers in three to five acts and six in one to three acts, not including the required opera every other year by a Prix de Rome winner. By 1915 this number had risen to seventeen new works of which fourteen had to be by French composers.

As a corollary to these nationalist efforts, many French musicians and administrators sought to achieve progress in musical education. For Bourgault-Ducoudray, improvement in the public's 'state of musical indifference' was a 'patriotic obsession'.[13] As early as 1869 he formed the Société Bourgault-Ducoudray to encourage people to sing choral music. And he was not alone. In the first decade of the new century there were increasing numbers of amateur choral groups, serious music societies and popular concert associations not only in Paris but also in the provinces (Lyons, Nancy, Montpellier, Angers, Le Havre, Nantes, Orléans). In Paris there were five symphony orchestras. A reviewer in 1908 admitted that a significant advance in French musical education had been made in the previous 30 years. Even the working class had its musical venues. With 'artists and amateurs having multiplied' and fashion now playing a role, at last one could speak of having 'democratized taste'.[14]

By the early twentieth century, composers as diverse as Maurice Ravel and Charles Bordes were fast at work transcribing and harmonizing folksongs from countries far and near. Public concert societies and private salons gradually welcomed the music of more times and places. But expanding the size and sound of orchestras, tolerating increasingly complex chords, incorporating musical elements from ever more distant musical cultures (while still protecting the interests of French composers) and even educating greater numbers of people in music represents only one concept of progress. And progress as boundless expansion was not an idea that could sustain itself. Armies had divided the world; the land was not endless. Composers had stretched tonality to its limits; the advantages of modality were not yet clear. Debussy, for one, was not even convinced that everyone should acquire a musical education.[15] Nationalist tendencies turned energies inward, and other notions of progress were needed.

PROGRESS QUESTIONED: THE DEBATE ABOUT VALUES

In spite of abundant material progress, it became apparent by the late nineteenth century that in many ways the nation was in decline. It has been argued that the concept of decline was 'conceptually inseparable' from that of progress in the nineteenth century and evolved as a reaction to urbanization, industrialization and democratization.[16] Artists and writers had long suspected that progress in science could only result in a decline in the arts and literature. Baudelaire felt that 'the purely material developments of progress have contributed much to the impoverishment of the French artistic genius which is already so scarce'.[17]

In 1892 Max Nordau gave a name to this sense of decline: 'degeneration', a word borrowed from psychiatric research. Nordau blamed the 'fin-de-siècle' decadence in the arts on mental illnesses that result from excess consumption of poisonous substances and the fatigue of modern life. He found such degeneration, or 'sick deviance', particularly dangerous for society in that, as a form of 'intellectual decomposition' it compounds itself with each successive generation and can lead to a 'twilight of the race [*crépuscule des peuples*]' (a reference, of course, to Wagner's opera *Götterdämmerung*, 'Le crépuscule des dieux').[18]

Nordau has been much criticized and ridiculed; George Bernard Shaw responded in 1908 with an entire book, *The Sanity of Art: an Exposure of the Current Nonsense about Artists being Degenerate*. But the observations about French society that gave rise to Nordau's crazy conclusions had some basis in reality. Those who enjoyed decadent art – 'only a small number of rich and distinguished people or fanatics[!]' – were often aristocrats. (The Société des Grandes Auditions de France which sponsored the first performances of Wagner's *Tristan und Isolde* and *Götterdämmerung* in Paris had many members with titles.) 'The end of an order of things that, during a long succession of centuries, satisfied logic, subdued perversity, and gave rise to beauty in all the arts' had begun for this class years earlier.[19]

Moreover, Germany's defeat of France in 1870 and its rise to great power provoked anxious reassessments of French national health.[20] And although Nordau's perception about the decline of the Latin race was exaggerated, the chief statistician of Paris published a series of studies in the 1890s on how the French population had been declining throughout the nineteenth century while, by contrast, that of Germany was rising. From 1700 to 1890 the number of French declined from 40% of the European population to 12%.[21] France's growth rate from 1872 to 1911 was a mere 10% as compared with Germany's 58%, Spain's 20%, Italy's 30%, Austria-Hungary's 38%, Great Britain's 43% and European Russia's 78%.[22] Some years there were even more deaths than births. The chief statistician advised remedying the problem with more babies, but other social scientists took seriously Nordau's complaint about urban diseases – alcohol, tobacco and drug abuse, insanity, suicide and venereal disease.

Musicians were not ignorant of these problems. In Charles-Marie

Widor's 'mimed legend' *Jeanne d'Arc* (1890) a chorus of soldiers sings an 'old song' to the words, 'War is a little expensive to the world, but it is love that will pay the bill. When one has depopulated the earth, one must then repopulate it afterwards'. In 1912 the modernist journal *Revue musicale S.I.M.* played with the idea in its 'Events of the month': 'Depopulation: With patriotic sadness, we have just learnt that in the sixth course [of the Schola Cantorum], three motifs from sonatas were recognized as inappropriate [*impropre*] for this genera-tion'. The word 'impropre' is used to mean not only inappropriate but also unclean or indecent.[23]

The country thus needed revitalization and a concept of social progress to keep up with its technological progress. To improve the quality of life it was advised in 1895 that: 'The duty of the statesman is no longer to push society towards an ideal that seems attractive to him, but his role is that of the physician: he prevents the outbreak of illnesses by good hygiene, and he seeks to cure them when they have appeared'.[24] When it came to the arts and literature, 'good hygiene' turned into a moral issue. Since Rousseau the arts had been thought of as responsible for corrupting morals. But others saw in them a different potential: 'In the chaos of ideas, one hopes that art will teach about the order that must follow confusion. The poet, the musician must announce, intuit, in which forms civilization will continue to expand. Tomorrow, what will be moral, what beautiful?'[25]

In music journals of the turn of the century, a new criterion of judgment appeared in response to such concerns: whether a composi-tion was 'saine' ('healthy'). No-one complained about folksongs, Mozart or even light opera, all of which provided the listener with 'the most healthy of joys'. But other music – Wagner's operas, Debussy's *Pelléas et Mélisande* and any that broke expectations – could lead to 'anaemia' at best, one's 'dissolution' at worst. Critics used health metaphors in particular to attack the validity of certain music, to warn the public against being seduced by it and to discourage them from supporting it. When Debussy's opera was first performed in 1902, conservative critics deemed it 'unhealthy', 'sick', 'harmful', and its music 'without life'; Debussy's 'craving for novelty' was 'unwholesome'.[26] Two of the most eminent and historically trained, Henri Curzon and Camille Bellaigue, made the same leap as Nordau had, assuming a connection between an artist's presumably decadent life, which the characters in his work have, and the effect such decadence could have on the listener. Curzon wrote that, like Debussy, the characters in *Pelléas* 'act as if in a vague stupor'; 'as if moved by some external and supernatural forces, they live, and we live with them, in the unconscious and the mysterious depths', those of a 'nihilism and negation of all faith, of all guide'. Bellaigue went even further: 'After listening to [*Pelléas*], one feels sick' and not unlike

74. Debussy's 'Pélleas et Mélisande', first performed at the Opéra-Comique, Paris, on 30 April 1902; design by L. Jusseaume for the final scene in Act 4

Pelléas, who sighs 'Nothing is left for me if I continue this way'; he continued, 'We are dissolved by this music because it is in itself a form of dissolution. Existing as it does with the minimum of vitality, it tends to impair and destroy our existence. The germs it contains are not those of life and progress, but of decadence and death'.[27] Later, when Debussy's music spawned imitators, critics called Debussysme an 'epidemic'. Even Satie called it 'a dangerous malaria' and warned his readers, 'you might catch it!'.

From this concept of music as capable of playing both a visionary and an educational role in society's moral development came two models of progress developed by musicians themselves. Both differed from the notion of progress as continual expansion of acquired knowledge in that they did not advocate sacrificing the old to the new, nor did they pretend the present was superior to the past. What was at stake for both was the preservation – indeed the survival – of a given set of values. Those committed to France's republican heritage were concerned about its future; those who still had loyalties to the *ancien régime* sought a form of progress that respected, and even took inspiration from, the great ideas of their predecessors. Both groups were acutely aware of history and their place in it. The notions about progress they thus formulated significantly affected their philosophies of education, their definition of the modern artist and, most important, their musical choices.

PROGRESS AS LINEAR EVOLUTION

The republican model for progress was linear, based on continuity with and evolutionary development from the ideas that flourished during the Republic, that is, the nineteenth century. At the Paris Conservatoire the idea was to 'conserve . . . to maintain a discreet but not exclusive cult around the charming works that have contributed to the glory of our country'. The institution had been founded with the aim of staying in contact with the spirit of the country, but at the turn of the century the director Théodore Dubois and the composition teacher Charles Lenepveu, among others, understood it as 'a conservative force, necessary to counterbalance the revolutionary forces that seduce talent toward new paths'. 'The law of continuity insists that progress have, as a corollary, a certain respect for the past.'[28]

Dubois, appointed to replace Ambroise Thomas after he died in 1896, based his philosophy of education on this idea of art as evolutionary, with each step forward necessarily built on the preceding one:

> Art evolves, progresses. It never develops by leaps [*saccades*]. And even if genius might be in some way spontaneous, it is not less true that the greatest innovators were in reality only the result, the product of lengthy efforts of which they, in personifying these efforts, are the highest manifestation. That is what knowledge and retrospective historical studies aim to show, and it is in this sense that teaching must proceed if its object is to train artists.[29]

Under Dubois' leadership, the Conservatoire continued its orientation toward dramatic music, espoused by Auber and carried on under Thomas, even though there was growing criticism that France had not yet produced any great symphonists. Students continued to write cantatas for the Prix de Rome competition, often imitating their teachers' music, and later for events that inaugurated statues glorifying the Republic.[30]

Most of the repertory taught and used for testing was from the nineteenth century. Even though, in Dubois' words, the study manuals were meant to 'direct the student towards a path more in keeping with the art of our time', they were grounded in the rules and values of the immediate past. Dubois' *Notes et études d'harmonie* (1890), for example, supplements H. Reber's 1862 treatise, which he edited and reissued in 1889. His intention was to 'complete, comment on, and modify in part' Reber's standard text, but in no way to replace it. His 'notes', appendices to Reber's chapters, merely clarify issues to which Reber gives short shrift – the use of diminished fifths, modulation to distant tonalities, the preparation and resolution of dissonant chords, suspensions and appoggiaturas. His subsequent *Traité de contrepoint et de fugue* (1901) expands F. Bazin's 1858 treatise, adding exercises and examples of 'the beautiful and healthy [*saine*] choral traditions of past masters' as models. But apart from two short excerpts from Palestrina and Lassus in which tritones appear in the counterpoint, given as examples of what not to follow, the only analysed works ascribed to specific composers are an eight-part chorus by Cherubini and the fugues that helped Dubois in 1857, Massenet in 1863 and lesser-known students of Massenet and Thomas in 1893, 1896 and 1900 win the Prix de Rome. Widor wrote his *Technique de l'orchestre moderne* (1904) as an 'appendix' to his predecessor Berlioz's *Grand traité d'instrumentation et d'orchestration modernes*. He considered 'one should, above all, religiously respect' Berlioz's work and therefore intended merely to clarify techniques made possible by recent instrumental improvements.

75. Title-page of 'Gloria victis' by Charles Lenep-veu (c1879), with a drawing of Antonin Mercié's sculpture of an angel carrying a dead soldier to heaven

Given this dependence on their predecessors, it is amusing to find Dubois describing his colleagues as musicians 'without prejudice, making art as they feel it' and not subscribing to any school or group.[31] When attacked by Wagnerians for being 'retrograde', Dubois defined the ideal artist as just the opposite of his antagonists who, from his perspective, seemed to repudiate all that came before their Messiah, to believe that serious study of harmony, counterpoint and fugue would do one harm, and to refuse to do whatever is in accordance with rules.

The subjects these composers set to music often promoted hope and faith in the republic's future, self-sacrifice and patriotism. The war with Prussia in 1870, in particular, motivated numerous patriotic pieces. Among the endless two-page harmonizations of simple strophic songs collected in *Chansons politiques et de circonstances* (bound in 1879), Charles Lenepveu's *Gloria victis* stands out for its length, the only ten-page piece. On the cover of this strophic variation in five parts is a drawing of a famous, prizewinning sculpture by Antonin Mercié, a member of the Académie des Beaux-Arts, depicting an angel carrying a dead soldier to heaven. Like the sculpture, the music and its text suggest that heroism and hope can come from apparent defeat. 'We thought her dead and frozen, the dear France of our forefathers', the song begins, with its straightforward two-plus-two-bar phrases in Eb . In its last section, as the poet J. Chantepie turns the soldier into a metaphor for France, the music slows to a Largo before returning to the dotted rhythms of its opening march. In a patriotic piece setting a poem by Victor Hugo (another republican hero) Lenepveu makes direct reference to the melodic and rhythmic shape of the *Marseillaise*. Commissioned in 1889 by the composer's home town of Rouen to inaugurate a mausoleum constructed in memory of their dead soldiers, this *Hymne funèbre et triomphale* was such a success that other French towns used it to inaugurate similar monuments throughout the 1890s.

Dubois, who wrote far more music than Lenepveu, also composed music with patriotic themes. In 1908 he chose a popular French tune as the theme of the second movement of his First Symphony and incorporated fragments of the *Marseillaise* in its third, calling the work *Symphonie française*. Lenepveu wrote little religious music besides a Requiem with which he fiddled throughout his life, but Dubois set an enormous number of religious texts – motets, masses, oratorios and religious melodies. His oratorio *Les sept paroles du Christ* (1867) rapidly became standard Easter music throughout the country and in 1894 helped him win a seat at the Académie des Beaux-Arts.

That a republican composer wrote so much religious music might seem surprising in the light of republican anti-clericalism and the law of 1905, which finally separated church and state. Yet one must remember that most French composers began as organists, perhaps because in the provinces the only serious music was heard in church. Dubois, like Gounod, Franck and Widor, as well as Paladilhe, Saint-Saëns, Fauré, d'Indy, Pierné, Messager and later even Schmitt and Büsser, supplemented his income by being an organist. First he worked as choir director and principal organist at Ste Clothilde (1858–68) then at the Madeleine, where he took Saint-Saëns' place and remained until 1896. Thus, republican composers embraced rather than rejected the church at the turn of the century.

The style in which composers like Lenepveu and Dubois wrote also harks back to that of their republican predecessors. Their music is essentially lyrical, built of recurring themes and, in the case of dramatic music, detachable sections. Lenepveu valued predictable, balanced movement within his phrases, four-bar groupings and little modulation. Ambroise Thomas was not only his teacher at the Conservatoire and the person whose seat he took in 1896 at the Académie des Beaux-Arts, but also his principal musical model. Dubois' music is more interesting contrapuntally and more complex harmonically, for Dubois had studied with César Franck and even once travelled to Munich to hear Wagner. But his music recalls that of Gounod more than Franck or Wagner. It won accolades for its harmony and unity, which were compared with the same traits in Dubois' life, rather than for its originality or daring.

By 1905 many of the public had grown tired of the music of Dubois, Lenepveu and other Institut composers, and their interest turned elsewhere. Performances that year of Lenepveu's 'La mort de Jeanne d'Arc', an excerpt from his 1886 opera *Jeanne d'Arc*, and a new *Stabat mater* by a fellow Institut member Emile Paladilhe, were received 'with deference, not more' and even 'coldly' at the otherwise arch-conservative Société des Concerts du Conservatoire. At the same time, Rimsky-Korsakov's Piano Concerto in C♯ minor and Debussy's *Prélude à L'après-midi d'un faune* had become standard repertory and were 'very applauded' even at the Société. The public was also growing increasingly receptive to French musical traditions of the more distant past, thanks to the new editions of Rameau's work, begun in the 1880s and 1890s, and a decade of early music performances by the Chanteurs de St Gervais.

PROGRESS AS A SPIRAL

For certain quasi-, would-be or real aristocrats, the notion of progress as building on the accomplishments of the republic was unacceptable. In the early years of the new century they found another philosophy of progress much more compelling. Like the one just discussed, theirs was based on continuity with the past and a sense of evolution from the past to the present;[32] however, they remarked, progress should not have to be linear. And the past from which it draws its force should extend well before the nineteenth century.

Charles Maurras, an arch-conservative member of this group, questioned whether 'progress in the knowledge of natural phenomena' had not occurred 'to the detriment of man's ability to generalize and to interpret . . . to the detriment of taste . . . to the destruction [*ruine*] of personality'.[33] 'To restore certain constant principles', like reason, order and balance, he advocated renewed study of the Greeks. In the musical world, like-minded reactionaries formed societies that performed primarily music on old instruments or exclusively music by Bach, Handel or Mozart.

Vincent d'Indy represented a related but slightly different concept perhaps better than any of his peers. An aristocrat by birth (unlike Dubois who was the son of peasants, and Lenepveu whose roots were bourgeois), he too believed that 'evolution signifies progress'.[34] But for him progress should take the form of a spiral. In a manifesto-like essay, published in the first issue of *L'occident* (1901), d'Indy wrote:

> I cannot conceive of progress as a straight road extending on a plain; but, to the contrary, I see the *monument-art* . . . in the form of a spiral whose volutes are linked to each other and strengthened by stays, reinforcements – the immutable human feelings on which each of the volutes relies, while stretching the spiral always ever higher towards the infinite.[35]

D'Indy's image of a spiral that turns back on itself to propel itself forward is more dynamic than Maurras' concept of mere return to the distant past and less deterministic than Dubois' of a line on which every aspect of the present can be traced back to something immediately preceding it. While it implies reactionary motivations, this idea also suggests a significant commitment to the future. It informs much of what d'Indy believed and tried to accomplish.

After reviewing for the state (on Thomas' death) which reforms were most crucial at the Conservatoire, d'Indy helped found a new music school, the Schola Cantorum.[36] There, in his composition lectures, he defined art as a means of progress (particularly for the soul); moreover, he saw the role of art as 'making humanity progress'.[37] In his speech at the opening of the Schola's new building on 2 November 1900 he explained how his view of progress underlaid his educational philosophy:

> Art, in its march forward throughout the ages, . . . is not a closed circle, but a spiral that always rises and always progresses. I would like to help students follow this development from one century to the next . . . they will leave even better armed for modern combat in that they will have lived, so to speak, the life of art and will have assimilated in their natural order the forms that logically followed one another in the diverse periods of artistic development.[38]

The two volumes of lectures d'Indy published as *Cours de composition musicale* provide a contrast to Dubois' pedagogic texts and shed light on what and how the Schola taught. First, d'Indy treats rhythm, harmony and counterpoint in the context of composition rather than as separate exercises. Second, he examines the 'conditions of art' – its educational role, its duration, its sincerity – even before addressing its techniques. D'Indy considered these volumes a 'treatise on the philosophy of Art'. Third, he teaches history and aesthetics alongside the elements of music, acoustics and the history of music theory in the first part and examines the study of musical genres in a historical manner in the second.[39] In presenting 'the progressive evolution of art' from the 'rhythmic-monodic period of the third to the thirteenth centuries' to the 'polyphonic period of the thirteenth to the seventeenth centuries', d'Indy aimed to 'give the student the synthetic notions necessary to understand how the first two periods relate to the third [the "metric period from the eighteenth century to the present"]'. His extensive examples range from Bach and Beethoven to Franck and Wagner. Madrigals and folksong receive extensive attention since d'Indy considered the first essentially a sixteenth-century aristocratic form and the second based on the church modes and therefore linked, in some earlier period, to religious music. Church modes embodied for him another way of using the past to reinvigorate the present and direct the future.

In their related publishing activities and in the concerts held at the Schola and their multiple branches in the provinces, members promoted the combination of old and new music. D'Indy worked on modern editions of Rameau and Gluck and conducted performances of them, while his colleague Charles Bordes and their student Déodat de Séverac collected, harmonized and published folksongs from many regions. The Schola's Edition Mutuelle, a type of vanity press, used advance subscriptions and the composers' own funds to publish their students' new works. Concert programmes too juxtaposed choral, organ or harpsichord masterpieces from the sixteenth to the eighteenth centuries with first performances of new works. D'Indy, in fact, considered the perfect formula for concert programmes was Bach, Beethoven and an 'advanced modern', as his friend Guy Ropartz had put into practice in Nancy.[40]

For d'Indy the ideal artist was a 'creator bringing to the old artistic edifice, eternally in construction, new materials that are solid and coherent with the old ones, materials taken from the life of his heart and shaped by his intelligence with the goal of serving the good of mankind and feeding the progressive life of humanity'.[41] He was neither a revolutionary, who 'wants to construct beside the monument and, finding no point of support, disappears, carried off by the centrifugal force [of the spiral]. One should feel sorry for him, while

76. *Vincent d'Indy conducting a rehearsal at the Schola Cantorum, Paris, in 1909*

blaming him for his useless audacity'. Nor was he an academic, who 'attaches himself to only one point of reinforcement and indefinitely turns around this same point without seeking to rise higher. These are never artists, they fade out, useless'.[42] Nor, in the case of performers, were true artists those who display their talents for their own sake. The Schola set out to make their performers interpreters and informed musicians in contrast to the virtuosos of the Conservatoire.

Again using the image of the spiral, d'Indy described what he considered the most important musical subject, human feelings: 'The artist worthy of the name, after endeepening his knowledge of the great earlier expressions of art, . . . will build on those immutable foundations a new cycle of the magnificent spiral, loyally expressing the ever-same human feelings as he perceives them and endures them'.[43] Only after this will he 'acquire personality and be able to serve lofty and healthy [*saine*] food to future souls – the supreme goal of art'.

With this focus on expressing feelings and on promoting certain traditions as healthy, it is no surprise that d'Indy gravitated toward subjects that also interested Dubois and his colleagues. Both valued religion, sacrifice and heroism rather than stories from the contemporary world or urban Paris (in this way they differed from, for example, Charpentier and Bruneau). Both were idealists. D'Indy's musical treatment of these subjects, however, was quite different. As early as 1886, in his *Symphonie sur un chant montagnard français* he chose a folksong as his principal theme; he also collected and harmonized two volumes of folksongs in 1890 and 1892. Throughout his works, moreover, d'Indy incorporated elements of Gregorian chant; the main theme of his opera *L'étranger* is one such example. As president of the Société Nationale de Musique after Franck's death in 1890, he promoted new chamber music and composed numerous chamber works.

The most important characteristic of much of d'Indy's music is its cyclical form. From a musical perspective the spiral recalls the cyclical formal principles espoused by Franck, d'Indy's teacher. Thematic return in cyclical works like the symphony cited above differs from the thematic interlacing that propels much of Lenepveu's and Dubois' music and from the rondo-like procedures they often use to insure coherence. In d'Indy's and many of his students' music, themes rarely return without substantial transformation of their melodic or rhythmic shape, their harmonic context or the feeling they express. Furthermore, in his four dramatic works, *Le chant de la cloche*, *Fervaal*, *L'étranger* and *La légende de Saint Christophe*, the themes function as Wagnerian leitmotifs, conceived as symbolic signs and continually developing according to the dramatic action.

Like the Scholists, Debussy was sympathetic to such a notion of progress.[44] Three months after hearing the Schola's performance of Rameau's *Castor et Pollux* in 1903, he wrote: 'Let us try to recapture the old traditions of the time when artists were proud of their masters and capable of devotion to one another'.[45] His piano piece *Hommage à Rameau* (1905) not only reminded listeners of his French heritage; it also allowed him to construct a place for himself in history. It is difficult to read Debussy's comment of 1915 – 'since Rameau we don't have any clearly French tradition' – without sensing his desire to be Rameau's successor. To stake a claim in the future, he must have reasoned, one must connect oneself to the past. In Debussy's music one finds elements that call to mind d'Indy's spiral. Only early works, like the *Fantasie* (1889), use strict cyclical form, but recurring material in most of his music helps to articulate significant points and almost never involves exact repetition. It has been argued that Debussy's forms often grow like spirals; Golden Section proportions characterize the internal proportions of works like *La mer* and *Jeux*, whether or not Debussy was aware of it.[46]

In the other arts, many echoed such ideas. At the Théâtre de l'Odéon in the first decade, and at the Théâtre des Arts and the Théâtre du Vieux Colombier in the second, revivals of Molière and Racine abounded. Presenting old writers interspersed with young modernists was the intention of both the Théâtre du Vieux Colombier when it began and the *Nouvelle revue française*. And besides the many painters who brought back ancient themes, such as Puvis de

77. *Ravel's ballet 'Ma mère l'oye', first produced at the Théâtre des Arts, Paris, on 28 January 1912, is an example of French fascination with the eighteenth century and with synthesizing the old and new*

Chavannes, solo female dancers like Isadora Duncan, Ida Rubenstein and Natalia Trouhanova virtually made careers creating dances inspired by Greek vase paintings. As often as not these dances juxtaposed classic masterpieces and modern music. From 1900 their performances in the salons and on Parisian stages helped to contribute to the rise of ballet as an increasingly important genre.

As these groups suggest, the quarrel between the 'ancients' and the 'moderns' had a new solution in the early twentieth century: why not have both? Such a notion of progress as the simultaneous presence, and even synthesis, of the old and the new became crucial to the definition of modernism in music at the time and underlies the neo-classicism following World War I (as well as the Domaine Musical concerts Boulez helped organize in the 1950s). The image of a spiral thus suggested to its proponents that yesterday's values can underlie today's, that return to the past is only possible in some transformed manner and that, in the case of independents like Debussy, the future inevitably demands innovation.

PROGRESS DENIED

Not everyone, however, believed in the idea of progress, especially those frustrated with the rate of change in society. In 1906 the Marxist Georges Sorel published a series of articles in the journal *Mouvement socialiste* that, two years later, became his book *Les illusions du progrès*.

The notion that the moderns could ever be superior to the ancients, he pointed out, is a circular argument (how can we know what we do not know?). Reality is nothing but a chaotic struggle, and the idea of progress is only a myth used to legitimize the status quo. Conceived as such, it is a conservative force that produces a passive mentality in its advocates.[47] Moreover, it is dangerous to assume, as seventeenth-century apologists did, that future generations 'are destined to have a fate that is automatically superior to ours'.[48] 'Moral rebirth is possible only under conditions that lie outside the idea of progress and the social institutions that foster the idea.'[49]

In 1909 the famed virtuoso harpsichordist Wanda Landowska devoted a large part of her book *Musique ancienne* to arguing for the impossibility of progress in the arts. She was not the first – Baudelaire rejected such a notion in his review of the 1855 Exhibition – and her primary purpose was to draw attention to forgotten masters, those whom she loved to perform. But she went much further than mere promotion of her musical tastes: she denied the evolutionary nature of artistic development. 'We're made to believe that all the old masters only existed to serve as seeds for the romantics, and these, in turn, to give rise to new geniuses', whereas in reality, she asserted, art, in its diverse historical forms, has only successive expressions of equivalent value. 'In art, there is no progress, only taste', she concluded.

Landowska was not alone in her thinking. In his *Musiciens d'autrefois* (1908), Romain Rolland contrasts the peacefulness and 'moral benefit' that music adds to life with the otherwise 'universal agitation' of the period's social and political history. While the latter 'is a struggle without end, humanity's push towards a progress ever being thrown into question', the former has no need for progress. In artistic history, perfection has already been attained many times, and still 'art is inexhaustible, like life'.[50] One critic attributed this lack of artistic progress to the unchanging nature of human emotions expressed by the arts.[51]

A NEW MODEL FOR THE TWENTIETH CENTURY

Many of those who felt sympathetic to Sorel or Landowska, who grew impatient or disenchanted with the protectivism of the republicans and the *ancien régime* loyalists or who were simply infected with what Mauclair called 'a prejudice for novelty' enjoyed the different attitude towards history and progress shown in the productions brought to Paris by the Ballets Russes. From 1909 until well after World War I these ballets espoused no continuity from one to the next. The first they presented was *Le pavillon d'Armide*, a love story about aristocrats set in eighteenth-century France. The purpose in choosing such a subject, according to the librettist and set designer Alexandre Benois, was to show that the Russians 'were not only supreme, but they could outvie the French on their own ground'.[52] The other ballets that year represented different intentions. *Les sylphides*, danced to an amalgam of Chopin's music, 'interpreted an epoch common to the whole of Europe'; *Cléopâtre*, Dyagilev's 'Russian salad of Russian composers', was 'a wonderful vision of the radiant beauty of the ancient world'; and the *Polovtsian Dances*, to Borodin's music, Benois saw as 'satisfying the thirst of Parisians for primitive unrestraint'.[53] These visiting foreigners had no reason to promote one period over any other, nor, like the anarchists and futurists, to try to deny or escape the past. In their play with bygone or imaginary cultures of diverse kinds and from many eras, the Ballets Russes subscribed to Landowska's notion of history. Like her, they proved that all periods, places and cultures can co-exist, can serve equally as stimuli for art, for beauty.

Furthermore, the impresario Sergey Dyagilev knew that, while presenting itself as a 'magasin de nouveautés' might incur criticism, this approach ultimately would be the key to the troupe's success. Whatever was billed as new had increasing appeal after 1909 and Gabriel Astruc, their astute manager and fund-raiser, excelled at selling culture to Parisian consumers. Among those who sponsored the troupe were the aristocrats Countess Greffulhe, her cousin Robert de Montesquoiu and Princess Polignac as well as the rich bourgeois Misia Sert. These patrons, like Nijinsky, wanted to 'be of tomorrow, to anticipate the future', if not to create it in their own image, according to their own tastes and values.

From this notion of the new as discontinuous with the past and valued for its own sake came a message that certain French people took as a lesson. In 1909 Robert de Montesquiou began to refer to his writing as 'leaping over intermediary ideas'. After collaborating with Reynaldo Hahn on *Le dieu bleu* (the first French ballet written for the Ballets Russes), Jean Cocteau changed his basic assumptions about art. The son of an *haut bourgeois*, Opéra-going family who never thought of 'astonishing' and who 'believed that art was undisturbing [*tranquille*] and calm', he was at first upset with Dyagilev's command, 'étonne-moi!'.[54] Eventually, however, he realized that the troupe wanted him 'to scorn everything that it shook up. This phoenix teaches that one must burn oneself alive in order to be reborn'.[55] From Stravinsky's music for *The Rite of Spring* and Jacques Rivière's review of it,[56] he concluded that each masterpiece must be the contradiction of previous ones, as indeed *The Rite* is to impressionist music. By 1919 Cocteau had expanded this perception into a general theory: 'One could say that the spirit of the new in every period is the highest form of the spirit of contradiction'.[57]

Numerous critics found in the Ballets Russes a new model for the creative artist. Henri Ghéon was taken aback by Stravinsky's *Firebird* in 1910: 'When the bird passes, it is the music that bears it aloft.

Stravinsky, Fokine, Golovine, in my eyes, are but one name'.[58]
Similarly, in 1913, Jacques Rivière wrote of *The Rite of Spring*:

> Who is the author of *The Rite*? Nijinsky, Stravinsky, Roerich? This
> preliminary question is unavoidable; yet it does not make sense to
> us Westerners. For us, everything is individual, a strong and
> characteristic work always carries the mark of only one mind. This is
> not the case for the Russians. If it seems impossible for them to
> communicate with us, while they are among themselves they have
> an extraordinary ability to feel and think the same thing at once.[59]

These critics were right. The two Stravinsky ballets, as many of the
others presented by the Ballets Russes, involved a creative process
that was indeed collective. In his memoirs, the choreographer Mikhail
Fokine recounts how he and Stravinsky together worked out the music
and the dance of *The Firebird* while improvising from their own first
ideas. After the initial vision that inspired *The Rite*, Stravinsky turned
to the set designer and amateur archaeologist Nicolas Roerich, with
whom he conceived the ballet's details and the succession of its
dances.[60]

To the many Wagnerians in their audience, these ballets presented
a fresh, new form of Gesamtkunstwerke, the symbolist ideal of total
theatre. In his review of Stravinsky's *Firebird*, Ghéon explains that the
dancers lost their appeal as individuals and became components of
the total work:

> Ballet centring on a star is finished, as is the reign of the star, like
> that of the tenor. To be fair to the Russian troupe, one should avoid
> discussing personalities. The troupe is superior to the many indivi-
> duals that make it up. It possesses the supreme quality of appearing,
> of becoming one with the work it represents even to the point of
> seeming to arise from the music and then melting into the colours
> of the set design. Now one should speak not of the 'dancer' but of
> the ballet.

An English critic wrote similarly of *The Rite* three years later:

> The functions of the composer and the producer are so balanced that
> it is possible to see every movement on the stage at the same time as
> to hear every note of the music. But the fusion goes deeper than this.
> The combination of the two elements of music and dancing does
> actually produce a new compound result, expressible in terms of
> rhythm – much as the combination of oxygen and hydrogen
> produces a totally different compound, water.[61]

In defending his generation against Max Nordau's attack, the writer
Victor Segalen pointed to the synesthesia that Ghéon, Rivière and
Colles perceived – of one sensation in terms of another – as just the
kind of progress the culture needed. 'Audition colorée', as he called it,

78. Scene (with Russian tribal elders and maidens) from the first production of Stravinsky's ballet 'The Rite of Spring' at the Théâtre de Champs-Elysées, Paris, on 29 May 1913; taking a subject so distant in time allowed the composer, the choreographer (Nijinsky) and the designer (Roerich) unprecedented freedom of expression

was 'compatible with the healthiest mentality' in that it involved synthesis. For Segalen, like d'Indy, synthesis was a critical aspect of progress.[62]

Imaginary subjects helped stimulate this synesthetic response. Even when communicating human feelings, as in *Le spectre de la rose* or the two middle tableaux of *Petrushka*, the object has something fairy-tale about it, allowing the artists to escape the real. In *The Rite of Spring*, for example, a past so distant as to be unknown allowed the composer complete freedom in what he might express. The story is merely a pretext for formal relationships among the arts – rhythmic mass movements or images that occur simultaneously on stage and in the music.[63]

In Stravinsky's ballets, discontinuity becomes characteristic of the musical style, not just the result of piecing together works by several composers (as in *Cléopâtre*). Beginning with *The Firebird*, Stravinsky presents themes first as fragments, sometimes (as Fokine suggested) to ensure a direct connection between stage events and the music. Similarly, eschewing transition between sections, he frequently juxtaposes or superimposes contrasting metres, motifs and harmonies. Each of these discontinuities depends on the listener to provide the conceptual continuity, to synthesize the succession of disparate events and to understand how the work coheres.

Some of the public saw in such ballets a revolution rather than an evolution. The Ballets Russes came from another culture: Sorel might have guessed that their attitude towards progress would be different. Others found in them a commentary on each of the kinds of progress discussed. Critics heard *The Rite of Spring*, for example, as part of 'the evolution toward increasing rhythmic, polyphonic and instrumental complexity' and therefore 'a premature specimen of the music of the future'.[64] In spite of its startling innovations, they also recognized in it the influence of Stravinsky's predecessors Glinka and Borodin, his teacher Rimsky-Korsakov and his friend Debussy.[65] They even traced its roots to the 'rhythmic and figurative symbolism' of ancient Greek dances. Nijinsky was praised for renouncing virtuosity and returning to this, 'the healthy [*saine*] and more glorious tradition of his art'.[66]

Still, what the Ballets Russes embody more than progress is an image of co-existence – of style, personality, discipline and even of men in society. There are works, as Rivière put it, to which one listens as one would the advice of a friend: they have a moral. But at the heart of the *The Rite* is a myth that refuses to speak to the individual in us:

> We are witnessing the movements of man at the time when he did not yet exist as an individual. People still hung together; they went in groups, colonies ... they were devoted to god ... Nothing individual appeared on their faces. At no moment during her dance does the young girl reveal the personal terror of which her soul must have been full. She accomplishes a rite, she is absorbed by a social function ... Man is dominated by what is most inert in him, most opaque, most limited, his society with others.[67]

With such a conclusion to his remarkable essay on Stravinsky's third ballet, Rivière unveils one of the critical issues underlying notions of progress at the turn of the century: whether it will be the individual (and therefore democracy) that ensures a better future or some collective state. Leaving the first performance of *The Rite*, Rivière was overwhelmed; for the first time he felt 'some sort of desperate possibility for evolutionist doctrines'.

*

That *The Rite* could embody multiple notions of progress, depending on the perspective from which one considers it, suggests that these notions were interdependent. All imply some relationship with the past, recognize the importance of the present and harbour some hope about the future. What created the debate about change and fuelled its intensity – which past to choose for inspiration, whether to resist or promote change, whether to tiptoe or leap into the future – was largely a social issue. With the society in flux, social groups sought distinction from one another and self-preservation. The republicans and *ancien régime* supporters had to fight for the survival of their values. Those of the former were continuously threatened; those of the latter were disintegrating. Because music was widely acknowledged as capable of having a profound effect on the listener, of rendering one healthy, many people saw it as a visionary and educational force. It is difficult to understand the music composed and supported in France before World War I without taking into account the values various members of society attached to it, and the future they hoped to shape through it.

NOTES

[1] This article is part of a larger study of the musical world of turn-of-the-century France. This forthcoming book will explain in more detail the issues raised only briefly here. I am grateful to the National Endowment for the Humanities for a University Teachers' Fellowship and to the University of California for a President's Research Fellowship in the Humanities that, in 1988–9, have generously supported this work. All translations are my own unless otherwise stated.

[2] Review of *Fervaal* from the *Revue socialiste* (Nov 1896); repr. in *Fervaal devant la presse* (Paris, 1897), 111–16.

[3] For a study of the methods republicans used to enforce their ideals and maintain control, as well as those the aristocrats used to exert influence, see J. Pasler, 'The Social Roots of Innovation in the Music of Turn-of-the-Century France' (forthcoming).

[4] For an excellent study of the topic, see R. Nisbet, *History of the Idea of Progress* (New York, 1980).

[5] Saint-Saëns, for one, was opposed to giving individual attention to such an instrument. In a letter of 3 Dec 1902 to the Conservatoire director Théodore Dubois he argued that 'the beautiful sonority of the instrument', 'the purity of its timbre', might be compromised by removing it from the context of the orchestra where traditionally it had been merely an 'ornament'. By contrast, Dubois was willing to fight with the minister over this issue.

[6] P. Valéry, 'At the Lamoureux Concerts in 1893', in *Occasions*, trans. R. Shattuck and F. Brown (Princeton, 1970), 198–9.

[7] P. Landormy, 'Debussy et le progrès de l'art musical', *Courrier musical* (15 June 1903), 182.

[8] E. Brody, 'Bourgault-Ducoudray', *Grove 6*.

[9] For the use Debussy made of the Javanese music he heard during the 1889 exhibition, see R. Mueller, 'Javanese Influence on Debussy's *Fantaisie* and Beyond', *19th-Century Music*, x (1986–7), 157–86.

[10] A. France, *Vie de Jeanne d'Arc* (Paris, 1908), p.lxxii.

[11] A. Bonaventura, 'Progrès et nationalité dans la musique', *Congrès international d'histoire de la musique: Paris 1901*, 226–39.

[12] See C. Abbate, '*Tristan* in the Composition of *Pelléas*', *19th-Century Music*, v (1981–2), 117–41; and R. Holloway, *Debussy and Wagner* (London, 1978).

[13] M. Daubresse, a review of Bourgault-Ducoudray's lectures on Russian music, *Courrier musical* (1 Oct 1902), 233.

[14] M. Daubresse, 'L'instruction musicale: progrès realisés, améliorations possibles', *Courrier musical* (1 Oct 1908). He nevertheless points out that 'the great masses are still largely ignorant of music'. To remedy this he argues for making instruction in the elementary principles of music 'obligatory in all the schools in France, no matter what their level (primary, secondary, superior) or their speciality' (547–8).

[15] In 1903 Debussy opposed the republic's efforts to increase the artistic education of the public at large: 'the most useless thing in the world . . . How, in effect, can anyone claiming to have some degree of artistic education be prevented from thinking himself at once able to take up art? It is that which makes me think that a too great diffusion of art will lead only to a greater

mediocrity'. Moreover, Debussy felt that 'the masses can no more be ordered to love beauty than they can be persuaded to walk round on their hands'; see *Debussy on Music*, ed. and trans. R. L. Smith (London, 1977), 141, 165.

16 R. Nye, 'Sociology and Degeneration: the Irony of Progress', in *Degeneration: the Dark Side of Progress*, ed. J. E. Chamberlain and S. L. Gilman (New York, 1985), 49, 51.

17 P. Bade, 'Art and Degeneration: Visual Icons of Corruption', *Degeneration: the Dark Side of Progress*, 221.

18 M. Nordau, *Dégénérescence*, trans. A. Dietrich (Paris, 1894), pp.vii, 8, 32, 62–3.

19 M. Faure, *Musique et société du Second Empire aux années vingt* (Paris, 1985), interprets Debussy's never-completed dramatic work *La chute de la maison Usher* as the representation, however unconscious, of 'a class haunted by the idea of its own end'.

20 Nye, 'Sociology and Degeneration', 52; note also that in the first decade of the century, nationalist movements in the colonies were gaining strength.

21 J. Bertillon, *Le problème de la dépopulation* (Paris, 1897).

22 R. Nye, *Crime, Madness, and Politics in Modern France* (Princeton, 1985), 134. I am grateful to Professor Allan Mitchell for pointing out this source.

23 Swift, 'Les faits du mois', *Revue musicale S.I.M.* (Dec 1912), 62.

24 E. Durkheim, *The Rules of Sociological Method*, cited in Nye, *Crime, Madness, and Politics*, 169.

25 Nordau, *Dégénérescence*, 12.

26 J. Pasler, '*Pelléas* and Power: Forces behind the Reception of Debussy's Opera', *19th-Century Music*, x (1986–7), 243–64.

27 C. Bellaigue, 'Pelléas et Mélisande', *Revue des deux mondes* (15 May 1902), 450–55.

28 X ***, former professor at the Conservatoire, 'Le Conservatoire national de musique et de déclamation', *Revue d'histoire et de critique musicales* (June 1902), 243.

29 T. Dubois, 'L'enseignement musical', in *Encyclopédie de la musique*, ed. A. Lavignac, vi (Paris, 1931), 3437.

30 Perhaps their teachers felt it was easier for students to 'transform ideas into feelings', as Dubois described the role of art, if these ideas were furnished by a text; or perhaps instrumental music – 'an ideal domain' which, he notes, 'all musicians consider the highest form of their art' – was still thought too élitist for students especially at the beginning of their careers. See the interview with Dubois cited in 'La musique à l'Académie de Médecine', *Le soir* (22 Jan 1895).

31 T. Dubois, 'A propos de ce qu'on appelle: les Wagnériens', MSS notes (Rés.F.1665 (14), Bibliothèque Nationale, Paris.

32 In an article published in the first issue of *L'occident*, A. Mithouard calls the West the 'land of continuity', though what he is espousing, along with other contributors to this journal, is a return to values that predate the Revolution.

33 P. Lasserre, 'Charles Maurras et la renaissance classique', *Mercure de France* (June 1902), 600–01.

34 V. d'Indy, 'L'artiste moderne', *L'occident* (Dec 1901), 11.

35 Ibid; d'Indy also gave this as a lecture at the Schola Cantorum on 5 Dec 1901.

36 The Schola Cantorum began in 1894 as a religious music society, whose aim was to reform chant for church services. Two years later, Charles Bordes, d'Indy and Alexandre Guilmant turned it into a school that taught not only liturgical music and Gregorian chant, but also solfège, counterpoint, harmony, composition, instruments, history and aesthetics. Unlike the Conservatoire, the Schola had no age limit and accepted students three times a year. Its students lived at the school where, according to Bordes, they had to submit to a sort of 'moral hygiene' and attend every class for which they had registered under threat of expulsion.

37 V. d'Indy, *Cours de composition musicale* (Paris, 1902), 9, 10.

38 Cited in R. Rolland, 'Le renouveau, esquisse du mouvement musical à Paris depuis 1870', *Musiciens d'aujourd'hui* (Paris, 1908, 9/1921), 250.

39 In his 'Souvenirs', published in *Cinquante ans de musique française de 1874 à 1925*, ed. L. Rohozinski, ii (Paris, 1926), d'Indy reveals that it was Liszt, whom he visited in Weimar, who suggested his courses at the Schola take a historical form (p.386).

40 Letter from d'Indy to G.-M. Witkowski (2 April 1899) in Y. Ferraton, 'Autour de la Société des Grands Concerts de Lyon', *RdM*, lxxii (1986), 246.

41 D'Indy, *Cours de composition musicale*, 9. In his 'L'artiste moderne' he defines the true artist similarly as one 'who, leaning solidly on old ancestral bases, knows how to find in himself the appropriate materials to consolidate, always higher and higher, the vertical line of the ever constant human feelings. There's precisely what makes the name artist a sublime title' (pp.11–12).

⁴² D'Indy, 'L'artiste moderne', 11. Among those d'Indy condemns to the status of academics are 'eclectic searchers after success, Jewish people and more or less talented imitators. These will never be creators'.

⁴³ Ibid, 15.

⁴⁴ Debussy and d'Indy were on fairly good terms, in spite of great differences in their character and music. D'Indy had argued vigorously for the inclusion of Debussy's music in the programme presented at the Universal Exhibition of 1900 and, on the basis of the human feelings he saw as the principal subject of *Pelléas*, if not for other reasons, he wrote a very favourable review in *L'occident* after its première.

⁴⁵ C. Debussy, 'A Consideration of the Prix de Rome from a Musical Point of View', *Musica* (May 1903), in *Debussy on Music*, ed. Smith, 201.

⁴⁶ R. Howat, *Debussy in Proportion* (1983); the Golden Section increases in size according to the Fibonacci number series $(0,1,1,2,3,5,8, n+[n-1])$ and in nature (shells etc) takes the form of a spiral.

⁴⁷ J. Stanley, 'Translator's Introduction' to G. Sorel, *The Illusions of Progress*, trans. J. and C. Stanley (Berkeley and Los Angeles, 1969), p.xxxiii.

⁴⁸ Sorel, *The Illusions of Progress*, 11–12.

⁴⁹ Stanley, 'Translator's Introduction', p.xxix.

⁵⁰ R. Rolland, 'Le rôle social et moral de la musique', *Musiciens d'autrefois*; repr. in *Courrier musical* (1–15 Sept 1908), 536.

⁵¹ P. de Stoecklin, 'L'anémie', *Courrier musical* (1 July 1911), 462.

⁵² A. Benois, *Reminiscences of the Russian Ballet*, trans. M. Britnieva (New York, 1977), 292.

⁵³ Ibid, 293, 296, 297.

⁵⁴ Cited in F. Steegmuller, *Cocteau* (Paris, 1973), 67.

⁵⁵ J. Cocteau, *Prospectus 1916* (Paris, 1924), 9.

⁵⁶ J. Rivière, 'Le sacre du printemps', *Nouvelle revue française*, v (1 Nov 1913), 706–30.

⁵⁷ J. Cocteau, 'Présentation d'oeuvres de musiciens nouveaux', *Institut des Hautes Etudes de Belgique* (19 Dec 1919); MS in the Harry Ransom Humanities Research Center, Austin, Texas. In J. Pasler, 'New Music as Confrontation: the Musical Sources of Cocteau's Identity', *Jean Cocteau and the Parisian Avant Garde: Irvine 1989*, it is suggested that Cocteau learnt how he could draw attention to himself and his work by following such an example; his subsequent interest in Satie, jazz and popular idioms derives from this desire to contradict his predecessors.

⁵⁸ H. Ghéon, 'Propos divers sur le Ballet Russe', *Nouvelle revue française* (1910), 210–11.

⁵⁹ Rivière, 'Le sacre du printemps'.

⁶⁰ For extended discussion of these collaborations, see J. Pasler, 'Music and Spectacle in *Petrushka* and *The Rite of Spring*', in *Confronting Stravinsky: Man, Musician, and Modernist*, ed. J. Pasler (Berkeley, 1986).

⁶¹ H. Colles, 'The Fusion of Music and Dancing', *The Times* (12 July 1913); repr. in *Le sacre du printemps: Press-Book*, ed. F. Lesure (Geneva, 1980), 63–4.

⁶² V. Segalen, 'Les synesthésies et l'école symboliste', *Mercure de France* (April 1902), 84–5.

⁶³ Pasler, 'Music and Spectacle in *Petrushka* and *The Rite of Spring*'.

⁶⁴ L. Vallas, 'Le sacre du printemps', *Revue française de musique* (June–July 1913); repr. in *Press-Book*, ed. Lesure, 29.

⁶⁵ In the last decade, scholars including R. Taruskin, P. van den Torrn and E. Antokoletz have shown how many of Stravinsky's most characteristic procedures (such as octatonicism) borrow and build on those of his predecessors.

⁶⁶ J. Marnold, 'Le sacre du printemps', *Mercure de France* (1 Oct 1913); repr. in *Press-Book*, ed. Lesure, 35–8.

⁶⁷ Rivière, 'Le sacre du printemps'.

BIBLIOGRAPHICAL NOTE
Primary sources

For a study of the social history of music in turn-of-the-century France, nothing substitutes for consulting primary sources. Most still lie buried at the Bibliothèque Nationale or the Bibliothèque de l'Opéra, Paris, or at the Harry Ransom Humanities Research Center in Austin, Texas, or in other libraries and private collections.

Among those which are published, the most important are composers' letters. Several large volumes have appeared: *Claude Debussy: Lettres 1884–1918*, ed. F. Lesure (Paris, 1980); G. Fauré, *Correspondence*, ed. J.-M. Nectoux (Paris, 1980), trans. J.A. Underwood as *Gabriel Fauré: his Life through his Letters* (London, 1984); A. Roussel, *Lettres et écrits*, ed. N. Labelle (Paris, 1987); and *Stravinsky: Selected Correspondence*, ed. R. Craft, 3 vols. (New York and London, 1982–5). A. Orenstein is preparing a volume of Ravel's letters that will supplant the earlier *Ravel au miroir de ses lettres*, ed. R. Chalupt (Paris, 1956). These volumes are not complete but are the largest and most accessible collections of composers' correspondence available.

Memoirs too can provide invaluable information and detail, though they sometimes contain a bias, especially those written long after the period being recounted. The interested reader should start with A. Bruneau, *Bruneau-Zola: A l'ombre d'un grand coeur: souvenirs d'une collaboration* (Paris, 1932); H. Busser, *De Pelléas aux Indes galantes* (Paris, 1955); M.-D. Calvocoressi, *Music and Ballet: the Recollections of M.-D. Calvocoressi* (London, 1933); A. Casella, *Music in my Time*, trans. S. Norton (Norman, Oklahoma, 1955); J. Durand, *Quelques souvenirs d'un éditeur de musique* (Paris, 1924); H. Février, *André Messager, mon maître, mon ami* (Paris, 1948); D.E. Inghelbrecht, *Mouvement contraire* (Paris, 1947); P. Lalo, *De Rameau à Ravel* (Paris, 1947); L. Laloy, *La musique retrouvée* (Paris, 1928); J. Massenet, *My Recollections*, trans. H. V. Barnett (Boston, 1919; first pubd 1912); *Ravel par quelques-uns de ses familiers* (Paris, 1939); C. Saint-Saëns, *Portraits et souvenirs* (Paris, 1900); and the special issues of the *Revue Musicale* focussed on Debussy (May 1926) and Ravel (December 1938).

Certain biographies must also be considered primary sources, for the authors knew their subjects personally. See V. d'Indy's *César Franck* (Paris, 1914); C. Koechlin's *Gabriel Fauré*, trans. L. Orrey (London, 1946) and his *Debussy* (Paris, 1941); Roland Manuel's *Maurice Ravel*, trans. C. Jolly (New York, 1972; first pubd 1947); L. Vallas' *Vincent d'Indy*, 2 vols. (Paris, 1946); E. Vuillermoz's *Claude Debussy* (Paris, 1957) and his *Gabriel Fauré*, trans. K. Schapin (New York, 1969; first pubd 1960).

Contemporary criticism illuminates society's perception of itself as well as current taste. The most important composers who wrote sometimes ironic but always perceptive criticism are Bruneau, *Musique de Russie et musiciens de France* (Paris, 1903); Debussy, *Monsieur Croche et autres écrits*, ed. F. Lesure (Paris, 1971), trans. and rev. R. Langham Smith as *Debussy on Music* (London, 1977); Dukas, *Ecrits sur la musique* (Paris, 1948); Saint-Saëns, *Outspoken Essays on Music*, trans. F. Rothwell (London, 1922); and Satie, *Ecrits*, ed. O. Volta (Paris, 1981). Influential critics who reissued their work in book form are H.-G. Villars, numerous volumes from *Lettres de l'ouvreuse* (Paris, 1890) to *Garçon l'audition* (Paris, 1901); J. Marnold, *Musique d'autrefois et d'aujourd'hui* (Paris, 1911); Romain Rolland, *Musiciens d'aujourd'hui* (Paris, 1921), whose last chapter, 'Le renouveau de la musique française depuis 1870', presents a particularly good overview; J. Tiersot, *Un demi-siècle de musique française, entre les deux guerres 1870–1914* (Paris, 1918); J. Cocteau, *Le coq et l'arlequin* (Paris, 1918); and those by J. Aubry, C. Bellaigue, A. Coquard, H. Imbert, A. Jullien, A. Pougin and E. Vuillermoz.

Music journals reveal the day-to-day functioning of the musical world as no other publications. Monthly or bi-monthly ones review the most important concerts, publish box-office receipts of performances at the Opéra and Opéra-Comique, announce competitions, list prizewinners and discuss analytical and aesthetic issues raised by the music being performed. The major music journals in Paris were the conservative *Le ménestrel*, owned by the publisher Heugel; *Revue d'histoire et de critique musicales*, orientated towards serious history, criticism and analysis; *Le courrier musical*, which later merged with *Le mercure musical* to form *S.I.M.*, one of the most progressive; and *Le monde musical*, owned by a piano maker and written for a broad public. Regular music criticism also appeared in intellectual journals, like *Revue des deux-mondes*, *Revue de Paris*, *Mercure de France*, *Revue blanche* and many others. For more information on the nature of these journals and their music criticism, consult C. Goubault, *La critique musicale dans la presse française* (Geneva and Paris, 1984), and J. Pasler, '*Pelléas* and Power: Forces Behind the Reception of Debussy's Opera', *19th-Century Music*, (1986–7), 243–64.

Secondary sources

Besides the work done by scholars outside music, like R. Shattuck and J. Siegel, the best study of music in its social context during this period is M. Faure, *Musique et société du Second Empire aux années vingt* (Paris, 1985). Although a Marxist ideology lies at its centre, the book is far from being pure argument. Its rich detail, thorough research and perceptive insights make it a landmark in turn-of-the-century studies. While Faure's attempts to find analogies between musical style and ideology are not always convincing, his descriptions of Saint-Saëns as a parnassian eclectic and a republican ready for combat, of Fauré as republican opportunist, of Debussy as a nationalist with monarchist sympathies, and of Ravel as an anarchist-bolshevek are as revealing as they are provocative. No other work comes close to Faure's. M. Cooper's *French Music from the Death of Berlioz to the Death of Fauré* (London, 1951) deals more narrowly with music and biography. E. Brody's recent *Paris: the Musical Kaleidoscope 1870–1925* (New York, 1987) offers an overview of the issues of principal concern at the time – exoticism, Wagner, relationships between the arts and the influx of foreign musicians in Paris, but without taking a critical stance. The strongest chapters are the two based on primary sources: the journal of the Spanish pianist Ricardo Viñes and contemporary documents concerning the Universal Exhibitions.

A number of composer biographies and monographs shed light on the period. E. Lockspeiser's *Debussy: his Life and Mind*, 2 vols. (Cambridge, 1962), explores the influence of painters, writers and other musicians on Debussy. In his *Debussy, Impressionism and Symbolism*, trans. R. Myers (London, 1976), S. Jarocinski argues convincingly that Debussy's music is rooted in symbolist theory more than impressionist painting. R. Orledge's *Debussy and the Theatre* (Cambridge, 1982) shows the composer's ties to the theatrical world. The biography that best places a composer in his social-political milieu is M. Marnat's *Maurice Ravel* (Paris, 1986). Although much of this book consists of citations of other published sources, Marnat goes further into Ravel's elusive life and his politics than previous biographers have. Nectoux's lengthy introductions to Fauré's letters unveil life in the salons; but for a detailed study of this subject, see E. Carassus, *Le snobisme et les lettres françaises* (Paris, 1966). New journals devoted to a single composer – *Cahiers Debussy (1974–)*, *Cahiers Roussel* (1978–81) and *Cahiers Ravel* (1985–) – continue to make available previously unpublished material.

For quick information on the more obscure composers during this period, there are no better sources than R. Dumesnil, *La musique française contemporaine*, 2 vols. (Paris, 1930), and O. Séré, *Musiciens français d'aujourd'hui* (Paris, 1911). In A. Lavignac, *Encyclopédie de la musique*, 6 vols. (Paris, 1931), *Cinqante ans de musique française de 1874 à 1925*, ed. L. Rohozinski, 2 vols. (Paris, 1925), and R. Bernard, *Histoire de la musique*, 2 vols. (Paris, 1961), one will find invaluable information on such broader issues as education, genre studies and institutions. Good bibliographies are contained in Brody's *Paris*, Goubault's *La critique musicale* and D. Pistone's *La musique en France de la révolution à 1900* (Paris, 1979).

Chronology

MUSIC AND MUSICIANS	POLITICS, WAR AND RULERS
1848 Ferenc Liszt (1811–86) appointed Hofkapellmeister at Weimar, instigating a modern movement in German music and completing his first symphonic poem *Les préludes*. Mikhail Glinka (1804–57) composes his orchestral piece *Kamarinskaya*. Donizetti (50) dies, Bergamo.	**1848** Year of revolutions: uprisings in Sicily, Paris, Vienna (3), Venice, Berlin, Milan, Parma, Papal States, Warsaw, Prague; all suppressed except Paris, constitution granted in Prussia. Abdication of Ferdinand I of Austria: succeeded by his nephew Franz Joseph (until 1916). Abdication of Louis Philippe and French Republic proclaimed (February); Louis Napoleon, nephew of Napoleon I, becomes President (December).
1849 Hector Berlioz (1803–69) composes his *Te Deum*. *Louisa Miller* by Giuseppe Verdi (1813–1901) given, Naples; *Le prophète* by Giacomo Meyerbeer (1791–1864) given, Paris. Richard Wagner (1813–83) exiled to Switzerland, where he writes *Kunst und die Revolution* and *Das Kunstwerk der Zukunft*. Fryderyc Chopin (39) dies, Paris. Frédéric Kalkbrenner (63) dies, Karlsruhe. Johann Strauss the elder (45) dies, Vienna.	**1849** Giuseppe Mazzini proclaims a republic in Rome, but Pius IX restored in July. Charles Albert of Sardinia abdicates in favour of Victor Emmanuel II. Frederick William IV declines title of German Emperor offered by National Assembly. Attempted German unity fails with the dissolution of German Assembly. Hungary and Venice submit to Austria.
1850 Wagner's *Lohengrin* given, Weimar. Berlin Conservatory founded. Václav Tomášek (75) dies, Prague.	**1850** The US Senate enacts 'The Compromise of 1850'. The Conte di Cavour appointed minister in Piedmont, where he inaugurates economic reforms. Taiping rebellion in China under Hung Siu-tsuen. Prussia agrees to Austrian supremacy in the revived Frankfurt Diet.
1851 Verdi's *Rigoletto* given, Venice. Wagner completes *Oper und Drama*. Théâtre-Lyrique, Paris, founded. Breitkopf & Härtel begin the first complete Bach edition (completed 1899). Gaspare Spontini (76) dies, Maiolati. Albert Lortzing (49) dies, Berlin.	
1852 Société des Jeunes Artistes du Conservatoire founded by Pasdeloup, Paris. New Philharmonic Society founded, London.	**1852** Second Burmese War; British forces annexe Pegu. New constitution for New Zealand. Louis-Napoleon proclaimed Emperor Napoleon III after a successful plebiscite.
1853 Verdi's *La traviata* given, Venice. Liszt completes his Piano Sonata in B minor.	**1853** In the role of protector of Christians of the Ottoman Empire, Russia invades the Danube provinces and defeats the Turkish fleet. Death of Maria II of Portugal; succeeded by Pedro V.
1854 Berlioz's *L'enfance du Christ* given. Eduard Hanslick (1825–1904) writes his influential book *Vom Musikalisch-Schönen*.	**1854** Crimean War (until 1856): Russia against Turkey, Austria, Britain and France. Allies gain victories at Balaclava and Inkerman. Commodore Perry negotiates the first US treaty with Japan. Murder of Abbas I, viceroy of Egypt; succeeded by Mohammed Said.
1855 Anton Bruckner (1824–96) appointed organist at Linz Cathedral. Crystal Palace concerts begin. Théâtre des Bouffes-Parisiens, owned by Jacques Offenbach (1819–80), opens.	**1855** Death of Tsar Nicholas I of Russia; succeeded by Alexander II. Taiping rebellion ends in China.

LITERATURE, PHILOSOPHY, RELIGION	SCIENCE, TECHNOLOGY, DISCOVERY	FINE AND DECORATIVE ARTS, ARCHITECTURE
1849 Matthew Arnold (1822–88) publishes his first volume of poetry, *The Strayed Reveller*. Charles Dickens (1812–70) writes the partly autobiographical *David Copperfield*. **1850** Pope Pius IX makes England and Wales into an ecclesiastical province of the Roman Catholic Church with its own hierarchy. Nathanial Hawthorne (1804–64) publishes *The Scarlet Letter*, a classic inquiry into the nature of American Puritanism. Alfred Tennyson (1809–92) publishes *In memoriam*. **1851** Herman Melville (1819–91) writes *Moby Dick*. Heinrich Heine (1797–1856) publishes *Romanzero*, written when facing death. **1852** First meeting of the Convocation of the Church of England since 1717. Harriet Beecher Stowe (1811–96) publishes *Uncle Tom's Cabin*, which stirs up great anti-slavery feeling. Charles Marie R. Leconte de Lisle (1818–94) publishes *Poèmes antiques*. William Thackeray (1811–63) publishes *The History of Henry Esmond*. **1855** Henry Wadsworth Longfellow (1807–82) writes *The Song of Hiawatha*. Anthony Trollope (1815–82) publishes *The Warden*, establishing the novel-sequence in English fiction. Elizabeth Gaskell (1810–65) publishes *North and South*, contrasting urban and rural England in the Industrial Revolution.	**1849** Armand Fizeau (1819–96) is the first to obtain an accurate determination of the velocity of light. Sir Edward Frankland (1825–99) isolates amyl in his pioneer work in organometallic chemistry. **1850** Rudolf Clausius (1822–88) formulates the second law of thermo-dynamics. **1851**. Isaac Singer (1811–75) patents his sewing machine. William Thomson (1824–1907) publishes a fundamental paper on the laws of conservation and dissipation of energy, *On the dynamical theory of heat*. **1853** Matthew Mavry (1806–73) publishes his *Physical Geography of the Sea*, the first textbook of modern oceanography. David Livingstone (1813–73) explores the Zambesi river. **1854** Georg Friedrich Bernhard Riemann (1826–66) writes *On the Hypotheses forming the Foundation of Geometry*, laying the analytical foundations for non-Euclidean geometry. Publication of *Mikrogeologie* by Christian Gottfried Ehrenberg (1795–1876), dealing with fossil micro-organisms. **1855** Completion of the electric telegraph between London and Balaclava on the Black Sea.	**1850** Gustav Courbet (1819–77) exhibits *The Stone Breakers* and two other pictures in the salon, establishing himself as the leader of the realist school of painting. Sir Joseph Paxton (1801–65) designs the Crystal Palace of glass and iron, the first example of prefabrication. **1851** John Ruskin (1819–1900) writes *The Stones of Venice*, an architectural study of immense original scholarship with moralistic overtones. **1852** Luigi Visconti (1791–1853) begins the New Louvre, the foremost monument of the Second Empire, completed by Hector Lefuel (1810–80). L. Vaudoyer (1803–72) begins Marseilles Cathedral, combining a Romanesque plan with a Byzantine elevation. John Millais (1829–96) paints *Ophelia*, a minutely detailed example of his early style. **1853** C. Mills (1810–83) completes the first equestrian statue to be cast in the USA, of President Jackson. James Renwick (1818–95), the leading American architect of the Gothic Revival, designs St Patrick's Cathedral, New York. **1854** Holman Hunt (1827–1910) paints *The Light of the World*.

The Late Romantic Era

MUSIC AND MUSICIANS	POLITICS, WAR AND RULERS
1856 Dresden Conservatory founded. Johannes Brahms (1833–97) accepts post as musical director at Detmold. Otto Jahn (1813–69) publishes study of Mozart. Robert Schumann (46) dies, Endenich.	**1856** Treaty of Paris ends Crimean War. Russians cede Bessarabia, Black Sea to be neutral, River Danube to be free to shipping and Danubian principalities guaranteed by the Powers. Massacre of Pottawatomie Creek; Kansas slavers murdered by free-staters. Second Anglo-Chinese War (until 1858).
1857 Verdi's *Simon Boccanegra* given, Venice. Budapest Academy of Music founded. Charles Hallé (1819–95) begins his Manchester orchestral series. Camille Saint-Saëns (1835–1921) appointed organist at the Madeleine, Paris. Liszt completes his *Faust Symphony*. Carl Czerny (66) dies, Vienna. Glinka (52) dies, Berlin.	**1857** Indian Mutiny against British rule (until 1858). Giuseppe Garibaldi forms Italian National Association for unification under Piedmont. Irish Republican Brotherhood founded in New York.
1858 *Der Barbier von Bagdad* by Peter Cornelius (1824–74) given, Weimar (under Liszt). *Halka* (four-act version) by Stanisław Moniuszko (1819–72) given, Warsaw. Händel-Gesellschaft edition begun. Chappell's Popular Concerts begin, London. César Franck (1822–90) appointed organist at Ste Clotilde. Brahms completes his First Piano Concerto.	**1858** More ports opened to British commerce and opium trade legalised in China. Transference of power from the East India Company to the British Crown. Commercial treaty between Britain and Japan.
1859 Verdi's *Un ballo in maschera* given, Rome. *Faust* by Charles Gounod (1818–93) given, Théâtre-Lyrique, Paris. Russian Musical Society founded. Birmingham School of Music founded. Louis Spohr (75) dies, Kassel.	**1859** War between France and Austria in Italy. By the peace of Villafranca, Austria cedes Parma and Lombardy, but Tuscany and Modena are restored and Venice remains Austrian. Ferdinand II of the Two Sicilies dies; succeeded by Francis II.
1860 Alexander Dargomïzhsky (1813–69) begins *The Stone Guest*, later completed by Nikolay Rimsky-Korsakov (1844–1908).	**1860** Garibaldi and Red Shirts capture Palermo and Naples; Victor Emmanuel invades the Papal States and is proclaimed King of Italy by Garibaldi. Election of President Lincoln.
1861 Bedřich Smetana (1824–84) settles in Prague after a period abroad. Liszt founds the Allgemeiner Deutsches Musikverein for the promotion of modern German music; he moves to Rome. Wagner returns to Germany by way of Paris, where a production of *Tannhäuser* is disrupted by the Jockey Club. Pasdeloup's Concerts Populaires de Musique Classique begin, Paris. Frankfurt Conservatory founded. *Hymns Ancient & Modern* published. Heinrich Marschner (66) dies, Hanover.	**1861** Death of Frederick William IV of Prussia; succeeded by Wilhelm I. Outbreak of American Civil War. Death of Sultan Abdul Mejid of Turkey; succeeded by his brother Abdul Aziz. Emancipation of Russian serfs. Prince Albert, husband of Queen Victoria, dies.

LITERATURE, PHILOSOPHY, RELIGION	SCIENCE, TECHNOLOGY, DISCOVERY	FINE AND DECORATIVE ARTS, ARCHITECTURE
1856 Gustav Flaubert (1821–80) publishes *Madame Bovary*, a novel of provincial life for which he is tried but acquitted.	**1856** Richard Burton (1821–90) and John Hanning Speke (1827–64) search for the sources of the Nile. Speke discovers Lake Tanganyika and Lake Victoria Nyanza the source. Hermann Helmholtz (1821–94) publishes *Handbuch der physiologische Optik*, a fundamental contribution to the understanding of the structure and mechanism of the eye.	**1856** William Frith (1819–1909) paints the immensely popular *Derby Day*, a huge panorama of Victorian society.
1857 Hippolyte Taine (1828–93) publishes *Les philosophes français du XIX siècle*, which is influential for the rest of the century. Charles Baudelaire (1821–67) publishes *Les fleurs du mal*, one of the great collections of French verse.	**1857** Louis Pasteur (1822–95) is the first to announce that living organisms cause fermentation.	**1857** Thomas Woolner (1825–92), the only sculptor of the Pre-Raphaelite Brotherhood (founded 1848), completes his bust of Tennyson.
1859 Edward Fitzgerald (1809–83) translates *The Rubáiyát of Omar Khayyám*, which is widely read. John Stuart Mill (1806–73) publishes *On Liberty*, examining the proper relations of society to the individual.	**1859** Charles Darwin (1809–82) publishes *On the Origin of Species*, establishing the theory of organic evolution and inaugurating a new era of thought. Edwin Drake (1819–80) strikes oil when drilling at Titusville, Pennsylvania, and launches the petroleum industry. Friedrich Argelander (1799–1875) publishes a work cataloguing *c*325,000 stars of the Northern Hemisphere.	**1859** William Butterfield (1814–1900) completes All Saints, Margaret Street, London, in the High Victorian neo-Gothic style. Francesco Hayez (1791–1882), the most important figure in the transition from Italian neo-classic to Romantic art, paints his *Romeo and Juliet*.
1860 Wilkie Collins (1824–89) writes *The Woman in White*, establishing the full-length detective story in English fiction. Paul von Heyse (1830–1914) publishes the *Italienishces Liederbuch*, later set by Hugo Wolf.	**1860** Robert Wilhelm Bunsen (1811–99) and Gustav Robert Kirchoff (1829–87) publish a fundamental work on spectrum-analysis. Jean Lenoir (1822–1900) patents the first practical internal-combustion engine.	**1860** Franz von Lenbach (1836–1904) paints the *Shepherd Boy*, one of the finest German naturalist works.
	1861 Max Schultze (1825–74) makes his most important contribution to the study of unicellular organisms, on the nature of the living cell.	**1861** William Morris (1834–96) begins to make hand-printed, hand-woven wallpapers and textiles. William Rimmer (1816–79), the most powerful and original American sculptor of the era, completes his *Falling Gladiator*.

MUSIC AND MUSICIANS	POLITICS, WAR AND RULERS
1862 Berlioz's *Béatrice et Bénédict* given, Baden-Baden. Verdi's *La forza del destino* given, St Petersburg. Mily Balakirev (1837–1910) founds the Free Music School, St Petersburg. Opening of the Provisional Theatre, Prague. Palestrina and Beethoven complete editions begun. Fromental Halévy (62) dies, Nice. František Škroup (60) dies, Rotterdam.	**1862** President Lincoln declares emancipation of all slaves. Otto von Bismarck appointed Minister-President of Prussia.
1863 Acts 3, 4 and 5 of Berlioz's *Les troyens* given, Paris. *Les pêcheurs de perles* by Georges Bizet (1838–75) given, Paris. *Jahrbuch für musikalische Wissenschaft* by Friedrich Chrysander (1826–1901) inaugurated. Brahms moves to Vienna.	**1864** Provincial councils established in Russia. War between Denmark against Prussia and Austria ends in Denmark ceding Schleswig, Holstein and Lauenberg. Archduke Maximilian of Austria accepts Mexican crown as emperor.
1864 Royal College of Organists founded in London. Giacomo Meyerbeer (72) dies, Paris. American ballad composer Stephen Foster (37) dies, New York.	
1865 Meyerbeer's *L'africaine* given, Paris. Wagner's *Tristan und Isolde* (under Hans von Bülow, 1830–94) given, Munich.	**1865** Assassination of Abraham Lincoln; succeeded by President Johnson. End of American Civil War. Meeting between Bismarck and Napoleon III who agrees to Prussian supremacy in Germany and a united Italy.
1866 Bruckner composes his Mass in E minor, influenced by the Cecilian movement. Smetana's *The Bartered Bride* given, Prague. Edvard Grieg (1843–1907) returns to Norway after a period abroad. Pyotr Ilyich Tchaikovsky (1840–93) begins teaching at the new Moscow Conservatory. Peabody Conservatory, Baltimore, founded.	**1866** Charles, Prince of Hohenzollern becomes King Carol I of Romania. Austria, at war with Italy and Prussia, is forced to cede Venezia to the Kingdom of Italy and is excluded from new German Confederation under Prussia, which now incorporates Schleswig-Holstein.
1867 Premières of Bizet's *La jolie fille de Perth*, Verdi's *Don Carlos* and Offenbach's *La Grand-Duchesse de Gérolstein*, all in Paris. Modest Musorgsky (1839–81) composes *Night on a Bare Mountain*. Bruckner becomes a professor at the Vienna Conservatory, succeeding his teacher Sechter. New England Conservatory, Boston, founded.	**1867** Austro-Hungarian Dual Monarchy established. Dominion of Canada established. US purchases Alaska from Russia. Execution of Emperor Maximilian in Mexico. Garibaldi marches on Rome but is defeated by French and papal troops at Montana.
1868 Premières of Wagner's *Die Meistersinger von Nürnberg* in Munich, *Mefistofele* by Arrigo Boito (1842–1918) in Milan, and Brahms's *German Requiem*. Max Bruch (1838–1920) composes his G minor Violin Concerto, Grieg his Piano Concerto and Henri Duparc (1848–1933) the earliest of his songs. August Ambros (1816–76) completes his history of music. Berlin Philharmonic founded. Gioachino Rossini (76) dies, Passy. Franz Berwald (71) dies, Stockholm.	**1868** Abolition of Shogunate in Japan and restoration of Meiji dynasty. Impeachment of President Johnson. Samarkand occupied by Russia. Revolt in Spain against Isabella II.

LITERATURE, PHILOSOPHY, RELIGION	SCIENCE, TECHNOLOGY, DISCOVERY	FINE AND DECORATIVE ARTS, ARCHITECTURE
1862 Victor Hugo (1802–85), the central figure of the Romantic movement in France, publishes *Les Misérables*. Ivan Turgenev (1818–83) writes *Fathers and Sons*, creating the first Nihilist hero.		**1863** Edouard Manet (1832–83) causes a scandal with his *Déjeuner sur l'herbe*, as nudity is only considered acceptable if sufficiently abstract in time and place.
1863 Ernest Renan (1823–92) publishes *Vie de Jésus*, rejecting the supernatural element in Christ's life, so creating a sensation throughout Europe. Leo Tolstoy (1828–1910) writes *War and Peace*.	**1865** The laying of the transatlantic cable is completed from Brunel's enormous ship *SS Great Eastern*.	**1864** Giles Gilbert Scott (1811–78) designs the Albert Memorial in Kensington Gardens.
1864 Jules Verne (1828–1905) writes the first of his books combining adventure and popular science, *Voyage au centre de la terre*.	**1866** Thomas Henry Huxley (1825–95) publishes *Lessons in Elementary Physiology* on his research into fossil reptiles. Robert Whitehead (1823–1905) designs the first torpedo.	**1865** Hippolyte Taine (1828–93), the leading exponent of positivism in 19th-century aesthetics, publishes *Philosophie de l'art*. Jean Baptiste Carpeaux (1827–75) creates the most famous of his large sculpture groups, *La danse*, for the Paris Opéra. Telemaco Signorini (1835–1901), a leader of the important Macchiaichi group of artists, paints the *Insane Ward at S Bonifazio*, a melancholy realistic work.
1865 William Booth (1829–1912) founds the Salvation Army. Lewis Carroll (Charles Dodgson, 1832–98) a mathematician, writes *Alice's Adventures in Wonderland*, a classic children's book.	**1867** Alfred Nobel (1833–96) patents dynamite which revolutionizes the explosives industry. Ernst Heinrich Haeckel (1834–1919) publishes *Natürliche Schöpfungsgeschichte* emphasizing the 'fundamental biogenetic law'. He disseminated Darwin's theory of evolution in Germany.	
1866 Fyodor Dostoyevsky (1821–81) writes *Crime and Punishment*. Algernon Swinburne (1837–1909) publishes his first book of *Poems and Ballads*, which influenced later generations of poets.		**1866** Winslow Homer (1836–1910) paints *Prisoners from the Front*, his first important work in oils, on the Civil War.
1867 Emil Zola (1840–1902) writes *Thérèse Raquin*, the first of his naturalistic fiction. Karl Marx (1818–83) publishes volume i of *Das Kapital* (volume ii completed by Engels, 1885). Louisa M. Alcott (1832–88) writes *Little Women*.	**1868** Publication of *Hereditary Genius* by Francis Galton (1822–1911) founds the science of Eugenics. Dmitry Mendeleyev (1834–1907) formulates the Periodic Law for the classification of the elements. Gustav Nachtigall (1834–85) is the first European to explore the central Sahara.	**1867** Japanese art is introduced to the West at the Paris World Exposition. **1868** A. Waterhouse (1830–1905) starts designing the neo-Romanesque Natural History Museum.

MUSIC AND MUSICIANS	POLITICS, WAR AND RULERS
1869 Wagner's *Das Rheingold* given, Munich. Balakirev composes *Islamey* (rev. 1902) and Tchaikovsky the first version of *Romeo and Juliet*. Wagner writes *Über das Dirigieren*. Liszt begins his annual stays in Budapest. Hector Berlioz (65) dies, Paris. Carl Loewe (72) dies, Kiel. Louis Gottschalk (40) dies, Tijuca.	**1869** Opening of the Suez Canal.
1870 Wagner writes *Siegfried Idyll* and his book *Beethoven*; première of *Die Walküre*, Munich. Léo Delibes (1836–91) composes *Coppélia*. Ignaz Moscheles (75) dies, Leipzig. Saverio Mercadante (75) dies, Naples. Michael Balfe (70) dies, Rowney Abbey.	**1870** Prince Leopold of Hohenzollern accepts the Spanish throne but is forced to withdraw. Further French protests result in the 'Ems Telegram' which sparks the Franco-Prussian war. Defeat of Napoleon III at Sedan. Revolt in Paris and proclamation of the Third Republic. Siege of Paris begun by Prussians. Italians march into Rome and declare it their capital city.
1871 Verdi's *Aida* given, Cairo. Wagner writes *Über die Bestimmung der Oper*. Royal Albert Hall completed. Société Nationale de Musique, Paris, founded by Saint-Saëns and others. Daniel-François-Esprit Auber (89) dies, Paris. Writer François Fétis (87) dies, Brussels. Writer Alexander Serov (51) dies, St Petersburg.	**1871** Wilhelm I of Prussia proclaimed Emperor of Germany at Versailles. Capitulation of Paris and armistice with Germany with harsh terms including loss of Alsace-Lorraine. Law of Guarantees in Italy allows the pope possession of the Vatican. Election of Thiers as President of the Third Republic.
1872 Smetana begins work on *Má vlast* (completed 1879). Franck appointed organ professor at the Paris Conservatoire. Trinity College of Music, London, founded.	**1872** The Emperors of Austria, Germany and Russia form an *entente* after meeting in Berlin; it becomes an alliance in 1873.
1873 Rimsky-Korsakov's *The Maid of Pskov* given, St Petersburg. J.A.P. Spitta (1841–94) begins his study of Bach (completed 1880).	**1873** Fall of Thiers and election of Louis MacMahon as President of France. Financial crisis in Vienna, which spreads to other European markets.
1874 Musorgsky's *Boris Godunov* (later revised by Rimsky-Korsakov) given, St Petersburg. *Die Fledermaus* by Johann Strauss (1825–99) given, Vienna. Musical Association (later Royal) founded, London. Peter Cornelius (49) dies, Copenhagen.	**1874** Socialist Working Men's Party formed in Germany. Alfonso XII of Spain comes of age.
1875 Founding of the Budapest Academy, the Music School at Harvard University and the Carl Rosa Opera Company. Hans Richter (1843–1916) appointed Kapellmeister at the Hofoper, Vienna. Georges Bizet (36) dies, Bougival, shortly after the unsuccessful first performance of his *Carmen*, Opéra-Comique, Paris.	**1875** Bosnia and Hercegovinia rebel against Turkish rule. Britain buys shares in the Suez Canal.

LITERATURE, PHILOSOPHY, RELIGION	SCIENCE, TECHNOLOGY, DISCOVERY	FINE AND DECORATIVE ARTS, ARCHITECTURE
1870 At the First Vatican Council the Roman Catholic Church declares Papal Infallibility in doctrine concerning faith and morals.	**1869** Walter Weldon (1832–85) completes his process by which manganese dioxide can be re-used, with enormous economic effect on the textile and paper industries.	**1870** Peter Carl Fabergé (1846–1920) takes over the Fabergé firm in St Petersburg and becomes the most fashionable jeweller and goldsmith in Europe until 1917.
1871 George Eliot (Mary Ann Evans, 1819–80) writes *Middlemarch*, one of the greatest novels in the English Language.		**1871** James Whistler (1834–1903) paints his most famous work, *Arrangement in Grey and Black: Portrait of the Painter's Mother*.
1872 Daniel Friedrich Strauss (1808–74) publishes *Der alter und der neue Glaube*, a negation of Christianity in favour of scientific materialism.	**1872** The *Challenger* Expedition explores oceanic temperatures, currents and the depths and contours of the great ocean basins.	**1872** Claude Monet (1840–1926) paints *Impression: Sunrise*, which, when exhibited in 1874, gave rise to the term 'impressionism'. Paul Cézanne (1839–1906) paints *The House of the Hanged Man*, his first work to be accepted by the Salon.
1873 C. Sigwart (1830–1904) publishes *Logic*, approaching logic through a study of acts of judgment.	**1873** James Clerk Maxwell (1831–79) publishes his celebrated *Treatise on Electricity and Magnetism*, propounding the electromagnetic theory of light which leads to the discovery of radio waves.	
1874 Henry Sidgwick (1838–1900) publishes *Methods of Ethics*, a study of moral philosophy along hedonistic lines. Pedro Alarcón y Ariza (1833–91) writes his best-known work, *El sombrero de tres picos*, which inspired a ballet (Falla) and an opera (Wolf). Juan Valera (1824–1905) writes *Pepita Jiménez*. William Stubbs (1825–1901) publishes *The Constitutional History of England*.		**1873** Gottfried Semper (1803–79), at the end of his long career, designs the Burgtheater in Vienna, executed by Karl von Hasenauer (1833–94). T. von Hansen (1831–91) starts to design the Vienna Parliament as part of a grandiose plan for the city.
	1874 The first typewriter, designed by C. Scholes and manufactured by E. Remington, is made available commercially in the USA. Henry Stanley (1841–1900) traces the course of the Congo from central Africa to the Atlantic.	**1874** Edgar Dégas (1834–1917) exhibits *The Dancing Class* in the first impressionist show.
1875 Foundation of the Theosophical Society in New York by Helena Petrovna Blavatsky, denying a personal god and personal immortality. Mary Baker Eddy (1821–1910) writes *Science and Health*.		**1875** Daniel Chester French (1850–1931) makes his name with *The Minute Man*, in Concord, MA.

MUSIC AND MUSICIANS	POLITICS, WAR AND RULERS
1876 First complete performance of Wagner's *Ring* opens the Festspielhaus, Bayreuth. Ibsen's *Peer Gynt* given in Oslo with Grieg's incidental music. Brahms completes the first of his four symphonies. Samuel Sebastian Wesley (65) dies, Gloucester.	**1876** China declares Korea to be an independent nation. Turkish massacre of Bulgarians. Sultan Abdul Hamid II comes to power. Serbia and Montenegro declare war on Turkey.
1877 Saint-Saëns' *Samson et Dalila* given, Weimar. Complete edition of Mozart begun.	**1877** Queen Victoria proclaimed Empress of India. Failure of powers to reconcile Russian and Turkish disagreements in the Balkans. Russia, Romania and Serbia declare war on Turkey.
1878 First edition of Grove's *Dictionary of Music and Musicians* begins to appear.	**1878** Death of Victor Emanuel II; succeeded by Humbert I. Treaty of San Stefano between Russia and Turkey. Bulgaria divided into three by Treaty of Berlin. British gain Cyprus for supporting Turkey. Anti-socialist law in Germany drives socialism underground.
1879 Tchaikovsky's *Eugene Onegin* given, Moscow. *The Pirates of Penzance* by Gilbert and Sullivan given, Paignton. D'Oyly Carte Opera Company founded, London. Grosser Musikvereinsaal, home of the Vienna Philharmonic, completed.	**1879** Britain occupies the Khyber Pass and later invades Afghanistan. Austro-German dual alliance. Proclamation of the Transvaal Republic.
1880 Edmund Gurney writes his book *The Power of Sound.*	**1880** Resignation of Benjamin Disraeli after electoral defeat on Irish Home Rule. Tahiti annexed by French. Tension between Italy and France in Tunis.
1881 Offenbach's *Les contes d'Hoffmann* given, Paris. Brahms's *Academic Festival Overture* given, Breslau University. Provisional Theatre, Prague, converted to the much larger National Theatre. Boston Symphony Orchestra founded. Musorgsky (42) dies, St Petersburg.	**1881** Assassination of Tsar Alexander II; succeeded by Alexander III. By a secret treaty, Serbia becomes a protectorate of Austria. Tunis accepts French protectorate.
1882 Premières of Wagner's *Parsifal*, Bayreuth, Rimsky-Korsakov's *The Snow Maiden*, St Petersburg, Gilbert and Sullivan's *Iolanthe*, Savoy Theatre, London. Glazunov's First Symphony completed. First edition of Hugo Riemann's *Musik-Lexicon* published. Joachim Raff (60) dies, Frankfurt.	**1882** Irish Ferrians murder the two chief government officials in Dublin. Italy joins Austro-German alliance, now the Triple Alliance. Britain occupies Egypt and the Sudan.
1883 Royal College of Music founded, London. Wagner (69) dies, Venice.	**1883** Paul Kruger becomes president of the South African Republic. Bismarck introduces the first sickness insurance scheme in Germany.
1884 Antonín Dvořák (1841–1904) conducts his music in England. Claude Debussy (1862–1918) wins the Prix de Rome with his *L'enfant prodigue*. Smetana (60) dies, Prague.	**1884** Germany occupies South West Africa, Togoland and the Cameroons. Berlin conference on African affairs provides for free trade in the Congo and the abolition of the slave trade.

LITERATURE, PHILOSOPHY, RELIGION	SCIENCE, TECHNOLOGY, DISCOVERY	FINE AND DECORATIVE ARTS, ARCHITECTURE
1876 Gerard Manley Hopkins (1844–89) writes *The Wreck of the Deutschland*, unpublished until 1918 when it has great impact. Mark Twain (Samuel Clements, 1833–1910) publishes *The Adventures of Tom Sawyer*.	**1876** Alexander Graham Bell (1847–1922) exhibits an apparatus embodying the results of his experiments in the transmission of sound by electricity, leading to the telephone.	**1876** Paul Auguste Renoir (1841–1919) paints *The Swing*, an early successful impressionist painting. Gustav Moreau (1826–98), a leading symbolist paints *The Apparition* (based on Salome). P. Abadie (1812–84) begins the Sacré-Coeur, a neo-Romanesque design with a cluster of domes.
1877 Stéphane Mallarmé (1842–98) writes the long eclogue *L'après-midi d'un faune*, which later inspires Debussy.	**1877** Thomas Edison (1847–1931), designs the phonograph.	
1878 Theodor Fontane (1819–98), writes the first of a series of novels, *Vor dem Sturm*.	**1878** Robert Koch (1843–1910) publishes *Untersuchungen über die Ätiologie de Wundinfektionskrankheit*, explaining his technique whereby bacteria can be stained and identified. Percy Gilchrist (1851–1935) and Sidney Thomas (1850–85) succeed in manufacturing steel from phosphoric iron ore. Adolf Erik Nordenskjold (1832–1901) accomplishes the North East Passage in the *Vega*.	**1878** Auguste Rodin (1840–1917) exhibits *The Age of Bronze*, inspired by Michelangelo.
1879 George Meredith (1828–1909) publishes his most famous novel, *The Egoist*. Herbert Spencer (1820–1903), the chief exponent of agnosticism in 19th-century England, writes *Principles of Ethics*.		**1880** Richard Shaw (1831–1912) designs Bedford Park, London
1880 Guy de Maupassant (1850–93) writes a short story, *Boule-de-suif*, which makes him a celebrity.	**1879** William Edward Ayrton (1847–1908) advocates power transmission at high voltage.	**1881** Dégas completes his sculpture of the *Fourteen-Year-Old Dancer*. Petrus Cuypers (1827–1921), builds the Central Station, Amsterdam, in the Dutch Renaissance style (–1889).
1881 Henry James (1843–1916) publishes *The Portrait of a Lady*.	**1880** Sir Joseph Wilson Swan (1828–1914) and Edison independently devise the first practical electric lights. Josef Breuer (1842–1925) uses hypnosis in treating a hysterical patient.	**1882** Wilhelm Leibl (1844–1900), completes *Three Women in Church*. Manet paints his last great picture, *A Bar at the Folies-Bergère*.
1883 Posthumous publication of *Prolegomena to Ethics* by Thomas Green (1836–82) who expounded the idealist philosophical doctrines of Kant and Hegel in English. Friedrich Wilhelm Nietzsche (1844–1900) writes *Also sprach Zarathustra*.	**1881** Sir Edward Burnett Tylor (1832–1917) publishes *Anthropology*, on primitive culture and the early history of mankind.	**1883** William Le Baron Jenney (1832–1907) designs the Home Insurance Building in Chicago. Its steel-skeleton structure paved the way for the first skyscrapers.
1884 Publication of the first volume of the *Oxford English Dictionary* (–1928), edited by John Murray (1837–1915).	**1884** Charles Parsons (1854–1931) takes out patents for his steam turbine engine, later developed for use at sea.	**1884** John Singer Sargent (1856–1925) exhibits his erotic portrait of Mme Gautreau, causing a sensation. Edward Burne-Jones (1833–98) paints *King Cophetua and the Beggar Maid*. Georges Seurat (1859–91) paints *Sunday Afternoon on the Island of La Grande Jatte*, using dots of unmixed colour.

MUSIC AND MUSICIANS	POLITICS, WAR AND RULERS
1885 Dvořák's Seventh Symphony composed for the Philharmonic Society, London. Gustav Mahler (1860–1911) completes the first version of his *Lieder eines fahrenden Gesellen*, Brahms his Fourth Symphony and Bruckner his Eighth.	**1885** The Sudanese forces under the Mahdi capture Khartoum and the British evacuate the Sudan. Crisis in Anglo-Russian relations over Afghanistan. Third Burmese War. Germany annexes Northern New Guinea and the Bismarck Archipelago.
1886 Saint-Saëns composes *Le carnaval des animaux*. Liszt (74) dies, Bayreuth.	**1886** Revolution in Eastern Rumelia against Turkey supported by Greece but condemned by the Powers. William Gladstone's third liberal government defeated over Irish Home Rule.
1887 Verdi's *Otello* given, Milan. Bruckner begins his Ninth Symphony (unfinished). Emmanuel Chabrier (1841–94) composes *Le roi malgré lui*, Hubert Parry (1848–1918) his *Blest Pair of Sirens* and Sir John Stainer (1840–1901) *The Crucifixion*. Debussy visits Bayreuth. Alexander Borodin (53) dies, St Petersburg.	**1887** Anglo-Italian agreement to maintain the status quo in the Mediterranean supported by Spain. First Colonial Conference; Britain, Austria and Italy sign treaty to maintain status quo in the Near East.
1888 Edouard Lalo (1823–92) completes his opera *Le roi d'Ys*, Franck his D minor Symphony, Gabriel Fauré (1845–1924) his Requiem and Rimsky-Korsakov his symphonic poem *Sheherazade*. Erik Satie (1866–1925) writes *Trois gymnopédies*, his earliest characteristic piano music. Mahler composes his First Symphony. Valentin Alkan (74) dies, Paris.	**1888** Death of Wilhelm I of Prussia. Succeeded first by his son Frederick III and then by his grandson, Kaiser Wilhelm II. Election of President Harrison. Germany gains permission from Turkey to build the first part of the Baghdad Railway.
1889 Richard Strauss (1864–1949) composes *Don Juan*. Oriental music heard (by Debussy, among others) at the Paris Exposition Universelle. George Bernard Shaw (1856–1950) becomes music critic of *The Star*.	**1889** Suicide of Crown Prince Rudolf of Austria; heir to the Austro-Hungarian Empire is now Archduke Franz Ferdinand. Granting of a constitution in Japan, but emperor maintains extensive powers.
1890 Acts 1 and 2 of Berlioz's *Les troyens* given, Karlsruhe. *Cavalleria rusticana* by Pietro Mascagni (1863–1945) given, Rome. Tchaikovsky composes *The Sleeping Beauty*. The Athenaeum School of Music (later the Royal Scottish Academy) founded. César Franck (67) dies, Paris. Niels Gade (73) dies, Copenhagen.	**1890** Bismarck dismissed by Wilhelm II. Cecil Rhodes becomes Premier of Cape Colony. Alexander III meets Wilhelm II but fails to secure a German-Russian *entente*.
1891 Chicago Symphony Orchestra founded. Léo Delibes (54) dies, Paris.	**1891** Triple Alliance of Germany, Austria and Italy renewed for 12 years. Franco-Russian *entente*.
1892 *Pagliacci* by Ruggero Leoncavallo (1857–1919) given, Milan. Tchaikovsky composes *Nutcracker*. Carl Nielsen (1865–1931) completes the first of his six symphonies. Dvořák becomes director of the National Conservatory of Music, New York. Lalo (69) dies, Paris. German lieder composer Robert Franz (77) dies, Halle.	**1892** Anglo-German convention over the Cameroons. Pan-Slav Conference at Cracow. Panama scandal in France.

LITERATURE, PHILOSOPHY, RELIGION	SCIENCE, TECHNOLOGY, DISCOVERY	FINE AND DECORATIVE ARTS, ARCHITECTURE
1886 Benito Pérez Galdós (1843–1920), writes his greatest novel, *Fortunata y Jacinta*. Publication of *Les illuminations* by Arthur Rimbaud (1854–91) one of the most revolutionary of 19th-century poets.	**1885** Karl Benz (1844–1929) runs his first motor car on a single cylinder engine. Gottlieb Daimler (1834–1900) runs his first in 1886. Sir Francis Galton (1822–1911) develops the system of identification by fingerprints. Heinrich Hertz (1857–94) establishes beyond doubt the electromagnetic nature of light.	**1885** Max Klinger (1857–1920) paints *The Judgment of Paris*. His etchings are considered forerunners of surrealism.
1888 Bernard Bosanquet (1848–1923), idealist philosopher, writes *Logic, or the Morphology of Knowledge*, in which judgment not concept is the fundamental form.		**1887** Building of the Eiffel Tower by Alexandre Gustave Eiffel (1832–1923), at 985 feet the highest structure in the world.
1889 Henri Bergson (1859–1941) publishes *Essai sur les données immédiates de la conscience*, subordinating the intellect to intuition, an idea welcomed by religious thinkers.	**1886** Completion of the Canadian Pacific Railway. Hydro-electric installations begin at the Niagara Falls.	**1888** James Ensor (1860–1949), Belgian artist, paints the huge satirical *Entry of Christ into Brussels*. He was one of the foremost influences on expressionism. Henri de Toulouse Lautrec (1864–1901) begins to illustrate the theatres, music halls and cafés of Paris. Paul Gauguin (1848–1903) paints *Jacob Wrestling with the Angel* in which he completely breaks away from impressionism. Founding of the Arts and Crafts movement in Britain to reassert the importance of craftsmanship in the face of growing mechanization and mass production.
1890 William James (1842–1910), American pragmatic philosopher, publishes his fundamental *Principles of Psychology*. Henrik Ibsen (1828–1906), regarded as the founder of modern prose drama, writes *Hedda Gabler*. Sir James Frazer (1854–1941) writes *The Golden Bough*, a vast comparative study of the beliefs and institutions of mankind.	**1887** Joseph Lockyer (1836–1920) writes *Chemistry of the Sun*, a pioneering work of astrophysics. **1888** John Dunlop (1840–1921) patents the pneumatic bicycle tyre, transforming the bicycle and making possible the motor industry. Etienne Jules Marey (1830–1904) produces his *chambre chronophotographique*, the first modern ciné camera, laying the foundations for scientific cinematography.	
		1889 Vincent van Gogh (1853–90) paints his *Self-Portrait with Bandaged Ear*, one of his greatest works.
1891 Thomas Hardy (1840–1928) publishes his penultimate novel *Tess of the D'Urbervilles*, which is badly received by the critics. Arthur Conan Doyle (1859–1930) writes *The Adventures of Sherlock Holmes*.	**1890** T. Curtius (1857–1928) discovers Hydrazoic acid, HN_3. **1891** Trans-Siberian Railway from Moscow to Vladivostok begun – 1916.	**1891** Auguste Rodin (1840–1917) designs a radical statue of Balzac (only cast and set up in 1939). Now regarded as the most original piece of public sculpture of the 19th century.
1892 Maurice Maeterlinck (1862–1949) writes *Pelléas et Mélisande*.	**1892** Rudolf Diesel (1858–1913) obtains the patent for his internal-combustion engine.	**1892** Victor Horta (1861–1947) builds the Hôtel Tassel in Brussels, the first Art Nouveau house.

MUSIC AND MUSICIANS	POLITICS, WAR AND RULERS
1893 Verdi's *Falstaff* given, Milan. *Manon Lescaut* by Giacomo Puccini (1712–1781) given, Turin. Dvořák composes his Ninth Symphony, 'From the New World'. Tchaikovsky (53) dies, St Petersburg, shortly after completing his Symphony no.6, 'Pathétique'.	**1893** Formation of Independent Labour Party under Kier Hardie. Second Irish Home Rule Bill defeated by House of Lords. French colonies of French Guinea and Ivory Coast formally established. Britain agrees to the annexation of Swaziland by the Transvaal.
1894 Debussy completes his innovatory *Prélude à L'après-midi d'un faune.* Establishment of the Music School at Yale University. Durand begins a complete edition of Rameau. Antonín Dvořák (62) dies, Prague. Chabrier (53) dies, Paris. Anton Rubinstein (64) dies, Peterhof. Hans von Bülow (64) dies, Cairo.	**1894** Japan declares war on China, having taken over Korea. Death of Tsar Alexander III. Succeeded by Nicholas II. Alfred Dreyfus tried for treason in France and unjustly sent to Devil's Island, causing furore in French politics.
1895 Mahler's Second 'Resurrection' Symphony given. Strauss composes *Till Eulenspiegel.* Melbourne Conservatory founded. Henry Wood begins the Promenade concerts at the Royal Albert Hall.	**1895** Chinese defeated at Wei-hai-Wei; both China and Japan recognize independence of Korea. Rhodesia formed from British South Africa Company territory. Massacre of Armenians by Turks. Organization by Lenin of the St Petersburg League of Struggle.
1896 Puccini's *La bohème* given, Turin. Isaac Albéniz (1860–1909) composes his opera *Pepita Jiménez.* Ernest Chausson (1855–99) composes his *Poème* for violin and orchestra. The Schola Cantorum founded in Paris by d'Indy and others. Bruckner (72) dies, Vienna. Clara Schumann (76) dies, Frankfurt. Ambroise Thomas (84) dies, Paris.	**1896** Crisis in Anglo-German relations over Jameson Raid into the Transvaal. New evidence for Dreyfus's innocence suppressed in France. Russia and China sign convention over Manchuria.
1897 Symphony no.1 by Sergey Rakhmaninov (1873–1943) given. Frederick Delius (1862–1934) settles at Grez-sur-Loing. Mahler becomes director of Vienna Hofoper. The Concerts Lamoureux (an outgrowth of earlier series) begin in Paris. Brahms (63) dies, Vienna.	**1897** Turkey declares war on Greece. Anglo-Russian agreement to maintain the status quo in the Balkans.
1898 *Louise* by Gustav Charpentier (1860–1950) given, Paris. Shaw publishes *The Perfect Wagnerite.* Guido Adler becomes professor of music at Vienna. Adelaide Conservatory founded.	**1898** Emile Zola writes an open letter to the French president on the Dreyfus affair. First German navy bill begins naval expansion over 16 years. USA declares war on Spain forcing them to cede Cuba, Porto Rico, Guam and the Philippines. Tzu-hs, Dowager Empress of China, seizes power and revokes the reforms of Emperor Te Tsung.
1899 Arnold Schoenberg (1874–1951) composes *Verklärte Nacht.* Maurice Ravel (1875–1937) composes *Pavane pour une infante défunte* (orchestrated 1910). Ernest Chausson (66) dies, Limay. Johann Strauss the younger (73) dies, Vienna.	**1899** Tsar Nicholas II suppresses liberties in Finland. Dreyfus pardoned by presidential decree, which helps to heal internal dissensions within France. Kruger's ultimatum on franchise in the Transvaal provokes Anglo-Boer War (until 1902).

LITERATURE, PHILOSOPHY, RELIGION	SCIENCE, TECHNOLOGY, DISCOVERY	FINE AND DECORATIVE ARTS, ARCHITECTURE
1893 F.H. Bradley (1846–1924) publishes *Appearance and Reality*, the most original work of the 19th century in British metaphysics.	**1893** Fridtjof Nansen (1861–1930) leads an expedition to the North Pole, designing a ship, the *Fram*, which can bear the pressure of ice and be carried along by it. **1894** Hamilton Castner (1858–98) develops his electrolytic process for the manufacture of caustic soda. **1895** William Ramsay (1852–1916) and Lord Rayleigh (1842–1919) jointly announce the discovery of a new gaseous element, argon. Ramsay discovers helium in 1896, and xenon, krypton and neon in 1898. Auguste (1862–1954) and Louis (1864–1948) Lumière construct the first satisfactory ciné-camera and projector. Sigmund Freud (1856–1939) publishes *Studien über Hysterie*, the starting-point of psychoanalysis. Wilhelm Konrad Röntgen (1845–1923) describes the properties of new X-rays.	**1893** Alfred Gilbert (1854–1934) completes the celebrated figure of Eros for Piccadilly Circus, cast in the new lightweight aluminium. Louis Comfort Tiffany (1848–1932) begins to manufacture his Favrile glass. After 1900 he makes Art Nouveau decorative glass. **1894** Aubrey Beardsley (1872–98) a leading *fin-de-siècle* aesthete, makes his name with illustrations to Wilde's *Salomé*. William Holabird and M. Roche design the Marquette Building, establish the Chicago School.
1895 H.G. Wells (1866–1946) writes *The Time Machine*, the first of his novels in the new genre of science fiction. Oscar Wilde (1854–1900) writes his masterpiece, *The Importance of Being Ernest*.		**1895** Edvard Munch (1863–1944) paints *The Scream*, an evocation of emotion which he translates into a lithograph. **1897** Camile Pissarro (1830–1903) paints *Boulevard Montmartre, Night*, an aerial perspective.
1896 Anton Chekhov (1860–1904) writes *The Seagull*, the first of his four great plays.	**1896** Guglielmo Marconi (1874–1937) takes out a patent for the first wireless telegraphy based on Hertz's discoveries. **1897** Joseph John Thomson (1856–1940) establishes the existence of eletrons. Sir Ronald Ross (1857–1932) identifies the malaria bacillus in mosquitoes. **1898** Pierre (1859–1906) and Marie (1867–1934) Curie recognize and isolate polonium and radium and discover the nature of radioactivity.	**1898** Joseph Maria Olbrich (1867–1908) builds the Sezession Halle in Vienna, with cubic walls and an open-work metal dome. Charles Rennie MacKintosh (1868–1928) builds the Glasgow School of Art, an asymmetrical design with an original centrepiece (completed 1909). Georges Minne (1866–1941), Belgian symbolist sculptor, produces his masterpiece, *Fountain with Kneeling Figures*. Cézanne paints *Grandes baigneuses*, continuing his study of the relationship of man to nature.

MUSIC AND MUSICIANS	POLITICS, WAR AND RULERS
1900 *The Dream of Gerontius* by Edward Elgar (1857–1934) given, Birmingham. Debussy composes his *Nocturnes*. First edition of Baker's *Bibliographical Dictionary of Musicians* published. Arthur Sullivan (58) dies, London. Zdeněk Fibich (49) dies, Prague.	**1900** Assassination of Humbert I of Italy; succeeded by his son Victor Emmanuel III. Boxer rising in China against Europeans.
1901 Rakhmaninov completes his Second Piano Concerto. Giuseppe Verdi (87) dies, Milan. Sir John Stainer (60) dies, Vienna.	**1901** Death of Queen Victoria; succeeded by her son Edward VII. Murder of Russian minister of propaganda to avenge repression of student agitation. Organization of the Social Revolutionary Party in Russia.
1902 Debussy's *Pélleas et Mélisande* given, Paris. Jean Sibelius (1865–1957) composes his Second Symphony. Mahler composes his Fifth Symphony.	**1902** Alliance with Japan ends Britain's diplomatic isolation. Russo-Chinese agreement to evacuate Manchuria. End of Boer War; Boers agree to British sovereignty with a promise of representative government. Australia gives women the vote in federal elections. Franco-Italian *entente*.
1903 Schoenberg composes *Pelleas und Melisande*. Igor Stravinsky (1882–1971) studies with Rimsky-Korsakov. Hugo Wolf (42) dies, Vienna.	
1904 Puccini's *Madama Butterfly* given, Milan. *Jenůfa* by Leoš Janáček (1854–1928) given, Brno. Alban Berg (1885–1935) and Anton Webern (1883–1945) study with Schoenberg. London Symphony Orchestra founded.	**1903** Russian Social Democratic Party splits into Mensheviks, led by Pecharoff, and Bolsheviks, led by Lenin and Trotsky.
	1904 Russo-Japanese War. Britain signs a treaty with Tibet by which the Dalai Lama will not concede territory to a foreign power. Entente Cordiale between Britain and France.
1905 Strauss's *Salome* given, Dresden. Debussy completes *La mer*, Delius his *A Mass of Life* and Ravel his *Miroirs*. Fauré appointed director of the Paris Conservatoire. Béla Bartók (1881–1945) and Zoltán Kodály (1882–1967) start their research into folk music. Juilliard School of Music, New York, founded.	**1905** Workers fired on in 'Bloody Sunday' massacre in St Petersburg. Nicholas II promises reforms and creates an Imperial Duma. Russian fleet defeated by Japanese. Norway separates from Sweden and Prince Charles of Denmark is elected King Haakon VII of Norway.
1906 Charles Ives (1974–1954) composes *The Unanswered Question*. Ralph Vaughan Williams (1872–1958) begins as editor of the English Hymnal. Anton Arensky (44) dies, Terioki. Influential Russian critic Vladimir Stasov (82) dies, St Petersburg.	**1906** J. Franco becomes premier of Spain with dictatorial powers. Pyotr Stolypin becomes premier of Russia and introduces agrarian reform. Dreyfus rehabilitated.
1907 *Ariane et Barbe-bleue* by Paul Dukas (1865–1935) given, Paris. Ferruccio Busoni (1866–1924) composes his *Elegies* for piano and writes his *Entwurf einer neuen Ästhetik der Tonkunst*. Reger appointed professor of composition at the Leipzig Conservatory. English publishing firm Stainer & Bell founded. Emile Hertzka becomes director of Universal Edition.	**1907** Second Duma in Russia dissolved by Tsar under pressure from reactionary party. Signing of the Anglo-Russian convention on Persia, Afghanistan and Tibet, aligning Russia with France and Britain against the Central Powers.

LITERATURE, PHILOSOPHY, RELIGION	SCIENCE, TECHNOLOGY, DISCOVERY	FINE AND DECORATIVE ARTS, ARCHITECTURE
1900 Bertrand Russell (1872–1970) begins his long career with the publication of *A Critical Exposition of the Philosophy of Leibniz*.	**1900** Freud publishes the *Interpretation of Dreams*, perhaps his most original and important work. Max Planck (1858–1947) develops the quantum theory.	**1900** G. Sommaruga (1867–1917), the leading Art Nouveau architect in Italy, builds the Palazzo Castiglione, Milan.
1901 Rudyard Kipling (1865–1936) writes his masterpiece, *Kim*, a picaresque novel of India.	**1901** Marconi transmits the first transatlantic wireless message from Cornwall to Newfoundland.	**1901** Gustav Klimt (1862–1918) paints *Judith I*, one of the archetypal images of the *femme fatale*.
1903 George Bernard Shaw (1856–1950) writes *Man and Superman*, a paradoxical version of the Don Juan story.	**1902** Oliver Heaviside (1850–1925) states his belief in a layer in the upper atmosphere responsible for reflecting radio waves back to the ground. Sir William Bayliss (1860–1924) and Ernest Starling (1866) together discover the hormone secretum.	**1904** Louis Sullivan (1856–1924) completes his major building, the Carson, Pirie & Scott store in Chicago. Henri Matisse (1869–1954) paints one of his first major works, *Luxe, calme et volupte*.
1904 Hugo von Hofmannsthal (1874–1929) writes *Elektra*, the first of his texts set by Richard Strauss.		
1905 Edith Wharton (1862–1937) is established as a leading novelist with the publication of *The House of Mirth*. George Santayana (1863–1952), speculative philosopher, publishes *Life of Reason*.	**1903** Wilbur (1867–1912) and Orville (1871–1948) Wright make the first flight in an aeroplane with a petrol engine.	**1905** Gustav Vigeland (1869–1943), the most famous Norwegian sculptor, begins his massive project for Frogner Park, Oslo, with *The Man in the Wheel*. E. Saatinen (1873–1950) builds the Central Station, Helsinki, in a highly original version of the Vienna Sezession style.
1906 Albert Schweitzer (1875–1965) writes *Von Reimarus zu Werde*, a life of Christ that aroused great opposition but also influenced European and American Protestant theology. Maksim Gorky (1868–1936) writes *The Mother*, later taken as the model for the Socialist Realist novel.	**1904** Ernest Rutherford (1871–1937) and F. Soldy (1877–1956) postulate their general theory of radioactivity.	
	1905 Albert Einstein (1871–1955) publishes four papers, each containing a great discovery: the special theory of relativity; the mass-energy equivalence; the theory of Brownian motion; and the photon theory of light.	**1906** Pablo Picasso (1881–1973), the most prolific and versatile artist of the 20th century, paints *Les demoiselles d'Avignon* a violent revolt against the form of traditional impressionism, which inspires cubism.
1907 August Strindberg (1849–1912) writes *The Ghost Sonata*, which has great influence on later psychological and symbolic drama. Raines Maria Rilke (1875–1926) writes *Neue Gedichte*, poems influenced by Rodin.	**1907** The Lumière brothers introduce the Autochrome process, the first successful direct-colour process in photography.	

MUSIC AND MUSICIANS	POLITICS, WAR AND RULERS
1908 Alexander Skryabin (1872–1915) composes his *Poème de l'extase*, Schoenberg his Second String Quartet, Berg his Piano Sonata and Bartók his *Bagatelles*. Nikolay Rimsky-Korsakov (64) dies, St Petersburg, shortly after completing *The Golden Cockerel*.	**1908** Revolt of Young Turks in Macedonia. Sultan Abdul Hamid II restores constitution of 1876. Declaration of Independence of Bulgaria: Annexation of Bosnia and Hercegovina by Austria.
1909 Strauss's *Elektra* given, Dresden. Vaughan Williams completes his *Sea Symphony*, Mahler his *Das Lied von der Erde* and Ninth Symphony. Schoenberg composes *Das Büch der hängended Gärten*, Five Orchestral Pieces and *Erwartung*, Webern his Five Movements for String Quartet op.5. Ives begins work on his *Concord Sonata* (completed 1915). First visit of Dyagilev's Ballets Russes to Paris.	**1909** Tension between Austria and Serbia over Bosnia. Young Turks depose Abdul Hamid who is succeeded by Mohammed V. Juan Gomez seizes power in Venezuela.
1910 Puccini's *La fanciulla del West* given, New York. *The Firebird*, Stravinsky's first ballet for Dyagilev, given. Debussy composes his first set of *Préludes* and meets Stravinsky. Vaughan Williams composes his Fantasia on a Theme of Thomas Tallis. Mily Balakirev (73) dies, St Petersburg.	**1910** Death of Edward VII; succeeded by his son George V. Union of South Africa becomes a dominion of the British Crown. Japan annexes Korea. Portugal declared a Republic. Russia withdraws opposition to the Baghdad railway in return for German non-interference in Persia.
1911 Strauss's *Der Rosenkavalier* given, Dresden. Stravinsky's *Petrushka* given. Bartók composes his opera *Duke Bluebeard's Castle* (première 1918). Sibelius composes his Fourth Symphony, Enrique Granados (1867–1916) his piano suite *Goyescas*. Schoenberg writes his *Harmonielehre*. Reger appointed music director at Meiningen. Gustav Mahler (50) dies, Vienna.	**1911** A German gunboat off the coast of Tangier creates international tension. Italy declares war on Turkey and has a decisive victory in Tripoli. Suffragette movement starts in Britain.
1912 Strauss's *Ariadne auf Naxos* given, Stuttgart. Debussy composes *Jeux*, Ravel his *Daphnis et Chloé*, Schoenberg his *Pierrot lunaire*, Busoni his *Sonatina seconda*.	**1912** Manchu dynasty abdicates in China and a provisional republic is established. Russo-Japanese agreement on spheres of influence in Mongolia and Manchuria. Balkans war between Turkey, Serbia, Bulgaria and Montenegro.
1913 Stravinsky's *Rite of Spring* given, Paris, to a riotous reception. Skryabin composes *Prometheus*, Rakhmaninov his symphony *The Bells*.	**1913** Poincaré elected president of France and remains in power throughout World War I. Second Balkan War with Bulgaria attacking Serbia and Greece. Russia and Turkey enter war against Bulgaria. Defeat of British women's-franchise bill.
1914 Ives completes his *Three Places in New England*, Berg his Three Orchestral Pieces op.6. Josef Hauer (1883–1959) experiments with tropes, an early form of 12-note writing.	**1914** End of Balkan war. Britain acquires control of oil properties in the Persian Gulf. Assassination of Archduke Franz Ferdinand and his wife at Sarajevo on 28 June by a Bosnian revolutionary. On 28 July Austria-Hungary declares war on Serbia. 1 August Germany declares war on Russia. 3 August Germany declares war on France and invades Belgium, starting World War I.

LITERATURE, PHILOSOPHY, RELIGION	SCIENCE, TECHNOLOGY, DISCOVERY	FINE AND DECORATIVE ARTS, ARCHITECTURE
	1908 Hermann Minkowski (1864–1909) arrives at a conception of a four-dimensional manifold in which space and time are interlinked – the mathematics of relativity.	**1908** Frank Lloyd Wright (1869–1959) builds Robie House, Chicago, the most famous of his low-lying, prairie-style houses. Rene Lalique (1860–1945) acquires a factory to make moulded glass.
1910 E.M. Forster (1879–1970) publishes *Howards End*, which establishes his reputation as a novelist.	**1909** Thomas Morgan (1866–1945), author of the gene theory, begins his research in genetics. Louis Blériot (1872–1936) makes the first overseas flight in a 'heavier-than-air' craft, from Calais to Dover.	**1909** R. Ostberg (1866–1945) designs Stockholm City Hall, influential in England in the 1920s.
1911 Katherine Mansfield (Katherine Beauchamp, 1888–1923) publishes her first collection of short stories, *In a German Pension*.	**1911** Charles Wilson (1869–1959) produces his cloud chamber, which becomes an indispensable tool of modern physics. Roald Amundsen (1872–1928) reaches the South Pole in December, one month before R. Scott (1868–1912), all of whose party die in the attempt.	**1910** Adolph Loos (1870–1933) builds the Steiner House, Vienna, of unrelieved cubic shapes. Wassily Kandinsky (1866–1914) paints *Composition no.2*, an early abstract expressionist work. Constantin Brancusi (1876–1957) creates *The Kiss*, fusing stone form and concept.
1912 Anatole France (J. Thibault, 1844–1924) writes his finest novel, *Les rieux en soif*, a study of fanaticism in the French Revolution. Thomas Mann (1875–1955), influenced by Nietzsche and Schopenhauer, writes *Der Tod in Venedig*, discussing the nature of the creative artist.	**1912** Loss of the world's largest-ever ship, the *SS Titanic*, through striking an iceberg on her maiden voyage.	**1911** Marc Chagall (1887–1985) paints *I and the Village*, dreamlike images from his Russian childhood. Georges Braques (1882–1963) paints *The Portuguese*.
1913 Alain-Fournier (H. A. Fournier, 1886–1914) publishes *Le grand Meaulnes*, one of the outstanding French novels of the 20th century. D. H. Lawrence (1885–1930) publishes his first major novel, *Sons and Lovers*. Marcel Proust (1871–1922) begins *À la recherche du temps perdu*, in which the narrator discovers that the past is eternally alive in the unconscious.	**1913** Niels Bohr (1885–1962) carries out research into the structure of the atom but his theory, a combination of classic mechanics with quantum theory, is slow to be accepted by physicists. Hans Geiger (1882–1945) introduces the first successful electrical device for counting individual alpha rays, the 'Geiger counter'.	**1912** Jakob Epstein (1880–1959) creates his innovatory tomb of Oscar Wilde, inspired by Assyrian sculpture. Aleksandr Archipenko (1887–1964) creates his *Walking Woman*, inspired by Cubist paintings.
		1913 Marcel Duchamp (1887–1968) becomes notorious for his *Nude Descending a Staircase*, combining cubism and futurism. Cass Gilbert (1859–1934) completes the Woolworth Tower, New York.
	1914 Sir Arthur Eddington (1882–1944), publishes *Stellar Movement and the Structure of the Universe*.	**1914** Oskar Kokoschka (1886–1980), paints his masterpiece *The Tempest*.

Index

Page numbers in *italics* refer to captions to illustrations

437